A User's Guide
to Saskatchewan Parks

— Other books in the Discover Saskatchewan Series —

Discover Saskatchewan: A Guide to Historic Sites
Discover Saskatchewan: A User's Guide to Regional Parks
Canoeing the Churchill: A Practical Guide to the Historic Voyageur Highway
Fishing Saskatchewan: An Angler's Guide to Provincial Waters

The support of the following organizations is gratefully acknowledged:

SASKATCHEWAN PARKS

Saskatchewan Heritage FOUNDATION

REGIONAL PARKS OF SASKATCHEWAN

A User's Guide
to Saskatchewan Parks

Michael T. Clancy & Anna Clancy

Series Editor
Dr. Ralph Nilson

2006

UNIVERSITY OF REGINA

CANADIAN PLAINS RESEARCH CENTER

Copyright © 2006 Michael Clancy and Anna Clancy
Copyright Notice
All rights reserved. No part of this work covered by the copyrights hereon may be reproduced or used in any form or by any means—graphic, electronic, or mechanical—without the prior written permission of the publisher. Any request for photocopying, recording, taping or placement in information storage and retrieval systems of any sort shall be directed in writing to the Canadian Reprography Collective.

Canadian Plains Research Center
University of Regina
Regina, Saskatchewan S4S 0A2
Canada
Tel: (306) 585-4758
Fax: (306) 585-4699
e-mail: canadian.plains@uregina.ca
http://www.cprc.uregina.ca

Library and Archives Canada Cataloguing in Publication

Clancy, Michael T., 1956–
A user's guide to Saskatchewan parks / by Michael T. Clancy & Anna Clancy.

(Discover Saskatchewan series 1484-1800 5)
Includes index.
ISBN 978-0-88977-198-7

1. Parks—Saskatchewan—Guidebooks. 2. Campsites, facilities, etc—Guidebooks. 3. Saskatchewan—Guidebooks. I. Clancy, Anna, 1957– II. University of Regina. Canadian Plains Research Center. III. Title. IV. Series.

FC3513.C538 2006   917.1204'4
C2006-903148-7

We acknowledge the financial support of the Government of Canada through the Book Publishing Industry Development Program (BPDIP) for our publishing activities.

Cover design: Donna Achtzehner, Canadian Plains Research Center
Cover photo: Pine Cree Regional Park (courtesy David McLennan, Canadian Plains Research Center)
Index: Patricia Furdek (www.userfriendlyindexes.com)
All photographs included in this book are courtesy of Michael and Anny Clancy, unless otherwise specified.

Contents

Acknowledgments vii
Introduction ix

SOUTHWEST SASKATCHEWAN
Antelope Lake Regional Park 3
Assiniboia Regional Park 5
Bengough Regional Park 7
Cabri Regional Park 9
Dunnet Regional Park 12
Eston Riverside Regional Park 15
Hazlet Regional Park 18
Herbert Ferry Regional Park 20
Jean-Louis Legare Regional Park 22
Lac Pelletier Regional Park 24
Lemsford Ferry Regional Park 27
McLaren Lake Regional Park 29
Notukeu Regional Park 31
Ogema Regional Park 33
Oro Lake Regional Park 35
Palliser Regional Park 37
Pine Cree Regional Park 40
Prairie Lake Regional Park 42
Rockin Beach Regional Park 44
Shamrock Regional Park 46
Sylvan Valley Regional Park 48
Thomson Lake Regional Park 50
Wood Mountain Regional Park 53
CYPRESS HILLS INTERPROVINCIAL PARK 56
BUFFALO POUND PROVINCIAL PARK 69
DANIELSON PROVINCIAL PARK 76
DOUGLAS PROVINCIAL PARK 80
SASKATCHEWAN LANDING PROVINCIAL PARK 85
ST. VICTOR PETROGLYPHS PROVINCIAL HISTORICAL PARK 93
WOOD MOUNTAIN PROVINCIAL HISTORIC PARK 95
GRASSLANDS NATIONAL PARK 97

SOUTHEAST SASKATCHEWAN
Carlton Trail Regional Park 103
Ceylon Regional Park 105
Craik and District Regional Park 107
Esterhazy Regional Park 109
Grenfell Regional Park 111
Kemoca Regional Park 113
Mainprize Regional Park 116
Moose Creek Regional Park 120
Moosomin and District Regional Park 122
Nickle Lake Regional Park 124
Oungre Memorial Regional Park 126
Oyama Regional Park 129

Radville Laurier Regional Park 131
Saskatchewan Beach Regional Park 133
Welwyn Centennial Regional Park 135
Woodlawn Regional Park 137
CANNINGTON MANOR PROVINCIAL HISTORIC PARK 140
CROOKED LAKE PROVINCIAL PARK 142
ECHO VALLEY PROVINCIAL PARK 146
KATEPWA POINT PROVINCIAL RECREATION PARK 152
LAST MOUNTAIN HOUSE PROVINCIAL HISTORIC PARK 155
MOOSE MOUNTAIN PROVINCIAL PARK 157
REGINA BEACH PROVINCIAL RECREATION SITE 165
ROWAN'S RAVINE PROVINCIAL PARK 168

WEST-CENTRAL SASKATCHEWAN
Atton's Lake Regional Park 175
Biggar and District Regional Park 178
Brightsand Lake Regional Park 180
Clearwater Lake Regional Park 182
Eagle Creek Regional Park 185
Elrose Regional Park 188
Emerald Lake Regional Park 190
Glenburn Regional Park 193
Kindersley Regional Park 195
Macklin Lake Regional Park 197
Martin's Lake Regional Park 199
Meeting Lake Regional Park 202
Memorial Lake Regional Park 204
Meota Regional Park 207
Outlook and District Regional Park 210
Redberry Lake Regional Park 213
Sandy Beach Regional Park 216
Silver Lake Regional Park 218
Suffern Lake Regional Park 221
Valley Regional Park 223
Unity and District Regional Park 225
Wilkie Regional Park 227
THE BATTLEFORDS PROVINCIAL PARK 229
BLACKSTRAP PROVINCIAL PARK 234
FORT CARLTON PROVINCIAL HISTORIC PARK 238
FORT PITT PROVINCIAL HISTORIC PARK 241
PIKE LAKE PROVINCIAL PARK 243

EAST-CENTRAL SASKATCHEWAN
Fishing Lake Regional Park Authority 251
   K.C. Beach Regional Park 251
   Leslie Beach Regional Park 252
Hudson Bay Regional Park 254
Ituna and District Regional Park 256
Kipabiskau Lake Regional Park 258
Lady Lake Regional Park 260
Lake Charron Regional Park 262
Last Mountain Lake Regional Park 264

Leroy Leisureland Regional Park 267
Lucien Lake Regional Park 269
Manitou and District Regional Park 272
McNab Regional Park 275
Melville Regional Park 277
Nipawin and District Regional Park 279
Pasquia Regional Park 282
St. Brieux Regional Park 285
Struthers Lake Regional Park 287
Sturgis and District Regional Park 289
Wakaw Lake Regional Park 291
Waldsea Lake Regional Park 294
Wapiti Valley Regional Park 296
Whitesand Regional Park 299
Wynyard Regional Park 301
York Lake Regional Park 303
DUCK MOUNTAIN PROVINCIAL PARK 305
GREENWATER LAKE PROVINCIAL PARK 313
GOOD SPIRIT LAKE PROVINCIAL PARK 320
TOUCHWOOD HILLS PROVINCIAL HISTORIC PARK 327
WILDCAT HILLS PROVINCIAL WILDERNESS PARK 329

NORTHERN SASKATCHEWAN
Canwood Regional Park 333
Little Loon Regional Park 335
Morin Lake Regional Park 337
Sturgeon Lake Regional Park 339
ATHABASCA SAND DUNES PROVINCIAL PARK 341
ANGLIN LAKE PROVINCIAL RECREATION SITE 343
BRONSON FOREST RECREATION SITE 346
CANDLE LAKE RECREATION PARK 348
CHITEK LAKE RECREATION SITE 353
CLARENCE-STEEPBANK LAKES PROVINCIAL WILDERNESS PARK 355
CLEARWATER RIVER WILDERNESS PARK 358
CUMBERLAND HOUSE PROVINCIAL HISTORIC PARK 360
EMMA LAKE RECREATION SITE 362
LAC LA RONGE PROVINCIAL PARK 366
MAKWA LAKE PROVINCIAL PARK 375
MEADOW LAKE PROVINCIAL PARK 380
NARROW HILLS PROVINCIAL PARK 392
HOLY TRINITY ANGLICAN CHURCH PROVINCIAL HISTORIC SITE 406
STEELE NARROWS PROVINCIAL HISTORIC PARK 407
PRINCE ALBERT NATIONAL PARK 409

Recommendations for Selected Stays 421
Index 430

Acknowledgments

This book would never have been written without the hard work and support of some very special people. The authors are grateful for financial assistance from the Saskatchewan Heritage Foundation (SHF) and the Canadian Plains Research Center (CPRC); without these grants we simply could not have afforded to research this material in only two summers.

Saskatchewan Environment and Resource Management (SERM) provided free camping and park entry passes as well as proofreading expertise by a host of busy people; I personally want to thank them for taking the time out of their schedules to make certain I got it right! The Saskatchewan Regional Parks Association (SRPA) assisted with park passes and expertise on the changes that system is undergoing.

The editors and staff at CPRC deserve further accolades for their patience and professionalism. Deadlines can be cruel mistresses for part-time authors yet never once did I hear so much as a murmur of discontent; the end product is as much their child as ours. The quality is all due to their professionalism; the errors are mine.

Speaking of which, while every attempt was made both during visitations and during follow-up mailings to ensure the material in this book is correct, there is always the chance that some quirk of the universe has created an alternate reality. For this I apologize as only my mistakes are truly mine; my successes must be shared with all who took part.

Last, and certainly not least, is my family. For the last two years they supported me in all my petulant moods as I pecked at this infernal machine; that support has kept me sane (even though there are those that question my sanity).

For Anna: your support for me is my strength; your love for me is my inspiration.

Michael T. Clancy
RR#5, Site 515, PO Box 2
Saskatoon, SK   S7K 3J8
Ph: (306) 384-2643

Email: mclancy@sasktel.net

Introduction

My family and I first drove around this province in an organized fashion in the summer of 1997 when we Discovered Saskatchewan while researching what became our "User's Guide to the Regional Parks." Once that project was done, we became infatuated with the idea of expanding that project to include the Provincial Parks and the National Parks under the same volume. Our friends at the Canadian Plains Research Center (CPRC) offered us a chance to update the regional park material as well as research a user's guide to the provincial and national parks, all to be published under one cover. We partnered with Saskatchewan Environment and Recreation Management (SERM), who provided a letter of introduction and free camping during our two summers of travel, and with the Saskatchewan Regional Parks Association (SRPA), who gave us park passes. The first time we went off on such an odyssey our three boys were young teenagers who offered us their keen insights to all the parks we visited; this served to make the final product "seen through a family's eyes" as it were. This time around we had to do the bulk of it by ourselves as their careers kept the lads from coming with us everywhere. Mind you, they did join us when they could and took their adventurous spirit into the wildest back-country to report on hiking trails and wilderness parks, for which I am grateful.

There are three park systems in Saskatchewan: the Regional Parks, the Provincial Parks, and the National Parks. The Regional Parks were originally formed by three or more municipalities pooling their resources to build a recreational facility based on local needs. In very general terms, these parks tend to be smaller and to specialize on one or two things; they generally have good golf courses, for example. They simply do not have the resources to provide a recreational opportunity for every need, so they concentrate on what they do best. The regional parks' charm is due to the local flavor and flair that is incorporated at every level. This is their park—they built it, they maintain it, and they are very proud of it (and rightly so). Again, in general terms, each regional park must be self-sufficient and cost-recover all their expenses, so there can be some variation in camping costs and fees between each park. They have standardized the annual park sticker costs, and it is still accepted at every regional park in the system though—a great bargain when you consider the number of parks you gain entry to! The Park system has undergone a major overhaul recently, moving towards an accreditation system which means all parks in the system must adhere to rigid quality standards. Safe drinking water, proper hygiene and waste management, playground safety, and food service are all things that the individual parks did to varying degrees of success; now they will adhere to provincewide standards. Some parks will find this process onerous and may not survive in the new environment; other parks have been leaders in providing quality camping experiences and so may not notice a change at all! Rest assured that through all this each park will still maintain its individuality, that home-style spark that has so endeared the entire system to all our family. This, the second edition of our written love affair with Saskatchewan's parks, gives you an updated picture in time, freezing the state of the system as it existed during our research phase of 2004–05. Things have changed as some regional parks have regrettably closed their gates while others continue to thrive and expand. There is even one new addition: welcome to Moose Creek Regional Park!

The Provincial Parks operate in a somewhat more standardized fashion. The shower house you find in one park is exactly the same as you'll find half the province away. Park fees and prices are standardized as well, so you know what to budget for. The provincial parks are, in general terms, larger than their regional park sisters and try to provide a more diverse camping experience because the camping public expects it. They have better hiking trails, more extensive and expansive camp sites and generally more services. They also provide a huge seasonal employment opportunity for local youth, which is evidenced by the real pride taken in the cleanliness and appearance of the parks. These young people take their work seriously, from John up at Wadin Bay to Meaghan at Duck Mountain and all the others in between, and their hard work shows in how eager they are to ensure your camping experience is a positive one. I can honestly say that all the people I spoke with in the parks were well-informed and very personable; I applaud them all.

The Provincial Parks fall into four broad categories: Historical, Recreational, Natural Environment, and Wilderness. The historical parks often have few amenities and will not be considered at length here. I have included a write-up on what to expect, but you probably won't be camping at them. The recreational parks are just that—they are intended to be a vacation destination with abundant and varied recreational opportunities, and extensive infrastructure such as modern washroom facilities and showers. There is some local flavor at each park but it can be subdued, as the approach to policy and pricing is standardized. This is comforting, though; you know what to expect. Natural Environment parks work at bringing the surroundings into the park experience—here you'll find hiking trails with information on plants, animals and landforms to be seen on the trail, interpretive programs—often with park staff to guide and facilitate learning. These parks might have a more rustic approach to camping as they expect you want fewer filters between you and nature. This is not to say that comforts do not exist in Natural Environment parks, far from it; there may be fewer fully-serviced camp sites, for instance. Natural Environment parks are a kind of bridge between the recreational parks and the wilderness parks. The wilderness parks are also just that; few if any amenities and only the most experienced and self-sufficient campers will be able to take advantage of the recreational opportunities showcased in the park.

The National Parks, and there are only two of them with campgrounds, are considered here as they have a bigger advertising budget globally, and Prince Albert National Park is rightly a jewel in the crown of the federal park system. Extensive camping, interpretive programs, and built-up shopping make Waskesiu more of a resort town than a wilderness park, which is very surely exactly what it can be—you just have to reach out your hand for the experience. Where else on the planet could you canoe peaceful backwaters and catch your own piscine lunch, then finish the day dining on fine china with a gourmet meal and fine wines? Prince Albert National Park is truly a remarkable resource. Grasslands National Park, on the other hand, occupies the other end of the spectrum entirely. There is no structured camping and little organized hiking within the park boundaries. You must be completely self-sufficient to camp in these prairies, but you will find a sense of wonder if you do. The starry night hems you in with a silence you swear you can hear, with only the strange yowling of coyotes to break the spell, and the Milky Way seems so close you think you can scoop it up in your cup. By day, it is an endless vista of rolling hills covered in waving grass with the stoop and fetch of hawks as they hunt their next meal; you can get a real appreciation for the lives lived here in the preceding thousands of years in this seemingly unchanging land.

Through all of this it became clear that this project is much more than the sum of its parts. The parks provide, individually, wonderful recreational opportunities to just about every community in the province. Collectively, these special places are preserving an astonishing natural resource for future generations. They are much more than campsites, beaches, and golf courses; they are a natural habitat for birds, mammals, and us. They are facing great pressure to provide all this for as little cost as possible, which means we, the camping public, are facing user fees for amenities we once enjoyed for free. Some regional parks charge for showers, the provincial parks charge for campfires (although the firewood is still free), and both systems have to increase camping and entry fees almost annually. Modern motor homes and vacation trailers have better amenities and can be larger than my first apartment; they require 30- and even 50-amp electrical service, not to mention larger campsites simply to accommodate them! Yet the parks are trying very hard to improve themselves by modernizing their campgrounds and with new initiatives such as the Dark Sky Preserve, where provincial parks are trying to get away from streetlamps and superfluous lighting; the first one was Cypress Hills Inter-Provincial Park. The regional parks are getting on board as well, with Rockin Beach near Rock Glen becoming the first such dark sky preserve in the system. The darkness of a forest night should be broken only by the soft silver light of the moon and her night sky companions the stars, or the flicker and glow of a campfire. This is, for one thing, more natural to the birds and animals that make the forest their home, particularly at night when they are normally active; it also allows us ever more urbanized campers to revel in the beauty of the Milky Way.

Another change is the advent of the information age; many parks have websites and email addresses, so I have incorporated that information where it is known. Those with internet access can benefit from the more up-to-date information these addresses will give you, such as pricing and interpretive programming—the things that might change annually.

The SRPA itself has an excellent website from which you can get updated information on individual parks by following links from their URL at: http://www.saskregionalparks.ca. The Provincial Parks have a wealth of information on their website at: www.saskparks.net. The National Parks have their own website at: www.pc.gc.ca/. From here you can find information on both the national parks in our province as well as the historical parks not included in this book as they have no camping facilities.

My intent in writing this book is threefold. First, I wanted to get people interested in visiting the natural beauty we have right here. Ask just about anyone, anywhere in Canada, and they'll tell you that Saskatchewan is flat, boring, and lifeless. You may indeed get this mistaken impression if all you ever do is drive across the province on the Trans-Canada Highway, but even a short side trip to any of our parks will show you a substantially different picture. Our sport fishing is among the best in the world, our hiking trails will test the hardiest of wilderness walkers, and our canoe routes follow the footsteps of this continent's history. Everywhere you will find the echoes of our First Nations people and in many places you will find those drums still beating at pow-wows, dances, and tribal celebrations and ceremonies. These are people who take pride in their culture and heritage, and are showcasing that to the world. Be it the grasslands, aspen parklands, or boreal forest, our many parks have preserved pieces of this province's remarkable natural diversity and celebrate it with campgrounds and the easy laughter of children at play. Interpretive programs are in place to educate and delight audiences of all ages in all of this activity, and usually at little or no cost. Truly, our tourism dollars belong right here at home—there's so much to see and do that our two years of research is but the beginning for us.

Secondly, I want visitors to our parks, be they from the far side of the planet or from the next town over, to have in one book a tool to assist them in finding a park that will meet their individual family's camping needs. Even the short list in the previous paragraph is somewhat overwhelming in that there is so much to do, and (if your family is anything like mine) you have limited vacation time—which park of so many will have just what you're looking for? Which park is the best? Now that's a tough question! You have to decide for yourself what it is you want from your vacation—fishing, golfing, swimming, hiking, discovery, or whatever; we've put some ideas at the back of the book that offer choices for selected amenities. This is by no means an exhaustive list, nor is it intended to be a "best of" chapter. Think about what you'd like to do, flip through the suggestions, and then go check out the individual park write-ups to see if that meets your needs; I've included contact information with each park so you can get advance information or reservations.

Thirdly, I want to get people involved with our park systems. There is a ton of things you can do besides camping for a week or two. Every park in the province is looking for interested people to volunteer time and energy in some capacity or other, particularly the regional parks. Whether it is with a "Friends of the Park" volunteer group or on one of the committees, energetic people will always be welcome and I hope this book gives you some ideas of where you can invest your valuable time to help preserve something so worthwhile for future generations to enjoy.

It was great fun for us to go and look at all these wonderful places, and I hope this go-to guide helps you in your travels. Thanks for supporting these people, and HAPPY CAMPING!

The Clancy Clan
Email: mclancy@sasktel.net

Southwest Saskatchewan

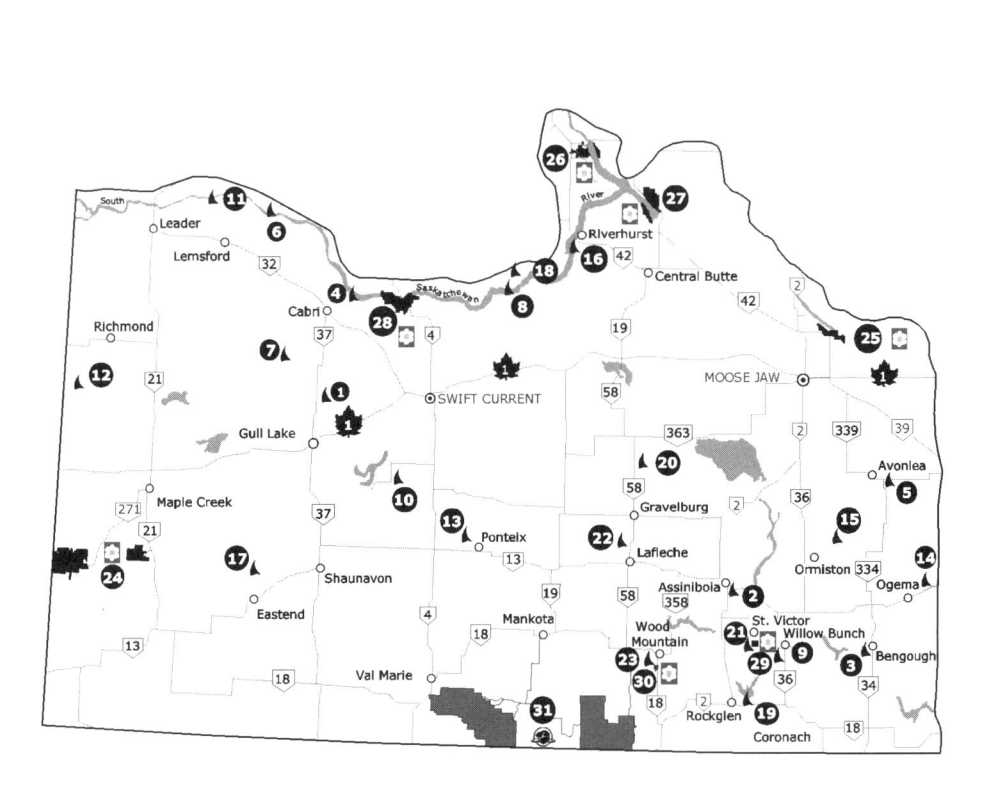

ANTELOPE LAKE REGIONAL PARK

Located 18 km northeast of Gull Lake, the road is paved right into the park as far as the hall and office. This is a quiet park that features family camping and a lake for water sports. The hillsides bordering the park are covered in typical prairie fashion, and in spring are ablaze with colorful wildflowers. The park is open from the Victoria Day weekend in May until the end of September, and costs $4 per day or an annual Regional Park sticker to enter.

SITES

There are 80 electrified sites that cost $10 per night; weekly, monthly, and seasonal rates are available on request and are subject to yearly change. The sites are located in several loops that back onto tall cottonwood groves and are separated by poles laid sideways. Electrical service is provided at the rear of each site and well water is piped to central taps. The sites are adequate for even the largest of units, and the roadways are well graveled. All sites have pole BBQs and picnic tables; the park no longer provides firepits or firewood so you must be self-sufficient. All the sites are open from the front and side, sheltered only from the rear by tall groves of poplars and elms. An overflow campsite area has been built. Equipped with power, it can be used for group or individual camping. The park has also built a new bathroom and shower house in this area. Sites can be reserved with one week's notice by calling the concession at (306) 672-3933.

WATER SPORTS

The swimming hole is a man-made pool resulting from a dam on a small creek feeding the lake. The outflow runs over a stone containment under an arched footbridge leading to the campgrounds (pictured above). Surrounded by cottonwoods, the large pool supports some canoeing by the cabin-owners at the far end, but no motor boating. The beach has plenty of soft, fine sand, and a rope hung from a stout limb to swing out into the water— a most popular toy on a hot day! The park office and canteen are located beside the pool in the park manager's cabin. A group of picnic tables separates the canteen from the shower house and change rooms; showers cost 25¢ per timed use. The canteen is open from 1000–2200 hr daily, and offers the usual array of snacks, pop, and iced treats, plus grilled foods such as hamburgers. The canteen closes one day every week, usually on a Tuesday. No boat launch is available as the lake has receded past the old boat launch area. The park has established a trout pond costing $4 per day, and a daily limit is in place.

GOLFING AND OTHER SPORTS

A 9-hole, sand green golf course is located at the top of the hill, to the left as you drive in. It is a par 34 course, 2566 yard in length, and costs $3 per day to play; a seasonal family pass is only $30! It is naturally watered and will usually show wear later in the year, but at $3 per day, it's worth the play. The course can be rented for tournaments for $60 per day, so you may want to consider that if planning a family reunion or other such gathering. A dining shelter is available to operate a tournament from. Greens fees can be paid either at the concession or in the honor box on the first tee. A score card is available but it has no course map so finding your way about for the first round can be a bit of a chore. Normally, the course isn't busy enough to warrant booking tee times, but you can phone the park office for details on booking a tournament or to see if the course is busy.

The park has a nice playground with slides, swings, merry-go-rounds, teeter-totters, and a climber, all on a lovely grass lawn in the day-use area. Well shaded with tall trees, this is a restful spot for an afternoon outing. All the park equipment was freshly painted the year of our visit, and in very pristine condition. The park has a ball diamond free to use, with grass in- and outfields. The backstop is made of wire mesh on tall wooden poles and there are benches for players to rest on.

SERVICES

The town of Gull Lake is an 18-km drive away, and it has all the amenities from excellent shopping to treating medical emergencies. The park has a hall capable of seating 200 people which can be rented for $110 per day, $35 of which is refunded if the hall is cleaned. The hall can host such things as dances and cabarets, reunions, and ecumenical services. The park hosts slow pitch and golf tournaments annually and so is busy most weekends of the year. If you'd like to enjoy this lovely park, you'd be well advised to call ahead. For information on the park, contact the Secretary-Treasurer at:

Antelope Lake Regional Park
c/o Secretary Treasurer,
PO Box 493,
Gull Lake, SK S0N 1A0
Park Office (in season): (306) 672-3933.

ASSINIBOIA REGIONAL PARK

This is a delightful municipal park located on the southeast edge of Assiniboia on Empire Road. It can easily be reached from either Hwys 2 or 13, as Hwy 13 becomes 1st Ave through town; turn south on Center St. then southeast on Empire Road. Follow the signs through town if you are entering from the north on Hwy 2, as it becomes Empire Road as you travel through town. The park is in three sections: the campgrounds, aquatic center and picnic/playgrounds in town, the golf course 3.2 km south of town on Hwy 2, and the reservoir, stocked with fish, is located 8 km east on Hwy 13. The town of Assiniboia has many things to offer the weary traveler including an aquatic center, excellent golf, spacious day-use lawns and playgrounds and easy access to the many natural wonders in the area, including the St. Victor Petroglyphs and the Wood Mountain Provincial Historical Site. The park is open from the Victoria Day weekend in May to the September Labor Day weekend, and does not charge entrance fees.

SITES

There are 15 electrified sites, and two non-electrified sites. The sites cost $16 per night or $13 if you have a Regional Park sticker. There is no daily entry fee, but you can purchase an annual sticker. All sites were naturally leveled and drained, and well grassed. Shade is provided by planted trees and shrubs, varying from elms to cottonwoods to carraganas. The result is a delightful, arboretum-like effect, and plenty of privacy from one's neighbors. The fact that Hwy 2 runs just past the park does cause some road noise, but not as much as I imagined it would. The roadways in the park are all paved and in excellent condition. All the sites had picnic tables, pole BBQs, and were large enough for even the noblest of campers. We did not find a firewood supply in the park, but several local merchants had bundles for sale; prices varied a bit. The toilet facilities were modern, located in the nearby Aquatic Center. Registered campers had 24-hour access from outside to the facility, which included free showers. Both showers and washrooms are wheelchair accessible, and the paved roadways will make park access a lot easier. Assiniboia municipal water is supplied from taps located between each site, and available at all times. There are no gates or a booth at which to register, so see the Aquatic Center staff; if you arrive after their hours, set up your camp and register in the morning. No reservations are accepted, so simply take the empty site you like best.

WATER SPORTS

The Assiniboia Aquatic Center is a fine outdoor pool with a well-laid-out design. It is a popular place on hot summer days. Patrons will pay $4 per adult, $3.50 per student, and $3 for children for the afternoon or evening public swims; a family pass is $10. The lifeguards also run an aquatic program with various events through the day besides their lesson sets. Four lesson sets are offered in the season, 2 in July and 2 in August. Lessons cost $20 to $44 for Red Cross levels, and $85 for RLSS levels, plus extra costs for books and exam fees. The pool offers 2 diving boards, a 1m and a 3m board, has lockers, showers, and a concession service outside the pool on the northeast corner of the building. The pool is open from 0630–2200 hr daily in season. The concession offers the usual snacks, pop and iced treats, and is open from 1400–1730 hr in the afternoon and from 1900–2030 hr in the evening. For more information on the pool or to register for lessons, contact the pool manager at (306) 642-5620 in season. The Willow Dam reservoir, located 8 km east of town on Hwy 13, has a boat launch and offers interested anglers stocked walleye and perch; provincial angling regulations apply. Canoeists will also enjoy these normally calm waters as motor boats are not allowed.

GOLF

A fine 9-hole, grass green golf course is located just 3.2 km south of the campgrounds. Well treed and complete with a driving range and a practice putting green, the course boasts an intricate layout. An irrigation canal wanders through the course, so water is in play on 5 of the nine holes. The course is 2768 yards long on a par 36. The tee boxes are all raised and well manicured. The abundance of water means the course is well irrigated and lush throughout. The greens are smooth but pin placement can make each hole an individual challenge. A concession and pro-shop offer patrons simple snacks and pop, as well as golf sundries and cart or club rentals. Greens fees are $13 for 9-holes or $20 for 18-holes, and the course is open from May 1 to September 30, longer if the weather allows. Tee reservations are not normally required as even weekend play rarely has a delay longer than 30 minutes.

SERVICES

The park has a large day use area with a good sized playground complete with teeter-totters, merry-go-rounds, rocking horses on springs, and a creative play center, all in sand pits to break falls. The picnic area has benches, tall shade trees, picnic tables and pole BBQs scattered about. Two paved tennis courts are available free of charge in a fenced enclosure; rackets are available from the concession for a $5 deposit. A sand volleyball court is also available, with equipment rented from the concession. A "Welcome Wagon" of sorts comes around to the campgrounds about 1900 hr nightly, and the deputation of one is a wealth of local information as well as free passes to the Aquatic Center. As the park is so diverse, its popularity is difficult to assess, but it is a safe bet that it has a steady stream of camping traffic. We found it a gentle oasis on our travels, and hope you will too. For more information on the park, contact the Park Manager at:

>Assiniboia Regional Park
>PO Box 1224,
>Assiniboia, SK   S0H 0V0
>Aquatic Center (in season): (306) 642-5620.

BENGOUGH REGIONAL PARK

Located in the town of Bengough on Hwy 34, this busy municipal park serves one of the busiest agricultural hubs in the area. Because of the business interest in the area, funds have been made available to build up an impressive array of recreational possibilities. Open from the first of May to the middle of October, the park was built in 1975, and revisions have been ongoing as more equipment is added. The park is located at the end of Main Street, and the gates are open from 0800–2300 hr; a $3 daily fee or an annual Regional Park sticker gains you access.

SITES

As you drive in the park gates you see a large painted map of the entire Regional Park, complete with park rules. There are 17 electrified sites available, and an "unlimited overflow" just to the west of the shower house, itself to the west of the campgrounds. A tenting area is available just to the south of the shower house. Sites cost $20 per night for an electrified site, or $12 per night for a non-electrified site. All sites are naturally leveled and drained, and have pole BBQs, picnic tables, and trash bins between every second site. The sites are large enough for the largest RV unit, although electrical service is 15 amp so units with air conditioning won't be able to take advantage. Shade is provided by dense, 12 to 15 foot tall stands of ash and poplar, particularly from the north; some have shade from the east or west, depending on geometry, but none have shade from the south. Firewood is available from a central bin, and drinking water (Bengough municipal) is available from a central tap at the shower house. Toilet facilities range from primitive biffies (on the golf course) to modern flush toilets at the shower house. Showers are free, and the facility was clean and neat. A large dining shelter or cook house is available beside the tenting area. Group camping is available; maximum group size is 25 units, but that is an arbitrary number and depends on the size of the units involved. Reservations are not accepted unless 5 or more sites are required; contact the park manager for details.

GOLFING

The Bengough Regional Golf Club offers a 9-hole, sand green golf course. Featuring raised tee boxes, the par 36 course follows 3265 yards in total. Although there is no practice putting area, a driving range is available. The course is very reasonable to play, as greens fees are $4 per day, collected on the honor system in a box on the first tee. A seasonal membership costs $40 for an adult. The condition of this naturally watered course was adequate during our visit, and would be a delightful play during the late spring and early summer. As this was a wet year, the course was very green and lush, but the fairways were well mowed and the course in generally good condition. Normally, tee reservations are not required. An open golf tournament is held towards the end of June; contact the Recreation Office for details.

SWIMMING

East of the campgrounds (pictured above, along Main Street) is the solar-heated swimming pool, part of the ice rink where both skating and curling is held in the winter. Swimming is popular as daily admissions are modest; adults and students pay $3, preschoolers $2, infants are free, and a family pass is $10. Swim lessons cost as little as $30 per level for all Red Cross and RLSS levels; call the Recreation Office for details. The pool has two diving boards, a 1 m and a 3 m, and varies from 4 m to 1 m in depth; it can also be rented for private functions at a cost of $50 per hour. A concession selling pop and snacks operates in the mornings, during lessons only. The pool personnel also co-ordinate the Summer Playground Program. This innovative enterprise costs $2 per day per person, and is divided into two age groups: ages 3 to 7, and ages 8 to 15. Activities are varied, and one popular venue is the Summer Story Hour; check with the Rec. office for details and registration. There are two playgrounds, one at the campgrounds (built in 1980), and a smaller one beside the pool (built in 1985). Between them they have swings, slides, merry-go-rounds, and teeter-totters. The campground site also has a creative play center. All equipment is in good repair, and built on large lawns. The park also has tennis courts and horseshoe pits for use; check with the Recreation Office for equipment rental.

BASEBALL

Located just to the north of the campgrounds, the ball complex is built in the fashion of spokes radiating out from a hub. During tournaments, the hub is comprised of the concessions, washrooms, and beer garden. There are 4 excellent ball diamonds with shelters for the players, stands for the fans, and tall wire mesh on metal poles. Dirt infields are complemented by the grass outfields, and baselines are limed during tournaments. Ample parking is available near the complex, so there is plenty of space for patrons. Several tournaments are held every year, most notably the minor ball, held in late May, and the slow pitch tournament, held in early to mid June.

SERVICES

The town of Bengough can meet all your traveling needs, be they shopping, mechanical, medical (Bengough has a Health Center), or religious. Several restaurants are available in town, a short walk from the campgrounds. The Bengough Heritage Museum is open as well, asking for a silver collection to view local historical artifacts. If you're planning a trip into the Big Muddy, you may wish to begin here! Besides all the sporting and cultural activities listed above, Bengough is considered the gateway to the Big Muddy and all the scenery to be found in these badlands. Bengough celebrates Heritage Day on the Canada Day long weekend, and has a street market, sort of a municipal flea market, in the middle of July. They also have a farmer's market at the end of August. As one can see, this is a busy place to visit; there's always something to see or do! Should you wish more information, contact the park manager at:

Bengough Regional Park
PO Box 340,
Bengough, SK   S0L 0K0
Rec. Office: (306) 268-2909/Fax: (306) 268-2988.

CABRI REGIONAL PARK

Located 20 km northeast of Cabri from the junction of Hwys 32 and 37, this park is located on the South Saskatchewan River just west of Lake Diefenbaker. The drive in is quite scenic due to the tall, steep hills and the river view is excellent. Open from the Victoria Day weekend to the middle of October, the park is serviced by 18 km of gravel roads which are somewhat twisting and steep at the last. At one time they were treacherous when wet, but recent road construction has made it passable in even the heaviest of downpours. Daily entry fees are $4, or free with an annual Regional Park sticker.

SITES

There are 106 electrified sites with 15 amp service and 5 river front tenting, non-electrified sites. As many as 60 sites are reserved for seasonal campers; contact the park manager for details. Sites cost $12 per day for an electrified site, and $8 per day for a tenting site. The electrified sites are built into 6 loops having a variable number of sites in each. No site map is available, so check in at the park office to register before you take a site. All sites are naturally leveled and drained, and well grassed to keep mud and dust down. Each site has a picnic table, pole BBQ, and a trash can. Firewood is provided in central bins. Washroom facilities are modern, with flush toilets and free showers. There are also centrally located trash bins in day-use areas. The sites are generally large enough for even the largest unit, but some areas have larger sites than others. Site cover is adequate, with both natural and planted trees of many species providing deep shade in the tenting and day use areas. Planted trees such as aspens, willows, and maples provide perimeter shade in the campsites, with brush filling in the spaces. Group camping is available in Area "F," with a maximum of 20 to 25 units. The area features large open firepits as well as all the other equipment, so group campfires are allowed. These are always a treat for the little campers, as the artful telling of late-night stories around a campfire's glow is the stuff of summer magic. A dining shelter in the day-use area provides some relief from the elements for casual picnickers. Drinking water is available from the blue-painted hand pumps; water provided is Cabri Municipal, and held in cisterns at each pump station. The water available in the pressure system taps is untreated river water and must be boiled prior to consumption. No reservation system exists, but it would be wise to phone head and ask if the park is filling up; call the park manager at (306) 587-2755 in season for up-to-the-minute information.

WATER SPORTS

The river provides a focus for all sorts of watery fun, and a fine man-made marina (pictured above) protects your boat from a summer storm. The boatlaunch costs $2 per day or $15 per season to use, and that includes use of the marina docks. A buoyed swimming beach is located just to the west of the boatlaunch, and has a floating dock with diving board for the adventurous. There is no lifeguard on duty, and no lessons are taught as the town of Cabri has a swimming pool that offers these amenities. The beach is small but well sanded, and surrounded by a well-shaded lawn for relaxing. Pets are allowed in the park if they are kept on a leash, but are restricted from the beach area. Both the boatlaunch and swimming area are protected from currents and storms by a large breakwater so one needn't worry about young swimmers being swept away by treacherous undertows. Mind you, I wouldn't care to attempt a crossing of the river past the breakwater; stay in the buoyed area and you'll have no trouble at all. The river itself has fine fishing for walleye, pike, and several other game fish. Skiers and jet boaters also find the river a play pen for miles in either direction, so the water can be busy at times! A Fun Derby is held in August, offering family-oriented fun and prizes for the young anglers in your crowd; contact the park office for details.

SPORTS

Besides water sports, the park offers young naturalists the opportunity to go bird watching and hiking in the hills surrounding the park. No trails are established or marked, but you can hike at will otherwise. You'd be well advised to take water with you as the hills seem to hold and magnify the heat, and little if any water will be found in the coulees. As no trails are established, you may want to organize your own adult-led exploration party to keep younger members from losing their way in the possibly bewildering coulees. For bird watchers, notable species include orioles, jays, finches, and humming birds. The park manager informed me that songbird species have been on the rise in recent years as the large amount of watering done on the lawns in the park increases food and shelter for them. A large playground is built to the west of the swim beach in the day use area, and features swings, slides, merry-go-rounds and teeter-totters as well as horseshoe pits and a volleyball court. Equipment for the last two is available at the Park Office. The playground has plenty of shade and is well grassed.

SERVICES

The park offers quiet family camping, so the focus is on activities for small campers. There is no golf course or ball complex for adult fun, and rules regarding quiet time are becoming more strictly enforced. The Park Office also houses the canteen, where iced treats, pop, and snack foods can be purchased. Hours for the canteen are variable, based on demand. The camp kitchen, located across from the Park Office, offers Pancake Breakfasts on occasion as the local service clubs put them on. There is no shopping in the park except for the treats; all laundry, grocery, mechanical, medical, and worship services are offered in Cabri, about 15 minutes away. The last weekend in July features a "Frolic in the Park," the big celebration in their year. As many as 200 to 300 people come for each day's entertainment of live performers in the afternoon, and DJ dance music in the evening. There is a beer garden and children's entertainment as well. The stage, built behind the camp kitchen, becomes the center of a swirling mass of dancers on into the night. Perhaps for this reason you may wish to attend the park on a different weekend if you've small children that may be disturbed by late-night music. We found the park lush and green, quiet and peaceful, and that is how it should be for all. For more information on this delightful oasis, contact the park secretary at:

Cabri Regional Park
PO Box 494
Cabri, SK   S0N 0J0
Park office: (306) 587-2755 (in season), or (306) 587-2435 otherwise.

DUNNET REGIONAL PARK

Built by a dam and reservoir that constricts Avonlea Creek, this park is located 3.2 km south of Avonlea on Hwy 334, then 3.2 km east on a grid road. It covers 50 acres of naturally treed valley, and is officially open from the Victoria Day long weekend in May until the end of September, but the season may be extended if weather permits. The park has much to offer, and costs $8 per vehicle per day to enter, or an annual Regional Park sticker.

SITES

There are 58 electrified sites (15 amp service only) and 180 non-electrified sites, costing $20 and $15 per night respectively. Weekly rates are also available, costing $120 for an electrified site, or $90 for a non-electrified site. All sites have picnic tables, firepits, and trash cans. Drinking water is available from central taps, and firewood is available for sale. A new potable water system was installed in 2002. Generally speaking, the sites are large enough for most units, but some of the newer, larger campers will have difficulty backing around in the farther reaches of a few of the camping loops. Shade trees abound; this is one of the most heavily treed parks in the area with many fine elms and maples plus a healthy stock of lilacs, evergreens, and cherry trees. Some of the farther non-electrified sites feel as though you are in a deep forest! A brochure with maps of all sites, areas, and equipment is available when you check in. The non-electrified areas also function as the group camping area in that the sites aren't as well demarcated so you can put several units together around a couple of firepits. Washroom facilities range from primitive biffies to a modern shower house with flush toilets. A new washroom/shower facility was built in 2003. The trailer dump station is in front of the old shower house, and is free to registered patrons. This park is unusual in its approach to the party crowd in that quiet time is enforced 24 hours a day. The park manager stated "If I can hear your radio, it's too loud!" This park wants families to come camping, and so they take a fairly stern line with any rowdier element. This park was in excellent condition when we visited; everything was clean, neat, and well painted. A lot of very hard work went into keeping it so clean, and is in large measure responsible for the increased interest in recent years. The park is busy, particularly on weekends, so you may want to call ahead; contact the park manager for details at (306) 868-4410.

WATER SPORTS

The damming of the creek has created a fine reservoir that has been liberally stocked with walleye. In fact, a breeding population has been established so fishing is popular among patrons. A boatlaunch is available, free to registered campers, and there is a large parking area for trailers beside the reservoir. An outdoor swimming pool, heated, with change rooms and showers keeps young campers busy, and is a focus of attention during lessons. There are two lesson sets offered in July, costing $45 to $50 per entrant, depending on swim level. Public swims are offered daily from 1300–2000 hr, with lifeguards on duty throughout. Pool fees are $2 for pre-school children, $3.50 for adults, and $10 for a family daily pass. A two week family pass is $90, and an annual family pass is $130. To register in the swimming program, call the concession at (306) 868-2151. A full concession operates beside the pool from 0830–2100 hr, longer if demand warrants, and sells the usual pop, snacks and iced treats as well as light meals. A covered dining shelter between the pool and the concession provides a quiet place for a cup of coffee while lessons are on, or a dry place to wait out a storm during lunch. Between the pool and the day use or picnic area is the playground, with slides, swings, teeter-totters, and a creative play center, all built on a fine lawn with plenty of space to run and play in. As with all park equipment, the playground toys are brightly painted and well maintained.

BASEBALL

The park has a total of 8 ball diamonds, 5 on top of the hill as you drive in the park, one by the pool, a fastball diamond in the overflow area, and a hardball diamond by the reservoir. All diamonds have grass outfields with dirt infields, tall mesh backstops on metal poles, and benches for players. Ample parking is provided, but there is little shelter so be prepared. These diamonds ring to the sound of the annual Canada Day celebration, the Avonlea Lions Club Funanza, with ball tournaments, a beef supper and games of chance for all. There is also the Dunnet Park Ball Tournament on the August Long Weekend with a pancake breakfast. The ball tournaments also usually have a cabaret, held in the "Blue Building." This is the Recreation Hall located between the pool and the picnic area, available for rent for any private function for $200 per day, less for local renters. This is a very popular venue for local events, so you'd best book as early as April to ensure you get your choice of dates! Contact the Park Secretary for details at (306) 868-4673, or in writing at the address below.

SERVICES

Besides all the other sports listed above, the park has a nature trail to the campgrounds which crosses the river on a swinging bridge (pictured on opposite page). A mountain bike trail is being built through the hills on the south edge of the park. One can also hike extensively in the local badlands, seeking native landmarks like the Painted Rocks. If you intend to seek these things, I recommend you stop at the Heritage House Museum on Main

Street in Avonlea. The displays of local history range from the prehistoric to present day. It is open from 1300–1700 hr Thursday, Friday, and Saturday, and costs $1 to enter. Here one can get information on where to wander and what to see in the badlands. A very challenging municipal golf course awaits in the Long Creek Golf and Country Club only 3 km east of Avonlea. It has 18 holes with grass greens and a licensed clubhouse. For more information or bookings, call (306) 868-4432. As this isn't part of the Regional Park, we did not stop to play but it is highly recommended locally. Of interest are the changes to the old shower house; it has been refurbished into a sort of "teahouse" which offers a sound stage for local talent to showcase music, poetry and other entertainments, all free to registered guests. This will be a highly variable event as one will never be certain when something is "on," but why wait—get up on the stage yourself! The town of Avonlea also offers a full range of services including shopping, mechanical, medical, and worship. The Palliser Regional Library is also available in town, operating on summer hours. Pets are allowed in the park, but they must be on a leash, and they are restricted from the playground and pool areas. For more information on this wonderful park, contact the Park Secretary at:

Dunnet Regional Park
PO Box 247,
Avonlea, SK   S0H 0C0
Call them at (306) 868-2252 or call the Park Manager at (306) 868-2250 in season.

ESTON RIVERSIDE REGIONAL PARK

This park is located on the South Saskatchewan River just 21 km south of Eston, on Hwy 30. Open from late May until the end of September, the golf course may stay open longer if the weather cooperates. The park has all the beauty of the river valley plus some fine old elms to add charm. The park managers have added something extra by reviving an old school house as the local recreation center, complete with patio and enclosed deck. It can be rented for your private function. The park entrance fees are $4 per vehicle per day, waived with an annual Regional Park sticker.

SITES

There are 20 serviced sites, all of which have power, water and sewer; electrical service varies from 20 to 30 amp. There are also 20 non-electrified sites as well as group camping. The sites cost anywhere from $10 per day for a tenting site to $20 per day for full hookup with a 30 amp service. All sites can be rented for weekly or monthly rates; contact the park manager for details. The tenting and non-electrified sites are naturally mounded and graded, while the full hook up sites have graveled pads for the units and a small lawn upon which to place your picnic table. All sites have picnic tables, pole BBQs or firepits, and trash cans. Firewood is available free from central bins, but water taps in the campgrounds do not provide drinking water; that is available from a central tap by the concession. Water from all other taps must be boiled before it can be consumed. Site size is generally adequate for even the largest unit, particularly the fully serviced sites as they are pull-through style. Mind you, the serviced sites have no trees between them, depending on one line of elms for shade. The unserviced sites are on a lower road, and have excellent shade and tall trees everywhere. Toilet facilities are generally excellent, with modern facilities in the shower house and biffies on the golf course. All the facilities are wheelchair accessible, from the bathrooms to the hall, canteen, and mini-golf. The showers operate on quarters, and were spotlessly clean when we visited. Pets are allowed but must be leashed at all times, and no reservation system is in effect. Quiet time is from 2300–0700 hr, and is strictly enforced.

WATER SPORTS

A fine outdoor swimming pool is available offering swim lessons and waterslides for park patrons. There are two lesson sets offered in July; costing $16 per week (Aquaquest, 1 or 2 weeks) or $100 for the Bronze series (5 weeks of lessons). Contact the park office for details regarding registration. A sandy beach can be found along the riverbank, but I cannot recommend swimming in the river due to unpredictable currents. The pool has change rooms and showers which require loonies to operate, and reasonable rates for public swims. There are also bleachers available for the parents to use while lessons are on, and during the public swims for spectators. Just beside the fenced pool enclosure is the playground, with swings, slides, and a 6-seat rocking horse, all on a huge lawn that includes the day use picnicking ground. Beside this is the park concession, open from 1100–2100 hr, depending on pool use. It offers the usual iced treats, snacks, and soda pop, as well as a selection of grilled and fried foods, plus home made pies! A small cement patio beside the concession allows patrons to share a meal with wheel chair bound companions in the comfort of the shade trees that surround the area. Both the pool house and concession have been renovated recently.

The river flows beside the park, and offers decent angling to camping fisher folk. There is no boatlaunch, but one can put boats in at the ferry, some 10 or 12 km away. There are no docking facilities, but one can simply beach the boat beside the park as needed.

GOLFING

There is a fine, irrigated 9-hole grass green golf course available for patrons. Its par 36 covers 3341 yards over the hills and coulees of the river valley so there is plenty of vertical change to keep one interested. A licensed clubhouse will serve light lunches and snack foods for its patrons, and is open from 0700–2400 hr, depending on demand, season, and available light. There is a putting green and a driving range (balls are $3 per bucket) to hone your skill, and a pro-shop to rent clubs and carts. Greens fees are $10 for 9 holes, $15 for 18 holes, and $6 for students. For this quality of course, the price is a steal! The course is varied, scenic, and not all that easy for duffers like myself. The tees and greens are immaculate, the fairways would be the envy of my block, and there is even parking available! Tee reservations aren't really necessary, unless there's a tournament under way on this popular course, as you should be able to get on in a matter of minutes. You can call the club house for more information or to discuss booking your own tournament at (306) 962-3845. A new feature is the golf cart shed, in which space can be rented to house your cart during your stay.

BASEBALL

There are 2 ball diamonds in the park, both with red shale infields and grass outfields. They have bleachers, tall mesh backstops on tall metal poles, and short mesh home run fences. Although they lack player shelters, they are excellent facilities, and the scene of the August long weekend Slow Pitch tournament every year. The old school house becomes the scene of the cabaret and beer hall during this venue, and is available for rent for $80 plus GST per night. No deposit is collected, but the facility is popular for weddings and reunions, so book early; contact the park office for details.

SERVICES

The town of Eston is about a 15-minute drive away, and offers the camper all the amenities including shopping, mechanical, medical, and worship services. A trailer dump station is available in town as well. The hall can be rented for private functions, costing $100 per day plus a $100 damage deposit. This is a quiet little park that is only rarely busy, and which tries hard to attract families to share its many splendors. The party crowd is discouraged, although you can expect revelers to enjoy themselves into the small hours when the ball tournaments are on. For more information, contact the park office at:

Eston Riverside Regional Park
PO Box 883
Eston, SK   S0K 1A0
Call the park office at (306) 962-3937 or fax at (306) 962-3907.

HAZLET REGIONAL PARK

This park is located about 4 to 5 km from Hazlet, just off Hwy 332 in the bottom of a coulee. As you make the turn, the first thing you see off the highway is a ball diamond complex; this is not the Regional Park although it is quite busy with various events. The Regional Park is a further distance on that grid road, and a much more pleasant destination. Built in 1960, the park is open June 1 to the end of December. Park entry fees of $4 per vehicle per day are waived if you have an annual Regional Park sticker.

SITES

There are 12 electrified sites, all with 15 amp service, and 20 non-electrified sites. A very large field can hold any number of overflow vehicles, so the park will never be thought of as full. Site rental is $10 per night for electrical, and $5 per night for non-electrical. All sites are equipped with picnic tables, some of them new and very sturdy, pole BBQs or firepits, and trash cans. The sites are not numbered; simply pull into a likely spot and the caretaker will collect the fees from you on his evening rounds, or you can deposit them in the "self-registration" box. The campsites line the west road of the park and are quite open between as there are no interposing trees. Shade is provided by a mature stand of parklands forest behind, however, so you will have evening shade as the sun sets. A couple of sites on the north end are more sheltered, as they are set in planted trees. Firewood is available from central bins, but the water in the central taps was not treated, so I cannot recommend it unless it is first boiled. There are two dining shelters available, both needing a bit of work but still serviceable. They have excellent wood stoves in them, and would serve to feed quite a crowd for pancake breakfasts and the like. One large shelter constructed of white plastic sheets with a tin roof is used for storage only. Washroom facilities are vault toilets but clean and free of odor. I doubt very much if you will need to reserve a site, but should you wish to arrange a reunion or the like, contact the Park Secretary at (306) 678-4818.

GOLFING

The local golfers are proud of their course, and rightly so. Set among the jumbled hills of the coulee the park is built into, the Hilltop Golf Club has named each hole; names like Calamity, Nobody's Friend, and The Ravine sum up the degree of difficulty this course offers. It is a 1935-yard, sand green course with 9 holes over a par 31. It is a short course but a difficult one, particularly if you play my hook! A small clubhouse has been put near the first tee, but isn't likely to be open except for tournaments. The $5 per day greens fees are collected on the honor system at a box on the first tee, where you will find the scorecards to keep record of your accomplishments. A major tree planting occurred in the spring of 2004, and the course is receiving ongoing improvements to its fairways and greens. The course hosts an open golf tournament on the 2nd weekend in June. The course will not be busy, so you needn't bother with reservations, although you can contact the Park Secretary about arranging your own private tournament.

SPORTS

The park built a spray pool beside the playground in 1995, to keep little swimmers from trying their luck in the pond. The playground itself is a nice one, with swings, slides, merry-go-rounds, and teeter-totters. There is also a creative play center, all merrily painted and sure to be a pirate's ship today or a space station tomorrow, depending on the children's whims. With the exception of the play center, which is built in a sandbox, the playground equipment is all built on a huge, closely mowed lawn. All the equipment was in good repair and brightly painted when we visited. There are also a couple of horseshoe pits, with horseshoes placed in a rack beside them for those interested. The lake or pond is a small one, too shallow to support fish over a prairie winter so there will be no fishing stories at this park! Boating is allowed, but the boat launch isn't a big one, so you may not want to try launching huge boats. Still, water-skiing or tubing would be popular here as the pond is large enough to support that activity.

SERVICES

The town of Hazlet has grocery shopping and gasoline and mechanical services, and the town of Cabri (about 20 minutes north) has medical services as well. The park has no regular concession; something may open up during special events, but you cannot count on that for normal camping. We thought this to be a pleasant little park, with a fun golf course and some interesting things to see for a day or two. I would certainly recommend it if you want peace and quiet as there seemed to be little organized activity in the park so you should be largely left alone. The park was neat and clean, and the basic equipment in good repair. For more information or to arrange a reunion or the like, contact the Park Secretary at:

Hazlet Regional Park
PO Box 62,
Hazlet, SK   S0N 1E0
Telephone: (306) 674-4818.

HERBERT FERRY REGIONAL PARK

Located 26 km north of Herbert, this park can be difficult to find as the roads wander a bit and some of the Regional Park signs had fallen down when we visited. The roads are all gravel and a bit rough in places; just go slow and you'll do fine. As you approach Diefenbaker Lake the road turns sharply right and rapidly descends to the shore. This is a very scenic part of the trip with tall, steep hills crowding the sky and the vision of the deep blue lake ahead. In fact, the scenery is perhaps this park's greatest feature. The building housing the park gate and office (pictured here) has a large map painted on one side that details the purpose of several buildings seen dotted around as you drive in. Of particular note is the old ferry dry-docked just behind the park office, which used to ply these waters in bygone days. A large teepee-like structure rises to the left of the gate, and dominates that side of the park. It is used as a picnic shelter and as a meeting place for the local church groups' vacation schools. No park entry fees were levied during our visit.

SITES

It's hard to say this park has sites as such, for they don't exist in the organized sense. Instead, there are 5 different camping areas and 4 dining shelters. Each area has tables and a fire pit, as well as primitive toilet facilities. When we visited in May we could find no firewood bins or garbage cans in the areas, but we may have been ahead of the park managers' maintenance schedule. The toilet facilities were in need of paint, but they had little odor. The sites themselves had little litter or broken glass to detract from their natural beauty. The roadways serving the sites were mostly dirt tracks and a few low spots may get marshy in inclement weather. Although shaded by the towering hills around them, the park has few trees. Some, near the main playground and dining shelter, have been planted some years before and are now quite large, but most of the park has wolf willow and wild rose as cover.

WATER SPORTS

The park surrounds a natural cove so deep and sheltered as to be safe against the most vicious of storms. Diefenbaker Lake runs west to east just here, and only winds from the northeast can get at boats anchored in the cove. A good boat launch and dock system are complemented by a fish-cleaning shack and another outdoor bench. A large, square-fronted building down by the waterfront has a deep stream running beside it, allowing boaters good access to the snacks and pop on sale. I doubt the building is open on a regular basis, though. Because of the shelter provided, this park is a haven for anglers seeking the sport fishing Lake Diefenbaker offers. I am told whitefish can be caught in the bay, and all the other species are available only a few minutes' boating away. The beach area, beside the playground to the right of the park gate, is nice and shallow, with a sandy bottom. The sand is of variable nature, running from fine to coarse within a few meters. To the right of the swim beach are some clay boulders, remnants of a bygone glacier. There are no buoys to demarcate the swim beach or lifeguards on duty, so swim at your own risk. Still, this is a better area to wade about than the more treacherous lake itself.

HIKING

The hills and valleys of this scenic park beg to be explored. Ruggedly beautiful, the scenery is reminiscent of the Alberta foothills except that there are few trees. Wildflowers abound as does wildlife. Deer signs are everywhere, and antelope often visit the park. Elk are a rarer visitor, and the mournful howl of coyotes praising the moon will add a plaintive note to the evening's campfire. No organized trails have been developed, but there are many game trails to lead you into the hills. Wild cacti are everywhere, so do watch where you sit down for a breather! The park managers don't want motorized vehicles off the roadways, so keep motorcycles, all-terrain vehicles, quads, and trikes back at the camp and leave only your footprints on the hills.

SERVICES

A pay telephone is available at the park gate as is a water tap. The water had a pronounced metallic taste, so you may wish to bring your own drinking water. If you choose to drink the lake water, you may wish to boil it first, just as you would with any unknown water source. There is no concession or store, so you must shop in Herbert, some 20 minutes away. A Heritage Museum is open to the public in Main Center, 13 km away. Although the park offers primitive camping, it is very beautiful and well worth the trip if you enjoy peace and quiet coupled with a chance to hike unhindered. For more information on this park, contact the park manager at:

Herbert Ferry Regional Park
PO Box 190,
Herbert, SK S0H 2A0
Telephone: (306) 784-2921, Fax: (306) 784-3149.

JEAN-LOUIS LEGARE REGIONAL PARK

Located just 1.6 km south of Willow Bunch, off Hwy 36, this park is open from the Victoria Day long weekend in May until the middle of October. The park is dedicated to the memory of Jean-Louis Legare, a pioneer instrumental in maintaining peace during the Sioux crisis after they fled the United States in the aftermath of the Little Big Horn. Set in a small valley filled with tall trees, this is a shady oasis locked away from the world. The road is paved right up to the park entrance with prominent gate signs and a well maintained fence. The park levies a $7 per day vehicle entry fee, waived if you have the annual Regional Park sticker.

SITES

There are 27 sites with 15-amp electrical service and 18 non-electrified sites as well as 6 tent pads as shown in the photo above. The sites cost $18 per night for an electrified site, or $11 per night for an unserviced one. The sites are all built up and drained by a mounded surface. All have picnic tables, firepits with excellent grates, and access to central trash bins. Firewood is delivered to your site upon request; the first armload is free and further armloads cost $3 each. Drinking water is available from central taps. The sites are somewhat variable in size, but in general terms should be big enough for larger units. The tenting pads are all about the same size, about 8 feet by 8 feet, and built up on fine gravel. They are probably the best we'd seen in our travels; really well done. Trees abound in this beautiful park, mostly elm and various cherry with some poplar. Spacing is dense, and most of the trees are over 30 feet tall. Most of the sites are so protected by the bush that you get the feeling of living in a dense forest, not the prairies. Privacy and shade are assured! Three modern washroom facilities serve the campgrounds, flush toilets in the two modern coin-operated shower facilities. As with all things in this park, the facilities were well maintained when we visited. There are two dining shelters, one of which is a gazebo. The gazebo contains a large, gas-fired BBQ that can be rented for $15 per use; the park supplies the propane. There is also a concession that can be rented for your special event for $30 per day or $50 for the whole weekend. Reservations for camp sites are now accepted and various facilities can be rented for private use; contact the park office for details at the address below or by telephone at (306)640-7268.

SPORTS

Since the previous edition, much work has been done on the golf course and its amenities. Grass greens have been installed as well as fairway watering. It is a 9-hole golf course that covers 2949 yards over its par-36 fairways. There is now a pro-shop with equipment rental, and the clubhouse offers a kitchen and concession. They now have golf carts for rent as well. The greens fees are paid there: $14 for 9 holes or $24 for 18 holes, and well worth it for this delightful course. The scorecard also has a map on it to guide newcomers about the heavily treed fairways. You will need tee reservations on this popular course; contact the park office for details. Besides Men's and Ladies' nights, the course hosts many tournaments annually, including the Men's, Women's, Junior's, and Mixed; contact the park office for information. The course is used in winter by cross-country skiers, although nothing is organized by the park managers.

There are also horseshoe pits available, and you can ask the park attendants for one of their two sets of horseshoes. One baseball diamond is available, with a tall mesh backstop and grass infields. There is no charge for use, just go and play and you will usually be joined by other interested players! A well-equipped playground is built under the trees in the day-use or picnic area. It has slides, swings, teeter-totters, merry-go-rounds and a large rocking horse and sand pit. A well-maintained creative play center provides a final touch, with all the equipment built under the trees for plenty of shade, and a generous helping of picnic tables for resting weary bones. There are two hiking trails established to lead the wanderer up onto the prairie to explore the grasslands. The trails are clearly marked by many feet, with short side trails leading off of the main to see items of particular interest. Both trails begin and end in the campgrounds, but no water will be available on the hike, so take plenty with you. The park now operates the swimming pool and ball diamonds in the town of Willow Bunch. The pool offers lessons and public swims; contact the park office for current pricing and availability.

SERVICES

The park itself has a canteen at the golf course, and relies on the town of Willow Bunch to provide for the traveler's remaining needs. A good range of shopping is available in town, as well as the local Health Center and mechanical services. A Heritage Museum showcases local color and history, including the famous Willow Bunch Giant. This is a beautiful, quiet park, well maintained by a staff both caring and proud. They deserve great credit for their hard work in keeping everything so clean with huge expanses of lawns to mow frequently. We thought this park was a good destination, perhaps not for the huge range of physical activity available but rather for the peace, hiking, and golf. It's usually busy on weekends and sometimes during the week as well. For more information on this oasis, contact the Park Secretary at:

Jean-Louis Legare Regional Park
PO Box 93,
Willow Bunch, SK   S0H 4K0
Telephone: (306) 640-7268.

LAC PELLETIER REGIONAL PARK

This park is located 29 km south of Swift Current on Hwy 4, then 11 km west on Hwy 343. It is open from early May until mid-September. The park is situated along the east bank of the 6-km-long lake, but there is development of various sorts all around the lake so this resort is both busy and popular. The park levies an $8 daily entry fee, waived if you have the annual Regional Park pass. They also offer a 3-day pass for $12 that covers the weekend.

SITES

There are 120 electrified sites with 30-amp service and water hookup, and 50 non-electrified sites, renting for $18 per night per unit or $11 per night, respectively. Electrified sites rent for $115 per week or $750 for the whole season. Note that any other unit sharing your site must also pay an extra fee. There are numerous campgrounds to choose from: The Point, Darling's Beach, Lakeside, Meadow, Ona's or Glade camping areas. Register for a camp site at the new park office at Darlings Beach. You can't miss it; it's across from the golf course, just to the west of the road as you drive in. There are two park gates, one at each entrance, that have new brochures with maps. All sites are naturally leveled and drained, and have picnic tables, firepits, and access to central trash bins; firewood is available fro sale at $3 per bucket (it's a big bucket!). Chlorinated drinking water comes from deep wells and is piped to central taps in each area. Sites are shaded by many tall poplars that have been planted over the years. Generally speaking, the sites should be large enough for the biggest unit although some sites are larger than others, the majority of which are the "back in" type. Washroom facilities vary from primitive biffies in the camping areas to modern flush toilets in the shower house where coin-op showers cost a loonie per use. The trailer dump station is located on the east side of the road between the Meadows campground and the driving range. There are 4 dining shelters available in various campgrounds, used on a first-come, first-served basis. There is family or group camping available, but the park office requires notice beforehand. Note that reservations for individual sites are not normally accepted but accommodation will be made for large groups or travelers; contact the park office for details at the address below. A large hall is also available for rent, annexed to the golf clubhouse. It costs $200 per day, and is rented by the Lac Pelletier Park Office. The hall features an electrified sound stage and a 300-person capacity. As it also hosts many functions throughout the year, such as the "Annual Opry" in July, reservations for this popular venue start early in the year, with choice weekends booked as much as a year in advance.

GOLFING

There is a 9-hole, sand green golf course set among the hills to the east of the road as you drive past the hamlet of Darlings Beach. Construction of grass greens will begin in 2004, making this a very interesting course indeed! It has 2618 yards of watered fairways over its par 34, with plenty of vertical change to challenge the unwary. Greens fees are modest, costing $10 for 9 holes or $18 for 18 holes. The course was in excellent shape when we visited, well mowed and with a fine view of the resort from the hills behind. There is a driving range with a simple pro-shop renting clubs and carts as well as retailing a small line of balls, tees, and needful items. A fully licensed clubhouse offers light meals as well as beverages to complement its fine view of the first tee. Tee reservations are recommended during the peak season, by calling the pro-shop at (306) 627-3419. This is a popular course, evidenced by the number of local tournaments on offer during the season. The hall annexed to the clubhouse is operated by the Park Office, so contact their management for bookings. The arcade/mini-golf/gift shop across the road also has a mini-golf course costing $3 per round as well as a line of movie rentals, souvenirs, local crafts, Lac Pelletier postcards, etc.

SPORTS

The spring-fed lake is an obvious magnet for anglers, swimmers, and boaters. It is about 6 km long and about a half-kilometre wide on a north-south axis. There are two boat launches with single docks to get your boat into the water, and parking for trailers in behind the boat launches. Anglers will enjoy the perch, walleye, whitefish, and pike-fishing this stocked lake offers. Bathers will enjoy the three sunny, sandy beaches and the buoyed swimming areas provided. There is one set of swimming lessons offered in July, with all the Red Cross Aquaquest levels taught, as well as Bronze Cross and Life Saving 1–3. For prices and registration, contact the park office. All lessons are taught at the Darling's Beach site, as it is closer to the store, washrooms, and arcade. There are 5 playgrounds in total in the park, spread out over the major campgrounds. Among them, they have slides, swings, teeter-totters, merry-go-rounds, a sand volleyball court, and horseshoe pits. Baseball is popular, with many tournaments both private and public hosted throughout the season. There is one permanent diamond and 4 temporary ones available for slow pitch. Although the park doesn't maintain any hiking or cross-country skiing trails, both activities are popular in season. Birding is also prominent as this basin is home to many bird types because of its trees and water.

SERVICES

The park has a fine store that sells a wide range of camping needs from grocery to small hardware. Fresh bread and buns are sold every Friday at 1500 hr, plus the usual iced treats, snacks, candy and pop are available. The grill serves hamburgers, sandwiches, and a daily breakfast special. The store hours vary with changing demand, being open from 0800–2200 hr on weekdays or from 0700–2400 hr on weekends in July and August. A new development is "Clancy's On The Beach," a full-menu restaurant that will also cater your private function; contact them directly at (306) 627-3206. They are open from 0700–2100 hr daily in season. Campers requiring more extensive purchases, or services like mechanical, medical and worship, are invited to Swift Current where local businesses await. The Hackers Lounge and hall is the scene of much that makes this park so special, from dance lessons to live entertainment and dances as well as cash bingos and crafts, bake sales, and flea markets. It seems there is always something going on in the hamlet of Darling's Beach, and the natural beauty of the hills and lake combine to make this a popular park. For more information on this park or to book your special event, contact the park office at:

Lac Pelletier Regional Park
PO Box 12, Site 6, RR1
Wymark, SK   S0N 2Y0
Telephone: (306) 627-3595 in season or (306) 627-3622 (winter);
Fax: (306) 627-3582.
E-mail address is lacpelletier@t2.net.

LEMSFORD FERRY REGIONAL PARK

The park is located 21 km north of Lemsford or 26 km south of Glidden on Grid Road 649. The park is located in the South Saskatchewan River valley, just past the south ferry landing. It has plenty of river fishing, quiet campgrounds, and a swimming pool. It is open from the Victoria Day weekend in May until the beginning of October. The park levies a daily park entry fee of $6.50 per day, waived if you have an annual Regional Park sticker.

SITES

There are 60 electrified sites with 15-amp service and 20 non-electrified sites. The rental fees are $11 per night for an electrified site, $8.75 for a non-electrified site, or $6.50 for a tent. The non-electrified sites are located to the left of the pool, down the slump and onto a wide glade bordered by tall trees to the south and the willow brush-covered riverbank to the north. All sites have picnic tables, trash bins, and pole BBQs. Some of the unserviced sites had firepits as well, but we could find no firewood. The central drinking water taps were disabled so the river water available had to be boiled before consumption. Except for the pool house and its modern toilets and showers, the washroom facilities were vault toilets. The serviced sites were somewhat close together, but still had a border of trees and were large enough for a good-sized unit. The unserviced sites were large enough for a bus! To register, simply drive in and set up; the manager will be along later on his evening rounds. If you wish to contact the manager, his trailer is just east of the park office, on the first right turn.

WATER SPORTS

During our original visit in 1997 we noted the pool wasn't open due to a problem with the pool liner. Special fundraising paid for the necessary repairs and the pool reopened in 2000. Since then, however, the park has fallen on hard times and had to cut back expenses so the pool remains closed although they plan to reopen it in the future. When open, normally late June to mid-August, the facility offers swimming lessons and public swims, and has change rooms and showers. The showers are usually free to registered campers, but the facility was closed during our visit so we couldn't verify that. There is a playground just behind the pool that has a mini-golf course and a trampoline, both available for a modest fee payable at the booth. The playground itself has swings, slides, teeter-totters, and a creative play center, all in reasonable repair. There is a canteen beside the pool that operates when the pool is open and offers the usual iced treats, pop, snacks, and candy. As the pool was closed, so was the canteen when we visited. The river running along the park is fast and treacherous, and I cannot recommend any one swim in it, or even wade in it as the currents can be deceptively swift. Fishing is excellent as walleye and pike abound, and goldeye, sturgeon, and black mariahs can also be taken. The ferry landing doubles as the boatlaunch, but there is no space to park your trailer so you must bring it to your site. There was no fee for this service when we visited.

SERVICES

The park has a hall just behind the playground that can be used as a beer garden and cabaret venue. There are several horseshoe pits in front of the hall, maintained by a local horseshoe club, and tournaments are held regularly, with entertainment provided at the hall. For rental information, contact the park office at the address below. The park is situated among the coulees and hills of the river basin, so there is plenty of hiking to be had. There are no trails or guides, but there are many flowers, plants, and animals to see in the hills. Much of it will be on private property, though, so you should ask permission before you set out. There will be little drinking water on the hike, so take plenty with you. The park has no shopping amenities outside of the canteen, depending on local towns to provide that. Leader, about a half-hour's drive south and west of the park, has a full range of shopping, medical, mechanical, and worship services, as well as a trailer dump station at one of the local service stations. This park is a quiet one and although reservations are accepted they generally won't be needed. If you want peace and quiet and prefer to amuse yourself, then you'll enjoy this park; if you want plenty of activities and lots of infrastructure, you probably won't. For more information on the park or to arrange a private function, contact the park secretary at:

Lemsford Ferry Regional Park
PO Box 97,
Abbey, SK   S0N 0A0

MCLAREN LAKE REGIONAL PARK

Located 29 km southwest of Richmound, the park can be difficult to find if driving up from the Golden Prairie access. We found Grid Road 637 to be difficult to follow and the park poorly signed if coming through that community; the park is much easier to find when coming from the Richmound access. It is open from the Victoria day long weekend in May until the middle of September, and features water skiing, jetboating, and peaceful camping. The park levies a $5 daily entry fee, waived if you've purchased an annual Regional Park sticker.

SITES

There are 25 electrified sites, with 15-amp service, and two large open spaces used for groups and non-electrified camping. Sites cost $10 per night for an electrified site, or $8 per night if you do not plan to use the power. The sites all have picnic tables, trash bins, pole BBQs suitable for charcoal cooking, and firepits. Drinking water is available from central taps, and is chlorinated well water. Firewood is available free from central bins. The electrified sites are bordered by groves of tall willows that provide shelter on three sides; the non-electrified sites have shelter on one side. Planted elms and shrubs provide some greenery for relief, and the park is extensively grassed. The sites are all naturally leveled and drained, and sufficiently large for most units. Washrooms vary from primitive biffies in the campgrounds to modern flush toilets in the shower house. Showers are provided free to registered campers, and a free laundry service is available in the utility room behind the concession; just bring your own soap. There is a dining shelter available, with a large, sturdy charcoal BBQ outside. Located near the beach, it is admirably suited as a focal point for family gatherings or private functions. The park allows site reservations, although they will seldom be needed. To reserve a site, call the Richmound Rural Municipality office at (306) 669-2000, or the park manager's office (in season) at (306) 669-4824.

WATER SPORTS

Although the lake had receded in the past few dry years, it is now refilling its basin and is once again safe for water-skiing. A boat launch with a single dock provides access to the lake, and there is plenty of trailer parking just beside the boat launch. Anglers can try their luck with the pike and perch that breed in the lake. A buoyed swimming area is backed by a large expanse of lawn, upon which the playground equipment (built in 1985) is located. Unfortunately, lack of interest has meant there are no swim lessons offered, but with the lake reviving the managers are planning to offer them again if demand warrants. The playground has the usual slides, swings, teeter-totters, and climbers, all brightly painted and in excellent condition. There are horseshoe pits as well, with equipment loaned from the park office. Just behind the playground is the canteen and park office which is usually open from Friday to Monday, 1100–2200 hr, depending on demand. The canteen offers the usual iced treats, snacks, and pop, as well as a selection of grilled fast foods including some great onion rings, according to one of my experts!

SPORTS
There are two baseball diamonds, one of which has a tall mesh backstop on wooden poles and an elevated announcer's booth, and the other of which is the overflow camping area and so it isn't as well maintained. The main diamond has bleachers, plastic mesh home-run fencing, and is in excellent condition. Both have grass infields and outfields and benches for the players.

A 1500-yard, par-3 "pitch and putt" golf course has been built along the road as you drive in. It has 9 holes with sand greens and an honor box on the first tee to pay the greens fees of $1 per round. This is an excellent facility to teach children to play golf, as it is within the range of most kids to hit a short iron into play. The fairways are naturally watered, somewhat narrow, and fairly straight. There is no scorecard as yet, but the managers hope to have one printed soon. There is very little challenge for an experienced golfer, but plenty of fun for a children's tournament or workshop.

SERVICES
Beyond the food sales at the canteen, there is very little to purchase in the park. The nearest hospital is in Maple Creek, about an hour away. Richmound offers a complete range of shopping, mechanical, and worship services. The park hosts an annual Slow Pitch tournament on the second weekend of July, and an annual July Sports Day. The park is rebuilding its clientele after several dry years and so it is a peaceful place. Many residents of Alberta enjoy this park for its quiet charms, particularly on weekends when boating and bird watching are the main activities. For more information on this park, or to reserve a site, contact the Park Secretary at:

McLaren Lake Regional Park
PO Box 150,
Richmound, SK S0N 2E0
Telephone: (306) 669-2000; Fax: (306) 669-2052.

NOTUKEU REGIONAL PARK

Adjacent to the town of Ponteix, the park is open from May 1 to October 15 annually. It is a small municipal park with tennis courts, a golf course and a swimming pool. The park levies no daily entry fees, but campers are expected to have an annual Regional Park sticker.

SITES

There are 18 electrified sites in the park, plus a large, non-electrified group camping area. Sites rent for $20 per night for an electrified site, and $8 per night in the overflow or group camping area. All sites are naturally leveled and drained, and have picnic tables and trash cans. There were no pole BBQs or firepits in the sites. A large fire pit in the picnic area can be used only with the written permission of the park manager. A central water tap provides Ponteix municipal drinking water. A trailer dump station is available free for registered campers. The sites are all well shaded with tall poplars on three sides. They are all "back-in" style, and should be large enough for the latest campers. Washrooms in the shower house to the right of the pool are modern, with flush toilets and free showers and are wheel chair accessible. Registration is easy: simply pull into the site of your choice and set up, then pay all applicable fees at the swimming pool just beside the campgrounds. No reservations are accepted, except for groups or reunions; contact the park secretary at the address below for details.

WATER SPORTS

The swimming pool is open from mid-June until the end of August, from 1300–1700 hr, and from 1800–2100 hr. There are two swimming lesson sets offered in July, with all Red Cross and RLSS levels costing between $15 and $23, depending on level desired. For information on lessons, contact the pool at (306) 625-3587 in season, or the park secretary at (306) 625-3724. The aquatic program also includes various "Fun Days," where participants can bring water guns, have their faces painted, or other fun stuff. Daily pool entry costs $2, with annual family passes being $75. There is a 1 meter diving board, shade trees lining the secure fence, and a large expanse of lawn to rest upon while waiting for swim lessons to finish. A well-treed playground has teeter-totters, swings, climbers, slides, and merry-go-rounds. As with all equipment in this park, it is well maintained and brightly painted.

GOLFING

The Ponteix Town 'n Country Golf Club is a fine, 9-hole grass green golf course available just behind the campgrounds. The course covers 2383 yards over its par-33 fairways, with many watered holes where local creeks and rivers cross the fairway. The fairways themselves are irrigated and well mown, so they are a treat to play. Greens fees are modest at $14 for 9 holes or $24 for 18 holes; a cart trackage fee of $2 per 9 holes is also levied. Fees are paid on the honor system, with a drop box on the first tee. A scorecard with course map is available from the clubhouse near the first tee or in the drop box. Although a concession is open during tournaments, one will usually have to make do with the clubhouse pop machine. Tee reservations are not normally needed; if the first tee is busy just hang on a bit and you'll be away! The park hosts many tournaments locally throughout the season, as well as provincial tournaments like the High School Sand Green Golf Championships. If you'd like to make your own arrangements, contact the park secretary at the address below, or by telephone at (306) 625-3882.

SERVICES

The park also has two tennis courts and a ball diamond. The diamond has a tall mesh backstop on wooden poles but no other equipment. The town of Ponteix has all the shopping, worship and mechanical services you'll need, as well as a health clinic. This is a quiet park that enjoys it's pool and golf course. The park will rarely be full, except when a reunion is on, and even then it will be a quiet place. The golf course is delightful, and I'm sure your little ones will appreciate the outdoor pool on a hot summer's day. For more information on this park, contact the park Secretary at:

Notukeu Regional Park
PO Box 513,
Ponteix, SK S0N 1Z0
Telephone: (306) 625-3587 in season; Fax: (306) 625-3204.

OGEMA REGIONAL PARK

Located on the south side of Ogema on Hwy 13, the park opens on the Victoria day long weekend and closes in the middle of September. This is a municipal park that has tried to maintain some of the local history, as evidenced the large covered grandstand pictured here; it has been given a new coat of paint and roof since our last visit. Daily park entry fees of $3 per vehicle are waived if you have an annual Regional Park sticker.

SITES

There are 8 electrified and 25 non-electrified sites in the park, renting for $12 and $8 per night, respectively, and another 6 electrified sites with water have been added. Fees can be paid at the pool if open, or wait for the manager to visit about supper time. All sites are naturally leveled and drained, and shaded from at least one side by willows and cottonwoods. All sites had picnic tables and pole BBQs, some in need of repair, and access to Ogema municipal drinking water from a central tap. Each electrified site has its own water supply. Firewood was provided free from a central pile, although it needed to be cut to length. Trash cans are centrally located. Washrooms are modern, with flush toilets and free showers in the shower house, all wheelchair accessible. A small laundry was also available in the building; there are no charges for its use. Generally, the sites needed some cleaning and we though the cover was sparse. The shower house has been renovated recently and is clean, neat and brightly painted. Reservations are accepted for sites but generally won't be needed. More importantly, the park has a huge indoor recreation facility that (in winter) has artificial ice for skating, hockey and curling. In summer it can host up to 1000 people for weddings, reunions and the like. For more information, contact the park board at the address below.

BASEBALL

There are 5 diamonds in the park, with the biggest facility in front of the historical grandstand pictured above. Built decades ago, it has been meticulously maintained so it is still quite useable to this day and is the most striking building of its sort in the park system. The other diamonds have smaller bleacher sets for spectators, and all have dirt infields and grass outfields. Home-run fences are wooden rails on short wooden poles. As one can imagine, this is a popular facility locally for ball tournaments, drawing players and spectators alike from communities all over the region.

SPORTS

The town of Ogema has a municipal golf course with 9 holes and sand greens just south of town, but as it is a municipal facility it isn't discussed here. There is a mini-golf course just beside the heated swimming pool that costs $1 per round; equipment can be rented from the pool staff. The pool itself is open from late June to late August, depending on weather conditions. It offers two sets of swim lessons, with all Aquaquest levels costing $15 per level if you've a season's pass; $20 without one. The season's pass costs $75 for a family and $40 for an adult. The pool is open from 1300–1800 hr daily on weekends for public swims, and 1300–1700 hr and 1800–2030 hr on weekdays. There is also a 0630–0830 hr Early Bird swim. The pool has change rooms, showers, and a small line of chips, pop, and iced treats for sale. For more pool information, or to register a student, contact the pool office at (306) 459-2557 in season. A fine playground is located between the pool and the campgrounds with slides, swings, teeter-totters, merry-go-rounds, and a large creative play center. All the equipment is in good condition, and some of it appeared new when we visited.

SERVICES

The indoor recreation complex has a grill that is open during ball tournaments and during the Fair Day. This is usually held on the second weekend in July, and features pet shows, a parade, games for the little ones, and various displays in the rink. A similar event is the Museum Day, where the local historical society puts on active displays of pioneer activity at the excellent museum on the north end of town. This miniature village has various shops and buildings complete with the hardware and displays of materials that existed when this province was young. During the Museum Day these displays come alive as practitioners invite the curious to help make rope from twine, or work the bellows at the blacksmith shop. This is a fascinating time to visit, but the times will vary depending on other events. The town of Ogema has a wide range of shopping and mechanical services for the traveler, and I thought it a nice touch that a local church held its service in the park picnic area the Sunday we visited, and followed it with a picnic cookout. This is a quiet family park in a community that prides itself on its history. We enjoyed our stay, and I hope you do as well. For more information, contact the park managers at:

Ogema Regional Park
PO Box 342,
Ogema, SK   S0C 1Y0
Telephone: (306) 459-2709.

ORO LAKE REGIONAL PARK

This park is a phoenix, rising anew from the ashes of neglect. Abandoned in the late 1980s due to a receding waterline, a new park board has been formed and the park is gaining a new life of sorts. Located 3 km east of Ormiston, off Grid Road 606, the park keeps irregular hours. In its rebirth, the park board decided to reduce usership and thereby expenses at the park. Thus, the park sees campers when local events warrant—a good thing really, as the current buildings and equipment are in good condition; it would be a shame to see it simply waste away. There is no daily park entrance fee as no one manned the park when we visited.

SITES

The park is very scenic but has almost no shade. There are 18 sites, 6 of which are electrified with 15-amp service. Sites rent for $5 per night although there was no fee collection system in evidence. A safe assumption is that the manager will come around in the evening to collect site rental fees. The sites are on the west side of Oro Lake, with toilets and water spigots centrally located. The sites have pole BBQs and new picnic tables. Piles of waste wood were available for fuel, and most needed to be cut into suitable lengths. Trash bins were centrally located and consisted of recycled oil drums. The sites were placed in brush thickets for shade, as this predominantly grasslands park has few trees of its own except for the tall cottonwoods in the concession and playground area. The brush is mostly hawthorn and chokecherry, tall enough to provide some shade but very little for most of the day. The sites are not bordered, being more open, so it really feels like one big group site. The toilet facilities have flush stalls draining to septic tanks, but they are in need of some maintenance. There are two dining shelters in the campsite area to the right as you drive in. Both are in fair condition with cement floors and open sides. Reservations are not accepted, nor will one be required in this park, as the only time it sees real traffic is during the annual events.

WATER SPORTS

The swim beach has suffered from the shrinking water table and is now bordered by rotting vegetation. A beach concession has not opened in several seasons except for special events. The beach change rooms and showers have not been serviced in a long while and so are not useable. The attendant washrooms are in poor shape but still functional. A well-built playground (pictured above) with slides, swings, teeter-totters, merry-go-rounds and climbers sits in a large sand pit. The mini-golf and paddling pool have been removed.

SERVICES

A ball diamond near the beach concession has a tall mesh backstop and a grass infield. The equipment is serviceable but somewhat age worn. A line of tall poplars offers shade and benches offer respite for spectators and players alike. Currently, the town of Ormiston has no services, so you must shop in Crane Valley, Ogema, Avonlea, or Bengough; all are about a half hour drive away. The park runs a few roping events throughout the summer, a ranch rodeo on the August long weekend and a sports day on the second weekend of June. The hall can be rented for private functions for $200. For more information on this park contact the park board at:

    Oro Lake Regional Park
    PO Box 25
    Crane Valley, SK   S0H 1B0
    Telephone: (306) 475-2264

PALLISER REGIONAL PARK

The park is so named because Palliser and his group camped in the spot in 1857, according to his diary! Situated in a coulee on the east shore of the old South Saskatchewan River system (pictured here), this park's glory is the scenery that abounds. If one travels along Hwy 219 from Saskatoon, you cross Lake Diefenbaker using the large, 18-place Riverhurst Ferry. This marvelous service was launched on July 14, 1967, the same day that the Park itself was opened by Premier Ross Thatcher. Those using the ferry should note that it is a 24–hour, free service. It travels from the west shore to the east hourly on the half hour, then from east shore to west every hour on the hour. It departs promptly, so don't be late! As you drive in from the entrance gate, the first thing you see is a modern resort village, the Diefenbaker Cottage Development. 104 lots were leased from the Palliser Regional Park Board, and 100 summer homes adorn the plateau above the lake. A permanent trailer court has been established for persons wishing a seasonal lot, and the spaces fill quickly, creating a waiting list for the tardy! Daily park entry fees of $7 per vehicle ($16 for a 3-day pass) are waived if you have an annual Regional Park sticker.

SITES

There are 106 electrified sites and 44 non-electrified sites, with water pumps dotted throughout the campgrounds. The water is potable without treatment, but it does taste faintly of the plastic used to pipe it about. The cost of the sites is $16.50 per night for an electrified site and $12.00 per night for an unserviced site. Full serviced sites cost $19.50 per night. Sites can be rented seasonally as well; contact the park office at (306) 353-4604 for more information. It is of particular note that no firepits or BBQs are available in the sites for evening campfires or cookouts. Campers are expected to provide their own firepits and must be prepared to cook with their own camp stoves, although firewood is available. The sites themselves are predominantly naturally drained, and quite a few are naturally leveled and so may not be suitable for trailers; the gate staffers are aware of this and will assist you in choosing a suitable site. They have site plans available for their campers so finding your site is made easier. If you'd like our advice, we thought that sites numbered in the high 50s and 60s were the nicest for shade and proximity to the many features this park offers. One even had an old tractor wheel for a fire pit! There are 3 group camping sites available, one holding 16 units, the other 8 units. A new one has been built holding 24 fully serviced sites. With the popularity of family reunions and other such activities, these sites are best booked well in advance, as the camp kitchen is integral to that kind of fun! The camp kitchen can be rented for $50 for the first 3 hours, $10 per hour after that.

The sites are screened with bushes like saskatoons or chokecherries, and the majority of the planted species are poplars and doing very well. They are about 20 feet tall now, and well placed to provide the maximum in sun and wind relief. Not every site will have them, though, and the planting continues so be prepared for a bit of variety! Instead of having all their playground equipment placed in one large area, several small playgrounds dot the camping areas so that a set of swings and a slide are never far away. The toilet situation is handled in a similar fashion as many "His and Hers" duets are scattered throughout. They are well maintained, clean, and odor-free, but you should take a flashlight with you at night as the ones we looked in had no electrical lighting. A new shower house/ laundry facility was built in 2003; the showers are free and the laundry is coin-operated.

GOLFING

My own golfing experience is not great, but I do know that the Riverbreaks Golf Resort, built on 157 acres of land leased from the Regional Park, will gladden the heart of any golfer from basher to pro. I didn't have a great deal of luck on the course as it favors the straight tee shot and mine is anything but, and I did have some difficulty with finding the hole, but all in all I thoroughly enjoyed my visit. The course is built right into the texture of the coulee so you will find a motorized cart to be a useful addition. You can walk the course, but I think you will enjoy the scenery much more if you don't! The course can be very steep at times, but the view from atop the coulee is spectacular, particularly as the shadows of evening herald the setting of the sun; the sunset vistas in this park are special as you face the width of Lake Diefenbaker with the far shore to frame the sun's rays. Definitely bring your camera! The greens fees are $19 for 9 holes or $30 for 18, but the challenge of the course more than makes up for it. Golf carts can be rented for the same price as the round of golf chosen. The course can be booked for tournaments, and reservations can be made by calling the pro-shop at (306) 353-2065. The resort boasts a restaurant and bar, and serves an excellent hamburger and fries combo. Although it can be narrow, the course is well maintained and has excellent grass greens and well-mowed fairways. The rough is nasty, though, as the natural shrubbery masks errant golf balls with incredible speed. My overall impression is that this course is a must for golfers who would camp as well.

WATER SPORTS

Another feature of this park is the heated swimming pool. It offers lessons during July and August, is well staffed and maintained, and has a large lawn area for lazy afternoon sunning and Frisbee games. The pool costs $3 per day per person, and lessons cost between $15 and $20 per set. Sufficient space exists for a pickup game of baseball, and an old school house has been moved onto the park to serve as a canteen or tuck shop. The hours will be about the same as the pool keeps, and that will vary according to season and lesson plan. Just beside the pool complex is a miniature golf course. No fees were posted at the time we checked, but all equipment and rentals were dealt with at the canteen.

Not to be forgotten is the admirable beach that seems to run the entire circumference of the lake! The sand quality varies widely, as with any natural setting, but the majority is good fine sand. Some clay deposits will help in keeping the sand castles together, and a few pebbled areas were evident. The beach was in good shape with few firepits and broken bottles to be seen, a comment that favors the whole park, really; everything was kept well tidied. There is no cost to using the beach, but no facilities are available.

Last but not least of this park's charms is Lake Diefenbaker itself. Long, wide, deep, and filled with 30 varieties of fish, this lake can be dangerous to the novice boater, but it is an angler's dream! Every Father's Day the park hosts the Walleye Classic. Sponsored by the Riverhurst Recreation Board, this catch and release derby is very popular, having been written up in Sports Illustrated. To take advantage of this, the Regional Park Authority now includes the Rusty Coulee Marina, a natural inland port. It has boat launches, 120 host docks, and an aquatic service station for fuel and the like. Boat and sea-doo rentals are not always available, but check at the marina for more details.

SERVICES

The park has food services at the pool concession and at the clubhouse restaurant. Telephone service is available in the park as well. The Mainstay Inn is now within park boundaries. It is a hotel-motel convention center that also offers great family dining. Contact them directly at (306) 353-2077. The town of Riverhurst has shopping and mechanical services, as well as a small museum depicting local history, fossils and Native artifacts. They can be viewed at the Fossil House and F.T. Hill Museum. Boat tours can be arranged with Sask. River Tours by calling them at (306) 353-4603. The Riverhurst Lions Club has provided a large playground across from the pool and organizes pancake breakfasts every Sunday morning starting in July. This is a busy park with many activities to accommodate a wide variety of interests; for more details about the park or arranging a site, contact the park Secretary/Treasurer at:

Palliser Regional Park
PO Box 89,
Riverhurst, SK S0H 3P0
Telephone: (306) 353-4064, Fax: (306) 353-4644
Website: www.saskparks.com/palliserpark.htm

PINE CREE REGIONAL PARK

Located 19 km east of Eastend or 32 km west of Shaunavon, this park is open from the Victoria Day weekend in May until the middle of September, although the main campground never really closes as cross-country skiers enjoy the challenge presented in the hills. The park levies entry fees of $6 per day, waived if an annual Regional Park sticker is purchased. Pine Cree Regional Park started out as Bakers Coulee; Everett Baker was instrumental in starting the park and helped with the formation of the regional park.

SITES

The Pine Cree Main campgrounds are truly magnificent. If you've ever camped among the Cypress Hills and wished for peace and privacy, then this is your campground. There are 27 deliberately unserviced sites in this area; the managers decided to preserve as much as possible the natural beauty of this area. As you drive down from the plateau you are confronted with a split in the road; turn left and you camp along the creek, turn right and you'll camp beside the towering hill. All sites are naturally leveled and drained, which can be a problem in a heavy rain, although the soil will soon soak up the excess. The narrow steel bridge you must cross to get to the right-hand campsites has been widened but it may still be a barrier to large motor homes. All sites have steel-framed picnic tables, trash bins, and firepits. The latter are made from half-inch thick steel pipe donated by the firm that put the oil pipeline through here, and will "outlast the next ice age," according to the park secretary. They have a swinging grate on top and are very user friendly. Firewood is sold for $3 per 10 "sticks," some of which are 24 inches across, so definitely bring your ax! The woodpile is found just to the right as you drive in on the plateau. All sites are shaded by huge lodgepole pines, poplars, and various willows and alders, offering almost complete cover and total privacy. The sites are arranged in small groups so you have at most 3 neighbors, or you can have a very private function. There are two dining shelters with stoves and picnic tables, and the drinking water is from a deep, cold well. It may be untreated but it is wonderful! If I may be so bold, site #13 (to the right) has a dining shelter and the well pump just across from it, and so it has almost all the amenities. Washrooms are "Port-a-Potty," pumped out regularly, and can be a bit of a walk from your site, depending on where you are. They were clean and odor free, so we had no complaint. Registration is easy; simply pull into an open site and wait for the manager to collect the fees around supper time. There is group camping available; contact the park office for details. Sites can be reserved by calling the park secretary at (306) 297-2038.

SPORTS

Baseball is popular throughout the province, and this area is no different. There is one ball diamond on top of the plateau at the main campgrounds, to the left as you drive in. It has tall metal mesh on steel poles for backstops, and all the equipment is in excellent shape. Infields are dirt, with grass outfields and benches for players. Hiking is popular in the park, as there are tall hills with sub-alpine pastures in which to roam at the main site, plus hiking along the creek to find those elusive trout! A major paleontological dig that unearthed a dinosaur skeleton can be viewed about 5 km from Eastend; follow the signs to the dig. One can wander about a bit as well as see what a dig looks like. All the hikes have no watering points, so be sure to bring some with you. None of the hiking trails are marked, but foot paths have been worn in the hill sides to guide you. You may wish to purchase a topographical map of the area to assist your wandering feet, particularly as the hills behind the park beckon. Of immediate interest in the main campground is the old Hermit's Cave (opposite page). A re-creation has been dug into the hillside on the east face of the hillside as the original was in danger of caving in. The story is that a university researcher made the original cave as his home while he studied the local area; people hardly ever saw him, hence his nickname "The Hermit." There are 2 playgrounds in the main campgrounds with a swing set and a slide each. Although the playgrounds are in good shape, you may wonder why the paucity of equipment? This is due to the huge hills and the lodgepole pines that live on them. What child can resist climbing among the exposed tree roots or clambering up the hills? Add to that the babbling brook in which to throw stones, and you soon see that building a playground is largely unnecessary! Adults can enjoy the park by wandering the hills by day looking for birds or sub-alpine plants or lying on a blanket in the upper meadows star-gazing, all in a quiet, natural environment. The stars, by the way, seem so close you can reach out with your mug and scoop up the Milky Way; it was a fine night!

SERVICES

The town of Eastend has all the shopping, mechanical, medical, and worship services that the traveler can ask for, as does nearby Shaunavon. The local historical museum is well worth the price of admission for the insights into local legends that it offers. I personally found the story about the home-built aircraft particularly interesting. Anyone spending time in the area would be well advised to visit the local paleontological site, about 5 km out of town, as the Tyrannosaurus rex skeleton found there is a popular artifact at the moment. Those wanting a quiet, natural setting and need few amenities will find the main campground to be all they could hope for. It is our belief that this park is a destination in itself for the peace and natural beauty captured for all to enjoy. For more information on this wonderful place, or to book your own function, contact the Park Secretary at:

Pine Cree Regional Park
PO Box 428,
Shaunavon, SK   S0N 2M0
Telephone: (306) 297-2038.

PRAIRIE LAKE REGIONAL PARK

Located just 20 km (12 miles) south of Beechy on Lake Diefenbaker, this park was built in 1984. It is open from the May long weekend until the September long weekend, and features bountiful water sports on beautiful Lake Diefenbaker, including a deep marina capable of taking fixed-keel sailboats. Hiking and scenery among the hills surrounding the park also make this a special place. The road into the park winds a bit, but is well marked and graveled so it shouldn't pose a problem. Daily vehicle charges of $5 per day are levied, waived if you have an annual Regional Park sticker.

SITES

The park is naturally divided into two discrete areas by the folding of the shoreline. The south campground has the fully serviced sites, while the north campground has the marina, beach, picnic grounds, and daily sites. There are 5 serviced sites with 15-amp electrical supply and 8 unserviced sites, with 10 more planned for the next year. These sites rent for $12 per night or $50 and $40 per week respectively, and include a picnic table, pole BBQ, and trash can. All sites are mounded with gravel pads for drainage, and the roadways are in excellent condition. The water supply is not safe for human consumption and must be boiled prior to drinking. The sites on the northern tip of the park will be an amateur astronomers dream as you'll have the endless vista of stars above and to the north with no light pollution! In addition, there are 84 fully serviced, seasonally rented sites in the south area that cost $450 per year; at this price it's no wonder that most of these sites are rented annually! All trees in the park are planted ash and poplar, so shade is variable depending on where you stay. Mind you, give the park a few more years to mature and you won't lack for tall trees! Washroom facilities are modern, with two shower houses (one in each area) complete with flush toilets. Showers are free to registered patrons, and are now wheelchair accessible. A trailer dump station is available, free for registered patrons. A dining shelter is available in the day-use area near the beach, with picnic tables and a large charcoal BBQ. Groups are welcome, and reservations are accepted by calling the park secretary at (306) 859-2067.

WATER SPORTS

Lake Diefenbaker is the focus of this park's activities, as evidenced by the fine marina and boat launch. The park has built a jetty out into this deep water harbor that allows for almost any craft that plies the lake to find safe harbor. A large parking area just behind the boat launch stores boat trailers, and the lake itself offers many adventures. There is plentiful fishing for all anglers, including many spots to land the big one from shore. There's a fish-filleting shack near the boat launch. A small cove hides the buoyed swim beach from boaters, and offers swim lessons in the first two weeks of August. Contact the park office at the address below for details or to register a swimmer. The swim beach has fairly coarse sand with many small pebbles, but is deep enough to hold many sunbathers. Although the beach is a bit small, the water quality is great; clean and sheltered, there is little danger from waves or sudden dropoff. Pets must be kept leashed and are strictly prohibited from the beach. There is also a large cement fire pit available for a beach fire and singsong, and firewood is available from a central bin. For those wishing a more extensive package, "Betty Lou" boat tours can be arranged by calling (306) 846-2005. Although tours vary depending on scope of rental, you can see the Sand Castles and Sunken Hill, among other wonders. A playground was built in 1993 in the day-use area, and includes slides, swings, and climbers, all in a large sandbox. There is some shade, and the proximity to the picnic area, beach, and shower house make this a busy place!

HIKING

Although there are no established trails as yet, the park is working on marking the most popular ones for all to enjoy. The scenery is wonderful, and wildlife is plentiful. Deer and elk are common sights in the park, and there are many plants to see in their natural habitat. Drinking water will not be found on the trail so bring your own supply, and you may want to bring a topographical map of the area. Sunsets over the lake can make for stunning photography, and many an amateur has taken calendar-quality shots from this area. As the park secretary writes "If you have a bleeding heart you can cure it in one week in this beautiful park." Another popular naturalist hobby in the area is bird watching, as many species either travel through here or make this their summer home. Bring your binoculars, hiking boots, a day pack for water and trail eats, and be prepared to enjoy some of Saskatchewan's famous Silent Space!

SERVICES

There is a concession and grocery store in the park that sells summer needfuls including ice, and people needing further shopping, medical, mechanical, and worship service can get them all at Beechy. The park is a busy one on most weekends in July and August, particularly during the Canada Day celebration with its fireworks, beer garden and supper, and musical performances. Another popular annual event is the August Long Weekend, where a stage is set up for Karaoke, a beer garden and bandstand. The park is a quiet one at night, but the lake and hills are very busy by day. Everything is in excellent condition, brightly painted and well maintained, all to make your stay enjoyable. For more information on this park, contact the park secretary at:

> Prairie Lake Regional Park
> PO Box 406,
> Beechy, SK   S0L 0C0
> Telephone: (306) 859-2067, Fax: (306) 858-2069.

ROCKIN BEACH REGIONAL PARK

Located 6 km east and 3 km north of Rockglen, the park occupies 200 acres on the south shore of Fife Lake. The road serving the park is paved but in disrepair, as are so many of Saskatchewan's highways. Fife Lake had been receding in the past few years, only recently refilling its basin. With the shrinking lake, park usage had dropped and many of its facilities lay unused. The park is once again rebuilding, and is working with the rural municipality to mow and grade the park's grass and roads. Of interest is the fact that this is the first Regional Park to declare itself a "Dark Sky Preserve," reducing the amount of light pollution it gives off such that amateur astronomers can enjoy the vastness of our night skies. Hopefully, the rest of the province's parks will follow suit! The park is open from the Victoria Day long week end in May to the middle of September, and levies a $5 park entry fee, waived if you have an annual Regional Park sticker.

SITES

There are 25 electrified and 50 non-electrified sites in the park, costing $12 and $10 per night respectively. The electrified sites are supplied with 30-amp service for operating motor home air conditioners. A simple site map showing park facilities is available. All sites have picnic tables and pole BBQs, and a few sites have firepits as well. No firewood is provided by the park, so bring your own. Trash cans are centrally located, as are drinking water taps. Washroom facilities are modern, with flush toilets and hot showers available in two shower houses. They may not be electrified as yet, so bring your flashlight for any night-time visits! Shade is provided by groves of elms, poplars, and carraganas throughout the camping areas. All sites have some shade, and all should be big enough for the largest unit.

WATER SPORTS

The lake had been receding in the 1980s drought years but is now refilling its basin. Windsurfing, kayaking and canoeing, jet boats and water-skiing are once again popular. A boat launch is available, but the dock is out of the water at the moment. The low water levels resulted in serious fish loss due to winter kill, so the park and the province are restocking the lake with pike and perch. The beach is groomed so that weeds are kept back and the sand is coarse with many small pebbles. There is no swimming area buoyed off, nor are there any swimming lessons offered. A waterfront concession is open during tournaments, and can be rented for private functions. It has a kitchen for grilled food as well as fridge and freezers for pop, snacks, and iced treats. A playground is located beside the concession with fancy climbers (one is shaped like an octopus), rocking horses on springs, and the usual swings, teeter-totters, slides, and merry-go-rounds. All the equipment is built into a well grassed area with a large parking space.

BASEBALL

The park has five ball diamonds with wire mesh backstops and benches. The fields have grass in and outfields, and there is ample parking for spectators. Although it has simple equipment, the park hosts several large celebrations in July when 15 teams compete for the top prize. A quonset hut with a cement floor functions as a dance hall, cabaret, or beer hall, and a large marquee tent can be erected beside it to accommodate extras. The hall rents for $40 per day, as does the concession nearby.

SERVICES

Besides the above mentioned sports, the park also hosts a Ranch Rodeo and a CCA-sanctioned rodeo, in mid July and in mid August, respectively. The trees planted in the park offer local bird life a place to feed and nest, so birds congregate here from all over. No hiking trails have been established but you can wander for a long distance over the low, rolling hills in the park, observing birds as they go about their business. The town of Rockglen has a Health Center as well as food and fuel services. More extensive shopping can also be had in Coronach, about 20 minutes away. This park has lain dormant the past while due to a dropping water table, but it is making a comeback. For Rockin Beach, 1997 was a rebuilding year and the managers thank their patrons for the patience shown. Since then, the park has removed the golf course and, as mentioned above, declared itself a Dark Sky Preserve; they are concentrating on bird watching, water sports and quiet family camping. As the park revitalizes itself, it will once again be the summer's source of fun it was in the 1960s and 1970s. They are now hosting Family Fun Days, Youth Dances, and an "Arts in the Park" weekend where you can watch decorative benches being built, then bid on your favorite (among other artistic endeavors). For more information on this park, contact the Park Manager at:

Rockin Beach Regional Park
PO Box 13
Rockglen, SK   S0H 3R0
Telephone: (306) 476-2388, Fax: (306) 476-2503 Winter Contact: (306) 476-2505
E-mail address is: haywir@sasktel.net

SHAMROCK REGIONAL PARK

Located 20 km (16 miles) north of Gravelbourg off of Hwy 58, this park is open from the Victoria Day long weekend in May until the Labor Day long weekend in September. The 8 km of gravel road had been freshly resurfaced just before our visit, so the trip is a pleasant one. First built in 1961 on 55 acres of land beside the Wood River (pictured here), the park has seen constant revision every year since. It features a natural wooded area with a pool, golf, and ball diamonds. The park charges a $5 daily entry fee per vehicle, waived if you have an annual Regional Park sticker.

SITES

There are 100 electrified poles in the park and about 40 non-electrified sites. There really aren't assigned sites with numbers as such; simply drive in and find the site you want then set up. Sites rent for $12 for an electrified site or $10 for a non-electrified site. You can also rent weekly ($50 per week), monthly ($175 per month), and seasonally ($300 for the whole summer). The idea of sites that aren't arranged into numbered order seems a bit confusing at first, but it really reflects the concept that families and small groups often travel together. In this way, the entire park is like a group site; it just depends on how cozy you want to be. This way, you can all share a sense of community among the mature forest in this scenic park. Sites have picnic tables, pole BBQs, and trash cans. Firewood is available free from central bins, and drinking water is available from central taps. Washrooms are modern in the two shower houses, with several primitive biffies in the various camping areas. A pleasant note is that the ladies' washrooms all have baby change tables as part of their equipment. The shower house near the pool also contains the park laundry, which costs $1 per load, payable at the concession. Pets are allowed but they must be leashed at all times. A fine map of the park is drawn on the back of their brochure, complete with a map key. There is no reservation system available as there is no way to keep track of non-numbered sites.

SPORTS

The park has a wonderful river running through it, but there is little fishing to be had. The outdoor swimming pool opens in the last weekend of June, closing on the Labor Day weekend. There are change rooms and showers in the pool house. The rectangular pool has a 6 foot maximum and a 3-foot minimum and offers two lesson sets in July. Swimming lessons cost as little as $15 to $40 per child, depending on which Aquaquest or Lifesaving level is needed. Public swims cost between $1.50 and $5, depending on age, or you can purchase a family season pass for $75. Contact the pool office for details at (306) 394-2028. There are 4 playgrounds in the park with most of the regular equipment among them, including some very nice creative play centers. There are 3 ball diamonds in the park in one field, with mesh backstops on wooden poles, benches for players, and bleachers. The infields are grass, and there is plenty of spectator parking. A popular local tournament occurs on the second weekend of July with the Annual Sports Day. Perhaps the most popular activity in the park is wandering along the river, berry picking or bird watching among the trees that line the banks of the Wood River. One can also canoe the river, but there are small shallow areas that can cause trouble. There are many birds that make this park their home, and their glad song fills the day as you go about your business.

GOLFING
There is a 9-hole golf course in the park, the Parkview Golf Club, with sand greens and a clubhouse. The course covers 2130 yards over its par-34 fairways, and keeps the river or its ravines in play for as much of the game as it can. There are no pro shops, cart rentals, or other amenities, but the greens fees are $5 per day, so this is a great course to begin teaching your own Tiger Woods on! The fairways are in good shape, and the bush lining them is very rough in places. Mind you, there are berries to be had, so knocking a ball into the bush isn't quite the penalty it first seems! The course hosts a tournament that draws well locally on the third Sunday in July. There will normally be no need for tee times, so there is no method to reserve one. If you wish to discuss your own private tournament, contact the park office at the address below.

SERVICES
The park has a fine concession that offers three meals a day; this is the first time the park is trying this for the whole year! It is open from 0700–2200 hr, with breakfast served from 0800–1000 hr daily, and also serves the iced treats, snacks, and pop one expects in the summer. Persons wishing to make larger purchases must go either to the village of Shamrock or to Gravelbourg. Either community will have grocery and mechanical services, and Gravelbourg has medical and worship services as well. This park had an interesting time of it during the spring flooding of 1997, and the people we talked to during our visit had many adventures to discuss; if they hadn't been so specific about the damage I wouldn't have known any had occurred! This speaks volumes about how well the maintenance people did their jobs, and the pride the park takes in its appearance. We found it to be a pleasant, peaceful place, and we hope you do as well during your visit. For more information, contact the park office at:

    Shamrock Regional Park
    PO Box 113,
    Shamrock, SK   S0H 3W0
    Telephone: (306) 394-4269 (concession, in season), Fax: (306) 648-3594
    Website at: www.shamrockpark.ca

SYLVAN VALLEY REGIONAL PARK

Located 2 km south of St. Victor and 1 km west of St. Victor's Petroglyphs Provincial Historic Park, this park is open from the Victoria Day long weekend in May until the Labor Day long weekend in September. The park is in two parts; the campgrounds set among the hills and woods in back of the town, and the museum, pool, and shower house in the town itself. The park levies a $5 per day vehicle entry fee, waived if you've purchased an annual Regional Park sticker.

SITES

There are 20 electrified and 30 non-electrified sites in the park, costing $7 for the first night and $5 for each following night for the electrified sites, and $5 for the first night and $3 for each successive night for the non-electrified sites. Registration is by drop box, with envelopes available at the entrance. The access road is paved right into the park, and the parks roadways are in good shape. All the sites have pole BBQs, picnic tables and firepits made from steel wheels. The sites are naturally leveled and drained, and aren't really established as to boundaries, so it is difficult to say how large they are. They are spaced sufficiently so that they should house the largest units, but that is variable. The mature willows and elms that shade the park are over 30 feet tall, and offer a constant forest feel to the entire park. Firewood and drinking water are available centrally, as is trash disposal; you'll need to split your own firewood. The washrooms are primitive biffies and in excellent condition, although there are hot showers in the town park site, with modern flush toilets in the shower house which is fully wheelchair accessible. There are no family or group sites available in the park; groups will simply be accommodated as needed. With the exception of the motorcycle rally in June, site reservations won't normally be a problem so no method exists to accept them.

SPORTS

The park has two ball diamonds with tall mesh infields and benches for players. A fine, large beer garden is available, as well as two booths labeled "Hot" and "Cold," open during tournaments or private functions only. The town venue has a small pond known as Jubilee Beach in behind the shower house with a diving board, a good sand bottom, and free showers in the shower house. There are no swim lessons offered, nor are there any lifeguards in attendance. Pond use is free with a Regional Park sticker. There are two horseshoe pits in the main campgrounds, but no equipment is available. There are two playgrounds in the park, one by the pool and the other beside the day use or picnic area in the campgrounds. The campground play area had a set of swings and a large merry-go-round. That there isn't much equipment reflects the fact that many children will climb the trees like squirrels anyway, so why invest heavily in equipment when Mother Nature has provided! The Petroglyphs are a short walk away and well worth seeing. Not only is the scenery worth a long look, but the rocks are covered with ancient drawings of animals and people. The hills also beckon wandering feet as there is a lot to see in the many draws and coulees. There are no established hiking trails, nor will there be any water service so remember to bring your own.

SERVICES

Most services are available in Assiniboia, about 30 km to the north. The town of St. Victor has few services or visitors, except when the Motorcycle Rally is on during the second weekend of June. At this time, over 1,000 bikers make the park one of the largest towns in the area. 1997 marked the 18th consecutive year for this event, so you know it will be continuing. The park also operates the Angus McGillis Heritage Site in town, a reconstruction of the homestead built in 1870. You can go on a self-guided tour through the old house and see artifacts from that era. There is no entrance fee, and I thought it to be very interesting. The shower house also functions as a meeting place where locals can play cards of a weekend, or gather for functions. The park is quiet, well maintained, and very pretty for the hills and valleys it highlights, as pictured above. For more information, contact the park office at:

Sylvan Valley Regional Park
PO Box 61,
St. Victor, SK   S0H 3T0
Telephone: (306) 642-4049

THOMSON LAKE REGIONAL PARK

Located 8 km north of Lafleche, or 12 km south of Gravelbourg on Hwy 58, this was the first park in the Regional Park system. The lake was created by the PFRA dam on the Wood River in 1958, and the park is located on 110 acres of gracefully treed, well grassed lake side land. Park info is available on a local FM band radio station; tune in as you enter the park for up-to-date information. It is open from the Victoria Day long weekend in May until the Labor Day weekend in September. The park levies an $8 daily vehicle entry fee, waived if you have purchased an annual Regional Park sticker.

SITES

There are 125 electrified sites in the park, costing between $21 and $17 per night, depending on whether or not you will need full hookup; non-electrified sites cost $12 per night. There are also 133 seasonal sites; they are very popular in this pretty resort, so you'd be well advised to call the park office for details on seasonal renting. "C" loop has 35 electrified sites for daily rentals, and 25 full-service sites are also available. "A" loop has sand pads for tents, improving drainage should the rains come on. One large family or group site is available on a private loop, capable of holding 200 people. There is one dining shelter in the picnic or day-use area just beside the pool. There are many privately owned cabins in the park, and some owners are willing to rent; make your needs known to the park office and they may be able to help. All sites are leveled and drained with gravel pads, and an excellent map to the sites is available as you drive in. The sites have picnic tables, firepits with grates, and access to central trash cans and water taps. Firewood is available for sale at the concession. The sites are heavily treed, with many mature elms and poplars growing between them, and thousands more planted throughout the park. Washroom facilities are modern, with flush toilets in the areas and in the coin-operated shower house. All the washrooms and the shower house are wheelchair accessible. The shower house also holds the park's coin operated laundry facility. A trailer dump station is available just to the right as you drive in the main gates. This park is very popular and quite busy; call ahead for reservations at (306) 472-3752 in season; 24 hours notice is the minimum normally accepted.

WATER SPORTS

The park has a fine marina with a boatlaunch, a filleting station and washroom facilities. There is a large parking lot for boat trailers, and ample dock space. The lake is stocked annually with pike, walleye and perch so angling is popular. Water-skiing, jet boating, and canoeing are also regular pastimes on this busy lake. The sand beach with a dock has eroded away, and the boat docks have changed due to erosion, but the marina is still in good shape. The center of aquatic fun is the swimming pool. Built in 1975, it is a half Olympic-sized pool with change rooms and showers. There are 2 diving boards, one of 3 feet and another of 6 feet. The pool ranges in depth from 3 to 12 feet, with a grass border running around it. There is one playground beside the pool, with swings, slides and a creative play center, and another playground beside the shower house with teeter-totters and climbers. There is a wading pool on the side, and an old pool has become an open-air auditorium which hosts Wednesday night bingo. It is large and has an excellent roof, making it quite popular for family gatherings; contact the park office for rental details. A volleyball net is available in front of the pool house. The concession by the pool offers the usual lines of treats, snacks, and pop, as well as light grilled meals like burgers and fries. A video arcade, the park library, and a line of camping supplies complete their services. They are open from late June to mid August, keeping pool hours of 1000–2200 hr. Three 2-week lesson sets are offered in July and August; contact the pool office for more details at (306) 472-5685 in season.

GOLFING
The park boasts one of the best golf courses in the area, with a 9-hole, grass-green course complete with a fully licensed clubhouse. The clubhouse restaurant is open from 0900–2100 hr and offers a range of meals for the hungry golfer. The Thomson Lake Regional Park Golf Course covers 3500 yards over its par-36 fairways, with practice putting greens and equipment rentals. The pro-shop has a line of golfing accessories as well as clothing with the park logo; you can also rent clubs and carts. The course itself is a gem, relatively flat but with water in play and curved fairways to keep the shanker unhappy. The fairways are clearly bordered by a variety of planted trees, some of which are very mature. It is well groomed and watered and worth the greens fees of $13 per 9 holes or $21 for 18 holes. Many golf tournaments are run annually with dates somewhat variable, so call ahead for details. Reservations are recommended; call the pro-shop at least one day in advance at (306) 472-5686.

SPORTS
There is one ball diamond in the park, with a tall mesh backstop on metal poles, gravel infield, and benches for players. Ball isn't as popular as it once was, so the space occupied by another ball diamond has been turned into a sports complex with volleyball courts, basketball half courts, and horseshoe pits, all fenced by new tree plantings. A BMX bike track has been built just behind the ball diamond, with many humps and valleys to challenge the contestants. There is one hiking trail along the lake that is about 1.6 km long. Marked with a sign, you should have no trouble following it.

SERVICES
Besides all the above activity, the park offers bingo every Wednesday night, as well as a rec. program for kids; they can register at the old campground office. A monthly jam session is held in the shelter built over the old paddling pool, and has become quite popular. There may not be enough seats, so bring your lawn chairs. Several of the local families have earned high praise for their singing voices, so this is a real treat. The park runs a "Park

Day" where the usual park pass is invalid and a special levy of $3 per adult is charged. There will be BMX races, stage shows, a fish derby, ping-pong ball drop, and fireworks. Besides the concession, the nearest shopping is in either Lafleche or Gravelbourg, with museums, mechanical, medical, and worship services available in both communities. This is a busy park, and popular not only locally but in an increasing area as well. For more information on this park, contact the park secretary at:

Thomson Lake Regional Park
PO Box 520
Lafleche, SK   S0H 2K0
Telephone (306) 472-3752 in season; Fax: (306) 472-3113
Website: www.thomsonlake.com
E-mail: tlrp@lincsat.com

WOOD MOUNTAIN REGIONAL PARK

Located 8 km south of the village of Wood Mountain, this park began as a lease to the Wood Mountain Turf Club in 1927. The lease was extended to the Wood Mountain Recreation Club and now hosts one of Canada's oldest rodeos. The rodeo grounds are pictured here, as seen from on top of the hill in back of the Rodeo Ranch Museum. The park is open from May 1 to the Labor Day long weekend in September, and is the camping gateway to the Grasslands National Park (East Block). The park charges a $6 daily vehicle entry fee, waived if you have an annual Regional Park sticker.

SITES

There are 60 electrified (15-amp service) and 27 non-electrified sites in the park, costing $16 per night and $10 per night, respectively. There are also a few sites with both electricity (30-amp service) and water, renting for $22 per night. Most sites are very large and built into natural tree shelter comprised of poplars, birch, willow, native cherry and saskatoons. Some of the trees are quite tall, and the cover is fairly dense, giving the camper a sense of privacy. Some of the newer sites are built into the field a bit and bordered by the brush only at the back. The park has planted trees between the sites, but they will take a few years to catch up to the rest. The group camping or overflow area is essentially unlimited as the field surrounding the rodeo grounds will fill. All sites have picnic tables, pole BBQs, and access to central trash bins. Water is piped directly to some sites while most have access to central taps. The water supplied is from a deep well and very refreshing. Washroom facilities vary from primitive biffies in the camping area to modern flush toilets and coin-operated showers in the shower and laundry house. Showers cost 25¢, clothes dryers cost 50¢, and the washers cost $1 in quarters. A trailer dump station is located beside this facility as well. There are two dining shelters available in the park, and firewood is available for sale. Reservations are no longer accepted.

WATER SPORTS

The outdoor heated pool originally built here was the first one outside a major city in southern Saskatchewan. It is open from mid-June to the September long weekend and offers three sets of lessons in July and August. Lessons cost $20 to $70, depending on which level (Red Cross or RLSS) desired; contact the pool office at (306) 266-4936 for more details. The pool has daily public swims, priced by age, and a seasonal family pass is also available. The facility is being expanded to accommodate a paddling pool for the younger folk as well. The pool is rectangular and varies from 3 to 8 feet deep; the diving boards have been removed. The pool provides the park's only access to recreational water, and was filled with happy, shrieking children the day we visited! There is a crafts program available free to registered campers, operated beside the museum. The playground is beside the pool, and was extensively renovated in 1990. It has teeter-totters, slides, swings, climbers, and fanciful rocking horses. As with all equipment in this well-maintained park, the playground features bright paint and neatly trimmed lawns.

SPORTS

Hiking is popular in this park, with a well-groomed trail worn through the prairie to the Wood Mountain Provincial Historical Park a kilometer or so away. This is a partially restored North-West Mounted Police post originally built to monitor Sitting Bull and the Sioux who sought refuge here after the Little Big Horn battle. The museum showcases NWMP history as well as the Sioux who visited. It is free and well worth the afternoon you'll spend walking over and about. A cairn on top of the hill behind the Rodeo Ranch Museum commemorates the work of Jean-Louis Legare, who was instrumental in keeping the situation between the Sioux and NWMP peaceful. There are various meanders through the park's hills and coulees that will show you some wonderful vistas as well as the short grass prairie. There are many plants, animals, birds, and berries for you to discover in this interesting park. For those wishing more extended hiking, the Rodeo Ranch Museum has information on the Grasslands National Park, the East Block of which is only 20 km south of the park. In any case, there will be little water and no amenities at all on the hike, so do take the usual precautions of taking extra water, some food, and a map and compass.

There are also several horse trails for those so inclined, although there are no rental animals available in the park. Some of the local ranchers may have horses for rent, so do ask at the park office if you're interested. There are facilities to corral and feed horses in the park if you wish to bring your own, and feed can be purchased locally if you need. As this park is very proud of its rodeo heritage (this is the site of the Wood Mountain Stampede, held annually on the second weekend of July since 1908), one would expect that there be an emphasis on maintaining livestock. The annual rodeo is a major affair in the area, with musical performances in the large hall, a beer hall, and a major rodeo with all the excitement and color that brings.

The park has a ball diamond with a tall mesh backstop on wooden poles, benches for players, and grass infields. A well-attended local tournament is held on the second weekend in August. There are also horseshoe pits available.

SERVICES

The park operates a concession that sells the usual iced treats, snacks and pop, as well as a selection of light meals from their grill. A diner also sets up operation in the hall during rodeos. The hall is a large one, complete with stage upon which various entertainers thrill their audiences. A George Fox concert played to a full house in late August! The park also hosts a Cowboy Poetry Festival on the last Sunday in July. The Rodeo Ranch Museum is well stocked with memorabilia from the many years of the Wood Mountain Stampede, as well as offering a glimpse into the colorful local history. What school child has not heard of Sitting Bull and his Sioux warriors? Entry fees are $2 per adult, $1 per child, and pre-school children are free. There are guides to answer your questions, and I found them to be veritable fountains of local lore; if you intend to walk over to the Provincial Historical Park, you'll do well to begin your tour here. This museum also has much information to assist you if you intend to enter the Grasslands National Park, so do take a look. The town of Wood Mountain has few services, as they depend on larger communities like Assiniboia, about 70 km away, for medical, mechanical, and larger shopping services. We very nearly ran out of gas, but a bulk fuel dealer filled up a gas can for us that allowed us to find a service station! Limerick, 50 km north of the park on Hwy 358 has groceries and fuel. For more information, contact the park office at:

Wood Mountain Regional Park
PO Box 7,
Flintoft, SK S0H 1R0
Telephone: (306) 266-4208
Website at www.woodmountainpark.ca

CYPRESS HILLS INTERPROVINCIAL PARK

This is the only Interprovincial Park in Canada as it crosses the border with Alberta. Although the two provinces do not share park administrations, they clearly share a unique and truly beautiful resource, the Cypress Hills. Rising 600 meters above the surrounding plains, these are the highest point of land between the Rocky Mountains and the Laurentian Mountains many miles to the east. As such, they house plants and ecosystems unique to Canada, and offer a wealth of recreational opportunities that remain as valuable today as in 1931 when the Saskatchewan government legislated this special place be put aside for future generations. Since then, this park has become the "crown jewel" in the provincial park system, offering an incredible array of cultural, historical, botanical, paleontological, and recreational opportunities for the discerning visitor. There are three distinct areas: East Block, Center Block, and West Block. The East Block is located around Eastend and is not part of the Interprovincial Park system. The Center Block is the most heavily developed with lakes, electrified campgrounds, swimming pools, 4-star resort and extensive cottage developments. The West Block, extending into Alberta, is considered a wilderness area and although it has campsites, none are electrified. The Center Block is located 30 km south of Maple Creek on Hwy 21 and then west on Hwy 221, the park access highway. The West Block is accessed from Hwy 227 (turn west at the Maple Creek Hospital); more will be said about this access in the West Block section. The campgrounds are open from the Victoria Day long weekend in May and close on the Labor Day weekend. Some fall camping is available and the park remains open during the winter for cross-country skiers.

CAMPING

The park has an amazing range of sites available, from truly rustic to full service; whatever you want by way of camping experience, this park can make it happen! Interestingly, there is a payphone at the entrance to each campground. There are a total of 6 camping loops as well as 8 group camping areas to discuss, comprising an impressive 394 single-unit campsites; the number that can fit in the rustic and group sites is difficult to enumerate but is probably another 240 or so sites. Yet the park is so busy that they are developing one of the old overflow areas to accommodate the new style of larger units! As the two Blocks (Center and West) are so disparate, I will consider them separately.

CENTER BLOCK

This is the most heavily developed part of the park, home to most of the amenities and the trappings of civilization. As one drives along Hwy 221 past Loch Lomond (home to a private cottage subdivision) one comes up to the park entry gate and kiosk, just at the entrance to the resort community; here you will pay your entry fees and be given a map to the area. Driving past the swimming pool and up the hill to the left of the entry booth you see a road to your right, just at the corner, with a mini-golf and gas station; that road is Pine Avenue, which provides access to the hotel/resort complex as well as several residential summer camps that operate in the park, and terminates in the campground entry office. Here you will be assigned your campsite, assuming you haven't already reserved one, and pay the camping fees for your stay. There are 4 main campgrounds accessed from this entry, beginning with the Pine Hill Campground off the main road to the right as you drive by. All four share the main sewage dump station located along the main road just before the Main Core Area. The park has a total of 145 sites available for reservation by calling (306) 662-5484 after the first Monday in June, or by email, fax and letter after January 1 each year; see the contact information in the "Services" section. As a generality, the park is changing over to metal-framed picnic tables so you'll only see the older wooden ones in the overflow camping if at all. They're also in the process of changing over to firepits from the older pole BBQs, another excellent idea if you ask me; I prefer the functionality of the firepit to the smaller pole BBQ. There is a secure trailer storage compound across the road from the campground office. Should you require this service, all arrangements can be made at the office; a nominal daily fee is levied.

Pine Hill Campground has 85 non-electrified sites, mostly of the "V" type wherein your unit is parked on one branch and your tow vehicle on the other. They all have picnic tables and firepits, are built onto gravel pads, and have little undergrowth between the tall pines. For this reason the campsites are somewhat open with little privacy, although you'll have excellent shade from above. The campground shares three water taps and several vault-style toilets, and has access to several firewood bins; trash bins are also centrally located. The campground shares a new service center with the Warlodge Campground a short distance away. The service center features 6 showers and three flush toilets per side; two of the showers are wheelchair accessible. There is ample parking in front of the service center as well as a large lawn to rest on while waiting for the rest of your party to clean up.

The Warlodge Campground is located a short distance south of Pine Hill; simply continue past the Amphitheater Parking access (where one turns for Pine Hill) and turn right into the campgrounds. This one is laid out in a doughnut shape, with an outer ring and an inner ring connected by a gravel road. All 79 sites in this loop are electrified with 30-amp service, and most of the sites are of the "V" style. This loop has 5 "double" sites, large enough for two units to park, and a Campground Host at site 75; it even has a small playground behind site 50. All sites are cut from the mature aspen, spruce and pine forest, and as such have much better privacy although the trees are a tad shorter than the taller lodgepole pines found elsewhere. The sites are leveled with gravel pads and have picnic tables and firepits; potable water taps, vault toilets, trash and firewood bins are all shared. As stated above, this campground shares the Pinelodge Service Center (shown here) with the Pine Hill campground; you can drive over or walk the well-established trail which starts from between sites 9 and 11.

TERRACE

Continue past the Warlodge entrance to the Terrace Campground; you'll drive past the exit to Rainbow campground first. This campground is built on the side of the hill in four terraces (hence the name) and has 90 camp sites, seventy of which are electrified. Although tall lodgepole pines provide adequate shade, there is little ground cover or underbrush so the sites are quite open. Built predominantly in the "back-in" style, they are large enough for most modern units. Each site as been leveled with gravel and has a picnic table and firepit. Flush toilets, firewood and trash bins, and potable water taps are all centrally located. The campground has its own playground (across the road from site 40) and its own service center with hot showers and washroom facilities. The service center has hot showers and flush toilets and isn't as wheelchair accessible as is the Pinelodge facility. Of particular note is that the electrified sites #1–9 (odd numbers only) are the most generously spaced in the campground while sites #71–90 at the top of the terrace are all non-electrified.

RAINBOW

The Rainbow Campground entrance is located a short distance along the road past the Terrace entrance. There are 70 sites here, of which 38 are electrified with 30-amp service, plus a further 10 are full-service sites. Two of the electrified sites (#7 and #8) are wheelchair accessible, and the campground host can be found at site #4. Nine of the full service sites are pull-through; the remaining sites are all "back-in" style, with leveled gravel pads and firepits. The flush toilets (with sinks), firewood, trash bins, and water taps are all centrally located. The unisex service center has 3 flush toilets and hot showers, one of which is wheelchair accessible. As with most of the camping in this park, there is plenty of shade from the tall pines but little side-to-side privacy. One swing set has been placed behind site 16, and all the non-electrified sites are located along the outside (eastern) loop of the campground so they are a bit more spacious. All 70 of the sites in this campground can be reserved by calling the park office at (306) 662-5484 after the first Monday in June or by email, fax or letter after January 1 each year.

LODGEPOLE
The other two campgrounds in the park are located outside the campground entry office road; you must still stop and register before setting up your site, however. The Lodgepole Campground is accessed from Pine Avenue by continuing past the campground entry office then turning right on Valley Trail. As with most of the other camping available, there is good shade but little ground cover so the sites, although large enough, have little privacy. There are 20 electrified and 5 non-electrified sites in this campground, sharing potable water taps, firewood and trash bins, and flush toilets. The campground host is located at site #20. Lodgepole has no service center but it is by far the smallest and therefore quietest of the park's campgrounds.

DEER HOLLOW
The last of the park's campgrounds is Deer Hollow, located a short distance past Pine Avenue; there will be a left turn just before the golf course. This campground is best suited for tenting, small trailers or truck campers only, and has some of the most unique sites in the park. There are 35 non-electrified sites built onto gravel pads, some of which are elevated; all the sites have firepits and picnic tables. Sharing the same tall pines found elsewhere, this area also has some ground cover so the sites are a bit more private than you might expect. Although the roadways are gravel there is little dust. The sites all share vault toilets, potable water taps, firewood and trash bins; interestingly, the otherwise impeccable campground map this park offers does not include Deer Hollow! Should you decide to stay here, and I highly recommend you do, we thought the sites numbered in the teens were the best of the bunch. This campground, by the way, is the one used for fall camping as it offers the best tenting sites in Center Block.

THE MEADOWS
The Meadows Campground deserves special mention for two reasons: it is being transformed into another electrified campground with up to 80 more sites. The construction of Phase One should be complete by the start of the 2005 camping season, with further sites, a service center and playground planned for future construction. A trailer dump station across the Bald Butte Road from The Meadows will be on line for the 2006 camping season. It also hosts the largest enclave of amateur astronomers in western Canada. The

annual Saskatchewan Summer Star Party gathers nearly 200 stargazers yearly, with many wonderful telescopes set up to capture the heavens. One fellow had the good fortune to find a comet (and the wits to recognize it as such) in 2001, for which remarkable event the park has erected a monument at the entrance to The Meadows Campground. It was this gathering of amateur astronomers that led to the naming of the Cypress Hills Interprovincial Park as the first "Dark Sky" preserve in the province; the remaining provincial parks will follow suit in time. Although The Meadows is reserved entirely for the astronomers during their August gathering, the public is welcome to walk in and see what all the fuss is about. If you ask politely (and never, EVER shine a flash light about) they will let you see some truly wondrous things through their telescopes. The problem is keeping it all straight after a while! For more information and the dates of future star parties, check out the society's website at: http://duke.usask.ca/~ges125/rasc.

GROUP CAMPING

That's only the registered campsites; there are 7 group camping areas available, none of which is shown on the campground map although they are all itemized on the park map. They all share the same basic features, though; with the exception of Valley Trail Group campground which has 11 electrified sites as well as several non-electrified ones, none have electrified sites. They have drinking water taps throughout as well as shared trash and firewood bins. All the group sites have a dining shelter, picnic tables and firepits or pole BBQs scattered around a central gravel roadway. All the toilet facilities are vault style, and none of the group sites have service centers so you'll have to drive over to one of the other campgrounds to use theirs—I'd recommend the Pinelodge Service Center as it is the largest. The largest group sites are on top of the hill along Bald Butte Trail: (listed from south to north) Sunset Campground (14 sites), Aspen Grove Campground, and Horseshoe Campground (both with 8 sites). These are still linked to all major amenities by paved highways or excellent pedestrian walkways (for more on those, see the section on hiking trails). The Hidden Valley Trail links Loch Lomond and its private cottage subdivision to the rest of the park, and dotted along this road are three more group sites: Shady Nook Campground, Hidden Valley Campground, and Lone Pine Campground. These three group sites are capable of hosting up to 40 to 50 people in reasonable comfort. The last group site is also my favorite for the quality of shade and privacy offered in a scenic hilltop package: Valley Trail Group Camping, located just across the road from Lodgepole Campgrounds, with 11 electrified sites and several non-electrified ones. The group camping sites can all be reserved for your gathering by calling the park office at (306) 662-5484 after the first Monday in June for the current calendar year or up to two years in advance at any time. Just a note, though: these very popular group sites will go quickly, so you'd best reserve yours early!

WEST BLOCK

There are three rustic campgrounds available in the West Block, accessed by gravel road. The drive in is an adventure itself, as the paved part of the road is very steep and winding; I cannot imagine how the truly big units would fare here, particularly those in tow. None of the sites are electrified, there are no service centers, all the toilets are vault style, and the camping is somewhat more relaxed as there are no "sites" per se; there are a number of pole BBQs and picnic tables scattered in each campground, but they are not the limiting factors here. What you will find in the West Block is peace and quiet; there is none of the crowding, hustle and bustle, or noise you may experience in the much more heavily developed Center Block. Here you can hike in the hills and see nobody else all day, fish the Battle Creek population of sassy brook, brown and rainbow trout for your supper, and listen to the coyotes howl their loneliness while the stars dance about. Yes, I really enjoyed my stay in the West Block and so will you, but be forewarned: you must be self-sufficient. Drinking water can be boiled from Battle Creek, or you can obtain potable water from the Ranger Station where the payphone is located.

The Equestrian Campground is just that: reasonably extensive corrals with 12 or so picnic tables and pole BBQs in a semicircle around the perimeter of a small clearing. The self-registration kiosk is located just beside the corrals. There is a large firepit in the middle of the clearing near which is the firewood bin. There is adequate shade and excellent ground cover in the dense aspens, but all sites are very open to the front. I was told of the many trails that weave their way through the forests and hills from this spot, making trail riding a popular pastime with this spot as the terminus. You'll have to make your own fodder arrangements though (pelletized commercial feed only permitted).

Just at the bottom of the hill, not far from the Ranger Station, is the first of the tenting campgrounds. There are several picnic tables and pole BBQs scattered in a small clearing, sort of a group site if you will, as well as a number of walk-in sites along the creek just past a small line of trees. You can see these from the road, but just barely! There are two vault toilets here as well as shared firewood and trash bins; drinking water is only available at the Ranger Station. Set yourself up and then self-register at the kiosk beside the entrance.

Following the Elkwater Road west, one finds the second campground just past a small wooden bridge. Turning north into this area, one sees the wooden arch of the old Boy Scout camp which this camp once was. There are a scattering of 14 or so picnic tables and pole BBQs as well as two vault toilets and one dining shelter; these are drive-in sites and end at the fence. Water can be drawn from the creek but you must boil it before you use it; cattle abound in this part of the park and they use the creek as well! Firewood and trash bins are centrally located, and you self-register at the kiosk as you drive in. I found the walk-in campsites right along the creek to be among the best in the park; shady, cool, and scenic with the tall hill to the north across the creek and access to a fishing pond a short distance down stream.

SPORTS

The park is well aware of its unique natural surroundings and works very hard to offer a wide range of activities while still preserving the fragile environment. They do a remarkable job of it, as there is something here for just about every outdoor enthusiast except the motorized ones; there are no off-road vehicles allowed. Snowmobiling is permitted in a designated area in the Center Block but not until adequate snow accumulates to protect the fragile native prairie environment. Due to rapidly changing weather conditions, the area is opened or closed on very short notice. Otherwise, you can get just about anywhere with "two feet and a heartbeat."

HIKING AND CROSS-COUNTRY SKIING

The park has built up an impressive repertoire of hiking trails, some of which are wheelchair accessible and some which require greater mobility. Obviously, the same trails one can hike by summer are for the cross-country skier in winter. The park offers 28 km of trails, of which 15.5 km are regularly groomed. The system wanders throughout the Center Block with excellent scenery amid the towering pines and snow-bound valleys. You should know that the park can receive up to 2 meters of snow each year, often followed by warm chinook winds out of the Rocky Mountains; it was for this reason that early First Nations people wintered here. Because of the dramatic shifts in weather and trail conditions, you should contact the park office prior to your winter visit to check things out. The park office number is (306) 662-5411; on weekends call the Cypress Hills Resort Inn at (306) 662-4477.

Threading through all the campgrounds, for instance, is the Woodlands Trail, which terminates just behind the beach change house on Loch Leven in the heart of the Main Core Area. Just before that terminus, a side loop called the Windfall Trail leads one off to discover that natural feature over approximately 1 km on the loop. One can use the Woodlands Trail from all four main campgrounds to access the Amphitheater and the Firepit when those facilities are hosting one of the many special events or programs the park offers from July to mid-August. It is well marked, wide, and very easy to follow, but it is not wheelchair accessible.

There is a paved Pedestrian Walkway that begins just behind the swimming pool and runs for about 3 km up to the ball diamond on top of the hill. Two lanes wide, well shaded, and complemented by benches at strategic rest spots, this trail is well suited to the casual walker. The native prairie trail begins on the west park boundary road just past the Bald Butte turnoff, after the road turns from pavement to gravel. There is parking available at the trail head.

Just off the Loch Leven picnic grounds near Valley Trail Group Camping, one finds the entry to Whispering Pines Nature Trail, which leads one off to a couple of scenic viewpoints overlooking Belanger Creek. You also get to see how the park protects itself from wildfires as you cross the fireguard near the far end of the loop. There is a parking lot at the entrance as well as a pretty picnic spot at which to enjoy your lunch.

At the other end of the park beside the Lone Pine Group Campground one finds the parking lot and entry to the Highland Interpretive Trail which allows you to take a self-guided tour of the rich diversity this part of the park offers. Approximately 1.5 km long, the trail has many signposts that explain the surroundings and lead you to more fully understand your surroundings. The trail itself, while easy to follow, is a bit marshy in places and certainly not wheelchair accessible.

One can also challenge portions of the Trans Canada Trail in this park, with approximately 16 km in the Center Block and a further 15 km in the West Block. You can also hike The Gap Road between the two, roughly 30 km (one way). The gap road is a municipal trail crossing private land; hikers require landowner permission before leaving the gap road and entering private land.

The West Block has its own map detailing the many hikes that have been catalogued for the area. All of these hikes are better suited to more active adventurers as they are more strenuous and require you carry in your food and water; you'll find none on the trail and from my own experience you should double what you thought you'd need; the sun can really beat down on you when you're on top of the hills. You will be rewarded with some astonishing views as well as a chance to see parts of the park so far removed from the masses of visitors that you wouldn't think you're in the same park! As mentioned above, trail rides are a popular way to see this park, and hikers will doubtless find themselves sharing some of the trails. Two 1:50000 scale maps may be of use to you: Hungerford Lakes 72 F/12 and Fairwell Creek 72 F/11, both available from the provincial Information Services Corporations website at: www.isc.ca.

If you'd rather not walk in the park, there are two "Auto Tour" maps published by the park, one for each of the two portions, Center Block and West Block. They offer a chance to see some of the more scenic panoramas the park has to offer as well as take in some of this special place's history. The more extensive tour is the Center Block one, with 10 points of interest along a circuitous route. The West Block tour, although with fewer stopping points, is the longer one as it takes you across The Gap Road (30 km one way) from the Center Block and back again. In the West Block you really must see the Fort Walsh National Historic site with its museum and colorful reproduction of Farwell's Trading Post (see previous page). Take the bus from the museum to the trading post and take the part of a wolfer trading pelts for a season's supplies; it's a fascinating look at the history of this area and the way life was lived in centuries past. One thing to note for both tours, though, is that the roads can be rough at times as they travel over cobblestone beaches from an ancient lake bed. In fact, I cannot recommend you take a motor home over the Gap Road even in good weather as it will rattle you to pieces, particularly over those cobblestone sections. The weather can play nasty tricks on you if you get caught in such places, so take every precaution when traveling these roads. Check for the latest weather reports and forecasts at the park administration office in the Center Block.

GOLF
The Cypress Hills Golf Resort offers an exceptional game, literally at the top of the province! It's obvious that golf isn't the only thing on people's minds as they travel this pretty course, as the back of the scorecard has pictures of prominent local flora and fauna along with some information to edify your trip around the course. The course plays 3362 yards over its 9 holes on a mature course with lush greens and excellent fairways. The pro-shop has a line of branded merchandise as well as clubs and carts for rent. There is no golf pro so there are no lessons. The licensed clubhouse offers a line of light snacks and cold refreshment as well as a place to brag about the days' accomplishments (I've yet to meet a golfer who didn't!). You can also rent tennis equipment here for the two courts at the top of the hill just past the riding stable. Call (306) 662-4422 for more information and to book your tee times and tournaments; you can also get more up-to-date pricing by checking their website at: www.saskgolfer.com/cypress/. For those wishing more luxurious accommodation, contact the Cypress Hills Resort Inn for stay-and-play packages at (306) 662-4477, or check out their website at www.cypressresortinn.com for more information.

Mini-golf is also popular in the park, with a fine course located at the intersection of Pine Avenue and Hidden Valley Trail, across from the Poplar Picnic Area. Reasonably priced at $3–$4 for 18 holes (depending on age), you can even find an ATM machine in the entry booth. Parking is ample in the grassy verge beside the course, and you'll find a gas bar and confectionary a few meters past the fence line; fuel prices were the same as in Maple Creek during our visit. The picnic area is well-lawned with pole BBQs and tables scattered in shady nooks; parking is across the road beside the mini-golf and beside the Hidden Valley Trail.

BEACHES, SWIMMING, BOATING AND BIKING: LOCH LEVEN

As with most other amenities, the Core Area in Center Block is home to the Loch Leven Marina, where you can rent paddle or row boats, canoes, surf bikes, bicycles, movies and vcr's. They even offer a line of bait and tackle as well as bicycle parts! They are open from 1000–2030 hr daily in season, from the May long weekend to the end of the Labor Day long weekend, and welcome group or school bookings. Contact them directly at (306) 662-2992 (in season) or at (306) 545-3614 (off season) for current prices and booking information. The beach volleyball court is located right beside the Marina booth from which equipment can be rented.

There is no boat launch on either Loch Leven or Loch Lomond as neither lake is large enough to support motor boats, so there will be no water skiing, tubing, wakeboards or the like; indeed, there is a 5 hp or 3.74 KW limit on motorized boats. You will find an almost idyllic calm and the chance to catch some of the park's brook or cutthroat trout, for which I wish you better luck than I had! By the way, the provincial record for both species has come from Loch Leven.

Just up the one-way road from the Marina is the Beach Picnic Area which anchors the south side of the beach. The public swim beach (pictured here) is relatively small but the sand is clean and there is ample shade behind on the lawns. There is also an excellent change house right beside the parking lot. The change rooms are bright and clean but there is no running water; vault toilets are available right beside. The swim beach is buoyed and shallow so there is plenty of room to splash about.

While we're talking about the lake, it must be noted that Loch Leven has cottage developments running all round it, and the paved roads serving the lake are so narrow that one-way traffic is all that is allowed. Ben Nevis Drive runs north along the west side of the lake, past the Marina and beach area. As it crests the top or northernmost part of the lake it becomes Ben Viorlich Drive and runs south along the east side of the lake. Right at the top part of the lake you'll find the Loch Leven Picnic Area, also the entrance to the Whispering Pines Nature Trail.

Located right in the heart of the Core Area is the swimming pool with its expanse of lawn and dining opportunities. The swimming pool itself offers lessons from the July long weekend to the August long weekend; check with the pool cashier about times and fees.

There are also public swims, lane swimming and aqua fitness times, pool games for families, and generally a good time for all. The pool is open from the weekend prior to the July long weekend to the Labor Day weekend, generally with classes in the morning and public swimming in the afternoon and evening.

RIDING STABLES, TENNIS AND BASEBALL

At the top of the hill, beside the intersection to the Bald Butte Trail and Fort Walsh Road, one finds the Riding Academy with its stables and trails. Horse rides can be arranged for individuals or groups, by the hour or for more extended trips, depending on what you want. Now, when I say hour I mean a 45-minute ride; as they must sort out which horse for which person you can adjust the amount of time accordingly. They also request that you make arrangements in advance for team or group rides. All trail rides are guided; you cannot simply strike off on your own! Contact them at (306) 662-3512 in season, which runs from the May long weekend to the Labor Day long weekend.

There are two tennis courts located beside Aspen Grove Group Campground. Equipment can be rented at the golf course if you didn't bring your own; the courts are free to use. The courts themselves are paved and have mesh screens to keep errant balls out of the gallery! Just past this facility is the baseball diamond, with grass infields and a tall mesh backstop on metal poles as well as benches for players; there is no equipment rental but the field is free to use although it may be reserved for special events. Both facilities share the vault toilets and potable water tap at Aspen Grove Campground.

SERVICES

You cannot discuss this park without speaking about the Core Area. You already know about the marina, pool and lake amenities, but there is a wealth of other things to see and do here. Right beside the pool (go figure!) is the park café. While the Cypress Park Resort Inn café serves brunches and full meals (at resort prices), the park café outlet offers a "food court" atmosphere and a variety of choices. There is also a selection of summer favorites like fries, rings, ice cream and the like. A wider selection of ice cream is available just across the road at Dar's Little Dipper, which offers burgers and other grilled items and is complemented by a large, roofed verandah with tables and benches to rest while enjoying your snack. Right beside Dar's Little Dipper is the Cypress Hills General Store with a reasonable line of groceries, hardware, camping supplies and branded merchandise.

Beside these buildings is the Park Office and Nature Center. No visit to Cypress Hills would be complete without a visit to this center for the wealth of information on display as well as the very competent staff at the information desk. Across from the Nature Center is a teepee and small picnic area, set amid tall trees on a lush lawn and anchored by a large conglomerate boulder.

While I'm on the subject of First Nations and their impact on this special place, the local First Nations communities are working together with the park to provide an interpretive program in the park. Through the summer months they will provide special events such as a teepee-raising ceremony with drummers and dancers; contact the park office for dates and times and plan your holidays accordingly—the color and majesty of ceremonies like these are not to be missed! If you are interested in Saskatchewan history, you really must visit Fort Walsh in the West Block. A National Historic Park, the museum and surrounding area comprise an interesting look at the early life in this place. Take the short bus trip from the museum to Farwell's Trading Post and be a "wolfer" for an afternoon, trading pelts for your winter supplies. The young people re-enacting the life of the post do a remarkable job and are very informative; that and it's a whole lot of fun! Learn more on their website at: www.pc.gc.ca or www.cypresshills.com; follow the links!

The park also offers a very extensive summer program schedule with some activity on literally every night from July to September. Most of these activities are free, taking place either at the Recreation Hall beside the Café in the Core Area, or over at the Amphitheater and Firecircle near the campground entrance office. This excellent venue has open-air bench seating for about 270–300 people in front of an electrified and illuminated stage. There is no sound amplification system, but none is needed as it's a pretty cozy atmosphere. It can be rented for private functions but availability is restricted; check with the park office for rates and bookings. Availability is restricted because the venue is booked pretty much every night of the summer; there's always something going on! Some activities are fun for the whole family, some feature local musicians such as "Ole Time Dancing," some activities are educational, involving archeology, anthropology, and botany; there's literally something for everyone. Be sure to pick up a current brochure when you arrive and check in with the information staff for updates; you'll be glad you did!

Travelers in the area can check out portions of The Great Canadian Fossil Trail, notably the T. Rex Museum at Eastend and the Notukeu Heritage Museum of Archaeology and Paleontology in Ponteix. Also on the list are the Fort Walsh National Historic Site and Cypress Hills Interprovincial Park. Pick up a brochure and explore this fascinating aspect of the area's prehistory.

Stay a while in this park and sooner or later you'll need a laundromat, which will be located adjacent to the gas bar on Pine Avenue beginning in 2006. The machines are all coin-operated, and change can be made at the Gas Bar if necessary; you'd be wise to bring a supply of quarters and loonies though, as you can't guarantee suitable change will be available.

For those wanting or needing a roof over their heads, the 4-season Cypress Hills Resort will suit your needs. From more rustic cabins to condo-style suites to standard hotel rooms, they have it all, as well as an indoor pool, a licensed beverage room and a four-star restaurant. For more details or to book your accommodation, contact them directly at (306) 662-4477 or check out their website at: www.cypressresortinn.com.

For more extensive shopping, medical and mechanical services you must go to Maple Creek. A church service is offered in the park every Sunday morning from July through to early September; check the activities brochure for times and places. As you can see from these pages, there is truly something for everyone in this park. From the self-sufficient solitude of the West Block campgrounds to the luxury condo accommodation in Center Block, there is an experience for every taste: educational and recreation programs galore; hiking and biking in a surprising range of terrain; hills, water, forests, birds and plants to marvel at. The stunning scenery at Bald Butte and the Conglomerate Cliffs, and the peace and crisp solitude of the cross-country ski trails make this special place truly a miracle.

To gather more information, contact the park office at (306) 662-5411 (year-round) or by post at:

Cypress Hills Interprovincial Park
PO Box 850
Maple Creek, SK   S0N 1N0
Website at: www.cypresshills.com
E-mail: cypresshills@serm.gov.ca

Remember, if you want to reserve a site, you must mail, fax, or email them with your request after the first of January each year, or call them at (306) 662-5484 beginning the first Monday in June. Go; you'll be glad you did!

BUFFALO POUND PROVINCIAL PARK

Located 36 km north of Moose Jaw on Hwy 2 (or 16 km south of Chamberlain), this park is open year-round for your recreational enjoyment. The park is very spread out, with two core areas approximately 1.5 km apart, and the trailer dump station almost 2 km away near the park entrance. Thus, you will see bikes and pedestrians almost everywhere; please be cautious. Fishing, boating, biking and hiking, interpretive trails, mini-golf and a heated outdoor swimming pool offer summer recreation for the entire family, while the ski hill operated by the Moose Jaw Alpine Ski Association offers t-bar and rope tows for its groomed runs. You can also see many ice fishing shacks on the lake in the winter, and the hiking/biking trails offer cross-country skiing enthusiasts a place to go. The park is named for ancient First Nations hunting practices, and evidence of that culture still echoes through the hills and coulees. A small herd of bison (and a bison observation tower) can be found near the eastern end of the lake, and you can find the Nicolle Flats Interpretive Area nearby. Truly, something for the entire family!

SITES

There are 156 sites in total (not counting the overflow sites), spread over 5 main campgrounds which will be considered separately. All roadways are paved throughout the park which is very spread out; watch for cyclists everywhere and deer at night. Definitely go slow! A trailer dump station is available just past the park entrance booth.

Hilltop Campground: The first, to your left as you drive past the park gates, is the Hilltop Campground. There are 54 unserviced but very scenic sites here, although the trees are short and far apart. The sites are very open, poorly shaded, and all are naturally leveled and drained. This is actually their overflow area, and you rarely see anyone here except on the busiest weekends. The sites are arranged as drive-beside with a central grass area around which you will camp. The sites all have pole BBQs, wooden picnic tables, access to firewood, central water and vault toilets. Mind you, if the park is full, the staff will doubtless bring a supply of firewood up if asked. The sites may be rustic, but they have an almost unadulterated view of the horizon in all directions with very little light pollution. If you intend to do any stargazing during your stay, these sites may well be your first choice!

Lake Side Campground: Driving down from the park gate you descend to the lake shore, somewhat disconcerting if you expect the prairies to be bald and flat! There are only 7 unserviced sites here, all back-in style, with tall aspens and elms for shade from the lake side but little between sites. You've a tall hill in front of the site and tall trees behind, but almost nothing for privacy. Having said that, the glory of this campground is that the lake is but a few meters from the back of your site. If you're boating or fishing, you'll enjoy landing your boat so close to your site. All sites are large, certainly large enough for modern units, including tow vehicle and boat trailer. They are built on gravel pads, drained front to back, with metal-framed picnic tables and excellent culvert-style fire grates. There is a parking lot in front of the campground and a grassy area as well, making this an alternative group camping area for school groups and the like. There is access to a central water tap, trash bins and vault toilets. Firewood is available from Elm View Campground.

Elm View Campground: Located just across the road from Lake Side Campground, there are 36 unserviced sites winding back from the road into the coulee. Heavily treed and very private, some of these sites are really too small for modern units (although sites #3, 4, 6, and 8 are larger), but are excellent for smaller motorhomes or tents. You might, for instance, find things a bit crowded if you try to park your boat trailer in the same lot as your camper and tow vehicle. There are shared water taps, vault toilets, trash bins and firewood piles. Sites feature metal-framed tables, pole BBQs and gravel pads, although each site's parking area is paved. The vault toilets, particularly near sites #26 and 27, are wheelchair accessible, and have a grey-water pit. Indeed, sites #24–27 themselves could be considered wheelchair accessible although there may be better choices in Maple Vale Campground, discussed later. Traffic flows in both directions on the shared road, which could be a problem if two large units meet. Hot showers are available in the service center near the pool a short distance away, free to registered patrons. Both Lake View and Elm View campgrounds share the distinction of being the closest campgrounds to the pool, boat launch, mini-golf, and day-use playground area (including the concession!)

Maple Vale Campground: Turn left at the bottom of the hill and drive about a km or so (just past the maintenance yard entrance) to Maple Vale, the first of the electrified campgrounds in this park. There are 61 sites here; all but 11 (#36–46 inclusive) are electrified. All the sites are fairly large, with excellent shade but little ground cover for privacy, for the most part. The sites have metal-framed picnic tables and pole BBQs, and are well laid out. The unserviced sites (#36–46) are considered the tenting loop and are located at the far end of the campground. Water taps, trash bins, wheelchair-accessible vault toilets and firewood are all centrally located. Of particular interest in this campground is the attention paid to providing wheelchair access. Three electrified sites are fully paved (#54, 57, and 62) and reserved for those requiring wheelchair service; one of these sites is offered as a seasonal campsite. There is a service center across from these three sites with free hot showers, flush toilets, and a grey water pit for wash water disposal. There is also a recycling center here where you can properly dispose of cans and bottles. There is one small creative playground in a grassy field beside the main entrance, with a slide and sturdy climbing structure. Maple Vale is quite a jaunt from the pool area to the east, so a small but serviceable beach (pictured here) is located just past the campground entrance. It is unsupervised and change rooms are provided in the adjacent mini service centers.

Shady Lane Campground: Located farthest west in the park, this campground is distinguished by having several small loops before the main area, which has 25 seasonal camp sites. In total, this campground has 52 electrified sites, of which 2 are full-serviced. The first loop (sites #1–10) is laid out such that all sites are drive-along with the metal-framed picnic tables and pole BBQs in the center of a small wooded and grassed area. There is good shade but little privacy. The loop has a central water tap, trash bins and vault toilets. Continuing on, there is a second loop with 4 electrified sites (#11–14) which are smaller but offer much better privacy. They are also "drive-along" style, with metal-framed picnic tables and pole BBQs. There is a water tap and trash bins but no vault toilets in this small loop. A third loop (#15–22) is similar to the first in that the sites all run along the perimeter of a small wooded area in which the sites have their wooden picnic tables and pole BBQs. There is a central water tap, trash bins and vault toilets. All three of these loops can use the service center in the main loop, with its hot showers and flush toilets. The last loop is also the largest (Sites #23–50) and has metal-framed picnic tables, pole BBQs, and well-shaded sites. You'll find a payphone and firewood pile just at the entrance. Water is shared among several taps, and a grey water disposal is located near the service center in the middle of the grassy area near site #25. There are 25 sites for seasonal rent here, including 2 full-serviced sites with water, sewer and electrical hook-ups.

There are two group campgrounds available for rent, Rankin's and Lower Chalet. Rankin's is closest to the lake but smaller, whereas the Lower Chalet site is closest to the mountain bike trail system that runs for quite a distance behind the ski hill area. Both areas have 14 sites with pole BBQs and wooden picnic tables, a set of vault toilets and water taps. There is a large fire pit in the center and a firewood supply. The sites are all naturally leveled and drained, and generally have good shade but little ground cover.

WATER SPORTS

The park has made excellent provision for water enthusiasts of all sorts. There is an excellent boat launch with two floating docks and ample parking behind for trailers; you are expected to retrieve your boat nightly and park it in your site. There is a fish cleaning shack beside the boat launch. As the lake is long and relatively thin it isn't as prone to big winds so there are many tow boats to be seen enjoying the weekend with skiers and tubes of all sorts. Anglers are not forgotten as there is excellent fishing to be had in the lake, with 2.5 kg walleye and 4–5 kg pike commonly taken. The park has also made a barrier-free trout pond available in a small but well-shaded picnic area just behind the entrance booth. There is a well-built fishing pier, fish cleaning station, and paved picnic area with 3 wooden picnic tables, pole BBQs, wheelchair-accessible flush toilets and potable water taps; there was no firewood supply. There is no charge to fish here, but you must have a valid Saskatchewan fishing license and park entry permit. An aeration system ensures trout survive the winter, but the pond is also stocked prior to the May long weekend, weather permitting.

There is a circular, heated outdoor swimming pool between the Elm View day-use picnic area and the boat launch. There is a daily admission charge to use the pool, although the showers are free to use. Red Cross swimming lessons are offered in July and August; contact the park office for dates, fees, and availabilities. There are two small but clean beaches, one near Elm View Campground, the other near Maple Vale Campground. The sand is fine with a few small pebbles, but no evidence of beach parties. There are buoyed swimming areas but no supervision, so parents are expected to watch over their own swimmers. You can use the change rooms at the swimming pool if you are using the picnic grounds or staying at either Lake Side or Elm View.

SPORTS

There is a ball diamond behind the boat launch parking area, with a tall mesh backstop and grass infields. There are several trash bins and wooden picnic tables available, but no pole BBQs for your pre-game tailgate cooking! Up the hill a short distance one will find a disused tennis court with basketball half-courts at either end. The facilities are free to use but they don't appear to have seen much use in a few years at least; there are bushes growing through the fence and the pavement is cracked with grass growing through. There is an 18-hole mini-golf course available behind the boat launch parking lot as well. Rates vary with age, and are payable at the booth entrance to the facility; group rates are available. It is open most weekends, weather permitting, from 1200–1800 hr.

The White Track Ski Hill is operated by the Moose Jaw Alpine Ski Club, with 4 or 5 groomed runs (depending on the weather) and a T-bar and handle tow bar. The upper chalet houses the concession and rental shop; the lower chalet is no longer used. They start making snow in mid-November, weather permitting, so they usually open for business in early December. Call (306) 610-0100 for current conditions in season; they open for Friday nights, Saturday and Sunday. The hill often hosts corporate nights and fun events like steak nights on Saturdays throughout the season; call ahead to find out if there's anything on! Nordic skiers can use the hiking and biking trails for their winter amusement; there is a warm-up shack midway along the Canada Cup trail but few other amenities; the trails will not be groomed. The park is planning on building a "Terrain Park" for snowboarders that should open in the winter of 2005–06. There are a lot of dedicated volunteers who labor long and hard to keep this operation open, and I salute their efforts.

BIKING/HIKING

This park is unusual in the province in that it has an extensive and comprehensive mountain bike trail network behind the ski hill. Part of the trail system is used in winter for Nordic skiing, and part of it was developed for the 2000 and 2002 Canada Cup Mountain Bike competitions. There is no fee for using the system, and a pamphlet with trail map is available. There will be no water or services once you're on the trails, although there is a warm-up shelter partway along the Canada Cup course. There are basically two directions in this park: "Up the Hill and Down the Hill"! If you like mountain biking, you'll enjoy this park, and the best of luck to you!

The park has also established several interpretive trails in an area known as the Nicolle Flats Interpretive Area. You can access a series of trails, some more extensive and arduous than others; maximum length (one way) is 8 km for the Dyke Trail/Trans Canada Trail, while the Marsh Boardwalk Trail is 0.5 km long. You can access the system from either end, driving through the park past the Ski Hill and group camping areas to the trailhead and parking lot near the Bison Viewing Tower, or you can drive around the park to the Nicolle Homestead parking lot. Here you'll find self-guided trails and the observation deck. There are vault toilets and trash bins at both trailheads and parking lots. The drive through the park is very scenic on a smooth, wide road which might be slick after a summer rain as there are places where the gravel has been washed off. Still, the drive is most pleasant with a plethora of wildflowers and wildlife. The drive around the park is scenic but in a different way; the scenery is all hills and vales, particularly as you descend into the lake valley.

The Bison Observation Tower, located near the Nicolle Flats trailhead, has its own parking lot and an imposing 2-story wooden structure from which you can observe the bison in this growing herd. The population is doing so well that the park must manage it by relocating members to new herds elsewhere in the park system. From the top observation platform you've quite a vista of the lake, far shore, and the bison herd on the near hills. There is a hiking trail, the Bison View Interpretive Trail, that begins here and loops back over 2.9 km. Bring water and sun protection as there will be little shade, although there are benches at strategic rest stops. As with all the trails in the park, there are brochures available to guide and instruct you.

SERVICES

There are is a food concession and store in the park. The concession is located in the Elm View picnic area beside the creative playground near the beach and pool, and the store is located between Maple Vale and Shady Lane campgrounds. They both offer the usual treats and sweets, although the store between the two campsites has more extensive shopping with a line of simple groceries and a restaurant offering grilled meals and a patio. There is an arcade for those rainy day activities, as well as a payphone. The park offers a Saturday Interpretive Program in July and August; check out their website or contact them for more details about program availability. They also offer an educational package running from late May to late June for school groups wishing to investigate the historical and natural aspects of the park; contact the park office directly for more information. The city of Moose Jaw is about 25 minutes away and offers a full range of shopping, mechanical, medical and worship services. There are also museums, golf courses, a mineral spa and a casino, and the world-famous Tunnels of Moose Jaw for the interested; check out the city's website at: www.citymoosejaw.com. There is a lot to see and do in this park and in the area around it. For more information about this park, contact the office at:

Buffalo Pound Provincial Park
#206-110 Ominica St. W.
Moose Jaw, SK   S6H 6V2
Telephone: (306) 694-3659
Fax: (306) 694-3743
Website: www.saskparks.net

DANIELSON PROVINCIAL PARK

Located on the north end of Lake Diefenbaker (formed by Gardiner Dam) approximately an hour's drive south of Saskatoon, this park is open from the May long weekend to the Labor Day weekend. It features one of the best boat launches on Lake Diefenbaker and provides fishing access to the northern portion of the lake as well as Coteau Bay. Interestingly, the lake level can rise and fall by as much as 10 meters each year! An excellent Visitor's Center just west of Gardiner Dam provides interpretation of the creation and impact of the lake on central Saskatchewan, and the center's restaurant provides hearty meals at reasonable cost. Driving south on Hwy 219 you stop at the T-intersection at Hwy 44; turn right and continue a short distance until a left turn takes you to the campgrounds and boat launch—driving straight west on Hwy 44 takes you across the dam and then the Visitor's Center.

CAMPING

There are three camping loops in Danielson Provincial Park: Bayside and Shady Lane to the left as you drive west, followed by Elmview to the right. There are a total of 49 electrified (30-amp service) and 43 non-electrified sites; all sites are back-in style. All sites have sturdy picnic tables built on metal frames, and a culvert-style fire pit or pole BBQ. Trash bins and potable water taps are centrally located, and a woodpile is located across from the trailer dump station as you drive in. Toilets are vault style in the campgrounds and flush-type in the modern shower facility located across from site 137 (pictured here) in Elmview campgrounds. The shower house is also the recycling station. If the park gate is manned when you arrive (on weekends; reduced hours on weekdays), they will direct you to your site; if unmanned there are two self-reservation kiosks, one at Bayside and the other at Elmview. Sites can be reserved for group camping by calling the park office. Only 25 electrified sites are available for seasonal reservation; all 43 non-electrified sites can be reserved seasonally, however, should demand warrant. All the sites are graveled and leveled and should be ample enough for the largest unit. The sites in the Elmview campgrounds have a bit better cover; the non-electrified sites at Shady Lane are larger but have less cover between sites and are therefore a bit less private although more open and roomy. There is one presentation area in Shady Lane campgrounds which functions to host evening programs when scheduled; otherwise it can be reserved for a private gathering or used as a camp kitchen in inclement weather. Although it does have picnic tables it lacks a woodstove or BBQ so you'll have to provide your own. The park is planning a new playground along the Bayside/Shady Lane road to be completed by the summer of 2006.

Elmview, by the way, also has the "Campground Host" (site 147) and the only playground equipment in the campgrounds. The campground host functions as unofficial park staff, particularly after hours. If you are experiencing problems, these volunteers will try to assist you; they also function as a sort of neighborhood watch, keeping an eye on seasonal units while the owners are at work. They are not a security service, nor are they expected to quell disturbances. They are friendly and knowledgeable, however, and provide a valuable service when troubles appear—inflating your mattress or helping fix a leaky tent, for example. Elmwood site #113 is wheelchair accessible and reserved for those requiring this amenity.

BOATING

No doubt about it, Lake Diefenbaker provides a lot of recreational opportunities to the province—just look at all the parks and resorts along both sides of the lake! Danielson Provincial Park's two boat launches provide access to the northern part of the lake with the fluctuating water level inherent within their design. There is one just past the campgrounds at the main site, and another just past the turnoff for the visitor's center. Built on expansive cement aprons, each boat launch has a floating dock on a sloped rail that adjusts itself to the variable water level so you are always assured of water access. There is ample parking behind each launch for tow vehicles and boat trailers, but neither boat launch has a marina system and the park recommends you bring your boat and trailer into your campsite nightly. Having said that, many patrons take all their watery toys with them and spend the day on one of the innumerable small bays or sand spits that adorn the lake, finding their own private beach! From such a private hideaway you can play in the water, go fishing, suntan, play beach sports, cook a shore lunch or work on your bird-watchers "Life List." In the evening, pack up and return to your campsite. The lake is so large that even on the busiest days it can appear quite empty. The visitor's center has information on local fishing derbies, and anglers can boat up to the beach in front of the restaurant for their morning coffee, if they've a mind to; just moor your boat outside the marked swimming area! There are no rentals here, but you can make arrangements at the Lakeside Marina Service in Elbow, about 20 minutes' drive south on Hwy 44. Call (306) 854-2211 for pricing and availability; see the section on Douglas Provincial Park for more details.

ACTIVITIES

Besides boating, there are two beaches in the park, one near the campgrounds and the other protected in a small bay in front of the visitor's center. The best of the two is the visitor's center beach as it is cleaner, groomed, has beach change rooms and flush toilets, a wide expanse of lawns and a well-treed picnic area as well as sturdy picnic tables right on the beach, built of recycled material and sure to last a long time! There is also a beach playground with swings and teeter-totters, and trash bins for your refuse. There are no open fires, overnight camping, or firewood, so picnickers must be self-sufficient. Please note: the lawns are watered during the day, so please leave your car windows up, particularly if you are parking in the first row right beside the grass!

The visitor's center deserves special mention as it functions as an interpretive museum with static displays and a small gift shop. It has an excellent movie that plays at regular intervals in the theatre, depicting the construction of Gardiner Dam (one of the largest earth-filled dams in the world) and its smaller sister, the Qu'Appelle River Dam which created Lake Diefenbaker. If you've never seen this film, I highly recommend it as it's well worth your time. You'll also find the "Top of the Dam Café" in the visitor's center, offering a tempting line of ice cream and frozen treats as well as a line of grilled meals, all at a reasonable price. Check the menu board for daily specials; the café is open from 1000–1900 hr (Monday to Friday) and 0900–1930 hr on weekends from May to September; they also have a small line of fishing tackle and bait.

There are two hiking trails established at the campground or main site; the Trans Canada Trail runs directly through the park from top to bottom, continuing all the way down the length of Lake Diefenbaker. Although there are no amenities along the trail is it wide and well marked. Remember to bring water, bug repellant and sun screen! The other, shorter trail runs off the north end of Elmwood camping loop and back to the main road just behind the wood pile. The trail winds around through low trees and scrub but is well marked and fairly short at about 2 km. You see many animal signs, particularly deer, although moose and antelope have been seen of late. Pay particular attention to the elms for signs of feeding porcupines that have stripped the bark off (seen here). The provincially rare Piping Plover nests on the banks of the Coteau Bay; please heed all warning signs about their delicate ecology—the visitor's center has an excellent brochure on the topic, or see Environment Canada's website at: www.pnr-rpn.ec.gc.ca/pipingplover.

SERVICES
Except for the café and gift shop at the visitor's center, there is no shopping to be had in the park. Patrons must depend on nearby Elbow for all their shopping, mechanical and worship needs. This park rarely has trouble with a noisier crowd, being thought of as a "slower" park—just what the doctor ordered! In July and August the park can be quite full; the park entry gates will display a "FULL" sign if no sites are available. There are summer tours available of the Coteau Creek Power Station; check at the visitor's center for details. The Riverhurst Ferry Crossing allows you to drive down to Riverhurst then cross on the largest ferry still operating in the province. Boat tours of the lake can be arranged from Palliser Regional Park with the Sask River Tours; check out their website for more info at: http://www.saskrivertours.ca/, or call them at: (306) 353-4603. You can get your summer swinging with excellent golf at Palliser's River Breaks Golf and Country Club, or at Elbow Harbors championship 18-hole golf course. A driving tour of the area simply must take you to the Sand Castles near Beechy, where the local landscape resembles huge sand castles, remnants of a beach thrown up by receding glaciers millennia past. There are many ways to let this park give you rest; contact them for more information at:

Danielson Provincial Park
P.O. Box 39,
Elbow, SK   S0H 1J0

Telephone: (306) 857-5500 (Tuesday, Wednesday) or (306) 854-5510 (Thursday to Monday) during the summer hours.

DOUGLAS PROVINCIAL PARK

There are many fine recreational opportunities in this province, but none quite like Lake Diefenbaker. Here there are resort communities, regional and provincial parks aplenty, and 800 kilometers of bays and beaches—so many that you can find a private place even when the lake is at its busiest. The anchor to this huge playground is Douglas Provincial Park (named for T.C. Douglas, a Premier of this province) and its attendant marina at the Elbow Recreation Site. Located 11 km south of Elbow on Hwy 19, this park is the administration center for Danielson Provincial Park and the Elbow Recreation Site. The park's 7,300 hectares surround the southeast part of the "T" of Lake Diefenbaker, right at the Qu'Appelle Dam, and encompass a land of rolling hills, sand and scrub that was home to First Nations people for as much as 9,000 years. The local resort community of Mistussinne was named for a huge boulder that was used as a gathering place in the Qu'Appelle valley prior to the dam. An impressive cairn at the Elbow Harbor commemorates and recognizes the importance of the rock to the culture and history of the land's earliest people. The park is open from the Victoria Day weekend to the Labor Day weekend in September and features camping as well as boating access to this huge lake.

CAMPING

There are a total of 150 campsites in this park, spread among 3 camping loops. Of these, 92 are electrified with 30-amp service; none are fully serviced. The sites are generally smaller than some modern units will require, and the roadways, although paved, are quite narrow; one-way traffic is the norm in this park. Having said that, the sites are built into mature aspen parklands and they are all well shaded and very private. They feature pole or culvert BBQs, sturdy picnic tables, and are leveled with gravel. Some sites in the 100 loop are drive-through style; most of the remaining sites are two-stage, with a parking spot for the unit and a picnic table area beside it. Potable water is piped to central taps and firewood is available in one central area to the right as you drive past the 100–loop entrance. There are two service centers in the park, both wheelchair accessible, with hot showers and flush toilets. The other toilet facilities are vault style with flush toilets, clean and odorless. In general, the 100–loop sites are somewhat larger while the 200–loop sites are available for the "Reserve-a-site" service. The 300 loop has sites that can also be reserved, although fewer are electrified; it also has a few "A and B" mini-group sites. The 300 loop also has access to 4 walk-in tenting only sites. These are set well back in the woods, a 2 or 3 minute walk from the small parking lot available for your car. The paths are well worn and easy to follow and the sites are easy to find. They feature privacy, pole BBQs and picnic tables but no water or toilets. These are wilderness sites, if you will, and require that you be self-sufficient; definitely a neat feature, though.

There is one playground in the campgrounds, in a small field behind site #354. A very sturdy, paved walking trail runs through the campgrounds, particularly the 300 loop, leading one to the beach and picnic area. Well shaded, it provides a gentle walk from your campsite to the beach. There are two wheelchair accessible sites reserved specifically for that use in the park, sites #107 and 314. Both are hard-surfaced and situated beside water taps; site #107 is electrified. Site #314 is located beside one of the service centers and is perhaps the better of the two. There is no laundromat service in the park; for that you must depend on nearby Elbow. A secure trailer storage compound is available just before the 100 loop; check with the park office for costs and availability.

There is a group camping area as well as a large overflow capable of holding 35 or so units, exclusive of the group sites. These are generally more open with lower shade trees and fewer amenities. There are two water taps and two sets of vault toilets serving this area; the sites have pole BBQs and picnic tables and there is a large field around which the sites are spread. Known as the Aspen Grove Group Camping Area, it has room for 15 units in a semi-private loop; contact the park office for reservation details and availability. A well-worn path leads from the field to the road terminating in the parking lot in front of the café and grocery store anchoring the beach. A trailer dump station is available just past the park entry kiosk, just after the turnoff to the boat launch and fish filleting shack.

The park has begun using the reserve-a-site system, with all of the 200 loop open for reservations. No seasonal sites are currently offered, although you can rent a site by the month; discounts were offered for multiple month rentals. Your park pass is also honored at the Elbow Lakeside Marina and the Elbow Recreation Site.

BEACH AND WATER SPORTS

There is one beach access in the park with change rooms and flush toilets. The parking lot for the beach is paved and huge, with some shade trees around the perimeter. There is one picnic shelter in the park just north of the parking lot, set in a large expanse of lush lawn. There are two playgrounds near the beach, a large fairly new creative playground beside the beach, and a set of swings and teeter-totters beside the dining shelter. The trail mentioned above runs beside the picnic area, which is interestingly set amid the mature aspens in a series of private bays or clearings accessed by a short trail off the walkway.

A wide set of terraces offers easier access to the beach, just behind the concession. Here, one could purchase the usual selection of summer treats as well as more complete meals. Breakfast seemed well attended, for instance. The grill was doing a brisk business with the usual line of hamburgers and fries as well as a couple of lighter meals. The store also offered a simple line of camping supplies and merchandise with the park logo on it; for more extensive shopping one is directed to nearby Elbow. To contact the store about hours of availability or specialty items, call them at (306) 854-4630 in season.

The beach itself can be monstrous, depending on water levels; when we visited the water was down approximately 5 meters and the beach could have held several thousand people. The sand was deep and fine with few pebbles and little evidence of vandalism; the swimming area is buoyed but unsupervised and no swim lessons are offered. Mind you, this is just the main beach complex. If you desire, the entire 20 km of shoreline inside the park is one giant beach. Pack up the wieners, kids, and water bottles in your boat and go find your own pristine, private beach—it's there for you!

SPORTS

No doubt about it, the lake is a big magnet for anglers and rightly so. There are 26 species of sport fish to test your ability, including some of the best walleye fishing in the province. Now, I know there are those anglers who would contest that statement, but the truth of the matter is that the fishing on this lake can be great, if you know where the holes are! Douglas Provincial Park has a fine boat launch, built of cement and leading into a small bay. Lamentably, the launch was closed during our visit due to low water levels but 2004 (when we visited) was an abnormal year for runoff. Even though the water level can fluctuate by as much as 10 meters from year to year, the spring usually has higher levels than we saw! No matter, as mentioned elsewhere, your park pass is honored at the Elbow Lakeside Marina (pictured on opposite page), as fine a marina as can be found in the province. They will charge slip fees to park your boat there overnight, but you can use the launch without charge. They are also one of the three fueling points on the lake, the others being at the Saskatchewan Landing Provincial Park Marina and at Rusty's Coulee. As you can see from this picture, it is quite an impressive facility. The operator can rent boats, motors, and arrange guides if you need. They also sell a line of boating merchandise as well as snacks and offer a full marina service. Contact them directly for more information at (306) 854-2211. You can also charter the 30-foot yacht "Dream On" and "experience the romance of sailing as she rides the gentle wind and waves."

Golfing enthusiasts will enjoy the panoramic view offered at the Harbor Golf Club and Resort in Elbow. The 6273 yard, par-71 course challenges you with its 67 sand traps and water hazards, and amazes you with scenic vistas of the lake and its seemingly limitless horizons. Lush, manicured fairways, elevated tees and expansive greens make this a luxurious course. The clubhouse offers all the amenities, with club and cart rentals, a line of golfing equipment and clothing for sale, and a full-service restaurant. The outdoor patio is a grand way to end the day, as you can enjoy the spectacle of the sun bleeding away across the lake. They also offer hotel services in the resort, with "stay and play" packages popular as gifts. For more details, contact them at (306) 854-2300, or check out their website at www.harborgolfclub.com.

HIKING

The park has built several excellent hiking and interpretive trails for your summer pleasure, the most impressive of which is the Dunes Interpretive Center, where you can wander through the area and see how wind and an ancient beach have combined to make this area unique in the province. I strongly recommend you begin with a tour of the center, as you'll find the information there very handy when you're out on the trails. From there you have access to a series of three trails: Juniper Trail (2.5 km), Cacti Trail (6 km) and the Dunes Hiking Area which has no established trails and can take 3 or 4 hours, depending on how much exploring you want to do. This is all dry land and there will be no water along the trail so bring plenty of your own. There is relatively little shelter for some parts, so bring sunscreen and a hat. This is sand and it shifts underfoot, so sturdy boots are also a good idea. Having said that, the trails are easy to follow, and the self-guided information posts along the way provide insights into the land you see.

There is another trail running through the forest along the lake, called the Sunset Trail (2 km). It demonstrates the changeable nature of this land by providing contrast to the sand dunes so short a distance away. Here, wetlands and forest provide a lush, rich environment with plenty of shade and birdsong. The moister environment attracts more insects and so more birds, so bring your binoculars! The trail loops around from its starting point at the parking lot for the 4 primitive tenting sites between sites 319 and 325 in the Homestead Campground.

Part of this trail is also part of the Trans-Canada Trail system of which 12 km (one way) parallels the shoreline; in fact, Lake Diefenbaker has 65 km of the trail running along its northeast shore from Danielson Provincial Park all the way to the Qu'Appelle dam and on to Tugaske. You can hike a long loop by using the Wolf Willow Trail (11-km loop), starting at the boat launch. A brisk 2-hour or so walk brings you back to the TransCanada Trail; turn left for home. All of the trails are well blazoned and a very serviceable line map and brochure will help you choose the trail for you. There is also a wonderful 28-page pamphlet "Douglas Provincial Park Nature Guide" which I highly recommend to you. It covers topics as diverse as geologic and human history as well as biodiversity.

SERVICES

The park naturalist offers interpretive programming throughout the summer months in a series of guided hikes, talks, and skits; keep an eye on the bulletin boards for times and places. The Dunes Nature Center is open from 1000–2200 hr daily in season, and the park naturalist is on hand to answer questions (if not involved with programming). With the exception of Lakeshore Foods (the beach concession and shop), there will be little in the park to part you from your dollars. The town of Elbow offers a full range of shopping, banking, mechanical, and worship services. Although there is a rural 911 service, the nearest health care facility is in Central Butte, approximately 30 minutes away by car. While in the area you may want to take in some of the local attractions; check out what's coming up on their website at www.elbowsask.com. Tourism enquiries can be made by calling the Village of Elbow at (306) 8554-2277 during office hours, Monday to Friday 0900–1700 hr. You can also consult Lake Diefenbaker's own tourism site at www.lakediefenbaker-tourism.com for other events and attractions in the extended area. This park and Danielson Provincial Park a short distance away share the same administration, which can work to your benefit when reserving a site; tell them how large your camping unit is and they'll try to steer you to whichever park can best accommodate your needs. As you're sharing the same lake (just a slightly different part of it), the choice becomes one of which park will be best for you; Danielson's more spacious sites or the amenities at Douglas. No matter which, you still get to choose! You can contact the park office directly at:

Douglas/Danielson Provincial Parks
Box 39,
Elbow, SK   S0H 1J0
Telephone: (306) 854-6266 in season. Website: www.saskparks.net

SASKATCHEWAN LANDING PROVINCIAL PARK

Located 50 km north of Swift Current on Hwy 4, at the westernmost end of Lake Diefenbaker on the South Saskatchewan River, the park commemorates the history of this rugged area with interpretive hikes and the artifacts displayed at Goodwin House. The bridge spanning the river uses the same shallows that made this place into a ford for the old Battleford Trail which brought freight and settlers from the railhead in Swift Current all the way north to the Battlefords. The river cut steep coulees which are still rich in wildlife, contrasting with the sere plains above. In the park you will find many interesting animals from bobcats to pronghorn antelope, pheasant to white pelicans, coyotes to rare prairie falcons. The park is open from the May long weekend to the September long weekend although camping is allowed year round; there will be no potable water in the off-season though. With excellent camping, a wondrous lake for water sports and fishing, golf, and hiking in the hills and coulees, there is much to keep patrons busy—come see for yourself!

CAMPING

There are 5 camping loops in the park with 279 sites, of which 135 are electrified with 30-amp service; there are no full-service sites. A further 20 non-electrical sites are under construction in the park, for a total of 299 sites available by spring of 2006. All roadways are paved except for the last few meters into Sagebrush campground, and all sites are leveled on gravel pads. Site geometry varies between "V"-shaped, bays, or terraced. A trailer dump station is located across the main access road from the Bearpaw campground. All camping areas have some shade trees, extensive lawns between sites, and are large enough for most modern units. There are 46 sites in Bearpaw campground available for reservation, with a minimum 4 days per reservation, and another 46 sites which can be seasonally rented in Bearpaw; contact the park administration for details. There is a trailer storage compound located north of the main access road just past the marina complex. Space in this locked compound can be rented by contacting the park office.

BEARPAW CAMPGROUND

Located about 1.5 km northeast of the campground entry booth (past the golf course, marina and cottage subdivision), this is the largest of the 5 campgrounds with its 172 sites in 5 sprawling loops. Of these sites, only 36 are non-electrified; all the remaining sites have 30-amp service—none are fully serviced. Moving east along Bearpaw, the first loop can be accessed either from first access off Hwy 261, or from the campground's main access road which runs parallel to Bearpaw campground. There are 23 electrified and 19 non-electrified sites here as well as some of the shadiest sites in the campground; the firewood bin is located near site #24. The next loop east has 47 electrified sites, of which #43 and #44 are best suited for wheelchair access as they are hard surfaced and closest to the barrier-free service center; the firewood bin is near site #89. Just past the service center, the next 2 loops have 23 and 24 electrified sites, all fairly open but also some of the largest in the park. The last loop has 36 sites, 18 non-electrified, all of which are fairly open except for the non-electrified sites along the lake which are quite well shaded. The firewood bin is located next to the fish cleaning shack between the lake and site #169.

All the sites are leveled on gravel pads and have either culvert or pole BBQs and picnic tables. Drinking water taps and trash bins are scattered throughout the loop, as are vault toilets. There are modern washroom facilities available in the two service centers serving Bearpaw campground; these are the only two such centers in the park. A mini-center is located along the road between sites 159 and 161, with 4 unisex barrier-free washrooms. A much larger barrier-free complex is centrally located near site #43, with 3 shower stalls, sinks and flush toilets per side as well as the coin-operated laundry facility. Bring lots of quarters for both washers and dryers; some change can be made at the camp store and confectionary which is beside the service center. Offering a line of iced treats, candy and pop as well as some groceries and camping items, they also sell used paperback novels and rent bocce and horseshoe sets. There is ample parking in front of the complex, as this is the main shower facility for all the campgrounds. The self-registry kiosk has been relocated to the mini-service center's meridian and is used only in the shoulder season when the park entry office is closed.

Bearpaw has the only two playgrounds in the camping areas, the largest of which sits in a large bed of soft sand south of the store, behind sites #99 and #101. There is a large creative play structure built of treated beams, including colorful slides and climbers. A smaller playground is also set in a sand pit behind site #162, near the mini service center. This playground has swings, teeter-totters, and climber with slide attached, and an open field for wide games. There is also a wonderful walking trail running through the woods between the campgrounds and the lake. It begins behind the fish cleaning shelter and runs for about half a km or so, ending at the beach between Bearpaw and the Sandy Ridge Cottage Subdivision. Wide and well shaded, it is paved for its whole length and suitable for wheelchairs.

Sagebrush campground, located just past Bearpaw's fifth camping loop on the campground access road, has 41 non-electrified sites in 4 small loops. Although all 4 loops share several features such as pole BBQs, wooden picnic tables, and spacious sites, there is a wide disparity between shade and privacy. Sites #1–9 are all set in deep brush and among the most private in the entire province while the remaining ones are all fairly open with a few shade trees and little underbrush for privacy between sites. There are two sets of flush toilets serving the campgrounds as well as 3 excellent firepits with bench seating, sure to host your campfire stories in style. The firepits and camp kitchen are all available free of charge on a first-come, first-served basis; note that the camp kitchen has no wood stove but the park will provide briquette BBQs to be used in the camp kitchen for group gatherings. One firewood pile is available near site #10, and potable water taps are available beside the camp kitchen and the toilets. There is ample lawn, well tended, throughout Sagebrush; the roadways are graveled but very serviceable.

This loop also shares the new Sagebrush Amphitheater with Bearpaw. The campground access road is paved right up to the parking lot for the amphitheater, and the path leading to the sturdy benches is barrier free. The amphitheater has sound and lighting, and has bench seating for 60 or so patrons. There is a large firepit behind with bench seating. Both venues are used by park staff in hosting various interpretive programs, all free to campers of all ages; check with the park entrance information kiosk or on bulletin boards throughout the park for more details and timings on all interpretive programs.

Nighthawk campground is reached by continuing past Bearpaw campground on Hwy 261 approximately 1 km or so, to an intersection (Riverside campground to the right, and Nighthawk campground to the left). There are 29 non-electrified sites here and, like Riverside, they are used as an overflow campground only. All the sites have wooden picnic tables, pole BBQs and access to a set of vault toilets, trash bins and a wood pile. The park has removed the old pump well and installed a new potable-water line to both Nighthawk and Riverside campgrounds; Nighthawk has 2 water taps and Riverside has 3. Although the roads are graveled now, they were previously paved as this was once the original campground in the park. Although there is little shelter, the facilities have been upgraded with new potable water and refurbished toilets; this loop is now used regularly by the younger generation.

Riverside campground is located across the main access road from Nighthawk, currently used as an overflow area. All 37 sites are located off the graveled access road, and share the vault toilets, trash bins, and wood pile. The sites back into the woods so there is some shade but little cover between sites for privacy; site #23 is the best of the bunch. As mentioned above, a new potable water system supplies drinking water to three taps in the loop.

Of note is the scenic drive one can take by continuing past the Nighthawk/Riverside intersection on the main access road. The paved road ends in somewhat rough gravel just past the intersection and travel is limited to 40 kph but there is much scenery to enjoy, so one wouldn't want to go much faster anyway. The drive ends in a very tight loop, returning the same way you came in. As you are skirting the lake you'll have tall hills and coulees just to the north and a scenic lake view at the turnaround point. There are no amenities along the way or at the turnaround loop, but the scenery makes the drive enjoyable all the same.

Prairie Meadow group camping's day-use area is located across the highway from the main part of the park, and includes beach, picnic area and playground, with the group campground at the far end of the paved road. There is no real upper limit to the size of group or number of groups which can be accommodated, although park policy regulates a minimum of 6 camping units to a group reservation. There are 4 electrical panel boxes spread out through the campground, supplying power to 40 camping units. There are tall cottonwoods for shade, pole BBQs and picnic tables scattered throughout. Two sets of vault toilets (one at either end of the area) also have trash bins, woodpiles and potable water taps. There are no camp kitchens, and the sites are all naturally leveled and drained. As there is little underbrush, there is little privacy in the very open sites, but there is plenty of grass for tents and games. Group area patrons have access to the shower facilities in Bearpaw campground, and are within easy walking distance to the main swim beach and its extensive playground and day-use picnic area. For more details or to book your own group, contact the park office.

BEACHES AND BOATING

There are several beaches in the park, two in the day-use area and one between the cottage subdivision and Bearpaw campground. The largest and nicest of them all is the main swim beach in the day-use area. There are 4 large, paved parking lots anchoring the area, as the picnic ground is huge, set amid tall cottonwood trees on a large, lush lawn. Although there is ample space for picnickers with pole BBQs and picnic tables, there is no firewood supplied so bring charcoal briquettes for the BBQs. The swim beach itself is monstrous, with clean, fine sand and a modern change room and washroom facility. Besides the change house, there is one set of barrier-free toilets located along the paved walking path on the west end of the day-use area. There are no showers, but there is a payphone available here. The buoyed swimming areas are non-supervised, and there are no swim lessons offered. A paved walking trail runs among the trees a short distance to a smaller (but still quite large) buoyed swim area. The lake is quite shallow in this spot, so there is ample room for splashing about. The trees form an interesting dichotomy to the beach: there are ardent sun worshippers tanning themselves on the beach proper while other folk seek the cool shade and lawn nearer the trees. The beach is so large that both groups are accommodated with ease, including the ubiquitous sandcastle-building among the wee folk. There is also a wonderfully large, colorful play structure set in a sand pit between the two beaches.

The third swim beach, between the cottage subdivision and Bearpaw is the smallest of the three, as well as the sunniest. It has two sets of non-wheelchair accessible flush toilets and trash bins but no picnic area. It does have buoys marking the swimming area, which isn't as wide as the main beach, and deep clean sand. Although the main beach is better in my opinion, the path draining happy campers from Bearpaw to this beach and it's proximity to the cottagers will make it more immediately used.

Boating on this entire basin is very popular, as are all forms of water sports, and the marina here does the lake justice. Situated in a sheltered bay with 110 slips available for rent daily or seasonally, this full-service marina rents fishing boats, kayaks, canoes and pedal boats. It also sells a full line of marine supplies, including fuel. Operated by Anchor Marine in nearby Kyle, the marina can service boats and motors at the Kyle location. Fishing tackle, bait, licenses, camping supplies, ice and a line of pop and candy are available in this modern facility. The hardened boat launch beside the marina is wide and deep enough for just about any boat and comparable to the Elbow Marina at the east end of Diefenbaker Lake for capability. There are only three marine fueling points on the lake: this one, Elbow Marina on the eastern end, and Rusty's Marina at Palliser Regional Park near Riverhurst. Sport fishing is popular on the lake, with 21 species of game fish regularly taken. As the lake is so large, there is adventure around every point and in every bay. You can find secluded places where your own private beach awaits, or you can sit on the open deck overlooking the marina and enjoy a cup of coffee as you watch the windsurfers dance in the waves. Contact the Marina directly at: (306) 375-2822 or by email at anchor.marine@sasktel.net; check out their website at www.anchormarine.ca.

GOLF

The Marina Mini-Golf is an 18-hole adventure offered beside the Marina, 9 holes of which are barrier-free. The fanciful holes are decorated with huge wooden carvings of birds and beasts, lined with white crushed rock, and very pretty to look at. Don't let looks deceive you, though: the course is not easy to par, no matter how "hot" you think your putter is! With an elevation change of 12 feet, sand and water traps and some rough greens, this is a challenge for the most seasoned of golfers, not to mention a whole lot of family fun. Contact the Marina directly to arrange a mini-golf tournament; they rent all the necessary equipment along with your greens fees.

Saskatchewan Landing Golf Resort is a pretty 18-hole grass green championship course set amid the hills and coulees of the north shore of Lake Diefenbaker. So rugged is the terrain that the only level lie you'll find will be in the fully licensed dining room! The pro-shop has a full line of club and cart rentals and sales, as well as branded clothing for sale. Those bringing their own golf carts will be charged a trackage fee. The course pro can assess your swing and give private instruction, and there is a putting green and driving range to help hone your swing. The barrier-free clubhouse has an excellent restaurant featuring the famed "Wooly burger," named for the wooly mammoth which is the course logo. The licensed dining room features a panoramic view of the lake and the 18th hole, serving a full menu and offering daily lunch and supper specials. The restaurant is open from May through to the end of September; contact them directly for catering information. Tee reservations are recommended for this busy and popular course; you can reach them at (306) 375-2233 in season or by mail at:

Saskatchewan Landing Golf Resort
PO Box 147
Kyle, SK S0L 1T0
Website: http://www.sasklandinggolfresort.com

HIKING

This is one area that Saskatchewan Landing Provincial Park excels in. Anyone who thinks Saskatchewan is flat and boring has never hiked the coulees and hills of this park! There are items of historical interest such as bison rubbing stones, tipi rings, and evidence of the Battlefords Trail. Self-guided interpretive hikes detail the rich and varied natural diversity as well as local history. These hikes are not for the faint of heart; several feature a 100-meter vertical change and there will be no water or real shelter along the way. Mountain bikers will rejoice to discover that they are welcomed on the backcountry trails, although I cannot imagine pedaling up some of those steep hills! Only one of the trails is not maintained in the summer months and the reward is as vast as the prairie horizon, limited only by your own vision. The sun and wind have little to play with but your unprotected skin, so bring a hat, sunscreen, and plenty of water … oh, and your camera. There are plenty of memories to capture, from stunning scenery to rare wildlife; check in at the Goodwin House office for more information.

From Goodwin House, home to the park administration office and interpretive center, you'll find trailhead for the Coulee Trail, either 1 km or 3 km (depending on your choice of loop) with interpretive signs to match. You'll discover the diversity of the terrain, wildlife, birds and flora, all of which will tempt you on to greater discovery. A gravel road leads about 2.5 km west from Goodwin House to trailhead for three loops. At the trailhead you'll find two sets of vault toilets and some trash bins, as well as signs depicting the trails waiting for your feet. Smart Trail follows the river and slumps on a 6-km loop; Brunyee Trail leads you around the coulee on a 2-km loop; and Prairie Vista Interpretive Trail (the newest of the three) leads you up and over the coulees on a 3.5-km loop. Prairie Vista is perhaps the most physically demanding of the three trails, as it takes you up and down 100-meter-deep coulees several times, with steep slopes (slippery when wet, watch your step) and no rest or water points along the way. I would recommend checking in with the park staff at Goodwin House before departure on any of these hikes so they know who is out on the trails in case of inclement weather.

Across the highway from Goodwin House is the Equestrian Camp with its paddock and trailer parking; there will be no feed or stables, so you must make your own arrangements locally. A set of vault toilets completes the facilities, which are available for reservation; contact the park office for details. From here you can hike the "Rings, Ruts, and Remnants" hiking trail, a 2.6-km self-guided interpretive hike. Here you will learn about early human habitation in the area with its varied successes and failures, from First Nations to the early homesteaders and ranchers. You'll see dim echoes of their lives in the impressions they left behind on this land, and see some of the rugged beauty that they came to know. Although the road into the Equestrian Camp is rugged and somewhat overgrown, we had no trouble taking our mini-van in; just go slow and you'll be fine.

Across from site #1 in Bearpaw is a small parking lot and the trailhead for "Ridges and Ravines Interpretive Trail," a 1.2-km self-guided interpretive hike that leads you into the hills to discover the nature of the very rocks and hills themselves. This hike concentrates on the geology and ecology of the coulees and offers some magnificent views of the lake as well; at the height of trail you'll find a couple of sturdy benches, from which vantage point you'll be rewarded with the sun rising over the far hills, spreading a rosy glow to the sleeping world below you—truly a sight never to be forgotten and well worth all the effort.

For those unwilling or unable to take in one of these hikes, you really should check out Lookout Point, just off the main access road as you drive to the main beach. The road leading to the scenic overlook is rough but serviceable, and the view is well worth the time. You'll have the lake spread out in front of you and (particularly in the spring) the hills painted with wildflowers. Of particular note is the prickly-pear cactus in blossom from May through late June, when this spiny plant covers the hills with yellow flowers.

SERVICES

The park office is located in historic Goodwin House (pictured here), faithfully restored from when it served as the house for the Goodwin family who settled in the area in 1898. You'll find a wealth of information here in brochures and displays, and in the park staff who are very knowledgeable about all matters pertaining to the park and its environs; I thought the displays of birds and reptiles found in the park to be of particular interest. You'll find a brochure here published by Nature Saskatchewan, *The Field Checklist of Saskatchewan Birds*, which lists 430 species of birds which have been recorded in the province. While I will not say you'll see them all in this park, the woods and water are most definitely a source of food and habitat for a bewildering array of birds of all sorts: songbirds, shorebirds, waterfowl, and birds of prey among them.

The park has two shopping venues, Papa Joe's Convenience Store in Bearpaw, and the Marina, offering short lines of confectionery, grocery and camping items. For more complete shopping consider Kyle (about 20 minutes north on Hwy 4) or Swift Current (about 30 minutes south on Hwy 4). Both communities offer full shopping, mechanical, medical and worship services. There is much to offer the camping enthusiast in this park: scenery, hiking, beaches, camping, and water sports. For more information or to reserve a site for your own adventure, contact the park at:

Saskatchewan Landing Provincial Park
Box 179
Stewart Valley, SK   S0N 2P0
Telephone: (306) 375-5525 (park office) or (306) 375-5527 (for campground reservations)
Website: linked from www.saskparks.net.

ST. VICTOR PETROGLYPHS PROVINCIAL HISTORICAL PARK

Located 2 km south of St. Victor and 1 km west of Sylvan Valley Regional Park, this park was established to protect the petroglyphs (rock carvings) created by the First Nations people who saw the spectacular landscape as a place of great beauty, perhaps even with spiritual power. Those people used to come here over many years and have left their mark upon the very rocks of the land. Who they were, how long they came to this place and the meaning of the carvings are all long lost, but what is certain is that this is a very special place. Archeological research suggests that the original carvers were ancestors of the Dakota and Nakota peoples, and that the carvings were made sometime between 500–1700 AD. They were probably carved by tribal shamans or medicine men as part of a religious ceremony, but the actual meaning of the carvings is a mystery. They must be preserved though, so please do not climb over the fence to get at the glyphs. There are a set of recreated carvings on the stone at the park entrance; use these to make rubbings and not the originals.

These carvings are unique because they are mostly on the horizontal clifftop cap stone; this is only one of 5 such sites in all of Canada. Carvings may have existed on the softer cliff faces, but centuries of erosion have eradicated them. The same forces of nature are slowly erasing these carvings as well, making them increasingly difficult to see. The best time to see them is on a cloudless day in the mid-morning or mid-afternoon when the angle of the sun increases shadows, outlining the edges of the glyphs.

There are no facilities in the park except for a small parking lot just beside the road. A well-marked but not wheelchair-accessible path leads from the parking lot up to the top of the hill where the views can be spectacular. Sylvan Valley Regional Park is only a kilometer away and there is a fine hiking trail from the regional park's campgrounds to the historical park's entrance. The regional park offers camping with some electrified sites as well as picnic tables and pole BBQs; free showers are available in the town of St. Victor.

While in the town, check out the Angus McGillis Heritage Site, a re-creation of an 1870s homestead; entrance is free and there is a lot to see. You should also see Le Beau Village Museum on Main Street in St. Victor; an entrance fee of $1 for adults accesses the displays of pioneer life, early local history, and the Petroglyphs. Tours of the Petroglyphs can be arranged by contacting:

> The Friends of the Petroglyphs
> PO Box 1716
> Assiniboia, SK   S0H 0B0
> Telephone: (306) 642-5386 in the summer months
>
> Email: st.victor@sasktel.net

More information on this fascinating park can be obtained from SERM at:

> St. Victor Petroglyphs Provincial Historic Park
> PO Box 850
> Maple Creek, SK   S0N 1N0
> Telephone: (306) 662-5411
> E-mail by linking from: www.saskparks.net

WOOD MOUNTAIN PROVINCIAL HISTORIC PARK

After the Sioux Nations had defeated General Custer and his 7th Cavalry at the Battle of the Greasy Grass River, better known as the Little Bighorn, they feared retribution at the hands of the "Long Knives," the American cavalry, so they fled north with all their families and possessions. In 1876 Chief Sitting Bull led his large band of followers to the Wood Mountain area, where the fledgling North-West Mounted Police (NWMP) would reopen a small outpost. It was up to the intrepid men of the NWMP to keep the peace between Sitting Bull's warriors and local people as well as deal with the politically sensitive issue of the American desire to have the Sioux returned to the United States. There were many people pulling the few NWMP officers in several directions at once, as the Sioux needed food, water, hunting privileges, and the ability to move through this territory, an area that they once traveled freely. Without the courage and steadfast honesty of men like Superintendent James Walsh and a local trader, Jean-Louis Legare, the situation could have devolved from serious to possible open warfare. To men like these fell the seemingly daunting task of convincing Sitting Bull and his 4,000 or so followers to voluntarily return to the United States. I cannot imagine how they did it, but they succeeded. The turning point was the loss of the buffalo, which were kept in the Montana territory by grass fires; the American military kept all hunting parties north of the border, so the Sioux became increasingly desperate as they were starved into submission over the course of 5 long winters. Finally, Sitting Bull and the last of his followers surrendered at Fort Buford, Montana in July 1881.

This was not the last of the stories told about this place, however; the border areas south of the Canadian Pacific Railroad were sparsely populated and thus a safe haven for criminals from both sides of the border, so the little outpost became an important symbol of the new Canadian nation, more than just a deterrent to crime. Patrols dealt with whisky traders, rustlers, cattle management, provision of assistance to incoming settlers, and a host of other duties. At one time the post boasted 41 officers and as many Métis scouts and guides, and one of the few telegraph stations in the area.

Located south of the Village of Wood Mountain beside Hwy 18, the post is open from June 1 to mid-August. No entrance fees are levied, although a donation box is available for visitors. Other than the Interpretive Center buildings, park amenities include picnic tables, drinking water and outdoor toilets; camping can be had at the Wood Mountain Regional Park a short walk away. Interpretive staff will be on hand from 1000–1700 hr daily in season, and group programs are available by prior arrangement. For more information, contact the park at:

Wood Mountain Post Provincial Historic Park
PO Box 850
Maple Creek, SK   S0N 1N0
Telephone: (306) 266-5525 (summer), (306) 662-5411 (year round), or toll-free at 1-800-205-7070 (Saskatchewan only)
Fax: (306) 694-3743
Link to their email from their website at: www.saskparks.net

GRASSLANDS NATIONAL PARK

Located south of Val Marie, this park is so new to the system that they haven't even finished purchasing land for it yet! When complete, there will be approximately 900 square kilometers of mixed-grass prairie reserved for future generations. Home to 40 species of grass as well as rare or endangered animal species like the swift fox or burrowing owl, this habitat came under extraordinary pressure from the waves of European settlers that tried to farm and ranch in the Prairies. Although a great deal of the land now in the park was once considered unsuitable for agricultural production, much of the original habitat was destroyed under a plow. These two small blocks remain relatively undisturbed because of local landowners whose continued environmental stewardship allowed the creation of a grasslands park. There are two main areas, West Block and East Block, with West Block being larger and, at the moment, more developed, although that may be too strong a term. West Block has also seen the arrival of some new residents as a small herd of Plains Bison has been re-introduced into the park.

WEST BLOCK

West Block can be accessed by driving east from Val Marie on Hwy 18 about 14 km where road signs mark the turnoff to the south for the park; follow this road for about 4 km, and watch for the numbered signs for the ecotour route. There is a small parking area near the park entry kiosk; driving on the non-maintained park roads is dreadful if they're wet, and there is no off-road driving allowed. Camping is allowed in the park by both front country at the campsite listed below or by backcountry permit. If you intend to overnight in the backcountry, you must camp at least 1000 meters from any road, and 500 meters from a grouse lek (a lek is defined as a traditional courtship display area attended by a male). No open fires are allowed so you must use camp stoves only. There are no structured camp sites available, although there is one drive-in camp site if you must stay near your vehicle; contact the park office for details. There is one set of vault toilets near the drive-in campsite, otherwise you should practice "No-Trace Camping" and bring out what you took in, toilet paper included. The Frenchman River runs though the heart of the West Block, so you will be ascending and descending the steep hills as you criss-cross the park; there are crossing points on the river where it is shallow enough for hikers, but take care—the bottom can shift and what might have been safe last year might not be this year. The trails are marked, but one should have maps and know how to use a compass if you intend to hike at length in this park. As this park is still obtaining land when it becomes available, you may well walk out of the park and into private land. The park reminds hikers that they must obtain private landowner permission to enter their land before beginning their backcountry adventure; this is the visitor's responsibility, not the park's. After all, it is only good manners to ask their permission first; check with the park office about private ownership in the areas you intend to hike through. (The photos above and below are courtesy of David McLennan, Canadian Plains Research Center.)

The Village of Val Marie is located in the southwest part of the province, at the junction of Hwy 4 and Hwy 18. The park office is located here, as are some essential services. Val Marie has a service station with fuel and supplies, café, grocery and souvenir shopping, hotel, museum, and municipal campgrounds. There is a small library in the village office, along with public internet access. There is a post office, and potable water can be obtained at the park office year-round or at the village campground during the summer months. Drinking water may also be purchased at the store which is open from Monday to Saturday. Please note: there is no drinking water available anywhere in the park; visitors should take 2–3 liters of water per person per day that they intend to stay in the park. The park office is open daily from mid-

May to Labor Day, and on weekdays from September to May. Ask for details and a route map for the approximately 2.5-hr self-guided auto tour that highlights some of the major features of Grasslands National Park.

EAST BLOCK
East Block is accessed by traveling about 125 km east of Val Marie on Hwy 18 to the junction at Wood Mountain Provincial Historic Site (past Mankota and Glentworth), then south on Hwy 18 approximately 23 km. At the park sign, turn west and drive about 6 km to a speed curve where you turn south for another 6 km or so, then turn west again for the last 2.5 km to the park entry kiosk. Don't worry, the route is well signed and you can't stray too far. There is a small parking area near the entry kiosk which has brochures and trail maps but only one campsite, although the park is planning to develop some in the near future. The one drive-in campsite has a set of vault toilets located just down the hill from the entry kiosk, but you are otherwise generally expected to camp at least 1000 meters from any road, and at least 500 meters from any grouse lek. There are several small creeks that run though the park draining spring floods to the Frenchman River, south and west of East Block. From mid-May to the Labor Day long weekend in September you can camp at the Wood Mountain Regional Park, approximately one half- hour drive north of the park; they've got the Rodeo Ranch Museum, well worth an afternoon's visit. You'll also find park information and brochures there; for more information, see the article on Wood Mountain Regional Park in this book.

You must remember that both the East and West Blocks are accessed by dry weather roads; if you're driving in the park, you really should consider leaving at the first sign of summer storms. Wind is a constant, but the roads can quickly become dangerous when wet. For the adventurous, try a horseback expedition in the park; arrangements can be made from the ranches near Wood Mountain Regional Park. Cycling is possible on many of the old roads, and nature photography is also quite popular. Please note, however, that park rules expressly forbid moving teepee stones or disturbing the prairie in any way to improve your shot. School tours are available in late May and June and park staff can also provide educational extension programs as well as adult group tours; contact the park office for more details on content and cost. Park staff also present special events such as:

"East Block Party": sleepover and hike (early August) and the "Have Yourself a Prairie Little Christmas": lantern hike and Christmas concert (usually late November)

For information on these or other aspects of this new park, contact the park staff at:

Grasslands National Park of Canada
P.O. Box 150
Val Marie, SK   S0N 2T0
Telephone: (306)298-2257
Fax: (306) 298-2042
TDD: (306) 298-2217
E-mail: grasslands.info@pc.gc.ca
Website: www.pc.gc.ca/pn-np/sk/grasslands/index_e.asp

Southeast Saskatchewan

Map of Southern Saskatchewan

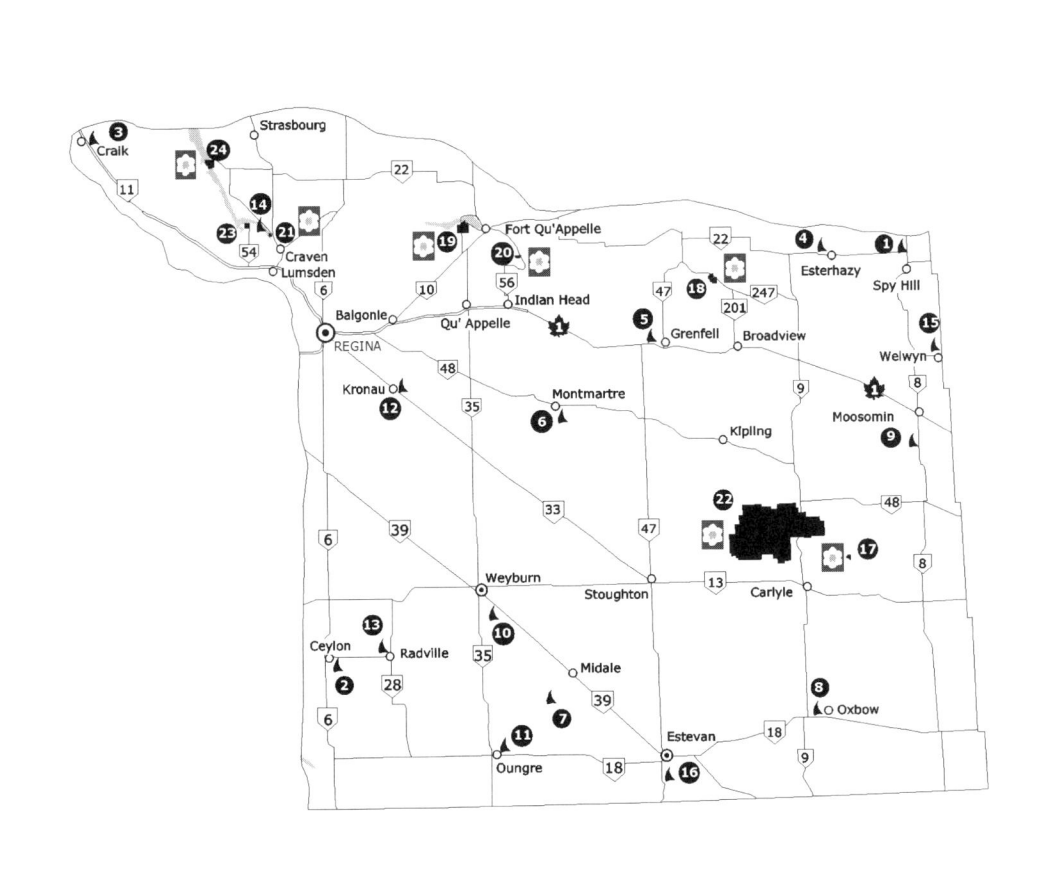

Locations shown on map:

- Craik
- Strasbourg
- Craven
- Lumsden
- Balgonie
- Fort Qu'Appelle
- Esterhazy
- Spy Hill
- Indian Head
- Qu'Appelle
- Grenfell
- Broadview
- Welwyn
- REGINA
- Kronau
- Montmartre
- Kipling
- Moosomin
- Weyburn
- Stoughton
- Carlyle
- Ceylon
- Radville
- Midale
- Oungre
- Estevan
- Oxbow

Highways: 11, 22, 6, 54, 10, 56, 247, 201, 47, 22, 8, 48, 35, 9, 33, 39, 28, 18, 13

CARLTON TRAIL REGIONAL PARK

Built in 1972, this park is located 20 km south of Langenburg on Hwy 8, and 6 km north of Spy Hill. It is located along one of the more important overland routes from Fort Garry (modern Winnipeg) to Edmonton House. Red River carts brought trade goods from the Fort Garry warehouses to the many trading posts strung along the way, including stops at places like Fort Carlton near Prince Albert. A recreational facility has been on site since the 1950s. Developed by a local landowner and professional landscaper to provide a pleasant place for locals and miners, it was then known as From's Lake Resort. It was purchased from the owner, J.H. From, when he became ill in 1972 and the Carlton Trail Regional Park Authority was formed. The Carlton Trail can still be seen weaving a ghostly path through the local area, with artifacts and local history captured by the Wolverine Historical Society. The roads are paved up to the entrance gate, which is open from early May to early October. The park has two man-made lakes in its boundaries, one reserved for swimming; the other, South Lake, has summer cabins and is stocked for anglers. Park entry fees of $4 per day or an annual Regional Park sticker are levied at the gate.

SITES

There are 75 electrified sites—18 with water in East campground, 57 watered ones in West campground and 20 non-electrified sites in the two campgrounds, costing $11 and $8 per day respectively. The electrified sites all have 30-amp service and cost $60 per week, $195 per month or $350 per season; non-electrified sites are $40 per week. All sites are leveled with gravel pads which are graded for drainage. All sites feature pole BBQs, and some have firepits as well. There are also picnic tables and trash cans at every site. The drinking water is piped to six central taps, and firewood is available free of charge from three central bins. The sites are cut out of mature Parklands forest, so aspens and willow dominate the campgrounds although spruce trees have been planted to help mark sites. The roadways are well graveled and should accommodate the largest campers, particularly in the East campgrounds. Toilet facilities vary from primitive to modern, depending on proximity, but all are clean and odorless. Three sets of showers are available for campers, one in each campground and one in the clubhouse. All are free of charge and wheelchair accessible. The East campground doubles as a group site and in a pinch the picnic area can be used as well. There are two picnic areas available, one to the west of the clubhouse, the other across the swimming lake from the clubhouse. A fine, grassed playground is available near the first picnic area as well, and was extensively renovated in 2004. When we visited there was a long waterslide on the hill coming down towards the swimming area. A trailer dump station is also just west of the clubhouse. Reservations are accepted; contact the park at 534-4724 for details.

SPORTS

Judging by the number of people tromping the wide beach, this is a popular swimming destination. Lesson prices may be one reason, as all Red Cross levels are taught for $10 per person or $25 per family. Contact the park office at 534-4724 for details or to register your swimmers. The beach sand is fine and plentiful with a level area covered in picnic tables for spectators. A diving platform is anchored in deeper water to augment lessons and tempt the adventurous out. The beach is unsupervised except during lessons, so swim at your own risk. A beach concession opens during special events, but is normally closed and is not available for rent. There is no boat launch in the South Lake, nor are power boats allowed. The lake is small so canoes, rowboats and paddleboats are all that is required. Stocked annually with walleye, you must obey all provincial regulations when angling.

Among its other charms, this park has developed three hiking trails totaling about 1.6 km (1 mile) that lead you to explore the Marsh/Parklands ecozone. No maps are available but signposts will assist you; the trails are wide and well mowed to differentiate them from the surrounding forest. Three volleyball courts, one on the beach and two on the west picnic area, are available; ask for the ball at the concession in the clubhouse. There are two ball diamonds available with tall wire mesh backstops and turf infields. Team benches are available but no bleachers. A new playground has been built adjacent to the campgrounds.

GOLFING

A 9-hole golf course dominates the hill to the north of the entrance road, featuring automatic watering on fairways, tees and greens, so the course is always green and ready. New PGA-style greens were installed in 2002. The 2800-yard, par-36 course can be tricky as it has a 100 ft. vertical on a rolling terrain, so a level lie only occurs in the clubhouse! Greens fees are $9 on week days for adults and $11 on week ends, for nine holes. You can golf all day for $12 on weekdays or $14 on weekends; juniors get cheaper rates. The club has a practice green and a free driving range, and a fully licensed clubhouse. The clubhouse is divided into two areas: the main area (open 0800–2300 hr) is the diner and concession as well as the pro-shop for booking tee times and renting clubs and carts. The lounge is to the right, up a short flight of stairs. Call the pro-shop at (306) 534-4724 for the course schedule; tee times are not normally reserved.

SERVICES

The town of Langenburg, 20 km north on Hwy 8, has police and health services, as well as shopping and mechanical services. Spy Hill, 8 km south on Hwy 8, has shopping, laundry, mechanical and fuel services available as well as a small museum featuring local history. There are two potash mines close to the park, and tours can be arranged with sufficient notice. As one can imagine, this is a popular park. It hosts eight golf tournaments annually and ball tournaments as well. A big event is the Canada Day celebration with sports, games and contests for the children, and fireworks. For more information on this park, contact the park manager at:

    Carlton Trail Regional Park
    PO Box 3
    Spy Hill, SK   S0A 3W0
    Telephone: (306) 534-4724 in season
    E-mail: carlpark@sasktel.net

CEYLON REGIONAL PARK

Located 3 km east of Ceylon on Hwy 377, this 20-acre park is open from the Victoria Day long weekend in May to the Labor Day long weekend in September. Situated on man-made Ceylon Reservoir, the park features water sports and camping. A fee of $5 per day or $30 for an annual Regional Park sticker is levied for park entry.

SITES

There are 21 electrified and 14 non-electrified sites, costing $15 and $8 per night respectively. Electrified sites can be rented weekly for $90. The sites have picnic tables and pole BBQs, plus access to central water taps. Trash bins and the free firewood supply are located centrally as well. All sites are leveled and drained naturally, and shaded on one side by Ash and Poplar. No trees are placed between the sites, so they are a bit open to the elements. A well-treed picnic area (pictured above) near the beach and playground offers better shade but sparse grass. In fairness, the weather when we visited had been hot and dry for several weeks, so the grass had suffered accordingly. Toilet facilities vary from primitive in the campsites, to modern in the beach shower and washroom complex. The beach shower house provides hot showers free to park patrons. The Lucky Duck is a canteen and grill built in the playground area near the beach. When open, it serves the usual iced treats, snacks, and pop, plus "the best burgers by a dam site" according to its billboard. When we visited, the concession was closed and so we couldn't verify that! The canteen is run separately from the park, so the hours of operation are up to the owner.

WATER SPORTS

The park has built a large sand-bottomed pool surrounded by deep, coarse sand. Little shade is available, so bring a beach umbrella! Two docks float in the deep end for diving and swimming lessons, the maximum depth being 3.5 meters (12 feet). A line of buoys separates shallow from deep. The water is clean and the bottom sandy. One set of swim lessons is taught in July, at a cost of $30 for any of the Red Cross Aquaquest levels, or $20 for Aquatots. There are beach change rooms and showers available. The beach will cost $3 per day per person to use, with seasonal passes costing $50 per family or $20 per single. Contact the park office for lesson information. A simple boatlaunch provides access to the lake, where anglers can try their luck at perch and pike. A beach playground has swings, climbers, slides, teeter-totters, and a merry-go-round all built into deep sand to break falls.

SERVICES

The park has two playgrounds, one by the pool and one by the diner which has a creative play center and rocking horses on springs, all in a huge sandbox. A ball diamond with a tall mesh backstop and bleachers for spectators is in good condition. The town of Ceylon has all the shopping, mechanical and worship services one could want, and the nearest health center is in Radville, 23 km east on Hwy 377. All in all, this is a fairly typical park with a few amenities to commend it. For more information on this park, or to reserve a site, contact the park manager at:

Ceylon Regional Park
PO Box 188
Ceylon, SK   S0L 0T0
Phone: (306) 454-2202
Fax: (306) 454-2627
E-mail: rmgap39@sasktel.net

CRAIK AND DISTRICT REGIONAL PARK

This park is located on the arterial route between Saskatoon and Regina, about 116 km south of Saskatoon. The park is 1.6 km east of Craik on a graveled access road. There are 26 acres of land currently fenced and used, with another 20 acres to be developed. Build in 1967, work is ongoing to upgrade and renew its facilities. The park is down in a small valley; the creek which cut it was dammed to make the Craik reservoir. Many tall elms and poplars grace the campsites, and have become the home for many birds. One notable species is a family of horned owls that lives in a grove just opposite site #2. Open early May to late September, daily fees are $5, waived with an annual Regional Park sticker.

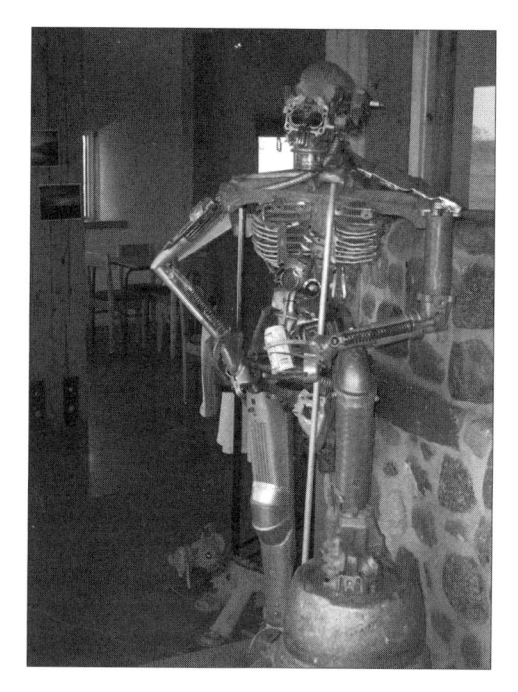

SITES

There are 48 electrified and 9 non-electrified sites, costing $21 and $13 per night, respectively. All sites had picnic tables and firepits made of culvert sections with a moveable grate. Fixed on a cement pad, I found this style handier than the usual pole BBQ. Trash bins were centrally located as were taps dispensing chlorinated well water. The sites varied in size from adequate to huge! The central block of sites are sufficiently large that one asks if each is a single site; I certainly did! An interesting note is the presence of gray water pits across the road from each site; one is asked to dump all dishwater in these pits. Although many of the electrified sites had taps which dispensed unfiltered water, there were none with sewer hook up. A trailer dump station is available. The campsite is surrounded by groves of aspens, but few trees shade individual sites. They have been planted though, and in a few years each site will reside in its own leafy bay. Toilets vary from primitive pump outs to modern flush facilities, with the pool washrooms providing free showers to registered campers as well as pool patrons. We found the sites clean and free of litter. There are two dining shelters available, both normally for casual use although they can be reserved for a special function. The newest one in the east campgrounds is large and completely walled in so it can be licensed for a liquor permit. A new fourplex wheelchair-accessible shower house is available nearby. Sites may be reserved by calling (306) 734-5102; based on the traffic we saw in our stay, this is a good idea! A maximum of 35 sites may be reserved for a special function such as a reunion.

SPORTS

The pool here is circular, asphalt bottomed, and ringed with a grass verge between water and fence. Built in 1968, it has a 200-person capacity. Lifeguards are on duty and two-lesson sets are offered over in July. Prices vary for the Red Cross and RLSS levels offered, and a season pass is also required, costing $25 per person or $65 per family. A 3-meter diving board is available, and plenty of safety equipment including a paddleboat reserved for pool staff only. Contact the park office for lesson information. Other sports offered include a mini-golf course, a badminton court, volleyball net, and two horseshoe pits. All the equipment is available from the concession free of charge except for the mini-golf which costs $1 per player. There are two playgrounds, one large one by the pool and one small one in the East campground. There are swings, slides, teeter-totters, merry-go-rounds and climbing equipment. A hiking trail was built in 1997, starting from an old highway bridge brought in to cross the small creek across from the park gates. About a half-mile in length, the trail leads you to the dam overlook, through the local slumps and flood plain. It may be extended in the future, and is marked with painted rocks. It is also well mowed and so is easy to differentiate from the surrounding grasslands. The dam creating the Craik Reservoir has a boatlaunch and docks to give motor boats access to the lake to try their luck on the 500,000 walleye and jacks that are stocked in there. The reservoir was quite shallow and fairly weedy with quite an algae bloom in effect during our visit, so I cannot recommend swimming or water-skiing here. The park also has a ball diamond for those interested in a pick-up game. A tall mesh backstop and benches are all that's there, but that's all I ever needed as a kid! As a final note, a municipal 9-hole, grass green golf course can be found across the road west of the park. Although not part of the park, one simply has to check it out! The clubhouse is fully licensed and offers a range of light meals, but more importantly it was built with energy conservation in mind. So detailed is the engineering of this facility that a local company offers tours of the building and surrounding grasslands. Contact Pelican Eco-Tours at (306) 734-7777 for details. You might enjoy a game of golf over the 2915 yards (blue tees) as well; call the clubhouse at (306) 7364-2364 for a tee time and current pricing.

SERVICES

The park has a fine pool concession that sells the iced treats, pop, and snacks so popular in summer. Open throughout the camping season, its hours are 1000–2200 hr, as business warrants. Craik, only two minutes away, has a full range of shopping, mechanical, medical, and worship services. Craik also has a museum that chronicles local heritage. Open upon request, it asks for donations as entrance fees, and the curator is only too glad to function as guide. Although the pool is a great draw locally, the Canada Day Celebration always plays to a packed house. The campgrounds are quiet, and there's always a chance to visit with folks from all over North America at this popular way station. A busy park, in part due to the traffic on the highway, this park is full to capacity during most of July, and about half capacity in June and August. For more information on this park, or to discuss swim lessons, contact the park office at:

    Craik and District Regional Park
    Box 431
    Craik, SK   S0G 0V0
    Telephone: (306) 734-5102 (in season)
    Fax: (306) 734-2688 (year round)
    Website: www.craik.ca/park/

ESTERHAZY REGIONAL PARK

Located on the northeast corner of the town of Esterhazy, at the intersection of Hwys 80 and 22, the park is open from Victoria Day to the Labor Day weekend. The golf course may be open longer, as weather permits, but the pool and campground will be closed. The park has a fine swimming pool and a wonderful golf course with a panoramic view of the Crescent Creek valley. No daily entry fees are levied, but campers are expected to have a Regional Park sticker

SITES

There are 25 electrified sites with water and 30-amp service and 3 non-electrified sites, costing $15 and $10 each, respectively. Surprisingly, the non-electrified sites are a bit larger than the electrified sites, and all have taps which supply Esterhazy municipal water. Every site has a trash bin and a picnic table. There are no pole BBQs or firepits, and no firewood is supplied. Sites are naturally drained and leveled and well grassed to reduce the dirt tracked into your camper. A sewer dump station is near the pool. There is no dining shelter or camp kitchen. The trees are all plantation poplars and evenly spaced. Shade is at a premium although the trees are 20 ft (6 m) tall. Modern toilet facilities are available at the pool, complete with free showers. Ask the pool attendant for a key when you pay for your site. Modern facilities are also available at the golf clubhouse, but these will be unavailable after hours.

GOLF

Esterhazy has a beautiful 18-hole course, a 5420-yard, par-69 that incorporates the Crescent Creek valley. The course is short, but the vertical change makes it interesting, and the view is excellent. A putting green is available to the right of the clubhouse, and a driving range is under construction. The pro-shop sells a full line of golf equipment, and will rent clubs and carts. No pro or lessons are available, though. Greens fees are $13 per 9 holes or $20 per 18 holes; a daily pass is $25. For tee reservations on weekends and holidays only, call the clubhouse at (306) 745-6456. The clubhouse hours are 0630–2130 hr; they serve light meals and are fully licensed. The adventurous may want to try their specialty, "Deep-fried Gizzards" (with Ranch sauce) which, so I am told, are quite delicious!

WATER SPORTS

A very nice, new pool has been built just across the access road from the campgrounds. Called the D.A. Mackenzie Aquatic Center, it opens in early June with its first lesson set soon after, and closes on the Labor Day weekend. The pool opens at 0630 hr on weekdays and closes at 2100 hr, with classes and public swims interspersed throughout. Lessons cost from $40 up to $100, depending on which Red Cross or RLSC level is desired. Register in person at the pool; no telephone registrations will be accepted. A public swim will cost as little as $2.50 per child up to $10 per family, with a family season pass costing $175. The pool can be rented for a private function; contact the pool manager for further information at (306)745-2844. Registered campers can get a key for the outside access washroom and shower facilities. Just beside the pool is a playground (pictured here) with swings, teeter-totters and climbing equipment. Altogether an impressive facility!

SERVICES
The town of Esterhazy has all the shopping, mechanical, medical and worship services a traveler could need. The park itself has no canteen or diner, except for the fully licensed clubhouse. The campground rarely sees a capacity crowd, so there is no reservation system. For more information on this park contact the manager at:

Esterhazy Regional Park
PO Box 490
Esterhazy, SK   S0A 0X0
Telephone: (306) 745-3942
Fax: (306) 745-6797
E-mail: town.esterhazy@sk.net

GRENFELL REGIONAL PARK

This municipal park is located on the western edge of the town of Grenfell just off the Trans Canada Highway. Because of this, the campgrounds can be quite full with people heading off on their own Canadian adventures. The park is open from May 1 to the middle of October, when the coming winter means the water lines must be blown dry. The park does not levy a daily entrance fee, but does recommend buying an annual Regional Park sticker for $30.

SITES

There are 32 serviced sites and 15 unserviced sites. The serviced sites have water and 15-amp electrical hookups, and cost $12 per night for electrical use, or $15 for full hookup. Two sites, #1 and #2, have been upgraded to 30-amp service. The unserviced sites rent for $10 per night. Only one unit is allowed per site; every extra tent or such will be levied an additional $2 per night. All fees can be paid at the pool booth in the recreation complex beside the campgrounds. All sites have picnic tables, pole BBQs and share central trash disposal. Two dining shelters provide wet weather relief. Firewood was not provided, and water was available from central taps, supplying Grenfell municipal water. Washrooms are located in the recreation complex and are accessible night and day except for the 2-hour period when they are cleaned. As they are down a flight of stairs they are not wheelchair accessible. The showers are free and the facilities modern with flush toilets and plenty of sinks. A trailer dump station is located to the right of the campground entrance, and is free to registered patrons. Pets are allowed but they must remain on a leash at all times. Reservations are accepted, but the bookings start in February, so you had best call early. Contact the Park Secretary at (306) 697-3055.

BASEBALL

There are 3 ball diamonds across the street from the recreation complex, capable of holding fastball, slow pitch, and minor ball types of play. The #1 field is home to the local fastball team, and is complete with limed red shale infield, grass outfields, grandstands, player's shelters, and a well-kept mesh backstop and home run fences. It can even be lit up for night play! Fields #2 and #3 have grass infields. The #1 field can be rented when not in use for league play, and costs $50 for the lights. The recreation complex has an arena and a top lobby that can be rented for an entire weekend (including one ball diamond) for $800. As one might imagine, this is a popular venue locally for tournaments, both private and public, so you'd best book early; contact the Park Secretary at (306) 697-3055 for details.

GOLFING

There is a 9-hole, sand-green golf course just across from the campgrounds. It has no pro-shop as such, but a gentleman in a booth at the first tee will take the greens fees and give you the scorecard and map. The course is reasonably priced at $5 for the entire day! It is built on a fairly flat piece of land, so it won't be terribly tricky to play; the biggest trouble you'll face is staying on your own fairway, if you play the slice I do! Just beside the golf course is the miniature golf course, with 18 holes of putting to occupy your afternoon. The course costs $1 for children or $2 for an adult, payable at the booth. The overflow campgrounds is located just behind the mini-golf, should the need arise.

SWIMMING

The recreation complex houses the change rooms and showers for the outdoor swimming and paddling pool that borders the campgrounds. There are 3 lesson sets offered in July and August, costing between $20 and $50 per registrant depending on level desired. Public swims are also offered daily with pool use costing $2 to $3 depending on age. Season passes are also available, with rates of up to $200 for a family pass. The entire pool facility can be rented for a private function for $75 per hour, including the lifeguard's wages; contact the park secretary for details. Just beside the pool is a large grassy area which houses the playground. It has a large sandbox, merry-go-rounds, a creative play center, slides, swings, and teeter-totters. All the equipment is in excellent condition, and there is a large field to run and play in as well.

SERVICES

The park has an interesting shop in the top lobby that sells crafts made by local people. The Grenfell Regional Park Craft Shop is a cooperative of sorts that opens from 1800–2030 hr daily during July and August, and offers a wide variety of items hand made by some very talented people. The park itself has no shop other than this one, although there is a pop cooler in the pool lobby. The Town of Grenfell offers a complete range of amenities, including shopping, mechanical, medical, and worship services. The park is host to golf and ball tournaments, most notably the Canada Day ball tournament. As one can see, this is a popular park with a lot going on. It was full the week we stayed there, mostly with people like ourselves who were en route to someplace else. We found the park to be quiet, well run and maintained, and busy with the joyful noise of the pool patrons. For more information on this park, or to book your event, contact the Park Secretary at:

Grenfell Regional Park
PO Box 1120
Grenfell, SK S0G 2B0
Telephone: (306) 697-2815
Fax: (306) 697-2484
E-mail: townofgrenfell@sasktel.net

KEMOCA REGIONAL PARK

Located on the edge of Main Street in Montmartre, the park is open from May 1 until the end of September. The Regional Park road signs show the way from Hwy 48, but the park is poorly signed in town; stay on Main Street and you'll find it on the south side of town. The park gets its name from the first two letters of its supporting towns: Kendal, Montmartre, and Candiac. The 40-acre park charges a $5 daily entrance fee, waived if you have an annual Regional Park sticker.

SITES

There are 6 electrified sites, with 15-amp service, that rent for $15 per night or $80 per week; pay at the pool house. There are also 10 non-electrified sites costing $12 per night or $65 per week. Firewood is provided free from a central bin, but the pole BBQs provided are quite a unique design and best for charcoal use. The sites also have picnic tables and trash bins. Although the sites are quite close together, on the left as you drive in, they have a line of tall trees planted between them, so you have the feeling of camping in a forest. Shade is obviously abundant, so the campsites are quite cool and private. They are all completely grassed, with drinking water (Montmartre municipal) piped between each two sites. Although you must back into them, they are spacious enough for the largest unit. Washroom facilities are modern, as the pool house has wheelchair-accessible flush toilets and free showers for registered campers. A trailer dump station is available by the park entrance, free for registered guests. There are two dining shelters available for use, one of which has removable canvas siding and a cement floor. This one doubles as the cabaret and dance floor during special events, and can be rented for yours. There is no reservation system in place; the sites rent first come, first served. Mind you, if you intend to rent the park for a private reunion or such, I'm sure the park will discuss reserving sites for the function. There are only 10 electrified sites, but a lot of grassy space for unserviced group camping exists around the many sports venues. Contact the park secretary for details at the address below, or contact the pool office in season at (306) 424-2232 for more information.

GOLFING

There is a 9-hole, sand-green golf course available in the park, with an old schoolhouse moved in as the clubhouse. The clubhouse won't normally be open except during tournaments, but you can rent it for your event; contact the park office for details. Just to show how much this park is supported by its many local patrons, the land for the golf course was donated by The Sacred Heart Parish. The course has no pro-shop, driving range, equipment rentals, or practice green, but it only costs $5 per day to play. Greens fees are payable on the honor system on the first tee. The course covers 2555 yards on its par-36 layout, with a score card including course map available from a bin on the first tee. Although it's a simple course, there has been much work done on it with literally thousands of trees planted to demarcate the fairways and shelter the greens. It is well maintained, as is all the park infrastructure, and worth the time to play. There won't normally be a need for tee reservations, even if there was a method to make them; simply show up and enjoy yourself!

SWIMMING

The park had a stroke of misfortune when the change rooms and canteen portion of the pool house were destroyed by fire in 1984. They have rebuilt it with a magnificent new design both interesting and functional, and have, since the first edition of this book, newly renovated it. There is a canteen that sells the usual treats and snacks as well as burgers and fries. It is open from 0900–1700 hr daily in season, and during the night when any special event is on. Swimming lessons are very popular here, with two pricing schemes based on the purchase of a season pool pass. Lessons are of two types, half-hour and one-hour sessions. If you've a season pass, lessons cost $30 for a half-hour set or $45 for an hour-long set; without a pass they cost $40 and $65. The lessons run daily in the morning for a week, and include all the Red Cross Aquaquest levels. The pool itself is a Junior Olympic design with a spray pool on the side for summer fun. Public swims take place daily in the afternoon and early evening, and vary in price from $1 for a pre-schooler to $3 for an adult. For more information on the pool's operation or to register a swimmer, contact the pool office at (306) 424-2232.

SPORTS

No question about it, the whole region has gone sports mad! There are 5 ball diamonds, with tall wire mesh backstops on sturdy metal poles (all installed by volunteers), dugouts, bleachers, and grass infields. The whole facility can easily hold a fairly major tournament, and has with zone and provincial playoffs held here over the years. The equipment was planned, organized and built by the Montmartre Baseball Club. A quarter-mile track has been built in the center of the park just to the left of the cabaret shelter that hosts an annual spring track and field event. There is a "2 on 2" basketball hoop and cement pad and a couple of horseshoe pits. The playground is in two sections, the old one with cement tunnels built into a short hill (pictured above), the new one with a large creative play center that includes a swinging rope bridge. Between them they have swings, slides, climbing structures and teeter-totters. As with all the park's equipment, the playground is in excellent shape, well maintained and gaily painted. A walking trail has been built, paved with crusher dust, around the park, running 1.35 km—perfect for the morning constitutional! In 2005 the park removed the football field and replaced it with 2 soccer pitches. They are also in the process of building a "Frisbee Golf" course. Any portion of the park or its equipment can be rented for your special function; contact the Park Secretary with your needs.

SERVICES
The park has the canteen but little else for your shopping pleasure. The town of Montmartre has a range of shopping, mechanical, medical, and worship services for the traveling camper. As one can imagine with all this equipment the park is busy with tournaments of all sorts. There are 4 ball and golf tournaments from June to August, with many other private and special functions as well. There are Country and Rock cabarets, and the Family Fun day, usually held on the second weekend of July. For more information on this delightfully busy park, or to book your function, contact the Park Secretary at:

Kemoca Regional Park
PO Box 330
Montmartre, SK   S0G 3M0
Telephone: (306) 424-2040.

MAINPRIZE REGIONAL PARK

Built in 1994, this is one of the newest parks in the system. It is located 15 km southwest of Midale off Hwy 39, on the banks of the Rafferty reservoir. The park is named for Dr. Mainprize, a local physician who worked for 50 years in the community, and in his memory a reconstruction of his little church has been built in the park; it seems to "bring a feeling of Doc's presence to the new park, because of his religious background." Since the park's opening it has seen major revisions to almost every aspect, making it one of the most dynamic recreation facilities in the province. It features a grassland and western theme with camping, a fine golf course, and access to some of the best fishing in the area. The park is open from May 1 until mid-October, although the season could be extended if the fall weather permits. The park levies a $6 daily entrance fee, waived if you have an annual Regional Park sticker.

SITES

There are four camping areas currently available, Camps A, B, C, and overflow. Camp A consists of 27 full-service sites with 30-amp electrical service, full sewer and potable water. Since our first visit the trees have grown and now provide some shade and wind protection. The trees are still young but will be magnificent when fully grown. A shower building is available on the west side of the area, beside which is a small playground. These sites, although smaller than the new ones, are pretty much reserved for seasonal campers; contact the park office for details.

Camp B has 35 sites, all electrified but only 10 of which have 30 amp service; the remainder have 20-amp supply. Potable water is centrally located and a shower/bathroom facility is located on the east edge of this area, shared between Camp B and Camp C. Grass-covered, the area has smaller sites for tenters as well as the larger motorhomes and trailers. The sites have tall fences between them for privacy, and all sites are the "back-in" style.

Camp C is a new development built to meet the expanding needs of this popular park. Begun in the fall of 2003, it will have 22 full-service sites open by the spring of 2004. When completed, it will have 46 fully serviced sites, some of which will have 50-amp service! As this is a new area, the trees are young and will in time provide ample shade. In the interim, be patient and enjoy the scenery! The campground supervisor lives in C12, and a small playground is located near C22.

The overflow area consists of 12 sites with 15-amp electrical service as well as 4 non-serviced sites. As it is the overflow, it is not placed near the shower/toilet center shared by the main campgrounds. Toilets are available nearby on the golf course and can be used by these sites' occupants.

All the sites have sturdy picnic tables and fire pits; firewood is available for sale at the park office or from the campground supervisor. A walking trail, approximately 1 km long and built on the old chandler rail bed, borders all three main campgrounds and links them to the beach area and ball diamond via a walk-through culvert. Potable water supplied is produced at the park's new water filtration facility. Prices for sites will change annually based on the rising costs of providing potable water, electricity and other services. As of this writing, a full-service site will cost $25 per night, $150 per week, $500 per month, or $1000 for the season. Sites with electrical-only service will vary based on amperage required, so call for details; non-serviced sites will cost $12 nightly, $72 weekly, $240 monthly, or $480 seasonally.

A trailer dump station is located just beside the main campgrounds. Washrooms are modern, with flush toilets and hot showers available free to registered campers in the shower house beside the main campgrounds or at the beach. Roadways are paved right up to the park gates, and in excellent graveled condition elsewhere. The sites have plenty of room for the largest unit, and are well drained and leveled. You can reserve sites by calling the park entry gate at (306) 458-2865 in season or the clubhouse (458-2452) in the off-season; have a major credit card available, and be aware that you will be billed for sites reserved that go unused unless you phone to cancel. Guests must be 21 years of age and will require a major credit card to rent a site; a campground supervisor is living onsite and will deal with all infractions of park bylaws. Pets are allowed but must be leashed at all times, and quiet times are enforced after 2300 hr.

WATER SPORTS

The Rafferty reservoir reached its full supply level in 1998, and as the reservoir filled so did the park. With such a large body of water (51 km long) and the warmer temperatures of southern Saskatchewan, the walleye population has matured substantially so that Rafferty has become known as one of the province's hot fishing spots. The pike population has also flourished, with specimens of up to 33 lbs being recorded! The park is the premier place to explore this lake, as it has a 4-place cement launch with docks. In 2002 the park instituted a boat launching fee of $3 per day or $15 for the whole season to help defray maintenance costs. Those wishing to keep their boat in the sheltered harbor may rent space to do so; contact the park office for rates. A filleting shack, parking area, and washrooms are all located nearby, as is a store supplying all the camping and fishing necessities, gasoline, and boat/motor rentals. Besides the excellent fishing, wake boarding, tubing, and water skiing are also popular pastimes. Canoeists can explore the Souris or Roughbark rivers, touching Nature by the hand, as it were. (This paragraph was supplied by Allan and Lorraine Clark, park managers.)

On the same small bay, but across from the boatlaunch, is the buoyed swimming area. It features a man-made beach, playground equipment, change/bathrooms including beach showers and a beach volleyball net. The beach is filled with smooth rocks and bordered by heavy sand so there is lots of material for even the most ambitious of castle builders. The picnic and day use area is located just behind the swim beach, and features a couple of sun shelters overlooking the harbor's boat mooring area. Because of the small bay, wind won't normally be a problem, and boaters are speed restricted until they enter the main body of the lake. As is normally the case, pets are restricted from the beach at all times. For those wishing swimming lessons, the municipal pool in Midale can help.

GOLFING

Quite possibly one of the most spectacular courses in the province, this is definitely one of the best in the Regional Park system. The facility consists of 21 holes; 3 practice holes plus an 18-hole, "links-style" challenge. Its 18 grass-green holes cover 7022 yards from the gold tees on a par-72 course. It has well watered and trimmed fairways, manicured greens, and graveled cart paths. A driving range and putting greens await your practice, and an amazing clubhouse compliments the course. It has a pro-shop with a full range of retail sales, including a stylish array of park clothing, as well as club and cart rentals. The fully licensed restaurant has a broad menu, and is open from 0700–2200 hr daily in season. Once you see the course, you will understand why it hosts more than 50 tournaments annually! The holes are winding, with plenty of vertical and a stunning view of the lake from several holes. An enclosed beer garden with an electrified stage has been built just beside the clubhouse, host to cabarets and private functions of all sorts. So popular is the course that in 1998 a 5,000 sq. ft. facility was built next to the clubhouse to host tournaments, reunions, cabarets, and private functions of all sorts. Called the Pederson Place Building, it honors a past board chairman. Greens fees are modest for this quality of course, and vary depending on time of year, time of week, group size, and age of golfer. Tee reservations are recommended, and can be made by calling the pro-shop at (306) 458-2452.

SERVICES

The park now boasts cabin developments totaling 48 cabins and homes, with 4 sites left to lease; contact the park office for more details. Indeed, with that amazing golf course and the awesome fishing to be had, the park is building itself into a "destination location," and rightly so. The park store, called "The Store and Shoreline Rentals" offers the usual line of summer treats as well as an 8-cabin rental facility known as "K 'n N Kabins." It is privately owned and operated, and can be reached at (306) 458-2225. The park's coin-operated laundromat is located near cabin #5. A new Bed and Breakfast operation also services the park, providing another 5 rooms. Located a short distance from the clubhouse, its games room and hot tub offers yet another relaxation mode; they can be contacted at (306) 458-2502. Located to the left as you drive past the park entry gates, local scale aircraft modelers often fly their creations from a hardened miniature airdrome surface known as Woody's Field, something every child (big and small) loves to watch. Air show dates and times vary a bit, so call ahead if this is of particular interest. A tiny church has been brought on site and can be reserved for services and weddings; there is a dining shelter and toilets nearby. The nearest major shopping is in Midale, about 15 minutes away, which also offers local history in its museum, and has mechanical, medical, and worship services for those traveling in the area. For a young park, Mainprize has much to offer. The reservoir beckons for water sports, and the golf course is a gem. Everything is in excellent condition, and I congratulate the park mangers on what they have built. For those wishing more information on this lovely park, or wanting to book a function, contact the Park Manager at:

Mainprize Regional Park
PO Box 488
Midale, SK   S0C 1S0
Telephone: (306) 458-2865
Fax: (306) 458-2559
Website: www.mainprizepark.com

MOOSE CREEK REGIONAL PARK

This is the newest park in the system, incorporated in 2002. The town of Oxbow still houses the old Bow Valley park, but it is now a municipal campground and won't be considered further here. The Alameda Dam created an excellent recreation opportunity and the visionary people of the area decided to capitalize on it. The campgrounds were built starting in 1998, boat launch and other amenities added, and the crowning touch is the brand-new 9-hole golf course. All this is located a short drive from the town of Oxbow; drive north off Hwy 18 about 8 km on Coldridge Road then turn west for about 3 km, following the excellent signs all the way. There is another route in, but the dirt road can be slick if wet; I found out the hard way! If driving from Alameda, it's about 12 km east from Hwy 9 on a grid road. The park is open from the Victoria Day weekend in May until the end of September, although the golf course may stay open after the campground lines are blown out, depending on the fall weather. The park levies a $5 entry fee, waived with an annual Regional Park pass.

SITES

There are 46 sites in total, 21 with 30-amp service, 6 with 15-amp service, 17 full-service sites, and 2 non-serviced sites. There are also 39 seasonal full-service sites available. The sites rent for $20 per night (full service), $18 per night (electrified), and $12 per night (non-serviced); seasonal sites cost $950. All sites are leveled on gravel pads and have metal-framed picnic tables and fire pits. Water taps are either shared between sites or centrally located, as are the trash bins. The park has its own water treatment facility beside the fish shack. Toilet facilities range from vault toilets in the camping areas to modern flush toilets in the shower house and clubhouse. The shower house is wheelchair accessible and brand new. There is a trailer dump station across the road from full service sites 1 and 4. The park has firewood available for $5 per bundle. Most sites back onto the woodlot so there is little shade or shelter between sites. Trees have been planted, but the park is so new they haven't had a chance to grow much yet! There is some gravel on the roadways but the park is so new it hasn't been worked in yet, so things can be a little slick after a summer's rain. Mind you, the park is working on that so it won't be much longer. The original campgrounds have become the seasonal sites, and having been built in mature aspen forest, they are a bit better shaded. Group camping is available in the field beside the campgrounds, with non-service pricing in effect. There is a campground map available in the park brochure. The park plans to build a dining shelter by the beach. There is one playground built on a sand lot within easy walking distance of the camping areas. There is a slide, climber and swings, and the park plans to expand the equipment as time permits. Reservations can be made by calling the office at (306) 489-4804. Not surprising with a park this new, everything was in excellent condition, clean and well maintained.

WATER SPORTS

The Alameda Dam created a reservoir about a km wide and roughly 28 km long. The reservoir has filled to a maximum depth of approximately 40 meters, so there is plenty of water to go around. The park has built a fine boat launch with two floating docks to provide boating access to the lake. There is no marina, so most folks either bring the boat into their site at night or dock it on the shoreline near the beach. A large parking area for trailers behind the boatlaunch is complemented by wheelchair-accessible modern flush toilets and a fish filleting shack. The lake has been stocked with walleye and perch, and a natural population of pike has been offering up specimens of 10 kg! There is an annual fishing derby hosted by the Alameda Rink Committee held in late June. Although the park is closed in winter, the lake is popular for ice fishing and snowmobiling.

The park has trucked in enough sand to make a man-made beach to the north of the boatlaunch. It has a buoyed swimming area but no lifeguards or swim lessons are offered. The park plans to build a dining shelter nearby but there is no shade for bathers as yet. The sand is somewhat coarse but clean, and the water is clean as well.

GOLFING

The Moose Creek Golf Club offers a stunning new 9-hole course built with $800,000 and countless volunteer hours. Elevated tees, bunkered grass greens, well-mowed fairways and enough vertical as you wind back and forth over the coulees of the reservoir banks all make this a very pleasurable course indeed. Moose Creek itself must be crossed so the course provides a cart bridge. The course stretches for 3338 yards (Gold tees) to earn its par 36 over a scenic play. There is a fine, fully licensed clubhouse which has a restaurant serving the usual grilled meals and snacks, pop and candy bars. A pro-shop rents carts and clubs as well as markets branded clothing and golfing accessories. The dining area is glassed in so you have a great view of both the first tee and the lake scenery. Greens fees are $16 for 9 holes and $22 for 18 holes of play. Tee reservations are recommended; call (306) 489-4804 for yours.

SERVICES

Besides the clubhouse, the park concession is available for the essentials of camping life. "Mickey's" is open from 0900–2200 hr in season (July to August and most weekends), and from noon to 1700 hr off season. It has the usual iced treats, pop, chips, a small line of camping needs and offers light meals as well. The towns of Oxbow and Alameda will meet most of the campers' shopping, mechanical and worship needs, and medical services are available in Oxbow. The park is neat, clean, well-maintained and quiet. The lake is teeming with fish and is an excellent recreational resource for skiers and water sports. The beach is a sure magnet on a hot summer's day, and the golf course literally must be seen to be believed. For more information on this delightful addition to the Regional Park system, or to reserve your site, contact them at:

   Moose Creek Regional Park
   PO Box 926
   Oxbow, SK   S0C 2B0
   Telephone: (306) 489-4804
   Fax: (306) 489-4804

MOOSOMIN AND DISTRICT REGIONAL PARK

Located 14 km southwest of Moosomin, off Hwy 8, this park is open from May 1 to September 30. It was first built in 1955 with the construction of the dam which now contains the reservoir beside which the park sits. A pretty summer resort with a cabin subdivision, the park levies a $5 daily entrance fee, waived if you have an annual Regional Park sticker.

SITES

There are 75 electrified sites (all of which are now full service), some of which have full 30-amp service as well as 15 non-electrified sites. They rent for $10 per night for an unserviced site, $15 per night for an electrified site with 15-amp service and $20 per night for a 30-amp site. All sites have picnic tables, firepits, and access to central water taps. All sites are naturally leveled and drained, and should be large enough for the biggest unit. Shade is provided by poplars and willows planted over the last 20 years. Drinking water is chlorinated well water in a modern pressure system. Firewood is available free from central bins. Washroom facilities vary from primitive biffies to modern flush toilets in the beach shower house; showers are free. A trailer dump station is available, free for registered patrons. There is family or group camping available, but there is no map of the campgrounds. There is no reservation system in effect, so first come, first served; the gates are manned from 1000–2100 hr daily, and the attendant will rent you a site as you drive in. Credit cards are accepted for campsite rentals.

WATER SPORTS

The Pipestone Valley reservoir is about a half-mile wide and about 8 miles long, and provides the focus for many boating and aquatic adventures. The swim beach is spectacular, one of the best in the system, and the swimming area is both buoyed and aerated. There are beach change rooms and free showers in the concession and store (more on that later), and diving floats anchored in deeper water. Swim lessons are taught and prices vary depending on the Red Cross level sought; contact the park office at the address below for details or to register. The beach concession is open from 0800–2200 hr daily, and offers daily breakfast specials as well as the regular selection of grilled meals and treats, pop, and snacks. There is also a video arcade and a pool table in the games room, and laundry machines in one room around the back. The concession also houses the park store which markets a small line of grocery and camping supplies. A small display on one wall depicts the local history of the park and the dam's construction. Boaters are not to be ignored in this park either, as they have two boat launches available to them with plenty of trailer parking. Little dock space is provided, as the majority of the boaters simply beach their craft. Anglers regularly try their luck at landing the pike, perch, and walleye that abound in the reservoir, both from the many boats that ply the waters, or from the fisherman's wharf built in one of the shallow bays.

GOLFING
There are two golf courses in this park, a little-used 9-hole pitch and putt course, free for the use just behind the park on top of the hill, and a much larger facility about 9.5 km south of the park. The second course features 9 grass greens over a 2716-yard, par-35 course. The course was in excellent condition when we visited, with well-trimmed fairways and manicured greens. The licensed clubhouse is spacious and serves the usual grilled fare. The pro-shop rents carts and clubs, and has a small line of golf equipment for sale. The scorecard has an excellent map to guide your first round. Set amid a low range of hills, the course offers some great scenery and enough vertical change to be challenging. The greens fees are modest at $10 for 9 holes or $22 for 18 holes. This is a popular course locally, so reserving a tee time will generally be a good idea. Call the pro-shop at (306) 435-3511 for details.

SPORTS
There are three ball diamonds just to the left as you drive in, at the bottom of the hill. They all have wire mesh on wooden poles for backstops, and benches for players and patrons alike. A local slow-pitch league plays here every Thursday night, and tournaments occur throughout the season. There are also horseshoe pits, a beach volleyball court, and fenced tennis courts with blacktop surfaces for patrons to play on. A playground has been built just beside the swim beach and tennis courts with slides, swings, and a creative play center. There is a new hiking trail system, beginning from the far end of the baseball diamond area, with trail loops covering 5 km amid the hills. A large map is available at the trail head, and the trails themselves are close-mowed and easily followed. There are benches along the trail, particularly at junctions, and picnic tables at points of interest like Matheson Point. There are no toilet facilities along the trail, and you must bring your own water.

SERVICES
The park has much to offer, and one usually won't have to go far to get everything you need. The beach concession has grocery and camping items, and automotive fuel pumps. For those needing more extensive shopping, Moosomin has shops, mechanical, medical, and worship services for the traveler. This is a deservedly popular park, with its fine beach and long reservoir, so it hosts many tournaments (both golf and ball) and reunions over the course of a year. The park begins to fill about mid-June, and remains fairly full until mid-August. For more information on this park, or to begin planning your own reunion, contact the park office at:

> Moosomin and District Regional Park
> PO Box 1044
> Moosomin, SK S0G 3N0
> Telephone: (306) 435-3531 in season.

NICKLE LAKE REGIONAL PARK

Created by a dam on the Souris River, Nickle Lake is located 11 km south of Weyburn on Hwy 39. It is entirely man-made and well treed, with many amenities. Open from the Victoria Day long weekend until the Labor Day long weekend, the park was built in 1985. The gates are open from 0900–2300 hr on weekends, and 1100–2300 hr on weekdays. Pets are allowed, but they must be leashed at all times; there is a $200 fine levied by the RCMP otherwise! The park levies a $9 per day vehicle entrance fee, waived if you have an annual Regional Park sticker.

SITES

There are 148 electrified and 8 non-electrified sites; 30 of the electrified sites are fully serviced with water and sewer hookups. Sites rent for $14 per day for unserviced, $19 per day for electrified and watered sites, and $25 per day for fully serviced sites (30-amp). So popular has the park become that 88 sites are now available for seasonal rent, although no over-wintering is allowed. All sites are naturally drained and leveled, and site size varies; although narrow, most should be big enough for the largest unit. Shade varies as the trees planted haven't reached full potential in all places. A block of electrified sites, #1–14 and #45–58 are very well shaded by tall cottonwoods. The newer sites, #59–126, have a hill to the east for morning shade, and smaller trees between sites. Mind you, give the park 10 more years and these sites will be set among towering trees as well. All sites have picnic tables, firepits, and access to central drinking water taps. Firewood is fire-killed pine, cut, split and sold for $5 per bundle. Washroom facilities are modern, with two shower houses built. One in each area, they offer flush toilets as well as free hot showers. There is one group or family area with 15-amp electrical service to the north and east; contact the park office for details. A wheelchair-accessible dining shelter is available just to the west of the Kayak Club building, and another dining shelter is available south of the water utility shed on the west side of the swim beach (pictured above). Reservations are no longer accepted, and the quiet time of 2300 hr is firm; the park patrol is very efficient and quite adamant about tossing noisy partiers out.

WATER SPORTS

No swim lessons are offered at the beach, as the community depends on Weyburn's pool for that. The buoyed swimming area has change rooms and free beach showers as well as an aeration system. A large, wide beach has volleyball and a small playground. There is also a larger playground beside the spray pool, with swings, slides, teeter-totters, merry-go-rounds, and rocking horses on springs. The wooden toys look new and all other equipment is in excellent condition. There are also lots of climbers with different degrees of difficulty, so there's always something to do! There is a fine marina on the other side of the point from the swim beach with two boat launches and there is an extensive docking system. Ample parking exists for trailers, and a filleting shack, sure sign of angling to be done! A collection of photos on the concession walls proclaims the pike and walleye fishing that is available, and adds a nice touch. Paddleboats can be rented from the beach store for $5 per half hour or $9 for a full hour, including life jackets. The concession is open from 1100–2100 hr weekdays, and 0900–2100 hr on weekends although the hours may be extended if demand warrants. The operation has the usual iced treats, snacks and pop as well as a variety of grilled and home-cooked meals.

SPORTS

There are three baseball diamonds in the park, complete with tall mesh backstops and mesh home-run fences. They all have gravel infields and grass outfields, and the main diamond has bleachers for spectators and benches for players. A large, covered beer hall occupies the center of the complex, and offers a stage for musical performances. Although the stage is electrified and has its own lighting, there is no seating for patrons; a large expanse of grass gives mute testimony to the need for lawn chairs! A fine mini-golf course is available for $2.50 per game, payable at a booth just beside the course. Each hole has an electrical switch on the start pole to operate that hole's equipment, so you're in charge of your opponent's shot! Although there are no hiking trails established, there is a lot of biking and wandering that can be done on abandoned roads around the park.

SERVICES

Apart from the diner there is little to purchase in the park as Weyburn provides all the shopping, mechanical, medical, and worship services the traveler will need. The park itself hosts an annual Co-ed Slow Pitch Tournament on the first weekend in June and a Country and Western Cabaret, put on by the Canadian Cancer Association in August. The park prides itself on being a quiet place to shed the cares of the world, and so it works hard at making life uncomfortable for a rowdier element. To this end, the local RCMP patrol the park nightly (twice on weekends), and the 2300 hr curfew is strictly enforced. Because of this, the park is always busy although it might not be entirely full. We enjoyed our stay, and we hope you will too! For more information, contact the park manager at:

Nickle Lake Regional Park
PO Box 1267
Weyburn, SK   S0J 2S0
Telephone: (306) 842-7144 in season.

OUNGRE MEMORIAL REGIONAL PARK

Located 70 km south of Weyburn on Hwy 35, this park sports one of the most varied indoor recreational facilities in the Regional Park system. The park is open year round but the campgrounds are open from the May long weekend to the September long weekend, with the gate booth open from 0800–2200 hr. Daily entrance fees of $3 per vehicle are waived if you have an annual Regional Park sticker. The park began its history as a recreation site in 1908 when homesteader Frank Foster and his family planted a grove of trees to be part of their farmyard. Although the Fosters left the area after Frank's death in 1926, the spot became known as Foster's Grove and was the home for annual sports days and picnics in the 1930s. In 1942 the RM of Souris Valley purchased the land and helped finance the construction of a cenotaph in 1947; a bandstand had previously been built in 1946. In 1963 this little grove of trees became a part of OMRP. A dam was built just west of the park along Long Creek, which was then used for swimming, and the golf course was built. In 1967 a building which serves as the concession booth, restroom and shower facility, and park meeting place, was erected to commemorate Canada's centenary. The community center was built in 1984; one year later an 18-hole mini-golf course was added. In 1989 a heated, covered swimming pool was built. Most recently, the campgrounds and centennial building have undergone major renovations to better serve the camping public.

SITES

There are 27 full-service sites ($25 per night) and 31 electrified sites costing $20 (30-amp service) or $17 (15-amp service) per day, respectively. Two of the sites are now drive-through and large enough for any unit, and the campground has been improved since the first edition of this book with new, larger sites. Three non-electrified sites cost $15 per night. There are also prices available for seasonal, monthly, and weekly camping; contact the park office for details when reserving a site. All sites are naturally leveled and drained, and have picnic tables, pole BBQs, and trash bins. Drinking water is available from central taps and firewood is available in central bins. Tall shade trees are abundant in the camping area, mostly willows and poplars. Larger units may have trouble fitting into some of the smaller sites, but in general one should have few difficulties. Washrooms facilities have been upgraded as well, featuring a new shower house addition to the Centennial Building in the campground, plus the modern flush toilets in the pool change rooms as well as free showers. A trailer dump station with water hydrant is located south of the main parking lot. Coin-operated laundry facilities are located in the Communiplex. Camping permit holders must be 21 years of age and must be onsite to obtain a camping permit. Family or group camping is available in the overflow area, capable of holding a dozen or so units. Reservations are accepted and can be made by calling the pool restaurant at (306) 456-2531.

COMMUNIPLEX

The Souris Valley Communiplex holds almost everything the park has by way of recreation, and is the main reason the park never closes. A 25-m indoor pool with diving board offers Red Cross swimming lessons through June, July and August. Lesson costs vary depending on level; contact the park for more information. The pool is open to the pubic between 1530–2100 hr in June and 1230–2100 hr in July and August. Public swims cost $3 per adult, $2.50 for students and $1 for those aged 5 and under.

Camping bundles are offered to campers and prices vary with the recreation package requested. Bundles include camping fees and unlimited use of the Dr. Brown Aquatic Center, ball diamonds, 18-hole mini-golf, and the 9-hole golf course! As they say "You won't find a better value for your leisure dollars." Contact the park office for an up-to-date price list.

The Communiplex also houses a two-lane, 5-pin bowling alley which costs $1.50 per game, including shoe rental. It has ping-pong tables, a large screen TV with VCR, billiards tables, video games, coin-operated laundry, and a post office! The restaurant is open from 0800–2200 hr daily all year and offers a full cafe service with a varied menu. The staff will also cater your private function. Besides meals, the diner also sells iced treats, pop and snacks. For more information, contact the park office through the restaurant at (306) 456-2531.

GOLFING

The park has two golf courses, an 18-hole mini-golf and a 9-hole, sand-green course. The mini-golf course is well maintained with many fanciful holes and a small creative play center just beside it. Equipment is rented from the "round house" or park gate and costs $3 per round. The 9-hole golf course covers 2900 yards over its naturally watered fairways and features some interesting "dog leg" holes. Greens fees are paid at the gate with scorecards available as well as club rentals. Golf costs $5 per round for adults, $4 for students, and between $40 (student) and $100 (family) for a season pass. The course may be reserved for a private tournament, but individual reservations won't normally be required; contact the park office for more details.

BASEBALL

The park has three ball diamonds, the most impressive of which is Larsen Field. This diamond has a gravel infield, night lights, player dugouts, and bleachers; tall mesh backstops on metal poles complete the facility. As with all the facilities in this park, everything is in excellent condition. Baselines are maintained in league play and during tournaments such as the slow pitch tournament held annually in mid-June.

SERVICES

Including the above-mentioned sports, the park also adds a beach volleyball court; ask at the gate for equipment. A reservoir near the park has pike and perch for anglers. There are two playgrounds, one by the mini-golf and one by the east campsites. Between them they have slides, swings, teeter-totters, climbers, and a sand digger machine in a large pit. The park will gladly host your private function, renting campsites, the rink ($150 per day), the Centennial Building ($135 per day), a large marquee tent ($100 per day), and grills ($40 per day). The nearest municipal services are in Weyburn, where you can shop and find most mechanical, medical and worship services. The restaurant sells milk, bread, and basic foods, but major shopping must be done elsewhere. All in all, the park is a busy one that tries to offer something for all age groups. Even in poor weather there is a lot of activity possible, all at reasonable cost. For more details or to book the facility, contact the park manager at:

Oungre Memorial Regional Park
PO Box 69
Oungre, SK   S0C 1Z0
Telephone: (306) 456-2531 or 1-800-730-6677 (toll free)
Fax: (306) 456-2404
Website: www.oungrepark.com

OYAMA REGIONAL PARK

Located 5 km east of Kronau, 30 km southeast of Regina off Hwy 33, this park is open from the Victoria Day long weekend in May until the Labor Day long weekend in September. It is situated on 100 acres of aspen parklands along the banks of the Kronau Reservoir. The park gates are open from 0700–2300 hr daily in season. The park levies a $5 per vehicle daily entry fee, waived if you have an annual Regional Park sticker.

SITES

There are 48 electrified sites and 50 non-electrified sites, renting for $15 per night and $10 per night, respectively. The serviced sites also rent for $150 per month or $600 for the entire season. Some are naturally leveled and drained, some are built up on gravel pads. The campsites are split into two areas, one near the shower house and concession, the other across an open field from the lake. Pictured here, it has 20 electrified sites plus an unspecified number of unserviced sites that serve as the group or family camping area. All sites have picnic tables, pole BBQs or firepits, and access to central water and trash disposal. Please note that the water was being tested for consumption during our visit and had to be boiled prior to drinking. The park suggested that you bring your own drinking water and use their supply for dishes and sewer functions only. The sites are generally large enough for most units, and are long, well-shaded, and fairly private. The trees are planted aspens and willows, and very mature. Washroom facilities vary from primitive biffies in the camping areas to modern flush toilets and coin-operated showers in the lakeside shower house. A fine dining shelter including a large, charcoal briquette-fueled camp stove is available beside the stage near the overflow area. Reservations are accepted by the park office at the number below beginning on May 15 annually—the sooner the better for any weekend, but moreso for any of the summer's three long weekends.

WATER SPORTS

The Kronau Reservoir is stocked annually by the provincial Fisheries Department with perch, and a special limit of 10 perch per angler is in effect on the lake; there are also a few pike taken every year. The reservoir is about 2 km long and fairly narrow, so no waterskiers or speedboats are allowed on the lake to minimize damage to the lakeshore from waves; trolling speed only is allowed. Boat size is limited to a maximum of 16 feet. A gravel boat launch and a small dock are available, with a fairly large parking area behind for trailers. The buoyed swimming area has change rooms just to the left of the beach. The beach is filled with somewhat coarse sand with many small pebbles, but the swimming area is clean and free of weeds. A fine beach concession is open from 0800–2200 hr daily in season and offers iced treats, snacks, pop, and a selection of grilled meals. Just to the right of the beach is the day-use or picnic area and a small playground (see next page) with slides, swings, teeter-totters, climbers, and rocking horses on springs. All the equipment is in good repair and brightly painted.

SPORTS
The park has three ball diamonds in the field between the two camping areas. All have tall mesh backstops on wooden poles, benches for players, and grass infields. No fee is charged for using them, and they are the site of two local tournaments at the end of July and August. The park has horseshoe pits and a beach volleyball court. Equipment for these can be rented at the concession for a $5 deposit (horseshoes), and $10 deposit (volleyball and net), refunded with the return of the equipment. A motorcycle cross-country race track is built on one end of the park, and is the site of an annual motorcycle rally called the Oyama Jam, held in mid-July. It also features live music on the outdoor stage. Seating is in the field, so bring your own lawn chairs. Another popular but more pastoral activity is bird watching. The trees and water here form an oasis in the grasslands for local birds which congregate here in large numbers, nesting and feeding among the trees.

SERVICES
The park depends on Regina for the majority of shopping, mechanical, and medical services, although some can be found in nearby Kronau. The highway between the park and the provincial capital is well maintained, so the trip is but minutes. The park is patrolled nightly to ensure that the quiet time of 2300–0800 hr is observed, although it isn't normally a problem during the week. The park hosts several activities annually, including the ball tournaments and the motorcycle rally. A musical performance called "Rave" is held here showcasing a varied array of local and professional talent. Dates vary, but generally it is the second weekend in August. As one can see from the number of summer weekends with activities planned, this is a popular park locally and you should book your site early to avoid disappointment. For more information on this park, contact the park manager at:

Oyama Regional Park
8 Garuik Crescent
Regina, SK   S4R 7E6
Telephone: (306) 781-2955 (in season), or (306) 569-8133 (winter).

RADVILLE LAURIER REGIONAL PARK

Located on the outskirts of Radville at the intersection of Hwy 28 and Hwy 337, the park was first built in 1965 and revised regularly. It can be found on the corner of Floren and Peterson streets, with a gate sign right at the park. Although the area was first settled in 1910 with the arrival of the CNR, the park was established in 1975 as a joint venture between the RM of Laurier and the town of Radville, and is completely manmade. History buffs will enjoy the self-directed tours to see the effects of the last ice age on this area, including The Big Muddy nearby. Buffalo rocks—large surface rocks that were exposed enough for animals to scratch their horns on—as well as buffalo wallows (hollows in the ground where buffalo rolled to add a coat of dust to protect themselves from flies and mosquitoes) are among the interesting sites you might spot in and around Radville-Laurier Regional Park. The park is open from May to October for camping, after which the water lines are cleared in preparation for the freeze-up. All vehicles entering the park are expected to have an annual Regional Park sticker; otherwise, a $5 per day entry fee is levied.

SITES
There are 16 electrified sites that rent for $15 per night or $75 per week. The park also offers 30 non-electrical sites at $8 per night and $40 per week for family or group camping. All the sites are naturally leveled and drained and set amid a heavily treed area. Many tall elms and poplars provide constant shade from almost every direction, and yet they don't interfere with the sites such that one cannot maneuver a large unit. All sites have picnic tables and trash bins, but only 4 of the sites have a pole BBQ or firepit, and firewood is not provided. Washroom facilities are modern, with flush toilets and free showers available in the pool complex. These facilities remain open 24 hours per day for the campers. Radville municipal drinking water is available from central taps. A dining shelter (pictured above) with picnic tables and a camp stove is available for use. Reservations can be made by calling the park manager at (306) 869-2231.

WATER SPORTS
The outdoor swimming pool (and attendant shower and change rooms) is open from June to late August, depending on the weather, and has a capacity of about 100. Rectangular in shape, it varies between 3 and 12 feet deep, and has a 1-meter and a 3-meter diving board. A full range of Red Cross lessons are offered twice in the month of July, and possibly a set

of Bronze Cross and Medallion lessons in August, depending on demand. Lessons vary in price from $20 to $40 depending on the level requested and the purchase of a season pass. The lifeguards organize various fun days and two midnight swims are held during the summer. A large playground built in a sand pit is located just to the side of the pool complex. First built in 1970 and extensively renovated in 2000, it is now "handicap accessible," and has slides, swings, merry-go-rounds, teeter-totters, and a creative play center. All equipment is in good shape, well maintained and brightly painted. Anglers aren't forgotten as Long Creek runs beside the town, a place where people can cast from shore for the pike and perch that live here.

GOLFING

Just outside the town (take Hwy 377 for 1.5 km west and turn north for 1.5 km) is a 9-hole sand-green golf course. The Robertdale Golf and Country Club is so named to honor A.R. Robertson, who devoted much of his time to the park and the golf course. The course is a par-35 that covers 2830 yards over its well-treed fairways, and there is a clubhouse available to run your tournament from; it won't normally be open otherwise. It has washrooms and a place to get out of the rain, but the bar isn't open except during tournaments. Be very careful where you park, as the first tee plays along the right side of the parking lot! The tees are watered, and the course is busy enough to keep two greens keepers at work mowing the grass. Greens fees are $6 per round, with student and family rates available, payable at the first tee. One won't normally need tee reservations as this is a friendly course; simply show up and you'll be on the first tee before you know it! As a popular local facility, the course hosts several tournaments throughout the summer.

BASEBALL

There are 4 diamonds here, one with red shale infields and three with gravel infields. All the diamonds have tall mesh backstops on metal poles and bleachers for the spectators. The one shale field has a shelter for the players as well. A pitching machine has been added for those who like to go out and practice. All the equipment is in excellent condition, a credit to the park as they host two major tournaments annually, the Minor Tournament in May and the Slow Pitch Tournament in August.

SERVICES

The park is a busy one for the many events it hosts. Besides the golf and ball tournaments, it hosts an annual rodeo in June, and the Kinsmen Mud Fling and demolition derby, a 4x4 race in mud pits held in mid August. The park has no concession or diner, but the town of Radville can supply all the shopping, mechanical, laundry, medical, and worship services the traveler could ask for. It is a favorite spot for local hunters to set up camp, as there is good pheasant, deer, upland game and duck hunting in the area. Altogether, there's a lot happening in the Radville Laurier Regional Park. For more information, or to reserve a site, contact the park manager at:

>Radville Laurier Regional Park
>PO Box 796
>Radville, SK   S0C 2G0
>Telephone: (306) 869-2231
>Fax: (306) 869-2533.

SASKATCHEWAN BEACH REGIONAL PARK

Located 11 km northwest of Craven, and only 1 km from the town of Silton on Last Mountain Lake, this park has little to offer the camping tourist. It does offer access to Last Mountain Lake and its watery resources, and so it is an important component of the Eastshore Rural Development Cooperative (ERDC). The ERDC is a collection of municipal, provincial, and national tourism interests devoted to developing Last Mountain Lake. The Regional Park is open from the Victoria Day weekend to the Labor Day weekend, although many cabin owners live here year round. First developed in 1906, the park joined the Regional Park system in 1963 to take advantage of the grants then available. As there are no overnight camping facilities, the park depends on its day-use sites for its livelihood. If you intend to camp in the area, the nearest sites are privately owned in Craven, 11 km away. Visitors are expected to have an annual Regional Park sticker.

WATER SPORTS

Last Mountain Lake got its name from a local Cree legend which said the Great Spirit built the hills near Govan (east of the lake) last of all; that legend lives on in the name of this lake. The Regional Park offers the cabin owners picnic sites, a boatlaunch and docks, 2 beaches and a playground. The resort village of Saskatchewan Beach divides the park into the east and west beaches, each with their own attractions. The east beach has the maintenance shed, half of which is a Recreation Hall that offers an evening program. This is also the larger of the two beaches in the park. The beach offers roomy washrooms and change facilities, and a tap to wash beach sand off your feet. A large sand pit beside the change rooms houses the play center. A well-shaded path leads from the parking lot to the beach area which is bordered by picnic tables and pole BBQs to the left along the lake. The beach fronts both sides of a short peninsula and is guarded by a buoyed swimming area all along. The sand here is quite fine and soft. Although the beach has little shade, the picnic area is well covered with natural trees and shrubs.

The west beach is just to the right of the boat launch on the other end of the park. The boat launch is well built, as are the two docks floating in support. Parking is plentiful nearby; all that is required to use the facility is a Regional Park sticker. The west beach is much smaller and has much coarser sand, although my two experts tell me the skipping rocks were great! There were two picnic tables with pole BBQs in the trees behind the beach, and a couple of rocking horses on springs for the little ones. There is a sand volleyball court to the right of the parking lot, but it appeared to have been little used of late so the weeds were taking over.

The lake is a destination in itself, as is the Qu'Appelle Valley, and has been since about 1906 when summer tourists took the train to a station on the east end of the resort. Many resort villages and parks line the shores of this pretty valley, particularly on the east side. Water sports abound, including sailing, boating, fishing, and swimming. Persons renting cabins in the resort as well as those attending local events like the Big Valley Jamboree will find this park's water access useful.

SERVICES

The town of Silton, about 1 km away, has shopping and simple amenities for cottage country. The town of Craven, 11 km away, has more extensive shopping, mechanical, medical, and worship services. The park has no concession or shops, nor does the resort village. The Last Mountain Sailing Club clubhouse is located in the west park area. In order to host the sailing venue for the 2005 Canada Summer Games, a breakwater was installed and the boat launch upgraded. Of historical interest is Last Mountain House Provincial Historical Park, a re-creation of an 1870s Hudson Bay Company post; it is about 3 km from the park on the Craven access road. Several municipal golf courses can be found along Hwy 20 to the north of the park. The ERDC's advertising motto is "You're among friends," and I hope you find the patrons of this park as friendly as we did. For more information on the park and its area, contact the park office at:

> Saskatchewan Beach Regional Park
> c/o Resort Village of Saskatchewan Beach
> PO Box 220
> Silton, SK   S0G 4L0.

WELWYN CENTENNIAL REGIONAL PARK

Located 1.8 km north of Welwyn off Hwy 308, this park is unique for the native oak trees that abound. The park is open from May 1 until the end of October and offers access to the 2-km-long reservoir created by the dam built on the Beaver Creek. The park levies a $5 per day park vehicle entry fee, waived if you have an annual Regional Park sticker.

SITES

There are 30 non-electrified sites arranged in two loops. The sites cost $5 per night, and fees can be paid at Harper's Store in Welwyn if there is no attendant in the park entry booth. All sites are naturally leveled and drained, and have picnic tables, firepits, and trash cans. Firewood is not provided, so remember to bring your own as cutting the park's trees is strictly forbidden. As a side note, there are a couple of large firepits with benches that are perfect for a group to sing up a storm around, or for the artful telling of a favorite story. It is of such magic that a small child's camping memories are made! The sites are not numbered, but are generously sized so you shouldn't have any difficulty parking your trailer. Washroom facilities are primitive, with biffies in the camping areas and on the beach. There is no shower or laundry facility. There are two dining shelters available, one in each loop; the farthest loop is the group site, and is fairly large. You should bring your own drinking water as there was no pump or tap we could find, and the reservoir water should be treated prior to consumption. The sites are well shaded by the splendid native oak trees that abound in the park, providing an interesting local ecology. There is no reservation system in place for individual sites, but you can make arrangements to hold a reunion or such by contacting the park at the address below.

WATER SPORTS

The reservoir is stocked yearly with walleye, pike, and perch by the provincial Fisheries Department. A fine, graveled boat launch provides access to the lake, with a small parking area behind for trailers. There is a T-shaped dock as well. The Beaver Creek runs through a pronounced valley; there is plenty of wind relief and few waves as a result. For this reason, the park is popular among water-skiers and other tow enthusiasts as well as anglers. The beach is deep and wide, and filled with fine sand. The swimming area is not buoyed, but it does have a floating dock to play with. Swimming lessons are taught here, with one set taught in the second week of July, 2 lessons per day for the entire week. All Red Cross levels are taught for $25 per swimmer, and registrations can be made by contacting the park office. The beach has change rooms and biffies, as well as a playground with swings, teeter-totters, and a merry-go-round. There are also sand pits up in the camping areas for the little ones to play in, as well as slides and swings.

HIKING
The reservoir is host to a number of migrating birds, including whooping cranes according to my source! The hardwood forest provides an interesting change from prairie or softwood forest for hikers, although there are no trails established. Simply wander at will along the banks of the reservoir; good berry picking can be found, so you won't go hungry! There is a trail from the campgrounds on top of the hill to the beach, but the steep and lengthy staircase suffered winterkill damage.

SERVICES
The town of Welwyn offers a range of shopping, mechanical, and worship services. There is a heritage museum, open on Sundays and free to the public, that highlights some of the local history and the people that made this place what it is. Those requiring more extensive shopping or perhaps medical facilities must go to Moosomin, 34 km south and west on Hwy 8. The park is busy during the swim lessons, and during its annual Canada Day celebration. Most long weekends will see the park filling, but only rarely at capacity. This is a quiet, family-oriented park that wants to remain as natural as possible. Once you see the forest, you'll understand why! You have to be more self-sufficient to stay here, but you are repaid with solitude and a chance to "recharge the batteries" without the bustle of a more developed park. For more information on this park, or to arrange a private function, contact the park manager at:

>   Welwyn Centennial Regional Park
>   PO Box 115
>   Welwyn, SK   S0A 4L0
>   Telephone: (306) 733-2155.

WOODLAWN REGIONAL PARK

Located 2 km south of Estevan on Hwy 47, this park incorporates the natural beauty of the Souris River Valley and a great many stately elm, maple, ash and poplar trees into one pretty park. An oasis of green, it has become home to a great many bird species as well as small animals. Built in the 1940s, the park has undergone many revisions since. Open from May 1 to September 30, the park has a lot to offer the traveler. Daily entry fees are $5, waived if you have the annual Regional Park sticker.

SITES

There are now 10 fully serviced sites with 30-amp service, water and sewer hookups. A further 69 sites have power (30-amp service) and water hookup, and there are 12 electrified sites with no water hookup. There are 11 unserviced sites as well, costing $15 per day; electrified sites cost $18 per day or $21 if they include a water hookup, and the full-service sites cost $25 per day. Weekly, monthly, and seasonal rates are also available; contact the park office for current prices. Reservations are accepted, and all campers must pay before entering the campgrounds. The roadways wind a bit, and the excellent campground map provided was invaluable. The sites are mostly built with a gravel pad for the camping unit, although some of the smaller sites are naturally leveled and drained. All sites have pole BBQs fashioned from a barrel cut in half lengthwise to which a grate is welded. Open from both ends, they are a functional design. Firewood (lumber cutbacks) is provided free in three central bins, and split firewood is available for $4 per bundle. Picnic tables and trash bins are also found in every site. Along with the elms, the campsites have maple, ash and poplars for shade and most sites are shaded from at least two directions. Toilet facilities range from primitive, along the trails and near the racetrack, to modern. The two main campground washrooms each have three showers, flush toilets, sinks and mirrors. The showers are free to campers, but the building closes from 2000–0800 hr daily for cleaning. The sewer dump station is near the main washrooms. Potable water is dispensed from a central tap near the west washrooms; water provided is Estevan municipal.

In general, the sites were spacious, particularly the double and fully serviced sites. We found them clean, well-trimmed, and shady. Group sites are available but there are no dining shelters. Sites may be reserved by calling (306) 634-2324. If you will be later than 1900 hr, you must call the park and notify them or else your site will be lost. A large, free picnic area is located on the northwest corner of the park, close to Hwy 47.

GOLFING

The park is home to the Woodlawn Golf Club. This exciting 18-hole golf course covers 6106 yards in a par 71 and has been upgraded with bunkers and raised tees, becoming one of the premier courses in Saskatchewan. The front nine holes play fairly straight forward, but the back 9 keep the water in play most of the way. To perfect your swing before the game, the course has a practice green and a driving range. Fully serviced, the pro-shop not only rents and sells equipment, but the certified CPGA pro will give instructions; contact the pro-shop to arrange your private lesson. A fully licensed clubhouse is attendant to the pro-shop, offering light meals throughout the day as well as a chance to brag over a cold beer. A strong juniors program keeps playership up, so tee reservations are a must; contact the pro-shop at (306) 634-2017 to book yours. For current prices and information on this course, check out their excellent website at: http://www.estevangolf.com/.

SPORTS

Although the park has no access to a swimming pool or pond within its borders, there is a fine facility just 2 km away. The Estevan Leisure Center includes a swimming pool, waterslides, library, and other recreational facilities. The Souris River can be canoed, but there is no boatlaunch for larger vessels. One can try fishing here, but better luck awaits at either the Boundary Dam or the Rafferty Dam reservoirs a short drive away. Several sports facilities have been built within the park, although they may not be of the park. The chuckwagon and chariot race track on the east end of the park has races on occasion, but these are not organized by the park. Met Stadium is part of an extensive ball complex with bleachers, team shelters, tall mesh backstops, mesh home-run boundaries, and an announcer's booth, and is slated for upgrading in the near future. The fields feature gravel infields, grass outfields and groomed pitcher's mounds. Although they can be used for a pickup game, any reservation has priority; contact the park office for details. A soccer field with net goals sits on a well-turfed pitch (it has underground sprinklers), also available for a pickup game. The two playgrounds have had extensive upgrades, with the large one beside the canteen in a treed grotto receiving modern equipment as well as restored original equipment. This one has wonderfully bent elms to climb, plus an assortment of fanciful merry-go-rounds and teeter-totters. Two new splash pools are also located near here, making the canteen area a magnet for children. The smaller one (pictured above), in the big picnic area, has swings and slides. Two trails have been marked for walking tours. One begins beside site # 37 and leads beside the river to the golf course. The other leads from the Rotary Park to Cassette Park, with two ball diamonds and the soccer field at the end.

Cassette Park and the soccer field have undergone extensive upgrades recently, so that the ball diamonds feature team shelters, tall mesh backstops, mesh home run boundaries and an announcer's booth. Complete with gravel infields, grass outfields, groomed pitcher's mounds and boasting lights for evening games, the facility awaits your tournament! As the park hosts an annual Estevan Bible Camp in July at the Rotary Recreation Hall complex, this trail leads the campers to their sports venues. When not booked by the Bible camp organizer, the complex can be rented for private gatherings for $200 per day. Many events both private and public are held at this busy complex; contact the park managers for bookings and availability.

SERVICES

The park boasts a wonderful diner and canteen, which markets the usual iced treats, pop and snacks, as well as light "home-cooked" meals. Tall trees and picnic tables dot the open area devoted to patron dining, a nice touch; a gazebo with picnic tables is also close by. A stall nearby advertises an evening coffee club which meets nightly at 1900 hr during the week. A baby-sitting service is advertised at the canteen for weary parents. A summer theater troupe, The Souris Valley Theater, gives live performances through July to early August in the Souris Valley Theatre (Frehlick Hall) on the edge of the free picnic area. Campers can walk from their site to the theatre for an evening's entertainment, a feature unique to this province! An old church has been moved into the park and restored as a historical marker. Free guided tours of the coal mines and power plants in the Estevan area can be arranged; brochures are available at the park gate. The town of Estevan has all the shopping, mechanical, medical and worship services the traveler could ask for. For more information on this park, contact the park manager at:

Woodlawn Regional Park Authority
PO Box 1385
Estevan, SK S4A 2K9
Telephone: (306) 634-2324 in season
Fax: (306) 634-2223.

CANNINGTON MANOR PROVINCIAL HISTORIC PARK

Saskatchewan is filled with stories, both successes and failures, and Cannington Manor is one such. The park has two themes, the first of which is more universal in appeal: the settling of the prairies. The lives of the settlers are commemorated by the careful reconstruction and restoration of the buildings and artifacts you'll see here. The implements, construction methods, and materials are as faithfully reconstructed as possible; many are the actual article, something of a rarity in such a display. The living conditions are also on display: there was no central heating—imagine winter with only a single wood stove! Yet the settlers persevered, commerce thrived, communities grew and our province was built. And then there's Cannington Manor, the other main theme!

Located northeast of Carlyle, the park can be accessed via gravel roads off any of Hwys 9 (running past Moose Mountain Provincial Park), 48, or 13. Secondary road 603 north from Hwy 13 (accessed east of Carlyle) is well signed and pretty much a straight run. The park is open from 1000–1700 hr daily from the Victoria Day weekend to the Labor Day weekend except for Tuesdays. Entrance fees of $5 per family, $2 per adult, $1 per child (6–17 years old; children aged 5 or less are admitted free) are collected at a self-registration kiosk beside the Visitor's Center.

At the time this community was conceived in the 1880s, the British Empire was in its heyday. Right or wrong, the ideals of British society were seen as simply the best model for aspiring colonies, and the social niceties of "merry old England's" farming communities would help transform the wilderness of western Canada into a piece of Britain. Or so the idea went! Nobody bothered with small inconveniences like hordes of mosquitoes, the prairie winter, or the sheer vastness of the continent and the distances goods must travel. All one had to do was keep a stiff upper lip and keep steadfast in the best British tradition, and all would be well. If only things were that simple!

The community of Cannington Manor was founded in 1884 by Edward Mitchell Pierce, although people had already begun moving into the area a couple of years prior. The village never really thrived as the world was going through an economic depression that kept wheat prices low while summer droughts and early frosts dealt farmers a harsh blow. The expected flood of European immigrants never materialized, so the village itself never really got much larger than 25 to 30 people, although the surrounding area had as many as 300 or so. Still, there were successes: the flour mill did fine business, winning first prize at the 1893 World's Fair in Chicago; the one claim to fame for the little village.

Perhaps another problem faced by the fledgling community was the importation of British social structure. The bachelors and "remittance men" (young men whose families in the Old Country paid them to stay away —you wonder why!) lived farthest from the heart of the village while the tradesmen (carpenter, blacksmith, shopkeeper) lived closer to the heart of the village, the church, store and flour mill. The choicest properties were the wealthier landowners' houses. As you look at the fine buildings you soon realize that the "gentry" had multiple-level houses; they could "look down" on their neighbors, as it were.

This is but a shallow sampling of the stories you'll find in this complex and interesting historical park. The park is quite busy in June with school groups enjoying the interactive programs guided by the capable park staff, but you'll find the park patronage lower in July and August, except for Sundays as the little church here (built in 1884—the second oldest church in Saskatchewan; only the Anglican church in Stanley Mission is older) is the property of the Diocese of Qu'Appelle and the congregation still gathers regularly. The highly knowledgeable interpretive staffers are a wealth of local history, and the hour or so you'll spend in their capable hands will pass quick away. You will have to ask them to tell the tale of how Maltby House came to be haunted, though!

Perhaps the most popular program offered at this park is the student education program, with two offerings: a half-day or full day program. Students will be guided through the village and will have a chance to partake in various "hands-on" activities such as stew or biscuit baking, various sports, as well as learn all about the village and its people. The day culminates in a stew and biscuit meal, prepared by the students themselves over wood stoves. The staff will generally do the dishes as well! Contact the park at the numbers listed below for more details.

Drinking water is available from a tap at the Visitor's Center where you'll also find the wheelchair-accessible flush toilets. No overnight camping is allowed but you will find picnic tables among the trees behind the All Saints Anglican Church. There is no shopping to be had in the park; the nearest will be either Kenosee or Carlyle, both approximately 50 km away. For more information on this park, contact the park at:

Cannington Manor Provincial Historic Park
Box 220
Kenosee Lake, SK   S0C 2S0
Telelephone: (306) 739-5251 (May–September) or (306) 577-2600 (year-round)
Fax: (306) 577-2622
From Victoria Day to Labor Day you can call their toll-free number: 1-800-205-7070
You can link to their email address from their website at: www.saskparks.net

CROOKED LAKE PROVINCIAL PARK

Located 30 km north of the Trans Canada Highway on the northeast end of Crooked Lake, the park is open from the May long weekend until the Labor Day weekend. The best access is from Melville; take Hwy 47 south for 40 km then 15 km east on Hwy 247. There are several resorts and cottage developments on this popular lake, as well as a scenic 18-hole golf course, all privately owned. The drive into the park on Hwy 247 is very scenic, although the driver must be wary on the winding, somewhat narrow pavement. The park is situated on the valley bottom, so the highway must wind along steep valley slopes in the descent from the upland plains. You will be rewarded with excellent camping liberally shaded by tall, stately cottonwood, maple and elm trees in this small (195 hectare) but pretty park. One of the wonders of this park is watching the sun set across the lake from your campsite; the steep hills on the west shore seem to frame the sun as the shadows sweep across the lake to envelope the world in their nightly embrace.

CAMPING

There are 39 electrified sites (of which 7 are reserved for seasonal campers; all have 30-amp services) and 54 non-electrified sites in two camping loops. All sites have picnic tables, most of which are metal framed; the park is in the process of changing over to the new style, so some wooden tables were still found during our visit. All sites have firepits with swinging grates for cooking, and a couple of large firepits are available for evening campfires and the artful telling of stories as moonbeams weave a silver skein among the evening shadows; of such things are summer memories made! Sites numbered 52–72 are generally kept for overflow use until late June or early July after which they are opened for general use; non-electrified sites numbered 73–93 (#82 seen here), nearest the boat launch, are more open and can serve as a group camping area if required. Most sites were generously spaced, well shaded amid mature stands of elm and maple trees, and fairly private due to the dense underbrush between sites. Some sites, notably electrified sites 31–37 (odd numbers, along the lake shore) have lake access and thus offer the opportunity to tie up your boat beside your campsite. Potable water is available from central taps and firewood is available in one bin near site #8. Toilet facilities range from vault toilets in the camping loops to flush toilets in the modern, wheelchair-accessible shower facility located behind the main beach and day use area. One set of wheelchair-accessible flush toilets is located in a small open area near site #4 but this facility has no showers. A self-registration station near the payphone booth at the park entrance asks you to find an empty site, drop off your camper or tent, then return to pay your access fees. A trailer dump station has been built to the left of the registration booth. From June to August a Campground Host will be available to assist you with information and support during your stay; their site is generally #8.

BEACHES AND BOATING

A boat launch is available at the far end of the park's main camping areas. There is a reasonably spacious parking lot for trailers immediately behind it, as well as wheelchair-accessible vault toilets and a fish-cleaning shelter. The expectation is, though, that you store both boat and trailer in your site nightly. As mentioned above, however, some sites have lakeside access so you can tie your boat up at your site and not retrieve it nightly. The anglers we spoke to said the lake had good fishing for pike and walleye, but can you ever really trust a fisherman's tales? You'll have to find out for yourself! Crooked Lake itself is long and narrow, surrounded by tall hills, and reasonably well protected from winds and storms. The same tall hills can mask the approach of storm clouds, however, so always keep a "weather eye" on the horizon, particularly the northwest, the lake's main axis.

A reasonably large, unsupervised swim beach is located just to the northwest of the boat launch. No swimming lessons are available in the buoyed swimming area. The sand is somewhat coarse, with many small pebbles and rocks, and lots of wind-blown twigs and so on—perfect for summer sand castles! A large expanse of well-mowed lawn gives ample room for sunbathers, and there is a wheelchair-accessible change room facility at the day-use parking lot. The building also houses free showers and flush toilets and has a potable water tap.

There is a fine, well-shaded picnic area as you continue to the northwest, with wooden picnic tables, trash bins, firepits and firewood supply, and a bottle/can recycling station.

Potable water is available from the beach change house or from water taps near the playground behind the picnic area. Of special interest is a monument dedicated to Acoose, a famous First Nations athlete from a century ago. He was noted for his long distance running ability; legend has it that he ran a herd of antelope down! You'll find a hardened, asphalt walking path running from the boat launch parking lot through the lawn and into the picnic area. You'll also see a few old concrete foundations, evidence of cottages from the period before the park was established.

HIKING

The hills and coulees of the Qu'Appelle Valley simply beg to be explored by foot or pedal. The land is rich in wild plants and animals, and birds abound in this prairie oasis. There is some stunning scenery from the hilltops and a wealth of wild flowers waiting for you; bring your hiking boots and see for yourself! As mentioned above, the beach area has a wheelchair-accessible trail running through it, and the park has built a trail connecting to the Trans Canada Trail system which runs through the Qu'Appelle Valley. There are seven kilometers of trail already established and maintained by the Crooked Lake Parks and Recreation Board, a group dedicated to promoting the recreational opportunities of this scenic area. These trails provide a safe cycling and walking path; no trail map is currently available, although benches have been installed at some of the more scenic stops along the trail and a pavilion or shelter has been built west of Cedar Cove resort. For more information on this trail system, contact the Trans Canada Trails at their website (www.tctrail.ca/), or visit the Saskatchewan Parks and Recreation Association website (www.spra.sk.ca/). The Campground Host will also be able to show you where the trails are. Remember to bring your own water supply and sunscreen; a hat and sturdy walking shoes are also a must—the trails will be steep!

SERVICES

The park does not offer an activities program so you must be prepared to entertain yourself. A fine, creative playground has been built in a huge sandbox behind the picnic area, fairly close to sites 50 and 51.

Golfers will find their pulse quickening when they see the first tee box on the Last Oak Golf and Country Club. The 18-hole, championship course covers 6,636 yards on its manicured fairways as it winds through the hills and coulees on the west side of the lake about 4 km west of the park. There's a creek wandering through the course that adds a hazard to 12 of the holes! The pro-shop has a complete line of golfing paraphernalia and offers club or cart rentals. After the game you can relax in the air-conditioned clubhouse with its licensed dining room and simply drink in the view of Crooked Lake from the deck or lounge. For more information or to book your tee time, contact the course directly at (306) 696-2507.

There is no shopping in the park but you will find that Cedar Cove Resort, about 3 km west of the park, offers a full range of services including a coin-operated laundromat, limited grocery and convenience shopping as well as fuel and propane. There's mini-golf for the children while you're doing the laundry, and the store also operates a small restaurant service with ice cream treats. Contact them directly at (306) 794-4926.

The nearby town of Melville (50 km north on Hwy 47) offers a complete line of shopping, medical, mechanical and worship services.

For more information on this park, contact them at:

Crooked Lake Provincial Park
PO Box 220
Kenosee Lake, SK   S0C 2S0
Telephone: (306) 696-6253 or (306) 577-2600
Website: www.saskparks.net

ECHO VALLEY PROVINCIAL PARK

Located along Hwy 210 approximately 8 km west of Fort Qu'Appelle, this park is built on the waterway between two of the Calling Lakes chain that are the heart of cottage country in the Qu'Appelle Valley. Situated on Pasqua Lake and Echo Lake there are two main swimming beaches, over 300 campsites plus 4 group camping areas, and access to excellent fishing and boating in the two lakes. There is truly something to offer the entire family in this pretty park! It is open from the May long weekend to the September long weekend, although the park remains open for limited spring and fall camping, cross country skiing, and ice fishing.

SITES

There are three main campgrounds in the park, which will be considered separately. There are also several group camping areas which can accommodate many more units on an overflow basis. Sites can be reserved by contacting the park office at the numbers given below or by linking from the SERM website. There are also a total of 100 electrified sites which are available for seasonal rent, 50 in each of Valley View and Aspen View campgrounds. They are let on a lottery basis; contact the park office in January for more information.

ASPEN CAMPGROUND

There are 80 electrified sites in this loop, all built on gravel pads with paved roadways throughout. The park saw heavy rainfall before and during our visit, and the campsites were, for the most part, still quite livable; a tribute to their drainage and design. Each site features 30-amp service, metal-framed picnic tables and fire pits made of sturdy steel culvert with a swinging cook grate. Firewood, trash and water are all shared from central areas. Most of the toilets in the loop are wheelchair-accessible modern flush facilities, as is one modern service center with hot showers between sites #256 and 254. There are two sites reserved for wheelchair-bound patrons, #255 and 253, which are close to water and the service center. There is one trailer dump station located near the campground entrance. This loop also has a horseshoe pitch located behind site #235, complete with benches for spectators. A volleyball court has been built in the grassy area beside the flush toilets and small playground between sites #231 and 229. For the most part, the park is well treed although there is little ground cover; you will have excellent shade but little site privacy. The sites are generally quite large, capable of housing the largest unit plus a boat and trailer.

VALLEYVIEW CAMPGROUND

Continuing past the entrance to Aspen Campground and up the hill, you'll find the entrance to Valleyview Campground, the largest of this park's camping areas. There are 141 sites here, 73 electrified and 68 non-electrified; 50 of the electrified and 10 of the non-electrified sites can be rented seasonally. The sites are large but there is little ground cover or privacy although there are adequate shade trees (maple and elm). There is an overflow area bordering an open field just past the last camping loop; you pass through it on your way to the scenic overlook for which the campground gets its name. The sites are built with gravel pads for the camping unit, paved roads throughout, and have metal-framed picnic tables and pole BBQs. Firewood is available from a pile near the trailer dump station at the campground entrance. Potable water taps and trash bins are found throughout the campground, and toilets vary from modern, wheelchair-accessible facilities near sites 50 and 17, and in the service center, to vault-style biffies elsewhere. Patrons requiring wheelchair access can rent either of sites 50 or 17, which have hard packed surfaces and easier access to water taps, trash bins, and the modern toilets. The service center also houses the park's coin-operated laundromat; bring loonies and quarters. There is a playground available on the lawn beside the service center, across from site #70, and a horseshoe pit beside site #56 across from the service center. This campground is unique in the province for the bike storage boxes located in non-electrified sites #165 and 167; bring your own lock. A Campground Host is located in site #55; drop by if you've any questions. As you drive to Valleyview you'll pass by an interpretive area and campfire ring where park staff will host events throughout the summer. So popular are these events that the campfire ring has bleachers for patrons to enjoy stories, songs, and skits; check with park staff at the campground entry booth for the current schedule. Last but certainly not least is the campground's namesake, the scenic overlook. Driving past the campground entrance a short distance you'll find a large parking lot past which is a pavilion with benches for patrons to drink in the scene as well as interpretive material describing the vista spread out at your feet. This is not a place you can simply see once and turn your back on; from this vantage point the entire Qu'Appelle Valley is laid out in front of you; on a clear day you can almost "see forever" it seems! It is a place of peace, filled with birdsong and the drowsy sound of insects in the grass; to borrow a phrase from Robert Service: "The still peaks above, the shadows below, and the lake like a petrified dream"!

LAKEVIEW CAMPGROUND

You can access this campground just east of the intersection of Hwy 210 and the Fort San/Fort Qu'Appelle highway. The campground is divided into two sections, the trailer campground and the tenting campground; there is a separate campground entry booth for this area. The first loop you'll see are the 23 electrified campsites of the trailer campground. The sites are built into mature willows and aspens which provide excellent shade and privacy, and have gravel pads for drainage. All sites have metal-framed picnic tables and "washtub" BBQs. All roadways are paved, and there is one set of modern flush toilets. Water taps and trash bins are scattered throughout the loop, and a woodpile is located behind site #117. There is a small playground on the lawn behind the centrally located toilet house, and a trailer dump station across the road from the campground entrance.

The tenting loop is located a short distance past the trailer loop. Here you'll find 63 non-electrified sites, all featuring gravel pads and paved roadways. Water taps and trash bins are scattered throughout the loop, and firewood is available from a pile across the road from site #35. There is one set of wheelchair-accessible flush toilets; as with the trailer loop, you'll have to use the beach showers or drive up to the service center at Valleyview, particularly if you've laundry that needs doing. There are some interesting features about this loop and the way it was built. There are two smaller areas comprised of sites #34–42 (even numbers) and sites 63–65 inclusive which form their own mini-group camping loops. The former is walk-in only, a matter of a few meters from the small parking area, while the latter is right at the end of the road on the traffic loop. While not group campsites as such, they would suffice if you require. Sites #6 and #8 are reserved for patrons in wheelchairs as they are just across the road from the larger modern toilet house and thus nearer the potable water taps as well. There is one set of swings at the entrance to the tenting loop, but no other playground equipment.

GROUP CAMPING

There are innumerable opportunities for hosting groups in the park, with 4 main group sites. They can be booked in advance for groups of five or more units by calling the park office. The bulk of the group camping is located on the Pasqua Lake side of the park, as follows:

Tee-Pee Group campsites are located adjacent to the Tee-Pee (electrified, it can also be rented). There is a pedestal providing four 30-amp breakers and four 15-amp breakers. Campers would park on the paved parking lot while tents could be pitched on the large lawn. Toilets are vault style but modern flush units are nearby in the Hole-In-The-Wall Group site or beside Pasqua Beach. There is potable water, firewood, four pole BBQs, picnic tables and benches and streetlights. This last item may be of concern if you intend to stargaze.

Hole-In-The-Wall Group Camp is divided into three non-electrified areas. The area is quite large and suitable for school, scouts or church groups. Campers would set up in the parking lot and tents would be pitched on the large lawn among the trees beside the parking lot. The choice spots down by the water are for tents only; trailers and all vehicles must stay on the pavement. As the area can be accessed by foot or water, this is the preferred camping area for those teaching canoeing skills. There is one set of modern flush toilets with an outside electrical outlet serving all three group sites. Group sites have fire rings, pole BBQs, potable water taps, a central firewood pile and trash bins, and wooden picnic tables. Group site #1 has 20 individual unserviced sites with wooden picnic tables, pole BBQs, a vault-style toilet, and shared potable water taps. This area is preferred for those with truck campers or tent trailers wishing to camp as a group.

Located across Hwy 210 from the access to Aspen Campground is Little McLean Group Campground. It is generally closed off unless rented out, as it has its own entry booth. There are three electrified camping areas here, each capable of holding a dozen units around a central electrified pedestal. There is a ball diamond near sites #13–36. All three areas have wooden picnic tables, a firewood pile, potable water taps, and vault-style toilets; there are streetlights at each pedestal. You can use the showers at the service center in Aspen Campground or at either beach.

WATER SPORTS

As this park is built on the connecting river between two lakes, there is two of everything! You'll find excellent beaches at both Pasqua and Echo Lakes, complete with beach change rooms. The beach sand is clean and free of debris, and both beaches have large expanses of well-kept lawn for picnicking and day-use. There are metal-framed picnic tables and pole BBQs scattered among the trees, but there is no firewood supplied; bring your own charcoal briquettes. Both beaches have a buoyed swimming area, but there are no lifeguards and no swimming lessons. Although they are somewhat narrow, the beaches extend quite a distance so there will be no crowding. There are huge paved parking lots anchoring both beaches and a wheelchair-friendly promenade running the length of the beach between sand and lawn, with metal-framed benches to rest upon. The Echo Lake beach has the volleyball net and a playground whereas the Pasqua Lake beach has the Echo Valley Mini-Golf course, a privately run operation which also operates the park store. Here you'll find confectionary items as well as a small line of grocery and emergency camping supplies. Ask park gate attendants for a coupon for $1 off for groups of 2 or more golfers.

There are two boat launches, one at either lake at the far end of the beach parking lot. The Echo Lake facility has two docks and a double-wide boat launch whereas the Pasqua Lake facility has a single dock and a modern fish filleting station. There is ample parking in the beach parking lot for trailers, although you are expected to retrieve your boat nightly and store it on your campsite. Fishing is excellent on the lake system, with pike, walleye, and perch commonly taken; ice fishing is a common winter activity. Marine fuel and repair facilities are available in Fort Qu'Appelle, about a 10 minute drive east of the park. Also popular in the Qu'Appelle Valley is recreational boating, waterskiing, canoeing, and sailing. There are no boat rentals available although there is a canoe instructional program; check with the park staff for more details as it may not be offered every year.

HIKING/CROSS-COUNTRY SKIING
The Qu'Appelle Valley Trail offers a 3-km, self-guided hike through the coulees and hills behind Pasqua Lake. Trailhead is beside the toilets for the Hole-In-The-Wall group campground, and ends in the picnic grounds just to the southwest of the parking lot. An excellent brochure is available at the trailhead or from the park entry booths, with information corresponding to numbered signposts along the way. There is no water along the route so bring your own supply as well as sturdy walking shoes as the trail is quite steep in places. There are staircases to help you over the worst verticals but you should be prepared for a good workout nonetheless. You can phone the park office if you'd like to arrange a group hike, and the park offers guided hikes over the course of the summer; check the bulletin boards for timings.

Winter is not forgotten in this pretty park as over 10 km of groomed trails have been laid out to test novice and expert alike. There are two warm-up shelters on the trails, one near the Little McLean Group campground entrance and one farther out at the junction of Fox and Ermine trails. Both shelters have a firewood supply and a wood stove; campfires are forbidden elsewhere.

SERVICES
Except for the simple shopping available at the mini-golf, there is no other shopping in the park. Standing Buffalo Service Station is a convenience store and gas bar approximately 400 meters north of the park boundary, adjacent to Hwy 210, which offers more extensive shopping. The town of Fort Qu'Appelle is about 10 minutes east of the park and offers a full range of shopping, medical, mechanical and worship services. You simply have to check out the Provincial Fish Hatchery about 4 km east of the park; all those fish the province stocks into all those lakes all over are grown right here! The facility is open to tours 7 days a week (May 1 to Labor Day) from 1300–1600 hr; contact them directly to arrange a tour at (306) 332-3200. Their fax number is (306) 332-3203.

The park offers an extensive summer program during July and August, with something on every day of the week. These events change from year to year, so check with the park staff for a current list and to check what fees (if any) may be paid. The Visitors Center offers a self-guided look at the effect glaciers had in creating the valley, and you may learn about local history or about indigenous wildlife. Schools and other groups can organize an educational program with the park staff, including canoe instruction; contact the park directly to plan and schedule your program or tailor one to your specific needs. With all the camping, boating and swimming, hiking, and bird watching, there is something for everyone in this lovely park; come and explore this marvelous valley. Site reservations can be made by contacting the park office at:

Echo Valley Provincial Park
P.O. Box 790
Fort Qu'Appelle, SK   S0G 1S0
Telephone: (306) 332-3215
Fax: (306) 332-3221
You can link to their email address from the SERM website at
www.se.gov.sk.ca/saskparks

KATEPWA POINT PROVINCIAL RECREATION PARK

There are four lakes in the Calling Lakes chain: Pasqua Lake, Echo Lake, Mission Lake, and Katepwa Lake. Together these lakes form the heart of the Qu'Appelle Valley whose name itself is an interesting story. Legend has it that the early Cree inhabitants heard the voices of spirits inhabiting the lakeshore while paddling their canoes, particularly in the last of the lakes. They named the lake *Katapwao*, meaning "What is calling"; early French fur traders with the North-West Company translated the word to "Qu'Appelle" (who calls) and applied the term to the entire valley. The legend has given rise to tales of young Cree lovers that Death separated, a tale captured in a poem by E. Pauline Johnson entitled "The Legend of the Qu'Appelle Valley"; you'll find a copy reprinted in the Fort Qu'Appelle Visitors Guide.

No matter what the legends say, the same things are attracting people today that brought hunters and their families for centuries past: a beautiful valley, narrow, protected lakes, and fine sandy beaches. Birds and animals make this watery oasis their home, enhancing the area's natural beauty. You'll find this day-use-only park located 10 km SE of Lebret on Hwy 56, or 26 km north of Indian Head on Hwy 1, less than an hour east of Regina. The park is open from the May long weekend to the September long weekend, and charges no entry fees.

SITES

There are no campsites here, although Echo Valley Provincial Park is approximately a half-hour west. There is a privately owned campground called "Katepwa Campground and Family 9" which has a full range of amenities as well as a 9-hole golf course, all about 2 blocks from the beach; call them directly for prices and availability at (306) 332-4264. The resort village of Katepwa Beach also has a full range of year-round hotel accommodations with the Katepwa Hotel (Tel: (306) 332-4696) or Sundays Log Cabins (Tel: (306) 783-7951); call either facility directly for current pricing and availability.

WATER SPORTS
The lake is everything to this park, so they take advantage of it with every breath! There is a fine boat launch and docking facility with a huge parking lot for trailers and tow vehicles. There is no marina so you must be prepared to retrieve your boat nightly. Water skiers and towing sports of all sorts abound, as do anglers trying for the pike, walleye and perch that live in the lake. There is a fine, groomed beach with change rooms and a service center with flush toilets; there are non-wheelchair-accessible vault toilets by the boat launch. Ice fishing is very popular in the winter, with an annual Ice Fishing Derby held in March.

The south-facing beach (pictured here) itself has deep, fine sand with a large lawn behind, upon which is set the picnic grounds. There is a buoyed swimming area but no diving platform or swimming docks. There are prominent signs warning of a sharp dropoff, so keep your younger splashers close to shore! Swimming lessons are offered in July and through the first two weeks of August; contact the park office for dates and prices. There is one small playground set in a sandbox centrally located in the picnic grounds near the beach. There is a modern washroom facility with change rooms and flush toilets.

There is an excellent paved walking path running from the parking lot behind the boat launch all around the point upon which the beach and picnic area is set. There are tall trees for shade, and metal-framed picnic tables spread out among them. You'll find pole BBQs and trash bins with every table, and one potable water tap. Please note: there is no firewood provided so picnickers are expected to use charcoal briquettes. There is no dining shelter in the park.

HIKING
There are two self-guided hiking trails available, both starting from the interpretive exhibit which explains some of the significance of the valley. The Cutout Coulee Trail winds for 1.6 km up to the hilltop for a panoramic view of Katepwa Point and the lake. There are interpretive signs to explain what you're hiking through. Trust me—you'll want to stop and read these signs, drink some water, and perhaps drink in the scenery; this is one steep trail! The second trail, the Hillside Nature Trail, actually forms part of the Trans Canada Trail. It winds for about 8 km back to the start/finish point and leads you to some beautiful views of the lake and its surrounding valley.

GOLFING

There is no golf course that is actually part of the park so they won't be discussed at length here, but there are several courses in the area as well as an 18-hole mini-golf course. The "Katepwa Campground and Family 9" offers a 9-hole, grass-green golf course for walk-on golfers. Contact them directly for fees and tee times at (306) 332-4264. For those wishing a greater challenge, one of the most scenic courses on the prairies has got to be the Katepwa Beach Golf Club. A new course, every hole features some spectacular shot or scenic vista. It has a fully licensed dining room and a pro-shop. If you golf, this course is something you have to see once in your life! Call them directly for tee times and fees (and to rent a cart!) at (306) 332-2582, or check out their website at www.katepwabeach.com. You'll particularly like the photos they've put on the web of the views from each tee!

SERVICES

The resort village of Katepwa Point has pretty much everything the traveling adventurer could want for grocery, souvenir, and restaurant shopping. There are hotels and campgrounds literally across the road from the beach and picnic area, with licensed dining and walk-up fast food. The village organizes family events such as the fireworks show on the Canada Day weekend as well as golf tournaments and fishing derbies. More extensive shopping is available in Lebret or in the local major center of Fort Qu'Appelle with most medical, mechanical, and worship services one could require. For more information on this park, contact the park office directly at:

Katepwa Point Provincial Park
Box 790
Fort Qu'Appelle, SK   S0G 1S0
Telephone: (306) 332-3215
Fax: (306) 332-3221
E-mail them from their link on the SERM website at: www.saskparks.net

LAST MOUNTAIN HOUSE PROVINCIAL HISTORIC PARK

Located about 45 minutes' drive northwest of Regina (about 8 km north of Craven on Hwy 20), this park keeps alive the memories of what life was like in a winter trading post. The remnants seen today of this tiny outpost of the Hudson's Bay Company were originally built in 1869 as an outpost of the much larger Fort Qu'Appelle trading post. The purpose of Last Mountain House was twofold: first, to take the fur trade to local First Nations people in an attempt to head off competition from free traders, and second, to function as a provisioning source by hunting the vanishing herds of bison. It was a winter post, as the men would hunt bison themselves as well as trade for furs, pemmican, grease and dried meat from the local people. The site for Last Mountain House was carefully chosen for the wood to build and heat the post, grass for animal fodder, lake for fishing (dog food back then), and the quantities of white clay used to chink the squared timbers used in construction. The First Nations people also wintered in this area for the same reasons as the Hudson's Bay Company built here: access to food and fuel. The post did well for only a short time, and was essentially abandoned in the summer months when little to no trading was done; only a caretaker remained then. When the buildings caught fire and burned the post down sometime in the 1870s, it was never rebuilt. By then the bison herds had moved far to the west, heralding the influx of settlers and farming on lands that once thundered to the hooves of thousands of wild bison.

The park is open from the first of July until the Labor Day weekend; admission is by voluntary donation. There is an interpretive staff at the park through the summer months, and the park reopens open in the winter for school children who come to learn about life as a winter trader. The full-day program is very intensive and offers students hands-on classes in fur grading, bannock baking, trade goods and an imaginary dog sled trip. As part of this, they will visit each of the park buildings to learn of how things worked in a winter trading post, as well as take a trip into the coulee to take part in the Trappers Quest game, an orienteering-based game that students use to find animal tracks and decide which animal made them. Teachers and classes interested in these fascinating activities are encouraged to book a reservation early (preferably no later than mid-December) by contacting the park staff at: (306) 787-1475 or (306) 787-2080.

Besides the educational programs, the self-guided summer walk through the buildings is quite interesting, and the park staff is very knowledgeable when answering your questions. Although the buildings are largely barrier-free with a boardwalk around the perimeter, the toilet facilities are not wheelchair accessible. There is also a hike down from the large parking lot down to the coulee and over to the lake. It is not wheelchair accessible, and the hike back up the steep hill can be quite arduous. You must bring your own food and water as there will be none for purchase in the park. Groups wishing to have tours in the summer months can make arrangements with the park staff; there will be a fee for group interpretive programs. The park can be contacted at:

Last Mountain House Provincial Historic Park
146-3211 Albert Street
Regina, SK   S4S 5X6
Telephone: (306) 787-1475
Website: www.saskparks.net. You'll find a link for their email address there.

MOOSE MOUNTAIN PROVINCIAL PARK

Located between the Trans Canada Highway (Hwy 1) and the town of Carlyle on Hwy 9, this park is one of the oldest in the provincial park system. The park office, for example, is housed in a fieldstone building dating back to 1931, used then as a hotel. It is now one of the prettiest and most incredibly picturesque park offices in the system, in huge demand for wedding photos amid the beautifully flowered lawns and for conferences in the "Grate Room." You'll find huge beaches, excellent camping, a water slide complex, and some of the prettiest golfing in the province. There is a wealth of hiking and biking trails, new volleyball courts, and a hotel with cabins and an indoor swimming pool for your winter stay. Although the park is open year-round, the core operation is open from the May long weekend until the September long weekend. The golf course will be open longer, weather permitting; the hotel is open year-round.

SITES

There are 331 sites in two sections of the same campground in the park; 30 electrified sites in the Lynwood loop and 301 sites in the Fish Creek loop; as it is larger, we will consider the latter first. There is a reservation system in place, and there are 33 electrified and 10 unserviced sites available for seasonal rent in the Fish Creek Campground. Contact the park office for more information; they will explain the rules. All camping is located about 3 km from the main beach area where the bulk of the park's amenities are located; there is a paved biking/walking trail running from the parking lot at the core area to the campgrounds.

FISH CREEK LOOP

There are 301 sites in two loops. The older sites are located to the west as you drive in, the newer sites are to the east where you'll also find the overflow and volleyball area; more on that later. There are 168 electrified sites, 11 full-service sites with water and sewer service, and 122 unserviced sites. All sites are built among mature aspen, elm and birch trees, and all roads are paved throughout the park. The sites are large, well-spaced and shady but ground cover is variable. The electrified sites have metal-framed picnic tables and fire pits; the unserviced sites currently have wooden tables but they are being changed over as time permits. Potable water taps and trash bins are spread throughout the campground, and there is one wood pile and recycling station beside the road as you enter the main loop. Toilet facilities vary from simple vault toilets (not wheelchair accessible) to modern flush toilets (wheelchair accessible) in the campgrounds, to the fully modern, barrier-free service centers near sites #8 and 9, and across from site #73. The service center near site #73 has a coin-operated laundry; bring quarters and loonies. There is one trailer dump station beside the road near the campground entry booth. There are two wheelchair-accessible sites, #8 and 9, both near the barrier-free service center. Of note are the uneven-numbered sites from #201–223, which have a lake view although they do not have lakeside access. We found the Campground Hosts in site #15; stop by with any questions you may have about the campgrounds or the park.

A sharp eye will note that there are no sites #156 and 158; they were removed to make room for the presentation area with a large fire pit and seating for the summer's interpretive programming. You'll also find the Lakeview Hiking Trail starting between sites 86 and 87 and running along Little Kenosee Lake for 0.9 km. The trail is hardened and wheelchair accessible; you exit the trail between sites #33 and 34 and can return to your campsite on the road. There are two playgrounds in the campground, one beside each of the service centers. Both playgrounds feature large, colorful creative play structures built in sandboxes as well as grassed areas in which to frolic. The park has built a new volleyball area with sand courts in the campground overflow, accessed from the turn beside site #232. This area is normally gated to preclude access except for when the park is full or when the Annual Volleyball Tournament is in full swing. It also functions as a group camping area as well as the other two such available: Group A to the north of the road a kilometer or so past the main campgrounds, situated on Little Kenosee Lake; the other is Group B, located between the main campgrounds and Group A, but situated on Christopher Bay of Kenosee Lake on the south side of the road. Both have the same amenities: pole BBQs, wooden picnic tables, a central grass area, and vault toilets; Group A has a dining shelter. They can be reserved by contacting the park office.

LYNWOOD LOOP
Located to the south of the main road transecting the park, Lynwood campground has 30 electrified campsites of which two, sites #5 and 6, are wheelchair accessible. The generally large sites are well shaded amid stately elms and birch, and have metal-framed picnic tables and fire pits. The campground has a modern service center with barrier-free hot showers, flush toilets, a potable water tap, and a firewood pile; trash bins are scattered throughout the campground. There is also a camp kitchen in the same large lawn, but no playground equipment. As with Fish Creek Campground, grey water is to be disposed of in the vault toilets or at the dump station.

SWIMMING/BOATING

The main beach and surrounding area forming the core of the park is quite the place! The beach is quite large and filled with groomed, clean, coarse sand. A building right on the beach once held the swimming lesson and water safety equipment, but lessons are no longer taught at the moment so the building now has other uses. The beach has a buoyed swimming area but there are no lifeguards and all swimming is unsupervised. Beach volleyball courts are also available. There is a large beach shower and change room facility with modern flush toilets, all barrier-free. Large though the beach may be, it is dwarfed by the lawned day-use area in between it and the huge parking lot. There are picnic tables and pole BBQs for picnickers, but no firewood so bring your own briquettes. Trash bins are placed on the paved walking path as are restful memorial benches, and swing sets are found all over. A large, colorful creative play structure has been built along the woods beside the parking lot. There is also a fenced tennis court with 2 basketball half-courts; ask park staff for equipment rental.

To the east of the parking lot is Allison's Store, where one can find just about any summer treat you could need, including an outdoor fast food restaurant. They also carry a surprising line of grocery items including fresh produce and meat as well as camping sundries and souvenir clothing. To the west of the parking lot is the only 36-hole mini-golf course in the province (that I'm aware of!). Master's Mini-golf is lit for night golfing and usually has some sort of daily special. It can host your private tournament or group function; contact Allison's Store for more details at (306) 577-2234. There is a recreation hall beside the golf course; available for rent, it is very popular for hosting wedding banquets and dances. Contact the park office for details. Of particular interest to the history buffs is the fieldstone foundation of the old Hudson's Bay wintering post located on the lawn behind the beach, just east of the store and south of the hotel. A cairn describes the significance of the structure to the early local economy.

There is one boat launch in the park, located inside the Sunnybank cottage subdivision at the end of Manitoba Street; here you'll find vault toilets and ample parking, although you are expected to retrieve your boat nightly and store it in your campsite. The boat launch itself is quite large and there are floating docks to assist you, but no marina system although there is a fish cleaning station. Boating and tow sports are very popular, though, and excellent fishing is to be had at the nearby Alameda Dam. The park rents canoes during July and August, but there is no other boat or motor rental available. The previous lake access, located between the campgrounds and group areas, has been turned into a day-use area with vault toilets, water tap plus a dining shelter with picnic tables and pole BBQs. There is a small playground with a set of swings and teeter-totters but no firewood supply.

Under the heading of water sports one simply has to mention the Kenosee Superslides and all its watery fun. It's a private venture located a few km from the gates, just east of Hwy 9, but still inside the park boundaries. Open from mid-June to late August, you'll find an adventure for just about any level of enthusiast on the 10 waterslides, from the 8-storey free-fall to "Kiddie Slides." There is a picnic area, "Cruisers Family Restaurant," showers and change rooms with rental lockers, a souvenir shop, and a huge parking lot. For current pricing, reservations or group bookings, call them directly at (306) 577-2343, or check out their website at: www.kenoseesuperslides.com. One can only imagine the happy shrieking and joyful glee from all the children splashing about on a hot summer's day. Oh, to be young again! There is a camping/waterslide package available; contact the park for more information.

HIKING/BIKING

There are three main hiking trails in the park, the Beaver Lake/Youell Lake Trail, the Lakeview Trail, and the Birch Forest Trail. All of the hiking trails can also be used by mountain bikers, but are banned for ATV drivers—such vehicles are not allowed in the core area of the park and only on designated backcountry trails!

Beginning from east to west, the first trail is the Beaver Lake/Youell Lake Trail. Trailhead is located at the northwest corner of the ball diamond, where you'll find the warm-up shelter for cross-country skiers. The 4.5 km-long trail loops around Beaver Lake, where you can see evidence of the beavers' lifestyle by all the stumps along the lake; you'll also see beaver lodges but only rarely will you see the animals themselves as they are quite shy. The Youell Lake Trail is a 2-km addition which adds to the hiking enjoyment of these lovely woods.

Lakeview Trail begins at either Site #33 or #86 in Fish Creek Campground. It is wheelchair accessible for its 1km length and is quite an enjoyable hike, particularly when you watch the sunset from the benches built into the boardwalk on the marsh.

Birch Forest Interpretive Trail is located at the terminus of a 3-km road known as

Church Camp Road; there's a parking lot and trailhead sign at the end of the road. Please note that this road is very slippery when wet so you might want to wait a day or two after a summer rain! The trail runs around Pickerel Point for a 2.1-km loop, and the brochure available is quite informative about the many things of note in a predominantly birch forest, which is a rarity in southern Saskatchewan; all the more reason to go for a walk in the woods!

The park has built an extensive 50-km trail system for use in winter, north and west of the riding academy. In summer, however, it offers an interesting backcountry adventure. The brochure mapping the trails shows several winter shelters where one can stop and use the stoves, but overnight camping is not allowed at the winter-use sites. The trails are all cut out of mature forest so there is plenty of wind shelter and shade, but there will be no drinking water along the trail; bring your own supply and be prepared to boil further supplies from lakes or streams along the way. Should you wish to camp out overnight along these trails, please contact the park office beforehand. Not only is it proper etiquette, it is just plain good common sense to let someone know where you're going and what your expected return time will be.

CROSS-COUNTRY SKIING/SNOWMOBILING

The park has built an extensive system of trails for backcountry winter access, with one side of the trail groomed for classical skiers and the other side screened for skate skiers. It is noteworthy that the park has reserved a large tract of land for non-motorized winter sports. The entire park northeast of the riding trails, formed by the Gillis Lake Road on the west all the way to Hwy 9 on the east, and from the Center Road (running right through the park) all the way to the park's northern boundary is posted as "No Snowmobiling," so your peace will not be disturbed. Just to be certain, however, the park prohibits ski and snowshoe use on any of the trails reserved for motorized use. The cross-country ski trails are cut into many small loops, and there are 5 warm-up shelters on the trail with wood-burning stoves and a fuel supply; no overnight camping is permitted at these shelters. For more details, ask the park for a copy of the "Moose Mountain Provincial Park Cross-Country and Snowmobile Trails" brochure.

Snowmobilers are not forgotten; they have 120 km of trails reserved for their use as well. In fact, almost the entire park except for the northeast quadrant detailed above has been marked with groomed and natural trails running throughout the park, off to several out-of-the-way little lakes. There are 4 warm-up shelters for snowmobile use, with wood-burning stoves and a firewood supply. Again, overnight camping at these shelters is discouraged. Snowmobiles can be unloaded at either the riding academy parking lot, or at the Village of Kenosee Lake.

GOLF
Golf Kenosee Inc. is an 18-hole grass-green course set among rolling hills north of the main road. Open from April to mid-October, the course plays for 5483 yards over its par-72 fairways, with elevated tees and bunkered greens; well manicured and set among tall trees, the course is simply sensational! The clubhouse, Club 19, offers a full range of meals in its fully licensed dining room or on the deck overlooking the magnificent first fairway. The view from there, particularly at sunset, will simply take your breath away! There's a pro-shop with equipment and cart rentals, as well as a line of merchandise for sale, including branded clothing. A putting green and a driving range are also available. The clubhouse can accommodate up to 150 people, and can cater large or small events. For more details or to book a tee-time, contact the facility directly at (306) 577-4422, or by checking the website at www.saskgolfer.com/kenosee. For those interested, the nearby White Bear Golf and Kenosee Inn have partnered to make an attractive golf-and-stay package available. Contact the Kenosee Inn for details at the number below. The park has also partnered with White Bear Lake Golf Course and Golf Kenosee to arrange an attractive golf-and-camp package; contact the park office for more details.

The White Bear Lake Golf Course has well-manicured fairways, elevated tees and bunkered greens on a relatively new course, built in 1987. Not in the park or affiliated with the park I won't go into great detail about it here, but if you're a golfer you really should check it out. Contact them directly for more information at (306) 577-4902, or check out their website at www.tee-off.ca/courses/sk199.htm.

SPORTS
As mentioned elsewhere, the core area includes beach volleyball courts, and the park has newly built volleyball courts in the overflow area, part of the Fish Creek Campground. There is a tennis court, fenced and paved, near the mini-golf venue, and there are two basketball half-courts in the same enclosure. Ask the park staff for rental equipment if you didn't bring your own. As for the privately owned mini-golf venue, contact information is listed in the beach section; just a reminder, though—it is the only 36-hole course we found in our rather extensive travels! The park has a baseball diamond with bleachers, a sound booth, concession stand (open only during events), and score board. You'll find the Beaver Lake trailhead in a corner of the parking lot for the ball diamond, and the park does try to organize weekly pick-up games of slow pitch through the summer months although you can have your own game for free if the diamond is otherwise unoccupied. There is a cenotaph near the ball diamond commemorating the servicemen and women who made

the ultimate sacrifice for our country; honor them when you pass by.

Worthy of special mention is the Kenosee Lake Riding Academy which operates west of the group campgrounds. They offer one-hour guided trail rides departing from their stables several times each day; they prefer advance bookings, please. They will also provide overnight trips into the northwest corner of the park upon request. Wedding planners should note that they will also provide horse-drawn carriages or winter sleigh rides. For more information, or to book a trail ride, contact them directly at (306) 577-2278 or (306) 739-2273. You can also email them at: jadams@serm.gov.sk.ca

SERVICES

Foremost among the services found here will be the Visitor's Center and Park Office. You really have to see this place, particularly in mid to late summer when all the flower beds are in bloom. I was told you really should book an appointment for wedding photos, as it gets so busy and I can certainly see why—it's beautiful! The fieldstone building was originally a hotel in the 1930s and still offers a stunning view of the lake to the south. The Grate Room has been extensively refurbished and can be rented for conferences or meetings; you'll find it both well-appointed and yet serene. You'll find a self-guided interpretive center here, and the grounds are well treed and filled with flowers and birdsong. This is also the place where the park interpretive staff hang out, preparing all the fun events they host through the summer months. They will also provide educational programs for school groups in the months of May and June. For a nominal fee they will provide school groups with canoe lessons, orienteering (the art of map and compass use) lessons, as well as natural history programs that showcase the forest, its plants and its inhabitants. A campfire program after learning of First Nations herbal and traditional lore, perhaps a day of hiking and experiencing or perhaps canoeing and bird watching, all in a truly wonderful setting—where was this when I was a kid!?!

Just to the east along the lake is a picnic area known locally as McNaughton Heights (no signs) with a fieldstone dining shelter, picnic tables and pole BBQs but no firewood; bring your own briquettes. There's also a scenic overlook and picnic area just to the left of the main road as you enter the park. It has picnic tables and one of the best views of the lake to the south and east.

There is plenty of hotel accommodation as well, at the Kenosee Inn Resort Hotel. Open year round, there are 30 hotel rooms and 23 light-housekeeping cabins for rent, as well as an indoor pool and hot tub. The Lakeview Dining Room and lounge offers a full range of meals as well as beverages in a pleasant setting overlooking the lake (hence the name). There are conference rooms and banquet facilities for up to 150 people, and access to the excellent golfing across the road. Call them directly for rates and reservations at (306) 577-2099, or check out their website at www.kenoseeinn.com.

The nearby resort Village of Kenosee Lake offers more extensive grocery shopping and accommodation as well as several "watering holes"; for more serious shopping, mechanical and medical services one must travel to nearby Carlyle, approximately 23 km south on Hwy 9. Worship services are available in the Village of Kenosee, and during July and August a non-denominational service is held in the Moose Mountain Provincial Park Recreation Hall. There are numerous private businesses, ranging from cabins and motel accommodation to hairdressing or nightclubs. Try the Moosehead Inn—it's supposed to be haunted (question: do they serve "spirits" there?) or the Bar-Bar, the only place in the park that sells off-sale. There are so many private businesses that I don't have the space to do them all justice; consult the local website for more information at: www.wawota.com/rec_and_ent/Kenosee_Lake.htm. Nearby Bear Claw Casino offers the gamblers a chance at some real money, or more likely the chance to come back and visit their own money! You'll find it has all the games you know and love, with tables, slot machines and entertainment; check out their website for more information at www.siga.sk.ca/bearclaw/index.html. Cannington Manor Provincial Historic Park is roughly 50 km east of here; check the writeup elsewhere in this book for more details on this historically accurate re-creation of an early pioneer's village.

No doubt about it, the park is busy; you'll need reservations through the months of July and August and all the long weekends in summer. Keep in mind the two packages the park has arranged with its golfing and waterslide partners; if you intend to visit this park, this is a great way to save some money! For more information or to reserve a site, contact the park directly at:

Moose Mountain Provincial Park
Box 220
Kenosee Lake, SK   S0C 2S0
Telephone: (306) 577-2600
Fax: (306) 577-2622
Or link to their email from the SERM website at: www.saskparks.net

REGINA BEACH PROVINCIAL RECREATION SITE

Located approximately 32 km northwest of Regina on Hwy 11, then 18 km north of Hwy 54 on the south end of Last Mountain Lake, this day-use-only park is interesting for the dual nature it presents: is it a recreation site with a town attached, or is the town attached to the recreation site? Either way, the glory of this park is the beach, and what a beach it is: rich, deep, soft sand on a promontory with a small bay—exquisite! This particular resource has been popular with sun and sand enthusiasts from the earliest times of our provincial history; the park has been used in one way or another since 1913, perhaps earlier! Open from the May long weekend to the Labor Day weekend, this park's busiest day is definitely Canada Day when 5,000 to 6,000 people make this beach their home for the day's festivities.

BEACHES AND BOATING

The beach is definitely the raison d'être for this park, no doubt about it. You start with the huge paved parking lot from where you can see the shower house/beach change rooms/administration building, the picnic areas, and the playground set amid tall shade trees. Walking towards the beach, you cross a paved beach promenade which runs from the old pier just north of the beach to the Buena Vista cottage subdivision, approximately 3 km. Barrier-free, it runs along the lakeshore for its entire length, with restful benches and shady spots along the way to relax and enjoy the day. It continues past the subdivision all the way to Lumsden Beach, approximately 8 km in total, but only the stretch inside the park is paved. This is a scenic walk, not an interpretive hike but thoroughly enjoyable for the scenery, the fresh air, and a smattering of bird-watching.

The playground has a large creative play structure set in the deep sand, with many colorful toys to occupy many an hour's contentment for the wee folk in your group. The tall trees in which the structure is set provide shade for most of the day and some relief from the wind. There are picnic tables and trash bins in the play area, and a drinking fountain at the nearby shower house. The shower house has men's and lady's "Gang" showers, 4 flush toilets per side as well as sinks and mirrors. It is also the drinking-water access for the picnic grounds which essentially surround it. Just north of the shower house is the old pier, a remnant of the structure used in times past to greet the steamboats that once cruised the lake carrying freight and vacationers from the railhead at Craven to various points on the lake.

The picnic area is quite impressive, with its large expanse of well-kept lawn and five picnic stations. Each station has a large metal-framed picnic table set in a cement pad, a pole BBQ and a trash bin. There is no firewood provided and it is illegal to transport firewood into a provincial park, so use charcoal briquettes instead. Besides the picnic stations, there are other, slightly smaller picnic tables scattered throughout the picnic and play areas, but they do not have pole BBQs and trash bins are centrally located. During the Canada Day celebration, it is not at all uncommon to see people arrive early in the morning (0500 hr, I've been told!) and set up for the day. Later arrivals will set up dining shelters of their own, so many that the entire beach and grassed areas become festooned with colorful cabanas.

Boating is also very popular on this lake, with two yacht clubs open to members at the south end of the lake; the Regina Beach Yacht Club (RBYC, seen here) is located just north of the park's free-use boat launch and dock. The Regina Yacht Club has facilities across the lake just north of Craven and so won't be discussed here. The RBYC has an extensive marina, with excellent facilities including a licensed clubhouse and dining room open to members and guests. Contact them directly for membership information at (306) 729-2461 or check out their excellent website for more information at: www.rbyc.ca/. The RBYC has a fueling dock as well as the only pump-out facilities on Last Mountain Lake; both these services are open to non-members but you will be charged accordingly. The park operates a free-use boat launch with two docks as well as fish filleting and vault toilet facilities beside the extensive trailer parking lot serving the site. There are no boat slips available, so you will have to remove your boat from the lake nightly. As a side note, the lake is 80 km long, fairly narrow, and has excellent fishing (particularly at the north end) for pike and perch; with all the sailboats, anglers, and tow boats on the lake it can be a busy and colorful place.

SERVICES

There are no commercial enterprises allowed within the Recreation Site; however, the resort village of Regina Beach has many private businesses that exist to serve the visiting public, and some of them have been in business for generations. Noteworthy among this list is the Bluebird Café and Nelson's Fish and Chips, which has been serving essentially the same menu from the same location for 80 years, first opening their doors in 1928. Their fish and chips, available from either the restaurant or the walk-up concession, are legendary locally, and I strongly recommend you sample them during your visit. There are many other diners, restaurants, and concessions, enough to suit any palate; two beach concessions operate during the summer months and sell the usual fare of iced treats, chips, pop, and candy, and there are several ice-cream parlors that operate during the summer as well.

If you want to try some horse-riding, give the local stables a call at (306) 729-2218; R-BAR-B Ranch offers rides with gentle horses, guided or not (whichever you're comfortable with), from one hour to overnight. They also boast one of Saskatchewan's oldest go-kart rentals; check them out! There are two mini-golf courses in town, one right beside the stables and one downtown beside an ice cream parlor. A local 9-hole golf course is available with pro-shop, club and cart rentals and a licensed dining room and lounge. There are elevated tees, bunkered fairways and grass greens awaiting you; call them directly at (306) 729-4433 for more information or to reserve your tee time.

There are hotels, bed-and-breakfasts, and cottage owners willing to rent their summer homes out to you; look through the yellow pages or consult the website at: www.saskatchewan.worldweb.com/SoutheastRegion/ReginaBeach/WheretoStay/. There is no camping in the park although 2 private campgrounds are available: Kinookimaw and Regina Beach. Both are located on the top of the hill as you drive in; turn right and you descend the hill to the beach, but turn left to the Regina Beach Campground or continue straight ahead to Kinookimaw Campground. Of note are the mountain-biking trails at Kinookimaw Campgrounds which are very popular locally. The Regina Beach Campground will store your RV annually or for any period you require; contact them directly at (306) 729-2629.

Should you want more information on this park, contact them directly in season at:

Regina Beach Recreational Site
146-3211 Albert Street
Regina, SK   S4S 5W6
Telephone: (306) 787-1475
Website link from: www.saskparks.net

ROWAN'S RAVINE PROVINCIAL PARK

Located about an hour's drive north of Regina on the east side of Last Mountain Lake, the park is accessed by taking Hwy 20 north from Craven then turning west on Hwy 220. Alternatively, you can take Hwy 322 west and north from Saskatchewan Beach; both highways are paved and quite scenic. The park was established in 1960 on the site of a homestead dating back to 1901, owned by William Rowan (hence the name), and has an excellent marina and beach on southern Saskatchewan's largest natural lake. Coupled with the extensive campgrounds and rental cabins, this park has a lot to offer the boating patron. Of special note is that every tree you see in the park was planted by hand, and forest management is ongoing to this day. The campgrounds are open from the May long weekend to the September long weekend although the cabin rentals extend into the fall hunting season, keeping the park open a bit longer.

CAMPING

There are two main camping loops, Elmwood and Underwood, comprised of 200 electrified sites (30-amp service) and 98 non-electrified sites; none are full-service sites. Of these, 112 are available for seasonal rental based on a lottery system; contact the park administration office for details. There are two barrier-free sites in Elmwood campground for seasonal rent, one on either side of the service center, with pavement and suitable picnic table and pole BBQ. There are several other hardened sites that will be wheelchair accessible as well; all of them are held for patrons requiring that service unless the park is completely full; the park has no site reservation system with the exception of the seasonal sites. All roadways in the campgrounds are paved, and all sites are built on gravel pads. The trees are tall enough for shade although brush between sites can be a bit of a premium, depending on where in the loop you are located. The seasonal sites have a bit better privacy. All sites have wooden picnic tables, park-supplied BBQs (either pole BBQs or culvert-style units with a swinging grate), and access to shared potable water taps and trash bins. Vault toilets in the campgrounds are complemented by flush toilets in the service centers and comfort stations. The service centers also feature hot showers and modern washrooms; all are wheelchair accessible. Of note is that all toilets have a grey water dump station for dishwater. A trailer dump station is located just past the old campground office, a short distance from the campground host in site #297.

Firewood is available from one central compound at the entrance to each campground, and each campground has a small playground. In Elmwood campground, the play area with swings and teeter-totters is built across the road from the wood pile. In Underwood, the playground is built across from the large service center, which also houses the coin-operated laundry machines for the campgrounds. Underwood campground also has 11 pull-through sites, #1–11 inclusive, all electrified. As with most sites in the campgrounds, they are big enough for the largest modern unit. Two of Underwood's loops have lakeside campsites with stunning views of the lake. Some of these sites are electrified and available for seasonal rent. We thought them among the best of the sites in the park until we spoke to the occupants, who warned us of the myriads of tiny fish flies that blow into the sites from the lake. Although harmless, they can be quite a nuisance. Also, one of the sites has a trail along the side through which people can access the lake; they aren't supposed to cut through your lot to get to the lake, but they do. There are two small group sites in Underwood campground, offering 7 or 9 non-electrified sites; the smaller loop has a large firepit in the center for family sing-songs or campfire stories.

BEACHES AND BOATING

Last Mountain Lake provides an astonishing recreational resource to the central part of the province. Once known as Long Lake, it is 80 km long and only about 2 km wide at its widest. With its generally warm waters and extensive sandy beaches it is a natural magnet for families looking for a little water-based fun. The Last Mountain Lake National Wildlife Area (NWA) is the oldest bird sanctuary in North America and hosts 280 species of birds annually; it is located on the north end of the lake west of Govan. There is excellent fishing to be had in this basin, with pike in the 14-kg range, and walleye in the 7-kg range. Carp fishing is so popular among European visitors that an annual derby occurs in the fall along the east shore of the lake. Huge, lush lawns with groves of tall shade trees, a modern washroom facility (with potable water taps), and central trash bins, all within a few meters of a large beach and playground area. Truly a marvelous resource!

The beach in this park is fairly large and long, with two exceptional beach volleyball courts (complete with umpire's chairs) at either end. The sand is somewhat coarse with many fine pebbles, and is groomed regularly to keep it free of trash and soften it. The unsupervised swimming area is buoyed and fairly shallow, and there is a large playground just behind the beach with colorful climbers and tire swings. A barrier-free beach changeroom is located between the huge, paved parking lot and the beach; it features modern washroom facilities and free showers. In behind the beach is a massive picnic area with lots of tall shade trees and picnic tables. Pole BBQs are provided for patrons use, but no firewood is available; use charcoal briquettes instead. Just a note: there is parking for several hundred vehicles in the parking lot, and certainly picnic space for all of the people they would hold. Just north of the beach changeroom is a log dining shelter with wood cook stove, available on a first-come, first-served basis although it can be reserved for special events. Continuing north along the beach past the play area you'll find the picnic shelter and its large, outdoor campfire pit with bench seating. The enclosed shelter can be rented for private functions; contact the park office for details.

A paved walking path runs south from the beach to the park restaurant, RB's Diner, where happy campers can buy the usual iced treats, pop and candy; it has many other offerings which will be discussed later. After the Diner, the path is hard-packed gravel and may not be as wheelchair accessible. It leads to the extensive, privately run marina, G & S Marina Outfitters, which operates the facility from mid-May to freeze-up in late fall; they're open during the fall hunting season as well, offering heated cabins and fishing or hunting guides. The marina store offers a small line of grocery items as well as hardware, fishing tackle and bait, and branded clothing and souvenirs. There is extensive paved parking behind the marina for trailers; no charge is levied for the service but you park at your own risk. There are vault toilets and a fish filleting facility beside the parking lot. The marina has 85 boat slips for rent and is one of only two boat fueling points on the entire lake (the other is at Regina Beach). Please note that slip fees will be charged for all dock usage. The marina store also rents paddle boats as well as fishing boats and motors; guides can be arranged if you desire. They have 12 camping cabins for rent with electric heat, a four-burner counter-top stove, a refrigerator, and potable water. A service center behind the cabins has modern washroom facilities and hot showers, and a dining shelter on the large lawn in front of the cabin area are all reserved for cabin renters only. The cabins can be rented without bedding or kitchenware, or you can arrange for the proprietors to supply everything but your food and drink; contact them directly for details at (306) 725-4466. Check out their website for further information at www.gsmarina.com

SPORTS

Besides the fishing, boating, and beaches, the park has an excellent nature hike available. The "Prairie Whispers Nature Trail" is a self-guided walk around the trout pond and into the low hills along the lake; trailhead is at the marina parking lot. There are two loops: "A" is 1.2 km long and takes you around the trout pond and ravine, while "B" is 2.7 km long and leads you through the low hills to discover the plants and animals of this pretty park. Neither trail is wheelchair accessible, nor is there drinking water available, so bring your own. The trails are well blazed with a close-mow lawnmower and require a reasonable degree of fitness due to the steep ravines you must traverse. There is one set of benches on the scenic overlook near station 14 on Loop "B," a place to drink in one of the park's trademark sunsets.

A private operator has an 18-hole mini-golf course just east of the beach parking lot. Fanciful obstacles and lots of color make this fun for the whole family. The facility is open from 1000–2200 hr in season (mid-May to early September), and rents bicycles to enjoy the park with, or miniature electric carts for the wee ones in your group. They can only run inside the mini-golf enclosure on a special track, but they are sure to be a hit with your children!

The park has built a basketball half-court behind the restaurant, and a ball diamond with gravel infield and grass outfield is available just beside the restaurant. As with the beach volleyball facilities, play equipment is available during designated hours of operation at the recreation facility adjoining the main beach change house. There is no charge for using any of these facilities, though.

SERVICES

RB's Diner operates a wonderful restaurant between the beach and the marina. Besides that necessary staple of camping life—ice cream—the restaurant offers a full line of meals from breakfast to supper, opening their doors in mid-May until early September. Keeping pace with modern dining, they offer pizza nights, wing nights and an excellent Sunday brunch; many of their specialties can be enjoyed in their licensed facility or taken back to the campsite. They also do two things that nobody else does: a "dock and dine" and movie nights. Although they are located on top of a hill and thus offer a stunning vista for those beautiful sunsets, particularly on their deck, they've built a dock for their boating patrons who come over for a meal and can thus dock their boats and use the staircase to climb the hill. During the summer months, weather permitting, they offer "movie nights" where patrons are invited to see a free movie, projected on a screen outdoors, and enjoy a bag of popcorn for a mere 25¢; both of these services have given the restaurant quite a reputation among their patrons. They can also provide catering services for weddings, family reunions, etc; contact them directly for details at (306) 725-4371.

The town of Strasbourg, approximately 15 minutes away from the park, offers shopping, mechanical, medical, and worship services. The city of Regina is approximately an hour away and has museums, a casino, and more complete shopping and mechanical services, not to mention Taylor Field, home to the Saskatchewan Roughriders football club; no summer visit to Saskatchewan is complete without taking in a game at "the world's largest outdoor insane asylum"!

The park does not have a site reservation system in place, but they can work with you in arranging group sites or the rental of recreation halls or dining shelters for your private function. For more information, contact the park directly at:

Rowan's Ravine Provincial Park
Box 370
Strasbourg, SK   S0G 4V0
Telephone: (306) 725-5200
E-mail linked to the website at: www.saskparks.net

West-Central Saskatchewan

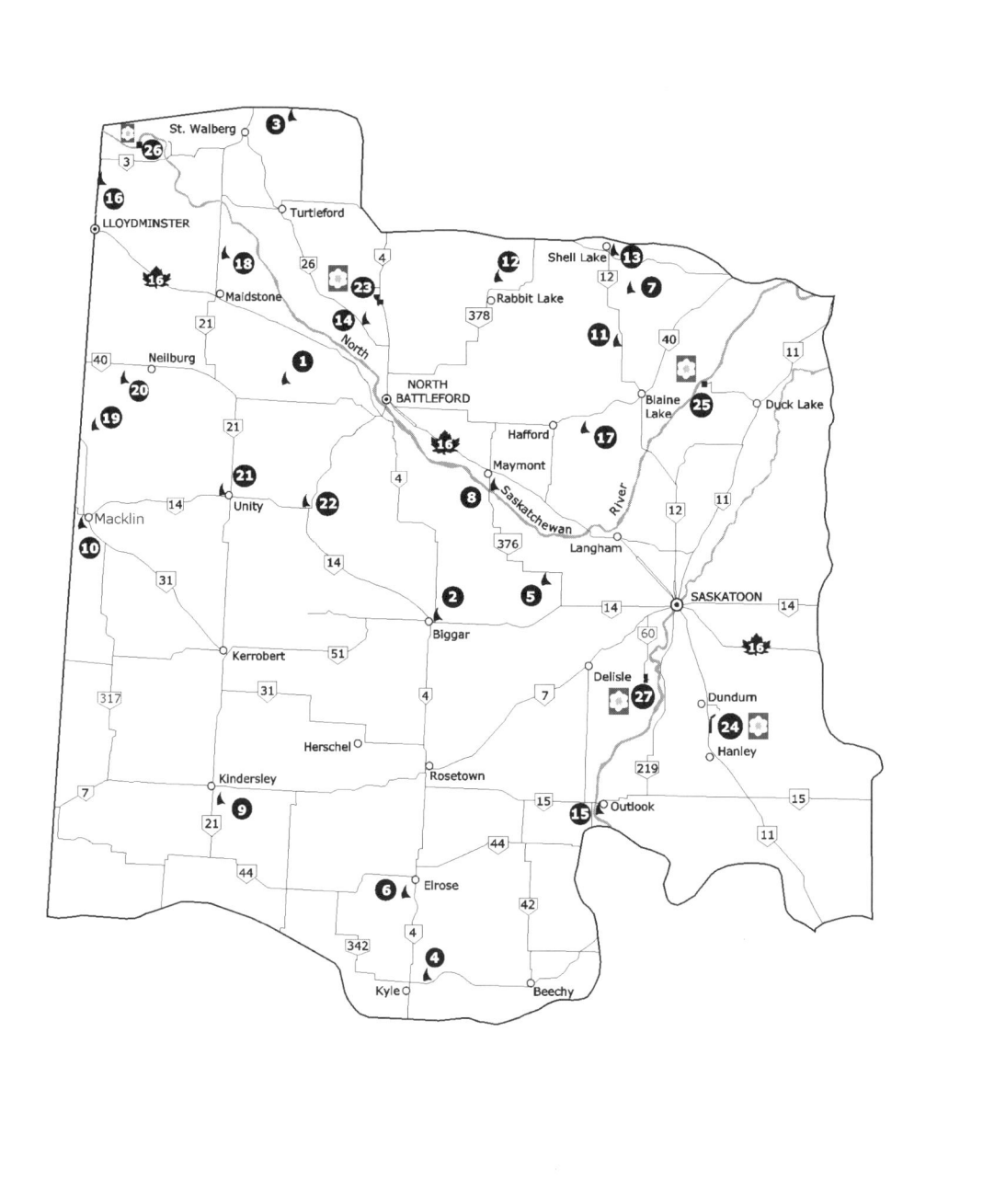

ATTON'S LAKE REGIONAL PARK

This park, first opened in 1953, is located 20 km (13 miles) north of the town of Cutknife, off Hwy 40. The access road is paved and well signed from the main routes by Department of Highways signs. The park is open from May through September, longer if the golfing season warrants. The park has an excellent waterfront and concession system as well as a lovely grass-green golf course; no wonder it's a popular resort lake in this pretty area. Entrance fees of $4 per day per vehicle, or $6 per weekend, are waived with an annual Regional Park sticker.

SITES

There are 60 electrified sites, some of which have the 30-amp service modern campers need for their air conditioners, and 40 non-electrified sites. The electrified sites cost $17 per night ($100 per week) for 15-amp service or $20 per night ($120 per week) for 30-amp service. Non-electrified sites cost $12 per night ($70 per week). Persons camping on a seasonal, leased cabin lot will have a 3-day grace period after which they will be charged the regular camping fees. This includes tents, trailers, campers, and motorhomes, and will be monitored by the Park manager; any unpaid fees will be billed to the cabin owner. All sites have picnic tables, pole BBQs and garbage cans; firewood can be purchased from the park. Washroom facilities vary from biffies in camping areas to modern flush toilets in the coin-operated shower house. A trailer dump station is located near the entrance registration booth. Drinking water is available from central taps at all times, supplying well water. As with many parks, the water tastes faintly of the plastic piping used. The roadways were bumpy and somewhat narrow, so meeting another large unit might be an adventure. Backing a large unit into one of the smaller sites might also be an adventure, but these units would normally ask for 30-amp service, and those sites were generally larger. Registration is an interesting process, as one is confronted by a large "mailbox" system just beside the manager's cabin as you drive in. Each box is labeled with campground location and electrical service. Simply fill out a registration form, found in a small box beside the 'mailbox' and place it in an empty slot. Pay the required fees in the envelopes provided and place them in the strongbox, and you are ready to go set up your site. Under no circumstances should you set up a site without first registering, as it can easily be taken by someone who registers first and asks questions later. Second units sharing a site are subject to extra fees ($10 per night or $50 per week), although pup tents occupied by children under 12 won't be billed. Group sites are also available; contact the park manager for details. Campsites are shaded by both natural and grove trees, poplars and evergreens predominant, although chokecherry and willow brush thicken the undergrowth in some areas. The gates are closed from 2300–0800 hr daily in season, and "quiet time" is from 2300–0800 hr as well. The park has no reservation system; contact the park manager at (306) 398-2814 for information.

WATER SPORTS

Atton's Lake has a fine beach and buoyed swimming area, and lessons are taught in the lake with 6 lesson sets offered starting the July long weekend and running weekly until the middle of August, based on demand. Lessons can be arranged through the concession a short walk from the beach. There are beach change rooms, and showers are available beside the concession; they cost 50¢ per timed use. Of interest to parents is that the shower house also holds the laundry service for the park. There are two washers and two dryers, costing $1 and 50¢ each respectively. Pets are welcome in the park, but they must be leashed and are absolutely restricted from the waterfront. The park patrol will levy a $25 fine should you wish to defy the rule. A boatlaunch allows access to the lake but motorboats are only allowed on the lake Monday to Friday as congestion on the lake due to park popularity has made weekend boating unsafe. Canoes, paddleboats, sailboats and the like are all welcomed as you wish, however. Boaters can take advantage of the pike fishing the lake offers, as well as the usual water-skiing and tubing during the week.

GOLFING

No doubt about it, golf is one of the more popular pastimes at Atton's Lake. The 9-hole Atton's Lake Golf Club has well-manicured fairways that stretch for 2797 yards on this grass-greened, par-36 course. There is plenty of vertical change in the rolling hills, and the fairly dense underbrush will penalize the unwary. The course is well irrigated so it is in excellent shape throughout the season, and a practice putting green is available while you make ready for your tee time. The course boasts a licensed clubhouse that serves light meals as well as the usual snacks and pop; the clubhouse hours are 0800–2130 hr daily in season. The capable staff can also rent carts and clubs for their patrons, as well as reserve tee times. Greens fees are $13 for 9 holes or $20 for 18 holes; annual memberships cost anywhere from $70 for students under 16 years of age to $525 for a family. Various tournaments are hosted through the year, but time can be made for a private tourney if you wish. This is a busy course, particularly on weekends, so you'd be wise to reserve tee times; call the clubhouse at (306) 398-4055. By the way, the course now charges a tracking fee, $50 per year or $5 per day for you to use your own motorized cart.

MISCELLANEOUS SPORTS

Two fine ball diamonds are grouped in front of the concession, each with tall mesh backstops anchored on metal poles. Shelters are available for team use, and bleachers are available to seat their adoring fans. Grass outfields are kept well trimmed, and the dirt infields have limed baselines during the tournaments that are held on the July and August long weekends. A fastball tournament is held in the middle of July. A hall located behind the golf clubhouse (which can be rented for private function; contact the Cutknife Elks for details) hosts dances accompanying the tournaments, and a beer garden is set up between "B" and "C" ball diamonds. Hiking is also popular in the park on the many walking trails and roadways. No trails have been established devoted to hiking only, but there are literally miles of varied walking to be had on the roadways around the lake. Birds of many sorts can be seen as you walk, so there is always something to charm your eyes away from the dusty trail. For the young at heart, a fine playground has been built near the beach. It offers slides, teeter-totters, merry-go-rounds, swings, and a large creative play center, all built on a large lawn. As with all the equipment in this park, it is neat and clean. Everything is well painted and free of litter; a source of pride I am sure!

SERVICES

The park's concession is open from 0900–2200 hr in July and August, and offers the usual iced treats, snacks and pop, as well as a fairly interesting line of fast food. My experts tell me the onion rings were particularly good! Meals can be eaten al fresco, or taken into the adjoining dining shelter. The concession also retails a good line of grocery items and small camping needs, and serves as a library in inclement weather. Many volumes have been donated by cabin owners and are free for the reading; all that is asked is to return them when you are done. The town of Cutknife offers more complete shopping as well as mechanical, medical, and worship services. It also has a museum chronicling local history and a souvenir shop. As one can imagine, this is a popular park, particularly on weekends. For more information on this delightful park, contact the park manager at (306) 398-2814 in season. Should you wish to contact the park out of season, write the park secretary at:

    Atton's Lake Regional Park
    PO Box 12
    Cutknife, SK   S0M 0N0
    Telephone: (306) 398-2814

BIGGAR AND DISTRICT REGIONAL PARK

Located between Hwy 4 and Hwy 14 on the outskirts of Biggar, the park is open from the Victoria Day weekend in May until the end of September, longer if the golfing season holds out! No fees are collected for park entry, and yet the camping areas are quite pleasant, set as they are in a small coulee just on the outskirts of town. The park has no lake or river access, and the irrigation pond used by the golf course is no longer stocked with trout. No daily or seasonal entry fees are collected at the moment.

SITES

There are 14 electrified (15-amp), pull-through sites and 12 non-electrified sites available, costing $12 and $8 per night, respectively. There is no park gate at which to register, so simply pull into the preferred site and wait for the park manager to collect the fee that night about supper time when he makes his rounds. All sites had picnic tables, firepits and trash bins, and are naturally leveled and drained. Drinking water, Biggar municipal, is available from central taps and firewood is provided from central bins. The campsites are in two areas, the first being unserviced and the second having the electrified sites and a dining shelter. The unserviced area can also hold a fairly large group, although it doesn't have a dining shelter. A trailer dump station is located on 8th Ave West in town, free for registered campers. Washrooms are primitive, with one his/hers biffy at each camping area. They were neat, clean, and free of odor, an obvious sign of daily care. There was very little shelter in the camping areas, with few trees for shade and none between the sites. Mind you, situated in a hollow as it is, the park will see little sun except at midday anyway. The trees available are all planted poplars, elms, and ash, and at least 20 feet tall. Pets are allowed, and there is no reservation system in place although you can contact the park's Secretary if you need to reserve a large space for family reunions and the like.

SPORTS

A fine grass-green, 9-hole golf course is located just 400 meters north of the campgrounds on Hwy 4, to the right of the highway as you head north. The course features raised tees, bunkered greens, and excellent fairways on its 3090 yards. A scorecard is available, but has no course map. A driving range and practice greens with sand trap are available to hone your game as you await your tee time, and the fully licensed clubhouse is open from 0900–2000 to serve your needs. The pro-shop has a small line of equipment for sale, as well as club and cart rentals. The restaurant serves sandwiches and light meals as well as chips and pop and offers a fine view of the first tee from its deck. Greens fees are $13 for 9 holes or $24 for 18 holes, and student rates are available. This is a pretty course and can be quite busy with many private and public tournaments over the year. Tee reservations are recommended, particularly on the weekend; call (306) 948-5488 to make yours.

SERVICES

The town of Biggar offers the traveler all the amenities, including shopping, mechanical, medical, and worship services. A municipally operated swimming pool is available, as is the museum which offers a glimpse of local heritage. Although this park isn't really a camping destination, the golfing is excellent. For more information on this park, or to discuss arrangements for a reunion or golf tournament, contact the park secretary at:

> Biggar and District Regional Park
> PO Box 297
> Biggar, SK S0K 0M0
> Telephone: (306) 948-2532.

BRIGHTSAND LAKE REGIONAL PARK

Located 27 km southeast of St. Walburg, this pretty park can be difficult to get to but it is worth the effort. A fairly large park, there are also private cabin owners who take advantage of this lake's natural wonders. Popular with bird watchers and for its watery delights, this park has something for everyone. Open from the Victoria Day weekend to the Labor Day weekend, park entry costs $5 per day or free with a seasonal pass.

SITES

There are 37 electrified and 75 non-electrified sites, including a new loop of 12 sites with 15-amp service. Premium sites command premium prices, so a site with 30-amp service and water will cost $25, while 15-amp service and no water costs $21; non-electrified sites cost $18 for one closer to showers and concession while more distant sites cost $15. Weekly and monthly rates are also available; call the park office for details. All sites feature picnic tables, pole BBQs, and trash cans. They are carved out of mature jackpine forest, so they are quite sheltered. The sites are naturally leveled and drained, and well spaced. Some sites are just along the beach, providing evening breezes to cool you down; #25 is one such. Water is available from central taps, and firewood is available for sale from the park office. The sites were free of litter and broken glass during our visit, and are suitably large. Washroom facilities vary from primitive biffies in the camping areas to modern flush toilets in the coin operated shower house. Three dining shelters are available as are 13 group sites. Space in the group sites varies, but each camping unit pays $10 per day. The roadways are of packed sand and quite firm. A new development in the park is the addition of two rental cabins, costing $100 per night (weekday) or $110 per night (weekend). They provide comfortable year-round accommodation for up to 7 people. Reservations will be accepted for all sites, private pavilions, ball diamonds and group sites; contact the park office for details.

GOLFING

A 9-hole, par-37 sand-green golf course is available to the right of the entrance road. Carved out of mature boreal forest, its 2890 yards weave around and over small sand hills. Its colorful sign is pictured above! A pretty course, bird song abounds and all for $5 a round or $9 per day. A clubhouse can be rented for tournaments, but there is no pro-shop or club rental service. A scorecard is available at the honor payment station near the number one tee.

WATER SPORTS

No doubt about it, this is one beautiful beach! A large, buoyed swimming area boasts a diving platform on floats. Changerooms are right on the beach and primitive toilets are nearby. An aquatic program teaches Red Cross and RLSS swim levels, costing $25 to $35. The lessons run two times daily, weekdays only, in the second and third week of July; contact the park office for details. The beach is huge, with coarse red sand deep and clean. A beach concession is open from 1000–2200 hr during the busy season, offering the usual iced treats, pop and snacks, plus light meals. It is also a well equipped store that offers patrons campsite necessities and simple groceries. An interesting souvenir is a wall clock made from an old leg hold trap; surely a more humane use for it! Besides its beach, the lake also offers boaters and anglers a place, as a new cement boat launch has been built to ease access. A large trailer parking lot is available nearby. The spring-fed lake is refilling its basin after the drought so fishing has been good with many fine walleye and pike finding their way onto the anglers' plates.

SPORTS

Besides camping and water sports, several trails have been built leading hikers through the boreal forest and muskeg that surrounds one end of the lake. The trails are well marked by signs and groomed with gravel making your hike enjoyable. Extensive work has been done to refurbish the trails by placing boardwalks over marshy areas and strengthening bridges. Increased signage and a trail map make the 28 km of trails an enjoyable and educational venture. Birders will particularly enjoy this park, as one enthusiast reported seeing forty species in one day. Notable species are ciskens, red tarts, and hummingbirds, and a pair of whooping cranes apparently nested on the far reaches of the park. Two baseball diamonds have been built along with a concession and beer hall pavilion which can be rented for $50 a day. The ball diamonds can be reserved for $10 each per day. The diamonds feature tall wire mesh backstops and large bleachers for spectators. A large playground has been built by the beach camp kitchen, with slides, swings, rocking horses on springs, and a creative play center. As a final note, this popular park is a stopover point for a wagon trek organized locally. For more details, contact the park office.

SERVICES

You can rent mountain bikes, canoes, and a host of sports gear for beach volleyball, etc., at the store; the office also has a small line of park-branded clothing for sale. Although simple grocery and camping items can be purchased at the beach store, one must go farther afield for larger needs. The town of St. Walburg has a full range of financial, shopping, medical, mechanical, and worship services. A world renowned artist, Count Imhoff, has his work preserved in a museum near the town; you simply have to see it. Groceries and fuel can be purchased closer to the park at the Brightsand Lake Store, 10 km from the park on the St. Walburg road. As a note to the unwary, quiet time (2300 hr) and local speed laws are strictly enforced by park security, and violators will be evicted if necessary. For more information on the park, contact the managers at:

Brightsand Lake Regional Park
PO Box 160
St. Walburg, SK   S0M 2T0
Telephone: (306) 248-3780
Fax: (306) 248-3329
E-mail: brightsandpark@yahoo.ca

CLEARWATER LAKE REGIONAL PARK

This quiet little resort park is located 3.2 km north of Kyle on Hwy 4, then 8 km east on Hwy 342. The park is open from the Victoria Day weekend in May until the beginning of September, although some portions of it may remain open longer depending on how long the water lines can remain open. The cabins, for instance, are available right through the fall hunting season, but without water service. Park entry costs $7 per vehicle per day, waived with an annual Regional Park sticker.

SITES

There are 22 electrified sites, 38 fully serviced sites, and 25 non-electrified sites in a group camping area. The sites cost $10 per night for an unserviced site, $15 for an electrified site only, and $18 per night for a site with power, water, and sewer hookup. There are several camping areas, depending on what service each area offers. All sites have pole BBQs and picnic tables in a central area that all sites back onto. Drinking water is available from central wells with pumps, and trash bins are centrally located. Firewood is available from the store and costs $10 per bundle. All the sites are naturally leveled and drained, and have nothing between them so they are big enough for the largest modern unit. Shade is provided by mature stands of poplars and elms with thick carragana hedges as borders. The campsites were well grassed and very pleasant, with well-demarcated paths leading to all the major spots such as the beach and store. A trailer dump station is available near the main park entrance, free for registered campers. There are two dining shelters, one in the day use area for picnickers, the other in the group area with 8 non-electrified sites about it. Washroom facilities are modern, with flush toilets and hot showers near each camping area; the showers cost 25¢ per timed use and are wheelchair accessible. There are trailers set up near the A-frame park office and manager's cabin that one can rent. They are on the small side, but reasonably priced at $35 per night for a two-bedroom cabin, and $30 per night for a one-bedroom cabin, plus applicable taxes. They have small decks and pole BBQs as well. Contact the park office at (306) 375-2726 for details or to rent these popular retreats; book early to avoid disappointment.

WATER SPORTS

The lake is a small, round one, which presents some difficulty as there are a large number of people using it. Water-skiing, boarding, and tubing are all popular activities, so people have developed a system where all motorboats go clockwise while towing so that nobody gets in anyone's way. As fishing is poor during the heat of the day, and that's when water skiing is at its best, the boaters take turns using the lake for various activities. It's actually something to see in action; there's no fuss, and everybody has a good time! A decent boatlaunch is available at the North East corner of the lake, accessed from either side by the gravel road which runs completely around the lake. Although there is plenty of space to park your trailer, there isn't any free dock space, so you'll have to anchor your boat in the shallows and walk out to retrieve it in the morning. Fishing is popular, and the lake supports a good population of perch; pike are also sometimes taken, but not as commonly. The waterfront is definitely the center of the summer's daily action, as there are 6 sets of swimming lessons offered every year, costing $12 per week. The lessons run each week from the first of July until the middle of August, and participants can register either at the park office by telephone or at the beach house. You must register the Sunday before the lessons start; contact the park office for details. Besides many lessons, the waterfront has a wide beach filled with fine, clean sand, a buoyed swimming area, and beach change rooms. There is also a good playground just beside the beach house with swings, teeter-totters, and a creative play center. The beach is well shaded, and has benches for parents to rest upon while their children leap and splash in the warm, shallow water.

GOLFING

A 9-hole, sand-green golf course adorns the west side of the park, and covers 2615 yards over its par 35. A practice tee is available, and greens fees are reasonable at $3 per round or $35 annually (family rate). There is no cart or club rental, and the fairways are naturally watered. The course is set among gently rolling hills and several of the holes play around these very hills, so the course can be a bit tricky at times. An excellent scorecard with map helps you through the trickier bits, and the course has little brush cover amidst which to lose your ball. There is no need to reserve tee times, as the longest wait will be 10 or 12 minutes. Altogether, an excellent way to wile away an afternoon!

SERVICES

The park has leased the rights to their store to private interests, who open the shop from 0900–2100 hr. They sell the usual snacks, pop, and iced treats as well as fast food such as burgers, fries, and the like. They sell a good line of camping sundries and grocery items, and have a line of T-shirts and sweats with the park logo on as well. The hotel inside the park, but not owned by the park, also has a restaurant that is licensed for the sale of alcoholic beverages. Wednesday nights the restaurant has a fish feed, a popular local event, as is the pancake breakfast every Sunday at the store. For those wishing more entertainment, a drive-in theater is open during the summer months at the junction of Hwys 4 and 342. A Quonset hut is used as the hall for dances and the like, and can be rented for private functions. It costs $100 for a dance, $75 for an all day function, or $35 for a part day, plus all applicable taxes. This is a very popular hall locally, so it is often rented up to a year in advance. For those persons requiring more in-depth services, the town of Kyle is only 10 minutes away, and offers shopping, mechanical, medical, and worship services. This might be a small lake, but what it lacks in size it makes up for in fun. There always seems to be something going on, and the many cabin owners see to it that their investment gains in value due to increased interest in the lake. Surprisingly, I found this park to be very peaceful, even with its busy state. The families who came here did not come to party but to relax, as we did. The park is busy most days of their season, particularly on the weekends, so reserving a site may be a good idea to avoid disappointment. For more information on this fun park, or to reserve a site, contact the park manager at:

Clearwater Lake Regional Park
PO Box 327
Kyle, SK   S0L 1T0
Telephone: (306) 375-2726 (in season).

EAGLE CREEK REGIONAL PARK

The road leading to this beautiful park is paved right to the very gate, so travel here is a breeze. Only 62 km (36 miles) from Saskatoon, the nearest major city, or 22 km (14 miles) from Asquith, this park is a hidden treasure for city folk tired of the crowds. Set among the Eagle Creek Hills, the 179 acres of parkland and grassland form a delightful oasis of green, home to many birds and mammals. The park has much to offer, including amenities like a shower house, concession, trout pond, and a golf course. It is open from the May long weekend until Labor Day, and levies a $5 per day park entry fee, waived if you have an annual Regional Park sticker.

SITES

There are 50 electrified sites and 50 non-electrified sites, costing $14 and $10 each per night, respectively. All sites feature the familiar pole BBQ and a picnic table, and some sites have a fire pit as well. Firewood is available for $2 a bundle. Most of the sites are quite large, and a few are downright generous in size! Some cover is provided in the main camping area by the tall bushes and planted trees, while stately cottonwoods provide deep shelter for the sites adjoining the river as well as in the picnic area. The picnic area is a real treat as the tall trees provide not only relief from the sun but real beauty in this day-use place. Lots can also be leased right on the river front for those persons wishing to make a long-term commitment to the park, with 5 cottages already built and 3 lots left for sale; contact the park manager at the address given below. One dining shelter is available on a first come, first served basis. If you like to park your vehicle and walk everywhere once the tent is up, then this is the park for you as the camping sites are a good distance from everything else due to all the open space available to play in. The ball diamonds and open area buffer the sites from the swim area and trout pond on the west side, and the east side of the river houses the golf course and stage, so there is a lot of space for a marquee tent if you intend to house a wedding or reunion. The washroom facilities vary from primitive biffies in the unserviced campgrounds to a modern, wheelchair-accessible service center in the main camping area. It has showers, flush toilets and sinks with hot and cold water. There is a trailer dump station near the service center.

GOLFING

The 9-hole, sand-green golf course is nestled away in the hills on the east side of the creek, so you must cross the steel bridge to get there. Newly installed outdoor carpets have replaced the sand greens. The park staff are happy to tell interested persons the tale of how the bridge was transported there from its old locale a mile away one cold and wintry day. Just ask; it's worth the listen! The course has no pro-shop, driving range or putting green, but it is pretty and quite challenging due to the vertical change on almost every hole. It costs $8 per round or $12 per day, paid on the honor system with envelopes and a drop box on the first tee; one can pay at the park entrance as well. The fairways are of average quality, as one would expect with a natural irrigation system. The greatest hazard facing the golfer is the placement of "islands" of bushes on the fairways to attract the unwary golfer's wrath.

A new 18-hole mini-golf course was built in 2002 near the concession booth and spray pool and is sure to delight the little campers. Ball and putter can be rented from the concession.

HIKING
Although there is only one hiking trail established on the west side of the park, starting near the picnic grounds, one can wander at will along the river bank in search of a "hot" fishing hole. The hiking/biking trail has also been recently upgraded to enhance your visit. The park is popular among trail-ride enthusiasts, as a corral is provided to keep horses for overnight stays. The horseback poker rallies and trail rides take place on land adjacent to the park, the participants returning to the park in the evening. A second corral has been built to accommodate the growing number of horseback enthusiasts and their mounts. The huge hill to the east of the park is an obvious challenge to the walker as it provides a panoramic view of the park and surrounding hills, as well as being an interesting place to look for wildflowers and birds. Mind you, as with all golf courses, casual walkers are discouraged from hiking the course as it disturbs the golfers. Lord knows they have enough on their minds already, poor things!

WATER SPORTS
Eagle Creek itself is too narrow for most motor boat activity, so the boat launch and dock is rudimentary. Canoes are easily put in, though, and are perfect for this type of water. There is calm, reasonably deep water to the south of the bridge, and shallower water approaching rapids to the north of the bridge, just after the beach area. The sand for this beach is trucked in and spread out, so there is a clay base to the swim beach, but it should not pose a problem. Some diving and slide equipment is put in the creek to increase enjoyment, as soon as the water warms up! The circular pool is too expensive to operate as a swimming center, but it will be used as a spray pool starting this summer. Between the pool

and the beach is a large playground, with swings, slides, teeter-totters, and a merry-go-round. There's lots of equipment so nobody has to wait for long. A concession stand sells the usual ice cream treats, pop, and snack foods as well as sunscreen and bug spray; the pay phone is also available here. Just to the west of the concession is the trout pond, stocked annually with rainbow fingerlings. Although there is no fee levied to use the pond, anglers are limited to 2 fish per person. No provincial license is required for the trout pond, but all regular regulations apply to fishing in the river system. An excellent outing is to canoe upstream for a kilometer or so, then drift back down fishing for pike as you slowly glide by the riverbanks. Pack a lunch and you're set for the day!

SERVICES

Asquith has all the shopping amenities for food and fuel, and Saskatoon has anything else you might wish for. The park itself has a concession for snacks and treats and a shower house for hygiene's sake; the concession has had a recent addition built. The United Church built in 1926 in Kinley was moved onto the park in 2004, together with the hall brought in from Struan. These two heritage buildings have been lovingly restored and can be rented for your private function or wedding; contact the park office for details. Of particular interest, I thought, was how this park made use of the east hill to create a natural amphitheater. They've built a stage to house their annual Jamboree, held on the last weekend of June, which features local as well as national country music talent (please bring your own chairs!). The Scouts hold an annual jamboree in the park, and two trail rides are held in this busy park as well. A "people mover" transports patrons to and from the camping area for free on a somewhat regular basis during those days when the park is busiest, such as the Jamboree. For further information on this or any other park activity, please contact the park office at:

Eagle Creek Regional Park
Box 359
Perdue, SK S0K 3C0
Telephone: (306) 329-4478.

ELROSE REGIONAL PARK

This municipal park is located on the southwest corner of the town of Elrose, and is comprised of the Uniplex center, which houses the indoor swimming pool, a hockey rink, and a curling rink. The park is open for camping from the beginning of May until the end of September, with daily entry fees costing $10, waived with an annual Regional Park sticker.

SITES

There are 6 fully serviced sites, with electricity (30-amp service), water, and sewer hookups, costing $10 per night. Four other electrified sites do not have water or sewer service. A small lawned area just beside the campsites can be used for tents as well, costing $2 per night per tent. Drinking water supplied is Elrose municipal, and available at all times. There are no dining shelters or group sites. It must be noted that the campsites are built onto the back of the Uniplex (pictured above), so you are camping in the parking lot. There is no shade, there are 2 firepits, and the washroom facilities are all inside the Uniplex—although a "port-a-potti" is available in the camping area. The door providing access to showers, etc. is open 0900–2100 hr. There are a few picnic tables and some benches, but very few amenities. The campsites are all graveled and gently slope away from the Uniplex for drainage. The golf course south of town has a picnic area beside it, with picnic tables and primitive biffies. There is no overnight camping allowed in the golf course's picnic area. This would not be a busy campsite under normal circumstances, seeing use only during ball tournaments. No site reservations would be needed, but they are available by contacting the rec office at (306) 378-2277.

SPORTS

The pool is open from mid-March to the first weekend in November. There are 3 lesson sets offered, one in April, one in August, and one in October. Family swimming is offered from 1800–2100 hr Wednesday and Friday, and from 1300–1600 hr on Saturday and Sunday. During July and August only, family swims are available Monday, Wednesday and Friday to Sunday from 1300–1600 hr. The pool has showers and change rooms, and is a center for local fun as it offers movie swims, "lights out" swims, and other special events; birthday parties can be booked as well. There are machines in the vestibule which sell chips, pop, and candy, but patrons are asked to refrain from bringing food into the pool area. A canteen in the Uniplex is open from the first of November to late March, and sells the usual treats, snacks, and pop, as well as light meals of burgers and fries. There is a licensed lounge which is open from late October to late March. It is also open during ball tournaments; contact the rec board for details.

There are 5 ball diamonds behind the Uniplex, 3 with shale infields and grass outfields. They have tall mesh backstops on metal poles, and are well fenced. Two others have dirt infields, grass outfields and no fences. The main diamond also has shelters for the players; other diamonds make do with benches for players. As one can imagine in such circumstances, the ball complex is very popular in the summer months with many local ball tournaments held throughout the ball season. As popular as it is, one should book the grounds early if you are planning a private ball tournament, so contact the town administrator as soon as you know what you'll need, at the address below. The Uniplex is well suited to host reunions, ball tournaments or a large group party as it not only has the pool but washrooms, showers, video games and vending machines. There is a large open area and kitchen which can also be rented; contact the recreation office for further details.

About a 5-minute drive south of town on Hwy 4 is the local golf course, known as the Elrose Golf Club. It boasts 9 holes on a sand-green golf course that covers 3061 yards in total. It is a naturally watered course but well kept, and it has a small clubhouse that would be useful in running your tournament. There is no club or cart rental, and little cover on what looks like a natural prairie setting. The course is set among a series of gently rolling hills, and has little trouble if you keep your ball on the fairway. Suffering from no such delusions personally, I doubt I'd have much trouble finding a wayward ball on most of these holes. Golf here is very reasonable, costing only $1 per round, or $25 for a family membership. A single adult season ticket costs a mere $15! A simple scorecard is available to keep track of your personal miracles, but no course map exists. There is an honor system on the first tee for payment of greensfees, where the scorecards are kept. No reservations are accepted or needed; if the first tee is busy, wait a bit and you'll be away. The golf course also houses the local picnic grounds, with simple biffies, picnic tables and pole BBQs. No overnight camping is allowed, though, and no firewood was available. There were a few trees for shade, and more pleasant surroundings than behind the Uniplex.

SERVICES

The town of Elrose offers all the amenities to the weary traveler, including shopping, medical, mechanical, and worship services. A small museum offers a taste of local history; check with the town office for details. In closing, fairness dictates that I reiterate the paucity of amenities the campground offers. There isn't much because the campground is not what the park is all about. The Uniplex is a marvelous facility that offers people in the extended community a year-round recreational outlet. If the campgrounds aren't pretty, it's because few people use them. Rest assured, it will be quiet at night except during ball tournaments! For more information on this park or to arrange your gathering, contact the Park Secretary in care of the town administrator at:

Elrose Regional Park
PO Box 517
Elrose, SK   S0L 0Z0
Telephone: (306) 378-2277
E-mail at elroserec@sasktel.net

EMERALD LAKE REGIONAL PARK

This park is located off the beaten path, as it is about 32 km from Leask on grid roads, and about 24 km from Shell Lake; the Shell Lake route is on a winding gravel road, some 21 km east of Hwy 12. The routes are well signed at the turns, however, and you should have little trouble finding your way here. The park has a good many cabins around the camping core, so there's always a steady stream of people driving to and from the park. Open from May 1 until September 30, the park levies a $7 daily entrance fee, waived if you have an annual Regional Park sticker.

SITES

You are provided with a park map when you register at the park office and gate, with a summary of park rules on the back. There are 15 electrified sites and 18 full-service sites, all now upgraded to 30-amp service, and 6 non-electrified sites. Sites rent for $20 per night for full service, $17 per night for an electrified site, and $15 for non-electrified; a full-service site rents for $600 for the entire season. There are also another 48 seasonal sites available, but the waiting list is so long they've established 3 temporary seasonal sites where you can only stay for a maximum of one year. All sites are naturally leveled and drained, and have picnic tables, pole BBQs and trash cans. Drinking water is provided from the centrally located, blue-painted taps, and is taken from a well. Firewood is available from the park gate and office for $3.50 per bundle. All the equipment was in good condition when we visited, although some of the roadways had been battered by the elements and traffic, so the 15 mph speed limit was needful. Most sites are "back in" style, but roomy enough for most campers' needs. Tree cover is natural parkland forest, with poplars and evergreens predominant, and good cover between sites in most areas. There is one camp kitchen in Area "E" available for use. Washroom facilities range from the primitive biffies located in the areas, to modern flush toilets in the shower house. The shower house bathrooms are wheelchair accessible, but the person may need assistance getting into the shower. The showers take quarters to operate the timer. A trailer dump station is located near the store and exit. Pets are allowed in the park, but they must be leashed at all times, and are restricted from the waterfront and beach area. Sites can be reserved by calling (306) 466-2089 and using a charge card to hold the site; a $5 service charge will apply.

WATER SPORTS

The huge beach is backed by a wide lawn with metal benches and a cement walkway providing a very pleasant place to spend a summer's day. The swimming area is buoyed, and has two floating docks to jump and dive off. There are change rooms and beach washrooms just to the right of the beach as you approach. The beach playground equipment has been extensively refurbished and will particularly suit children aged 8–10; a new playground behind the shower house near Campground C will suit children aged 10–13.

One set of swimming lessons is offered in late July, costing $30 per registrant for all Red Cross "Aquaquest" levels. You can register by contacting the park board at the address below, or by calling the park office at the number above. Beach parties have been greatly reduced since the cabin owners began a program of patrolling, and the Blaine Lake RCMP regularly patrol the park as well. Combined, these activities keep the noise and trash down. Indeed, there were no such problems at all last year—a good thing, as all equipment is in good repair and well maintained; the last thing anybody needs is for some fool to vandalize it. Of note for the future is that the back area of the beach is due to be leveled and sodded to increase the lawn area and stabilize the waterfront from erosion. This will not appreciably reduce the available play area but will keep it from degrading.

A boat launch on the east edge of the park provides boaters ready access to the lake. This is a sheltered lake, so skiing and boating of all sorts is popular, as is fishing. The lake is stocked with walleye and pike, and fishing was good last year. A small dock is available at the boat launch, and there is a small parking lot for trailers just behind the access road. There are no boat rentals at the lake, nor is there a filleting facility; patrons are asked to bag fish waste and place it in their regular trash.

GOLFING
A 9-hole, sand-green golf course can be seen just to the left of the road as you drive in. The 2900-yard course is listed as a par 36, but is considered very challenging because of the many hills upon which the course is built. The scorecard has a simple map on the back, provided when the fees are collected on the honor system on the first tee. There is no pro-shop or equipment rental. Greens fees are $7 for 9 holes, $10 for the entire day. Seasonal rates vary from $30 for a junior membership to $160 for the entire family. There is no tee reservation needed; wait a bit and the first tee will open up for you. The course hosts the Hector Duncan Memorial Golf Tournament every year; contact the park office for details.

SERVICES
There are two playgrounds, one in the picnic area behind the beach, the other, smaller one in Area "C." Between them, they contain slides, swings, teeter-totters, merry-go-rounds, and creative play centers. They are all built onto lawns so the children won't track sand

everywhere, although they seem to anyway when camping! A ball diamond is available in the overflow or group camping area, and is a big field in which to play. It has no equipment as such, but is free for use; simply go play and someone will join you! The park office doubles as the store and sells light grocery items as well as pop, chips, and candy. It is open from 0900–2200 hr daily, and doubles as the golf clubhouse as it is near the first tee. Across the road from the park office is the caretaker's cabin should you need anything. The towns of Leask and Shell River are a short drive away, and have all the amenities the weary camper could need, including laundry, shopping, mechanical, and worship. Medical services are available in Shellbrook, some 40 minutes away. Because it's a bit off the beaten path, this is a fairly quiet little park so it has attracted quite a faithful following, as evidenced by the fact that all 48 of their seasonal sites were booked for the whole season in 2005. The park is full on most weekends, so you may wish to place your trailer on the site you want in the middle of the week and pay the extra for the weekdays so you'll have a site for the weekend. For more information on this park, or to book your reunion, contact the Park Secretary at:

Emerald Lake Regional Park
PO Box 39
Leask, SK   S0J 1M0
Telephone: (306) 466-2089
Fax: (306) 466-4776.

GLENBURN REGIONAL PARK

Situated 100 km from Saskatoon, or 50 km from the Battlefords, this serene little park is one of the system's jewels. Located along the North Saskatchewan River, it encompasses both mixed-grass prairie as well as riverine ecosystems. The scenery enjoyed on the 8-km drive from Maymont on Hwy 16 is wonderful, and the road is paved right up to the park turn. The park access road is just to the north of the bridge. The park is open from the Victoria Day long weekend until the middle of September, with the gate being open from 0700–2300 hr daily in this time. Vehicles not having an annual Regional Park sticker are charged $6 per day for entry, with an extra surcharge levied on site fees; makes getting a sticker worthwhile, doesn't it!

SITES

There are 32 electrified sites and 14 non-electrified sites costing $16 and $11 per day respectively. Service varies from 15 to 30 amp. Persons wishing to tent in the overflow are charged $11 per site. All regular sites have pole BBQs, picnic tables, and trash cans. Toilet facilities are new and modern, as well as the modern shower and washroom facility near the pool. Well water is available from a central tap near the camp kitchen to the right of the entrance gate, and at the shower house. Firewood is available from a bin near the entrance gate, and costs $2 per armload. There are two firepits, large steel tubs, that can be used upon request; check with the park caretaker if you'd like one. There are two camp kitchens that can be used in inclement weather; they are a bit small but quite serviceable. The shower facility requires quarters to operate and has two showers and three washrooms per side. The sites are pretty well covered by dense brush, mostly poplars and diamond willow, with trails that join the outlying sites to the main area to allow walkers quicker access. These are pleasant trails due to the many wildflowers that brighten them. The roadways are graveled now. The sites are generally generous, some larger than others, but all capable of holding a modern unit. A trailer dump station is available for a $2 fee.

WATER SPORTS

The park managers have expanded an old pond that used to be here years back, added a berm, and made a very unique natural pool out of it. Generally shallow, it is about 8 feet deep in the center, and sports two floating platforms for divers to lark about on. Lessons are offered for two weeks in July or August; contact the park office for more details. Benches have been placed along the shore for sunbathers to enjoy, and the beach is more grass than sand. As a very large and extensive playground is just to the back of the pool area, the lack of beach sand is of little concern. The play area is well treed to provide shade to the children playing there, something lacking around the pool. The playground features a multi-level play center, swings, slides, teeter-totters, merry-go-rounds, a large sand digger, and several rocking-horse units. Taken altogether, children of all ages can find something to play on!

GOLFING

A 9-hole, sand-green golf course spills out of the park and across Hwy 376 as it winds across the slumps formed by the river basin. Over 2800 yards in length, it features a lot of vertical change, making the course look deceptively easy. There are no rentals, driving range or putting greens, and the tee boxes are simply shaded portions of the fairway. The course is naturally watered, so there can be rough spots on the fairways. Mind you, winter rules are in effect at all times, so one can provide relief from a bad lie at all times. The greens fees can be paid at the pool concession, and are $5 per round or $7 per day. A scorecard is available to keep track of your progress. Of interest is the road past the concession to get to the first tee; the old Maymont Ferry that used to ply the river is now in dry-dock, repainted and used as a practical display. Volunteers have placed flower boxes about the ferry, making it quite a nice display. The park hosts Night Golf Tournaments; contact the park for details.

SERVICES

There are 4 ball diamonds available, in good repair. The two nearest the concession are in the best shape, one complete with curved mesh backstop, bleachers, and dugouts for the players. The infields are of packed earth, and the outfields of well-mown grass. In good repair overall, they are a likely spot to host a pickup game of ball or a tournament. The park hosts a men's tournament here on the August long weekend annually. There is no boatlaunch in the park, but the road past the entrance turn runs to the river, where light boats like canoes can be launched. It is a favorite spot for anglers who try for walleye, goldeye, and pike both here and by the bridge. The concession is open from 1100–2100 hr daily, longer if activity warrants. It sells a full line of treats as well as snacks, pop, and light meals like burgers and fries. Every Friday night in season it offers a Ukrainian Smorg which is often followed by a jam session. One also pays for wood, camping fees, greens fees, and so on here. The nearest town of Maymont has more complete shopping, and the Battlefords are a half hour away should you need more serious matters. There's no doubt about it: this park thrives on peace and quiet. The noisiest place in the park is the playground, and the children love it. The pool serves well, and the golf course is a great place for budding players to hone their skills. The campgrounds are peaceful and cool, and the river is there for those who want to fish. Truly, this park has a lot to offer! For more details or to reserve a campsite, contact the park at:

   Glenburn Regional Park
   PO Box 76
   Maymont, SK   S0M 1T0
   Telephone: (306) 389-4700
   Fax: (306) 445-4611.

KINDERSLEY REGIONAL PARK

This municipal park is located on the west edge of Kindersley, just off Hwy 7. Open from May 1 to September 30 (longer, if the golf season permits), the gates are open from 0700–2200 hr daily in season. The park features a golf course, camping nearby, and fishing in the reservoir. No daily entry fees are collected although you can purchase an annual Regional park sticker.

SITES

There are 48 electrified sites (30 amp service), costing $18 per night or $125 per week, payable at the clubhouse just across from the campground. Major credit cards are accepted for payment, and if you arrive when the clubhouse is closed simply put your camper in an available site and register the next day. No reservations are accepted, so you won't have to worry about taking someone else's spot. The sites are all well constructed, with pads for your unit made either of gravel or sod; some are even paved! The roadways are all paved so road noise is reduced as is dust and mud. All sites have picnic tables, pole BBQs, and access to central trash bins. Firewood is available free from central bins, and water (Kindersley municipal) is piped to central taps. Not all sites have tree cover, and some are "pull through"; all should be large enough for most modern units. Trees in the park are all planted elms and poplars and quite tall. There is one dining shelter with a wood-burning stove available just behind the campgrounds in the day use or picnic area. Washrooms are modern, clean, and located in the shower house. They are never really closed except for brief periods in the day for cleaning. The showers are provided free to registered campers, and there is a pay phone just outside the building. A trailer dump station is available just across from site #12, free for registered campers. The campground operates on a first come, first served system, and there are no family or group camping sites available.

GOLFING

The 9-hole, grass green golf course (pictured here) is complemented by a fine clubhouse and pro-shop. The course covers 3127 yards over its par 36, and winds around a creek, some small ponds, and planted trees. The course was in excellent condition when we visited, with close cropped greens and immaculate fairways. The raised tee boxes, gravel cart paths, and footbridges combine to make this a pleasant course indeed. The fairways are all straight, except for #6, and the course has few difficulties due to terrain, so the placement of bunkers and water hazards provides challenge. Greens fees are $14 for 9 holes or $23 for 18 holes. The scorecard provided is excellent and has a good map of the course. The pro-shop is well equipped with a complete line of retail sales as well as equipment rentals. There is a practice green and a driving net behind the clubhouse to practice your swing. The clubhouse is built on two levels, with an elevated deck providing a panoramic view of the first and ninth fairways. Many flowers have been planted about the area to make it very pretty. Fully licensed, the clubhouse is open from 1000–2200 hr, based on demand. It can serve a full range of meals for your dining pleasure, from the mundane to the sublime. The clubhouse also has a stage in the basement, in a hall capable of holding 50 people for your special event. The restaurant can also cater the function; contact the park office for details. This is a very popular local golf course, so tee reservations are recommended. Call the pro-shop at (306) 463-2788 to book yours.

SPORTS
There is a reservoir just behind the campgrounds that has been stocked for the past few years with pike and walleye. There is no boatlaunch, and motor boats are not allowed. Canoes and rowboats can ply these waters, and fishing success has been reported as fair; provincial regulations apply. Kids who like BMX biking will enjoy the trail built around the reservoir, and it is a restful place for a walk as there are trees and shrubs around the pond for shade. There are two ball diamonds on the far side of the picnic area, both in excellent repair. They have tall mesh backstops on metal poles, red shale infields, and bleachers that can hold dozens of spectators. Benches are available for the players, and there is plenty of parking. The picnic area has a playground built on the grass beside it, featuring a large creative play center with slides and swings built right in, all a short walk from the campgrounds. In winter, cross-country skiing is allowed on the golf course, although it isn't organized by the park managers.

SERVICES
The park has no canteen except for the clubhouse diner, which also sells a line of chips and pop. The town of Kindersley is well suited to meeting the needs of the traveling camper, as it offers a full range of shopping, mechanical, medical, and worship services. The park is a busy one, mostly due to the golf course, but also when the town puts on its annual July 1 rodeo or a trail ride happens to pull in. The park also hosts ball and golf tournaments at various intervals. We found this park to be clean, well maintained, and proud of its golf course. You may not consider it a destination, but it most certainly is a pleasant stop enroute. For more information on this park, contact the Park Secretary at:

> Kindersley Regional Park
> PO Box 1843
> Kindersley, SK   S0L 1S0
> Telephone: (306) 463-2788
> Fax: (306) 463-4292.

MACKLIN LAKE REGIONAL PARK

Located adjacent to Macklin Lake, just 1 km south of the town of Macklin at the junction of Hwys 14 and 31, this park has more to offer than a simple municipal park would generally be thought to. It is open from May 1 to September 30, although the golf course may stay open longer if weather allows. The roads are paved right up to the gates of the park, and the park is very easy to find. Park entry fees of $3 per day are waived if you have an annual Regional Park sticker.

SITES
A fairly large campground, the park has 30 electrified sites, 95 sites with electrical, water, and sewer hookup, and 14 unserviced sites. They rent for $19 for a serviced site or $10 for an unserviced site per day. Group camping is allowed, but by reservation only. Sites are leveled and drained with gravel pads, and all have trash bins. Picnic tables, firepits, and firewood in central bins round out the equipment list. Sites without water hookup have access to Macklin Municipal water in central taps. Some sites are larger than others, but most should be big enough for the largest camper. Shade is provided by tall groves of cottonwoods along the rear of the site, but there is almost no growth between sites. Washroom facilities are modern, with flush toilets in the camping areas, and hot showers in the beach shower house. There was no map to the park available, but the park entrance booth had one on its wall and could give clear instructions to your campsite. Major credit cards are accepted for site fees, although only groups could reserve sites. Contact the park office for more information at the address below.

WATER SPORTS
Macklin Lake has no fishing but ample boating, boarding, and skiing. The swim beach (pictured above) is protected from the lake proper by a grassy dike and swim lessons are taught. Prices and times vary, so contact the park office for details. The sand is fine and clean, and the beach change rooms and showers are clean and well maintained, making this a popular facility for all. There are no docks at the boatlaunch, but there is a fairly large area for vehicles and boats. A beach side playground is built into a large sand pit with swings, slides, and a creative play center. The beach shower house and change room also houses the laundry; it costs $1.50 per wash and $1 per dry cycle. A pop machine outside the building has cool drinks for a loonie.

GOLFING
The Lakeview Golf Club is a 9-hole, grass-green golf course that covers 2953 yards over

its par-36 course. The clubhouse will rent clubs and carts, and has a small line of balls, caps, tees, and gloves for sale. A practice putting green and a driving net are available to practice your swing, and a fine scorecard with map shows you the course. Greens fees are modest, $12 for 9 holes and $20 for 18 holes, with a $5 student rate. The clubhouse is licensed and has a small line of grilled fare. A deck with tables offers a fine view of the lake as you relax over coffee after your round. This was a busy course when we visited, drawing patrons from all over the area to play its irrigated fairways. Tee times are recommended and can be reserved by calling the clubhouse at (306) 753-2175.

BASEBALL

There are 5 ball diamonds in the park, with tall mesh backstops on metal poles. Home-run fences are in place on the grass outfields, and there are bleachers, players' shelters, and baselines maintained during tournaments. A concession is also opened during tournaments, offering burgers, drinks, and various snack foods. The entire complex can be rented for private functions; contact the park office for details.

SERVICES

The park hosts ball and golf tournaments, both private and public throughout the season, as well as the World Bunnock Championship on the first weekend in August, a hotly contested sport of skill and control where players toss horse knuckle bones to knock over a row of bones. The last championship attracted 1000 players! Although the organizers are considering building Bunnock courts, they currently use the ball diamonds just to the west of the clubhouse. As the park is located so close to Macklin, it doesn't have much shopping. The town of Macklin is well suited to provide all the shopping, mechanical, medical, and worship services the traveler could need. For more information on this park, or to organize your own Bunnock Tournament, contact the park office at:

Macklin Lake Regional Park
PO Box 275
Macklin, SK   S0L 2C0
Telephone: (306) 753-2175
Fax: (306) 753-3234.

MARTIN'S LAKE REGIONAL PARK

Located 24 km northwest of Blaine Lake off Hwy 12, the park is open from the Victoria Day long weekend in May until the middle of September. The park is built into mature parkland forest, so poplars and willows abound and berries are available in season. Swimming, fishing, golfing, and camping are all popular in this quiet, family-oriented park. It levies a $3 per day vehicle park entry fee, waived if you have an annual Regional Park sticker.

SITES

There are 40 electrified and 32 non-electrified sites, costing $18 per night and $14 per night respectively. Note that some of the electrified sites have 15-amp service—make your needs known regarding electrical service at the time of booking. There are also 74 seasonal sites available; contact the park office for details. There is no map handed out to patrons, but a large, well-painted sign on the entrance booth details the park quite nicely. All sites are naturally leveled and drained, and have picnic tables, pole BBQs, and trash cans. Drinking water is provided from wells in central locations, and free firewood is found in central bins. Shade is provided by mature stands of poplars and willow that border the sites on three sides. Some sites may only have a rear border of trees, some will be almost completely surrounded; all will have some. A trailer dump station is available near site 52, on the southeast corner of the campgrounds. Roadways are in good condition generally, well graveled and drained. Modern washroom facilities with showers are available to campers in the shower house. The showers cost $1 per use, and are not wheelchair accessible. There are family or group camping sites available as well as a few double sites that offer more room and privacy for small groups. All equipment was in excellent condition during our visit, a tribute to the maintenance people's hard work. Reservations are accepted by telephone beginning May 1 yearly, with the first night's fees due upon reservation.

WATER SPORTS

The lake is an obvious magnet on a hot summer's day, particularly as it has a large, fine beach. The water table has been down in recent years so the buoyed swimming area is quite shallow, but this hasn't affected the quality of the water. There are two swimming lesson sets offered, bookings for which can be made by contacting the Park Secretary at the address below. The unsupervised swimming area, pictured above, has three floats moored in deepening water to play on. Open from 1000–2200 hr daily, the beach concession offers a small line of grocery and items needful for camping, as well as the usual array of treats, snacks, and pop. Grilled foods can also be purchased, the video arcade is popular, and paddleboats can be rented. They cost $10 per hour, plus a refundable $20 deposit; the price includes lifejackets. A boatlaunch and dock is available for boaters, with a small parking area behind the boatlaunch for trailers. A sign beside the boatlaunch advised boaters to watch out for the floating signs marking scuba divers, the only park we found with this activity. This is likely due to the lake reaching a depth of 45 to 90 feet! Fishing is also popular, as evidenced by the fish-cleaning plant near the boat launch. The Park Manager was telling me that the lake's anglers regularly land pike with average weights of 3 to 5 pounds. Walleye and perch can also be taken, so bring your fishing tackle when you come! A boat dock and launch are located beside the fish filleting shack, which has running water and an underground septic tank for fish waste.

GOLFING

The Martin's Lake Regional Park Golf Course is located to the right of the main road, north of the camping areas. It features a 9-hole, par-36 sand-green golf course that twice crosses the main road over its 2842-yard fairways. It is naturally watered and has no driving range or practice green. It is generally a gentle course, but only if you stay out of the dense brush that lines some of the fairways! The clubhouse sells balls and tees, as well as rents clubs and carts. Greens fees are modest at $9 for 9 holes or $15 for 18 holes; carts rent for $12 per round ($24 for 18 holes). The clubhouse features the "Kozy Kitchen," a full service diner that serves three meals a day; it is open from 0800–2300 hr daily. Tee reservations are not generally required; even on the busiest day you won't have time for a second piece of home-made pie before the tees are open. If you'd like to arrange a private tournament, contact the Park Secretary at the address below for details.

SPORTS

Besides golfing, swimming, boating, fishing and water skiing, the park has some walking trails that wander through the camping areas, mostly leading bathers to the beach. As there is a small creek, two bridges have been built to carry foot traffic. Baseball enthusiasts haven't been forgotten: a large field that doubles as the overflow has a backstop and benches for a pickup game. A large, recently built creative play center has plenty of toys for children of all ages, with slides and swings, teeter-totters and tubes, all waiting to become the next starship or whatever the wee folk decide. Built into a huge sand pit, there is plenty of room for literally dozens of children. The beach has a volleyball court, and equipment can be rented at the beach concession for $5, of which $3 is refunded upon the return of the ball.

SERVICES

Besides the grocery shopping at the concession, the park has little to keep shoppers happy. The town of Blaine Lake, about a 20-minute drive away, has all the shopping, mechanical, medical, and worship services the traveler might want. A beach volleyball tournament is held every August (contact the park for dates and costs). As you might expect, the golf course hosts several tournaments annually, notably the David Howe Golf Tournament as well as private ones for reunions and the like. A local antique car club hosts a car show in the park, but usually the park is quiet and peaceful. It is busiest on the May long weekend and most electrified sites are taken on all weekends thereafter, but the park is rarely booked full during the week. If you'd like to make sure you have a site for the weekend, the simplest solution is to drive in Thursday night and place your trailer or tent on a site. You'll have to pay for the extra night, of course, but you'll certainly have a site for the weekend. This is a family-oriented park, and the park patrol has developed a good working rapport with the local RCMP so noise-makers are warned then evicted; the quiet time of 2300 hr is strictly enforced. Should you wish more information on this pleasant park, contact the Park Secretary at:

Martin's Lake Regional Park
PO Box 488
Blaine Lake, SK   S0J 0J0
Telephone: (306) 466-4438

MEETING LAKE REGIONAL PARK

Located 10 km north of Rabbit Lake, off Hwy 378, this park takes its name from local lore that has this lake used historically as a native meeting place. Because of this, all the picnic tables and general-use buildings are built in a circular form. Particular attention has been paid to providing wheelchair access in the shower house, chapel, and hall. The park is open from May 1 until the middle of September, and levies a $4 per vehicle daily entrance fee, waived if you have purchased an annual Regional Park sticker.

SITES

There are 83 sites in total, most of which have been converted to electrified sites with 15-amp service. They rent for $18 per night for electrical and water service, or $15 per night for an unserviced site. Sites can be rented annually for $600 for an electrified, watered site, or $850 for a fully serviced site. Some of the sites (#8, for example) are best restricted to tenting as they resemble a leafy tunnel, but generally the sites are large enough for any unit; specify your need when you register at the entrance booth and they'll fix you up. There is no map to the sites currently available for patrons, but the park managers hope to have one professionally done in the near future. All the sites are naturally leveled and drained, and most are equipped with circular picnic tables and pole BBQs. Drinking water is either available from taps at each site or central taps in the unserviced sites. Firewood is available for $2.50 a bundle. Shade is adequate for the most part and provided by natural stands of poplar and willow, although some sites are so overgrown that they are almost invisible from the roadways; these are best left to tents, but are great for that purpose! There is a dining shelter available between sites 71 and 72, to the left of the ball diamonds, near the group camping area. This is a very popular venue locally for reunions and the like, so you'd best book it a year in advance! The group area is quite large, has some serviced sites on the perimeter, and is capable of holding quite a number of units. Washroom facilities vary from primitive biffies in the areas to modern flush toilets in the shower house; showers cost 25¢ per use, and the shower house is wheelchair accessible. It also houses the coin-operated laundry machines. A trailer dump station is located beside the road to the boat launch and marina. The big hall, circular in shape, can be rented for private functions for $150 per 24-hour period or $275 for a weekend. It includes the use of the kitchen, steam tables, and a large dance floor. It is also wheelchair accessible, and is very popular so book it early to avoid disappointment. All sites can be reserved by calling the park office at (306) 824-4812.

WATER SPORTS

The lake is somewhat shallow, but there is a wide, magnificent beach bordered by a well-treed picnic area. Swimming lessons are offered in July, costing $35–45 per swimmer; contact the park office for details or registration. The swimming area is buoyed and has a floating dock with a diving board. Beach change rooms and showers (costing 25¢) are available in a large, clean building just behind the beach. A small playground borders the picnic area with swings, teeter-totters and a climber. A much larger playground has been built just beside the concession, about a block away from the beach. This playground has two campsites inside it, both of which can be reserved, but you'd better book early! The larger playground is a must-see for small children as it is a fairyland of bright colors and well-maintained equipment, including a large sandlot with 4 digger machines! Boaters enjoy this lake as it has one of the most extensive marina facilities in the area. Plentiful docking beside the cement boat launch and a large parking area for trailers at the end of a long breakwater make this a wonderful harbor. Anglers enjoy the pike, walleye and perch fishing the lake provides, although the park managers are pressing for "catch and release" tournaments to preserve the fish population.

SPORTS
There are two ball diamonds beside the group camping area with tall mesh backstops and grass infields and outfields. There is very little other equipment, and the diamonds can be used by anyone; just start playing and other folks will show up to join in! The diamonds may disappear if large groups have appeared, though, as they are part of the overflow area. An 18-hole mini-golf course has been built between the hall and the concession, costing $3 per adult or $2 per child to play; equipment can be rented at the concession.

SERVICES
The park operates a diner and concession in a fine facility just beside the large playground, near the big hall. It is open from 1100–1900 hr on weekdays, and 0900–2100 hr on weekends. It has the usual line of iced treats, snacks and pop as well as light meals and breakfasts. There is seating for 20 or so around the tables in the diner, and the home-made pie is an excellent accompaniment to a cup of coffee. One can also purchase automobile gasoline, a small line of postcards, souvenirs, grocery and camping supplies, as well as rent paddleboats here. The park has a small chapel, managed by the Rabbit Lake Heritage Society, that can be rented for weddings and the like; contact the park office for details. There are many cabin owners that are willing to rent their second homes for weekends or longer, with prices and available dates fluctuating. None of these are owned by the park, but the managers have a list of cabin owners willing to rent, which they will forward so that you can make arrangements privately. The town of Rabbit Lake has a larger range of services, with shopping, mechanical, medical, and worship services available to meet the traveler's needs. Rabbit Lake annually hosts the Carlton Trail Jamboree, a country music cabaret, in July; many patrons of this event stay in the park. This is a busy park, particularly on weekends when most sites are filled. Reservations are recommended for any weekend during their season, starting with the Victoria Day weekend. For more information on this park, or to reserve sites, contact the Park Secretary at:

> Meeting Lake Regional Park
> PO Box 40
> Rabbit Lake, SK   S0M 2L0
> Telephone: (306) 824-4812
> Fax: (306) 824-2076

MEMORIAL LAKE REGIONAL PARK

The Village of Shell Lake adorns the park, or maybe the park adorns the town; one is never quite certain as the symbiosis between the two helps make this park unique. Located 70 km west of Prince Albert on Hwy 3, the park is situated on picturesque Memorial Lake and is open from the Victoria Day weekend to mid-October. The camp gate is closed from 2300–0700 hr, and quiet time is strictly enforced; violators will be warned once before eviction. The park charges a $5.50 entry fee, waived with an annual Regional Park sticker.

SITES

There are 145 electrified sites costing $16.95 per night, spread out in six areas. Tenting patrons will pay $14.20 per night. Thirty of the sites are reserved for seasonal patrons. The park has undertaken a campsite rejuvenation project which made things more attractive. Most of the sites are leveled with gravel pads, and have a gentle slope back to front for drainage. A few sites appeared to be naturally leveled and drained, but they are being graveled as time and resources permit. All sites have pole BBQs, picnic tables, and trash cans. The picnic tables are all chained or lashed to steel pegs. Drinking water is available from central taps. Tree cover is provided by the mature stands of pine, fir, poplar, and a few birch trees; tree plantings are mostly done on the golf course. Toilet facilities vary from primitive pump-out biffies in the camping areas, to modern flush facilities at the coin operated shower house in area "B." Firewood is available for sale at $2 per bundle. There are two trailer dump stations, one to the right of the ball diamonds as you drive past the park gate, the other in area "B." An excellent map of the park is provided with your registration at the park gate. Make reservations by calling the park office at (306) 427-2281, May 15–September 6 yearly or every Monday from 1000–1600 hr. You can also download their reservation form and fax it to (306)427-2081. The park levies a $5 fee for all reservations and your credit card will be billed for the fee plus your first nights accommodation. No reservation will be accepted without pre-paying the site. Another concern is that pets are increasingly bothersome, so the restriction that all pets must be leashed and kept 100 feet from all waterways and beaches is increasingly enforced by the park patrol. The campsite is beautiful and water sports plentiful, so this is a popular retreat, particularly on weekends, making reservations a good idea.

There are two group camping areas available, The Sports Ground Area and "The Hollow" Camp Kitchen. The Sports Ground can easily accommodate groups of 50 or more units. It has ball diamonds, a kitchen with grill, fridge and freezer and large serving doors.

A large covered building can also be rented. The area also boasts a new completely barrier free washroom and shower facility as well as a large grassy area and a fire ring. Tall shade trees offer relief from the summer sun, and picnic tables can be moved to accommodate your group. "The Hollow" is a much smaller area with space for 5 or so units; tents can be placed around the open-air kitchen. Located at the bottom of a natural round hollow, it is a great place to gather for campfire stories of an evening.

WATER SPORTS
The beach has unsupervised swimming and is divided into three distinct areas, the most prominent being the swim beach. The beach erosion is managed with a sturdy cement retaining wall. Buoys demarcate the swimming area, and a fine floating dock assists swimmers for pleasure and during lessons. Two lesson sets are offered during July; each set lasts for 2 weeks and prices vary for the full range of Red Cross levels and Bronze Cross and Bronze Medallion classes. Contact the park office for dates and space. The beach sand appears trucked in; it is clean and coarse with a few small stones, and bordered with a large grassy sward and many benches. Just behind the beach is the day-use area with many choice picnicking spots and the playground. A beach change room is available; there is no waterfront concession.

A boat launch about 500 meters to the left of the swim beach has a cement launch, a large parking area, and an excellent fish-filleting facility. Anglers try for pike and walleye with variable success. Motorboats are popular as is water-skiing, proven by the separate water-ski landing on the shore between the boat launch and swim beach. Fishing boats and motors can be rented in town. The lake is fairly placid, and canoeing is popular. All water craft are forbidden from entry to the swim area; other boating restrictions are posted by the boat launch.

GOLFING
The 18-hole, grass-green golf course is very popular as it is both pretty and challenging. Covering 6002 yards over a par-71 course (blue tees), players must cross a creek three times in a game. They've rearranged the course as part of the installation of the new holes, so the clubhouse is now to the north of the park/village entrance road. There is ample parking near the new fully licensed clubhouse. Greens fees are $15.60 for 9 holes or $22.85 for 18 holes. Special pricing is in effect for school groups. A practice green and driving net can be used. A pro-shop will rent clubs and carts and sells a line of branded clothing as well as the usual golfing essentials. The clubhouse features a full-service, licensed diner

which offers seated dining, light meals, and take-out food. The course is often busy, so reservations are recommended; call (306) 427-2124 for your reservations.

An 18-hole mini-golf course is available to the left of the park gate as you drive in, costing $3 for patrons above 13 years of age, and $2 for those 12 years or younger. It is not operated by the park but it always seems busy!

SPORTS

Two ball diamonds are available, with tall wire mesh and grass infields. Bleachers are available for spectators and benches for players. All the equipment is in good shape, as is an electrified cook shack between the two. All can be rented for a special occasion; contact the park office for details. A local business offers guided one- and two-hour horse rides along the lake; information is posted in the village. Two playgrounds have been built, a large one beside the beach and picnic area filled with slides, swings, teeter-totters, a merry-go-round on springs, and climbers. A smaller one is located in group A, and has a slide, swing, sandbox and a creative play center.

SERVICES

The Village of Shell Lake has most of the shopping services one could ask for, from grocery to souvenir. A great museum is right next to the park entrance, as is a licensed diner. A laundromat is available in town; fuel is available at the crossroads. The nearest hospital is in Shellbrook, about a half-hour away. This isn't a way stop on your way elsewhere: this park is a destination, and has all the amenities one could ask for. It is a popular park and deservedly so. For more information or to reserve a site, contact the park at:

Memorial Regional Park
PO Box 10
Shell Lake, SK S0J 2K0
Telephone (306) 427-2281
Fax: (306) 427-2081
Website: www.rkc.ca/shell_lake; follow the links.

MEOTA REGIONAL PARK

The park itself is located just on the outskirts of the village of Meota on the banks of Jackfish Lake north of North Battleford. Open from late May to early September (gates are open from 0700–2300 hr), it has undergone constant revision to reflect the changing needs of the communities it serves. The park is comprised of three pieces, the campgrounds, the waterfront and its playground, and a brand new golf course about a kilometer to the south. As one drives in, the village street bisects the park into the campgrounds and waterfront areas. Simply turn right into the campground with its ball diamonds, horseshoe pits and small playground. The camping area is covered with mature poplar forest providing some shelter from the elements, except for the new, fully serviced area that has freshly planted trees. Daily park entry fees of $2 per vehicle are waived if you have an annual Regional Park sticker.

SITES

There are 36 electrified sites as well as 8 non-electrified sites. A new addition is the placement of 14 sites to the left as you drive into the campsite; these are fully serviced with water, power, and sewer. They are well drained on graveled pads, and will be quite nice when the poplars grow in. All the sites appeared larger than usual, and many appeared to be formed in small "bays," so that several sites could be booked together to provide small group areas. A larger group site exists to the side between the ball diamonds and the campsites. The sites cost $10 per night for an unserviced site, $12 for an electrified site, and $15 for a fully serviced site. All the sites can be reserved; contact the park manager at the address below for details. The water provided is Meota municipal, and is very good. Only the fully serviced sites have individual water service; all others use central taps. All sites have the usual picnic table and pole BBQs, and several have steel firepits on cement pads as well; firewood is provided at no charge. No dining shelters are available.

WATER SPORTS

Jackfish Lake is but a 5-minute walk from the campsites, and has a delightful beach complete with play equipment, including one of the longest slides in the Regional Park system! Other beach play equipment includes teeter-totters, swings, and a merry-go-round. A new swimming area bermed off from the lake hosts swim lessons in July, although it won't have lifeguards outside of the aquatic program. A newly extended boat launch can be used by park patrons, costing $2 per day; it is free if the tow vehicle has a park sticker. A fish-cleaning hut has been built beside the boat launch. A large recreation facility near the beach houses a recreation program during July and August as well as the change rooms and wheelchair accessible shower facility. A concession may also be available, depending on demand, to sell the usual treats, pop, and snacks as well as a selection of delicious home-made meals. The cement boat launch and its dock provide access to this beautiful lake for motor boats as well as sail craft. The park hosts the annual Sailing Regatta on the August long weekend every year. Fishing is excellent, and pike are the usual prey. Standing on the beach and looking southeast, one can see the resort town of Cochin and a remarkable landmark, "The Lighthouse." Benches line the beach, as does a grassy sward and several large trees. A picnic ground is located just to the side of the access road.

GOLFING

The Meota and District Golf Club is becoming a real strength for this park. It has 9 holes with beautiful grass greens, a driving range ($8 per bucket), a practice putting range, a licensed clubhouse and pro-shop with all needful rentals. The clubhouse will also provide light lunches to hungry golfers. Because it is so new (its first full season was the summer of '97), the course is still growing in. The transplanted trees are maturing, the fairways are immaculate, the greens and tee boxes well built, and the water hazard quite a view when the aeration pumps are on. This hazard is a large irrigation pond that first enters play to the right of the second green. Small footbridges provide quick routes over narrow portions of the pond. The course is 3119 yards long, a par 36, with few real difficulties for those blessed with a straight shot. Being as I am not one of them, the course is somewhat longer! The course costs $14 for 9 holes, or $25 for 18 holes, with junior pricing as well. Call the clubhouse for tee reservations at (306) 892-2200.

BASEBALL AND HIKING

There are three beautiful baseball diamonds that feature red shale infields, tall backstops and 2 sets of bleachers per diamond. Although the baselines will be limed during tournaments only, the fields are a pleasure to use even if it should rain. As close to the campsites as they are, they form an admirable setting for a company ball tournament. There are also 8 horseshoe pits with benches and scoreboards just to the north of the ball diamonds. There are a number of wide trails that wind about the perimeter of the campsites, allowing one to hike about a bit. None of the trails are very long, but they do feature many berry bushes, including raspberry, saskatoon, and chokecherry. In total there is about an hour's worth of gentle hiking. Birds of all sorts abound due to the proximity to the water and bush. One can see waterfowl like shorebirds, ducks, or the odd loon, as well as perching birds like bluebirds and swallows. Hunting birds like hawks can also be seen trying their luck for an unwary gopher in the fields just to the west of the campgrounds. A volleyball court has been set up to the left as one drives into the park; equipment can be rented from the beach recreation complex.

SERVICES
Although no hall is available to house reunions or weddings, the town hall can most likely be rented for such things. The concession stand was doing brisk business with daily meal specials and some astonishing home-made carrot cake. The village of Meota has many shops to meet the casual needs of visitors, and North Battleford is but a half hours' drive away should anything more be needed. Museums and National Historic Sights are also available in the Battlefords should you wish to take in the sights one afternoon. The park offers many annual events such as golf tournaments, the Sailing Regatta, and ball tournaments. Persons wishing more information should contact the park secretary at:

Meota Regional Park
PO Box 84
Meota, SK   S0M 1X0
Telephone: (306) 892-2292.

OUTLOOK AND DISTRICT REGIONAL PARK

Located adjacent to the town of Outlook, near the intersection of Hwys 45 and 15, this 100-acre park is well suited to answering the recreational needs of the whole family. Very prettily located between the two bridges serving the town, the scenery here is wonderful as one can survey the South Saskatchewan River valley. Open from the Victoria Day weekend to the end of September, this park was originally built in 1922 as a memorial to the men who fell in the Great War. It joined the Regional Park system in 1961. The park can be found at the end of Progress Street, to the left of Mackenzie Drive, the main street as one drives in across the South Saskatchewan River Bridge. The roads are paved right into the park, and all the way to the entrance to the campgrounds. Daily park entry fees of $5 per vehicle per day are waived if you have an annual Regional Park sticker.

SITES

There are 51 electrified sites (each with water service), costing $18 per night, with special weekly and monthly rates. All sites feature picnic tables and pole BBQs; trash bins are centrally located. They are naturally leveled and drained, and are strung among one of the oldest stands of American elm in the province so they are well shaded. There are three campsite areas, the largest to the left of the main road. A wheelchair-accessible central modern washroom facility has showers and flush toilets. A trailer sewage disposal tank is also available just behind this building, as is the playground. Firewood is available at the park booth, costing $5 for a large bundle. To the right of the main road are two smaller areas; one area is reserved for smaller campers only, as the sites are large, but the roadway is too narrow to allow for safe maneuvering. These last two areas are quite close to the swimming pool, so you may find it a bit noisy if you like grabbing a nap in the middle of the afternoon. Mind you it is very handy if you intend to spend a lot of time at the pool. A large picnic and day-use area is found in the natural bowl to the right of the main road. Pole BBQs and picnic tables can be found at intervals under the tall elms, with potable water taps at strategic locations. As the underbrush has been largely removed, the end result is a seeming natural temple with the branches arched overhead. At times there seemed to be more children in the trees than squirrels! A small playground with new equipment and a dining shelter are also available in the day-use area. The pool concession sells snacks and pop; light meals are available in the golf clubhouse. One of the picnic areas can double as a group site should necessity present, although no services are available. A new group camping area has also been established; contact the park for details.

Campsite reservations are highly recommended at this popular park, particularly in July and August; call the park office for details.

GOLFING

The 9-hole, grass-green golf course here is a must-play for the golf aficionado, as many of the tees are shaded by the elms, making this 2865-yard course a delight on a hot summer's day. The course itself is well maintained and irrigated with river water. The fairways seem narrow to shaggers like myself, but the course is scenic and well worth a play. The well-equipped pro-shop can rent or sell you any piece of equipment you'll need from clubs to carts, including a colorful assortment of proprietary clothing. A small practice green is available just behind the first tee. The clubhouse serves snacks and pop as well as light meals of sandwiches and burgers. Just a note: if you bring your own power cart, there is a $5 trackage fee. That fee is built into the price of the rental carts. The greens fees are $13 for 9 holes or $19 for 18 holes. Lessons from the course CPGA pro are available; call for details. A children's program also runs in May, concentrating on course etiquette and rules of play; children 12 years or younger will need to have this training if they wish to play unsupervised. You can call the pro-shop for tee times, particularly recommended in the months of July and August, at (306) 867-8266.

WATER SPORTS

The swimming pool, originally built here to commemorate Canada's First World War veterans who died in the service of their country, was opened in 1922, making it only the second of Saskatchewan's outdoor pools. A modern Junior Olympic pool was built on the site and opened in 1989 to replace the aging facility. Swimming lessons are available, prices varying depending on the qualification desired. Public swims are also available, costing $10 per family per day. Punch cards are also available for Aquafitness classes, costing $25 for 10 sessions; the cards are good for the entire season, not just a two-week session. Complete with change rooms, showers, a paddling pool, and a panoramic view of the South Saskatchewan River, this is a delightful place to be on a hot summer's day. In addition, the pool can be rented for group use in non-peak times; call the park office for details. There is no boat launch in the park, but canoes are welcome; a shallow access can be found just to the left of the main road past the swimming pool. A small beach is also found here, but I cannot recommend it as many fishermen ply the banks casting for an unwary walleye or jackfish. During our visit we caught sight of a harmless bull snake in the willows by the river, something we'd only rarely seen. No animals are allowed down by the river, as the town of Outlook has their pump station here.

HIKING

There are three sections of the Trans Canada Trail transecting the park, including the Sky Trail which features Canada's longest pedestrian bridge. In the fall of 2003, the old CPR train bridge was converted to a walking bridge with the help of local volunteers and the 33rd Field Military Engineer Squadron of Calgary. This new addition to the Trans Canada Trail makes it the longest walking bridge in Canada at 3000 ft! Of the other two trails, one runs among the willows behind the large campsite area, and a second runs underneath the railroad bridge at the other end of the park. Both feature an interesting look at how these tall trees have built homes for many different creatures. Deer signs can be found along the banks, even in the town limits, and the older trees have hollow trunks that have become nesting places for many species of birds. The trails are not long, only 2 km or so, but one can still see much that is different on such a walk.

SERVICES

The town of Outlook is capable of dealing with any shopping concern you might have, as well as medical or worship services. The town also has school playgrounds to augment the two playgrounds found in the park. The park's trails are used in the winter for cross-country skiing, and the hills become tobogganing runs. The park hosts several golf tournaments in August and many reunions over the remainder of the summer. This is a popular park because of its natural beauty, its mature golf course, and the spaciousness of its campsites. Should you wish to visit here, call early to reserve a site. You can contact the park office at:

>   Outlook and District Regional Park
>   PO Box 1256
>   Outlook, SK   S0L 2N0
>   Telephone: (306) 867-8846
>   Fax: (306) 867-9898
>   E-mail: outlookregpark@sasktel.net.

You can also look at their website at: www.town.outlook.sk.ca and follow the links to the regional park page.

Top: Anglin Lake Provincial Recreation Site
Bottom: Bronson Forest Recreation Site (Little Fishing Lake)

Top: Buffalo Pound Provincial Park
Bottom: Candle Lake Recreation Park (Sandy Bay)

Top: Clarence-Steepbank Lakes Provincial Wilderness Park
Bottom: Crooked Lake Provincial Park

Top: Cypress Hills Interprovincial Park
Bottom: Danielson Provincial Park

Top: Douglas Provincial Park
Bottom: Duck Mountain Provincial Park

Top: Eagle Creek Regional Park (courtesy Jenny MacDonald, Regina, Saskatchewan)
Bottom: Echo Valley Provincial Park

Top: Fort Carlton Provincial Historic Park
Bottom: Good Spirit Lake Provincial Park (courtesy David McLennan, Canadian Plains Research Center)

Top: Grasslands National Park (courtesy David McLennan, Canadian Plains Research Center)
Bottom: Greenwater Lake Provincial Park

Top: Jean-Louis Legare Regional Park
Bottom: Lac La Ronge Provincial Park

Top: Lucien Lake Regional Park (courtesy David McLennan, Canadian Plains Research Center)
Bottom: Manitou and District Regional Park (courtesy David McLennan, Canadian Plains Research Center)

Top: Meadow Lake Provincial Park
Bottom: Moose Mountain Provincial Park

Top: Narrow Hills Provincial Park
Bottom: Notukeu Regional Park (courtesy David McLennan, Canadian Plains Research Center)

Top: Pine Cree Regional Park (courtesy David McLennan, Canadian Plains Research Center)
Bottom: Regina Beach Provincial Recreation Site

Top: Saskatchewan Landing Provincial Park (Goodwin House)
Bottom: Shamrock Regional Park (courtesy David McLennan, Canadian Plains Research Center)

Top: St. Victor Petroglyphs Provincial Historic Park (courtesy David McLennan, Canadian Plains Research Center)
Bottom: Sturgis and District Regional Park (courtesy David McLennan, Canadian Plains Research Center)

Top: Sylvan Valley Regional Park (courtesy David McLennan, Canadian Plains Research Center)
Bottom: Wood Mountain Provincial Historic Park, Sitting Bull Cairn (courtesy David McLennan, Canadian Plains Research Center)

REDBERRY LAKE REGIONAL PARK

Built in 1969, this park is located 13 km east of Hafford, just south of Hwy 40. It is open from the Victoria Day long weekend in May until the end of September, and features some excellent bird watching and sailing on the saline lake. It is also the only regional park located in a UNESCO Biosphere Reserve due to the pelicans nesting on the park's islands. Other activities in this park include golf, swimming, and some of the best berry picking I've had the joy of sampling in many years. As is usually the case, pets are allowed in the park if they are leashed but they are restricted from the beach area. The park levies a $9 daily entry fee, waived if you've purchased an annual Regional Park sticker.

SITES

There are 68 electrified and 34 non-electrified sites, as well as extensive group camping and "tenting only" sites. Rents are $18 per day for an electrified site, $11 for a non-electrified site, and all fees are collected at the park entry booth. Seasonal campsites cost $750 for the whole summer! All sites are naturally leveled and drained, and are well shaded as they are built in a mature aspen forest. There are picnic tables, pole BBQs, and trash bins at each site, and the individual site numbers are gaily painted with woodland motifs. An excellent map of the sites is available at the entry booth, detailing the drinking water taps and the free firewood bins. The sites are variable in size and shape, and some may not fit the largest units. Washroom facilities are primitive in the camping areas and modern in the beach shower house. Flush toilets and coin-operated showers can be had here, but the showers are not as yet wheelchair accessible; plans are in place to make the beach shower house wheelchair-accessible in the near future. One unisex, wheelchair accessible flush toilet has been built near the new campsites. A trailer dump station is available free of charge next to the ball diamonds. There is a dining shelter available beside the Rose Bowl, a natural amphitheater used for musical events, and a hall can be rented for private functions as well. Reservations are accepted but they prefer at least one week's notice; contact the park office at the address below for more details.

WATER SPORTS

The lake is very salty so it doesn't support a game fish population. The salt makes the water strikingly blue and clear, though, so snorkeling, swimming, canoeing, and boating are popular. A cement-padded boat launch is available around the lake past the golf course and trout pond. Sailing regattas are often held here, and the colorful sails of the many boats that ply these waters make for spectacular photographs. The lake's many islands are off limits for boaters, however, as the lake is a Federal Wildlife Sanctuary due to the number of birds that nest on them. Swim lessons are taught from the fine beach here, usually one set in late July. Fees are very reasonable; contact the park office for dates and prices. There is a buoyed swimming area with attendant change rooms, and a coin-operated beach shower. A waterfront concession operates daily, selling the usual iced treats, snacks and pop, as well as bread, milk, and other simple groceries. There is a large, enclosed eating area adjoining the concession. There are two playgrounds, one by the seasonal rental sites and the larger one on the beach. The beach playground has a large creative play center, swings, and a beach volleyball court. The equipment costs $10 to rent, but $5 is refunded when you return the ball. There is fishing in the park, as they have provided a stocked trout pond with drive-in access and a good pier system; the pond is closed to all boats. The Redberry Pond Trout Fishery has ample parking and a fish-cleaning table. One must have a valid Saskatchewan fishing license to partake and all applicable regulations are enforced.

GOLFING

There is a 9-hole, sand-green golf course stretching up from the lakeshore and playing over the hills in back of the lake. It covers 2304 yards over its par-35 fairways, and offers a lot of challenge for your $11.50 greens fee (9 holes), $20 for 18 holes. An interesting local rule is that there is no out of bounds on the course! Fees are paid on the honor system if the small clubhouse is unstaffed. A small line of balls and tees is on sale, and there are club rentals. The scorecard has a simple map of the course to guide you from green to tee. There is a lot of vertical change in the course, and the dense brush lining some of the fairways can be a problem if you spray the ball like I do. The fairways are well mowed, but naturally watered and so they can be a bit dry late in the year, depending on the weather. There is usually no need to reserve a tee time; simply show up and, if needed, wait a minute and you're on the first tee. For more information on the course, or to book a private tournament, contact the clubhouse at (306) 549-2337. There is also a mini-golf course beside the concession, where equipment can be rented for $2 per round.

SPORTS

Besides all the fun listed above, the park has a berry hill between the golf course and the trout pond that has to be seen to be believed. It must be one of the richest saskatoon-berry hills in the area, and yet locals also have their favorite "secret" spots. Our family delights in picking and preserving these berries, so that our winter toast holds a memory of the sun drenched hills we wandered. We have also found many edible mushrooms among the aspen leaf litter, particularly in the spring. Dried and put away for our winter's soups, stews, and sauces, they were a welcome addition to our cuisine. There are two established self-guided trails that display the many types of trees and plants that grow in this terrain.

SERVICES

Beside the seasonal campers there are a few ball diamonds, free for the use, that have mesh backstops on wooden poles and benches for players and spectators. Grass infields and wide open space make a pickup game a constant opportunity. The park offers a stage in the Rose Bowl and seating on the grass for up to 3000 people; the whole bowl is lit for night performances. The hall rents for $50 per day, and includes the camp kitchen. The park hosts several annual events, including golf tournaments and a Canada Day celebration on the July long weekend. They hope to be starting weekend dances in the coming year, featuring local musical talent. As one can see, this is a busy park and its proximity to Saskatoon keeps it so. It is full most weekends but rarely so during the week. The town of Hafford has much of the shopping, mechanical, and worship services you'll need, and medical service is available in North Battleford or Saskatoon. Their brochure has a pelican on it with the motto "Hope you enjoy your stay with us"! Well, we did and I hope you do, too. For more information on this park or to reserve a site, contact the park office at:

Redberry Lake Regional Park
PO Box 250
Hafford, SK S0J 1A0
Telephone: (306) 549-2149
Website: members.shaw.ca/mjfinley/rrp.html.

SANDY BEACH REGIONAL PARK

Located 19 km north of Lloydminster, just off Hwy 17 on grid road 798, this park is open from May 1 to September 30. There is a new entrance booth which combines the concession and golf rentals as well. The park has grown since our last visit, with more cabins, upgraded electrical service and a new playground with modern equipment. The park levies a $7 daily entry fee, waived if you have an annual Regional Park sticker.

SITES

There are 41 full service sites in the park and 15 unserviced sites, renting for $22 per night or $120 per week for an electrified site, $10 per night for an unserviced site. Seasonal sites cost $1,650 per year. The sites are all naturally leveled and drained, and have pole BBQs, trash bins, and picnic tables. Water is provided to each site, and firewood is provided in central bins. Shade is provided by aspens and willows that have been planted over the last 20 years; some are still growing, but give them time! Washrooms are modern, with flush toilets and coin-operated showers in the shower house. Simple biffies are located up on the Rancher's Road hill where the group camp sites are located. This is where the younger party crowd is allowed to congregate, so the main campgrounds are very peaceful. You can reserve the family or group site for a private function, but there is little equipment on top of the hill. Mind you, the scenery is panoramic! We found the campsites to be in excellent condition, well maintained and a fresh coat of paint sprucing things up. Pets are allowed in the park, but they must be leashed at all times and are restricted from the beach area. The quiet time of 2300 hr is strictly enforced in the main campgrounds by the park patrol. Reservations are accepted by the week by calling the park manager at (306) 825-2092.

WATER SPORTS

The lake is long, lined with private cabins, and the scene of most of this park's recreational activity. A fine boat launch and dock offer lake access to motorboats, and there is a large parking lot in behind the boat launch for trailers. The boat launch costs $15 per day or $45 for the entire season. There are fish in the lake, but fishing success has been poor of late due to the severe winters we've had recently. Water skiers, tubers, jet boats, and other watercraft ply these waters constantly, creating a blur of color on hot summer days. A fine beach is equipped with changerooms, free beach showers, and a large array of water equipment such as docks, diving boards, floats, and so on. The beach itself is filled with fine sand just right for sand castles, and two sets of swim lessons are offered in July and August. The beach was the site of the 1997 Alberta Summer Games beach volleyball and canoeing venues, so you know this is a great beach! The park rents equipment for volleyball, basketball, baseball, and horseshoes for a $5 deposit, refunded when you return the equipment. Ask at the concession for the gear and they'll fix you up.

SPORTS

There is a 9-hole, sand-green golf course just to the right of the main entrance as you drive in. It is a fairly flat course that plays for 3028 yards over its par-35 fairways. For the most part it isn't all that difficult although the narrow fairways can be a hazard to a shanker like me, and they do play long for the most part. The course is well maintained, with neatly trimmed fairways and tees. Greens fees are modest at $7 for 9 holes or $10 for the holes. Clubs can be rented at the concession, where one pays the greens fees, and a driving range is available. The scorecard has a good map on the back, available when you pay your fees. No reservations are likely to be needed; the course is friendly enough that you'll be able to walk right on for the most part. The park has one ball diamond set in a large grassy field. You can rent bats and balls at the concession for $5, refunded when you return the equipment. Simply go play and you'll soon find yourself in a pick-up game! A fine playground is set in the picnic or day-use area, with teeter-totters, slides, merry-go-rounds, swings, and a creative play center. Everything is brightly painted and well shaded by tall poplars. The dining shelter is quite close, and popular enough that it must be reserved to avoid conflict. A small basketball court is built on a cement pad just beside this, with equipment available at the concession.

SERVICES

The park concession also serves as the entry booth, where one pays their camping fees. It offers a range of iced treats, snacks and pop as well as a wealth of rental sports gear. Lloydminster is the place for shopping, mechanical, medical, and worship services, all about a 15-minute drive from your campsite. A hall can be rented for private functions; contact the manager for details. This is a popular park on weekends when many local businesses will run staff BBQs and campouts, but fairly peaceful as it considers itself to be a family park. For more information, contact the park manager at:

Sandy Beach Regional Park
PO Box 2275
Lloydminster, SK   S9V 1S6
Telephone: (306) 825-2092
Fax: (306) 825-8867
Website: www.sandybeachpark.com

SILVER LAKE REGIONAL PARK

Located 17 km from Maidstone on Hwy 16, this lovely park is easily found by the colorful signs park management has placed on the highway to mark the route. The access road is paved right up to the main gate as it leads to the park office past the ball diamonds. The park gates are open from April 15 to October 15, 0800–2200 hr. Built in 1963, it has seen extensive renovations in the years since then and it now boasts a remarkable golf course and pro-shop/lounge complex. Situated on the south shore of Silver Lake, a small creek also bisects the park, so a variety of terrain delights the hiker. The park itself is built on the edge of the old Fort Pitt Trail as it curves north of Maidstone, and the lake was probably named by the freighters or settlers that originally traveled the road. Daily entry fees are $3 per vehicle, waived with a $30 annual Regional Park sticker.

SITES

The park has 30 sites with electricity and water service, as well as 14 sites with electrical, water, and sewer service. There are unlimited unserviced sites as well. All the sites are naturally drained except for the fully serviced sites which feature leveled gravel pads. The sites vary from $12 per night to $20 per night, depending on the level of service requested. Sites can also be rented on a weekly or seasonal basis, costing $72 to $120, depending on the level of service you want. Built in the mature forest surrounding the south end of the lake, all the sites are well treed and fairly spacious. Each site has its own pole BBQ, a picnic table, and garbage can. Several of the sites adjoin one another to allow a couple of families to camp together. Larger groups can be accommodated at two sites, both of which feature large dining shelters and open areas for children to play. These dining shelters cost $30 per day, above the cost of camping here. These two areas are popular among local organizations and companies for staff and member picnics, so you must book them well in advance if you'd like to use them. The park has central bins filled with free firewood, and bathrooms with shower and laundry facilities are located on the north end of the camp. Reservations are accepted by telephone, with a major credit card. "No-shows" are billed for one night's accommodation, and the site is rented out the next day. Contact the concession operators at the address below for further information.

GOLF

The 9-hole, grass-green golf course is an interesting play as it features a natural creek meandering through; the swinging bridge found on the course is a trademark of the park. It is a par 36, being 3150 yards in length; RCGA rating is 35. The grass greens and irrigation system are fairly new, having been completed in 1986. The course is well treed, the fairways reasonably straight (except for that incredible dogleg right on #5!), and the greens well mowed. Playing the course fresh in the morning with the dew still on the greens is a treat that simply has to be tried to be believed. As a compliment to course play, a driving range is available, costing $3 per bucket. A mini-golf course is also available, costing $1 per round, so the little golfers have a place to go; check with the concession staff for rentals. The course costs $13 per round or $22 for 18 holes. Clubs can be rented, as well as pull carts and motorized carts. Seasonal memberships can also be purchased, which may be a bargain if you intend to golf while the children attend swim lessons, as an adult membership is $325. The clubhouse has an elevated deck overlooking the 9th hole and is a scenic place to end your game. It is licensed and serves light lunches. Many golf tournaments are hosted here over the year; one is best advised to call the park office for dates and prices. Although tee reservations are not normally needed during the week, it would be wisest to make them during the busy summer weekends. Contact the clubhouse at (306) 893-2831.

WATER SPORTS
In 1973 the park board decided to make the swimming area safer by enclosing it in an earthen dike, separating it from the lake proper. This certainly curtails problems with motorboats and waves, making the swim area much safer for the littlest users. Lessons from both the Canadian Red Cross and the Royal Life-Saving Society are offered in the first two weeks of July, the cost varying based on the swim level desired. Except for the swim lesson, no lifeguards are on duty. The beach is filled with lovely soft sand, with floating docks and slides placed in the water for summer fun. The beach features change rooms and bathroom facilities near the playground. The playground equipment features slides, swings, merry-go-rounds, teeter-totters and a climbing structure, and adjoins the picnic area to the west. Although canoes can be launched in the lake, no boat launch exists in the park. Fishing reports regarding this lake vary, so I cannot state what you may catch and when.

HIKING TRAILS
Taking full advantage of the variability in terrain, the park has established a Nature Trail into a marshy area to the northwest of the park, in partnership with Ducks Unlimited. A tower has been built to enhance the view, and waterfowl of all sorts can be observed going about their business. The trail is about 2 km in total length and wanders along lakeshore as well as estuarine terrain. The trail also allows one to see sign of many small animals and many interesting plant and geoform associations. Signs have been erected to guide you along the way.

SERVICES

As one drives into the park, the first thing to see is the ball complex comprised of 3 diamonds, each with their own bleachers. The main part is near the concession, and is the baseball diamond. The bleachers ar capable of holding a hundred or more fans. The other two diamonds, only marginally less grand, are sized for fastball or slowpitch. The Standard Hill Baseball Club holds their annual tournament in the park every Father's Day weekend. Maidstone offers a full range of shopping as well as medical and mechanical services. As one can guess from all that is written here, this is a popular park that serves not only the immediate area, but a wide range of travelers from afar. I am told that it is fairly busy nearly every weekend of the summer, and booked heavily for a total of 110 days out of the season; a remarkable tally, to be sure. I certainly suggest reserving a site in advance of your intended stay. Simply contact the camp office:

> Silver Lake Regional Park
> PO Box 307
> Maidstone, SK   S0M 1M0
> Telephone: (306) 893-2831.

Have your credit card handy, as it will be needed to hold your reservation. As their brochure says, "Come and Play!"

SUFFERN LAKE REGIONAL PARK

This park is located just off Hwy 17 on Grid Road 680, 28 km southwest of Marsden off Hwy 40. Manito Lake was once part of the park, but it has since withdrawn from the park system; please do not contact Suffern Lake for information on Manito Lake, as they have nothing to do with it anymore. The access roads are built of gravel, and sections were somewhat rough; slow down and you'll do fine. The park is open from April 1 to October 30, and levies a $5 daily vehicle entry fee, waived if you have the annual Regional Park sticker.

SITES

There are 14 electrified sites and 22 non-electrified sites in this resort park. The sites rent for $15 per day or $90 per week for an electrified site, and $10 per day or $60 per week for a non-electrified site. There are many cabin owners on the north side of the lake, and some are willing to rent their cabins privately; contact the park office with your request, as they may have a list of interested owners. All sites are naturally leveled and drained, and have picnic tables, firepits made from metal pipe with grates, and trash cans onsite. There was no park map available, and the roads were a tad confusing at first. Drinking water is available from a central tap and firewood costs $5 per tub. Washrooms provided are modern flush toilets in the campgrounds, with flush toilets and showers in the clubhouse. Shade is provided at all sites by the tall aspens and willow scrub into which the sites are built. Each site has a small bay with a large open area in front, and so will hold the largest unit. There are no dining shelters, but the golf clubhouse can be rented for private functions at a cost of $100 per day or $200 for the full weekend, plus a $100 refundable damage deposit. There is a wealth of family or group camping available, as the open space in front of each site extends for quite a distance. Reservations are accepted by calling the park caretakers at (306) 826-5410 and leaving a message on their machine.

WATER SPORTS

The lake is a small one, so there is a speed limit of 5 kph for all boaters. A boat launch is provided at the north end of the lake, with a fish filleting station as well. Parking is at a premium, so boaters are asked to park their trailers in their sites. The lake is stocked annually with rainbow trout, and the anglers I spoke to said fishing had been good that summer. There is a beach on the south of the lake with change rooms and biffies. A small parking lot along a line of saskatoon bushes provides shade and a quick snack. The park is extending the beach by spreading more sand, and has provided playground equipment at one end. There are no lifeguards, and no lessons are taught at the moment.

GOLFING

A 9-hole, sand-green golf course is available just on the right as you drive in. Its par-33 fairways extend for 2438 yards over low hills amid the poplar scrub, providing shade and varying terrain. A driving net is located just in front of the first tee. There is a very nice clubhouse with a broad, covered deck, flush toilets and showers, and a small hall for private functions. Greens fees are modest at $5 per round, payable in a drop box on the first tee. Tee reservations won't normally be needed; simply walk up and swing. Even if the tee is busy, you probably won't have finished your warmup before it clears. To book the hall or arrange a private tournament, contact the park office at the address below.

SPORTS

There is a ball diamond in an open space, with a mesh backstop on wooden poles, perfect for a pickup game of softball. The park has built a sand volleyball court just off the road in a sand pit; bring your own equipment. Bunnock pits are available at the clubhouse, but bring your own set of bones; for more information on this interesting sport, check out the Macklin World Bunnock Tournament website at: http://www3.sk.sympatico.ca/macklin/bone.htm. There is a series of bike paths off the north end of the lake, near the turn for the boat launch, comprising 15 km of trails for bikes of all types, although quads and motocross bikes are the commonest patrons; this area is not maintained by the park, however. There are two small playgrounds in the park, with swings and maypoles at both. Hiking trails have not been built, but the woods surrounding the lake are meant to be explored.

SERVICES

The park has no concession or canteen, so park patrons must visit Chauvin, Alberta for laundry and more extensive shopping, while groceries and mechanical services are available in Senlac, Marsden, and Macklin. More extensive shopping is available in Lloydminster, an hour's drive away. Medical services are available in Neilburg and Unity. We asked about quiet time in the park, and the caretakers told us this wasn't a concern as the park clientele is either families or the cabin owners, and so late night noise isn't a problem. That is perhaps one of the great charms about this park: the quiet atmosphere provides a chance to "recharge the batteries" without a lot of bustle and haste. For more information on this park, or to organize a private function, contact the park office at:

> Suffern Lake Regional Park
> Box 121
> Senlac, SK   S0L 2Y0
> Telephone: (306) 826-5410
> Fax: (306) 826-5410
> Macklin World Bunnock Tournament: http://www3.sk.sympatico.ca/macklin/bone.htm

VALLEY REGIONAL PARK

This park is divided into two sections roughly 27 km apart. The Rosthern site is more easily accessed as it is situated roughly halfway between Saskatoon and Prince Albert on Hwy 11. The Waldheim site is 27 km west of Rosthern on Hwy 312. Open from mid-April to mid-October (dates depend on the golfing season), the park gates open from 0600–2200 hr daily in season. A daily pass costs $5 or free with an annual Regional Park sticker.

SITES

The Rosthern site is the larger of the two campgrounds, with 11 full-service (seasonal) sites, 45 electrified (30-amp service) and 11 non-electrified sites; Waldheim has 12 full service sites costing $10 per night. Electrified sites in the Rosthern Park cost $20 per night; seasonal sites are $850 per season. The Rosthern sites are larger and better shaded with tall poplars; both parks' sites are naturally leveled and drained. Rosthern's roadways are well graveled and in excellent condition, with a map available to identify facilities. Waldheim's park has none. Campers register at the park gate in Rosthern, at the golf clubhouse in Waldheim. Drinking water is available at central taps, one for every three sites in Rosthern, one tap in Waldheim; all water is municipal in origin. All sites have pole BBQs, picnic tables (metal-framed in Rosthern's park) and trash cans on site; firewood is sold for $3 per bundle. The north end of the Rosthern campsite can have as many as 19 sites reserved for a group function, with two small bays (one east, one northeast) for smaller groups. The camp kitchen on the north end can be reserved for private functions if 19 sites are reserved as well. Site reservations can be made by phone by calling the park gate at the number below, but you must leave a 50% deposit. This includes the south camp kitchen and the A-frame clubhouse. Sites can be reserved for the Rosthern campground by calling (306) 232-5600.

GOLFING

Both parks feature golf courses, but the better of the two is Rosthern's. It has 18 holes with immaculate, manicured fairways and greens which are complimented by many tall trees and a fountain barricading the first tee. The Rosthern clubhouse offers a full range of service including light meals and snacks. Clubs and carts can be rented at the pro-shop and a complete line of merchandise is available for sale. An excellent putting green and driving range are available to hone your skills prior to your tee time. Greens fees are $14 for 9 holes and $24 for 18 holes (weekdays) and reservations can be made on Monday for the week ahead. Call the pro-shop at (306) 232-5272 for more details.

Waldheim's 2870-yard, sand-green golf course also has a clubhouse with a glorious view of the first tee and ninth green from the spacious raised deck. Waldheim's greens fees are $8 for 9 holes or $12 for 18 holes, with cheaper children's rates. The clubhouse can also be rented to host a private function. To reserve a tee time or for rental of Waldheim's facility, call (306) 945-2255.

SERVICES

Waldheim's park has a trout pond, stocked annually with rainbow trout fingerlings. It also has one of the finest ball complexes in the area, fully lighted for night use, and complete with large stands and a public address system. Dugouts for the players and red shale infields make this an impressive facility. Rosthern also has a ball diamond, but nowhere as well equipped as this! Mind you, Rosthern's park has an impressive day-use area with two camp kitchens, one available for rent, and one of the largest slides in the regional park system. As one drives in, the hill upon which the slide is built dominates the playground to the right. A fine mini-golf game is also found in Rosthern's extensive playground which includes a beach volleyball court. A shower facility complements Rosthern's north campgrounds; open to patrons 24 hours a day, it requires quarters to operate. Both clubhouse (Waldheim) and concession (Rosthern) can be rented for special functions, and both are open (in season) to sell simple meals, like breakfast and light meals or the usual summer fare of chips, pop, and candy. The local communities of Rosthern and Waldheim will provide most shopping one will need, and Rosthern boasts a swimming pool with lessons, public swims, change rooms and showers. Both communities offer mechanical and worship services, and a hospital for medical emergencies. The two parks are widely different in what they offer their patrons: golfing and camping in Rosthern, coupled with a huge creative playground; Waldheim's ball complex is a marvel, and the golf course is a nice play. The sites use different mailing addresses. For more information, contact the manager at:

Valley Regional Park
Box 998, Rosthern, SK   S0K 3R0
Telephone: Office (306) 232-5000, or Rosthern's Gate (306) 232-5600
E-mail: valley.reg.park@sasktel.net
Website (for updated pricing): www.valleyregionalpark.com

Valley Regional Park
Box 460, Waldheim, SK   S0K 4R0
Telephone: (306) 945-2255
Fax: (306) 945-2360.

They take reservations beginning April 1 annually.

UNITY AND DISTRICT REGIONAL PARK

Located at the junction of Hwys 21 and 14 in northwest Saskatchewan, the town of Unity houses an amazing park. Open from late May to late September (longer if the golfing weather holds), the park offers an amazing value for your recreation dollar. The park is divided into two areas, the main one in town with a museum, four baseball diamonds, a pool, playground and a tennis court, the second out of town comprising the campgrounds and golf course. Built in 1972, the park sees revisions yearly as local recreational needs grow. The latest addition has been the purchase of land from the province to build a campsite near the golf course. No daily fees are charged for park entry, although an annual Regional Park pass is mandatory if you wish to golf.

SITES

The campgrounds are located 2 km west of Unity, just off Hwy 14. The 14 non-electrified sites available are all free of charge on a first come, first serve basis. The roadway is paved right to the golf course, 500 m or so north of the campgrounds. The campsite access road is well graveled and follows a "figure eight" pattern, with most of the sites, #4–14, on the right loop. The sites are all on the roadway, with space for the largest unit in several. The central portion of the loop is in a natural shallow depression, and is filled with willow, native cherries, and saskatoon bushes. The picnic tables and pole BBQs are all down in this glade, with short trails feeding from the campsites down to them. Walkways have been mowed through this, making berry picking a pleasant task. Wood is available from a central pile, most needing to be split, but free of charge. Untreated well water is available from three central taps. It tasted fine and is quite potable. Trash bins are located on posts beside each site, and outhouse-style toilet facilities are available near the camp kitchen in the center of the campgrounds.

GOLFING

A fine, 9-hole grass-green course is located 2 km west of Unity on Hwy 14. The par-36, 3219-yard course is played on the hills and plateau above Sink Lake, so vertical change is a constant. The fairways, tees and greens are all heavily watered to make this a lush course. There has been constant improvement to the course, the most recent of which is the ladies' tees on several holes and the new signage. The fairways seem a bit narrow to a notorious shanker like myself and the rough (where I normally play) is lined with many planted trees. Elevated tees and manicured greens make this lovely course one of the best in the area. Greens fees are $10 for nine holes, or $17 for eighteen holes. A fully licensed clubhouse offers cool relief after a game, and snacks, pop and candy bars as well as sandwiches for hungry patrons. The clubhouse is also available to cater for private functions. A practice green and a driving range await your swing, and a pro-shop rents clubs and carts plus retails a line of balls, gloves, and the like. Normally tee reservations are not required as this is a good walk on course. Should you wish to call ahead or arrange a tournament, contact the clubhouse at (306) 228-3688.

WATER SPORTS

A fine municipal pool sits amid an extensive recreational area just off Hwy 21 to the north of the intersection of Hwys 21 and 14. A full range of swim lessons are taught four times yearly, with one set of advanced training offered. Lessons range from $19 to $65 per set, depending on level. Public swims occur daily, costing $6.50 per family or between $1 and $2.75 per day, depending on age. The pool is open from the beginning of June to late August, and has two diving boards for the adventurous: a one-meter and a three-meter springboard. Lessons can be arranged by contacting the pool in season or by contacting the recreation director at (306) 228-2621. Of note is the water polo team that runs every Thursday; the pool also has a Dive Club and a Swim Club. The park has no access to a lake or a river even though Sink Lake borders the west portion of the park, but fishing can be had in the area at the Scott trout pond.

SERVICES

The park has four fine ball diamonds with red shale infields, dressed pitcher's mound, tall mesh backstops and shelters for the players. Bleachers and tall shade trees provide comfortable seating for the spectators, and a concession is available near the main diamond. An ATCO trailer has been moved in for washrooms, and parking is abundant. This complex sits on the same parcel of land as the pool, modern tennis courts (with weather-resistant surfacing) and playgrounds, all on the northeast corner of Unity. A heritage museum also adorns the park with many old buildings and machinery given new life as static displays of pioneer life. Donations are accepted to tour the facility which is open from 1400–1700 hr, May 20 to September 05. Curators are available to guide and instruct in this interesting museum. Horseshoe pits are also available, near the picnic area and playground which has slides, swings, teeter-totters, merry-go-rounds, and climbers, all on a large lawn with tall shade trees. The town of Unity can provide all the shopping, mechanical, medical and worship services one could ask for. The park hosts several events annually, including rodeos, ball and golf tournaments. For more information on this excellent park, contact the Park Secretary at:

> Unity and District Regional Park
> PO Box 1030
> Unity, SK   S0K 4L0
> Telephone: (306) 228-2621
> Fax: (306) 228-4221
> E-mail: unity@sk.sympatico.ca

WILKIE REGIONAL PARK

Adjacent to the town of Wilkie, the park serves as a popular reunion center for local patrons, and a way stop for a host of other travelers. It is open from May 1 until the end of August, with the entry gate open 0630–2300 hr daily in season. There is a $5 daily vehicle park entry fee, waived if you have an annual Regional Park sticker.

SITES

There are 33 electrified and 10 non-electrified sites, costing $15 per night or $10 per night, respectively. They also cost $75 per week or $50 per week, respectively. All sites are naturally leveled and drained, accessed by excellent, well-graveled roads. All sites have picnic tables, pole BBQs, and access to central trash cans. Drinking water (Wilkie municipal) is supplied from central taps, and firewood is available free from central bins. Washrooms vary from biffies in the campgrounds to flush toilets in the shower house, as well as a modern facility in the ball diamond area; all are wheelchair accessible. A trailer dump station is available at the shower house as well. There are two dining shelters, one in the camping area, and the other in the ball diamonds which operates as a concession during tournaments or can be rented for a private function. The sites are bordered by tall stands of planted cottonwoods that provide close shade throughout much of the day. Most sites are back-in style, but a few are pull-through and large enough for the biggest unit. This park is popular for reunions, and must be booked a year in advance to guarantee the weekend you want. Individual sites can also be reserved by calling the secretary-treasurer at (306) 247-2033 or 843-2828 in season.

SPORTS

There are 4 ball diamonds in the park, all in excellent condition with red shale infields, a batting cage, and tall mesh backstops on metal poles. There are team shelters, bleachers for spectators, and ample parking for all. An octagonal beer garden and a concession are available to rent for private functions, but otherwise open only during tournaments. As with all the equipment in this park, everything is in excellent condition.

A 9-hole sand-green golf course is available on the other side of the town, about a 5-minute drive away. It covers 3165 yards over its par-36 fairways, without a lot of vertical but with a lot of bushes to capture errant golf balls. A fine clubhouse is available for rent for $100 per day to host a private tournament, although no pro-shop or equipment rental is available. Greens fees are $5 per day, payable on the honor system on the first tee with a drop box and scorecards. There are many public and private tournaments held during the season, but always room for one more! No tee reservations will normally be needed, but you can call (306) 843-2035 for more information.

The town operates a paddling pool and a swimming pool in a small park, but as they are not part of the Regional Park system we did not examine them further.

SERVICES

The town of Wilkie offers all the shopping, laundry, mechanical, medical, and worship services one could want. The park itself holds many golf and ball tournaments over the year, as well as many church and school picnics. This is a busy municipal park due to the many reunions booked every year. If you plan to stay here on a weekend, you'd be well advised to call ahead for reservations. For more information on the park, or to book a site, contact the park office in care of the RM of Tramping Lake at:

Wilkie Regional Park
PO Box 536
Wilkie, SK S0K 4W0
Telephone: (306) 247-2033
Fax: (306) 247-2055.

THE BATTLEFORDS PROVINCIAL PARK

Located 39 km north of North Battleford on Hwy 4, this park offers an interesting duality: you can awaken to the rustle of a morning's breeze in the aspens, birdsong filling the air, golf on a well-kept 18-hole course and fish Jackfish Lake, while only a few minutes away is the historical and cultural center of North Battleford with its museums and casino. Officially opened in 1961, the park receives patrons from the May long weekend until the September long weekend; although winter camping is allowed, there will be no amenities or staff. Jackfish Lodge Golf Resort will stay open as long as the weather extends the golfing season. Over the years the park staff has planted thousands of aspens, ash, maple, pine, and spruce as well as chokecherry and Saskatoon bushes, keeping the park green and lush. With the camping, golfing, cultural and historical opportunities this park has to offer, it is easy to see why this is such a popular summer retreat.

CAMPING

There are 317 campsites, of which 182 are electrified with 30-amp service, built in 3 main loops. All access roads are paved while the camping loop roads are gravel. The trees and shrubs in the campgrounds provide excellent shade and privacy; some of the sites appear to be built in green tunnels they are so verdant! Park staff clean the sites between patrons, so everything was tidy and litter-free during our visit. As with just about any place where children have been spending their summers, there are many trails winding through the trees leading ultimately to the beach and the ice cream concession. Although toilet facilities are modern in the campgrounds, not all are barrier-free; make your needs known when checking in so the staff will place you near one of the wheelchair-accessible facilities. On a separate note, this park has obviously attracted lots of family gatherings, as they have no fewer than 8 group camping loops for groups of 5–20; they will be covered separately. There is also a boat and trailer storage compound located just past the park entry gate; contact the park office for availability and fees for this secure site.

Following the curve to the right, past the campground permit office where you must check in, the first loop is South Campground. There are 121 sites, 64 of which are electrified, with metal-framed picnic tables and pole BBQs or fire pits. Firewood is available from the repository across the road from the trailer dump station near the entrance. All sites are built on gravel pads and are well drained. Drinking water is piped to central taps and trash bins are shared between two sites. Modern toilets are scattered throughout the loop, and one barrier-free modern service center with hot showers and sinks is centrally located. It also has a coin-operated laundry facility; you can get change at the Beachside Concession near the Centre Campground. The lawn surrounding the service center has a small playground with teeter-totters and a swing set; there is ample parking and you will also find the payphone booth here. Some of the sites are 'doubles', and big enough for the largest unit while others might be a bit tight; all sites have tall trees for shade as well as the chance to pick the berries for your morning's pancake batter right from the bushes in your site! The Recreation Hall is located just off the access road to the South Campground, a facility which can be rented for private functions as well as hosting some of the Canada Day celebrations.

The Hilltop Campground is located to the right of the park administration office and has 17 non-electrified sites, all of the pull-through style and suitable for large units. There are no showers, and there is one flush toilet facility beside a water tap near the Clearview Campground entrance. Firewood must be obtained at the communal pile across from the trailer dump station at the entrance to the Centre Campground. This loop is also home to Clearview Group Campground and Keeway Group Campground, both of which are opened only when demand warrants.

Continuing past the Hilltop Group Campground one comes to an intersection: to the left is the Jackfish Lodge Golf Resort, to the right is the North Campground and its 117 sites (62 of which are electrified). The sites feature metal-framed picnic tables, culvert-style fire pits and tall shade trees. With gravel pads and excellent drainage they are proof against the fiercest storm. Trash bins are shared between sites and firewood is available from one bin near site #17. Some of the sites are quite spacious, particularly #1–15 (all non-electrified) on the first right-hand loop. They are also spaced such that they are quite private and fairly quiet. Only three sites in this loop are "doubles," # 38, 47, and 117 (all electrified). One barrier-free service centre is available across from sites #30 and 31 with a small playground nearby; there is no laundry facility in this building, though—for that you must use the nearby Centre Campground coin-operated laundromat. There is a pedestrian/bike access path leading from the back loop (near site #36) across the road to that facility, providing easy access to the games area as well.

Centre Campground is closest to all the "action" as it were; the games area, store, beach and concession, boat/bicycle rental and recreation office are all nearby. Centre Campground has 79 sites, 51 of which are electrified. All sites feature culvert fire pits and metal-framed picnic tables amid tall shade trees; gravel has been used to level and drain the sites. Flush toilets and potable water taps are scattered throughout the loop. There is a trailer dump station across the road from the modern, barrier-free service centre and its coin-operated laundry facility and payphone. The communal firewood pile is located beside the trailer dump. There is a large playground in behind the back loop of this campground, across from the large parking lot used for beach patrons. There is also a picnic pavilion beside the parking lot, available for use on a first-come, first-served basis.

The park has taken extra measures to accommodate groups of patrons, having no fewer than 8 group campsites capable of accommodating 6–20 units; a minimum reservation is for 5 members in a group. Each group site will have central water, vault toilets and a series of picnic tables and fire pits or pole BBQs located around a central open space. Robinson Bay group campground is also closest to the second, smaller beach. South Campground has three group campsites, Willow, Aspen and Maple, of which Aspen is the smallest. As mentioned above, Hilltop Campground has two group sites, Clearview and Keeway, while Centre Campground has one: Ball Diamond Group Campground. To reserve any of these you must contact the park office at (306) 386-2212 or by email from the website: www.saskparks.net.

SPORTS

The beach anchors all the other activities available, as they are all within a short walk from here. There are beach volleyball courts, horseshoe pits, and a ball diamond with tall mesh backstop and grass infield. You can sign out a set of horseshoes at the entry gate; you must bring your own equipment for all other sports, although there are no other fees charged. Lakeshore mini-golf is available here as well, with equipment and fees to be paid at the booth beside the entrance. There is a small playground beside the beach volleyball court, and an excellent barrier-free walkway running behind the beach from one main parking lot to the other, perhaps 500 meters in length.

There are three self-guided hiking trails, Lakeside Trail, Wintergreen Nature Trail, and Mountain Bike Trail. The Lakeside Trail runs 1.5 km (one way) along the lake from the South Campground Recreation Hall parking lot south to Robinson Bay, across the road from which is the trailhead for the other two hikes. The Wintergreen Nature Trail is a 1 km self-guided loop, while the Mountain Bike Trail is a 4-km loop running through the hills between Hwy 4 and the lake. While it can be hiked, it is best enjoyed from the saddle of a bike.

Birding is a popular pastime in this park as the lake attracts a large number of migratory fowl each year, including the exceedingly rare Whooping Crane and the Osprey. You can borrow a Nature Backpack from the Administration Office to enhance your enjoyment of these hikes. Each backpack contains plant or insect identification books, binoculars and some bug magnifier viewers. While at the Administration Office, check out the Interpretive Centre and the informative displays describing local flora and fauna.

BEACHES AND BOATING

There are two unsupervised beaches for park patrons, Main Beach beside Centre Campground, and Robinson Bay near the Delorme cottage subdivision to the south. Both beaches have somewhat coarse sand, and with the lake level quite low there is more small rock in the play area than otherwise. The lake itself is quite shallow, only 17 feet at the deepest, so it is normally quite warm. Although there is a change room at the main beach, there are no beach showers. During the Canada Day celebrations the beach and Recreation Office become the focus for the day and a retractable stage is set up for musicians and dancers. The main beach also has an excellent concession offering the usual iced treats, pop and chips as well as a line of grilled items. The store offers a line of camping items, groceries and souvenirs; both shops can be contacted at (306) 386-2860 for details.

The park has two boat launches: the southern one in the Delorme cottage subdivision and the main beach boat launch. Both launches have trailer parking nearby, while the main beach launch also has a fish-cleaning station. You are, as always, expected to retrieve your boat each day and store it on your campsite overnight.

As the water is shallow and warm, boating of all sorts is quite popular in this basin, including water skiing, knee boarding, and tubing. The main beach rental shop, Beachside Rentals, offers paddleboats, kayaks, canoes and bikes for rent, as well as a line of tow equipment. They do not rent motorized watercraft, however. Their shop is open from 1200–1600 hr daily or upon request; contact them at (306) 386-2860 for details. Even though the lake is quite shallow and the water can be murky as a result, fishing is popular here, as evidenced by the regular restocking of pike, perch, whitefish and walleye that occurs here and at nearby Murray Lake.

GOLF

Jackfish Lodge Golf Resort offers an excellent facility with its 18-hole par 72 rolling over 6710 yards of undulating terrain, with elevated tees and bunkered greens. The seventeenth hole is considered the most challenging, while the twelfth is the most scenic as it runs alongside the lake. An excellent 58-room hotel complete with licensed fine dining and lounge is complemented by a pro-shop with club and cart rentals as well as a full line of golfing merchandise and clothing for sale. There is a practice putting area and a driving range available, and the course pro will provide lessons; contact the pro-shop for details. Altogether a remarkable facility, it is open from early May until the weather forces it to close in the fall (usually October)! Check out their website for more information at: www.jackfishlodge.com. Contact them directly to reserve a room or book a tee time at (306) 386-2877.

SERVICES

Among the unique things this park does is attract First Nations partners in its celebrations. The really big day in this park is Canada Day, when local First Nations artists and drummers perform traditional dances with all their color and excitement. There is music and song throughout the day, followed by fireworks at dusk; the best place to see all this is right from the main beach area. The park also hosts a "Show and Shine" where local antique car enthusiasts get together to showcase their restored vehicles. Another musical interlude is provided by Saskatchewan Express, a song-and-dance troupe that tours the province and makes an annual stop at the Recreation Office stage. For all these and other events, contact the park office for dates and details.

While in the area, there are a great many cultural and historic venues to check out in North Battleford: the Western Development Museum, the Allen Sapp Museum, the Chapel Gallery, the Fred Light Museum, and the Fort Battleford National Historic Park, to name but a few. There are also sports museums, nature centers and an outdoor adventure centre, all within a few minutes of this amazing park. For links to these and other noteworthy places, check out the Battlefords Tourism website at: www.tourism.battlefords.com/, or contact the tourism office at 1-800-243-0394 and request your free copy of the Battlefords Tourism Guide.

As you can see, The Battlefords Provincial Park combines a natural setting with proximity to many urban and cultural amenities. Although you cannot reserve a site at this time (except for group sites), you can contact the park office for further information at:

The Battlefords Provincial Park
PO Box 100
Cochin, SK   S0M 0L0
Telephone: (306) 386-2212
Fax: (306) 386-2155
E-mail by following the link at: www.saskparks.net.

BLACKSTRAP PROVINCIAL PARK

Located just 40 minutes south of Saskatoon off Hwy 11, the major feature seen as you drive up to the park will be the hill which rises 45 meters above the surrounding plains. Mount Blackstrap, as it is known, is a man-made feature built for the 1971 Canada Games, and is still used for downhill skiing and snowboarding to this day. Because of the ski area, the park is open the entire year, with some winter camping available as well as cross-country skiing; no park entry fees are charged during the winter months. Combined with the lake for water activities including fishing, boating or canoeing, and tow sports, one can see this park is full of recreational opportunities. One of the prettiest features of this park is the sunset which can be seen across the lake from both sets of campgrounds; the perfect end to the day!

CAMPING

There are two sets of campgrounds available, completely different in approach. Hazelnut Grove Campground, located just past the park entry booth, has 20 non-electrified sites on two loops of 10 sites each: loop A and Loop B. Although loop B has slightly larger sites than A-loop's predominantly tenting-only sites, they all have better privacy and shade than the electrified sites at the other campground. The sites are naturally leveled and drained, generally sloped back to the lake, and the roadways are quite narrow. You'll find parking at a bit of a premium for most of these sites with little room for even a tent trailer. You'd be better served parking nearby in the ample lots after setting up your tent. There are pole BBQs, wood picnic tables and central trash bins. Potable water is available from central taps only during the summer months; this campground remains open for winter camping although there are few amenities. Vault toilets are available in the campgrounds and picnic areas, with free showers available in the modern facility at the Kevin Misfeldt campground to the south. Recycling bins are available for bottles and plastics, and firewood is available near sites A8 and A9. The one overwhelming glory of these sites is that you have lakeside access for your boat. You can literally tie your boat up in front of your site for most of these campsites. Please note that if you'd like to try your hand at winter camping here, there will be no running water or showers and you are expected to self-register as you drive in. Discount rates will be in effect, however, and there will be little competition for sites.

Kevin Misfeldt Campground, located some 5 km south of the Hazelnut Grove campgrounds on a paved road, commemorates a conservation officer whose life was tragically ended in a helicopter accident, a reminder to us all of the dedication and sacrifice these men and women make to conserve and protect our peaceful spaces. There are 31 sites here, of which 12 are electrified with 30-amp service. The sites are ample, capable of holding modern units and leveled with gravel pads. Most sites are of the back-in style, although #2 is a pull-through site. There is good shade and some privacy, and all sites have metal framed picnic tables, firepits and access to central trash bins, water and firewood. There is a modern wheelchair-accessible shower facility with flush toilets available and vault toilets elsewhere in the campgrounds. It also houses a payphone and a recycling station. A trailer dump station is located beside the road about 500 meters from the campground. Six of the campsites are available for seasonal rent; contact the park office for details. There is a small group site/overflow area, very open, on a grassy area beside the self-registry station near the service center. Only 3 of these sites are lakeside: # 2 (electrified), 4 and 5 (both non-electrified). There is a small, buoyed swim beach available and a creative play structure in a sand pit beside the service center. This campground is closed in the fall, with only Hazelnut Grove camping available after the September long weekend.

Interestingly, there are 4 walk-in tenting sites located a short distance (about 2 minutes' walk to the farthest) from the small parking lot near site #26. Although not a strenuous hike, these sites are a bit more difficult to access and have no amenities. The trail accessing these sites is fairly easy to follow but definitely not wheelchair accessible. Bring your own water and note that there are no toilets serving these sites. There are pole BBQs but no picnic tables or trash bins. The sites are very small but well shaded and very private, naturally leveled and drained. There was some firewood in each site when we checked, but it was clearly carried in by previous campers. Please note: the mosquitoes back here had to be experienced to be believed—definitely bring your own "bug juice"!

PICNIC AREAS

You'll find three day-use areas in the park: Aspen Grove Picnic Area, Lakeview Picnic Area, and Mountain View Picnic Area. None of the day-use areas has a firewood supply, as patrons should use charcoal briquettes in the pole BBQs provided throughout.

The largest of these is Aspen Grove, with a large parking lot to serve its many amenities. Many wooden or metal-framed picnic tables and pole BBQs are scattered seemingly at random among the tall aspens shading this well-lawned expanse. Central potable water taps and trash bins can be found near the wheelchair-accessible change rooms with modern flush toilets. There is one dining shelter available, free to use as "first-come, first-served." The swimming beach itself is relatively small, filled with coarse but clean sand and complemented with a buoyed swimming area. There are no swim lessons or lifeguards in attendance; swim at your own risk. The beach may be small but the lawn behind it is quite large, capable of holding hundreds of sun worshippers, should the weather ever warrant. There is a beach concession available, offering the ubiquitous iced treats, pop, and snack foods as well as a line of grilled foods. Their hours of operation depend on the season: Saturday and Sunday in May and June, longer in July through to the September long weekend. There are vault toilets behind the concession as well, but there is no play area available.

Lakeview Picnic Area has a small playground, vault toilets, and central trash bins and water taps. The picnic area is the smallest of the three day-use areas and less open, so it is better for small, family-sized groups. You'll find odd little nooks with pole BBQs and wooden picnic tables, some of them right down at the water's edge for the boating patrons. All are well drained and built into excellent lawn with tall aspens above and willows between so privacy and shade are assured.

Mountain View Picnic Area is unique in the park as it is the designated water-ski base. Come for the day, leave your boat trailer at the boat launch, and operate from this picnic area for a day's entertainment. Most of the picnic tables and pole BBQs are located along the shoreline, although they are scattered from the large parking lot among the tall trees as well. This area, by the way, also had the greatest evidence of partiers, particularly near the water's edge. There are wooden picnic tables, pole BBQs, vault toilets, and central water taps and trash bins. The beach here is just a thin sliver of coarse sand, but that's all that's really needed for the sports.

WATER SPORTS

The lake is popular among tow enthusiasts, as it is a long, thin basin, so one has a long run if so desired. There is also a lot of sport fishing available, with pike and walleye taken regularly. The beaches border fairly shallow swimming areas, with two buoyed swim beaches available: the larger in the Aspen Grove Picnic Area, and the other at the Kevin Misfeldt Campgrounds. The only change rooms available are in Aspen Grove.

There is a fine boat launch located just past the ski area, with a large parking lot, wheelchair-accessible vault toilets, a fish-cleaning shack and two hard-surface boat launches—one to launch your craft, the other to retrieve it. There are no docks, marina, bait or fuel shops, and no shade to speak of in the area. There are no picnic tables, pole BBQs, or drinking-water taps; this is a place for you to begin your exploration of the lake. You will find a set of stairs leading you up from the lake to the parking lot, however—just the thing to stretch your legs after a day in the boat.

HIKING

Although the hills beckon your wandering feet, there is only one established hiking trail of approximately 5 kilometers. The start/finish point is adjacent to the downhill-ski pro-shop on Mount Blackstrap. There are two loops available, the Upland Trail of approximately 3.3 km, and the Lowland Trail of about 1.7 km. These trails function as groomed cross-country ski trails during the winter months. Please note that hikers may find themselves sharing the hiking trail with mountain bikers on occasion.

SKIING
Mount Blackstrap was built up to 45 meters in height above a small knoll that already adorned this park, partly to accommodate the 1971 Canada Winter Games and partly to provide winter recreation. There are two chairlifts, a pro-shop with equipment rental and lessons, a restaurant serving a selection of grilled meals, hot drinks and snacks, and a deck from where you can see the hillside action. The operators make snow as soon as weather conditions permit, and the hill is usually busy with snowboarders and skiers. For more information, consult their website at: www.skiblackstrap.com or call them at (306) 492-2400 in season. Cross-country skiers can use the 5 km of groomed trails or set out to find their own adventure. There are no warm-up shelters or watering points for cross-country skiers, so be prepared.

SERVICES
The only shopping access in the park will be the Aspen Grove concession in summer and the ski hill operation in winter. Those requiring more extensive grocery, mechanical and worship services are invited to the town of Dundurn, approximately 10 minutes away, and the city of Saskatoon can answer to any need travelers may require, from the mundane to the extravagant, about 40 minutes away by car. The roads are paved right into the park, and are in generally good condition. The lake may be shallow at points, but it allows one to fish from the shore with impunity. The campsites may be small, but many offer lakeside access (a rarity elsewhere in the province) and decent privacy. There may not be much shopping in the park, but that is the price of solitude. Come for the birds, water sports, and glorious sunsets; you'll be glad you did! For more information on this quiet little park, contact the park office at:

> Blackstrap Provincial Park
> 102-112 Research Drive
> Saskatoon, SK   S7K 2H6
> Telephone: (306) 492-5675
> Fax: (306) 492-5677
> E-mail: link from the website at: www.se.gov.sk.ca/saskparks.

FORT CARLTON PROVINCIAL HISTORIC PARK

Located 26 km west of Duck Lake on Hwy 212, this reconstruction seeks to tell the tales of the fur trade in this province. From 1810 to 1885 this post was an integral part of a thriving fur-based economy. Situated on the banks of the North Saskatchewan River, the post benefited from the canoe brigades bringing trade goods down from the isolated posts on Hudson's Bay. In 1859, it became even more important as a terminus of the Red River Cart trail from St. Paul, Minnesota, which brought trade goods north from that railhead. From the many buildings found during the archaeological digs in the 1960s, it was evident that the fort was much more than a glorified "General Store"; it was an integral part of the cultural and administrative life of the early North-West Territory. The reconstructed buildings, including a tipi encampment, faithfully represent the way lives were led for 75 years, long after a wooden fort such as this should have crumbled and been rebuilt elsewhere. It is due to the importance of the post locally that it was repaired in the same place for so long. Treaty 6 was signed in 1876 near Fort Carlton, between the new Canadian government and local First Nations bands. This important event is celebrated annually during the Treaty Day celebration in August, and coincides with the Beardy's Powwow. At the end of its life, Fort Carlton saw the opening shots in the Northwest Rebellion, after which it was abandoned and burned. As you can see from this short description, much of Saskatchewan's formative history took place in sight of this small outpost.

CAMPING

There are 12 non-electrified tenting sites in a meadow just south of the visitor's centre, costing $11 per night. There really are no boundaries on the sites themselves, so they are huge, almost a group site in size. The open meadow is surrounded by mature aspen forest so you will have some shade. Each site has a sturdy picnic table, and the pole BBQs are being replaced by firepits with moveable grates. Firewood is available free from a central bin, although there is a $3 per night campfire fee. Potable water is available from a central tap, and the vault toilets were clean and well-maintained during our visit. Wheelchair-accessible flush toilets are available in the visitor's centre. There is one dining shelter available in the picnic area between the visitor's centre and the camping area. Well treed with gnarled maples, this picnic area has its own water point as well as firepits. The dining shelter is cement floored and wheelchair accessible; it can be reserved for your private function at a cost of $20 if you require electrical service. There are no playgrounds or sports fields, although the large open area in front of the campsites would doubtless serve for a pickup game of ball or soccer.

HIKING

There are two trails maintained in the park, one leading off from the visitor's centre into the hills surrounding the park, the other leading from the fort down to the river. The longer of the two, the Carlton Trail Walk, is a 1.8 km-long self-guided hike that leads you to see the terrain through new eyes as you discover the ruts from Red River carts and learn more about the landforms and plants in the area. The park has made a series of signs that explain the sights to be seen, all relatively new and in excellent condition. This trail is not for the faint of heart, though, as the hills surrounding the park can be steep, and the staircases they've built to get you up and down from the highest points can be a challenge. The path itself is graveled and well built, but there will be no drinking water available along the way, so be sure to bring some. The River Walk leads north from the Fort to the North Saskatchewan River, and the signs along the way describe some of the history of this remarkable trail. Only .8 km long, it is a gentle walk in the woods, with the river landing as its terminus. Imagine yourself sweating under the hot sun with a pack of trade goods on your back, one of a group of packers paid to carry the freight to and from the Fort! You can fish from the shore here for walleye and pike, with all provincial angling rules in effect, but you shouldn't plan on launching a boat as the park discourages vehicular use of the road. Swimming is also discouraged in the river as it can be treacherous; no lifeguards or safety equipment will be available at any time.

INTERPRETIVE PROGRAMS

The visitor's centre is open from 1000–1800 hr seven days per week in season (May long weekend through the Labor Day weekend) and has an excellent set of static displays of the area which introduce the visitor to the fur trade and Fort Carlton. Admission is $6 per family, $2.50 per adult, and $1 for a youth (age 6–17), and is well worth the time and money due to the high educational quotient. Our province had its beginnings here and in other small places just like it; we must preserve our past in order to understand it and learn from it, and Fort Carlton does just that. The recreation of the Fort itself (open during the same hours as the visitor's center) also features a tipi just outside the fort's gates, in which are laid a number of artifacts from the park's collection to demonstrate key elements of life at that time. Inside the Fort are several buildings, each one demonstrating one part of the way commerce worked and people lived in those times. The guides working here are goldmines of information, providing anecdotes as well as details on every artifact they handle as they show you around the many displays. The types of furs, the fur press and a fur bale, trade goods, living quarters, and a host of other details make the 2 hours or so pass in a blur. Go, live our history; experience the sights and smells firsthand!

This is a busy park, as many school groups spend part of a day here each year, experiencing our history. There are many events held annually here, most notably the annual Fur Trade Day celebration held on the third Sunday in July. Other special events include the Beardy's Powwow in August, which coincides with the Treaty 6 commemoration, and the Candlelight Tours in September. This is only a partial list; contact the park for a more complete list and to find which special event would interest you. The park has few shopping amenities, excepting the souvenir and gift shop in the visitor's centre, and the soda pop vending machine there. Locally, one can find most amenities at the town of Duck Lake, along with riding stables, art galleries, and a museum depicting local artifacts from the pioneering days as well as the history of the Métis people inhabiting the area. For further information on the park or its programs, contact them at:

Fort Carlton Provincial Historic Park
112 Research Drive
Saskatoon, SK   S7K 2H6
Telephone: (306) 787-2700, or 1-800-205-7070 (toll-free in Saskatchewan only)
Website: www.saskparks.net

FORT PITT PROVINCIAL HISTORIC PARK

"Ho! I like to see the sun get up that way—red, like blood. It's a sure sign of victory for the Indians, always." (Imasees, Cree war chief, before the battle of Frog Lake)

Even then, Fort Pitt was a small backwater of a once-great empire, a place where people gathered to trade furs for manufactured goods, perhaps a waystop and a chance to catch up on news or to see the tattered edge of civilization. For one terrible weekend Fort Pitt rose above these mundane concerns and became a battlefield during the North-West Rebellion. A detachment of North-West Mounted Police manned the post, though they were there more to keep Big Bear and his Cree warriors in check than to organize a defense. Unfortunately, the leadership of the band passed to Imasees and Wandering Spirit, two warriors who wanted the white government thrown out of the North-West Territory. The Métis resistance, centered at Batoche, was the spark for these men and they began by killing civilians at the village of Frog Lake on April 2, 1885. Word of the massacre reached the fort the next day, and the inhabitants worked to create defenses as best they could. Wandering Spirit and Imasees did not want the Hudson's Bay Company to leave the North-West; they only wanted the removal of the White government, so their intent was to kill all the police and Indian agents, as they were the hated face of that government.

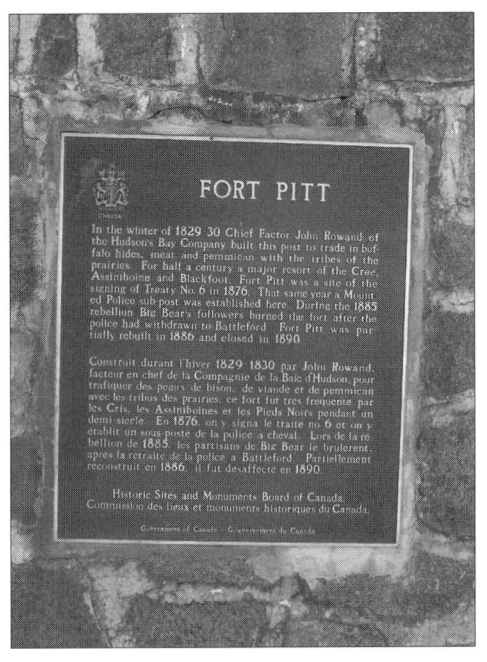

For 10 long days the two sides were poised on the brink of warfare, with negotiations between Inspector Francis Dickens (son of the famous writer Charles Dickens), Chief Trader W. J. McLean, and the marauding native warriors reaching a peak when two police scouts, Constables Loasby and Cowan, rode back between the fort and the warriors. Thinking the White police were either attacking or trying to escape, the natives opened fire, killing Cowan on the spot and wounding Loasby so badly he crawled to the fort and had to be helped in. One of the Cree warriors, Lone Pine, was riding his own horse in pursuit of the scouts, and probably shot Loasby in the leg and through his horse's neck. His horse shot out from under him, Loasby picked himself up and ran to the fort as best he could, but another shot from Lone Pine laid the scout out with a bullet near his spine. In an extraordinarily brave act, Lone Pine threw himself on the ground and coolly crawled to the wounded trooper's side, cut the ammunition and pistol belt from the trooper's waist, crawled to safety and then jumped on his horse and rode up the hill with bullets whizzing around him. At this time Loasby regained consciousness and staggered to the gate where welcoming hands pulled him in. These were the last shots fired during the siege of Fort Pitt.

Finally, through negotiation and trickery, the Hudson's Bay Company employees all surrendered to the Cree, leaving the 23 police troopers in the untenable position of trying to defend the fort. They had to beat a hasty retreat on the afternoon of April 15, 1885 by taking to scows on the Saskatchewan River, itself a daring feat as the spring break-up had occurred only a few days before and great chunks of ice still swirled in the icy spring flow; an overturned craft would surely have meant death by drowning or hypothermia. It took them 7 days in total to reach the relative safety of Battleford, finally landing at 0900 hr on April 22. The fort itself was burned to the ground after being looted of all valuables, including the gold watch given to Inspector Dickens by his father. The Fort Pitt hostages, some 28 men, women and children were later rescued unharmed when the Alberta Field Force caught up with the band at Steele Narrows.

Fort Pitt would be rebuilt and would serve as a Hudson's Bay Post for a few more years after these stirring events, but it was shut down completely by August 1890. All that remains today is a reconstruction of the trading post, and a fenced enclosure with a stone cairn and a plaque commemorating it as "God's Half-Acre." The park can be reached by taking grid road 797, located 17 km off Hwy 17 from Lloydminster, or Hwy 3 from Spy Hill. The access road is 6 km long and well signed, although it is down to one-way traffic for the last 1.5 km and I cannot recommend attempting the dirt road if it is wet; it would be very slippery.

As you drive up you'll see a large field beside the wooded river bank. Along the woods there are 4 wooden picnic tables and pole BBQs, and one set of trash bins. There is one vault toilet, but you may want to bring a supply of paper as there may not be any when you get there. There is ample parking and the grassy field is kept trimmed. There is no overnight camping allowed, and the path down to the river would be troublesome to bring a canoe down. There was no firewood supplied, as the park expects you to use charcoal briquettes, and there is no water supplied either. You can fish from the riverbank in the Saskatchewan River, but the trees and brush grow right down to the water's edge so you will have trouble casting.

We found the park to be peaceful during our picnic lunch, and the soft rustle of the breeze in the trees gave lie to the tumultuous events of the past. For more on the fascinating history of this place, you may wish to read William Bleasdell Cameron's first-hand account called *Blood Red the Sun* (Kenway Publishing Company, Calgary AB, ©1926). For more information on this park, contact the office at:

Fort Pitt Provincial Historic Park
Box 39
Loon Lake, SK   S0M 1L0
Telephone: (306) 837-2410
Fax: (306) 837-2415
Website: www.saskparks.net.

PIKE LAKE PROVINCIAL PARK

Located 30 km southwest of Saskatoon on Hwy 60, this recreation park offers great camping and excellent pool facilities. First built in 1960, the park has seen several major renovations to its pool, playgrounds, and (most recently) to the main office. The lake is a shallow pinch-back or oxbow formed by a shift in the South Saskatchewan River flow. While there is no flow between the lake and the river, water levels are maintained by a pumping system from the river. Having said that, there is a lot to do with all the camping, hiking, boating, and naturalist programs as well as all the fun of the pool and water slide; you needn't be idle here unless you want to be! This is evident in the number of private cottage subdivisions in the park. The park is open from the Victoria Day weekend in May to the Labor Day weekend in September, although there is off-season camping allowed in group camping site number one.

CAMPING

There are 225 campsites in one large camping loop, of which 125 are electrified with 30-amp service; none are full-service. One trailer dump station is located just across the road from the campground office. Thirteen of the electrified sites are pull-through style, and large enough for the biggest unit. There are 2 barrier-free sites (Wheelchair #1 and #2) which can be reserved by calling the campground office at the number below. These two electrified sites are located just around the corner from the wheelchair-accessible service center, which is across the road from sites # 76 A&B. All sites share common features, such as graveled pads for leveling and drainage, metal-framed picnic tables and pole BBQs, and access to communal flush toilets and potable-water taps. They are built into mature aspen forest with adequate brush to ensure privacy; the trees are generally tall enough for shade through the entire main camping loop. Roadways are paved throughout to keep the dust down. Firewood is available from a pile beside the service center and trash bins are also in central receptacles. Many of the sites are built such that two units share the same large bay, although each site would have its own table and pole BBQ—perfect if two families want to camp together. The other sites are built as a relatively large bay scooped out of the mature aspen forest and leveled with gravel pads. There are two service centers for the campgrounds; the larger one across from sites # 76 A&B has the coin-operated laundry while the smaller one is near a creative playground in the field beside the recreation hall and its parking lot. The toilets in the main loop are all barrier-free flush toilets, and both service centers are barrier-free as well. There is one overflow camping area used only during peak demand, located near the recreation hall, beside group site #3. The overflow is essentially an open field with picnic tables and pole BBQs around the perimeter; shade will be at a premium. There are 28 sites available for seasonal rent, 4 of which are non-electrified; contact the park office before April 30 for the site lottery in early May.

There are three group camping sites clustered near the campground office, numbered 1–3. Each is capable of accommodating a minimum of 5–11 units (or more), with a dining shelter, bonfire ring, and 11 picnic tables and pole BBQs around the periphery. All have a potable water tap and one set of flush toilets. Group sites #1 and #2 are electrified and available for off-season camping (no drinking water after the end of September) by self-registering at the booth provided. There is a fourth group site in a field beside Group Site #3 but it has none of the above-mentioned amenities; it functions as either an extension of #3 if the group size is large enough, or as a non-electrified group site if demand warrants. Groups may be interested in renting the recreation hall, located just beside Group Site #3 as well. Contact the park office directly to reserve a site for your group, or to inquire about prices and availability of the group sites or recreation hall. Pets are welcomed during your stay, but they must always be leashed and never left unattended.

BEACHES AND BOATING

There is a boat launch located north of the campground, just before the tennis courts and ball diamond. It isn't very large, and the dock beside it is also quite small, but the park limits outboard motor size to 10 hp so a larger facility will not be required. Fishing isn't all that popular here although some pike can be caught, particularly in the spring of the year, and with the motor restriction in place there isn't any water skiing or knee-boarding here, either. This makes the lake perfect for canoeists, sailboats, and those odd-looking pedal craft called "aqua boats." The lake is narrow and generally calm so there is ample opportunity to explore the shoreline from these peaceful platforms. "Irene's Boats" rents all such craft and the required safety gear from the beach near the pool; contact her directly at (306) 931-4994 for current prices and boat reservations. Her shop is open from 1000–2000 hr daily in season, from the Victoria Day long weekend to the Labor Day long weekend; be sure to call early if you're making group equipment rentals.

The swimming pool and waterslide are definitely a top attraction in this park; you can hear the happy shrieks of the children from the very end of the large parking lot! This is a large facility with picnic tables around the pool and extensive lawns outside for games and naps among the shady trees. Open daily from early June to Labor Day, there are lessons and public swim times and fees posted on the park bulletin boards. Daily, weekly, and seasonal passes are available for adults, children and families. Red Cross levels 1–10 are taught by qualified instructors from late June to mid-August, costing $25 per week per child; minimum age is 6. Check at the administration office or pool for registration times (usually early June) and requirements. The waterslide is well designed to suit most needs from the novice to the beginner, and has its own separate splash-down pool so as not to affect the swimmers. The pool itself goes from zero depth to about 1.5 meters so there is plenty of water for all needs. The entire pool facility is wheelchair accessible, and can be rented for private functions after hours by contacting the park administration office. Rental costs include certified lifeguards.

The beach is somewhat narrow and the lake is quite shallow in the park area, so the water can be dirty if it's been stirred up. There is a buoyed swimming area, and a large barrier-free beach shower and change room; use the same parking area as for the pool facility. No lifeguards will be on duty. The sand is coarse but deep enough for the favorite summer pastime of castle-building, and it is regularly groomed to soften it and remove trash. Sorry—no pets are allowed on either the sand or the grassed area; signs are posted. There are vast areas of grass behind the beach, and a paved nature trail runs south from the beach change rooms to near the campground. Pine Point picnic area is located just off this trail about halfway down its length, right at the end of the parking lot. Tall shade trees and lush lawns make this a very popular place at lunch time. Another picnic area, Shady Lane, is located at the other end of the parking lot, closer to the pool. There are picnic tables and pole BBQs scattered throughout both picnic areas but no firewood; I suggest you use charcoal briquettes instead. It is, after all, illegal to bring your own firewood into the park.

SPORTS

There are a great many things to do off the beach and out of the pool, if you've a mind to. There are four playgrounds in the park, the largest beside the concession near the pool and two in the campgrounds; the fourth is located beside the tennis courts north of the golf course. Although they differ somewhat in size, they all feature colorful creative climbers, diggers, teeter-totters and swings set into deep sand; all the equipment is well-kept and quite sturdy. There are two sand volleyball courts located near the campground office, with picnic tables on the lawn beside and benches for the players to rest upon. There are also two horseshoe pits in the area; horseshoes and volleyballs can be rented at the campground office.

To the north of the pool area just past the boat launch you will find a 9-hole, sand-green golf course, free for patrons. There are no club or cart rentals, no pro-shop, no tee reservations but (most importantly) no fees! Although regularly mowed, it is naturally watered and can be a bit dry in the late season. Still, it's a wonderful place to begin educating your wee "Tigers" about the life-long frustration known as golf! Besides, the fairways are lined with berries in season, and I've been known to pick more than a few edible mushrooms from the woods surrounding the course. Just a word of caution though: know your mushrooms before you eat them—not all are edible! There is no water or food service on the course, so bring your own. For those wishing a more challenging game, Moon Lake Golf and Country Club is available about 15 km north of the park. Contact them directly at (306) 382-5500 or check their website at: www.moonlakegolf.com/.

Just past the golf course are the tennis courts. There are two of them on paved courts inside a meshed compound. There are no equipment rentals, and the courts are free on a first-come, first-served basis. You'll also find the ball diamond here, with its tall mesh backstop and grass infield. There are benches for players and some trees for shade, but neither facility has potable water so you'd best bring your own. As mentioned above, there is also a playground in this area; something for the wee ones while you're showing the world how good you are!

There is a mini-golf built across the parking lot from the store and concession. It is open daily from late June through to the Labor Day weekend in September, with putter and ball rentals from the booth at the gate; the booth has the prices listed on the wall. It can be rented for a private function or for groups; contact them directly at (306) 220-3282.

HIKING

There are two hiking trails established, the first of which is the lakeside promenade with its paved, barrier-free walkway and timbered observation decks. If you enjoy bird watching, this is an obvious choice as there will be songbirds in the trees behind you, shorebirds in front of you, and waterfowl on the lake; there are over 200 species of birds that either pass through here or make the park their home! It is approximately 500 meters in length (one way) and a gentle walk.

The other hike is more strenuous as it carries you into the natural sand dunes in the southeast corner of the park. The "Gift of Green Nature Trail" is a self-guided 1.5-km loop that winds through woodlands, short grass prairie and into the dunes and back. Trailhead is the Nature Center behind the campground office. Bicycles cannot be used on the trail, and the sand alone makes it unsuitable for wheelchairs.

SERVICES

A new undertaking for this park is the construction of rental cabins known as Night Owl Camping Cabins. They have electric heat, a mini-fridge and 2 rooms which can sleep up to 6. Each cabin has a 2-meter covered deck plus picnic table, pole BBQ and outdoor potable-water spigot. The cabins all share a modern washroom and shower facility reserved for their use only. For prices and availability contact the park directly at (306) 651-0879, or toll-free (in Saskatchewan only) at 1-877-651-0879 (e-mail: nightowlcabins @sasktel.net). Persons renting the cabins may also be interested in renting the recreation hall for a private function; contact the administration office directly for more details at the address below.

The park offers a series of interpretive programs in the months of July and August, free for camping patrons. There is literally something on every day, with most activities beginning at the Nature Center behind the campground office. The Nature Center also houses the collection of mounted animals and birds collected over the years and presented as a naturalist display with informative placards. Campers interested in enhancing their stay in the park can make use of all four of the self-use nature packs, available at the campground office. The packs include materials and guide books to showcase the following areas: Bird-Watching, Insect Collecting, Orienteering, and Pond Dipping. Pike Lake Provincial Park offers an Education Package for teachers interested in bringing classrooms to the park as part of outdoor education. Contact the park directly for more information.

The park boasts a private concession near the pool which offers a wide range of groceries and camping items. Known as "The Huddle," it also offers a concession service with all the usual iced treats, pop, and candy. It has barrier-free picnic tables outside as well as wheelchair access to the store and restaurant. As a restaurant it offers indoor seating for patrons to enjoy grilled items such as burgers and fries. Open from mid-June to the Labor Day weekend, from 1000–1700 hr on weekdays and to 2000 hr on weekends; they can be reached in season at (306) 668-4910.

This is a popular park, mostly due to the pool amenities and camping so close to the major urban center of Saskatoon. Pike Lake is now part of the Reserve-a-Site program; you can contact the park beginning in January each year to book a site, contact the park office for more details. The park is also very busy during the period when swimming lessons are on, so plan accordingly. For more information on this pretty park; contact the park administration at:

Pike Lake Provincial Park
102-112 Research Drive
Saskatoon, SK   S7K 2H6
Telephone: (306) 933-6966
E-mail: pikelake@serm.gov.sk.ca
Website: www.saskparks.net.

East-Central Saskatchewan

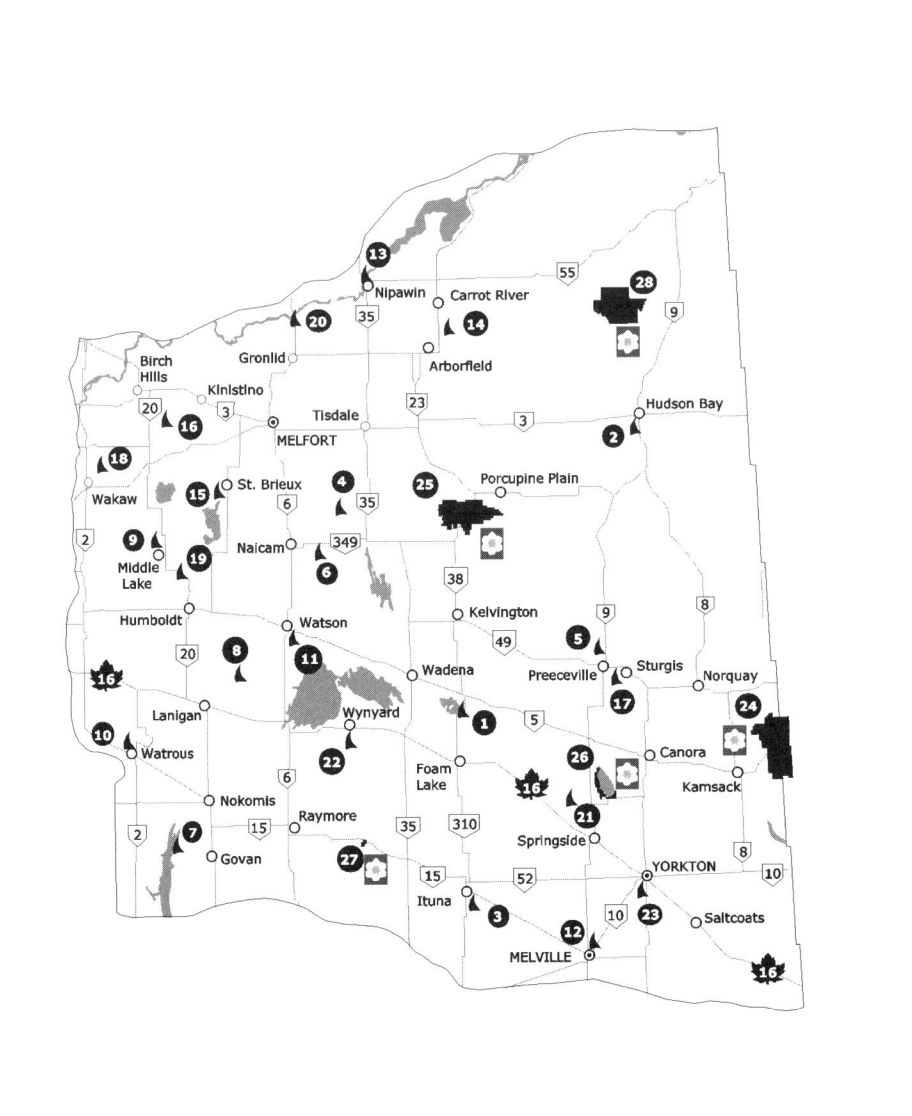

FISHING LAKE REGIONAL PARK AUTHORITY

The Fishing Lakes Park Authority takes in three distinct and (to a certain extent at least) autonomous groups: K.C. Beach Regional Park, Leslie Beach Regional Park and the Foam Lake Golf and Country Club. Saskin Beach is no longer part of the Regional Park structure as it was irretrievably damaged due to the unprecedented flooding of the lake in recent years. Fishing Lake itself is located just south of Kuroki off Hwy 5 on Hwy 310, which leads to Foam Lake on the Yellowhead (Hwy 16). Hwy 310 provides access to all the parks, and is in generally good condition although parts were damaged in the flooding.

K.C. BEACH REGIONAL PARK

This park is located 25 km north of Foam Lake on Hwy 310. Open from Victoria Day weekend to the middle of September, this 10-acre park boasts a wonderful campgrounds as well as serviced lots for lease. Vehicles require a $5 daily pass or an annual Regional Park sticker for entry.

SITES

This park has well-laid-out campgrounds with many open grassed areas among the tall poplars that shade its 75 electrified sites. The sites rent for $17 per night (or $120 per week) or $14 for a tent; 50 of the sites are reserved for seasonal campers, costing $575 for the period May through September. Mind you, the tenters may wind up on the lawn near the main shower house beside the horse shoe pits. A map is available to guide you to your site after you register. The sites are generally roomy, well sheltered amid mature poplars and pines, and graced with picnic tables and pole BBQs. Trash bins are centrally located and firewood is available for a nominal fee. Water is available from the park office/store as it must be brought in due to the flooding; the wells and water lines are unreliable at the moment although I'm sure that will change. Weekends tend to be busy, and reservations are recommended; call the park office for details.

WATER SPORTS

A fine boat launch can be found at the end of the entrance road with a dock to assist boaters. Persons renting seasonal sites will have dock space available to them, while others pay a $5 pier and boat launch fee. Anglers find the lake a haven for walleye and pike as evidenced by the new fully equipped, indoor filleting station. A tagged fish derby takes place on the August long weekend where registered anglers vie for cash prizes should they catch specifically numbered fish; contact the park office for details. Since the first edition of this book, the water level has receded to the point where the lake once again echoes to the sound of water-skiers and power boats towing tubes and kneeboards, and the happy laughter of children playing in the sand of the two swimming areas.

SERVICES
The Town of Foam Lake, about fifteen minutes away, has all the major services a traveler may need. The park office is also a general store where simple grocery items can be purchased as well as a line of fishing tackle. Open from 0800–2200 hr daily, the store offers the usual iced treats, pop and snack foods, videos, and carries a line of local crafts and candles for the discerning shopper. Two playgrounds are available, one placed to the left of the store entrance (by the tenting area), which offers a lawn filled with swings, teeter-totters, and a creative play center, and another new one on the main beach. Four modern washroom facilities are available with coin operated showers, flush toilets, and sinks as well as two newly renovated shower facilities. The park now boasts 40 cottage owners taking in "the greatest sunsets you've ever seen." For more information on this beautiful campground or to reserve a site, contact the park office at:

> K.C. Beach Regional Park
> PO Box 831
> Foam Lake, SK   S0A 1A0
> Telephone: (306) 272-3993 in season.

LESLIE BEACH REGIONAL PARK
Located about 22 km north of Foam Lake on Hwy 310, this park is open from early April until late October. The park gates are staffed from 0800–2200 hr on weekdays and twenty-four hours per day on weekends by security staff. Although the rising lake waters have wrought havoc with hundreds of cabin owners around this popular lake, this regional park's beach remains a wonder. Park entry is $6 per day or $30 for a seasonal pass.

SITES
The campgrounds are well organized with streets and avenues to make site-finding easier. There are 54 electrified sites costing $20 per night and $125 weekly. The park has also built 70 seasonal sites; contact the park office for rates and availability. The sites are naturally leveled and drained, and most offer tall poplars for shade. All sites have picnic tables and pole BBQs, with trash bins in central locations. Potable water is not supplied to the campsites so bring your own; drinking water is sold at the entrance office. We found the site size to be generally adequate, with well graveled roadways to maneuver even the largest trailer. The two modern toilet facilities are wheelchair accessible, and have coin operated showers. Firewood costs $3 per bundle at the entrance office. A spacious playground by the campgrounds has slides, swings, teeter-totters and a creative play center. A smaller playground is available beside the beach concession, near the camp kitchen and picnic area. A new, 18-hole mini-golf course has been built near the entrance office which rents clubs and balls. Groups wishing to camp here will be accommodated as needed in the main campgrounds. Sites can be reserved by calling the park office, particularly on the weekend as this is a popular park. Call the park gate at (306) 272-3968 for the latest information and to reserve a site.

WATER SPORTS

The beach in this park is a wonder: wide, deep, and filled with wonderfully even sand, this beach rivals some I've seen in famous resorts. A huge buoyed swimming area demarcates the safe zone from the water-skiers and "sea-doos," and is anchored by the beach concession. Pets are allowed in the park, but restricted from the waterfront area: park security regularly patrols the beach. One set of Red Cross swimming lessons are offered in mid-July; costs vary depending on level and applicants should call the park office to register. A boat launch is available with a large parking space for trailers; it is free for registered campers although others must pay a $5 fee. Walleye and pike can be caught here, and a tagged fish derby is held in the lake annually.

GOLFING

The Foam Lake Golf and Country Club has an excellent 9-hole, grass-green golf course located about 500 meters from the park gates. This gem of a course is thought of as one of the province's best 9-hole courses—a must-play! It is 2913 yards long and a par 35, and recently added a lake to its first fairway, using the soil from that to elevate some fairways. It has a fully licensed clubhouse that serves light meals. A pro-shop rents clubs and carts and offers a full range of golf equipment for sale. A well-groomed practice green and a driving net will hone your swing prior to the match, and all for $16 for 9 holes or $26 for 18 holes. Tee times can be reserved by calling the pro-shop at (306) 272-3801.

SERVICES

The town of Foam Lake is only 15 minutes away, and offers a full range of shopping, mechanical, medical and worship services. The beach concession sells the usual range of iced treats, pop, and snacks as well as light meals such as burgers and fries. The Fishing Lake Lodge, just to the right of the park gate, offers light house-keeping units, a licensed dining room, and a lounge with live entertainment on some weekends. For more information on this park, contact the manager at:

   Leslie Beach Regional Park
   PO Box 478
   Foam Lake, SK   S0A 1A0
   Telephone: (306) 272-3968.

HUDSON BAY REGIONAL PARK

Located 116 km east of Tisdale on Hwy 3, or 200 km north of Yorkton on Hwy 9, this park is open from early May to late September, although the golf course may be open longer as weather permits. The park was built in 1971, and its gates are open from 0900–2200 hr in season. It is located about a kilometer south of Hudson Bay on Hwy 9. The park features mature boreal forest as cover, and interesting terrain as the park is trisected by three rivers: the Fir, Red Deer, and Etomante rivers. Park entry fees are $5 per day per vehicle, or free with an annual Regional Park pass.

SITES

There are 30 electrified sites and 5 non-electrified sites in two areas. The sites cost $17 (30 amp), $15 (15 amp) and $12 per night. Four of the non-electrified sites are reserved for tenting only, and an overflow area to the left of the park gates has 13 very nice electrified sites. The sites in the main area, to the right of the park gates, are naturally leveled and drained, while the overflow sites are leveled with gravel. All sites have picnics tables, trash bins, and fire grates on cement pads. Drinking water is available from a central tap, and firewood is available free of charge from several central bins. The sites are generally roomy, and are nestled among tall pines which provide shade and the smell of the north. Toilet facilities vary from modern, in a new shower house, to basic in the campgrounds. All were in good condition with smooth, painted cement floors. One dining shelter is available in the upper picnic area beside the playground, and three areas of the park can be reserved for group camping. To reserve a site, contact the park office at (306) 865-4144, or the town office at (306) 865-2263; there is no charge for this service.

A new addition is the Ruby Lake recreation site about 8 km north of Hudson Bay on Hwy 109. It has 9 unserviced sites and access to Ruby Lake for recreational boating. There is a boat launch, beach, swimming area, and picnic area with pole BBQs, picnic tables, and vault toilets. There is no water supply, so boil the lake water before consumption. Alas, there are no fish in this lake but there are many other lakes in the area all teeming with fish for your angling pleasure.

SPORTS

The park has a wide variety of sporting equipment, including badminton and volleyball courts. The playgrounds have tetherball, horseshoe pits, log climbing equipment, swings, teeter-totters, merry-go-rounds, a playhouse, and a climbing tree. A trampoline is fenced into its own enclosure. All are gaily painted and in excellent condition. There are three hiking trails that explore the local terrain, covering a total of 15 km. The trails converge at the lower picnic grounds, where a map is painted on a sheet of plywood to describe them. They are well traveled and easy to follow. No guides have been written to describe the trails as they wander along the Fir River through mature boreal forest. An excellent slow pitch/fastball facility has been built in a natural amphitheater. The three diamonds in the Park each have two sets of bleachers and a tall mesh backstop on a metal frame. The complex complements the four municipal diamonds in Hudson Bay, and has a concession stand that operates during tournaments. Shooters may be able to practice at the Pasquia Gun Club, which has a rifle, trapshoot, and handgun range at the south end of the park. Their clubhouse features an indoor range, and they have a silhouette range within the Red Deer Downs. Anglers can try their luck for pike and walleye in the Red Deer River, or they can make the park their base for an assault on the many lakes and rivers teeming with fish in the area. Opened in 1982, the Red Deer Downs offers an annual rodeo with chuckwagon and chariot racing, gymkana and horse show events. The Downs also has a concession stand, clubhouse and a riding arena. A series of groomed cross-country ski trails can be found within the park. There are 30 km of trails with varying degrees of difficulty for the winter enthusiast. As you can see, there is a lot of activity in and about the park!

GOLFING

Deserving special mention, this 9-hole grass green course is a popular place for the amateur and skilled alike. The fairways are narrow but very pretty and lined with spruce and pine trees. The terrain has some vertical shift as the course is set among low rises, so the 2821-yard par-35 course is a pleasant play. The clubhouse is licensed and serves as a pro-shop as well. Clubs and carts can be rented, and a small line of balls, tees, gloves and the like are available for sale. A scorecard is available to show you the course, and greens fees are $12 per 9-hole round or $22 for 18 holes. Tee times may be reserved, or tournaments booked, by calling the clubhouse at (306) 865-2100.

SERVICES

There is no shopping within the park itself. The town of Hudson Bay has a full range of shopping, mechanical, medical, and worship services. The town operates a museum dealing with the local history, and a souvenir shop is available. Entrance fees are a silver donation. The park hosts a rodeo on the August long weekend. Ball tournaments are held in both July and August, and many golf tournaments are held throughout the season. For those seeking more information about the park and area, check out the website at www.townofhudsonbay.com. For more information or to reserve a site, contact the park office at:

>Hudson Bay Regional Park
>PO Box 69
>Hudson Bay, SK   S0E 0Y0
>Telephone: (306) 865-4144
>Fax: (306) 865-2800
>E-mail: hudson.bay@sasktel.net

ITUNA AND DISTRICT REGIONAL PARK

Located just a kilometer from Ituna, this park was first built in 1967. It's open from the Victoria Day long weekend in May until the middle of September. Its pride and joy is its new swimming facility, and the golf course draws a strong local following. The park levies a $7 per vehicle daily entrance fee, waived if you have an annual Regional Park sticker.

SITES

There are 12 electrified sites, with 15-amp service, and 5 non-electrified sites. They rent for $10 per night if you require electrical hook up, and $7 per night if you do not. All sites are naturally leveled and drained, with picnic tables, pole BBQs, and trash cans. Campsites are rented at the pool booth on a first-come, first-served basis. Firewood is available in central bins by the playing field, site #4, and the dining shelter. Shade trees are plentiful, both natural and planted poplars and some evergreens. There are no group or family camping sites, but there is an open field beside the dining shelter (built by the local Lion's Club) with a few extra pole BBQs that should suffice for extra campers. Washroom facilities vary from primitive biffies in the camping area to flush toilets in the golf clubhouse, and showers and flush toilets in the pool building. Drinking water is provided from one central tap in the camping area, and another in the kitchen facility. The kitchen facility can be rented for private functions, and has running water, a stove, fridge, freezer, and natural gas outlet. A building in back of it would function as a beer hall or garden, and its proximity to the ball diamonds would make it an ideal watering hole during a tournament. Contact the Park Secretary for details at the number and address below.

WATER SPORTS

A junior Olympic swimming pool was built in 1995 and is the cornerstone of this park's recreational ability. It offers 4 lesson sets, starting in late June, and may offer 5 sets in the years to come, so popular has this pool become. Lessons vary in price, depending on which level is desired, and cost between $27 and $37 per swimmer. Those wanting Bronze Cross or Medallion classes will pay $72. The pool is open from 0800 hr until 2100 hr, and is closed daily at noon. Public swim times are from 1300–2100 hr daily, and will cost $2 per person for the whole day. There is a 1-meter diving board for play, and a large grassy sward to sunbathe on. The pool house has 3 showers per side, free for registered campers, and large change rooms. A playground is built beside the pool house, and has the usual equipment young campers desire. For more information on the aquatic program, contact the lifeguards at (306) 795-2693 in season, or the park secretary if the pool isn't open.

GOLFING

A fine, 9-hole sand-green golf course, known as the Ituna and District Golf and Country Club, adds to the fun this park offers, covering 2311 yards over its par 34. The clubhouse is just to the right of the pool as you drive in, on top of the gentle hill. Built in 1980, it has flush toilets and a comfortable view of the first and ninth fairways. It's generally open, but rarely has anyone in it except for during tournaments. It has a kitchen as well, and can also be rented for private functions. There is no pro-shop, club or cart rentals, putting greens, or driving range. The course is set amid treed fairways in gently rolling hills, and is quite a delightful play. Greens fees are modest, only $10 per day, and payable on the honor system in the clubhouse. The course won't normally be busy enough to warrant tee reservations; simply show up to play and enjoy yourself!

SERVICES

The park has also built a ball complex, with three diamonds arranged in fan shape around a low hill that functions as spare bleachers. The diamonds each have tall mesh backstops on metal poles, bleachers for patrons, and benches for the players. The infields are of well maintained grass and there is plenty of parking although little shade. The park holds several ball tournaments yearly, mostly in June, complete with canteen and beer garden. There are golf tournaments as well, varying in date throughout the season. The park also celebrates Canada Day with sports, fireworks, and fun for all. Their big celebration, though, is the Carlton Trail Days, held on the third weekend in July. Sports, swimming events, a cabaret, and other events combine to make this a most popular weekend in the Ituna area. The park has almost no shopping at all, except during events, and all needful shopping can be done in Ituna. It also has mechanical, medical, and worship services for the traveler. There is a museum in town (not operated by the park) that helps explain the significance of the local history; ask the pool staff for details on operation and cost. This is a quiet little park, busy by day but not at night except for the listed events. One can wander the woods and pick berries, watch for birds, and generally relax. For more information on this park, or to book your event, contact the park secretary at:

Ituna and District Regional Park
PO Box 76
Ituna, SK S0A 1N0
Telephone: (306) 795-3460
Pool house: (306) 795-2693
Fax: (306) 795-2688.

KIPABISKAU LAKE REGIONAL PARK

Located 42 km south of Tisdale just 12 km off Hwy 35 on a grid road, this park's campgrounds are open from the end of May to the middle of September. As the resort village of Kipabiskau Lake is accessed just beyond the park boundary, the park itself never really closes. Featuring parkland forest along a long, narrow lake, the park has some wonderful hiking trails, decent berry picking, fairly large sites, and great water skiing! Indeed, water sports are a main feature of this parks many attractions. Daily entry fees of $7 per vehicle are waived if you have an annual Regional Park sticker.

SITES

There are 35 serviced sites in Areas A, B, and C and 12 unserviced sites. The serviced sites all have 30-amp electrical service and cost $18 per night. Most of the unserviced sites are situated along the lakeshore and so they cost $20 each. They are, however, prime sites as they combine tall trees with the chance to have your boat just beside your campsite. There are 4 unserviced sites to the left of the main road across from the beach playground, costing $14 per night. A new feature is the installation of 7 full-serviced sites. All the sites were naturally leveled and drained, although some of the new serviced sites have a lot of gravel on top of the sand base. Generally speaking, the sites are large, well shaded by tall poplars, and even the farthest an easy walk from the main beach and marina. We did find that the sites just by the shower facility were narrow, and getting a large trailer in may be a problem. No such trouble exists for the other two serviced areas, though. The toilet facilities are primitive in the areas, but the coin-operated shower facility is bright and new. Wood is available in central bins, and water is piped to central taps. All sites have pole BBQs, and a number of them have firepits on cement pads as well. All site equipment was in good condition, with most of the picnic tables freshly painted. Sites can be rented seasonally, costing up to $975 per season including the park pass. Only 5 sites are currently available for seasonal rent, though; call the park office for details. All other sites can be reserved by calling the park office at least three days in advance. Something new for the park is the rental cabin they have available; the upper floor can house 8 people comfortably, and the main floor can house 4. Both venues offer light housekeeping and are close to the beach and marina; contact the park office for details.

WATER SPORTS

Kipabiskau Lake is about 10 km long and 1 km wide. The Regional Park operates a marina and boat launch just to the east of the beach campsites, where you can rent paddle boats, canoes and kayaks, or purchase fishing tackle and aquatic supplies. Motor boats are also available for rent, costing $10 per hour for a boat and motor; gasoline is extra. Sport fishing is popular, as jackfish, walleye, and perch can be caught. Protected by tall hills on its major axis, the lake has become a haven for the water-skiing set. Indeed, two-time World Freestyle Champion Jim Clunie trains here. The water-skiing equipment is the property of the Kipabiskau Water Sports Club; only members of the club may use the equipment, for insurance reasons, but new members are welcome. Check with the people in the marina for details. They operate a water-ski clinic, usually in the first two weeks of July, and often have members of the national team as guest coaches. The waterfront extends to the east of the marina and includes an excellent beach and dock system where swimming lessons are offered in the summer months. Both Red Cross and RLSS levels are offered by qualified instructors; prices and times are available from the marina staff. The buoyed swimming area is large and the water quality excellent. The waterfront staff also operates an evening program for the children offering songs, skits, campfires, and the odd movie. Inquire at the marina for details. There are also modern, wheelchair accessible washrooms at the beach in the new laundry/change house and in the store. The store sells the usual confectionery items and light meals including pizza, lasagna and dry ribs. It also sells simple grocery items like milk, bread, and eggs. There are two playgrounds available, the largest being right on the beach, including slides, swings, teeter-totters, and climbers. The other playground is located to the east of the serviced sites, and has less equipment but more room to run about, including a ball diamond and a basketball hoop. Both playgrounds have sand to break the fall of unwary climbers, and the equipment is all in excellent condition.

HIKING
The park is set among some interesting hills, and the managers have taken advantage of that in planning the hiking trails. They have created 5 trails totaling 10 km that intertwine at various stages; they are well blazed and named, and one can wander peacefully without worrying about getting lost. The same trails offer the Nordic skier some challenges in the winter, and as the trails are closed to ATV's and snowmobiles you needn't worry about the peace being challenged by an unmuffled engine. The hike will take you back into the higher meadows where you can pick wild saskatoons and blueberries or maybe find some wild mushrooms in season. Many large rocks are encrusted with colorful lichens, which make for interesting photo opportunities. Across the lake from the park is another good berry-picking area, but no trails exist and you are off the park property so you may wish to ask about wandering about on the far side before you go.

SERVICES
The town of Tisdale is the nearest center for shopping and other services. Most small purchases can be made right in the park at the concession which is open from 0800–2100 hr daily. Due to the interest in water-skiing this park is famous for, it can be busy, particularly for the Canada Day celebrations. A fish derby, sand castle competition, fireworks, and other activities make this weekend one of the park's busiest. Although pets are allowed, they must be leashed and they are barred from the waterfront. Quiet time is 2200 hr, enforced by patrol and eviction. Mind you, this is generally a quiet park, and few such problems have occurred. For more information on the park or to make a reservation, contact the managers at:

Kipabiskau Regional Park
PO Box 325
Tisdale, SK   S0E 1T0
Telephone: (306) 873-4335; Fax: (306) 873-4785; E-mail: kippark@sasktel.net

LADY LAKE REGIONAL PARK

Located 8 km north of Preeceville on Hwy 9, this park is partially administered by the Sturgis Regional Park Board. The Lady Lake managers are working at building their own park board, and they hope for autonomy soon. The park is open from the Victoria Day long weekend until the end of September, and offers one of the most spectacular floral displays in the province. Park entry fees of $3 per day are waived if you have an annual Regional Park sticker.

SITES

There are 37 electrified sites and 7 non-electrified sites. Of the electrified sites, 8 have 30-amp service and the remainder have 15-amp service, costing $17 and $14 per day, respectively. Unserviced sites cost $6 per night (prices are subject to change without notice). Depending on where the site is, it may be leveled with a gravel pad or naturally leveled. All sites are carved out of aspen parkland forest, and shaded from at least two sides. The sites all have picnic tables, firepits with swinging grates, and access to central trash bins. Firewood is provided free, and drinking water is available from a central well. The same water is pumped to the shower house where metered showers (costing $1 per use) with wheel chair access are provided. Washroom facilities vary from primitive biffies in the camping areas to modern flush toilets in the shower house. A new bathroom has been built with sinks and toilets. There is no area set aside for family or group camping. A map is available of the park detailing campsites and building function, and is provided when you register. Simply set up in the site you desire and the park manager will be around in the early evening to collect the fees. There is a hall with a stage available for rent for $150 per day, and a beer hall or open seating area in a natural amphitheater called "The Circle" that rents for $50 per day. The kitchen rents for $75 per day and includes running water and all the stoves, etc. Walk-in coolers rent for $1 per hour to cover the cost of electricity, and the park now offers two new gas BBQs for $10 each per day, fuel included. As you can see, this park is admirably set up to host your reunion! All the buildings are in excellent condition and special access has been made for wheel chairs throughout. Reservations are accepted for any or all of these buildings and the campsites by contacting the park manager at the address below; deposits are required.

WATER SPORTS

Lady Lake has been stocked with two types of trout—rainbows and tigers—and anglers report good fishing with 4 pound trout common. The lake is part of the provincial aeration scheme, so it won't freeze in winter. The trout population can breed and grow in the lake, making fishing popular. A boat launch and filleting table are available, but no motorboats are allowed. Trolling motors (electric), rowboats, and canoes are all that you'll need on this lake. A swim beach just below the hall complex has the playground in behind, complete with swings, slides, merry-go-rounds, teeter-totters, and several dome-shaped climbing structures. All these are brightly painted, built of metal to last, and situated in a large lawn. The swim beach is small so few sand castles can be built, but the shallow area has a dock to play on. The water is clean and the lake has a fine, sandy bottom in the swim area, with a large shallow area to splash about in. Swim lessons are taught in July or August, depending on instructor availability; contact the park manager for details and registration. There are change rooms and the shower house is quite close.

HIKING

No doubt about it, this park is in a class of its own for the sheer number of flowers planted here each year by the many volunteers. Broad walkways are lined with perennials and annuals in huge beds, with benches to rest upon and tall trees for shade. The walkways are broad enough for wheeled traffic so persons in wheelchairs can be brought right out to the picnic site. Because of the variety of flowers and the colorful way they are laid out, each turn in the path is another delight. Birds of many sorts have chosen this park as their summer home, so they add their cheerful song to the scent of flowers wafting in the air. There are no established hiking trails, but there are many walkways that wind about through the picnic and day-use areas, and along the lakeshore. The mature parklands forest also offers its own charm, with plentiful saskatoon and cherry picking in season, and mushrooms for those who can identify the edible ones. The picnic areas have tables, trash bins, and large stone firepits set in private bays in the aspens that offer shade and privacy for the day. Here too you will find flower beds to delight the eye although there are also cautionary signs asking patrons to keep from chasing errant balls into the bush! The floral array in this park is a testament to the years of dedication, hard work, and vision of a handful of people who have labored long for our benefit, and I want to thank them for that work; it is appreciated.

SERVICES

Besides the above mentioned sports, the park also has a ball diamond with a tall mesh backstop on wooden poles, benches for the players, and bleachers for spectators. The facility is in a large grass field with plenty of parking, and there is no charge for using it. The park has a canteen selling the usual treats, ice, and fresh coffee. For larger purchases, Preeceville will have all you need, including shopping, mechanical, medical, and worship services. A trailer dump station is also available although there may be a charge for using it. The park hosts an annual jamboree on the second weekend of August with many events for patrons of all ages. Events include local musical talent, an Old-Time Fiddlers competition, a beer garden, and more. Last year it was attended by over 700 people! The park won't normally be full, although the long weekends are busy. This is a quiet park that has worked hard at its beauty. If you like a quiet walk among flowers and birds, some peaceful trout fishing, and quiet campgrounds then Lady Lake is for you. It is well situated to host your family reunion, a wedding, or just a week of recharging your batteries. I hope you enjoy your stay! For more information on this charming park, or to make reservations, contact the park manager at:

Lady Lake Regional Park
PO Box 274
Endeavour, SK S0A 0W0
Telephone: (306) 547-3242; Fax: (306) 547-2793.

LAKE CHARRON REGIONAL PARK

Located 13 km from Naicam, the park is on an island in the middle of the lake. Open from mid June to early September, the park can be a bit difficult to find. The Department of Highways sign south of Naicam on Hwy 6 directs you to the park on 13 km of grid roads. Hwy 349 east of town has a small white sign that states "Lake Charron 3 km" and points south. The grid road is in good shape, but the highway is better. One recent development is that the park is renting cottages by the day or week. Daily park access fees of $2 per vehicle are waived if you have an annual Regional Park sticker.

SITES
As one drives in, a large open space has ball diamonds to the right, along with a large beer hall and concession used during tournaments. To the south of this is the beach, playground and picnic area. The park has 34 electrified and 24 non-electrified sites, most of which are in behind the ball complex. There are also 12 tenting sites available. The park is removing the stone fire pits and replacing them with pole BBQs. A major refurbishment and cleanup program has been instituted, so the sites are much cleaner than our previous visit. They are also refurbishing all the picnic tables, repairing and painting as needed. The sites are located in tall aspen and birch trees so are well shaded, and are naturally leveled and drained. Sites cost $5 for a non-electrified site, or $25 a week, or $7 per day and $35 per week for an electrified site; you can have one for the whole season for only $250! No garbage bags were provided for the 45 gallon drums used as trash bins in each site. Firewood is provided free in central bins, some of which were empty in our visit. Water must be boiled before it can be consumed, and is available from a central pump by the beach. Naicam municipal potable water is provided in a container beside the beer hall. Washrooms are primitive and not wheelchair accessible; a trailer dump station is available in town.

WATER SPORTS
The lake had dried up a bit during the dry 1980s, but has made a comeback in recent years. A swim beach with change rooms lies on one side of the island. The men's change room is one large room, and the ladies is subdivided into separate cubicles. The beach sand is coarse but high in clay and so should be good for little construction engineers. The water seemed clean, and the beach had been recently cleaned. A fine floating dock was moored in deeper water to tempt swimmers. Two large stone-ringed firepits anchored one end of

the beach, and both were scenes of active parties although there was little broken glass. The playground in behind the beach had slides, swings, climbers, and a merry-go-round. Most of the equipment was in working order and there was sand underneath to break the falls of the unwary. The picnic area nearby was dotted throughout a wooded area behind the beach. A boat launch can be found to the east of the main campsite area, with a large trailer parking area in behind. The park levies a $1 per day or $5 per season fee for the use of the boat launch. The floating dock hadn't been put out yet, during our visit, and reports of fishing success vary widely (as for most lakes!). The problem is that the lake had receded a few years back and although making a comeback it still isn't at full capacity. The cement part of the boat launch does not reach the water, for instance.

SERVICES

The park has several private cabins to the west of the beach area, and is used in winter by the Naicam Snowmobiling Association, who have a warm-up shack near the beach. It appears to double as a beach concession, but it wasn't open when we were there. It is a canoe rental as well, when the concessionaire is about. The park has four ball diamonds, three of which had small backstops and no other facilities. The main facility is impressive due the large beer gardens, concession, and dance hall beside it. The hall has an electrified stage, ceiling lights, and cement floors. It can probably hold about 500 people on a busy night, but only has two bathroom facilities so bushes may get busy! The seating is currently picnic tables, and the open walls will keep fresh air circulating. A hiking trail off the west of the boat launch leads along the lakeshore. Berries and, in season, hazelnuts line the trail, which forks about 500 meters down. The left fork leads to the park dump and the right fork leads around the island. The town of Naicam has all the shopping, mechanical, medical and worship services the camper could ask for, should the need arise. I must admit that this park has a lot of potential; the island is covered with tall, stately trees and a wealth of shrubs. The beach is a good one and the park board is making every effort to clean things up and keep it so; I wish them well. For more information on the park or to see about renting a cottage, contact the manager:

Lake Charron Regional Park
PO Box 24
Naicam, SK   S0K 2Z0
Telephone: (306) 874-8187
Fax: (306) 874-5516.

LAST MOUNTAIN LAKE REGIONAL PARK

The oral history of the Plains Cree states that the hills to the southeast of Duval were the last things that the Great Spirit built during creation; the name Last Mountain Lake commemorates that tradition. Located 14 km west of Hwy 20, between Govan and Nokomis, this 80-acre park is a bird watcher's dream. The park is located inside the Last Mountain Lake National Wildlife Area (NWA), the oldest bird sanctuary in North America. The NWA is home to thousands of birds because of several unique circumstances; mixed prairie and marshland meet in the only wooded area for miles around. This creates a myriad of habitats for all types of birds, including several species seldom seen elsewhere. The Regional Park is home to the only public bird banding station in the province, a place where you can volunteer to be part of this important work, or simply learn more about this fascinating topic. The banding program is regularly open to the public in May, August, and September. The park itself is open from the Victoria Day weekend to the Labor Day weekend. The gate hours are from 0800–2300 hr daily; vehicle charges of $7 per day or $15 per weekend are waived with an annual Regional Park pass.

SITES

There are 84 electrified sites and 30 non-electrified sites costing $20 (30-amp), $16 (15-amp) per night and $12 per night respectively. They've built 12 new campsites by the bird banding station, and have set 15 electrified sites aside for seasonal campers; these sites cost $770 per season. All sites come with picnic tables and fire grates on cement pads or pole BBQs. Water is available from central taps, and trash bins are available at key locations. Firewood is provided free of charge from a roofed bin in the camping area across from site #39. The sites are quite large, well treed with tall cottonwoods, and naturally leveled. Reservations are accepted with a major credit card by calling the park office; there is a $5 fee. The roadways are well graveled and in good condition. There are two dining shelters in the picnic area along the beach, complete with cement floors, picnic tables and pole BBQs. A large area to the east of the entrance road holds the group camping site and the spacious picnic hall, available for rent for $70 per day, with site rental. This hall is perfect for reunions, weddings, and the like because it has separate toilet facilities, is well electrified, and as plenty of room to hold your group. In the campgrounds are "His and Hers" primitive toilets, some in the shape of teepees, and there are modern facilities in the shower and laundry house near the beach concession. The showers, coin operated, as is the clothes washer and dryer set. A trailer dump station is available beside the boat launch entrance. None of the washroom or toilet facilities can really be considered wheelchair accessible.

WATER SPORTS

The north end of Last Mountain Lake is a haven for trophy pike and walleye, so much so that a sign prominently displayed by the boat launch details the maximum size of fish you are allowed to keep! The park has built a cement boat launch with floating dock and an enclosed fish cleaning station. An ample parking lot is available to hold your trailer during your visit, immediately adjacent to the boat launch. A trailer dump station can be found just to the east of this area. The lake is relatively narrow here, and fairly shallow; reports have it at only 12 to 15 feet deep (about 3 or 4 meters) although it is much deeper to the south of the park. The relatively small beach is covered with fairly coarse sand containing many small pebbles. A floating dock is placed out in the buoyed swimming area for more serious splashing about. A new outdoor swimming pool was completed in 1997 and operates three-lesson sessions in July and August. Both Red Cross and RLSS levels will be taught; contact the park office for dates, times, and prices. As an added benefit the pool is available for private rental to accommodate your function; the pool number is (306) 484-2071! Pool hours will be 0800–2000 hr daily. Note that the waterfront is unsupervised; only the pool will have lifeguards on duty, and only during regular hours. A very nice touch is the extensive flower beds near the beach and picnic area. A fine playground has also been built here, with slides, swings, merry-go-rounds, and climbers, all on a large expanse of grass.

GOLFING

A 9-hole, sand-green golf course is available just to the east of the entrance road. Built and largely maintained by volunteer labor, it is a tribute to the community spirit of the cabin owners and local townsfolk. It is fairly flat, fairly straight, and not that long at 2785 yards. Greens fees are $3 for 9 holes or $5 per day, with a family membership costing $45 per year! The course is in good condition, the fairways well mown, and the ancillary equipment in good repair. All in all, it's well worth the price of admission. There is no clubhouse, driving range, or rental, and no need to arrange tee times unless you wish to host your own tournament. A very popular event locally is the Annual Golf Classic held in mid June with its Texas Scramble format and longest drive competition.

HIKING

Let there be no doubt, this place is a birders dream. I was very impressed with the sheer numbers of birds I saw in my stay, most of which I couldn't identify. The regional park has one hiking trail established which begins at the Nature Center (maps are available for the roughly 2-hour hike); the NWA has two self-guided trails and a driving trail. More information is available from the park office or the NWA Information Kiosk. The NWA is a

20-km drive to the north, from which the two trails lead you to explore the region. The driving tour takes about an hour, and a cassette monologue is available from the park office or the NWA to guide you through. The banding station can be accessed during the months of May, August and September, coinciding with the spring and fall migrations. Not only can you help with your volunteer spirit, a 6-part course is available in bird identification called "Bird Quest." Check with the park office for details.

SERVICES

As you can see by now, there is a lot to do in this busy park. The park hires a recreation director who puts on a craft oriented day program, costing $3 per day per child; check at the recreation hall for details. Two music festivals are held, an old-time music festival as part of the Canada Day celebration, and a rock music concert at the end of the year. Two ball tournaments are also held that attract a wide following among the local sportsters. On these two weekends, one in June, the other in July, the normal quiet time of 2300 hr is allowed to lapse as the revelers can last until about 0400 hr. Mind you, the quiet time is strictly enforced on all other occasions by patrol and eviction, so you needn't worry otherwise. The beach concession will sell the usual snacks, pop and treats, as well as light meals of burgers and fries. Starting in late May every year, the concession offers a popular Sunday smorg, and has supper specials though the rest of the week. There is also a convenience store that sells the usual goods required by campers. More substantial purchases must be made at the nearby towns of Govan or Nokomis. These towns also have medical, mechanical, and worship services available. The park also has about 100 privately owned cabins, some of which may be for rent from time to time; contact the park office for a list of available rental properties. The entire east shore of Last Mountain Lake has a motto: "You're Among Friends." I certainly thought so, and I hope you do too. We always find the park to be well maintained and tidy, a sign of the obvious pride the park employees take in its appearance. To find out more about this park, contact the park manager at:

Last Mountain Lake Regional Park
PO Box 308
Nokomis, SK   S0G 3R0
Telephone: (306) 424-4483
Fax: (306) 484-2081
E-mail: lmrp@sasktel.net

Website at: www.govansk.com/park.htm

LEROY LEISURELAND REGIONAL PARK

The first thing one notices about this park are the colorful highway signs which have been painted to mark the park. The park is 8 km from Leroy, 24 km east of Hwy 6, south of Watson. Seventy acres in size, the park follows a natural creek bed and is built in a mature aspen forest. Open from the Victoria Day weekend in May until the middle of September, the gates are open from 0800–2100 hr daily in season. The park costs $3 per day to enter, or an annual Regional Park sticker.

SITES

A small campground has 20 electrified (some with 30-amp, some with 15-amp service) which cost $20 and $15 respectively. The 30-amp sites are all full-service with sewer and water; the 15-amp sites have electricity and water only. A trailer dump station is available beside the access road to the second camping loop. The sites have pole BBQs and picnic tables, but are not numbered and so can be confusing to differentiate, particularly as no site map is available to assist. Trash cans are centrally located, and a single water tap serves the electrified sites; firewood is available in central bins. The campsite roadway leads down into a marshy area and so has fist-sized rocks on top of gravel to ensure suitable drainage. All sites are naturally leveled and drained, and well grassed. The perimeter of the camping area is well treed, but there are no trees between sites and so the campgrounds lack a sense of privacy. Toilet facilities are modern, including free showers at the clubhouse and at the beach a short walk away. A log-sided camp kitchen is available with a stone fireplace, a cement floor and a pole BBQ outside; it can be rented for $30 per day. These picnic grounds also double as the non-electrified sites, and are well grassed although no organized or mapped sites are listed. Alas, the beautiful stone picnic fireplaces are gone, the victims of time and the fact that volunteer expertise to maintain them is extremely hard to come by. Sites can be reserved by calling the park office at (306) 284-3437.

WATER SPORTS

The pool is a man made one with a sand bottom and an excellent beach and playgrounds. Beach change rooms and wheelchair accessible showers are available free of charge. Several floating docks allow the eight-feet-deep center of this circular pool to be exploited, as well as serve as instructional aids during lessons. Although there is no natural shade at this pool, several roofed beach shelters provide relief from the sun. To the right of the pool is a large picnic area beside a sand volleyball court. The playground has a sand digger, swings, and teeter-totters, plus two slides which empty into the pool. All the equipment is in good condition, particularly the creative play center which was built in 1993. Pool fees are $3 for adults and $1 for children. Swimming lessons are offered twice, in early July and in early August. A full range of Red Cross levels are offered: contact the park office for details. Tennis and volleyball equipment is available at the concession, free of charge.

GOLFING

A par-36, 9-hole, sand-green golf course completely encircles the park. The first tee is home to the field-stone starter's box, pictured above. The course's 2975 yards criss-cross the little stream seven times. Only two holes are without water hazard, which makes this an interesting course indeed! The clubhouse is open from 0900–2200 hr daily, and has excellent modern washroom facilities free of charge to registered campers. Although naturally watered, the fairways are well cut and play well. The tees are slightly raised and an excellent scorecard guides you through this watery maze. The fairways are bordered by tall aspens and many new trees add to the greenery. Greens fees are $13 for nine holes or $22 for eighteen holes. The concession also rents clubs and pull carts, and will make arrangements for tournaments or to rent the clubhouse for private functions. Normally, tee reservations are not required but you can call the concession at (306) 286-3437 to find out how busy the course is.

SERVICES

Besides the pool and playgrounds, an excellent baseball diamond occupies the west end of the day-use area. Along with a tall mesh backstop and home run fence, the field has ample parking and bleachers for spectators. The park office and concession is open from about 1200–2200 hr daily in season, and sells the usual iced treats, snacks, and pop, as well as light meals. The town of Leroy offers shopping, mechanical, and worship services. There are medical first responders locally and hospital care is available in Watson. For more information on the park, or to make arrangements for a reunion or such, contact the park office at:

>   Leroy Leisureland Regional Park
>   PO Box 305
>   Leroy, SK   S0K 2P0
>   Telephone: (306) 286-3437
>   Fax: (306) 286-3377
>   E-mail: leona.wakelam@leroy.cu.sk.ca

LUCIEN LAKE REGIONAL PARK

This park is located beside Middle Lake on Hwy 20, about 45 km north of Humboldt. If you are driving up from Saskatoon, only the last 26 kilometers are graveled, the remainder is paved. The route is winding, through hills and around a surprising number of small lakes. The first thing you see as you drive in is Bethany Seniors Lodge to your left. Although not a part of the park, it is a wonderful idea to have such easy and free access for the seniors to the park. Indeed, right in the boundary between the two is a dining shelter, very near the huge playground (pictured here) so that proud great-grandparents can sit in the shade and watch all the life around them as the picnic is prepared. Someone had a truly marvelous idea there! The park is open from the May long weekend until the middle of September; gate hours are 0700–2300 hr daily. Park entry fees of $5 per vehicle per day are waived with an annual Regional Park sticker.

SITES

The park has 55 electrified sites and 15 unserviced sites, costing $15 (15 amps), $17 (30 amps), and $10 per night, respectively. So popular is the park becoming that they are building 5 more full service sites! The entire rate sheet is available on request but consider this: a 30-amp serviced site rents for $500 for the whole season; an unserviced site is a mere $200! Two group-sites are available just beside the north corner of the ball complex, capable of holding 70 or so persons. No services are available to each camper, but there will be some water and electrical outlets to serve the group as a whole. All the sites are well treed as they are cut out of mature aspen forest. Interestingly enough, the park has spaced the unserviced sites out by rather a distance, so you really get a feeling of solitude. The unserviced sites are just that, though, so you'd best be self-sufficient. These sites are quite a ways from the main area, so you will have to walk a bit to get to the main attractions. Most of the choice sites (34 in total) near the main swim beach are rented on a seasonal basis, which seems quite reasonable as it is a lovely beach area. We found that all the sites in the 20s were large enough for the majority of campers. Site #15 is a choice site as it is electrified, situated near the outhouses and had a delightful, if small, playground right beside it. All sites have a picnic table (a few are still wood but most are metal-framed now), and either a fire pit on a cement pad or a pole BBQ. Water is piped into central areas, except for the unserviced areas which have no water service at all. Each site has its own garbage can. Wood is available beside the concession, costing $1 for four blocks, or free if you block it yourself. Toilet facilities range from primitive vault-style in the camping areas to modern, newly renovated facilities with hot showers which cost $2 per use or free to registered campers. There is a trailer dump station near the shower building. Sites can be reserved by calling the park office, but you must be 20 years of age or older in order to rent a site.

BALL DIAMONDS

No question about it, the art of baseball in its many forms is something this park takes great pride in. There are 4 ball diamonds each with its own home run fences colorfully decorated with advertisements for the local merchants, bountiful bleachers, an announcer's booth, and very adequate fencing. The two diamonds nearest the concession had roofed dugouts built in 1997; all currently have benches for the players. Tall poles with purple martin condo's are strategically placed to keep the mosquito population at bay, as well as entertain the patrons with their flight. The infields are of grass, and very well kept. Parking is spacious, not only for ball patrons but for those interested in the nearby swim beach. A "beer garden" area can be rented should you wish that service during your tournament, or for reunions, weddings, and the like; it is located to the north of the ball diamonds. Small wonder that provincial championships have been played here, and I can see why private tournaments take up so many summer weekends as companies from as far away as Saskatoon come here.

WATER SPORTS

The beach and attendant playgrounds have got to be seen to be believed! Children will take one look and that will be all; you'll never have to wonder where they are again! The climbing structure, built in 1995, is among the most extensive I've seen, all on wonderfully soft sand to break the falls of unwary users. The beach is buoyed, and has a floating dock with springboard for diving and general larking about. A floating dock separates a wading portion of the lake from the more serious swimming portion. The area encompassed is generous, about 30 feet by 8 feet in dimension, and about 2 feet at maximum depth. This dock allows for both sides to be used in teaching lessons to interested swimmers, usually in the first 2 weeks of July. Both Red Cross and Royal Life Saving Society classes are taught, and family rates are available. Except for the times that lessons are being taught, no lifeguards are in attendance, so swim at your own risk. The beach is filled with fine sand, although a small area has been cleaned away down to the base clay so that young artists can make clay figurines to keep guard on their sandcastle's watchtowers. A beach changeroom is available, and washrooms are close at hand, both on the beach and at the concession. A short walk north along the beach finds the paddle boat rental shack, boats renting for $3 per hour; numbers are limited, so book early! There are two boat launches available, the main and the north dock. Both have fish-cleaning stations in attendance so please use them instead of bringing your catch back to the campsite. Local fishermen catch perch, walleye and pike in the lake, but they can be difficult to catch on account of fishing pressure, so patience is a must!

SERVICES

The park's concession sells the usual summer-time treats, snacks, and pop, as well as rents the mini-golf equipment, for $1 per 9 holes. The dining area in front of the concession is covered by an arched fabric roof to provide shade from the sun and shelter from the rain; as such it promises to be a popular place! The concession not only serves ball patrons, but the swim beach and playground just to the south of it. Prices are reasonable, and I highly recommend the coffee! Two dining shelters are available, one just beside the playground, and one near the paddleboat rental shack. They offer pole BBQs, picnic tables, shade, and shelter from inclement weather. A building beside the ball complex serves as a beer gardens, available for rent during tournaments, weddings, and reunions. Middle Lake is the nearest community and offers a wide range of services including shopping, mechanical and worship. Medical service is available either in Wakaw or Humboldt, both about 45 kilometers away. There are always nurses on duty at Bethany Senior's Lodge, and they will gladly help out in an emergency. As one can imagine from all that goes on here, this park is busy most weekends in July and August. One should consider reserving a site well in advance, giving at least one week's notice. To place a reservation or for more information on this beautiful park, contact the park manager at:

Lucien Lake Regional Park
Box 2
Middle Lake, SK   S0K 2X0
Telephone: (306) 367-4300, Fax: (306) 367-4300.

MANITOU AND DISTRICT REGIONAL PARK

The resort village of Manitou Beach is the overwhelming reason for this park's continued popularity. The mineral waters of Little Manitou Lake are unique for their chemical composition, believed to have healing powers for a bewildering array of ailments. The village is well suited to taking advantage of this natural bonanza as it caters to the post-treatment relaxation of the many visitors. Restful parks, spas, drive-in movies, golf and Danceland (among other features) combine to make this an enviable resort indeed. Situated 6 km north of Watrous on Hwy 365, the lake's very name is rich in Saskatchewan history. The word *Manitou* means God to First Nations people, and they have believed for centuries in the healing powers of this lake and its oily mud. Various ceremonies were performed to increase the healing ability of the water, ranging from drinking the salty water to bathing in the lake or mud, or the full treatment in a sweat lodge. If you stop to think about it, the village still has the same resources! The Regional Park is comprised of 3 parts: the campgrounds, the golf course across the highway and about 500 meters past the park gates, and the beach front. The campgrounds are open from May 1 to October 15, including the Thanksgiving long weekend. Daily park entry fees of $4 per vehicle are waived with the purchase of an annual Regional Park pass.

SITES

The campground is well suited to dealing with large motor homes or trailers as it features more electrified sites than non-electrified. There are 205 electrified sites, with more being built to accommodate the demand; 111 of these sites are fully serviced with 30-amp electrical service, water, and sewer. Nine of these sites are pull-through and cost $21 per night. The other 102 full-service sites cost $19 per day. There are 94 more electrical sites with 15-amp service costing $16 per day; water is available for these sites from central taps. There are also 22 non-serviced sites, costing $13 per day. Weekly rates are available for May and June, and September and October; contact the park office for details. Three sites are available for monthly rental but please note that none of the pull-through sites can be reserved. Other sites can be reserved with a deposit but you'd best do so well in advance; due to its central location and many amenities, this park fills quickly. The sites are all spacious enough to fit the most discerning camper, well treed with tall aspens, and well leveled and drained. The pull-through sites, and those large enough to allow it, all have graveled pads to "park the house" on, with a grass lawn beside. The others feature a lawn upon which to park. Please note that park policy states these sites must have the trailers removed once every week to save the grass; those with a gravel pad have no such problem. There is a trailer dump station between sites 115 and 116. Each site has a picnic table (many appear new this year), a pole BBQ; trash bins are centrally located. There are two camp kitchens available to any camper on a reservation basis: one in the new area on the eastern edge of the campgrounds and the second one by the playgrounds. Other cookhouses can be found in town along the beach for day use. There are three modern shower/washroom facilities in the campground: one near site 50, another between sites 104 and 105, and the newest one by site 195. All are clean, odorless and free to registered campers. Firewood is available for sale at the park office, costing $4 per bundle; some burning barrels are available behind the maintenance shed which can be put on your site if you wish to have a campfire; check with the park office. Except for the fully serviced sites, water service is by central tap; the water supplied is Manitou Beach municipal, and is reverse-osmosis treated. A walking trail leads off the campgrounds to the spa, starting between sites 104 and 105, allowing access to this popular attraction without having to move the house. Sites can be reserved up to three years in advance; there is no charge for this service. You must be at least 18 years of age to rent a site.

WATER SPORTS

The lake is very salty, having a specific gravity similar to sea water so it is much more buoyant than fresh water. Floating is no problem, so sailing and boating are popular past times. A boat launch is available to the west of the village, just past Danceland. As the water is so salty, fishing is nonexistent. Freshwater showers have been erected at intervals along the beach to wash the salt off. The beach equipment is all courtesy of the Regional Park, so playgrounds seem to sprout up on the grass at 500 meter intervals along the beach. Benches and shade trees are everywhere, so adults can have a visit while the children splash about. The beach sand is somewhat coarse, but it should hold together just fine for castle building. A band shell (pictured above) hosts musical performances featuring local talent during the summer months; dates and times are uncertain, so watch for postings on the billboards along the beach. A very colorful beach house and change room can be found at the west end of the beach, near Camp Easter Seal. Recently painted with sea monsters and other fanciful murals, it is a natural draw for the child in us all. Two tennis courts are also free to the public near here, but you must bring your own equipment as only the nets and court are provided. There are no swimming lessons offered in the Regional Park, but a freshwater pool in Watrous does offer lessons in the summer months.

GOLFING

A 9-hole, grass-green golf course can be found just a short walk from the park gates. It is a 3000 yard par-36 course with elevated tees, bunkered greens, and a fully licensed clubhouse with pro-shop. The greens fees are $14 for 9 holes or $24 for 18 holes; some special rates apply based on the season. Reservations are accepted for tee times up to 48 hours in advance without fee, and a service charge of $2 per person is levied for those wishing to make long-term arrangements. The pro-shop carries a full line of merchandise for sale, and can also rent pull carts, clubs, motor carts as well as buckets of balls for the driving range. The clubhouse can be rented for tournaments, including catering and bar rentals, and can accommodate 150 people in the lounge. For details on this or any other aspect of the golf course, including tee times, contact the pro-shop at (306) 946-2861. You can also fax them at (306) 946-2697. Should you wish to contact them out of season, write them at:

Manitou Beach Golf Club
PO Box 1122
Watrous, SK   S0K 4T0

SERVICES

The park does not have a concession or restaurant, except for the golf clubhouse. With the village so close, it doesn't seem necessary! The park does have campgrounds particularly suited to the recreation vehicle, an outstanding golf course, and a wonderful beach complex brimming with play equipment. Mind you, it is strung out over a ways so it reduces strain on any one area. The village offers many other recreational delights such as mini-golf, a weekly flea market, and the world-famous Manitou Mineral Spa. One of the last remaining drive-in theaters in the province is just beside the campgrounds, and one cannot forget Danceland. This amazing dance hall has a wooden floor cushioned with coils of horse hair, so one can dance the night away with greatly reduced foot and ankle strain. Walking in the area will introduce you to the many shore birds that inhabit the area, and the National Wildlife Area of Last Mountain Lake is only a half-hour drive away, where you can partake in the only public-access bird banding station in the province (in season). Small wonder that the park is a busy one! RV clubs regularly congregate here for a jamboree, and family reunions are common as the park is central in the province. For more details on this wonderful park, check out their website at www.manitouregional.com or contact the park office at:

Manitou and District Regional Park
PO Box 1193
Watrous, SK S0K 4T0
Telephone: (306) 946-2588 or (306) 946-2028 (off season)
E-mail: manitouregional@sasktel.net

MCNAB REGIONAL PARK

Located along Hwy 6 on the south edge of Watson, this small park packs a huge recreational punch in its fifty or so acres. The campgrounds are open from the May long weekend to the Labor Day weekend; the golf course may stay open longer as weather permits. Park entry costs $4 per day, waived with an annual Regional Park sticker.

SITES

There are 13 full service sites in this park and one non-electrified site in the picnic area, costing $25 and $7 per night, respectively. All sites feature picnic tables, some of which are metal framed and set into the ground, and pole BBQs. The electrical service is 15-amp, and available on poles between every second campsite. These power stands also have water service on them, with Watson municipal water piped in. Trash bins are available on poles between every second site, and liberally scattered in key locations elsewhere. Toilet facilities are modern and a fine shower house can be found on the road to the pool and golf clubhouse. Showers are free for park patrons and the facility is clean and spacious. Waste water pits can be found in the bush between each site, but no trailer dump station is available in the park. All park sites are surrounded on three sides by mature aspen trees with many varieties of bush, including red dogwood and diamond willow. Thus, shade is assured through most of the summer's heat, and the small campgrounds make for a quiet, friendly atmosphere. All sites are built up on sand and gravel pads, so they are quite level and drain well. Firewood is provided in a bin to the east of the campgrounds. Check in to an open site then walk over to the new golf facility to register.

WATER SPORTS

The park sports a fine outdoor pool, built in 1998, that has a separate paddling pool and creative playground for wee folk. The pool varies from three feet to twelve feet deep and has one diving board. Of special interest is a viewer's gallery where anxious mothers can watch their little treasures at their lessons. Behind the chain-link fence, it also provides shaded seating during the many aquatic events and demonstrations held during the short season—an obvious center for activity on a hot summer's day! The pool's entrance fees are modest at $4 for adults, $2 for children 15 and under and free for preschoolers. Season passes are available which will also reduce the cost of lessons from $45 per level to $20 per level. Four lesson sets are offered in the summer months teaching all Red Cross badge levels, as well as RLSS Bronze Medallion and Bronze Cross. Shower and changeroom facilities are provided along with modern toilets. Although no eating or drinking is allowed in the pool area, a concession is available at the golf clubhouse. For more information on the pool or to book lessons space, contact the pool manager at (306) 287-3648.

GOLFING

A 9-hole grass-green golf course awaits the traveler. It has been extensively revised since our last visit, and the clubhouse has been moved as well. The course is a 3174-yard, par 35 with new tee boxes. The fairways are well trimmed and cared for, so you should have a fair lie; a scorecard with map is available. Greens fees are modest at $13 per nine holes or $22 for 18 holes (adult rates), $9 per nine holes or $15 for 18 holes for grade eight students and under. A family season pass is $600 a year! A new, fully licensed clubhouse is available where chips, pop, and snacks can be purchased, as well as a selection of grilled items. Clubs and pull carts can also be rented here, as can a fully enclosed camp kitchen. Costing $25 per day, this building allows for family functions and features a large gas BBQ, spacious grounds, plus horseshoe pits and two tennis courts. Equipment for these two sports is available free of charge at the clubhouse. The concession can be contacted at (306) 287-4240 to book a tee time.

SERVICES

The town of Watson can provide all the shopping amenities plus mechanical, medical, and worship services. The ESSO service on Hwy 6 has a laundromat and the town has a heritage museum downtown. The park may have a small campground, but it has many recreational opportunities based on the pool and golf course. For those interested in more information on this park, contact the park office at:

McNab Regional Park
PO Box 314
Watson, SK S0K 4V0
Telephone: (306) 287-4240
Fax: (306) 287-3465
E-mail: daniel.loehr@sasktel.net

MELVILLE REGIONAL PARK

Located within Melville at the junction of Hwys 10 and 15, this interesting park is open from May 1 until October 1 annually. A novel land use idea is that the park was built over an old nuisance grounds, providing ample green space over what might once have been considered an eyesore. It now features one of the best golf courses in the region, and plenty of quiet camping. The park no longer levies an entrance fee, but expects campers to have an annual Regional Park sticker.

SITES

The park has 124 electrified sites with water and 12 non-electrified sites, costing $20 per night ($100 per week) and $14 per night ($70 per week), respectively. The electrified sites all have gravel pads for the trailers to park upon, whereas the non-electrified sites are naturally leveled and drained. A map to the sites is painted on a large sign at the entrance, between two of the largest prairie lilies I've ever seen! All sites have picnic tables, trash bins, and firepits made of culvert sections with swinging grates. Firewood is provided free from central bins. Several of the sites have mutual access to large firepits suitable for group bonfires. Drinking water, Melville municipal, is available from central taps. Shade is provided by plantation poplars, spruce, and willows, although some sites have greater shade than others. Most sites will be adequate for even the largest unit. Washroom facilities are modern flush toilets, available in the shower house as are free showers. As the facilities are down a short flight of stairs, they cannot be considered wheelchair accessible; they open from 0700–2100 hr daily. More modern shower houses are being developed in the near future. One dining shelter is available in the large picnic or day-use area. Group camping is available in the center, lawned area of the campgrounds, and group numbers will be large. No reservations are accepted, except for large groups, nor will they generally be needed.

SPORTS

The park itself doesn't maintain the pool, but the city has one adjacent to the park. As it isn't part of the park operation, it isn't considered here, but it is a fine facility with huge lawns, shade trees and a playground—well worth the visit. Besides public swim times there are a full range of lessons open to all. A playground was originally built in 1967 and has been extensively revised this year. It features slides, swings, teeter-totters, and a large creative play center; all the equipment is now maintained by the town. A cross-country ski train runs through the park in winter months, and the city wants to build a paved biking trail through the park.

Of particular pride in this park is the extensive baseball complex. The seven diamonds are anchored by Pirie Field with its tall mesh backstop and players' dugouts. All the diamonds have crushed shale or gravel infields, grass outfields, and short mesh home run fences. A large expanse of lawn is the parking lot, and concessions will open during tournaments. Bleachers for the fans and modern washroom facilities are on site, and a beer garden tent can be raised if desired. This is also the only park in the system with batting cages and mechanical pitchers; the machinery operates on loonies, and is maintained by the Terry Gould Foundation. All the equipment is in excellent condition, and is an excellent venue for a private tournament; contact the park office for details at the address below.

GOLFING

The Melville Country Club is operated by the park, and is one of the best-kept secrets in the area. It is located about 500 meters north of the main park, across the highway. It has 18 grass-greens on a 6100-yard, par-71 course plus practice putting greens but no driving range. The pro-shop has a full line of equipment for sale or rent, and the clubhouse is fully licensed. It also serves light meals and is open from 0800–2000 hr daily in season. The scorecard available has no map to guide you on your first trip around, but you won't get lost! The real glory of this course, besides its obvious beauty, is the greens fees; 9 holes will cost $16, 18 holes are only $24, and you can golf for the entire day for $32! As you might guess, the course is busy, and tee reservations are recommended, particularly on weekends. You can reserve your tee time by calling the pro-shop at (306) 728-3931.

SERVICES

Besides all the above activities, the park has a museum that showcases local history; there were no entrance fees when we visited. The park is a busy one with many golf and ball tournaments, both private and public, as well as reunions and the like. There is little shopping as the town of Melville has all the shopping, mechanical, medical, and worship services you could want. Although the highway through town runs just past the park, it is fairly quiet as little road noise penetrates the trees. It certainly isn't a wilderness park, but you will find it comfortable, quiet, and friendly. For more information, or to plan your own event, contact the park office at:

Melville Regional Park
PO Box 1358
Melville, SK   S0A 2P0
Telephone: (306) 728-4111
Fax: (306) 728-2103.

NIPAWIN AND DISTRICT REGIONAL PARK

Located on the northwest corner of Nipawin on Hwy 55, this is one of the few truly four-season Regional Parks. Over 300 acres in size, the park never closes as modern cabins can be rented for winter use even if the campgrounds are locked in winter's icy grip. The access road is paved right up to the park gates, and the route is well marked with Department of Hwy signs and the park's own colorful signs. Park entry costs $7 per day, waived with an annual Regional Park sticker.

SITES

There are 114 electrified sites (30-amp service) and 16 full-service sites (30-amp, water and sewer), costing $21 per night. Innumerable non-electrified sites are available in overflow areas as every effort is made to turn no one away. A group site is available capable of holding 14 trailers in electrified sites and many more on its central lawn. The group site has its own camp kitchen, fire rings, pole BBQs and toilets. Two camp kitchens are available in the large day-use and picnic areas, and two more are available: the chalet and a kitchen near site #31. Two shower houses are available to patrons: one near each of sites #78 and #28. Water is piped to every serviced site, and central taps are available to overflow campers. Firewood is also available for $2 per bundle. All sites feature fire grates, picnic tables, and trash bins. They are leveled with gravel and packed sand, and so don't retain water for long after a downpour. The park has built 20 full service seasonally rented sites, removing the two ball diamonds to make room. All camp sites in the park are generous with many being the "pull-through" style. The tree cover is great: most sites are sheltered from at least two directions by mature stands of pine, spruce, birch, and aspen. A trailer dump station is available near site #14. MacSwaney's cabins are available for rent, costing $59 per night, based on double occupancy; contact them directly at (306) 862-4544 or check out their website at www.macswaneyscabins.com. As one can see from this description, this is a popular park and reservations are recommended; call the park office at (306) 862-3237 for yours, or email them at the address below. Reservations must be called and confirmed or they will be lost. Pets are welcomed but must be leashed at all times and the site must be raked upon departure. As a note, checkout time is 1300 hr, but you can pay to extend your stay: $8 for the period 1300–1800 hr; after that you'll be charged for another day's stay.

WATER SPORTS

The park borders the Saskatchewan River, and has some of the best fishing in North

America in the channel. A private business, Twin Marine Boat, has been licensed in the park to rent boats and motors to visiting anglers. Lakewoods Store sells fishing equipment plus snack foods just beside the two fine wheelchair accessible boat launches the park has on the river. New boat launch fees are being levied: $5 per day or $25 for a season's pass. There is a large area at the base of the toboggan hill for boat trailer parking. A fish cleaning plant has one of the few gray water grinders in Saskatchewan. Designed to reduce the smell and nuisance of fish guts, the unit grinds fish waste into minute particles for disposal. A houseboat charter, Aurora Houseboat, also resides on the waterfront, taking parties of anglers out on the river for a scenic cruise and to try their luck. Besides the river, the reservoirs of Tobin Lake and Codette Lake are excellent fishing grounds. To celebrate the art of angling, several tournaments are held annually. The Vanity Cup attracts anglers from as far away as the United States, all trying to catch a walleye bigger than the 17 lb. 6 oz. record caught only a half-mile from the boat launch. Besides the excellent river fishing, a trout pond has been stocked beside the Lakeland Leisure Shop at the top of the hill behind the boat launch. For the smaller camper, a spray pool has been built in the playground, and the town of Nipawin has a swimming pool.

GOLFING
The park has another treat in store: the Evergreen Golf and Curling Club (EG&CC). This 18-hole grass-green course plays a par 72 over 6539 yards. A driving range and a practice putting green will hone your skills prior to the game, and the pro-shop has a full line of retail and rental equipment for patrons. Greens fees are $18.25 per 9 holes and $32 for 18 holes, adult rates. A CPGA pro offers private lessons, all in the mature boreal forest covering the course like a skin. The fairways and elevated tees are immaculate and the heavily bunkered greens near perfection. Altogether, this is one of the most impressive courses in the Regional Park system. The facility also houses six sheets of artificial ice for curling enthusiasts. A well-appointed, fully licensed clubhouse serves both facilities with its dining room, one of the town's best restaurants. Experts have claimed this to be one of Saskatchewan's premiere golfing facilities, and I won't disagree. It is busy, and tee times are required. Contact the pro-shop at (306) 862-4811 to reserve yours.

MISCELLANEOUS SPORTS
There are 10 km of hiking trails waiting to lead patrons on an exploration of the boreal forest. Well blazed, they provide insight into the complexity of this wonderful ecosystem. The trails are also groomed for cross-country skiers in the winter, and a further 14 km of

trails are groomed on the other side of the river. The Twin Lakes Trailblazers have developed 250 km of 4-meter-wide trails for snowmobiles. The park has an extensive playground (zip-line pictured above) with swings, slides, teeter-totters, merry-go-rounds and a creative play center, all near the picnic grounds. The big hill behind the boat launch serves as the local tobogganing and alpine ski center, but no ski lift or rentals are available. A stock car racing oval is also part of the park, but the local racing club is in charge of all events. A new mini-golf course has been built beside the park entry booth, which currently rents the equipment although they plan to build a separate booth for that. Another new feature is the petting zoo, built beside the Ochre Trail head. Horseshoe pits and a volleyball net round out this park's sports list.

SERVICES

The park will rent its facilities for private functions, the chalet, amphitheater (natural seating for about 500 people), the Nipawin Wildlife Federation (NWF) building (holds 100–200 people), and the E.G. and C.C. can cater events in its hall for up to 450 people. The park has several enterprises to sell or rent many items the patron will need. Diners, concessions and boat rentals will ease your stay, and Nipawin's many shops provide all the shopping, mechanical, medical, and worship services one can require. In conclusion, many people have looked very hard at the recreational needs of this region, and labored long to build an integrated system to meet those needs. The golf course is awesome, the campsites worthy of a National Park, and the staff open to a visitor's needs. Truly, "a park for all seasons and reasons"! For more information on this or any other aspect of the park, contact the park manager at:

Nipawin and District Regional Park
PO Box 1499
Nipawin, SK S0E 1E0
Telephone: (306) 862-3237
Fax: (306) 862-4722
E-mail: nipawinregionalpark@sasktel.net
Website at: www.nipawin.com/regionalpark

PASQUIA REGIONAL PARK

Located 10 km from both Carrot River and Arborfield on Hwy 23, the Pasquia Golf Course has been drawing avid golfers from the far corners of the province. Set in the hills and valley surrounding the Carrot River as it winds along, the park has a great deal to offer the golfing family. The highway is paved right up to the gates of the park, which are well marked with a large sign. As you drive up, you can see the first two fairways of the golf course, and probably a few golfers enjoying this popular attraction. The old rodeo grounds have been moved from the park, and the remaining space used to build softball diamonds; the park now hosts several ball tournaments annually, usually on the August long weekend. The park is open from May 1 to October 31, and charges $6 per day to enter, waived with an annual Regional Park sticker.

SITES

There are 61 electrified sites, costing $18 per night, and 7 non-electrified sites that cost $14 per night. Most of the sites are leveled and drained naturally, but the terrain is generally flat; some of the sites bordering the mature stands of cottonwood that adorn the valley sides have leveled camper stalls. All the sites are huge beyond belief! They could easily contain two large units, and sometimes will hold three in a pinch. Small wonder that some people move a motor home onto a favored lot and park for the season! To allow for casual campers, though, the park limits site reservation. The golf course is festooned with purple martin condominiums, so these hungry birds make short work of mosquitoes, keeping the need for pesticides to a minimum. The mature forest allows the naturalist the opportunity to go mushroom hunting and berry picking as well as bird watching; the purple martins are quite acrobatic as they feed in the evening. Across the stream from the main camping area is the group camping site, called The Island. It has fewer trees, but does offer relief via its openness to breezes. It offers groups up to 200 persons the chance to get away together. It has 8 serviced sites available, a large gazebo, a fire pit, and a sense of togetherness for your family reunion. It costs $400 per weekend to rent, and that allows you to put as many campers on the lot as it will hold, which can be quite a saving. Groups can also book the golf course's restaurant facility for special catering, although advance notice is necessary. All sites have picnic tables, and pole BBQs; trash bins are centrally located. Firewood is available from central bins, and drinking water is piped to central poles between sites. Washroom facilities are modern, with flush toilets in the shower house and at the diner. Simpler facilities are available in the campsites.

GOLFING

The golf course is well maintained and boasts an excellent restaurant, which is open from 0700–1900 hr daily. It offers a variety of hot meals as well as ice cream, pop, and snack foods, and hosts a number of buffet suppers on special occasions. The course itself is a 9-hole, 2876-yard par 37 with excellent elevated tee boxes and grass-greens; scorecards are available to show you the course. The fairways are wide and well manicured, and the tree cover is plentiful. Of particular interest is the manner in which the design keeps the hills in play from the tee boxes, necessitating the use of tower mirrors to ensure that the fairways are free to drive to. My favorite hole is #3, where one shoots from the top of the hill to a well-protected green that slopes left to right and top to bottom. Pin placement is everything, and typically it is wiser to play short and chip on than to try and "go for the hole." The course is not heavily bunkered, nor is there much water except for #4, where "Cavanaugh's Creek," a man-made hazard, is a magnet for any errant ball. Everywhere on this popular course one can hear songbirds and see squirrels chasing through the trees. If you are fortunate, you may find edible mushrooms in the forest bordering the course. I claim it is for this reason that I play the woods so often; the other members of my foursome will tell you a different story, I'll wager! The course is very reasonable to play on, costing $13 for 9 holes or $22 for 18 holes—a bargain on this remarkable turf. A driving range and a practice putting green are available to hone your skills. Motorized golf carts are available for rent, as are clubs, but the selection is limited so you are well advised to bring your own equipment. For more information or to reserve a tee time on this popular course, contact the pro-shop at (306) 768-2880.

WATER SPORTS

The river allows for canoeing, and there is a boat launch. The fishing in the park is very poor, probably nonexistent, although nearby Tobin Lake and the Saskatchewan River abound with trophy fish, all about a half-hour drive away. A playground has been built for the little campers, featuring slides, swings, climbers, merry-go-rounds, and teeter-totters. The parks' swimming pool, built in 1990, features regular public swims as well as lessons. The public swims cost $4 per adult, $5 per teen per day, with children at $2 per day. The lessons are between $35 and $40, depending on the person's age and ability, and are given by a qualified staff of 8 lifeguards. The pool, a junior Olympic design, has 2 diving boards, change rooms, and shower facilities. A mini-golf course is being built beside the pool. One will quite often see families camp in the park for the entire duration of the lessons, golfing, swimming and hiking. For more information, contact the pool office at (306) 768-2855 in season.

HIKING

The park's latest feature is the discovery ten year's ago of a large fossilized crocodile-like dinosaur. In conjunction with the Royal Saskatchewan Museum in Regina, the park managers have established the Andy Jumalt Hiking Trail to and from the site. The trial is marked, and tours are available in July and August. It is 12 km (7 miles) in length (return trip) though, so do bring a supply of water, some bug repellent, and perhaps a snack or two for any little travelers you bring along. If you'd prefer to ride, a tractor-towed wagon has a daily, guided run to the fossil bed, costing $6 per person with a minimum group of 10. The trail follows along the river bed and includes a look at some interesting fauna and landforms along the way. The Dickson Hardie Interpretive Center is open Monday to Friday in season; contact the park office for details.

SERVICES

The park is well serviced as the nearby towns have all amenities from hospital service to excellent shopping. Medical emergencies can be treated at the Carrot River Health Center. Gasoline and mechanical services are available at one of the local service stations, and a laundromat is available in Carrot River as well. The RCMP have a detachment in Carrot River, and consider Pasquia Regional to be a quiet, peaceful place as they very rarely ever have any calls to the park. In closing, I find this park caters to the whole family on a first-rate basis. The golf course is challenging, the pool is deliciously cool on a hot summer's day, the hike well worth the effort, and local amenities serve to accentuate the positives in this fine park. Bring your family and enjoy! For more information on this park, contact the park manager at:

Pasquia Regional Park
PO Box 339
Arborfield, SK S0E 0A0
Telephone: (306) 768-3239
Fax: (306) 769-3258
Website: www.pasquia.com

ST. BRIEUX REGIONAL PARK

Located a kilometer west of St. Brieux, just off Hwy 368, the park is open from the Victoria Day long weekend until the first weekend in September. It was built in the 1970s and features excellent camping beside a lovely lake and a great golf course. Check-out time is 1300 hr, and quiet time is 2300–0700 hr. The park charges $5 per day for park entry, waived if you have an annual Regional Park sticker.

SITES

There are 54 electrified sites and 14 non-electrified sites, costing $20 per night or $14 per night, respectively. Electrified sites can also be rented by the season, which costs $700. Most sites are "back-in" style, but sites 41, 42, 43, and 44 are pull-through and big enough for a small group! An overflow campsite is located behind the beach in the day-use area. The sites here aren't as comfortable as the numbered ones, but they should be adequate. All sites are naturally leveled and drained, and cut out of the aspen forest so there is plenty of shade and privacy. All sites have picnic tables (some made of cement), firepits or pole BBQs, and trash bins. Another nice touch is that all sites have gray water pits for you to dispose of wash water. Firewood is offered free for the first time this year, available from a bin by the park office. Washroom facilities are modern, with flush toilets and coin operated hot showers in the campgrounds and a washroom facility near the beach. The washrooms are wheelchair accessible, with some assistance as there is a bit of a hump to get into the facility; once in, there should be no difficulty. There is one dining shelter in the picnic area behind the beach, open for general use. Drinking water (St. Brieux municipal) is available from central taps located at the washrooms. The campsites are very pretty and you get a wonderful sense of privacy amid the poplars and birch. Hiking trails connect the sites with the beach, golf course, and a walking trail leading south of the park. The stone entry gates are very nice, and the whole park is a gem. The park has an excellent map with the local rules printed on the back. Reservations are accepted by calling the park office at the number below.

WATER SPORTS

The lake has good fishing, a nice swimming beach, and a boat launch (pictured above). The park levies a $5 per day or $12 per season boat launch usage fee. A large parking area for trailers is located in back of the boat launch, as well as the filleting shack. The lake has good fishing for perch, walleye, pike, and whitefish, and is popular among water-skiers, sail boats and jet boats. There is a buoyed swim beach a short walk south of the campgrounds with changerooms and a wide expanse of sand. Swim lessons are taught with one set offered lasting for 2 weeks in July; contact the park office for details. One floating dock tempts the daring out, and a slide extends into the water. The beach is anchored by large lawns on either side, and has a playground just behind with a creative play center built into the woods. The playground also has swings, slides, teeter-totters, and climbers. There is a beach volleyball court, with equipment available at the park office.

GOLFING
The park boasts a fine 9-hole grass-green course. The fairways extend for 2818 yards over the par-34 course, built in the low, rolling countryside a short walk from the campsites. An excellent clubhouse offers the usual summer treats serving as the park concession as well as offering a licensed atmosphere for the golfing patrons. Light meals can also be purchased from the hard working staff! The concession is open from 1000–2000 hr on week days, and 0800–2000 hr on weekends. The pro-shop offers a small line of hats, balls and shirts, as well as renting carts and clubs. Persons bringing their own motor carts are charged a $2 tracking fee. There is a driving range, and practice putting greens are under construction. The course plays well from its elevated tees, and the greens keepers work hard to keep it in top condition. Greens fees are $12.50 for 9 holes, or $22 for 18 holes. Tee reservations are recommended for this popular course, particularly on weekends, and can be made by calling the pro-shop at (306) 275-4433.

SPORTS
The park has 3 ball diamonds located just to the left as you turn into the park access road. The diamonds all have wire mesh backstops on metal poles and dirt infields with grass outfields. There are washrooms and ample parking for spectators and players alike, but no seating so bring your own lawn chairs. There is a large concession building that is open during tournaments, offering meals and pop. This is a popular venue locally for various ball tournaments, and is available for a private function; contact the park office for details.

The park has many trails wandering from the campsites to the beach, golf course (and its concession!), and south along the lake. At one point the trail leaves the park property and crosses private land. Currently, park patrons are allowed to enter the private land, but you are asked to respect it and leave it as you found it. Berry picking is allowed, but they ask that you eat from the bush and not pick for later consumption.

SERVICES
The town of St. Brieux is a short walk from the park and offers a full range of shopping, mechanical, medical, and worship services. A museum chronicles local history and offers insight into the lives of the people who settled this area. This park has many charms, not the least of which are its pretty campsites. There are many recreational opportunities here, with something to suit just about anyone. With this much happening daily, plus golf and ball tournaments scattered throughout the season, it's no wonder that the park is a busy one. When you wish to visit, I strongly recommend you call ahead and reserve a site. They'll hold it for you until 1900 hr unless you've made prior arrangements, after which you may lose the site to someone who has been patiently waiting in line! The park prides itself on attracting families, so it deals quickly with noisy patrons; the police are but an eye blink away, and unruly patrons are asked to leave. Because of this, the park is a quiet, peaceful one where children laugh and play. We certainly enjoyed our visit to this park, and I hope you do, too! For more information on the park, contact the park office at:

St. Brieux Regional Park
PO Box 414
St. Brieux, SK   S0K 3V0
Telephone: (306) 275-2255
Fax: (306) 275-4838.

STRUTHERS LAKE REGIONAL PARK

Although it may seem a bit off the beaten path, that is the very reason one should go looking for this wonderful park. The lake is filled with fish (my son caught his very first here), and the woods are filled with trails to be explored. Kinistino is a 15-minute drive away over decent grid roads, and the park can also be reached by driving along Hwy 41 from Wakaw to Yellow Creek; the Regional Park sign on this paved road shows the turn left onto the grid road that, 16 km later, will see you turn into the main gates. The road follows a stream that has many beaver dams to explore, and offers some canoeing challenges as well. In the spring of 1996 there was quite a waterfall near the road as the spring flood overflowed the beaver's dam. The park opens on the May long weekend, closing in September. The gate hours are from 0700–2300 hr daily, with quiet time from 2300–0700 hr The park levies a $3.50 daily entry fee, waived if you have an annual Regional Park sticker.

SITES

There are 36 electrified sites (service varies from 15 to 30 amps) costing $15 per night, and 8 non-electrified sites costing $8 per night ($40/week). Some cabins are also available for rent, for $25 per weeknight, $30 per weekend night, or $120 per week. Bedding and utensils, including plates, cups, etc., are the responsibility of the renter, but the cabins are furnished and electrified. The sites were varied in setting, with some being naturally leveled and drained, and others being leveled by bulldozer and drained with a layer of gravel. All the sites have access to water standpipes which supply sand point well water to the park. The water is clean and fresh, although it tastes faintly of the plastic piping used. The roadways are all sand based, so will be passable in the wettest weather. Washroom facilities are modern in the shower house, with coin operated showers and flush toilets. Toilets in the campgrounds are biffies, and were odorless when we visited. The park's chief glories are its fishing and the hiking to be had among the poplars. The locals also claim that the park's solitude and quiet are among its many attractions.

A gazebo can be rented for special occasions, costing $20 for a daily event such as a church service, $50 per day for a reunion or other such function, and $100 for events requiring liquor permits. Speak to the park office to reserve this facility or a camping site. All the sites can be reserved but three days' notice must be given; contact the park office for details.

SPORTS

Struthers Lake itself isn't huge, being about 2 km in length and about a third of that in width. It is bordered by mature aspen parklands, so there is shelter from inclement weather. A boat launch is provided for a $3 daily fee or a $6 annual fee. Some dock space is also to be had, but it will be at a premium. The lake is stocked yearly with walleye, and a breeding population of pike is also to be had. Once famous for its large perch, the lake is now suffering a decline in that population. In order to reduce winter kill, an aeration project is keeping the lake oxygenated year round, which should improve the fishery. Filleting stations are in place near the boat launch, free of charge.

A small beach just down from the concession keeps the summer's heat from becoming too harsh. Although it has no lifeguards or swim lessons, the swim beach does offer some shade and benches to rest upon. Swim lessons used to be taught on the lakeshore, but have dropped off as demand itself waned. A floating dock is pushed out into the lake and tethered to provide a bit of noisy fun for the swimmers. Beach showers are provided in the concession stand and restaurant, costing $1 per timed shower. The beach itself was sandy with some clay, as are most lakes of this type, and fairly clean.

There are two ball diamonds in the park, with mesh backstops on wooden supports and grass infields. Kowalski Park is the home of the Mudhens, the local ball club, and it has bleachers for fans, benches for players, and wooden home run fencing. All the equipment is in good condition with ample parking for all. All bookings have priority on the field, but otherwise you may use them for your own pickup game.

SERVICES

Much work has been done recently to keep the little campers happy, as the large and excellent playground attests. Filled with swings, climbers and slides, all on a soft sand base, it is well situated beside the concession stand to take full advantage of the several picnic areas and roomy parking lot nearby. A welcome addition is the miniature golf course, rentals for which are available at the concession. For a somewhat older crowd, the sand volleyball court is a nice touch and sure to be popular in mid-summer. The concession itself (pictured above) is open from 0900–2100 hr daily in July and August, and offers iced treats, snacks, and pop as well as excellent homemade pie and light meals from their grill menu. It also has a small line of camping supplies and simple groceries, but more extensive shopping must be done in Kinistino. One can also find mechanical, medical, and worship services there. Annual events include the Canada Day celebrations, complete with fireworks, and two ball tournaments, one in July and one in August. For more information on this park, contact the park office at:

Struthers Lake Regional Park
PO Box 857
Kinistino, SK S0J 1H0
Telephone: (306) 864-3240 in season
Fax: (306) 864-3748.

STURGIS AND DISTRICT REGIONAL PARK

Located south of Sturgis town limits off Hwy 49, this small park enjoys the charm of its stream bank location. The town of Sturgis boasts "the province's largest one-day rodeo" on the July long weekend. There are many games offered such as ball tournaments, rodeo, fiddler's contests, and the like. The campgrounds are open from the Victoria Day weekend to early October. Park entry costs $3 per day or free with an annual Regional Park pass.

SITES

There are 10 electrified sites and 6 non-electrified sites costing $7 per night. A self registration booth is located just to the right as you drive in, with envelopes and a drop slot. All sites are built among the elms that grow beside the Assiniboia River, so shade is assured. All sites are leveled with gravel and drain naturally. They have picnic tables, trash cans, and a fire box with a moveable grate; firewood is available from central bins. The electrified sites are all close to the river, and a small waterfall (pictured above) will add its cheerful tinkle to your camping pleasure. The sites are large enough for most campers, but the access road to the smaller sites in the unserviced area may be a barrier to the largest campers. One dining shelter in the picnic area provides shade, tables, and a wood stove for day use. The smaller campgrounds, to the south of the electrified sites, can double as a group site as it has a circular roadway. Washroom facilities are modern in the shower house with flush toilets and showers costing a "loonie" per use, as well as primitive biffies in the campsites. The town has a trailer dump station for park patrons; inquire at the tourist booth in town or at one of the service stations.

SPORTS

The Assiniboia River runs through the park

and may offer canoeists a chance to explore, but I cannot recommend swimming in the river as there are no lifeguards, reaching assists, or any other safety equipment. The river bottom is unknown, and dangerous currents may exist. A short walking trail winds along beside the river, and people can fish from the shores if they wish. The playground in the day use area has swings, slides, and teeter-totters. A large open space behind the camp kitchen beckons for wide games or a pick-up game of ball.

The ski hill visible on the hill across the Assiniboia River valley from the town of Sturgis is the Sturgis Ski Hill, operated by the Assiniboia Ski Club. The facility is not operated by the Regional Park Authority and so won't be considered at length here. It is open on weekends and has a good-sized warm-up shelter with hot drinks. Access to the hill comes from the rope tow, with several runs available from the top.

SERVICES

The town of Sturgis has many of the shops and services one could immediately need, including grocery, mechanical, and worship services. Medical services are available at Preeceville (10 km west), or at Canora, 30 km south. For more information on this park, or to begin planning your private function, contact the park office at:

Sturgis and District Regional Park
PO Box 520
Sturgis, SK   S0A 4A0
Telephone: (306) 548-2108
Fax: (306) 548-2948.

WAKAW LAKE REGIONAL PARK

A lot of work has been done in this park of late, partly to refurbish its assets, and partly to refurbish its clientele. Located 10 km east of Hwy 2 just north of the town of Wakaw, this spacious park is home to many people who are renting seasonal campsites for large fifth wheel campers. Why do they come? Because the park is working very hard to make these people feel at home. The road into the park is paved right up to the ornate dressed stone entrance, and well labeled with Department of Hwys signs as well as the parks own colorful signs. To the right as one drives in is the beautiful golf course and clubhouse; the restaurant is directly ahead. To the left is the miniature chapel and the gazebo, both available for rent, and a miniature golf course. A stage and the driving range are also found in this area. South of this is the beach and the majority of the camping areas. Daily park entry fees of $5 per vehicle are waived if you have an annual Regional Park sticker.

SITES

A large park by anyone's standards, there are 257 serviced sites, of which 122 are electrified and 135 fully serviced with water, power, and sewer. The costs for these sites are $15 per day for a regular site and $20 per day for a fully serviced site. The sites can also be rented by the week, month, or year; prices vary, so contact the park office for a complete, up-to-date price list. There are 5 camping areas in the park, with Groups "A," "B," "E," and "F" reserved for permanent rentals. Group "D" sites ring the gazebo (available for rent), mini-golf and miniature church and are generally a bit larger than the Group "C" sites. This last group is located just to the south of the main beach and is remarkable as some of the sites are lakefront so one can dock a boat almost beside the campfire! The coin-operated laundromat and showers are also located near Group C, as well as the overflow and picnic area. The park itself is carved out of mature parklands forest, so the trees are all poplar and birch with a heavy undergrowth of various berry bushes, saskatoons and chokecherries predominant. Most sites have excellent shade and good privacy, particularly in Group C. A great many trails wander through the wooded areas, mostly made by children whose unerring navigational instincts have cut the shortest routes through the brush to either the beach or the concession! Groups A, B, E, and F are all well drained with graveled pads to park the trailers on, while groups C and D are naturally drained and leveled. All sites have the usual pole BBQ, but a few also have a metal fire pit; every site had its own picnic table. A good many people rent a site for two weeks so that their children can take swim lessons at the excellent beach as well as have a summer holiday filled with golfing and fishing—an excellent idea, I think! Reservations are preferred for all sites as the park can be very busy, particularly on long weekends. Although reservations commence on May 1 for the current year, you must call at least 7 days in advance unless you require the site for a longer period (for instance, monthly rentals require more notice); a $5 reservation fee is charged. Contact the park office at the number below.

WATER SPORTS

Wakaw Lake is a long, narrow lake with over 800 cabins ringing it, particularly on the south and east shores. None of these are in the park, but there will be a lot of water traffic nonetheless. The beach inside the park is filled with fine sand and is large enough to hold hundreds of sun bathers. The lake is quite shallow in this area, so the diving platform seems to be a terrible distance from shore. An aquatic program offers swim lessons in both the Canadian Red Cross and Royal Life Saving Services qualifications; contact the park office for dates and prices. The aquatic program personnel also offer an evening program of songs and stories on the beach free of charge. The program will be posted on the swim shack and at the beach concession. This fine building not only sells the usual treats, snacks, and pop, but offers grocery and other staple items as well. It houses the beach showers and changerooms and has a good parking lot in front. The park has a beach shack that rents out canoe equipment and colorful paddle boats, complete with all safety gear. A cement boat launch is available for visitor use, with a good-sized area just back of it to park your boat trailer. The lake is filled with fish, much to the delight of my boys, all of whom have mastered the perch population here. Pike also abound as do walleye, although they can be more difficult to invite to dinner!

GOLFING

The greatest surprise for me during my visit here was the work that has gone into the golf course. The fairways were immaculate as always, but the tee boxes and greens have all been built up. The tees are elevated on field stone boxes (pictured above), and the once-flat greens are now elevated and somewhat less than level! Sand bunkers have sprouted in the fairways, usually about where I can hit to! I will never be accused of being a golfer (or at least a good one!), so take my judgments with a grain of salt but I must say I found this course to be very attractive indeed. The view from the fourth tee is stunning, shooting from an elevated tee in a treed tunnel down a long hill onto the fairway below. A good drive seems to hang in the air forever! Green fees are reasonable, adult rates being $14 for 9 holes, $25 for 18. Juniors play for $7 per 9 holes or $12 per day! A full season membership is $330. The small pro-shop is well equipped, with all the golfer's needs for sale. One can also rent pull or motor carts, bash off a bucket at the driving range or practice putting on the excellent green just off to the side. The restaurant across the parking lot will place a cold beer in your hand as you wait for a light lunch, or it will serve you a wonderful Sunday brunch for a mere $7 per adult. Prices are most reasonable and the staff is most friendly. The restaurant is open from 0700–2200 hr daily. If you are contemplating staying here for a couple of weeks to let the children take their swimming lessons, the course PGA pro will give lessons. To make arrangements for lessons, tee times or queries regarding tournaments, contact the pro-shop at (306) 233-5955.

SERVICES
The town of Wakaw offers all amenities including shopping, and a hospital and mechanical services should they be needed. There are two museums, the Heritage Museum and the John Diefenbaker Law Office, and the municipal airport offers parachute training for the bold. The shower and laundry facilities here are among the best we've seen in our travels. Clean, spacious and modestly priced, they are centrally located in the open area behind Group C. Another shower facility is available beside the concession near the beach, serving beach patrons and Group A sites. The park also has two gazebos or dining shelters that can be rented for special occasions, one between the chapel and stage (to the left as you drive in), and the other in back of the restaurant. The second location is unique in that it is fully enclosed, making it eminently suited for private functions wherein alcohol may be served. Both these shelters are popular for hosting weddings (as is the mini chapel) and staff golf tournaments, so do book early. As a side note, the restaurant staff will cater functions held in the park; for more information on renting these facilities contact the park office at:

Wakaw lake Regional Park
PO Box 730
Wakaw, SK S0K 4P0
Telephone: (306) 233-5744 (front gate) or (306) 233-4644 (park office)
Fax: (306) 233-5666
Website: www.townofwakaw.com//regionalpark.html

WALDSEA LAKE REGIONAL PARK

Located about 10 km northwest of Humboldt off Hwy 5, the park is open from the Victoria Day long weekend in May until the middle of September. The park also has a Scouts and Guides camp by its western end, and 49 privately owned cabins. The park levies a $5 daily park entry fee, waived if you have an annual Regional Park sticker.

SITES

There are 5 electrified sites with 20-amp service, 10 full-service sites with 30-amp service, and 9 non-electrified sites in the park. The sites rent for $25 per day for a full-service site, $19 per day for a 20-amp site, and $12 per day for a non-electrified site. Weekly, monthly, and seasonal rates are available upon request. All the sites have been recently modified, mostly to enlarge them and to enhance amenities. Pole BBQs and metal-framed picnic tables, trash bins, and non-potable water taps are available, and drinking water is available near the concession building. This is a new development: Lakeview Place is the concession, diner, and entrance booth as well as the nerve center of this park. Firewood is available for $4 per bundle from Lakeview Place. All toilet facilities are modern flush units, and there are coin-operated showers available. There are some rental cabins in the park, costing $35 per night or $250 per week; contact the park office for details.

WATER SPORTS

Waldsea Lake is very saline; it is one of only two lakes in North America with this particular chemistry, so there are no fish in the lake. The park has two simple boat launches, one at either end, to allow motor and sail boats access to the lake. The water table has dropped recently (although it appears to be making a comeback) so the boat launches may not actually be in the water; call ahead to make certain. Water-skiers and tubers will love the lake, and swimmers will appreciate the huge public beach. There are shower stands on poles at intervals along the beach to wash the salt off. There are wheelchair accessible changerooms near the playground. A nice touch is the boardwalk and deck that allows wheelchair access to the beach where one can watch the children at play. There are no lessons taught as the town of Humboldt offers them at their indoor pool. A very good idea was for the park to contact the local schools about their old playground equipment, which has found a new life as one of the most extensive playgrounds in the regional park system. The old ball diamond has been removed and replaced with an astonishing assortment of playground equipment, now known as Play Land. Another small playground is built right on the beach with swings, slides, and climbers. As the park day-use area is right beside the beach path, you can park, picnic, and play in a huge, well-treed area with a boardwalk to get a wheelchair right down to the waters edge.

SPORTS

There is a hiking trail established that leads from the hall area to the Buffalo Pits. Well blazoned and wide, it can also take bikes as well as pedestrians—no ATVs or motor bikes, though. There are approximately 20 km of trails available, color coded and well maintained, that offer parkland forest and prairie plus lake ecosystems. There is a ball diamond with a short mesh backstop on wooden poles in a grass field; just start playing and you'll attract other players! There is a volleyball court right on the beach, and horseshoe pits beside the hall. Equipment for both of these is available at the concession free of charge. A fine grass-green golf course is available in Humboldt, but it is not of the park so we didn't examine it further. A mini-golf course located near the concession rents for $1 per child or $2 per adult.

SERVICES

Lakeview Place offers a line of snacks, treats, and pop, as well as light meals from their grill. They are open from 0900–2100 hr on weekdays, and 0900–2200 hr on weekends. The large hall can hold up to 75 people, and can be rented for $60 on weekdays or $100 for Saturdays, Sundays, or holidays. This is a very popular venue for reunions and the like as it has 30 or so fine electrified camp sites in the same area, so it books early. The park will also cater your private event; contact the park office for details. The town of Humboldt offers a full range of shopping, mechanical, medical, and worship services for the traveler, all with German hospitality. With the huge playground, excellent beach, and lakefront camping that is peaceful at night and offers a glorious view of the sun setting over the park, this is a pretty place to find some summer fun. For more information or to reserve a site, contact the park at:

Waldsea Lake Regional Park
PO Box 2094
Humboldt, SK S0K 2A0
Telephone: (306) 682-3528
Fax: (306) 682-2510
Website: www.waldsealake.com

WAPITI VALLEY REGIONAL PARK

Situated on Codette Lake, a man-made reservoir formed on the Saskatchewan River by the Codette Dam, this park is only a 16-km (9-mile) drive north of Gronlid on Hwy 6. Built in 1983, the park is famous for its skiing and has built an electrified campgrounds for summer use. The ski hill opens in early December and stays open as long as the season allows, usually the end of March. The marina and boat launch facilities open as soon as weather permits in spring, usually by late May or early June, and remain open until early September. Although no park entry fees are collected in the winter months, patrons of the campground, marina and boat launch are expected to have an annual Regional Park sticker.

SKIING

As one drives in from the highway, you first see a large maintenance shed, then the ski patrol hut to the left, and the main lodge. A large parking lot is capable of holding a hundred or so vehicles, and one can see the chalet that is available for rent. The lodge itself is an impressive structure, built of logs and featuring a large stone fireplace complete with a mounted elk's head (*wapiti* means elk in Cree) above the mantel. The Wapiti Lounge is a licensed facility which offers patrons an alternative to bringing their own liquor onto the slopes, a practice to be discouraged on all ski slopes. The lodge's main section offers tables, chairs, and a place to sample the newly renovated restaurant's many wares as you warm up. Meals are simple but well prepared and very reasonably priced; a burger with fries and a pop will cost about $6. All their food is tasty and quickly prepared as the proprietors know you'd rather be back on the slopes than waiting in line! Restaurant hours are 1100–1900 hr in season. The park is open weekends and holidays only until January 30, then open daily for the remainder of the season. The resort opens at 0900 hr and the lifts begin operating at 1000 hr. The lifts run until 1630 hr on weekdays, and on Friday nights from 1800–2100 hr. Generally speaking, the park will not be open if the air temperature is -30°C or colder.

The hills that buttress Codette Lake are covered with mature aspen and spruce trees. Combined with the naturally steep slopes, one feels little wind chill which makes for a pleasant stay. There are 11 runs, totaling 5 km (3 fi miles) falling over a 90-meter (300-foot) vertical. The runs vary from a beginners' slope to the much more challenging "Wapiti Way." There are three lifts providing access to the top, a rope tow on the "Bunny Slope," the main 550-meter-long chair lift, and the Owl's Nest Handle Tow. There is a series of groomed cross-country ski trails available just 5 minutes south of the park, operated by the Melfort Cross-Country Ski Club. A fine brochure is available from them, and a supply is also available at the park chalet. The facility has 20 km of groomed trials and a warm-up building at the main entrance. As they are not part of the park operation I won't go into much detail about them. Contact the club for more details by writing for one of their fine brochures at:

> Melfort Cross-
> Country Ski Club
> PO Box 3813
> Melfort, SK S0E 1A0

RENTALS
The lodge also houses the ski rental shop, offering 450 sets of skis, poles, boots and bindings to their patrons, as well as 60 snowboards. A full set of ski equipment rents for $15 for adults and $12 for children and students. Snowboarding is also popular, with full sets renting for $25 per day. A family of four can get a full day's equipment rental and lift ticket for $109 or $79 for a half-day. Lift tickets are similarly affordable, costing $21 per adult per day, $19 for those 13 to 18 years of age, $17 for students, and free for those 5 years of age and younger. School rates are available; $15 per student gets them rentals, lift tickets, and lessons for the day. Lessons are provided by CISA trained and certified staff, and cost $25 for an individual 1-hour lesson, $16 per person in pairs, $14 per person in groups of three, and $12 per person in groups of four or more.

Hilliards' Four Season Resort offers 5 three-bedroom wheelchair accessible cabins for rent just to the left of the main parking lot, with modern flush toilets and hot showers as well as a large, covered deck on each cabin. The cabin rental includes all cooking utensils, dishes, and linens; rentals start at $100 per night plus GST. Contact the resort directly at (306) 862-3242 for more details, or check out their website at www.hilliardsresort.com; you can link to their email address from there. The Heritage Inn in Melfort offers a ski and swim package, giving two free adult lift tickets per room plus access to Melfort's Northern Lights pool complex; contact the hotel at (306) 752-5961 for more details.

SUMMER FUN
There are 10 camp sites available right at the marina, all with 30-amp electrical service and potable water, costing $20 per night. A trailer dump station is available near the shower house. There is a fee for using the showers, payable at the concession when you get the shower key. The sites are rather small, but you can leave your boat in the marina as a registered patron. There are no trees in the campground so there is little shade or ground cover, but people come here for the fishing! Sites are naturally leveled and drained, and have wooden picnic tables and pole BBQs. Firewood is available for a small fee, payable at the concession. A small playground is available in the picnic area, with a climbing structure and sand box. There are also 16 unserviced sites available in a provincial campground located just across the river from the ski area (approximately 2 km away), which has been leased by the Four Seasons Resort. These sites are naturally leveled and drained but are

much larger and have been built into mature aspen forest so there is excellent shade and ground cover. Toilet facilities are vault-style, there is one well with pump handle, and the sites all have wooden picnic tables and pole BBQs. There is a dining shelter here, beside the picnic or day-use area. All sites have two interesting features: the wood piles are built in small, roofed bins and all sites are pull-through style. The first bank of sites is very picturesque as they look over the Wapiti Valley. Sites can be paid for at the self-registry kiosk at the campground entrance, or at the concession, and cost $10 per night.

The marina features a sheltered bay with a boat launch, a concession and boat rental, a dining shelter and a fish cleaning shack. The main store sells fishing tackle and bait plus a line of confectionery items. One can also rent boats and motors for $85 per day or $15 per hour; fuel is included with the full-day price, but is extra with the hourly rental. You can call the marina operators for reservations, but the boat will typically only be held for about an hour after your expected arrival, so don't be late! The marina hours are evenings and weekends in May and June, and from 0900–2000 hr daily in July and August. Contact the Four Seasons Resort directly for more information on boats, camping, and accommodation at:

Four Seasons Resort
PO Box 105
Gronlid, SK   S0E 0W0
Telephone: (306) 862-3242
Website: www.hilliardsresort.com

SERVICES

The park is popular for school outings and with local skiers. With its facilities and snow-making machinery, the park offers an excellent alpine skiing experience for prairie patrons. One cannot claim they offer the same experience as to be found in the Rockies, but they don't have the price tag and crowds either! The addition of the campgrounds and extension of the marina/concession operation make this a true year-round park with something for all patrons. Fishing is excellent on man-made Codette Lake both in winter and in summer, the campgrounds are a welcome addition, and the skiing is wonderful! There are two main events held here annually: the Peace 100 Snowmobile Rally in February and the Walleye Derby organized by the Melfort Mustangs Hockey Club on the August long weekend. The winning walleye taken at last year's derby weighed an impressive 13.2 lb. (6 kg)! Every time I hear of such a prize being taken, I think of the fact that there are even larger fish waiting to be caught! For more information on this fascinating park, or to book its impressive facilities, contact the manager at:

Wapiti Valley Regional Park
PO Box 181
Gronlid, SK   S0E 0W0
Telephone (306) 862-5621 in season; (306) 863-4143 any time (863-4141 evening)
Fax: (306) 862-2828
Website: www.skiwapitivalley.com (you can link to their email from there).

WHITESAND REGIONAL PARK

Located 8 km northeast of Theodore, just off the Yellowhead Highway, this quiet little park sits on the Theodore Reservoir. Over 10 km long, the reservoir was created when the Whitesand River was dammed in the 1960s. The park access is paved right up to the gates, and the route through the town is well labeled with white and red painted signs. Built in 1965, the park is open from early May to mid-September—longer if the golfing weather holds out. Daily passes are $5, waived with an annual Regional Park sticker.

SITES

There are 23 electrified, 10 non-electrified sites, and 8 fully serviced sites (two of which are pull-through). Costs vary with the length of stay, with non-electrified sites costing $10 and electrified ones costing $15 per night, respectively; fully serviced sites cost $22 per night. So popular is the park becoming that 7 more fully serviced sites are under construction. Several of the choicest sites are booked seasonally, costing $525 for a full-service site, $330 per month or $110 per week. The sites are spacious, with tall poplars for shade and the chance of picking fresh saskatoons for your breakfast pancakes from the shrubs surrounding your own site. All sites have pole BBQs and freshly painted picnic tables. Trash bins are shared between every two sites, and water is available from a central tap near the concession. Water supplied is from a spring-fed well and is regularly tested to ensure quality. There are four primitive toilets serving the campsites, and one modern toilet with two showers, free for registered campers, in behind the concession. A trailer dump station is available free of charge to registered patrons. One dining shelter is available free of charge behind the playground. Two large group camping sites can be reserved by calling the park office at the number below.

WATER SPORTS

Although the original plan was to have a sand beach, over the decades the sand has all but disappeared. Fist-sized rocks are all that remain so swimming from the shore cannot be recommended, particularly for smaller swimmers. A fine boat launch and new dock is available, and the concession will rent boats and motors for $8 per hour or $40 per day, gas included. A major attraction for this park is its fishing with pike and walleye in the reservoir, and the provincial fisheries stocking it with perch this year. To date, the largest pike registered at the concession is 9.5 kg., and the largest walleye is 1 kg. A fishing derby is held annually on the August long weekend, and the local Wildlife Federation holds one on the reservoir in July. Water-skiers often grace the lake with their antics, although no equipment is made available by the park.

GOLFING

A well-manicured 9-hole par 34, sand-green golf course is another popular attraction in this park. Recent improvements include new sand traps and the construction of 10-cart storage bays for seasonal or yearly storage. Costing $8 for 9 holes or $12 for 18, this is one of the least expensive 2600-yard courses you'll play. Parts of the course are cut into mature aspen forest, so a lost ball may mean a short berry-picking delay! The concession rents clubs and power carts, and score cards are available. The course is naturally watered and can get a bit dry, but the cheerful chirp of bird song and the quiet rustle of the trees whispering in the evening's breeze still make this course a lovely play. In fact, it's so popular that eleven tournaments are held here annually! The course can be reserved for your own tournament, costing $100–$150 per event depending on size.

SERVICES

Besides golfing and boating, the Poplar Leaf Hiking Trail was developed that runs around the perimeter of this 120 acre park. Besides berry picking, the 4.25-km trail winds around the golf course and camping areas and gives great views of the lake and river. A playground is situated on a large grassy area with swings, slides, monkey bars and a seesaw. The park concession has a variety of sporting equipment on request, such as volleyball, tennis, etc. A 9-hole mini-putt course is available for the younger enthusiasts, costing a silver collection.

The town of Theodore is a short drive away, and it has a full range of shopping, mechanical, and worship services. Two doctors work out of the medical center should emergency arise, and Yorkton is only a half-hour away should you wish to make a major purchase. Theodore also boasts "Mrs. Bee's Doll House," a wonderful collection of antique dolls, and Diana May Clay, which features Ukrainian pottery that is shipped worldwide. The park concession is open from 0900–2100 hr weekdays or 0800–2100 hr on weekends in season, and offers the usual iced treats, snacks, pop, and light meals. The walls are covered with various golfing trophies and fishing information and the tables seem filled with patrons chatting over a game of crib and a coffee. The charm of this park, to me at least, was the easy friendliness of the managers and its quiet atmosphere. No loud parties, no hustle and bustle, just golf, fishing, a quiet campgrounds and homemade berry pies! Check out the website at www.saskregionalparks.ca. For more information on this park, contact the managers at:

Whitesand Regional Park Manager
Box 406
Theodore, SK   S0A 4C0
Telephone: (306) 647-2191
Fax: (306) 647-2089, Winter Contact: (306) 647-2089
E-mail: whitesandregionalpark@sasktel.net

WYNYARD REGIONAL PARK

Situated 2.5 km south of Wynyard on grid road #640, the park has an interesting history. The lake, currently used for a trout pond, was originally constructed in the 1920s by the CPR as a reservoir to provide the water needed by the steam engines that plied the area. A wooden canal still brings water to the town where it is used to irrigate the municipal golf course and boulevard medians, among other uses. The park itself is built on top of the old municipal landfill, used in the 1950s and 1960s. Completely covered with lush grass and tall cottonwoods, little evidence of this use remains. The park is open from the Victoria Day weekend in May to the end of October, as goose and duck hunters often use the park during the fall hunt. A $5 entry fee is waived with an annual Regional Park sticker.

SITES

There are 22 electrified sites, of which 8 have the 30-amp service required by large modern trailers and RV's. The cost is $20 per site per night or $10 for a tenting site, collected by the park manager as he makes his evening rounds. Simply pull into the site of your choice and set up camp; the manager will take care of the rest. There is one shower facility with a shower and a flush toilet on each side. The park has two trailer dump stations for patrons. The sites are fairly large, some naturally leveled and some leveled with gravel pads. All sites feature picnic tables, pole BBQs, and garbage cans. Water is provided from a large holding tank supplied with Wynyard municipal water. All the sites are shaded by tall cottonwoods with some diamond willow. Only sites 15 to 22 have planted trees for cover, but these poplars are quite tall so cover is assured. There is one camp kitchen with a wood burning stove, available on a first-come, first-served basis. Firewood is provided free of charge in bins by both camp kitchens, the shower house, and site #14. Reservations are not accepted.

WATER SPORTS

The large trout pond is, as mentioned above, actually a reservoir built by the CPR in the 1920s and still used to irrigate the municipal golf course. It is stocked with 2,000 brown and speckled trout fingerlings every two years, with some of the trout surviving in deep holes through the winter. The largest brown trout caught here weighed 5.5 pounds, and measured 23 inches from nose to tail. A daily fee of $5 is levied to fish at the pond; all anglers are expected to have a provincial angling license and are limited to 2 fish per day. A small boat launch and dock are available to allow canoes and rowboats access to the pond; no motorboats are allowed. The park doesn't have a pool or swim beach, but the town of Wynyard has a pool with lessons, public swims, and lifeguards. Contact the town office for details.

HIKING

Although no organized trails have been built, many trails run from the sites around the lake to allow the walking angler access to the dam at the far end. A small stream winds around the park, and footbridges have been built to facilitate access. The trail running from the campgrounds to the trout pond is well marked and about 1.5 km long. The surrounding forest is a haven for songbirds and small animals like rabbits and foxes. The trails are narrow, but there is an abundance of life to make the walk worthwhile.

SERVICES

The town of Wynyard has all the amenities one could ask for, including shopping, medical, mechanical, and worship services. A municipal golf facility has 9 grass-greens on a 2598-yard, par-34 course with putting greens and a pro-shop. Greens fees are $12 for 9 holes or $20 for 18 holes, and tee times can be reserved by calling the licensed clubhouse at (306) 554-2154. The local museum, situated right on Hwy 16, is a storehouse of tourist information as well as local history. It also has a small souvenir counter. The park itself has no concession or shopping, so all purchases must be made in town, mind you the showers are free! For more information on the park contact the park manager at:

Wynyard and District Regional Park
PO Box 734
Wynyard, SK   S0A 4T0
Telephone: (306) 554-3661
Fax: (306) 554-3224.

YORK LAKE REGIONAL PARK

Located 5 km south of Yorkton on Gladstone Ave., this park is one of the city's best kept secrets. Originally built in the 1920s, it has a wealth of recreational opportunities awaiting the traveler, from the exotic to the expected. Open from the Victoria Day weekend to early October, the park levies a $4 daily entry fee, waived with an annual Regional Park sticker; campers can access the park free.

SITES

There are 30 electrified sites (six of which are 30-amp) and 5 tenting sites, costing $20 and $15 per night, respectively. All the electrified sites are pull-through or slip-in with a grass verge and are large enough for any camper. The sites are all carved out of mature Parklands brush, so campers have the opportunity of picking saskatoon berries for breakfast right in their own site (we did!). As the sites are curved, you really have shade on four sides, although that stretches the case a bit. All sites have a picnic table, fire grates on cement pads, and trash bins. Iron-filtered well water is available at all sites, and firewood is available from the concession; the first bundle per day is free with subsequent bundles costing $5 each. Toilet facilities vary from "Porta-Potty" in the campgrounds, to modern in the shower house behind the concession. The shower house is free to registered campers; ask for a key when you check in. A sewer dump station is also available to registered guests. Reservations are accepted with a minimum of two days notice by calling the park office at (306) 782-7080.

WATER SPORTS

The park is popular for Kin Point with its beach complex comprising swim beach, playground, picnic and day-use area, and beach concession. No swim lessons are offered but the beach sees heavy use for its fine building sand and clean water. The playground has swings, slides, teeter-totters, merry-go-rounds, and a creative play center. A boat launch is available to the right of the Sask. Wildlife Trap Club on the southeast corner of the park. The lake is so shallow that fishing is non-existent at the moment, but water-skiing is popular. The Yorkton Canoe and Kayak Club have a presence on the lake, with an annual canoe regatta, and the Navy Cadets have a field day here as well.

SLOW-PITCH

A fine, modern complex has been built as home to the Yorkton Slo-pitch League, comprised of four diamonds in a wagon wheel design with two lighted diamonds. Bleachers for spectators, shelters for players and ample parking are complemented by concessions which are open during tournaments. Visitors can watch a free game of league slow-pitch almost every night during the summer. Understandably busy, you may still be able to book your tournament if you call early. Annual ball tournaments hosted are the Co-Ed Qualifier, Men's Qualifier, and the All-Native Fastball Annual. Contact the park office for details.

SPORTS
A 3-km self-guided hiking trail has been built along the north edge of York Lake. Follow the road leading past Kin Point about 500 meters and you'll see the sign for the start point of the trail just past the railroad tracks. You can get a brochure describing the plants and animals at each of the 15 stations marked along the trail; just ask for one at the canteen. The Sask. Wildlife Trap and Skeet Club have a clubhouse and range on the other edge of the lake, and host shoots every Tuesday throughout the summer; visitors are welcome to check it out. Two sets of horseshoe pits border the left side of the picnic area, with equipment available at the concession.

GOLFING
The York Lake Golf and Country Club is built about 5 km northwest of the park gate along a grid road. It is a gorgeous 18-hole, par-72 course that covers 6034 yards. Practice greens and a driving range wait to hone your skills, and a fully licensed clubhouse lets you brag about your prowess. The restaurant is open from 0700–2100 hr daily, and serves three meals a day from a varied menu. A fully equipped pro-shop retails a complete line of golf equipment, and will rent clubs and carts as well. Greens fees are $15 for 9 holes, or $24 for 18 holes. The course is in excellent condition, with lush fairways and immaculately groomed tees and greens. Built in a set of low rolling hills, this is a course no golfer should miss! As one can imagine, this is a popular course hosting many tournaments in the season, including the Men's Open, Ladies' Open, Senior Open, and Junior Open. To reserve a tee time, contact the pro-shop at (306) 783-8424.

SERVICES
The city of Yorkton has a complete range of shopping, mechanical, medical, and worship services available. The concession at Kin Point is open from 1000–2100 hr on weekends, 1600–2100 hr on weekdays, and offers a full range of iced treats, snacks, and pop. Simple grocery items and ice are also for sale. The shower house adjoining the concession is locked but each campsite is given a key upon registration. A television is suspended from the ceiling in the day room between the two shower sets, allowing patrons to catch up with their favorite shows. For more information on this park or to reserve a site, contact the park at:

> York Lake Regional Park
> PO Box 1166
> Yorkton, SK   S3N 2X3
> Telephone: (306) 782-7080
> Fax: (306) 782-6507
> E-mail: yspl@sasktel.net

DUCK MOUNTAIN PROVINCIAL PARK

Located 23 km east of Kamsack on Hwy 57, this park is home to the southernmost reaches of the northern boreal forest. There is a wealth of hiking, biking, golfing, horse riding, skiing and snowmobiling opportunities in this remarkable four-season park as well as the main lake, called Madge Lake, for swimming, sunning, boating, and fishing. The campgrounds are open from the Victoria Day long weekend in May until the Labor Day weekend in September. The park will remain open through the off-season, operating from self-registry kiosks until approximately the end of October, offering a fall camping experience at a reduced rate. Duck Mountain Lodge offers a modern hotel, townhouse-style condos and cabin accommodation year-round. The main area if the park is more heavily developed with cottage subdivisions, the golf course and resort, and other amenities listed below. Pickerel Point is home to all the major campgrounds as well as an excellent beach and wheelchair-accessible nature trail. Truly, this part of Saskatchewan awaits your visit; come for a day and you'll want to stay a week. Come for a week and you may not wish to leave!

CAMPING

When driving east from Kamsack on Hwy 57 you'll find the Pickerel Point campground turnoff to the left about 7 km from the west park entry booth. If you're driving west from Manitoba it will be to your right about 2 km or so west of the park gate. This campground has its own office where your site will be allocated and payments made, and where you can find information on hiking, interpretive programs and all park activities. There are 3 camping loops: Birch, Poplar and Spruce, offering a total of 353 sites.

Located right of the campground office past the store and playground, Birch campground is the largest of the camping loops with 211 sites, 143 of which are electrified with 30-amp service. Of these electrified sites, 15 (#192–207 inclusive) are full service. One section (#139–152 inclusive, all electrified) is available for seasonal rental. The non-electrified sites in the single-digit loop are lakeside and offer evening breezes as well as an excellent view of Madge Lake. All sites are built into mature aspens and pines with plenty of shade and ground cover for privacy. All sites are leveled with gravel and are supplied with a picnic table and firepit. Generally they are huge, large enough for most big modern units; some sites are pull-through although most are back-in style. Trash bins are centrally located in wire-meshed enclosures, and the toilets are either flush or vault-style in the camping loops. Drinking water is supplied in central locations, and firewood is supplied in one huge pile to one side of the Pickerel Point General Store parking lot; the wood is free but you must obtain a camp fire permit. Birch has one service center for the entire loop, with 4 showers and flush toilets per side, male and female. It is fully wheelchair accessible, and has adequate parking. The roadways are mostly gravel and the traffic is bidirectional. When we visited there was new construction and some of the roads were soft in places; that should be all fixed by now, though.

Poplar campground has 59 electrified sites, all reserved for seasonal campers. The loop is accessed immediately left of the campground office, just past the trailer dump station. The sites are large, well spaced and fairly private, with gravel pads and tall trees. They are all of the "back-in" style, and share one service center with 4 unisex showers. They have picnic tables and firepits, and share potable water taps in central locations. Toilets are all modern in this loop, and trash bins are secured inside meshed enclosures. One interesting feature of this loop is that several of the sites back onto the paved biking/hiking trail used to get over to the core area; just a hop away is the pedestrian highway to walk over to the main beach and cottage subdivisions.

Spruce campground is accessed from a left turn just before the store and playground area. This is the loop for the boaters and anglers as you have Madge Lake essentially on either side of the loop; some of the sites are quite pretty for the lake view. The boat launch and trailer parking lot is also in this loop, as is the boat rental shop with its dock and fueling point; these are private facilities, mind you—you'll have to pay if you wish to use them. The loop has 83 sites in total, of which 26 are electrified with 30-amp service. Built amid tall pines, there is less ground cover here so the sites are more open. They are quite large however, and feature the ubiquitous picnic table and firepit. You'll find a filleting table near the public boat launch and dock. Spruce loop has its own service center with 4 unisex showers and flush toilets. There are flush toilets strategically scattered elsewhere in the loop. The trash bins are located inside those same mesh enclosures; one wonders about the raccoon population!

There are also 3 group camping loops: Moose, Elk and Deer are located off a short road just right of the campground booth, or you can access them from behind sites #157 and #158 in Birch loop. Moose and Elk loops are circular with one shared water tap, vault toilet set and meshed trash bins all located around a dining shelter. The loops each have 10 sites with picnic table and firepit although they could accommodate more units than that; none of the sites are electrified. A large grassy area is available between Moose and Elk group sites for wide games; there is no playground equipment available. Deer group campground is square and doesn't have as many sites although it too has firepits, picnic tables and a dining shelter. Vault toilets, drinking water and trash bins are all located near the entrance to Deer Group Campground; the campsites themselves are all open. A fourth group site is located past St. Michaels Camp (a residential summer camp), past Benito cottage subdivision. This is Whitegates Group Site, with 12 non-electrified camp sites. They have picnic tables and firepits and share a potable water tap and central vault toilets. There is no dining shelter here but you do have your own firewood supply. This group area is used as an overflow, and fall hunters prefer this locale. When the park is completely full (on a long weekend) the picnic grounds in the core area will be used as extra sites. The non-electrified sites will have picnic tables and pole BBQs, but will generally not be very large. Having said that, some of the overflow sites will be very large and surprisingly private; some people request these sites for this very reason! There is a ball diamond and tennis courts nearby, and you are close to Ministik beach and all its amenities.

There is also a wealth of backcountry camping opportunities for the adventurous. When exploring the extensive hiking trails in behind Batka Lake you are welcome to camp along the trail. There are also several warm-up shelters along the trail as they are part of the winter cross-country ski trail system. Batka Lake itself has a camp kitchen with picnic tables, firepits, trash bins and vault toilets for day use, as well as a boat launch and dock for anglers; firewood is provided but there is no potable water. As always, you must obtain a free back country use permit at the administration center in the core area prior to your departure as well as check back in upon your departure. This is more for your protection than anything else; the park officials need to know you're there in case of emergency.

HIKING

The park is justifiably proud of its trail system. Indeed, Duck Mountain Provincial Park is the trailhead for the Trans-Canada Trail which enters Saskatchewan from Manitoba approximately 2 km east of Pickerel Point on Hwy 57. The park boasts many trails, rated for degree of challenge, ranging from broad, paved full-access trails to arduous backcountry hikes better suited for the fit and adventurous; a brochure with simple map is available to help plan your travels through the backcountry. The park has also made provision for those wishing to camp in the wilderness; check with the park office about permits prior to departure. For backcountry hikers they also recommend purchasing a 1:50,000 topographical reference map: Kamsack 62N/12, Edition 3, NTS 1927, which is available from:

> ISC Geospatial Data Products
> 300 - 10 Research Drive
> Regina, SK
> S4P 3V7
>
> E-mail: ask@isc.ca
> Home: 1-866-275-4721
> Fax: (306)787-922

Several of the trails offer excellent biking due to the width of the trail itself and the paving that has been done. Those wishing more rustic trails are invited to the Batka Lake trailhead. We hiked the majority of them during our stay and were particularly impressed with the Boreal Forest Interpretive Trail, the Woodland Nature Trail, and the Pelly Point Nature Trail. The Boreal Forest Interpretive Trail is located at the north end of Birch campground and is completely barrier-free throughout its 1.0 km loop. There are numerous signposts on this self-interpretive trail that describe the unique natural surroundings. It is a very easy walk, well suited to strollers and small children, with shady trees and a scenic look at the lake which offers a glimpse of life along a shoreline marsh. The Woodland Nature Trail is paved for its entire length and is wide enough to accommodate mountain bikers and hikers alike. It begins behind Poplar Campground and runs all the way to the Madge Lake core area, a distance of some 6 km one way; the Woodland Trail is a 2 km loop which is part of this system. With tall trees, wide trails and some fairly steep albeit short hills to travel, the trail is wheelchair accessible for sport chairs. Please observe all traffic signs, particularly on the steep downslopes as you can build up quite a head of steam with a mountain bike! The Pelly Point Nature Trail is a 4.4 km loop devoted to hikers although we saw bike ruts along several stretches. To access this wilderness trial, take the road past Madge Lake Riding Stables and the nature center; turn southwest onto Old Park Road—trailhead is well signed with adequate parking, approximately 1.2 km down the road. This trail is much more challenging for the roughness of its terrain, the slippery nature of its slopes, and the narrowness of its trail. You will be rewarded by stands of old growth balsam fir and maple as well as lush fern meadows. The turnaround at Pelly Point has a warm-up shelter with picnic tables and pole BBQs, vault toilets and trash bins. Lake water should be boiled before consumption; there is no potable water but firewood is provided for the camp kitchen. This is a true wilderness hike so you should be prepared with food, water, appropriate footwear and bug repellant.

SKIING AND SNOWMOBILING
As you can see from these short descriptions, there are many adventures waiting for the hiking enthusiast, and these are but a few of the trails that showcase the natural wonders to be found in this park. The same trails offer excellent cross-country skiing in the winter, with a total of 150 km of groomed trails located in and around the park. There are several warm-up shelters along the trails which offer overnight shelter on a first-come, first-served basis; check with the park office first if you plan to overnight in the back country. You can contact the park office for a copy of their "Cross-country Ski and Snowmobile Trails" winter information brochure, or download it from the SERM website.

All this covers just the southern half of the park; there are over 80 km of groomed snowmobile trails surrounding the northern part of the park, all anchored in the park's core area. Add to this the excellent ice-fishing to be had, and you see why this park is popular year-round.

BEACHES AND BOATING
Madge Lake offers the water enthusiast excellent fishing, swimming, skiing and tubing, and boating. There are two main public-access beaches; the largest is in the core area (seen here) and the other at the Pickerel Point campgrounds (seen in introduction). Both have buoyed swimming areas with large creative playgrounds as well as a service center nearby. The Pickerel Point beach is the smaller and narrower of the two, and its service center is across the road beside the store parking lot. The playground is surrounded by tall shade trees and has been extensively refurbished with a huge expanse of soft sand and a brightly colored creative play center. Pickerel Point beach is shaded by tall trees to the east and wooden stairs have been built to provide access to the beach from the playground and lawns. There is little grass to sit upon so you may wish to bring your own chairs. A short walk away is the Pickerel Point store with its tasty ice cream and grilled snacks as well as the obligatory pop, candy and chips. The beach faces west and so offers a better vista of the setting sun.

The Ministik beach is larger, has a huge beach shower and changeroom building with modern toilet facilities and a paved walkway running from the expansive parking lot along the beach front. There are tall trees for shade and benches to rest upon as well as a huge expanse of lush green lawn. The playground here has also seen major upgrades with its own creative play center in a bed of deep, soft sand. A beach concession offers iced treats, grilled foods, and the usual pop and candy. Facing north into the main body of Madge Lake one has a seemingly limitless watery vista from this beach, almost the perfect place for summer star-gazing. The core area also holds the other main sporting venues with golf, ball diamonds, tennis courts, and so on, but those amenities will be covered more extensively in another section.

Spruce campground in Pickerel Point has a boat launch and dock near sites 66–69, with a parking lot behind the sites. There is also a filleting table and a potable water tap beside the boat launch. Past site 83 at Spruce campground is the boat rental and dock, a concession owned by the Duck Mountain Lodge. Here one can rent boats and motors, paddle boats, canoes, and all the attendant safety gear. Current prices can be obtained by contacting the Lodge at (306) 542-3466 or the marina in season at (306) 542-3493.

A larger and much more elaborate marina is available in the core area in a secluded bay just west of the park office. There is an excellent boat launch here as well as boat slips for rent; contact the park office for details. There are vault toilets available for boating patrons but no filleting table or drinking water. The marina is somewhat small but definitely a safe haven in even the roughest weather. It is part of the Kamsack cottage subdivision and has a small picnic area in behind the parking lot with lush green grass and picnic tables with pole BBQs. A third boat launch is available a bit west of this one on a larger bay called Ranger Bay; one must access the launch and picnic area through the Kamsack cottage subdivision. The three main fishing basins in the park, Madge Lake, Jackfish Lake and Batka Lake, are all regularly stocked with walleye and rainbow trout although both Jackfish Lake and Madge Lake have successfully breeding fish populations and so may not be stocked annually; check the SERM website for details—information will generally be about a year behind—or you can download a copy of the most recent stocking list at www.se.gov.sk.ca/fishwild/anglersguide/Stocked%20Waters%2003.pdf. In 2003, for instance, only Batka Lake was stocked in the spring with 100,000 walleye fingerlings.

SPORTS

The park has a plethora of other sporting venues to attract visitors, with paved, fenced tennis courts in a large field behind Recreation Hall. There is also a ball diamond here with a tall, mesh backstop, grass outfields and benches for players. A drinking water tap and vault toilets are also available for patrons. You'll find a day-use area across the road with picnic tables and fire pits. There is no equipment rental for either venue, so bring your own games. No fees are charged for use which is on a first-come, first-served basis. Recreation Hall is quite large, fully enclosed and electrified, and can be rented for private functions by contacting the park office.

Golf is not to be forgotten as the Madge Lake Golf Resort offers the golfing public an excellent, lush 18-hole course with elevated tees, bunkered greens and undulating fairways over its 5522 yards. The licensed clubhouse has a full line of club and cart rentals as well as a pro-shop with golf equipment and clothing for sale. The clubhouse offers fine dining as well as a coffee and snack shop; they set up a large marquis-style tent for the summer months and offer regular steak nights as well as cabarets, local tournaments and league golfing. For more details or to book your own tournament, contact them directly at (306) 542-3485 in season, or check the website at www.teeoff.ca/courses/sk103.htm. They also have the "Log Shack," a warm-up shelter which offers cross-country skiers respite.

A mini-golf course is located beside Lakeside Service just north of Hwy 57 as you drive in from Kamsack. The "Fore Fun Mini-Golf" can be reached at (306) 542-4361, the same number as the store and gas station where you can buy delicious ice cream, coffee, food and fuel. You can also rent bicycles and movies, purchase fishing licenses and bait and, of course, ice.

For the horse enthusiast there is also Madge Lake Riding Stables, where you can arrange for trail rides or board your own horse. They offer hourly rates on guided trips or you can take more extensive rides lasting 4 hours which include a lunch. They also operate remote horse camps for large and small groups with overnight trips a specialty. They will buy and sell horses, board and train horses, and provide riding lessons—truly a full-featured riding stable! You can contact them at (306) 542-3439 or by email at trailrides@canada.com for further information and current pricing.

SERVICES
No discussion of Duck Mountain Provincial Park would be complete without mention of the Duck Mountain Lodge (see page 305). This full-featured, four-season resort offers hotel, condo, and cabin accommodation plus a convenience store for camping needs and souvenirs as well as licensed dining and a swimming pool. They also have "Golf and Accommodation" packages available; because of its popularity one should book groups and conferences early to assure availability. Contact them directly at (306) 542-3466 for prices and availability. The Pickerel Point Store sells a line of groceries including a meat counter, camping supplies, souvenirs and antiques. They also have an ice cream counter and concession offering a range of fast food items, located beside the laundry room. One rents the machines for loonies and quarters; change can be made at the store. You'll find some payphones located beside the store with shade trees and picnic table. You can contact the store directly at (306) 542-3469.

The park itself offers a range of activities throughout July and August, including Interpretive Programming that educates patrons about the natural wonders in which they are living. Such programming includes classes on edible wild plants, fish filleting, orienteering, crafts and much, much more. All the activities are free and can be accessed at various locations throughout the park; check with the Interpretive Center or on the posters found all over. Many of the activities take place at the Charles Harvey Program Center in Pickerel Point, also known as The Amphitheater. Capable of seating 150 or so people, with an illuminated stage, it is available for private functions; contact the park for bookings and fees. The Interpretive Center must also be mentioned as it is the source of all information for the park. Located in the Park Administration building in the core area, admission to this informative, "hands-on" center is free. It is here that you check in for backcountry permits as well as arranging a boat slip in the marina (if available). They have also built an impressive education package, "The Educators Guide to Duck Mountain Provincial Park," which assists classes and teachers planning educational trips to this remarkable place. All of the campsites can be reserved in advance, and it is recommended that you do so as this popular park can fill quickly, especially on long weekends; reservations can be made by written means (mail, email, faxes, on-line at www.saskparks.net) starting January 1 of the current year. Starting the first week in June they will take reservations by telephone at (306) 542-5513.

The town of Kamsack, 23 km west of the park, has a full range of shopping, mechanical, worship, and medical services. There is plenty to do in this marvelous, four-season park; stay and let this special place wash the worries from your mind! The park can be reached at:

Duck Mountain Provincial Park
Box 39
Kamsack, SK   S0A 1S0
Telephone: (306) 542-5500
Fax: (306) 542-5512
E-mail address is linked to their website at: www.saskparks.net.

GREENWATER LAKE PROVINCIAL PARK

Located 16 km south of Chelan on Hwy 38, this 20,700 hectare four-season park has a lot to offer the camping family. There is a lot of hiking, beach fun, free interpretive programs, fishing and boating and all in excellent Boreal Forest, part of the Porcupine Uplands. The campgrounds are open from the Victoria Day long weekend in May to the September long weekend although the rental cabins mean that patrons can visit any time of year. The golf course will be open as long as weather permits in the fall, and there are extensive cross-country ski trails as well as snowmobile trails serving the park and its large cottage subdivisions in winter. There's always something to do!

CAMPING

There are a total of 186 sites of which 144 are electrified with 30-amp service. The sites are spread through 4 main loops near the lake (discussed individually), and there is excellent group camping on the other side of the lake from the main beach area. None of the sites are full-serviced, nor are any specifically barrier-free. One-third of all sites can be reserved by contacting the park office or by using the "reserve-a-site" system; see below for details. All roadways in the campgrounds are paved, as is a barrier-free hiking trail leading from Hilltop and Lakeside campgrounds to behind the campground office. When reserving a site, state your need for such access and the park staff will ensure you get one of several hard-packed sites located near the barrier-free service center. All firewood provided is well-seasoned aspen; bring your own splitting axe, though. One trailer dump station is available just beside the campground office. All shower buildings also house a set of recycling bins for cans, bottles, and so on.

Aspen Grove campground is located just behind the campground office and service center. There are 14 non-electrified sites built into mature aspens with dense underbrush between each site. With the tall trees for shade and the dense brush for privacy, we found this campsite to be perfect for the tenting crowd, or those with smaller camping units. Sites #4–7 are located on a small cul-de-sac and thus form a small group campground although it isn't normally used for such. All sites are leveled with gravel pads and contain picnic tables, culvert-style firepits, and share central potable water taps, firewood and trash bins. There is one set of flush toilets serving this loop, and you have easy access to the service center behind the campground office a short walk away. The service center has a barrier-free washroom but not the showers; patrons requiring that level of access should use the Cranberry Campground service center. Both buildings have benches, and payphones are located at the Campground service center.

Lakeshore Campground is located on the right side of the intersection just past the campground office. All 36 sites are electrified and pull-through style, large enough for the big, modern units and are well shaded with tall aspens. All toilets are modern, flush units. All sites have well-drained, gravel-leveled spaces for the camper and an opening beside for the picnic table and firepit. They share potable water taps, firewood bins and trash bins from several locations in the loop. Of note is the barrier-free hiking/biking trail, accessed from behind site #26, which leads past the creative playground to the campground office. Broad, well-lit and paved, the trail features benches to rest upon and a gentle slope, never steeper than 5%. As biking is very popular in this park, you will be sharing the trail with hikers and cyclists of all ages. Patrons of this loop share the hot showers at the campground office service center; use the Cranberry Campground service center for barrier-free showers.

Hilltop Campground is accessed by taking the left turn at the intersection just past the campground office. All 87 sites are electrified and feature a "stepped" parking pattern, with a deeper spot to back in the camper beside a shallower one for the car, picnic table and firepit. All sites are well drained, leveled with gravel and very generously spaced in tall aspens. Combined with dense brush between sites, they are among the most private to be found in the province. All toilets are modern flush units, fully wheelchair accessible. The sites all share potable water taps, firewood, and trash bins scattered throughout the loop. Park staff will do their very best to accommodate requests for sites requiring wheelchair accessibility.

To access Cranberry Campground you must drive through Hilltop Campground and past the barrier-free service center the two camping loops share. There are 45 sites in this loop (#25 seen here), of which 21 are electrified with 30-amp service. All sites are well leveled and drained, and are built into the mature aspen forest. Excellent shade and privacy plus the usual amenities of picnic tables and firepits make these sites particularly nice. As always, they share low-volume flush toilets, firewood and trash bins, and the service center with its hot showers. There is a large parking lot for this service center as well as a large grassy area for wide games while you wait for the rest of the party to finish their showers.

There is one overflow campground up on top of the hill past the golf course, about 3 km from the main park area on the Marean Lake road. The sites have poorer cover and few amenities with vault toilets, no service center, one firewood bin and no drinking water taps. None of the sites are electrified, and most have picnic tables and pole BBQs. There is almost no privacy between sites to speak of, and shade will be at a premium. The sites here are serviceable, but you would be wise indeed to contact the park early and reserve a site at one of the main loops!

There are 6 group camping areas available with 33 sites in total, about 2 km on

Pheasant Road to the east and north of the main park area. Group sizes vary from 3 to 13 sites, and there are some interesting geometries to be had; some sites have stairs leading up to the tenting site while others have stairs leading down to the picnic table and pole BBQs; even here you have decent privacy! There are central vault toilets, firewood and trash bins, and large open areas in each group site with water taps in the "common" area. You will also be using the shower facilities in the main campgrounds. Call the park office for availability and prices on any of the group areas.

HIKING

There are over 125 km of marked trails established for four-season use in this park. By summer they provide hiking access to the farthest reaches of the park while in winter they are used for cross-country skiing and snowmobiling. Brochures with maps are available upon request by mail, or they can be picked up from the park Interpretive Center which is open year-round.

There are several trails worthy of special note, however, beginning with the Steiesol Lake Trail, approximately 6 km north of the park entrance on Hwy 38. This trail leads to the trout-stocked Steiesol Lake with its winter aeration system. There are a few small privately owned boats lined up on shore, so if you want to try your luck you'll have to portage a canoe up there, a long way uphill, if you ask me! The trail itself is quite pretty though, and well worth the time.

Trailhead for the Highbush Interpretive Trail is located at the south end of the parking lot near the marina. There are two loops: the Greenwater loop is 1.7 km long and offers a feel for what the park has to offer. The Donald Hooper Loop is 3.3 km long, and skirts the wetlands area. Although the trail is quite pretty, particularly in the evening when shadows are longer and the animals are a bit more active, it is boggy in spots and not really wheelchair accessible. There are benches along the trail for rest and lunch stops.

Marean Lake Birding Trail is designed with the birder in mind as the park, particularly its southern edge, is home to over 200 species of wild birds of which 147 species come to the park annually to nest and breed. Trailhead is at Marean Lake about 5 km past the golf course, at the parking area. The self-guided interpretive trail is 1.5 km long, wide, well packed with crushed rock, and crosses through several different ecosystems to maximize bird encounters. Although portions of the trail are wheelchair accessible, there are some very steep sections.

There are several other hikes established for the more robust hiker as they have no prepared hiking surface. The Hawkins Lake Hiking Trail (6 km loop plus an additional 3.3 km around the lake), the Birch Forest Hiking Trail (6 km one way, return on the same trail), and the Rough Fescue Prairie Hiking Trail (13 km return). Other trails are also available, all part of the cross-country skiing trail system; see the "Winter Information—Cross-Country & Snowmobile Trails" brochure for details. You can also take a 63-km driving tour of the area, beginning and ending at the visitor center. For more information on all these activities, please obtain an up-to-date copy of the park's "Hiking & Scenic Drive" brochure from the park office or at the Interpretive Center.

SKIING AND SNOWMOBILING

For winter patrons, whether you're staying in the park or at The Cove Resort just outside the park boundaries, all the hiking trails are used as part of an extensive set of groomed cross-country ski and snowmobile trails. There are several trail shelters and toilets provided for back-country use, and a very serviceable brochure and map to describe the routes and trails. As always when using back country trails, speak with one of the very knowledgeable park staff prior to departure for up-to-the-minute news on trail conditions, presence of maintenance vehicles, trappers lines, and so forth.

BEACHES AND BOATING

The beach here is a marvel: filled with deep, fine sand and anchored on a huge expanse of lawn with a promenade running behind a line of tall shade trees. There is ample parking for the entire complex, from the marina through to the picnic area. There is a brightly colored creative playground with swings, teeter-totters and slides between the beach and the marina. There is also a beach volleyball court, benches spread among the trees, a large beach change room and shower complex as well as a beach spray shower. The Beach Café offers the usual line of popular iced treats (try the Paintball Supreme!), candy, pop and snacks as well as grilled meals and barrier-free picnic tables. The restaurant offers full meals from the same kitchen, and has a seating capacity of 60–80 (if you include the outside seating). The buoyed swimming area is large and fairly shallow; no swimming lessons are taught. The picnic area has metal-framed picnic tables and pole BBQs but no firewood; they would prefer you to use charcoal briquettes here. All in all, the beach is a destination all on its own!

Boaters are not forgotten either, with an excellent marina, boat launch and slips available. The marina is very well protected from even the worst of summer storms as it is located on a small narrow bay. The Tackle Box will rent boats, motors, paddleboats and canoes as well as all the safety equipment required. They've also got a ski boat for rent, and can arrange an operator if requested. They sell a full line of fishing tackle, bait, and fuel, and have some pop and snacks for the anglers just heading out. They even rent a meshed trampoline beside the deck! Contact them directly for prices and boat availability in summer at (306) 278-2845. Of interest is that the back end of the marina, which goes completely around Norgrove Island, is a wonderful place for children to practice pedaling their watercraft in a safe, wind-free area. There are a series of numbered boat slips available for seasonal rent; contact the park office for details. Any of the non-numbered boat slips in the marina can be used on a first-come, first-served basis, free for 48 hours. A good-sized trailer parking lot is available just behind the boat launch.

The two large basins in the park, Greenwater Lake and Marean Lake, have excellent populations of pike, and are stocked annually with walleye fry. Steiesol Lake, approximately 6 km north of the park entrance on Hwy 38, is stocked with rainbow trout. The lake, as mentioned above, is aerated in winter so the fish overwinter quite well. This means that large trout are regularly taken, as large as 6 kg! As no motors are allowed on the lake, it is a quiet place to fish. Having said that, the trail up (although well marked) is approximately 1 km long and none of the boats along the shore can be rented; you must either hike a canoe up the trail or fish from shore. Fish filleting is discouraged in the campsites; use the filleting shack beside the marina boat launch to prepare your catch for the fry pan!

SPORTS

The park has one tennis court built behind Recreation Hall, as well as horseshoe pits. Equipment can be rented from the park store, which also rents all sorts of bicycles, from trail bikes to 4-wheelers. The park arcade is located beside the store as is the "Crazy Critters Mini-Golf"; balls and putters can be rented at the store. The park has one ball diamond located on Pheasant Avenue just before the group camping areas. There are grass in- and outfields as well as a mesh backstop on tall wooden poles. Benches for players, vault toilets, and a potable water tap round out the amenities. As mentioned elsewhere, the park is very popular among birders for the number of species that regularly make the park their home. The park offers a series of interpretive programs during the summer months that educate and amuse patrons with guided hikes, campfire sessions with stories and song, games, and naturalist-oriented programs. All of these are offered free of charge; just get a current copy of the week's events and plan to attend! Ask any of the park staff if you are unsure of where to meet for any of the programs; they'll be glad to help you! As I said before, there's always something to do in this park!

The Green Hills Golf and Country Club is an excellent championship 18-hole grass-green golf course, approximately 3 km from the core area on the Marean Lake road. With rolling well-kept fairways, elevated tees and bunkered greens, and a very scenic forest, this is a pretty course. It plays well over its 6717-yard, par 72 with many scenic holes, particularly since the completion of a $2 million renovation in 2001. The abundant animal life common to the park can often be viewed on the verdant fairways, particularly in the morning hours. The fully licensed clubhouse offers a line of light meals, and the full-service pro-shop provides club and cart rentals as well as branded merchandise and golf equipment. The course pro can provide private or group lessons and the driving range will help hone your skills. For more information, check out their website at www.greenhillsgolfresort.com. You can call the pro-shop in season to book your own tee time or arrange a private tournament at (306) 278-2489.

SERVICES

The park Interpretive Center houses displays about the ecosystems found in the park as well as information on the plants and animals to be found. There was even astronomical information, including the Perseid meteor showers. The displays are colorful, "hands on," and very informative. There is a lot of printed information, and the park staff is very helpful and informative as well. Any questions you may have regarding the park Summer Programming will be capably answered here.

The park has a total of 23 rental cabins available, some modern with fireplace and satellite TV, others non-modern. Thirteen cabins are winterized and can be rented year-round. There are two sets of modern cabins, cedar and log cabins on the hilltop behind the marina, and the cabins across from the beach; the non-modern cabins are all lakefront.

All modern cabins have hot and cold running water; the more rustic non-modern cabins share a washroom facility with flush toilets and sinks in a building behind the units, and patrons have access to the beach showers. All cabins are light-housekeeping style; all you must bring is your food and beverages, personal items, and clothing.

They can be reserved up to one year in advance by contacting the park office by phone or in person; email is for informational purposes only.

The park store is centrally located and calls itself "The Little Store With More," a motto it richly deserves. Besides the bicycle and equipment rentals, video arcade and mini-golf course, it also houses the park's coin-operated laundry machines. They require loonies and quarters to operate, and are very generous with their drying time. The store sells a fairly complete line of grocery and camping items as well as clothing with the park name and logo. With reading materials, a small hardware line, local crafts and souvenirs, and even movie rentals for those rainy days, this busy shop has a lot to offer. They can be contacted at (306) 278-3220.

The Cove is a private resort located just outside the park boundaries with hotel rooms, a swimming pool, an off-sale and grocery store, and a fully licensed dining room. They also have 8 electrified sites for their patrons; check out their website at www.greenwaterreport.com/cove.htm—there's a link for their email address there as well. They can be reached at (306) 278-2992 for information or reservations.

The towns of Porcupine Plain (about 25 km north) and Kelvington (about 40 km south) will meet all your shopping, mechanical, medical, and worship needs. For more information on this park, or to reserve a site (highly recommended) for your own coming visit, contact the park at:

Greenwater Lake Provincial Park
Box 430
Porcupine Plain, SK   S0E 1H0
Telephone: (306) 278-3515
E-mail: greenwater@serm.gov.sk.ca

Website: www.saskparks.net

GOOD SPIRIT LAKE PROVINCIAL PARK

Located 32 km north of Yorkton on Hwy 9, then west on Hwy 229 for 16 km, this park offers one of the better beaches to be found for many miles around. The park was first established in 1931 because of the excellent beach which remains its hallmark to this day. Excellent camping with barrier-free sites and hikes, abundant wildlife and cheerful birdsong combine to make this park a delightful oasis of calm in a sometimes frantic world. The park is open from the May long weekend to the September long weekend with all services, and offers a discount program for fall camping as the service centers will be closed—you must provide your own drinking water as well. The park remains open in winter with its 18 km of groomed cross-country ski trails, and the two cottage subdivisions provide vehicular traffic through the park gates as well. Interestingly, the park completely surrounds a private acreage, the home of one of the original pioneers in this area, Mr. Donald Gunn. A rancher and entrepreneur in the area, his descendants still live locally and regularly return to the old homestead. As it is private property, please respect their privacy when hiking in the area. The other thing of note in the park is the active sand dunes and the interpretive trail established to educate patrons about this remarkable natural feature.

CAMPING

There are three main camping loops with a total of 192 sites, 126 of which are electrified with 30-amp service. There are two trailer dump stations in the park, one near the park entry gates and one near Aspen Campground entrance. Roads are paved through the main camping loops. The campgrounds have all been built into mature aspen forest, so shade is above average and all sites are quite private because of all the bushes (saskatoon and cherry) growing between them. This, of course, means that you can pick the berries for your morning pancakes from your own site! Firewood provided is predominantly poplar and well seasoned; bring your own splitting axe, though.

Aspen Campground is the largest loop in the park with 86 sites, only 21 of which are non-electrified; it is also the nearest to the core area with its many recreational opportunities. Of the electrified sites, 13 (#47–59 inclusive) are reserved for seasonal campers. There are also two barrier-free electrified sites with cement pads, both quite close to the service center with its hot showers and modern toilet facilities; one of these sites is also available for seasonal rental. All sites feature culvert-style fire pits and metal-framed picnic tables; most sites are of the "back-in" style although a few are "drive-along." Some might be a bit cramped for modern units; let the staff at the gate know your needs and they will accommodate with an appropriate site. With the exception of the barrier-free sites, all sites are levelled with gravel pads and well drained. Trash bins and potable water taps are centrally located, and the service center has three showers per side. There is also a small playground set amid dense brush in the forested area across from the service center parking lot. Paths have been made through the brush leading from the campsites to the playground which features a deep sandbox filled with swings, teeter-totters, and climbers. The firewood bin is located across from the service center as well.

Continuing past the Aspen Campground entrance a short distance one finds Balsam Campground with its 62 electrified sites. Three of these (#123, 125, and 126) are held for seasonal patrons. The sites in this loop are a bit larger than in Aspen, being of a "vestibule-type" with a long trailer stall plus a space for tow vehicle in front of the picnic table. There are no specifically barrier-free sites in this loop although site #134, directly across from the service center, would do in a pinch. The service center is smaller than in Aspen, with two unisex showers complete with modern washrooms. Flush toilets in the loops have "Isogel™" waterless hand-washing stations. All sites have culvert fire pits and metal-framed picnic tables, and are levelled with gravel pads. Trash bins and potable water taps are centrally located; the firewood bin is located near site #147. A pedestrian walkway built from the Donald Gunn cottage subdivision runs along the lake behind this campground to the core area, and is accessed from beside site #121. With tall shade trees, excellent privacy and drainage, these sites are among the best to be found.

Sandy Ridge Campground is located a short distance away from Aspen and Balsam, on top of a local promontory (hence the name), just off the Donald Gunn cottage subdivision road. As it is on top of a sand ridge, trees are shorter so shade is at a bit of a premium for most of the 44 non-electrified sites found here. With picnic tables, pole BBQs and packed sand roads, the somewhat smaller sites are more suited to tenting patrons. The campground shares one set of flush toilets, central trash bins and potable water taps. There is a firewood bin beside the toilets near site # 176, but no barrier-free sites or service center. Patrons here can use the beach showers or the service centers in the other two loops. There is another overflow campground available further north along the main road in with the group camp sites.

There are 5 group campsites available in two areas. The first, Group Site #1, is located west of the main road past the Aspen Campground turnoff and has 8 electrified sites along the forest clearing as well as a huge open space with sufficient camping space for many more units. The sites are naturally levelled and drained, and have picnic tables and pole BBQs. There is a dining shelter available with potable water tap, central trash, firewood pile, and vault toilets. The ball diamond with mesh backstop on wooden poles is here, as is a set of horseshoe pits. With the sites mostly located along the forest wall, shade can be at a premium.

The other 4 group sites are north of the Donald Gunn cottage subdivision, in the overflow area. Each group site, numbered 1–4, has a set of vault toilets, a potable water tap, and central wood and trash bins. None of these group sites has a dining shelter, and all sites are naturally levelled and drained. All trees in the group areas are low trembling aspens, so shade is at a premium; if you're planning a family gathering you should be prepared to rig a series of tarps for shelter.

HIKING

The park has built a series of hiking trails running from the main beach south along the lake to Gunn Beach. The Dune Trail is an easy 1-km hike on a paved, barrier-free trail to Gunn Beach, terminating at the Water Control structure. Following the trail to the right at this structure takes you back to the main beach via the Woodland Trail, another easy 1.5-km hike. Both of these trails are also popular with cyclists who share the trail with hikers. From the water control structure down to Gunn Beach is a steep, sandy descent and not really wheelchair-friendly. If one follows the beach about 500 meters to the east you will find the Dune Discovery Interpretive Trail (pictured here), a 1.5-km loop built on a metal mesh walkway with self-guided markers to educate patrons about the fragile sand dune environment. As this area is very fragile, hikers are asked to stay on the metal path and cyclists are restricted. The Trans-Canada Trail is also available in the area with a hiking trail running through the south and east quadrants of the park. In winter, these 18 km are groomed for cross-country skiers; snowmobiles are banned from using the ski trails. There is no camping or open fires permitted in the backcountry, and you must be prepared for an arduous hike so take extra food and water, bug and sun screen, and sturdy footwear. As you walk back to the main beach on Woodland Trail you will see the Gunn family residence; please remember this is private property and respect it as such. The final trail of note is the barrier-free pedestrian walkway running along the lake from the Donald Gunn cottage subdivision to the paved streets of the Kitchimanitou cottage subdivision and the core area. With scenic lake vistas and tall shade trees for much of its length, this walkway is a popular hike just for the fun of it!

BEACHES AND BOATING

No doubt about it, the beach is very popular here and rightly so. The sand has been likened to sugar grains for size and it is regularly groomed to reduce trash, reeds and flotsam. As the lake is relatively shallow (a maximum of 20–25 feet) the buoyed swimming area at the main beach is unsupervised but very warm, just perfect for splashing about. Gunn Beach is also very shallow but the swimming area is unbouyed. There is a cement promenade running the length of the main beach but there is little lawn area. There are two beach volleyball courts behind the beach; balls can be rented with a $5 deposit at the beach concession.

A large playground with a tall, creative structure and swings is located in a deep sandy area near the beach showers and changerooms, beside the picnic area. There is an excellent camp kitchen here as well, although there is no firewood supplied. It can be rented for special occasions but is normally available on a first-come, first-served basis. There are two sets of toilets beside the camp kitchen, an older set of vault toilets that is not wheelchair accessible, and a newer set of barrier-free flush toilets. The picnic area is quite large and well shaded amid tall spruce trees. Metal-framed picnic tables and pole BBQs are available beside an ample parking lot; use charcoal briquettes in the BBQs. This is also the trail head for the Dunes Hiking Trail; you can park here and work up an appetite for lunch!

There are two boat launches in the park: a public-access one north of the Donald Gunn subdivision and a private one in the Kitchimanitou subdivision. The public boat launch has a fish-cleaning station, a water tap and vault toilets beside the ample parking lot, and a long dock for boaters. As the lake is very shallow here, most boaters anchor offshore and walk in. You should note, however, that boats are not allowed at this dock overnight—you must retrieve and store them at your campsite nightly. You can, if you wish, store them near the main launch in the Core Area by anchoring them offshore; there is no charge for this sort of boat slip. You'll find Jiggy's Rentals at the main beach, a full-featured boat rental shop with bicycles, canoes, kayaks, paddleboats and all the required safety equipment as well as fishing boats and motors. They are open from 1000–2000 hr daily in season; contact them directly for prices and availability at (306) 563-7165. Fishing is popular on this lake due to its breeding population of walleye and pike; even though the lake is low at the moment the province does not stock Good Spirit Lake. As the lake is quite large (approximately 54 square kilometers) it is popular for water sports as well: skiing, knee and wake boarding, and sailing—there's plenty of room for all!

SPORTS

Besides water sports and hiking, the park offers beach volleyball (rent equipment at the concession for a $5 deposit) and paved tennis courts beside the recreation hall. You must provide your own tennis gear, however. There is a mini-golf facility beside the recreation hall, with rentals available in a booth that also sells a small line of pop and candy. The park has also built a fine campfire pit in a small natural amphitheatre between Aspen Campground and the mini-golf parking lot. A wide trail runs from the small parking lot across from site #59 to the campfire pit where park staff hosts a "Cosy Campfire" session starting at 2000 hr every Friday night in July and August. This is the stuff of magic, really—stories and songs around a crackling campfire late into the night. Wonderful!

Golf is also popular for park patrons although the park does not itself operate a course. Only 1.6 km south of the park is Good Spirit Lake Golf and Country Club, which operates an excellent 18-hole course. A par-72 course travelling 6326 yards with elevated tees and bunkered greens, a creek in play and heavily treed fairways, it has a full-service restaurant and licensed lounge. The pro-shop offers a line of branded clothing and golf equipment as well as club and cart rentals, and you can book lessons with the course pro. The course is also affiliated with Good Spirit Lake Villas and Inn, a four-season resort offering accommodation for a wide range of patrons. For more details or to make your room reservation, contact them directly at (306) 792-4615. To book a tee time or arrange a private tournament, contact the pro-shop at (306) 792-4600. Further information is available from at www.goodspiritvillas-golf.com.

As this is the largest body of water for miles around, it is home to a large number of birds of all sorts. The forests attract songbirds while the lake attracts shore birds and waterfowl, and sits squarely in the middle of one of North America's largest bird migration routes. All this makes the park very popular among birders, so much so that one commonly sees hikers with binoculars and guidebooks throughout the park.

SERVICES

I must admit I was pleasantly surprised by the park store, the family-operated Manitou Concessions. They offer the usual line of iced treats, burgers, fries and the like, but they go an extra distance for their patrons as they host regular "Breakfast on the Beach" days with a hearty breakfast of eggs, bacon, toast and coffee for a modest $3. I also noted they serve a "Wild Mushroom Omelette" (in season) for the more discerning palate. Add to this the homemade baking they sell, including wild berry pies and crumbles, all served on picnic tables outside (weather permitting) and washed down with gallons of excellent coffee. They also sell a small line of fishing tackle, camping supplies and groceries, all at reasonable prices. They are open daily from May to September, with hours of operation varying based on demand; they're open a bit earlier and stay open a bit later on long weekends, for instance. You can contact them directly in season at (306) 792-4405.

The Spiritwood Market is located about 1.6 km south of the park on Hwy 229 and offers a larger line of groceries as well as liquor and fuel. For those with a sweet tooth, they sell a line of homemade fudge from their "Fudge Factory." They can be contacted at (306) 792-4608.

The city of Yorkton is approximately a half-hour drive away and offers all shopping, mechanical, medical and worship services as well as a casino for the adventurous. Check out the city's web page at www.city.yorkton.sk.ca/

The park offers interpretive programs in July and August with all program information available at Recreation Hall and the administration office. Although most programming is held in the great outdoors, it will be held indoors at Recreation Hall in inclement weather. The Hall can be rented for private functions as well; check with the park office for details. As you can see, this park has a lot to offer the camping public. The Sand Dunes Interpretive Trail is a "must-see" if you are staying in the park. The beach and its camp kitchen are wonderful, the campgrounds quiet and very private, many amenities and all a short drive from a major urban center. For more information or to reserve a site, contact the park at (306) 792-2110 (campground office, in season) or the administration office year-round at (306) 792-4750, or by email at goodspirit@serm.gov.sk.ca. You can also check out their website: www.saskparks.net. Their mailing address is:

Good Spirit Provincial Park
PO Box 38, Site 9, RR 2
Canora, SK   S0A 0L0

TOUCHWOOD HILLS PROVINCIAL HISTORIC PARK

Located 27 km east of Raymore on Hwy 15, Touchwood Hills Provincial Historic Park is noteworthy for several reasons: it housed the last of the Hudson's Bay Company trading posts built in the North West, it served as a way station along what was once the major overland route serving the old Canadian West, and it was once a telegraph station for the Dominion Telegraph company. Perhaps the park may be humble in appearance now, but it once saw the transition of a fledgling nation from Red River cart to steam engine, from open prairie to the beginnings of what would become a flood of emigrants.

Most people know that the Hudson's Bay Company once traded for furs all across Canada and through a part of what is now the United States, but few know that they also traded in the raw fuel of that trade, pemmican. Berries pounded with dried bison flesh and fat are stuffed into bags made of bison hides and stored for long periods of time. Pemmican became the food of choice for the fur trade, feeding the paddlers on the long canoe and York boat voyages as well as the Red River cart treks along the Carlton Trail. Posts like the Touchwood Hills were important in provisioning the fur trade, particularly in the final stages of the 1800s.

Little remains of the Carlton Trail nowadays, just a few ruts vanishing into the prairie landscape. There are places, though, where those ruts can still be seen and with them bring back dim images of a long line of Red River carts, those stalwart if squeaky vehicles with which provisions and trade goods moved west from the railhead and steamboat terminus of St. Paul Minnesota all the way to what is now Portland, Oregon. It passed through Fort Garry, then the hub of the overland trade route and from there cargo was trans-shipped to points all over Western Canada. Truly, the Carlton Trail was an important part of shaping Western Canada's settlement as people built outposts along the trail which grew into farming communities. Not many of those original communities exist, but for a while they were all linked together by the Carlton Trail, and together they were the seeds of Dominion in the West.

Part of shaping the Dominion of Canada was the ability to communicate, and the Dominion Telegraph constructed a line between Winnipeg and Edmonton to ensure settlers had access to the outside world. Many tiny outposts were started up, and one such was at the Touchwood Hills Post. When railroad construction was completed in the area around 1909, the post lost its reason for being and it closed. Today, all that remains of it is a sunken cellar surrounded by a concrete foundation and a stone cairn (pictured above) commemorating the special place of this post in Saskatchewan's early years. There is a smattering of picnic nooks including four pole BBQs carved out of the mature aspens, alongside a gravel road circling through the bluff, but there is no wood, drinking water or toilets. A small parking area beside the prairie grass enclosure in which the cairn and foundation are set completes the amenities for this park. There is no contact number or services available, with the nearest municipality being Raymore where you will find food, fuel, lodging, shopping, medical, mechanical, and worship services. The one thing you will find at Touchwood Provincial Historic Park is the tranquility to reflect on the history of a fledgling land.

For further information contact the park office at:

Regina Park Area manager
3211 Albert St.
Regina, SK   S4S 5W6
Telephone: (306) 787-1475

You can link to their email from the SERM website at: www.saskparks.net.

WILDCAT HILLS PROVINCIAL WILDERNESS PARK

There are three provincial Wilderness Parks in Saskatchewan: Athabasca Sand Dunes, Clarence-Steepbank Lake and the Wildcat Hills. You can only fly into the Athabasca Sand Dunes, or perhaps take a boat across Lake Athabasca if you don't mind boating across what looks like an inland ocean, but you can actually drive right up to the very edge of the Wildcat Hills; Clarence-Steepbank Lake is the only one you can drive into. You'll find the park located about 40 km north of Hudson Bay on Hwy 9 (and west about 14 km through the forest), or about 45 km east of Carrot River off Hwy 55. From there you'll have to walk, though, and make no mistake about it, these hills and the almost incredibly dense forest guarding them are not for the faint of heart.

You must be very well prepared and extremely well versed in wilderness movement. Your compass will only be a general guide—there will be no straight line you can walk to keep a compass bearing due to the trees. You will literally feel as though the forest has closed in behind you. When you do try to camp, there will be no place to adequately pitch a tent, except perhaps for a mountaineers bivouac tent—the trees are just too close together. Should you actually stand on top of the Wildcat Hills and look down, all you'll see is more forest; even the two lakes, Bankside and Firhead, are almost completely hidden amid the tall spruce and fir trees. Bankside Lake has an old bush plane dock, probably used at one time to assist a trapper with pick-up and drop-off, but there is no boat launch of any sort. The lakes apparently have northern pike but they are shallow and the expense of getting a boat in by float plane would dictate you try elsewhere. In short, this park has been set aside to preserve some of the most rugged, unforgiving terrain the province has left. There are logging operations in the area, and you can ask them to watch over your vehicle; they cheerfully did so for the team I sent in to explore. You are also well advised to contact the park office at Porcupine Plain before attempting to hike here; they can give you up-to-date information and it lets them know where to look for you should something go wrong. Let's face it, even a helicopter will have the Devil's own time setting down here—you are utterly, thoroughly on your own.

There are no campsites, so you are asked to practice "no-trace camping"; pack out what you pack in and leave the wilderness as wild as you found it. Water for hikers will be difficult to get to as the lakes are all bordered by marshy banks, and the clouds of voracious insects means you must take plenty of repellant and apply it often as you will sweat it off quickly. There is a snowmobile trail that allows access to Bankside Lake in the winter months but you must be an expert rider; this trail in neither groomed nor maintained. If you intend to explore this wilderness, obtain the latest topographical maps from the provincial office at:

ISC Geospatial Data Products
300 - 10 Research Drive
Regina, SK   S4P 3V7
E-mail: ask@isc.ca
Home: 1-866-275-4721
Fax: (306)787-9220

You'll need 4 maps at 1:50,000 scale: 63 E/1 Leaf Lake, 63 E2/ Fir River, 63 E7 Red Earth, and 63 E/8 Otosquen. These show all the main waterways through the area, including the Fir River and the Man River. If you'd like an out-of-the-way hiking trip but don't want to fight your way into the park, camping along the shores of the Fir River can be quite peaceful; the bridge at Hwy 9 over the Fir River provides an excellent starting point, simply hike upstream as far as you'd like.

For more information on this park, contact the park office at:

Wildcat Hills Provincial Wilderness Park
P.O. Box 3003
Prince Albert, SK   S6V 6G1
Telephone: (306) 953-3571
Fax: (306) 953-2502

Link to their e-mail from the SERM website at: www.saskparks.net

Northern Saskatchewan

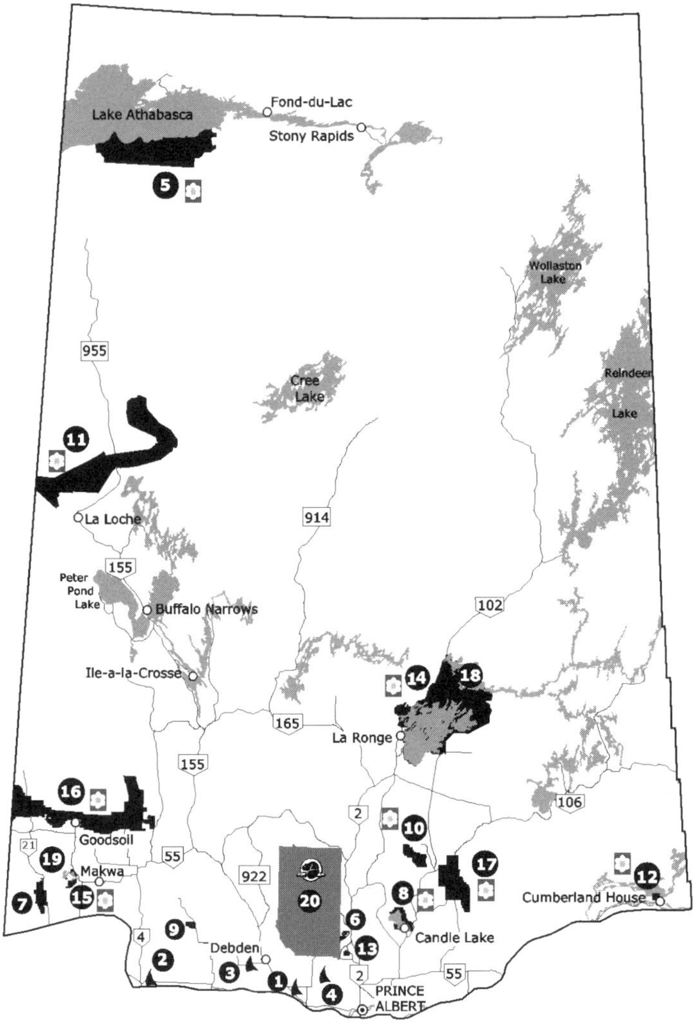
Lake Athabasca
Fond-du-Lac
Stony Rapids
5
Wollaston Lake
955
Cree Lake
Reindeer Lake
11
La Loche
914
155
Peter Pond Lake
Buffalo Narrows
102
Ile-a-la-Crosse
14
18
165
La Ronge
155
16
2
106
10
Goodsoil
21
19
55
922
17
Makwa
20
12
7
15
8
Cumberland House
6
9
Candle Lake
4
Debden
13
2
3
1
2
55
4
PRINCE ALBERT

CANWOOD REGIONAL PARK

Built in 1961, this park is located 4 km east of Canwood, off Hwy 55. The road from town is paved, but the road from the south of the park is graveled. The park is open from the beginning of May until the end of September, or longer if the golf season permits. A great effort has been made to keep the natural beauty of this boreal forest park as true to original as possible, so the park seems new and fresh, if rustic. The park entry fee is $3 per vehicle per day, waived with an annual Regional Park sticker.

SITES

There are 8 electrified sites with 15-amp service, and 12 unserviced sites. They cost $14 and $10 per night each, respectively. All sites are naturally drained and leveled, with a very sandy soil. This makes drainage less of a problem in even the heaviest downpour! Each site has a picnic table, some of which are metal framed, a pole BBQ, and a trash can. Firewood is available from central bins, and drinking water is available from a central tap. Shelter is available from the mature stands of pine and spruce that line the campsite areas. There is not a lot of shelter between sites, though, except for some sites near the golf clubhouse and shower house. There are two group or family camping sites, each about 100 m by 25 m in size. Two dining shelters are available for use in inclement weather or for central cooking for your special occasion. Washrooms vary from the rustic to the modern, as the shower house contains flush toilets and hot showers (they ask for a donation to help defray the cost of the heating), whereas the toilets in the campsite areas are biffy style. The shower house is wheelchair accessible, clean, and well maintained, and has the trailer dump station in front of it. We found the park to be clean, with little litter and no broken glass. Sites can be reserved by calling the clubhouse at (306) 468-2663.

SPORTS

The park has no water sports, pool, or other water access. There are three well-maintained ball diamonds, with gravel infields and grass outfields. There are no team shelters, but bleachers are available to seat hundreds of patrons. The back stops are tall mesh on steel poles, and the home run fences are mesh as well. This complex is the scene of the Elks and OORP ball tournament on the fourth weekend in June, a well attended local event. There are two playgrounds for the wee folk, built in 1988: one smaller beside the golf clubhouse and one larger beside the ball diamonds. Between them, they contain slides, swings, merry-go-rounds, teeter-totters, and climbers. Horseshoe pits are also available, and equipment can be borrowed from the park office. As the park managers try hard to preserve the natural beauty of the park, birds of many sorts can be found making their joyous noise in the park. I have no accurate record of the number of species, but one observer said "about 150." Apparently this referred to the number seen throughout the year, not all at one time!

Golf is another popular pastime in this park, with a 9-hole, sand-green golf course whose clubhouse combines with the park office. There are no practice putting greens or driving ranges, but the clubhouse does rent carts and clubs to patrons, and a scorecard with map will help you around the course. The par-35 course plays well with its gently rolling terrain and sweetly scented pines covering 2783 yards over naturally watered fairways, and is quite reasonable at $8 per round. The Canwood Golf Club clubhouse was built of logs in 1962 and is still in use today. The clubhouse hours are from 0900–2100 hr daily, and staff can serve light lunches as well as the regular pop, snacks, and iced treats. The course hosts the Canwood Open Golf Tournament on the third weekend in July. Tee reservations will not normally be required, but you can call ahead to find out how busy the course is by calling the clubhouse at (306) 468-2663.

SERVICES

The town of Canwood is only 5 minutes away, and will provide all the shopping, medical, mechanical, and worship services the traveler will need. An interesting museum in town also has the mini-golf course beside it. The golf course has a nominal charge, but the museum is free to enter. This park has few entertainments for small children, outside of the playgrounds, and yet we found it peaceful, clean, and a good place for a quiet ramble among the pines. The roadways are all firmly packed sand and the park as a whole in good condition. If you don't mind the fact that there are no water sports to be had, you will probably enjoy the peace and quiet of this naturally pretty park. For more information, contact the Park Secretary at:

Canwood Regional Park
PO Box 9
Canwood, SK   S0J 0K0
Telephone: (306) 468-2663
Fax: (306) 468-2388.

LITTLE LOON REGIONAL PARK

Located 10 km east of Glaslyn, 70 km north of the Battlefords on Hwy 4, this quiet little park features its friendly people most of all. The park was established in the 1960s by local volunteers who built the beach and swimming hole by removing trees, stumps, and sand from along the lake. The golf course was built by breaking the brush and working it down to eventually having grass; it had its grand opening in 1970. The clubhouse was created by renovating an old one-room schoolhouse. Open from May 1 to September 30 (longer if the golfing season permits), this park takes advantage of the lake by placing the majority of its campsites just along the shore. Situated on the west bank of the lake, the park regulars savor the peace and beauty of a quiet sunrise. Indeed, peace and quiet are the norm here and the park managers welcome families to come up and share it with them. Daily park entry fees of $5.35 per vehicle are waived if you have an annual Regional Park sticker.

SITES

There are 27 electrified sites, 21 with 30-amp service and 6 with 15-amp service, and 26 non-electrified sites costing $20 and $16 respectively. Most of the sites are near the lake although they are not actually on the shore itself. The exceptions are a series of sites atop a small hill near the boat launch. Some of these sites are quite nice and could be used as a group site in a pinch. Reservations are accepted and with a campground this small, you'd best call the park office early to book a site, particularly on a long weekend. There are also 51 leased lots available; quite large, with water and electrical service, they are very popular as the waiting list shows. All sites have a pole BBQ, picnic table and a trash bin. Drinking water is available from central taps and firewood is available free of charge from central bins. A new water treatment facility has been built behind the campgrounds. They've also built a wheelchair accessible full-service center near the beach area, with laundry, showers and flush toilets. Most of the sites, particularly those to the right of the entrance road, have excellent shelter among the poplars. Some, notably those to the left of the road (used as the overflow campgrounds), are quite open. A small playground with swings, teeter-totters, slides, and a merry-go-round can be found just beside the mini-golf course, equipment for which can be rented from the concession. A picnic area can be found near the beach or to the right of the main road, about halfway down. With tall shade trees and large rocks as a border, this small but charming spot is an excellent place to picnic and listen to birdsong or watch the sun rise.

GOLFING

The flower boxes on the #1 and #9 tees are a tribute to the many volunteer hours that have built and maintained this charming 9-hole, grass-green golf course. The 2218 yards are listed as a par 33, but its narrow fairways can be deceiving. The course is well watered so the fairways and tees are delightful. Greens fees are $12 per 9 holes or $22 for 18 holes per day. The clubhouse serves as the park office and concession as well, so it is a focus of events for park regulars. It is normal to see people lingering over a piece of pie and a game of crib while their tee-time slips away. The golf course will be there tomorrow; home-made cherry pie is harder to find! Open from 0800–2100 hr, the clubhouse offers home-made cooking and simple groceries as well as the usual iced treats, snacks and pop. Buffets are available at tournaments. The clubhouse will rent clubs and has some carts as well. The course is busy enough to warrant booking a tee-time; contact the park office for details. For smaller golfers, an 18-hole mini-golf course has been set up, costing $2 per adult and $1 per child.

WATER SPORTS

Little Loon Lake is stocked with walleye fingerlings every second year by the provincial Fisheries Department. Regulars say that the lake's deep holes are full of fish, but lament the difficulty in landing one! They blame it on the abundance of freshwater shrimp upon which the fish usually dine. To assist anglers there is a boat launch to the left of the main road, with a large parking lot in which to store the trailer. A small, buoyed swim beach is available just to the right of the camp kitchen and laundry/shower building. The beach sand is coarse but clean, and there is a bench and trash bin to the right in a shaded area. Swimming lessons are offered during the last two weeks of July, and the beach is unsupervised so swim at your own risk. Domestic animals are restricted from the waterfront, as can be expected.

SERVICES

The towns of Glaslyn and Medstead have any shopping amenities for food, fuel, and camping sundries; more extensive purchases can be made in the Battlefords. The town has a first responders' team for medical emergencies, with hospitals available in Spiritwood or the Battlefords. Horseshoe pits are available beside the golf course #1 tee. To the right of the playgrounds is the laundry/shower house. A camp kitchen with wood stove is also found here; it can be rented for family reunions or other such events; contact the park office for details. A trailer dump station is located on the entrance road just before the concession. For information on any part of the park, contact the manager at:

> Little Loon Regional Park
> P.O. Box 458
> Glaslyn, SK S0M 0Y0
> Telephone: (306) 342-2176
> Fax: (306) 342-2135.

MORIN LAKE REGIONAL PARK

Located 18 km west of Debden on grid road 793, this park was built in 1984. It is just a short walk away from the hamlet of Victoire, to which it provides a resort base. The park features a fine lake for various water sports and a quiet campground. Open from the Victoria Day long weekend in May until the Labor Day weekend in September, the park levies a $5 per day vehicle charge, waived if you have an annual Regional Park sticker.

SITES

There are 27 non-electrified sites available, costing $13 per night or $80 per week, and 18 electrified sites (with water service) costing $17 per night or $105 per week. They are leveled with gravel pads and have firepits and picnic tables; trash cans are centrally located and firewood sells for $2 per bundle. Drinking water is available from a central pump near the beach. Washroom facilities have been upgraded to modern facilities with flush toilets and hot showers; they are located by the playground. A new service center near site #9 is kept locked; ask for the access code when you register. Some of the vault toilets are wheelchair accessible, as is the beach shower house; the new service center is not. The manager is located in site #32. Shade is provided by mature stands of poplars and pines, with groves of trees planted as boundaries for various areas. The sites themselves are well built and spacious; all are the "back in" type, and a trailer dump station is provided just to the right of the park gate. Free to registered patrons, others can use it for a $3 fee. An overflow and group area is available to the right of the park entrance and is capable of holding 15 units for $9 per night each. There are many private cabins along the waterfront on Lakeview Ave., but none are available for rent. A map of the park is available from the park gate as you drive in, and sites are assigned as you enter. Reservations can be made by calling the park office at (306) 724-4955 after the first of March in each calendar year. There is a $5 charge plus one night's fee as deposit (non-refundable if canceled) which is applied to the total owing when you register. One can also reserve the group sites for a reunion or such; contact the park office at the address below for details.

WATER SPORTS

The lake provides the bulk of the park's recreation, offering a decent boat launch built of packed gravel, and is listed in the provincial fisheries' system as having the Morin Lake Spawning Shoal. The boat launch is complemented by the large trailer parking lot just to the right along Lakeview Ave. The park has decent fishing for pike and walleye, and perch are often taken as well. Water skiers, canoeists, and sailors also enjoy the lake so it is a busy place. The lake has an island and a sand bar, both inviting boaters for shore lunches or to enjoy a private beach. The park offers one set of swimming lessons in the middle weeks of July from the buoyed swim beach. All Red Cross aquasize and RLSS levels are taught. The price will vary depending on level desired, so contact the park office for details. The beach itself is just across the road from the playground and picnic area with parking lot, and has fair, coarse sand. They've built a beach shower near the volleyball court to rinse the sand off. A beach gazebo has been built, an excellent place to watch the sun sink away across the lake. There was no evidence of beach parties, and everything was clean and presentable during our visit. The playground beside the beach was built in the 1990s, and has been revised yearly since then. It now has slides, swings, climbers and teeter-totters, all built on a large lawn. As with all the equipment in this park, it was neat, clean and brightly painted when we visited, an obvious sign of the pride the maintenance staff takes in their work.

SPORTS

Although not part of the park, the village of Ormeaux (about 10 km away) has a privately owned 9-hole, par-35 grass-green golf course; the clubhouse has a pro-shop with equipment rentals. There is one baseball diamond beside the overflow/group camping area. The park is notable in the area for the birds that make it their home, and a 1.5 km walking trail explores the forest nearby. There are also other short hikes to lead one to the town or other local sights. A set of horseshoe pits is located by the beach, as is the beach volleyball net; bring your own equipment for both sports.

SERVICES

The park also operates the Morin Lake Reunion Grounds which cover a large area and include camping sites, two ball diamonds, horseshoe pits, outdoor dance area with a covered sitting/dining hall, large fire pit with benches, plus a large clubhouse with washrooms and cooking/dining facilities. Useful for reunions, tournaments and wedding receptions, they can easily accommodate 200–300 people; contact the park office for rental details.

The town of Victoire has the "Little Country Grill" open from May to September, which caters to the appetites of visitors. It offers a good range of home cooked meals for reasonable prices, as well as deep fried foods like onion rings or french fries. Grocery shoppers will approve of the Lucky Dollar Store in Victoire. Travelers needing more extensive medical, shopping or mechanical services will have to go to Debden, home to the Debden Community Center with its bowling alley, museum and library. This park is quiet but charming and won't normally be busy except for the Family Day celebration in the second week of August, scene of the annual relay races, and during the swim lessons in July. These events are co-ordinated by the Morin Lake Regional Park Board and are well attended. For more information on this park, contact the park manager at:

Morin Lake Regional Park
PO Box 503
Debden, SK   S0J 0S0
Telephone: (306) 724-4955
Fax: (306) 724-2220.

STURGEON LAKE REGIONAL PARK

Located 23 km north of Holbein off Hwy 3 on grid road 693, this park is open from the Victoria Day long weekend in May until the end of September. The park gates are open from 0800–2100 hr daily in season, and checkout time is 1200 hr. This pretty resort lake has lots of very nice cabins, all privately owned. The park levies a $5 per day vehicle entry fee, waived if you have an annual Regional Park sticker.

SITES

There are 28 electrified sites and 5 non-electrified sites, renting for $16 and $11each per night, respectively, and 6 full-service seasonal sites. A group or overflow area on the top of the hill, to the left of the park access road, has some electrified sites, horseshoe pits, beach volleyball, and biffies. They have also built the mini-golf course in a fenced compound in the group area. It is large enough for 20 or 30 units and although not as well shaded as the main campgrounds, it is still a very nice area for group use. As you can see from the picture above, all sites have picnic tables, firepits with grates, and are naturally leveled and drained. Trash bins are located on every site, and shade is provided by the mature spruce and pine trees in which the park is built. Some sites are pull-through style, but most are "back-in" style and generally big enough for most units. The roadways are wide and in good condition, so handling the big trailers isn't as bad as it could be. Washrooms vary from primitive biffies in the campgrounds to modern flush toilets in the fully wheelchair accessible shower house. The showers are coin-operated, requiring loonies to run, and are open from 0800–2100 hr daily. There is a sewer dump to the right as you enter, free to registered patrons. There is a dining shelter available in the picnic or day-use area with extra picnic tables and a camp stove. It has access to the beach-side playground and a large grassy area to play on. Drinking water is available from central taps scattered throughout the camping area. Quiet time is from 2330–0630 hr, enforced by the park patrol. Reservations are accepted and recommended for weekends particularly; contact the park office at the number below for details.

WATER SPORTS

Sturgeon Lake is stocked annually with pike, walleye, and perch. The lake has a boat launch with a large parking lot in behind for trailer parking, and a fish-cleaning table near the shore. The beach is filled with fine sand and small pebbles, and there is a buoyed swim area in front of the playground. A floating dock with a slide on one side and a diving board on the other is moored about 10 meters off shore. No swim lessons are taught, and there are no changerooms except for the shower house a short distance away. The beach playground has slides, swings, merry-go-rounds, and a creative play center built on a large expanse of sand. Pets are allowed in the park but they must be on a leash, and they are strictly prohibited from the beach area. As with all of this park's equipment, the playground toys are well constructed and maintained. The park also has horseshoe pits and a beach volleyball court up in the overflow area. Equipment for these sports can be signed out free of charge by registered campers from the store.

SERVICES

A hiking trail extends from the main camping area north along the lake to Pickerel Point, a favorite destination. There is no trail guide, but it is well traveled and easy to follow for its kilometer length. The park office is also the store and diner. As the store, it offers a line of snacks, pop and iced treats as well as simple grocery and concession items. As a diner it serves light meals and offers a place to meet for coffee and visit friends and neighbors. You can even phone ahead to order for either sit-down dining or to take away. It is open from 0900–2100 hr daily in season, and may stay open longer if demand warrants. Patrons wishing to make larger purchases may have to go as far as Shellbrook, 13 km west of Holbein on Hwy 3. This town offers banking, shopping, medical, mechanical, and worship services. The park hosts the annual Cabin Owners Potluck supper, a very well attended mass picnic, but has few other events. This park prides itself on being a quiet family park with a friendly atmosphere, and the fact that the park was honored by the Regional Park system as the "1996 Park of the Year" reflects this. It's a popular park, and full most weekends so reservations are a good idea; for more information, contact the park office at:

    Sturgeon Lake Regional Park
    PO Box 475
    Shellbrook, SK   S0J 2E0
    Telephone: (306) 747-3331.

ATHABASCA SAND DUNES PROVINCIAL PARK

Located on the southern shores of Lake Athabasca in northwestern Saskatchewan, this park offers a unique ecological and evolutionary ecosystem. Comprised of approximately 100 km of active sand dunes along the lake shore, you will find plants and landforms that exist nowhere else in the continent. The dunes found here are among the northernmost such landforms in the world and offer an almost alien vista; the pictures of desert pavement (seen here, photo courtesy of SERM) bear an eerie resemblance to the pictures sent from the surface of Mars. As they exist in the cooler temperate zone, the plants that inhabit these dunes have evolved to withstand extremes of temperature and moisture conditions. Add to this the stunning if somewhat surreal scenery and you can see why the park is gaining in popularity among the adventurous. There are no amenities here, and no way to access the park except by float plane in summer. Even if you do rent a plane and go, there will be no infrastructure to assist you in your stay when you get there; you must be completely self-sufficient and prepared for the wilderness. Excellent 1:50,000 topographical maps cover the area from William Point to MacFarlane River: 74N/3 William Point, 74N/2 Cantara Bay, 74N/1 Archibald Lake, and 74O/4 Helmer Lake. Obtain appropriate maps from:

ISC Geospatial Data Products
300 - 10 Research Drive
Regina, SK   S4P 3V7
E-mail: ask@isc.ca
Home: 1-866-275-4721
Fax: (306)787-922

Should you decide to go, be aware that there are only six authorized places to camp: three near the McFarlane River on the eastern edge of the park, and three around Thompson Bay and Beaver Point on the western third of the park. All have good water access, but you should be bringing cook stoves as gathering firewood will damage this fragile ecosystem. Fishing is excellent, particularly for pike, and there are many species of birds living or traveling in and through the area. You should also be aware of the manner in which the park is sub-divided as this will impact directly on your selection of camping area. There are three management zones listed as 1–3 with various strictures on use; Zone 1 is for day-use only, Zone 2 is restricted to no more than 3 days camping in one place, and Zone 3 is restricted to no more than 7 days of camping in one place. Campfires are not allowed in Zones 1 or 2, and not recommended for Zone 3. Hiking is allowed in most areas, but hiking across desert pavement is prohibited and must be avoided as your footprints will disturb the pebbles and erode the surface.

SUGGESTED RESOURCE READING

There are three other works I would suggest you obtain and check for more information prior to any trip into this fragile environment: for simple information on what and where to go and see, I suggest the Saskatchewan Environmental Resource Management brochure, *Athabasca Sand Dunes Provincial Wilderness Park*, available from SERM or from the department office in Stony Rapids; call 1 (306) 439-2062 for your copy. Although not as comprehensive as the other two suggested references, it does provide an overview of the history and geography of the area. The next book is much more graphic in nature, a photo journal of trips into the park made by Robin and Arlene Karpan. Entitled *Northern Sandscapes* (published by Parkland Publishing, 1998), this is a richly illustrated guide to their interesting visits of the park, their thoughts and impressions as well as some very useful data on traveling in the park; well worth the read if you're thinking of visiting here yourself. Lastly is the more academic work entitled *The Sand Dunes of Lake Athabasca* by M. Jonker and Stan Rowe (published by University Extension Press, 2001). The book is filled with data and photos from several visits made by research teams from the University of Saskatchewan, and describes in great depth the things one will find here. Endemic plants, animals, fish, landforms and geology are all discussed in layman's terms although scientific names are used for all the living things catalogued. The book is also filled with interesting sidebars, each with a factoid or native story, or anecdote about travel in the area. Well organized and extensively indexed, the book is full of invaluable information on this incredible place.

SERVICES

There are no services in the park whatsoever; in making this journey you must be mentally and physically fit, fully competent to live and travel in the area. This means you must know about wild animals, zero-impact camping, and non-motorized means of travel (canoe and sea kayak are preferred) as well as navigation with map and compass. You must also acquaint yourself with the rules and strictures in place that govern use of this park. For more information, contact the park office at:

Athabasca Sand Dunes Provincial Wilderness Park
Box 5000
La Ronge, SK   S0J 1L0
Telephone: (306) 425-4288
Or:
SERM
c/o General Delivery
Stony Rapids, SK   S0J 2R0
Telephone (306) 439-2062

Athabasca Eco Expeditions is a private organization which offers guides and expertise for travel in this special place; visitors are strongly recommended to allow them to make travel arrangements in the park. For more information, contact them directly at:

Athabasca Eco Expeditions
PO Box 7800
Saskatoon, SK   S7K 4R5
Telephone: (306) 653-5490, toll-free: 1-800-667-5490
Website: www.athabascalake.com/ecoindex.htm

ANGLIN LAKE PROVINCIAL RECREATION SITE

Located 65 km north of Prince Albert, follow Hwy 2 and turn left on Hwy 953. The paved highway is very scenic all the way through the resort community of Anglin Lake. Mature mixed woods and boreal forest make for a very pleasant drive, particularly in the early morning when wildlife abounds along the road. The first sign along Hwy 953 will be for the Scout camp, followed shortly by the turn into the North Campsite. Just past that is Anderson Point campgrounds, then the resort community of Anglin Lake. Carrying on past Anglin Lake brings you just to the border with Prince Albert National Park. The park has excellent camping, access to the amenities of the resort community, extensive hiking on the cross-country ski trails, plus excellent fishing and boating on the Anglin Lake basin. Could you ask for anything more!

SITES

There are three campgrounds and a day-use site in the Anglin Lake Recreation Site, two of which are non-electrified group sites. The Anderson Point campground is the largest with 25 electrical and 35 non-electrical sites. As we drove around the campground we noted several sites with orange marker tape across the entrance; these sites are for seasonal campers. As with most other provincial parks involved in this program, seasonal sites are available from the May long weekend to the September long weekend. Sites are allocated by a public lottery process in April at each park; successful applicants are notified soon after and sites not allocated are available on a first-come, first-served basis after the draw date. If you are interested, contact the park of choice or call (306) 787-2700. We found the campsites to be sparsely placed, with 10–20 meters between each, often more. All the campsites were very large, easily capable of holding a camper, vehicle, and boat trailer. All sites are built on graded gravel pads amid mature trees, and feature sturdy picnic tables and firepits with swinging grates. Potable water is available from central taps, and electricity supplied is 30-amp service. Bear-proof trash bins are centrally located. Firewood is available from a central bin; although the wood is free, campers are expected to pay a campfire fee. A new wheelchair accessible service centre with modern toilets, sinks, and free hot showers has been built down by the lake. New flush toilets have been built in the campgrounds although the old buildings are still there. A trailer dump station is available near the park entrance. A self-registration booth is available to the left as you drive in; set up on an open site, then go back and register it for your stay, placing the tag in the post beside your site.

The two group sites are available as economy camping for $13 per night, and can be booked for a private function by contacting the Christopher Lake SERM office at (306) 982-2002. Just before the Anderson Point campgrounds is the north site, with 8 non-electrified sites, all self-registered. Toilets are vault-style, clean and free of odor, and water is available from a central tap. The charm of this campground is the shore-side placement and its open, airy feeling. Most of the trees are behind the sites, so they are open to the north. The second group site, called the Spruce River campgrounds, is about 2 km past the cottage subdivision and includes a camp kitchen. This campground features 10 non-electrified sites, one set of vault toilets, and the same sturdy picnic tables and grated firepits found at the other group site. The sites are strung out amid jackpines whereas the North sites featured aspen and birch trees. Both campgrounds were neat, free of broken glass and rubbish, and naturally leveled and drained. Bear-proof trash bins are centrally located. For those looking for a slightly more adventurous camping experience, try canoeing from the north site to the Spruce River site, fishing as you go. It's a gentle day's paddle with no portages, and excellent camping at both locations. The return journey is no less pleasant, particularly if you hug the north shore as you travel; it may not seem like much of a difference, but the change in scenery makes it seem like two separate trips!

There is no camping at the Jacobsen Bay day-use area, but there are picnic tables on a large lawn, a boat launch, dock and fish filleting station, and swim beach. There is ample parking and the Jacobsen Bay Outfitters is just across the parking lot for ice cream!

SPORTS

A fine, colorful playground has been built in the Anderson Point campground, sure to be busy for the slides and climbers it offers. A fine beach has been built near the boat launch, with somewhat coarse sand but clean and free of broken glass. There will be no lifeguards or swimming lessons, so plan accordingly. An easy hiking trail has been built from site #48 to the Anderson Trapper's Cabin, a heritage site commemorating the very people for whom the campground is named. Only 5 minutes in walking length, the trail is wide and easy to follow, and the buildings you'll walk among at trail's end are an interesting injection of local color and history. As the park prides itself on its excellent camping and lake access, it makes no attempt to provide for ball players or other sports, but excellent golfing can be had at the Emma Lake Golf Course or the Elk Ridge Golf and Country Club, both approximately a half-hour drive away.

Fishing and boating are big sports in this park, as water is everywhere one looks. Many fine pike and walleye have been caught here, and the water table is stable as a dam moderates the flow out of the basin. The lakes are relatively small, so canoeing is popular among campers who choose their own muscles to explore the many small bays and reed beds. A fine boat launch is available at the Anderson Point campground, but it has very poor docking and landing facilities; please make every attempt to avoid undisturbed areas to land your boat as the damage can take years to repair. A filleting station is available just behind the boat launch, well lit and odor free. Just remember, this is bear country, and fish entrails would attract some unpleasant company so you would be well advised to use the filleting stations! Although water skiers and tubers will toy about on the lake, this is really fishing country, so boats and motors can be rented from Land of the Loon Resort at the Anglin Lake Cottage subdivision. You will also find food, fuel, a modest restaurant, and cottages or hotel accommodations for rent. Contact them for more information at (306) 982-4478 or visit their website at www.landoftheloonresort.com.

HIKING

This park deserves a special category for the quality of its hiking trails. They are essentially the same trails as used for cross-country skiing in winter, even though the park isn't open then, but one can rent ski gear from the resorts in the area. The 48 km of hiking trails are well marked, with a serviceable map available from SERM; pick one up from the local outfitters or order one from the park office. The glory of these trails is that they hook up with the extensive trails in the Prince Albert National Park; you can hike from one park to another. From the Anderson Point Campgrounds one only has to walk about 2 km to get to the trailhead at the Jacobsen Bay Outfitters. A gentle 3 km hike gets you across the bridge just past the Spruce River campgrounds; thus far the terrain has been forgiving, with tall trees and pleasant footing. Just past the bridge, though, things get interesting as you hike towards the fire tower. With an elevation of 1950 ft, and a very steep access trail, your hard work will be rewarded with a stunning view of the surrounding lake country. The Anglin Lake Recreation Area is spread out at your feet in glorious detail, and to your right you can see the beginnings of Prince Albert National Park. Just down and to the right from the fire tower is the 1-km access trail to the Spruce River Highland Trail, a loop covering 8.5 km of hills and woods in Prince Albert National Park. There is one shelter along this network, at the junction of the Moose and Jacobsen Bay trails. It has no amenities, and overnight camping is discouraged. There are no water points along this trail, and anyone attempting it is expected to be self-sufficient. With the exception of the steep, cautionary areas, most of the trails will be accessible by persons with moderate fitness. At a hiking rate of 2.5–3 km per hour, most of the trails can be done in one day's hiking, without requiring an overnight stay. As this is a mixed wood forest, you will walk among many different types of terrain and forest cover. The hills will carry you up to marvelous vistas, while walking along the valleys and wetlands will show you the diversity of this extraordinary place.

SERVICES

With the Resort Village of Anglin Lake a 2-km stroll from the Anderson Point campground, one needn't go far for simple purchases. The store at the Jacobsen Bay Outfitters has all the tackle, camping supplies, ice cream treats and simple groceries one could ask for. The Outfitters can also rent boats, motors, souvenirs and even serve simple meals in their coffee shop. Major shopping is available in Prince Albert, a 45-minute drive away, along with a full range of medical and mechanical services. The paved highway ends just after the Spruce River group campgrounds, but continues as a gravel road all the way back to Emma Lake and cottage country. The paved road is generally in better shape, though, even if it is a bit longer. For more information on this wilderness gem, contact the park office at:

Anglin Lake Provincial Recreation Site
P.O. Box 66
Christopher Lake, SK S0J 0N0
Telephone: (306) 982-2002.

BRONSON FOREST RECREATION SITE

Located 60 km north of Paradise Hill on Hwy 21, this 15,540-hectare park offers a pristine getaway for the angling enthusiast with its many lakes and rivers. There is good camping at the two campgrounds, and local lodges offer hotel accommodations. Travelers will also find the North-West Resistance left its mark in the area, with provincial historic parks at Fort Pitt and Steele Narrows. Nearby, St. Walburg once boasted Count Imhoff, a noted painter of religious works, among its residents and his studio is now a museum showcasing his astonishing work. Truly, there is much to offer in this pretty little park and its supporting communities.

SITES

There are two campgrounds in the park: Little Fishing Lake and Peck Lake; a third at Ministikwan Lake has been taken over by Johnson's Outfitters, who operate the lodge there.

Little Fishing Lake is the first campground you encounter as you drive north on Hwy 21. It has 33 non-electrified sites, 10 of which are reserved for seasonal rental. All sites are naturally leveled and set among mature jackpines which provide good shade but little privacy between sites. They have picnic tables, pole BBQs, and access to central water bibs, firewood and trash bins. Toilet facilities are vault style but clean and well-maintained. The campground operates on a self-serve basis from a kiosk beside the parking lot serving the beach; set up on a vacant site then register and pay at the booth in the envelopes provided. There is one camp kitchen near the beach changeroom and playground, with a water bib and trash bin. All trash bins, by the way, are sturdy bear-proof models. There is a trailer dump station just to the right of the first entrance as you drive up to the campground. Across the road from the campground is Little Fishing Lake Resort, where you can purchase fuel, groceries, fishing equipment and some camping essentials. The resort also has a shower/laundry house (all coin operated) as well as a diner and a payphone. You can call them directly at (306) 344-2276.

The beach, although narrow, is quite long and filled with fine, clean sand. The beach changeroom is Spartan but clean and the playground is small, having swings and climber with a slide, all set in clean sand. It also has (as does the beach) benches for patrons to rest upon while the children are playing. There is no buoyed swim area; swimming is unsupervised. The lake has a boat launch and simple dock but there is no marina; patrons are expected to retrieve their boat nightly and store it on their site. A fish-cleaning table is located near the boat launch; to keep bears away, please clean all your fish here, not in the site!

Peck Lake is a smaller lake and campground located a few kilometers north of Little Fishing Lake. There are 20 non-electrified sites here, 10 of which are reserved for seasonal campers. The seasonal sites, #1–10, are all back-in style and leveled with gravel pads. Of special note are sites numbered 12–20, all of which are lake-front. All are naturally leveled and drained and have picnic tables and pole BBQs. Potable water is shared from a bib near the camp kitchen near site #20. There are shared trash bins, vault toilets and firewood near site #5 and the beach changeroom and playground is near site #17. There is an overflow area just south of the campground entrance with its own water bib, vault toilets and firewood. The self-registration kiosk is located beside the parking lot that serves the camp kitchen and beach area. There is no shopping or other service at Peck Lake; the nearest will be at Little Fishing Lake.

The lake has a boat launch and simple dock but no marina; you must retrieve your boat nightly and store it in your site. There is a fish-cleaning table beside the boat trailer parking lot; please do not clean fish in your site. The beach is wider and filled with soft, fine sand, but the lake has receded a bit so there is a line of detritus along the water's edge. The water is clean and shallow enough for splashing about, but there is no buoyed swim area nor are there any benches; swimming is unsupervised.

SERVICES

The town of Paradise Hill has all the shopping, mechanical, medical and worship services the traveling camper could want, while the towns of Loon Lake (45 min. NE) and St. Walburg (45 min. SE) offer somewhat more extensive services. There are several hunting and fishing outfitters in the area: Little Fishing Lake Resort, Ministikwan Lake Lodge, and Johnson's Outfitters. As they are in the park but not of the park, they will not be considered at length here except for mention where they are associated with a campground as at Little Fishing Lake. They all offer a variety of hunting and fishing experiences, and they all have a lodge and cabins or campsites for rent. If you are interested in this type of service, contact them directly for more information at:

Little Fishing Lake Resort: (306) 344-2276
Johnson's Outfitters: (306) 837-4731
Ministikwan Lake Lodge: (306) 837-4962

There are no established hiking trails in the park although an ATV trail, used for snowmobiles in winter, wanders from lake to lake and offers the mountain biking enthusiast a chance to explore the park off road. The park may be small in listed amenities, but it is large for the experience it offers; peaceful northern nights and a chance to catch your supper in one of many small lakes in the area. At night, stories around a campfire while the Northern Lights dance offers the perfect end to a day in the Boreal Forest. For more information on this park, contact the park office at:

Bronson Forest Recreation Site
Box 39
Loon Lake, SK   S0M 1L0
Telephone: (306) 837-2410
Fax: (306) 837-2415
Website: www.saskparks.net

CANDLE LAKE RECREATION PARK

Located approximately 75 km north and a bit east of Prince Albert, this park is renowned for its sandy beaches and excellent fishing amid a boreal forest and parklands setting. Take Hwy 55 to Meath Park and turn north on Hwy 120. Open from the beginning of May to the middle of September, the park has two campgrounds available to serve your needs. The largest is the Sandy Bay campground, just past the Resort Village of Candle Lake, while Minowukaw campgrounds is located on the east side of the lake. Besides camping, there are many outfitters serving the cottage country around this beautiful lake; for more complete information on these private businesses, contact the chamber of commerce at (306) 929-2115. As a recreation park, one would expect to find a wide range of activities here, and you do: hiking, fishing, boating, berry and mushroom picking, birding, skiing and snowmobiling (in winter) and the chance to get back to the "silent spaces." Come and see for yourself!

CAMPING

There are two campgrounds, as mentioned above, which I will consider separately. The first (and largest) is Sandy Bay Campgrounds, located about halfway up the west side of the lake, past the Resort Village of Candle Lake. There are 146 campsites in total, all back-in style and none of which border the lake. Of these, 76 sites are electrified with 30-amp service and the others are unserviced; none are full-service sites. Each site has a pole BBQ, picnic table, and access to central potable water taps and trash bins. Toilet facilities in the campgrounds are generally vault style except for modern flush toilets in the service center. There is one firewood bin—bring your own axe as very little wood was split! Please note, there are no dining shelters in the campgrounds; the only one available is in the beach area right in the resort village. All roadways in the campgrounds are paved; the sites are leveled with gravel and should be large enough for just about any unit. A trailer dump station is located just north of the road as you drive in past the entry office.

Interestingly enough, tenting is so popular in this park that 6 sites (#40–45) are reserved for tenting only; there is a small parking lot in behind these sites for your vehicle. A further 8 tenting sites are located along the edge of the boat trailer parking lot; generally speaking these sites are used only as overflow when all others are full. Four electrified sites (#335–338) near the service center are reserved for wheelchair visitors. The sites are leveled with asphalt and are situated near water taps as well. The service center itself is fully wheelchair accessible, and includes the laundromat, showers, and recycling bins. There is also a payphone and information board here for your use. The laundromat requires loonies to operate both washers and dryers and the showers are coin-operated as well. There are several group camping areas, one just north of the park entry office and two others located at the Fisher Creek day use and picnic area. When we visited, the Fisher Creek group sites were occupied with a rather large family reunion so many of the picnic tables that would have been scattered throughout the wooded trails were gathered into the group sites.

The group site just past the park entry gate is also the terminus for the Musker Lake Trout Pond Trail. At about 1.5 km, it's an easy stroll through the woods and across the highway to an excellent resource in the trout pond. Stocked annually with rainbow trout, the pond is remarkably well suited to the wheelchair-bound angler, with paved trails running from the parking lot to the dock overhanging the pond itself. The dock has a complete bench and rail enclosure allowing anglers to safely cast and retrieve from the comfort of their own wheelchair—quite remarkable, really, even if it doesn't have a fish filleting shack; all provincial fishing regulations apply.

The second campground is the Minowukaw Beach Campground accessed off Hwy 120 just past the Torch River Bridge, about 10 minutes or so past the resort village of Candle Lake. The name comes from the Cree words for good (*mino*) and bend (*wukaw*); the beach has a gentle bend in it. There are 54 electrified sites (all in the 100 block) with 30-amp service, and 34 non-electrified sites; none are full-serviced. There are two main camping loops, the 100 block being closest to the store and café. These sites have taller trees but sparse ground cover so they are not as private as the sites in the 300 loop. All sites have pole BBQs and sturdy picnic tables. Firewood is available from a central bin near site 133 and potable water is available from central taps. All roadways are paved, and the sites are leveled with gravel and should be large enough for most units, particularly in the 100 block. Toilet facilities are flush in the 100 and 300 loops, vault elsewhere. One wheelchair accessible service center with free hot showers can be found south of the 100 loop on the road to the beach parking lot and the other camping loops. One walkway has been built running beside site 151 to the parking lot behind the boat launch, and many trails run throughout the loop, all of which ultimately lead to the store and its summer treats. It has been my experience that there are two great trail builders in the forest: deer moving from food to water and children finding ice cream!

The 200 block is very open with little shade as the trees were thinned out in 2000–2001 as part of the Dwarf Mistletoe Management Project. Because of this, and because none of the sites are electrified, the loop is rarely used except as an overflow when the park is full. The sites do have picnic tables, pole BBQs and access to two central potable water taps and one set of vault toilets. Firewood is available in a central bin shared between the 200 and 300 loops. The sites in the 300 loop, although non-electrified, are interesting as they are the most private in the park and those numbered 301–309 (odd interesting as they are the most private in the park and those numbered 301–309 (odd numbers only) back onto the lake so you can bring your boat right up to the site—very handy (see photo of site 309). As with the other loops, they feature pole BBQs, sturdy picnic tables and graveled sites. One set of flush toilets near site 313 (and a small parking lot) serves this loop, and potable water is available from central taps. There is a small trail leading off between sites 313 and 312 to take you to the dam and spillway that is part of the water table maintenance for this popular lake. Protected from the ravages of waves and wind by a deep, narrow inlet and large rocks, this is an interesting place to watch the sun set or (as we saw during our visit) catch minnows and bugs with hobby nets. The trail continues past the dam around the point to the park boundaries and Camp Tawow, one of several residential summer camps in the area. There are no sites specifically reserved for tenting or wheelchair use in this campground; for that you must use the Sandy Bay area. There is one group camping area to the north of the intersection that leads to the campground entry office. Used as an overflow under normal circumstances, it can be reserved for your group function by calling the park office at the address below. It has its own central open area surrounded by 10 or 12 pole BBQs and picnic tables, its own vault toilets, potable water and firewood supply.

Minowukaw Beach is served by Joe's Cabins which operates a store with café, cabin and boat rentals, and offers quite a complete four-season operation; for more details and current prices, contact them directly at (306) 929-4619, or visit their website at http://www3.sk.sympatico.ca/lucraw. I mention them here because it would be difficult to discuss this campground without telling you about this facility; the park and this operation are pretty heavily intertwined in providing service to the camping public.

BEACHES

As mentioned above, the vast expanse of sandy beaches is one of the trademarks of this park, and the beach at Sandy Bay is huge, certainly the best one in the park. There are vault toilets, changerooms, and a drinking water tap near the basketball and volleyball nets. The beach itself is deep and wide, approximately 1 km long and 50–55 m deep, filled with fine sand with few rocks or clay deposits. The buoyed swimming area is unsupervised, quite large and fairly shallow for the most part, just perfect for splashing and larking about! Running the length of the beach is a fine boardwalk, allowing a wheelchair quite close to where the family has pitched their beach umbrella. A very large parking lot provides vehicular storage, near which is the boat launch, dock and a large boat trailer parking lot; a fish filleting shack and drinking water tap round out the amenities near the beach.

Located in the resort village of Candle Lake is the day use and picnic area of Waskateena Beach. There are a scattering of picnic tables, benches, a set of vault toilets and a dining shelter, set amid tall pines. The beach itself is rather narrow and the lake is quite shallow, allowing waders to walk a long ways into the lake! This is more of a picnic and day-use area for wading and splashing rather than a beach for sunning and sand castles. There is no firewood supply so bring your own, and there is no drinking water at this site. On the busiest days the somewhat small parking lot fills quickly, so extra parking can be found in the grassy verges along the main road leading past.

The east side of the lake holds Minowukaw Beach, part of the park's facilities on that side. Although not as extensively supported as the Sandy Bay beach, it does have excellent parking and a boardwalk to bring you across the sand dunes behind the beach.

Interestingly, there is good hiking through these fragile dunes if one stays on the established paths. You may even find purple sand, a natural formation caused by the glaciers having ground up large amounts of garnet and depositing it as part of the ancient beach which is now the dunes—and yes, it really is purple! The beach itself is narrower than the Sandy Bay beach, but very long as it runs almost 2 full km from the boat launch south to the third camping loop. There is a basketball half-court just beside the parking lot, with a cement pad. There are no changerooms nor are there toilet facilities although one is available beside the parking lot as is a potable water tap. The buoyed swimming area is unsupervised and the water is fairly shallow for quite some way out. As with both the other beaches, the sand is reasonably fine with few pebbles, and clean with no sign of beach parties.

BOATING
The park has two boat launches for camping patrons: one at Sandy Bay and the other at Minowukaw Beach. Both of these facilities feature cement boat ramps, a small dock, fish filleting shacks and vault toilets. The Sandy Bay facility has a larger trailer parking lot than at Minowukaw Beach although both facilities recommend removing your boat nightly and storing it at your site. As mentioned above, some of the sites on the 300 loop at Minowukaw back onto the lake so you can bring your boat almost into your site! This is cottage country, and many businesses are there to rent you boats and motors. They can also suggest guides or make those arrangements for you, and rent tow boats and equipment if you want to try skiing or tubing; you can get a list of contact numbers from the resort village's website at www.candlelake.com. Just past the Waskateena parking lot is a public use boat launch accompanying Nobles Point Marina. The marina is a private facility and all docks, slips and parking have fees attached. You can rent boats and motors and there is a small line of fishing merchandise on sale; contact them directly at (306) 929-3362 for up-to-date prices and availability.

HIKING
There are several good hiking trails in the area, the best of which is the Hilltop Ski and Hiking Trail in behind Minowukaw Beach campgrounds. Turn north onto Torch St. at Joe's Cabins store and follow that road as it turns left into Candle Lake Road, terminating at the warm-up shelter and parking lot for the trail head. Although we found the trail to be well blazed and easy to follow once on it, the junction markers were a bit harder to find and follow. We also had no end of mosquitoes and flies tasting our flesh, so be advised that bug spray is mandatory! Bring lots of water as there is none at either the trail head or on the trail; sturdy hiking shoes and a hat are also a must. The trail runs a maximum of 5.8

km, depending on the route followed, and takes you across some fairly steep terrain. We made the round trip in just over an hour but we couldn't stop and enjoy the view from the hilltop at trail's end due to the voracious insects; perhaps you'll fare better! The Homestead Heritage Hiking Trail lies outside the park boundaries so it won't be considered here. The Musker Pond Trail begins at the group camping site in the Sandy Bay campgrounds and takes you over a very easy 1.5-km trail to the trout pond. As mentioned above, the campgrounds themselves are laced with undescribed trails that seem to lead little feet to the local stores; as they are unofficial, they won't be discussed at length here. Please note, though, that bikes of all sorts are very popular in this park, particularly at the Minowukaw campgrounds; take every precaution when driving the roads, particularly at twilight.

SERVICES

The resort village of Candle Lake has pretty much every amenity that could be wished for, with the exception of medical facilities; for that you must go to Prince Albert. There are restaurants, boutiques, crafts, cottage subdivisions, outfitters, golfing, mini-golf and arcade, worship and mechanical services. One thing you should know, though, is that the village hosts an annual Co-ed Beach Volleyball Tournament on the August long weekend, which draws as many as 5,000 extra people to the village and park. This places an incredible strain on just about everything up there, so you may want to keep that in mind if you're planning a family holiday! There are an astonishing number of services and outfitters that can help you make arrangements for your perfect holiday, certainly far too many to list here. You can get contact numbers from the resort village website at www.candlelake.com as well as basic information on all the amenities. Otherwise, the park is busy from June to mid-August although you should have little trouble getting a site mid-week; as the park isn't accepting reservations at this time, you may want to drive up a day or two early and leave your camper on the site to hold it for your weekend stay. There are two play grounds in the park, one at either campground. The one in Sandy Bay is larger but older although all the equipment is in fine shape. The Minowukaw Beach playground, near the service center, is newer and smaller. Both feature brightly colored creative play structures in large sand pits. For more information on this pretty and popular park, contact the park office at:

Candle Lake Provincial Park
Box 119
Candle Lake, SK   S0J 3E0
Telephone: (306) 929-8400
Website: www.saskparks.netParkInfo.

CHITEK LAKE RECREATION SITE

Located just past the resort village of Chitek Lake you'll find this interesting recreational opportunity. The village is located in the heart of Saskatchewan's boreal forest, where lakes abound with fish and large animals wander the forest almost at will. The area seems almost primeval; you get the impression the woods and water have seen the rise and fall of many such as you, and that some greater force exists that has made all this for you to enjoy. Mind you, I always "recharge my batteries" as it were when I'm camping among the pine and fir trees of the North Country; the sounds and smells of an evergreen forest are unique. Stay on the main highway through the village and you'll find the park access about 500 meters from the edge of town. It's open from the Victoria Day long weekend until the end of October; there is discount camping in September and October when the water has been turned off but the fishing is still excellent!

SITES

The campground is the second left turn past the park gate. You'll find 27 electrified sites and 18 non-electrified sites. The park reserves 10 sites for seasonal occupants awarded on a lottery system; contact the park for an application and deadlines. The sites are quite large, certainly large enough to house a modern motorhome plus tow vehicle and boat trailer. The sites are leveled with gravel pads draining front to back, and share potable water from central taps. There are metal-framed picnic tables and pole BBQs in each site, and the mature trees provide excellent shade and reasonable privacy. A firewood pile is located on the road just behind the fully wheelchair-accessible service center which offers free hot showers as well as flush toilets to patrons. Toilets in the campground are wheelchair accessible vault style, clean and free of odor. The park operates on a self-serve basis; occupy the vacant site of preference and then go back to register and pay for your site. The park tries to keep site #23 available to those requiring wheelchair access; please do not register for this site unless it is the last one available. The campground host is in site #13, who told us the best time to visit the park is from the end of May to mid-June, or from mid-August to Labor Day; the amenities are all functioning at 100%, but the park is generally only 50–60% full! The campground host will assist you with local information and help you with any difficulties you may encounter.

There's a walking path running in back of site #45 on the western edge of the campground, heading to the Pelican Picnic Area about 1 km away; you can also drive on the blacktop road to the picnic ground parking lot. Here you'll find the better beach, changerooms, wooden picnic tables and pole BBQs and a dining shelter. There are also two sets of vault toilets with the one nearest the large parking lot being wheelchair accessible. There's a small playground and drinking water taps but no firewood that we could see.

There are two camping lakes in the park: Chitek Lake and Shell Lake (located 15 km NE of Chitek Lake off Lac Eauclaire Road). There are 7 unserviced sites at Shell Lake which have picnic tables, pole BBQs, firewood and vault toilets but no potable water. There is a boat launch with a small parking lot and a fish-cleaning station. Shared trash bins complete the amenities.

WATER SPORTS

No doubt about it, this in an angler's paradise! So popular is fishing to this park that the boat launch has two floating docks and two (count them, two) fish-cleaning huts in the huge trailer parking lot. The park recommends you do not leave your boat and trailer here over night, but rather that you retrieve your boat nightly and store it on your site. The beach area in front of the campground is very thin with large rocks and little sand. It does have good lawns to play on and benches to rest weary bones. There is a large new playground with climbers, swings and slides in a big sand box beside the service station. The beach at Pelican Picnic Area is much better, so it has the changerooms and a smaller playground set; the lake will be the focus for the children! There is a large buoyed swim area, and all swimming is unsupervised. The swimming area is shallow for quite a ways so the water is warm for most of the season, making it very enjoyable for children and adults alike.

The surrounding forest, as mentioned above, has many small lakes all waiting to be explored by boat. They generally have a small boat launch at each so all you have to do is try to catch the big one (or at least tell outrageous lies about it getting away!). Many fish species are available, including pike, walleye, perch, various trout, whitefish and splake.

SERVICES

The resort village of Chitek Lake can meet most travelers' demands for shopping, mechanical services, and fuel. There are restaurants, handicraft shops, lodges and hotels, as well as an excellent 9-hole, grass-green golf course. The Chitek Lake Golf Course offers club and cart rentals and modest rates: $13.50 for 9 holes, $21 for 18 holes, or $21 per day (adult rates). Contact them directly for more information at (306) 984-4514. Those wishing more extensive shopping and other services should try Leoville, about 15 minutes south. The park itself offers a relaxing visit to a very special place: Saskatchewan's north. The campsites are large, well shaded and private, the area boasts some of the best fishing in North America, and the people are friendly. Come and see for yourself! For more information on this pretty park, contact the park office at:

Chitek Lake Recreational Site
PO Box 39
Chitek Lake, SK   S0J 2J0
Telephone: (306) 984-2343
Fax: (306) 984-2215
E-mail them by following the link from the SERM website at: www.saskparks.net.

CLARENCE-STEEPBANK LAKES PROVINCIAL WILDERNESS PARK

Located 150 km north and a bit east of Prince Albert, this park is a bit of an anomaly: it is 17,549 hectares of true wilderness and relatively easy to access; other wilderness parks are extremely difficult to get into. Take Hwy 55 to Meath Park and turn left onto Hwy 120 (the Candle Lake road). Drive past Candle Lake to Hwy 913 and turn left, heading north on this well-graveled road. A few kilometers north is Hwy 927, leading up to East Trout Lake; the turnoff to Clarence-Steepbank lakes is about a third of the way up this road. Turn left onto the narrow, winding access road and follow it to the main campsite area at Clarence Lake. You'll note the "road" really looks like a couple of ruts running between the trees—that's it, so go slow as it really is narrow and winding with several deep potholes. Our mini-van had no real trouble but I would be very leery of taking a motor home or trailer into the farther reaches of the park. The park does not levy entry fees and there is no kiosk to pay for sites in the park. This is wilderness camping, so do not expect many amenities—you must be self-sufficient.

CAMPING

There are two campgrounds in the park with a total of 6 sites; 5 at Clarence Lake and 1 at the terminus of the access road just east of Steepbank Lake. The campsites are very much wilderness camping at its best; excellent firepits and picnic tables delineate the sites and that's about it. There is no trash disposal system in the park—pack out what you pack in and be very aware that garbage left lying about will attract the wrong sort of forest creatures! There is one set of vault toilets at Clarence Lake and a single-seater at Steepbank Lake; you would be wise to have your own "butt fluff" supply as the park staff visits once a week. There is no potable water supplied so be prepared to boil lake water, and you must harvest your own wood supply from the surrounding jack-pine and spruce forests deadfall. This is the one true charm of the campgrounds, however; you are camping in one of the last true stands of old-growth boreal forests in the area. Fires and loggers have reduced other stands or thinned them out, but none of that here. The Clarence Lake sites are generously sized to say the least as they are spread out around a small clearing near the quagmire used as a boat launch. The site at Steepbank Lake is located at the top of the hill range just behind the lake.

ACTIVITIES

One hiking trail from the campsite at Steepbank Lake runs along the south and west side of the lake and provides access to the western end of the park as well as to Birch Lake. It isn't maintained as such and resembles a deer trail for most of the way. It is also quite steep in places, particularly down to the lake; it's not called Steepbank Lake for nothing! Once at the shore, though, the view resembles a fiord more than anything else as the narrow lake is dominated by the steep hills on both sides. This, of course, means that getting water is an arduous task, as would be portaging a canoe or boat down to explore the parks farthest reaches.

Still, that task is what makes this park so appealing. You will not need a large boat to fish these lakes so bring your canoe and relax with the knowledge that you'll most likely be fishing in peace. There won't be any outboard motors here, no wake boarding, "personal watercraft," speedboats or other motorized impedimenta—just you and a collection of small, pretty lakes that are stocked annually with a variety of fish. The fact that fishing pressure will generally be low means better fishing success for those hardy enough to portage in. Even the Clarence Lake boat launch is a challenge for a trailer as it is very shallow, boggy and soft. Getting a boat trailer through that and into water deep enough to launch a boat would be Herculean in nature; even a "car-topper" would be a problem.

There are no beaches to speak of, and all swimming activities are unsupervised and at your own risk; bring a shaker of salt to remove the leeches if you do decide to go for a dip. The lakes have a marshy bottom, so you'll have to go out a ways to find clean water. The park does not have any playground equipment, nor does it plan to build anything in the future; this is a wilderness park and will stay so.

There are several small lakes just off the road running from Clarence up to Steepbank Lake, each stocked differently; following the road north, this is what you'll find: Clarence Lake is stocked with walleye and has pike as well. Kit Lake (pictured here) is the only one stocked with rainbow trout. Ridge Lake (you have to climb up and over a sandy ridge to access the lake) is stocked with brook trout. Jasper Lake (accessed right from the road) isn't stocked but has good native populations of pike, walleye and perch. Steepbank Lake has good pike and is stocked with walleye and lake trout although the lakers haven't done too well. Birch Lake, the last in the chain and accessed only from the north end of Steepbank Lake, has good lake trout and pike populations. Birch Lake is also the most difficult to get into; that portage down the hill to Steepbank would be rough. In fact, you'd bleedin' well better catch some fish after all that work!

Snowmobiling and trapping activities occur in the park during the winter months, and cross-country skiing is also possible on the road. One trapper's shack can be found just off the road near Jasper Lake but it is private property so please respect it.

As this is old-growth forest, you can find plants and birds that would be rare elsewhere. The larger trees can support the nesting habits of larger birds, such as pileated woodpeckers, bald eagles, goshawks and owls, as well as a host of other, smaller songbirds. The varied terrain makes for wide variations in moisture which in turn shapes the forest cover, which also modifies the ground cover plants. Researchers have found provincially rare plants here, such northern twayblade, bog orchids, and adder's-mouth. I don't pretend to be botanist enough to make the distinctions among such plants, but the important thing to note is that they can be found by the observant. When you do find them, though, "take pictures and leave only footprints."

SERVICES

As mentioned before, this is a wilderness park and therefore has no services at all. The nearest store would be the outfitters at East Trout Lake, approximately 25 km north of Clarence Lake. Narrow Hills Provincial Park is only 30 km east of here, with access to the stores and outfitters at Caribou Creek Lodge and Lower Fishing Lake. Candle Lake Provincial Park and the hamlet of Candle Lake are both about 30 km south and a bit west of here and offer pretty much anything you could need by way of shopping, mechanical and worship services. The nearest hospital is in Prince Albert, 150 km away. For further information on this park, contact the park office at:

Narrow Hills Provincial Park
P.O. Box 130
Smeaton, SK   S0J 2J0
Telephone: (306) 426-2622 or toll-free at 1-800-205-7070 (in Saskatchewan only)
Website: www.saskparks.net

CLEARWATER RIVER WILDERNESS PARK

Make no mistake about it, this is not a journey for the faint of heart. The 63 km of Hwy 955 past La Loche were built of crushed rock over bedrock and muskeg; there are potholes and rough spots where you can barely crawl along. This road would rattle a motor home to pieces in short order! Mind you, we took the family car and drove up—the locals all thought we were nuts but we made it back. They all use fairly robust SUVs or 4-wheel drive pickup trucks and they don't go too fast, either! This road can be passable in clear weather at a maximum speed of 60–70 km per hour in a small passenger car. If the road is wet or it's stormy, you may want to reconsider! So then why should you bash axles and risk flat tires (or worse) to travel to this place? Simply put, because the river is clear and unpolluted. You will find peace and solitude, and perhaps the thrill of adventure if you want to try the Warner Rapids (pictured here, from the bridge) near which the campground is placed. This is a man's wilderness where the feet of voyageur and explorer have trod for centuries in the employ of the Hudson's Bay Company, and for uncounted hundreds of years by the inhabitants before that. To stay here a while is to touch the face of history. To highlight this you'll find a small turnoff just to the left of the north end of the bridge. There are two cairns here commemorating the many brave men who traveled this way in times gone by.

SITES

Finding the campground entrance was a little tricky; the signs were missing so we drove past it by 2 km or so. Driving north you'll see an access to your right about 200 meters or so beyond the Warner Rapids Bridge. There's a picnic spot here with a pole BBQ and a couple of picnic tables beside a bear-proof trash bin; a good idea if the tracks around it are any indicator! There are 17 or so unserviced sites spaced out along the road leading to the terminus at the river. This is where I will camp next time I'm up that way—there is better access to the vault toilet, fire pit and picnic tables. The firewood supplied was big blocks of spruce—bring a splitting axe. There is no water supply except for the river running at your feet. The only problem will be landing a canoe here as the rocky banks are quite steep. There is a lower spot a few meters east which offers better access but only for one canoe at a time. You'll camp with the roar of Warner Rapids to your right and a smaller set about a km or so to your left, with a large bay or widening between them. No reservations are taken, nor will any be required.

WATER SPORTS

The Clearwater is a Canadian heritage river, so named for its cultural and historic significance. As the river flows west it carves ever-deepening canyons, creating rapids varying from Class II to Class IV+. For more information, check out the SERM website on the canoe route, "From Warner Rapids to Ft. McMurray" (210 km long) at www.saskparks.netcanoe/trips/default.asp?TripNumber=40

For those with more peaceful activities in mind, the fishing here will be excellent with all northern species available, particularly pike and walleye. If you're canoeing and fishing, remember that a Saskatchewan license will not be valid in Alberta. There is no boat launch at all, so canoes are recommended. Just remember, the Warner Rapids are a Class III set, and can be very dangerous to the novice. Either launch below the rapids or stay well away—you'll drift quickly in the current.

SERVICES

The community of La Loche offers a complete array of services for the northern traveler, the most important of which is fuel—never, and I mean never, drive past a gas station in the north unless your tank is full. You'll be able to find lodging, shopping, medical, mechanical, and worship services in La Loche. Should you wish to avoid the roads and fly, there are several air services operating from here and from more southern places as well. It is, after all, about 14 hours by road from Saskatoon! Still, I will return here some day; there's a fish in that lake that owes me either lunch or my hook back! To find out more about this park, contact the park office at:

Clearwater River Wilderness Park
PO Box 40
La Loche, SK S0M 1G0
Telephone: (306) 822-1700
Fax (306) 822-2030
Website: www.saskparks.net

CUMBERLAND HOUSE PROVINCIAL HISTORIC PARK

Located 157 km north east of Carrot River, approximately 110 km past the E.B. Campbell Dam, the drive up to this village can be daunting as the gravel road can be hard on tires and nerves. You will be rewarded with some fine scenery in what must be one of the least despoiled parts of the boreal forest, as well as access to one of the largest inland deltas in the world. Covering almost 500,000 square kilometers this delta on the confluence of the Saskatchewan, Sturgeon-weir and Grass rivers provides the home for a stunning array of waterfowl and fur-bearing animals. Indeed, it was the sheer richness of the fur from this area that prompted the Hudson's Bay Company to establish a trading post here in 1774. For many years it functioned as a major focus of commerce and transportation in the fur industry. That trading post has survived as a village of nearly a thousand people whose lives are still closely tied to this magnificent land, making this the oldest established community in Western Canada. The only remaining portion of the old trading post is the stone-walled powder magazine in which gunpowder was stored as late as the 1890s; it is preserved as a static reminder of those old days, and self-guided tours serve to educate the visitor about the role fur played in early Saskatchewan's commerce.

The Cree name for this community, "Waskahiganihk," means "at the house" in reference to the Hudson's Bay post which used to be referred to as a "house." The history of this remarkable community is tied to the river which provided the main highway of commerce through this land for so many years. Riverboats used to make regular stops here, bringing trade goods from the railhead at Prince Albert and returning with the fur crop. One such steam boat, the HBC *Northcote*, played a role in the North-West Resistance, losing its funnels to the crafty Métis during the final battles of Batoche. Its boilers are part of the historic parks display, and there are self-guided tours to educate the visitor about the history of Cumberland House trading post as well as the role steamboats played on this river; brochures are available from several businesses in town (the *Northcote*'s cannon appears above, photo courtesy David McLennan, CPRC). After the Resistance, many families moved to the delta, making a living by hunting, fishing, trapping, and agriculture off the rich delta soil.

The construction of the E.B. Campbell hydroelectric project on the Saskatchewan River has changed the water flow past Cumberland House such that levels fluctuate greatly, which impacts fish, waterfowl and animal populations. The local people still enjoy a close relationship with nature as evidenced by the fact that the Northern Store (what used to be the Hudson's Bay Store) is still purchasing fur from local trappers. Guiding and outfitting is also popular with many persons employed in the tourism industry, using traditional skill and knowledge in maintaining their love for this land.

There is no camping to be had in this park, nor are there services offered by the park for patrons. Visitors can find lodging at the Cumberland House Hotel, a 6-room facility with 3 kitchenettes and 3 double rooms as well as a licensed beverage room. The Waskahiganihk Family Restaurant, located in the hotel, serves a wide range of meals from snacks to full course in an air-conditioned dining room. Hotel reservations can be made by contacting them at:

Cumberland House Hotel
P.O. Box 248
Cumberland House, SK   S0E 0S0
Telephone: (306) 888-2266
Fax: (306) 888-2220

For more information you can contact the park office at:

Cumberland House Provincial Historic Park
PO Box 70
Cumberland House, SK   S0E 0S0
Telephone: (306) 888-2077
Website: www.saskparks.net
Or check out the village's website at: www.geocities.com/inez_school/index.html.

EMMA LAKE RECREATION SITE

Located 41 km north of Prince Albert off of Hwy 2, turn west on Hwy 263 past Christopher Lake and Neis beach to Murray Point. You'll find that this park offers a chance to camp in mature stands of spruce and poplar beside a busy lake. Trails beckon the hiking enthusiast, while boating, skiing and fishing await the adventurous. The call of the loon, the silence of the night heightened by the crackle of a campfire, and the smells of the boreal forest are all less than an hours drive from Prince Albert; truly this area has a lot to offer! As you drive in, you'll note the trailer dump station to your left then see the right turn into the park gates. Should you continue past the park gates a short distance, you'll find yourself in the Murray Point cottage subdivision, filled with summer (and some permanent) private residences. Just past the cottages you'll find the Murray Point North Campground.

SITES

There are two campgrounds available: Murray Point and Murray Point North. Both have something different to offer, so I'll consider them separately.

Murray Point Campground is the larger and more developed of the two, having 136 sites of which only 54 are non-electrified. The electrical service is 30 amps, but none of the sites are fully serviced. There are 5 wheelchair-accessible sites: #110, #111 and #113 are electrified, and #81 and #85 are unserviced. Potable water is piped to central locations and a sewer dump station is located just west of the main access road. There are two group sites that can be reserved, the larger of the two with 30 sites, washrooms, an electrified dining shelter and its own potable water. The smaller area has 17 sites and none of the other amenities. Both will be used as overflow when necessary, and if they are not already rented to a group. We found all the sites to be ample for even the largest camping unit although the somewhat narrow roadways, paved as they are, may make backing a huge motorhome something of a challenge. The forest of spruce and poplar is mature so every site will be well shaded, and they are spaced approximately 10–15 meters apart. Those sites with low numbers will be closest to the park entrance and will back on a boggy area; the higher numbers will be nearer the main beach area; you receive an excellent map as you register. The sites themselves are well gravelled, and slope towards the roads. They feature a sturdy firepit with swinging grate (some still have a pole BBQ although they are being phased out) and a large picnic table. Garbage disposal is in bear-proof central bins, and firewood is available from a central depository. In general, we found the park to be clean, neat and quiet.

The Murray Point North Campground is situated approximately 1 km north of the main entrance, where you must register before heading over there. There are 33 campsites here, none of which are electrified, and the toilets are vault biffies. Water is available from central points, trash bins are central and bear-proof, and firewood is available from a bin near site #1. Although the sites are somewhat smaller than the larger campgrounds, they are still large enough for most units and seem almost buried in the forest, as it were. They too are well graveled and slope towards the paved road. With the same sturdy picnic tables and firepits one expects in a provincial park, they will serve admirably. As the campgrounds itself is smaller it will generally be quieter but you pay for that by being a bit farther from the beach and playgrounds. Staying here still allows you access to the service centre but you'll have farther to go!

Of interest is the fact that the park has reservable sites at both campgrounds on a first-come, first-served basis. It would be a very good idea to call well ahead to have a site held for you as they are only allowing 27 electrified and 22 non-electrified sites at Murray Point, and 4 non-electrified sites at Murray Point North. In fact, site reservations begin as early as January although phone-in requests are traditionally accepted beginning the third Monday in June! Contact them by fax, email or letter as soon as you can, or you can call the park gate at (306) 982-4741 in season. Be advised that they've also established a waiting list for the peak season which runs from the last weekend in June to the second week in August; it's for those campers requesting an electrified site on busy weekends. What they'll do is assign you one of the non-electrified sites and assign any available sites to those present in person each day at 1500 hr. You must check back with them for updates; just walk over to the park gate and inquire. However, if you aren't in front of the park gate by 1500 hr you have the option of remaining on the list and trying again the next day. Therefore, if you've reserved a site don't be tardy or at least let the park staff know your estimated time of arrival. Call the Christopher Lake office at (306) 982-2002 for further details. When speaking with the park staff, make them aware of any physical restrictions in your party as three of the electrified sites (and 2 of the unserviced sites) are better suited to wheelchair access. Those with small children may also request a site near one of the playgrounds in the campgrounds.

The group sites can be reserved for your private get-together, but not on long weekends; they need those sites for overflow as the park is usually full during those weekends. Furthermore, the group sites are often booked a year in advance so let them know your needs early on in your planning process. School groups and youth groups can rent the group sites for $1 per person per day; you can see why they book early!

SPORTS

The park has several self-guided hiking trails looping through and around the campgrounds. These trails are part of the local snowmobile association's 500 km of groomed trails although the portions open to the park are nowhere near that extensive. A map shows the available trials and the directions to follow on them. They are also well suited to mountain bikers as they are wide enough to share comfortably with pedestrians. The shortest trail would be the distance from your site to the beach; the longest would be a matter of a couple of kilometers. For those wishing a bit more fun, the park staff have collected an assortment of informative guide books, binoculars, and lenses into an "activity bag" which they will loan you for a refundable $20 deposit. As this is a recreational site there are no interpretive programs. There are three playgrounds in the park, two in the Murray Point Campgrounds and one behind the north beach. A horseshoe pit is available near the main beach; equipment can be borrowed from the park entry booth. There are no ball diamonds in the park and swimming will be in the lake, unsupervised; there is one set of lessons sponsored by the local cottagers association. Changerooms are available near the smaller north beach. A vast, lawned area lies between the two campgrounds, and is equipped with a variety of picnic tables, pole BBQs, toilets, parking, a camp kitchen and a small playground. The lawn lies between the lake and the Murray Point cottage subdivision, scene of many a garage sale during our visit! There are no ball diamonds as the parks natural wonders are the reason everyone comes here in the first place. Those wishing to view the forest from the back of a horse should contact the good folks at the Rothenburg Family Park, approximately 2 km west of Murray Point. They have a bookstore, coffee shop, pony rides and guided trail rides, with "horses for all—beginners welcome." Contact them at (306) 982-4805 for more details. Although the park itself does not have a golf course, the Emma Lake Golf Course operates a fine facility a short drive south of Murray Point. Their course now boasts 18 holes that wander a challenging 5600 yards through mature forest. Contact them for your tee time at (306) 982-2054.

The park closes for the winter season so it doesn't offer any structure for snow enthusiasts. It is a part of the very extensive local snowmobile trail system, however, and several resorts in the area do offer year-round adventures.

WATER SPORTS

Emma Lake is regularly stocked with many sport fish and is well suited to the fishing enthusiast. A fine boat launch is available just north of the main campgrounds, complete with dock and a trailer parking station. Boat trailers are expected to have a park pass as well. An enclosed, lighted fish-cleaning shelter is available in behind the boat launch area, as are a couple of picnic areas. Just north of the boat launch are a series of private docks; please do not use them without permission. For those wishing to rent boats and motors, the Emma Lake Resort at Macintosh Point (approximately 5 km south of Murray Point) has a complete line of fishing boats and party barges for rent by the hour or day. Contact them at (306) 982-3133 for details and availability. This is a busy lake with all the cottage developments, residential summer camps, resorts, and parks along both shores, so boating is exceptionally popular. Skiers, tubers, wake boarders, canoeists, and sailboats all vie for space with the fishermen, all delighting in the glory of a hot summer's day.

SERVICES

This is cottage country so things can be very busy; expect some services to be stretched a bit. Restaurants, for example, vary from simple confectionary-style to full-service, licensed family dining. The numbers and names of all such businesses would occupy a book of their own, so the local Board of Trade has commissioned a map of the Christopher Lake/Emma Lake area which details all the commercial outlets open to the traveling public. From the Murray Point Campground, however, Fern's Grocery will be closest. Located roughly halfway between Murray Point and Murray Point North campgrounds, it offers a line of groceries as well as the usual pop, iced treats and summer snacks. Their patio also has typical grill fare. Contact them at (306) 982-2006 should you wish more details. Christopher Lake has a more complete line of shopping amenities and worship services, and Prince Albert is about a half-hour drive away. Fire service is operated by the RM of Lakeland through 4 volunteer fire halls. A '911' service is available, with Prince Albert providing the hospital and police service. As increasingly seems to be the norm, thieves can be found anywhere so take appropriate precautions with your valuables. Wildlife can also pose a problem for the unwary, so take precautions with your food as well; there are bears in the forest! For more information on Emma Lake Provincial Recreation Park or to reserve a site, contact them at 1-800-205-7070 or check out their website at www.saskparks.net. They can be reached at:

Emma Lake Provincial Recreation Site
P.O. Box 66
Christopher Lake, SK   S0J 0N0
Telephone: (306) 982-2002/(306) 982-4741 in season
Fax: (306) 982-3031
E-mail will be answered from a Regina office at: inquiry@serm.gov.ca

LAC LA RONGE PROVINCIAL PARK

Located 236 km north of Prince Albert on the CanAm Hwy (Hwy 2), this is the largest park in the province's system at 344,740 hectares. There are over 100 lakes inside the park and access to one of the greatest historical canoe routes of the world, the Churchill River, just on the park's north boundary. In fact, if you include Lac La Ronge's 20,480 hectares in the total (approximately 6% of the park's area), it seems there's more water than woods in the park! Because of this, the park boasts some of the best fishing in the province plus excellent amenities at its 6 established campgrounds as well as true wilderness camping for canoe and hiking out-trippers. The park begins just outside the town of La Ronge and continues for 77 km north along Hwy 102. The highway is paved up to Wadin Bay, and is a four-season gravel road past that campground all the way up to South End of Reindeer Lake. The highway itself was cut through the Precambrian Shield, the bones of this rugged country, and offers many scenic vistas as well as roadside turnouts every few kilometers. Although the highway is well-traveled there are few mechanical services outside La Ronge, so please make certain your vehicle is ready for the trip—check your spare tire! The park is geared to serve pretty much any type of visitor; choose to be an active participant by cross-country skiing, canoeing, hiking, birding, fishing, boating, or camping either back-country or in a site at one of the established campgrounds. You can choose a somewhat less strenuous adventure by sight-seeing local vistas and history such as the Otter Rapids on the Churchill River just north of Missinipe, the first church in the territories at Stanley Mission, or Saskatchewan's version of the Grand Canyon at the Nipekamew Sand Pillars, among other fine sights. Finally, you can choose to be pampered by one of the local outfitters, relaxing lakeside with a good book or on a rental houseboat; let their capable guides show you where the real fishing is, and savour the taste of a shore lunch of freshly caught pike amid the smells of a pine and spruce forest. Truly, Lac La Ronge Provincial Park has it all, no matter what you want in a holiday.

WATER SPORTS

During the early history of this area, waterways were the prime movers of people and goods along the Churchill River to Hudson Bay and the trading posts huddled along those frozen shores. Later, the Montreal River was instrumental in moving goods from the railhead in Prince Albert north to many communities, La Ronge among them. Shortly after the first road was pushed through in the 1930s, the first fishermen came along to sample the incredible fishing to be had. The road changed the nature of travel in the area although watercraft remain to this day an important means of transport for local folks. Most people view the abundance of water in a recreational light nowadays, as the number of lakeside outfitters will attest. There are many businesses that rent boats, motors and guides for the lakes and streams for those wishing to fish them, travel them, or simply savour their natural beauty. In fact, there are too many such outfitters to list properly here, so I direct interested parties to the La Ronge Chamber of Commerce website at www.townoflaronge.ca. They've put out an extensive brochure entitled "Heading North 2004," which begins with the statement "Treat the earth well—it was not given to you by your parents but loaned to you by your children," a sentiment that resonates throughout this marvelous land.

HIKING/SKIING/SNOWMOBILING
Although the park doesn't have many established hiking trails, it does have some of the best in the system and you always have access to the backcountry. That, however, requires you be self-sufficient in all aspects of bush travel, and that you check in with park staff before you depart and when you return from the bush; common sense demands no less. For those who prefer more order in their hikes, the Don Allen cross-country ski trails near the Nemeiben Lake turnoff offer up to 7 km on a series of 4 nested loops, or 8 km if you take the Summit loop. The trail is groomed and easy to follow with excellent signage and a warm-up shelter, usually used in the winter months. Other trails exist, such as the Nemeiben Lake Interpretive Trail and the Nut Point Trail, both described in greater detail in the sections for those campgrounds. I can't recommend you bike the Nut Point Trail due to the rock scrambles, but the Don Allen Trails are favorites among local mountain bikers for the varied terrain and wide trail. None of the hikes provide drinking water, so be prepared; definitely bring some form of bug repellent—they will be intense!

At least the bugs aren't as bad in the winter, so the saying goes, and the park takes advantage of that with its 60 km of groomed cross-country ski trails. As the local snowmobile association takes care of their trail system outside the park boundaries, I won't go into great detail here; if you want more information, check their website at www.snowlaronge.ca. Of interest is the night skiing offered by the park at its Nut Point Campground. Here, all 4 loops are open to skiers every night, and the street lights are kept on to allow enjoyment of the park's natural beauty by night. With an army of volunteers (and a few very late nights on the part of trail groomers), the town of La Ronge hosts an annual Don Allen Saskaloppet, a recreational cross-country ski race. The event is named for Don Allen, who established the local ski club. The event draws hundreds of skiers from across Canada who participate in 8-km, 13-km, 35-km and 55-km races and tours as well as the Kupeswin, an 80-km overnight race. One of the highlights of this event is the themed checkpoints that exist along the trails, as local volunteers dress up to welcome skiers for drinks and snacks along the race. Pirates, ballerinas, and other wondrous sights can be seen, all part of the hugely popular event. For more information check the Ski Club website at www.saskaloppetlady.tripod.com.

CAMPING

There are six established campgrounds in the park, which I will consider individually beginning with the closest to the town of La Ronge and ending with the farthest north. Just as a side note, we found a small bug-proof shelter very handy during our visit—the bugs get hungry, too!

Nut Point Campgrounds, located just on the northern edge of the town of La Ronge, has 88 sites on three loops. The first loop (numbered 1–17) is electrified with 30-amp service; it is also the closest to the boat launch and boat trailer parking lot. The next two loops, although non-electrified, are built in such a way that the Precambrian Shield provides some of the prettiest camping in the province; this photo of site #77 is pretty much the norm. One site in particular, #39, has a rocky shelf beside the lake about 2 meters above the water. The firepit is built on this natural feature, and a wooden bench is placed such that you have a stunning panorama laid out at your very feet: the sun bleeding away across a vast expanse of water that can be as still as a petrified dream. A loon's weird, echoing tremolo and the gentle crackle of a camp fire reminds us that this province is truly blessed.

All sites feature metal-framed picnic tables and pole BBQs. Firewood, potable water and flush toilets are all centrally located. There is one service center with free hot showers located between the two far loops. All roadways are paved and although there is some variability in the size of individual sites, they should be large enough for most units. As many as 20 sites (at the park manager's discretion) are available for seasonal camping; call the park office for details and availability. Most of the sites are naturally leveled and drained although some are graveled and mounded. Trash bins, none of which are bear-proof, are centrally located. All sites are built into a mature spruce and pine forest so there is adequate tree cover everywhere, and the spacing between sites is generous so you often get the feeling you're alone. The campgrounds are well maintained, with very clean toilet and washroom facilities. Of particular note is site #63, located just beside a trash–drinking water–toilet nexus; it is wheelchair accessible and reserved for those in need of such amenities. There are no group or family camping loops available at Nut Point although every effort would be made to accommodate such requests where possible. One dining shelter exists behind site #31; it can be reserved for a private gathering. Sites can be reserved by calling the park office for dates and availability.

The Nut Point trailhead is at a parking lot about 1 km northeast of the park gate. This excellent trail is not suitable for those in poor shape, however, as we found one needed to exert a fair amount of energy, as you can see from this photo. You will be rewarded with some fine scenery, though, and the chance to camp alone at the terminus. You can make arrangements with one of the local outfitters to ferry you and your equipment to the small wilderness camping spot at the end of the trail, hiking back after a night or two of camping in this scenic place. I would recommend this route instead of arranging a water taxi to pick you up after hiking in; you cannot guarantee the weather and storms can change your plans in no time at all, it seems.

The Nemeiben Lake Campgrounds are located just a 15-minute drive north of La Ronge, 8 km on a winding, graveled road off a paved highway; this is still a substantial lake although it winds around a lot and can be a bit confusing to novice navigators. One should also be cautious about the many rocks and shoals that can be troublesome. Of particular interest is the small rapids and waterfall at the river outlet. *Nemeiben* is the Cree word for sucker, a type of fish common in the area, and the Sucker River drains Nemeiben Lake into Lac La Ronge. There is no shopping service available in the campgrounds although a payphone is located near the entrance.

The campgrounds are self-registered and no reservation system is in place for its 52 campsites. The people maintaining the campgrounds are usually found driving a utility vehicle as they make their rounds cleaning the sites and amenities, and can assist you in choosing a suitable site for your camper. There are 29 electrified sites with 30-amp service; there are no fully serviced sites. The sites themselves are a bit variable in size and contour as the campgrounds has been built over a small hill; most modern units will have little trouble fitting, particularly in the electrified sites. All sites are well shaded amid tall spruce, and the soil is generally sandy and well drained. Sites have metal-framed picnic tables and pole BBQs. Potable water, flush toilets, wood, and trash disposal are all centrally located. None of the trash bins were bear proof. One service center provides 4 unisex shower/washrooms; the showers are free and the facility was very clean and neat during our visit. There is a dining shelter centrally located between the service center and the beach parking area. It has several sturdy tables and a fireplace, and hosts interpretive programs when offered by the park. Although no sites can be reserved at this popular recreational lake, seasonal sites are available for those wishing longer stays; contact the park office for prices and availability as not all sites are open for seasonal use.

There is an excellent boat launch with vault toilets nearby, towards the north end of the campgrounds. There is no docking facility at the boat launch but a fine, multiple dock facility has been constructed near the small swim beach and playground at the south end of the campgrounds. The beach is clean although a bit small and the creative play structure is situated just beside the beach. These docks are free for the use of campgrounds patrons, as is the large boat trailer parking lot across the access road from the beach area. For those wishing longer term, secure storage of trailers or campers, a fenced and locked compound is available; space can be rented and arrangements should be made with the park office. It should be noted that local cottage owners also use the boat dock and parking facilities.

An excellent, graveled, self-guided interpretive trail has been built just north of the boat launch. Its 1.5-km wander through several different types of terrain and many sign posts offers insights into the rich forest around you—altogether a very pleasant way to spend a half-hour or so. The trail is easy to follow but not wheelchair accessible due to marshy sections and one rock scramble. I was particularly impressed with a small path that led off this trail down to the lake and a rocky ledge; that ledge sat a meter or so off the water and just begged for an angler to try his or her luck as the clear water dropped sharply to the depths below. Facing west, sitting on this ledge and fishing for supper as the sun drops behind the hills would be the perfect end to your day's hard work!

Wadin Bay Campgrounds, located 26 km north of La Ronge, just east of the highway, has 57 sites scattered over 5 loops. Of these, the first two loops (Birch Crescent and Willow Crescent) have larger sites and are electrified with 30-amp service, a total of 19 sites. An interesting feature of these two loops is that some sites are banked at the back with heavy timbers, ensuring a level site as well as enhancing privacy. The next loop, Spruce Crescent, was regrettably the focus of a short-lived tornado prior to our visit. Although it will be cleaned up and re-opened, its 13 non-electrified sites and the group camping area cannot be used at the moment. Aspen Crescent (13 non-electrified sites) and Pine Crescent (12 non-electrified sites) are located just past the service center. All sites have metal-framed picnic tables and pole BBQs. They are set amid mature spruce with an often thick understory; as the sites are generously spaced, privacy and shade are assured. Although the sites aren't generally as large as those at Nemeiben Lake, they should be large enough for most units; none are drive-through, though. Firewood, potable water, and trash bins are all centrally located. All toilets in each loop are wheelchair accessible, flush-type, very clean and odor-free. A trailer sewage dump station is located just before the entrance to Birch Crescent on the left side of the road. A wheelchair-accessible service center with free hot showers can be found behind the beach beside Aspen Crescent. A large and well-appointed picnic shelter can also be found here, anchored to the large parking lot servicing this excellent, buoyed beach and a creative playground. This dining shelter, by the way, also doubles as the campground's amphitheatre, where park interpretive guides will host events through the summer. Another dining shelter is located behind site #53 in Pine Crescent. Both of these shelters can be reserved for private functions.

This campground has a reserve-a-site system in place; contact the park office at 306-425-2580 for availability. As this campground also offers monthly and seasonal site rentals, electrified sites may be at a premium so call early! There is no park booth; simply pull into an available site and self-register at the kiosk provided. The park staff can assist you with finding a suitable site—you'll see them driving around servicing and cleaning the campgrounds. If you've reserved a site, you will have been given the site number and it will have a "site reserved" marker placed on it for the time period you've requested. The campsites are popular, being busy most weekends. Although you can gamble that a site will be open when you arrive, you would be wise to call ahead!

Wadin Bay also has an excellent boat launch; instead of turning left to the camping loops, continue on straight a short way to the lake. There is a reasonably large parking lot and fish filleting facility. The local outfitter, Wadin Bay Resort, has a marina here as well. The outfitter has a small store with a line of sundries, snacks, and fishing tackle located across the road from the park office and pay phone. They also rent boats, motors, and cabins, and can arrange guides if you wish; contact them at (306) 425-2292 for current prices and availability.

As you drive into the resort area, you will see the outfitters' store; a right turn here takes you past the cottage subdivision to the main beach and its amenities. Also part of the park operation, this is a larger beach both wider and deeper but with the same clean, fine sand. Also buoyed and unsupervised, it has vault toilets, a creative climbing structure, picnic area with pole BBQs, and a large parking lot. There is no charge for using the picnic area; no overnight camping is allowed. With its two excellent beaches, boat launch and docking, large, private sites and the wind whispering your name amid the trees, Wadin bay awaits your visit!

Missinipe/Otter Rapids (2 campgrounds) are located 80 km north of La Ronge. The last 50 km or so is accessed by an all-weather gravel road built right through the Precambrian Shield as the paved road ends just past Wadin Bay. Some of the gravel used is crushed rock, so slow down and save your tires! The road itself is somewhat narrow and heavily used as it is the motor vehicle access to Reindeer Lake, far to the north. There are many widened areas for one to pull over for scenery or a rest. Enroute past Wadin Bay you will see several lakes (Lynx Lake, Althouse Lake, Mulloch Lake, Lussier Lake) advertised as you drive along; these lakes are canoe route access points or stocked trout lakes. There may be no amenities to be found at these lakes: no toilets, trash disposal, picnic tables, or pole BBQs. Also found along this road are two small campgrounds: Mackay Lake and Little Deer Lake. These are great "get away" campgrounds more in the style of backcountry camping, perfect for canoeists or people with smaller camping units. Both have self-registration kiosks, pole BBQs, picnic tables, vault toilets, trash bins, boat launch and fish filleting facilities. There is no potable water supplied—boil lake water before use.

There is one camping loop with 14 electrified sites in Missinipe, plus one non-electrified site (#15). Off on a short road all by itself on a small promontory, site #15 is large, private, well-treed and totally awesome! If you don't need an electrified site, try this one—you won't be disappointed. All sites have metal-framed picnic tables and pole BBQs; water, and trash bins; firewood is centrally located and the vault toilets are all strategically located. The sites have been built on sand and leveled with gravel so they are well drained. Tree cover is at a bit of a premium, though, and there is little understory so the sites are fairly open. One fairly new service center has been built with free, hot showers and flush toilets. Sites are available by self-registry or reservation; call the park office for details and availability. An excellent boat launch and docking facility is available, along with a fish filleting shack and a large parking lot. Of interest is the floatplane anchorage seen just right of the boat launch; it services the fly-in fishing industry as well as the cottage subdivision.

Besides being the camping gateway to the Churchill River, the community of Missinipe offers many amenities including decent grocery and hardware shopping at the local store; fuel is also available there and propane can be purchased at the outfitters. Thompson's Camps offers complete resort amenities (including a hot tub suite and a swimming pool) as well as being a fly-in base camp. They can rent boats, motors as well as offer hotel services and guided jet boat tours of the famous Otter Rapids. Just a note about that tour, though—you WILL get wet! To arrange any of these activities contact them directly at (306) 635-2144 or 1-800-667-5554.

Just 10 km north of Missinipe is the mighty Churchill River, the original highway in this land. Use of this river dates back centuries before the Hudson's Bay Company sent its fur brigades over this route, as evidenced by the rock pictographs ancient First Nations artists left behind. The road crosses the river on a steel grate bridge which has a pedestrian walkway, and from which you get a bird's eye view of the wild and majestic Otter Rapids, also known as "a / mile of watery hell." Just before the bridge there are some vault toilets and a small parking lot for those wishing to fish these waters for walleye, while the road bisects the Otter Lake Campgrounds just past the bridge. There are a total of 13 non-electrified sites with wooden picnic tables and pole BBQs. There is no drinking water supplied, and all the toilets are vault style but even that is a luxury if you've been on the water for a week or so! Trash bins and wood are centrally located, and a well-used dining shelter offers some relief from the elements. There is no park entry booth, and the self-registry kiosk is just beside the west campgrounds entrance. One often sees anglers fishing below the rapids, and local outfitters will provide all the equipment and guides you'll need. Contact either

Thompson's Camps (1-800-667-5554) or Horizons Unlimited/Churchill River Canoe Outfitters (1-877-511-2726) for details.

There are several campgrounds along the road north of the river, but they lie outside the park boundaries and so I won't consider them in detail here. Check with the tourism office in La Ronge about current campground conditions for places like Dickens Lake, Reindeer Lake, Courtenay Lake, Geikie River, and Hidden Bay. There will be few, if any, amenities and the road will be rough; the fishing will be good, though!

CANOEING

It seems only fitting to mention this park's phenomenal canoeing opportunities in the same place as Otter Rapids. SERM has approved a series of documented canoe routes with excellent publications on each. These brochures detail water conditions, numbers and severity of rapids and portages, relative length (in days) of each trip as well as sights of interest along the way. These brochures can be obtained from the SERM office in Mistasinihk Place or off the SERM website at www.saskparks.netcanoe/. An excellent book, *Canoeing the Churchill* (2002), published by the Canadian Plains Research Center, discusses many of these in far greater detail than I can here. These trips can range from a day or two up to a major expedition, from novice level up to wilderness expert. You are asked to check in with the park office at Mistasinihk Place prior to your departure as well as upon your return to civilization; this is for your safety as well as in case of emergency. Once your trip is complete, you can apply for a voyageur's certificate which states when you canoed these famous waters, and which ones you challenged. Never forget that this country was first explored from the seat of a canoe; it is still the best way to experience it. A local outfitter, Horizons Unlimited/Churchill River Canoe Outfitters, offers a full range of services for canoeists, including rentals, instruction, guides, pick up/drop off, vehicle storage, and light housekeeping cabins, and complete package tours. Contact them by phone at 1-877-511-2726 or check their website at www.churchillrivercanoe.com.

As you can see, Lac La Ronge Provincial Park has so much to offer; these few pages hardly do justice to the hard work of the park's staff nor do they truly prepare you for the wealth of recreational opportunities that await you. Go North; adventure awaits!

SERVICES

The town of La Ronge has all the amenities one could ask for, including shopping, medical, mechanical, and worship services. Of particular interest is the number of excellent crafts produced by local First Nations artists. The local SERM office at Mistasinihk Place, for example, has an interesting series of displays showcasing local talent such as birch bark bitings. The town also hosts many festivals and tournaments over the course of the year, so contact the tourist information office (tel. 1-866-LA RONGE) for details on events bracketing the time you plan to stay and play in this wonderful wilderness. The First Nations population continues their close association with the surrounding wilderness, so fur trading and wilderness arts can be viewed and purchased at the local trading posts such as Paul Robertson Trading Post on La Ronge Avenue. One of the great shows during the year is the King and Queen Trappers event at the Winter Festival every February.

For more information on this beautiful park, contact the park office at:

Lac La Ronge Provincial Park
P.O. Box 5000
La Ronge, SK   S0J 1L0
Telephone: (306) 425-4234
E-mail: cfafard@serm.gov.sk.ca
Website: www.saskparks.netParkInfo

MAKWA LAKE PROVINCIAL PARK

Located 60 km west of Meadow Lake or 170 km north of North Battleford, Makwa Lake has much to offer the vacationing public with its 5 lakes, 3 campgrounds, 9-hole golf course and access to local history and culture. For history buffs there is Steele Narrows and Fort Pitt, scenes of the North-West Resistance, as well as rifle pits and encampments on the northwest shore of Makwa Lake dating back to 1885 and echoes of that resistance. Nearby St. Walburg houses the Imhoff art gallery with its exquisite paintings from that remarkable artist. There are swimming lessons in season, hiking at Stabler Point and on the Mewasin Trail, fishing in any of the 5 lakes, water skiing, camping amid pines, birch and poplar, and always the chance to hear the weird, echoing tremolo of a loon on the water. Makwa Lake is named for the Cree word for loon because of the number that make this area their summer home. I don't know about the rest of the world, but nothing signifies northern camping like a campfire with the loons calling on the water; there I will find peace! The park is open from the May long weekend until the Labor Day weekend although the golf course remains open longer (weather permitting) and there is always winter camping available as well as cross-country skiing on the hiking trails.

SITES

There are three campgrounds in the park, all situated around the Big Jumbo/Little Jumbo basin. The largest is the Stabler Point complex while the smallest is the Jumbo Beach Campground. I shall consider them separately. It is worth noting that the park sits on the side of the village of Loon Lake, so several of its amenities are tied closely to that community.

If you are driving to Jumbo Beach Campground from Hwy 21 you will use the grid road 699, paved for the last 20 km or so into Loon Lake. This takes you right past Little Jumbo Lake and the diminutive Jumbo Beach Campground. There are 17 unserviced sites here of which 9 are for seasonal rent, all relatively small although perfect for tent trailers or truck campers. Several are set right along the water's edge for you boaters! They are built into mature parkland forest and well drained with gravel pads. They are relatively private with decent ground cover and access to a central firewood pile and trash bins. Sites have pole BBQs and wooden picnic tables and access to 3 potable water taps; there is one set of wheelchair accessible flush toilets. There is good parking here and access to the lake from a floating dock but no boat launch. Launch your boat across the lake and park it near your site; bring the trailer back, however! There is no park entry booth here but the park is very close to Jumbo Beach where the swimming lessons take place, so this campground is very popular during lesson sets.

Stabler Point Campground is accessed by driving through the border of Loon Lake and down a paved road approximately 5 km, through the cabin subdivision, past the administration office, then the Loon Lake Golf Club to the campground office. You'll find this huge campground has some of the nicest sites in the province. There are 221 sites of which 84 are electrified; a total of 29 sites have been set aside for seasonal rental, of which 15 are electrified. All sites are built on gravel pads for drainage and have pole BBQs and wooden picnic tables although the park is changing over to the metal framed ones. Potable water taps are scattered throughout the campground and a firewood pile is located beside the boat launch road; firewood is provided free of charge but you must still purchase a campfire permit. All roads are paved in the campground, and you will find most sites adequate for the largest camper, particularly the electrified sites. Washroom facilities vary from wheelchair accessible modern flush units to vault toilets. One trailer dump station is available near the campground office. There are two modern, barrier-free shower facilities, one for each of the electrified and non-electrified loops. For patrons requiring wheelchair accessible sites, the park has reserved sites # 182 (electrified) and #19 (unserviced). Although the park does not normally reserve sites, if you contact them in advance they will hold one of these sites for you. Several sites have raised pads for your camping unit, built on stone bases; they are really quite nice (e.g., site #103 above)! Most of the sites are back-in style although there are 20 pull-through or drive-by sites, all in the unserviced loop. All the sites are well shaded amid tall birch, aspen, and some spruce and there is excellent ground cover; you generally cannot see your neighbors. There are two sets of horseshoe pits in the park; bring your own equipment. There are also two small playgrounds, one near site #185 (and the service center), the other on the beach behind site #59. They both have swings and creative play structures built into soft sand to catch your wee adventurers. The beach has a volleyball net. There is a picnic area behind the beach with picnic tables and pole BBQs but no firewood—use briquettes.

There are also 3 group camping areas available, numbered 1–3. They can accommodate between 7–10 camping units. They share a vault-style toilet and several water taps. Group site #2 has a dining shelter and a firering with benches, while #3 has sites right along the lake. All the sites are leveled on gravel pads and have wooden picnic tables and pole BBQs. There are tall, graceful birch and aspens for shade, and sufficient brush to provide some privacy. You'll share the service center in behind the boat launch, where you'll find the trash bins and firewood pile. Contact the park office to arrange a group site for your private function.

Just past the trailer dump station you'll turn left to drive to this small campground to camp at the bottom of Big Jumbo Lake. There are 24 non-electrified sites here, of which 4 are available for seasonal rent. The sites are set up in two loops: #1–12 to the right of the parking lot and the remainder to the left. Each loop has its own vault-style toilets, potable water, firewood pile and trash bins. There are more pines and spruce trees here so there is generally good shade but relatively poor ground cover. The sites are more naturally leveled and drained and have wooden picnic tables and pole BBQs. The left loop has a camp kitchen, and there is a changeroom between the parking lot and the beach. Several of the sites border the lake, which is a nice touch for the boating crowd! There is no boat launch so you must use the ones on Little Jumbo Lake and boat around; you should leave the trailer in your site, however. There is a small playground beside the beach, and a set of horseshoe pits. From the Mewasin Beach Campground you can access the Mewasin Hiking Trail; more on that later.

WATER SPORTS

With 5 lakes in the park, one can assume that boating is very popular, and you'd be right! There are two boat launches, one near the cabin subdivision near the administration office as you drive into the park and the other in the Stabler Point Campground. Both launches have cement slip ways and floating docks. There are large parking lots but patrons are expected to retrieve their boats nightly and park the boat and trailer in their campsite. There is a fish filleting station at the Stabler Point boat launch, evidence that the pike, walleye and perch fishery is excellent. For those requiring wheelchair assistance, there is a barrier-free fishing pier at Exner Lake, just past the Mewasin Beach Campground. Exner Lake is regularly stocked with trout, and the remaining bodies of water are stocked with walleye fingerlings, over 1.5 million in 2003 alone! There are no marina facilities although the resorts of Makwa Lake and Pine Cove will rent boats and motors; their numbers are listed below. As you might expect, ice fishing is a common winter pastime in the area.

Waterskiing is popular as evidenced by the docks which have been placed to accommodate this recreational use, both at Jumbo Beach Campground and at Stabler Point Campground (near sites #51 and 53). The docks are free to use, but these are shared facilities so please be respectful.

With three beaches in the park, swimming is also popular. The biggest and best of the beaches is at Jumbo Beach, between the cottage subdivision and Jumbo Beach Campground. This is where the swimming lessons are taught in July, and the only time the beach changerooms will be open; vandals will ruin them otherwise, unfortunately. The beach is huge, with excellent, fine sand and a small playground at one end and a beach volleyball net at the other. There is a picnic or day-use area on the lawn between the parking lot and the beach with tables but no pole BBQs. There are a few tall trees for shade but really the focus is the beach and so it should be; with its west face it catches all the summer sun and can be quite crowded on July weekends. The beach at Stabler Point is smaller, certainly thinner, but still has the same excellent sand. There is a volleyball net and a small playground here as well. Mewasin Beach is the smallest of the three, with poorer sand quality due to the tree roots and organic material that you'd expect. There is also a small playground here, with swings in a sandbox. Please note that the swimming lessons are not offered by the park staff; they are offered by a private operator who will take applications. The park office can give you the operator's contact information; it's best you start there.

The Northwest Canoe and Kayak Club offer lessons for the discerning patron, held at the Jumbo Beach boat launch. Lessons run at varying times depending on interest and weather. There is the summer racing team, focusing on competitions held throughout the province, adult classes in both kayak and canoe, fun camps (recreational, week-long camps) and learn to kayak/canoe (5 hours of instruction). Of note is that parents can attend for free if their children sign up for lessons! For more information, check with the park for up-to-date contact information, or try calling 236-5546 or 837-4762, the last contact numbers I had for the club.

HIKING/CROSS-COUNTRY SKIING

There is one established hiking trail at the Mewasin Beach Campground. Depending on the route you take, the Mewasin Hiking Trail covers 5 or 6 km and can take an hour or two to complete. You'll walk through a glacier-sculpted landscape shaded by stands of poplar and jackpine, to find a beaver lodge, the remnants of an old trapper's cabin, and picnic in the deep woods. There is no water supplied along the route so bring your own as well as suitable bug repellant; the mosquitoes can be voracious! There's a map available at the trailhead or at the campground entry booth.

There's a walking path that runs almost completely around Stabler Point, offering a scenic wander. There's no trail map nor would one normally be required. For those desiring more adventure, there is walk-in camping available on Big Jumbo Lake; simply follow the trail past the campgrounds and you'll find it after an hour or so. Please note that if you wish to camp at the walk-in site, you must make arrangements with the park staff beforehand. Canoeists will use these sites as well, particularly those wishing to make the 450-meter portage from Big Jumbo Lake into Tulibee Lake, canoeing over to the Steele Narrows Provincial Historic Site approximately 12 km away. Again, check with the park staff before you set out; they will definitely be able to inform you about conditions and required permits.

The park has set aside 30 campsites, all unserviced, for off-season use by snowmobile enthusiasts and cross-country skiers. All the summer hiking trails are groomed for use in winter, and several more trails are added so there is something for everyone from novice to expert alike. In total, there are nearly 20 km of groomed trails and one warm-up shelter near the parking lot just short of the Stabler Point Campground. There is a winter brochure available which outlines the trails and rates them by difficulty; contact the park office for a copy.

GOLF

No discussion of Makwa Lake Park would be complete without mentioning Loon Lake

Golf and Country Club, located about 2 km inside the park gates. This immaculate 9-hole course is built into mature aspen forest, and plays well over its 3197-yard (blue tees), par-36 fairways. With elevated tees and bunkered greens anchoring the somewhat narrow fairways (to my wandering shot anyway!) and a fairly good chance to see wildlife along the way, this course is certain to delight amateur and pro alike. There is a driving range to practice your swing, and the pro-shop offers a full line of rental clubs and carts as well as a line of branded clothing and golf accessories. The licensed clubhouse offers light meals and a lounge area with a splendid view of the first tee and 9th green. This is a popular course so tee times are highly recommended; make yours by calling the pro-shop at (306) 837-4653.

SERVICES

The village of Loon Lake offers many of the shopping, mechanical, and worship services the vacationer could need. More extensive shopping and medical services are available in Meadow Lake, approximately 70 km west. The park has no interpretive staff, and the lessons offered are not taught by park staff. There are two operations renting cabins, boats, and motors for interested persons: Pine Cove Resort on the north side of Makwa Lake has 10 modern, all-season cabins for rent as well as laundry, store and tackle shop and other amenities. For more information, call them at (306) 837-4612. Makwa Lake Resort, on the south side of the lake, has 17 seasonal cabins for rent. Call them in season at (306) 837-2133.

As you can see, there's a lot going on in this park. The village of Little Loon and the cottage subdivision run many fun-filled events through the summer—check with the public notice boards for details. There's excellent golf, wonderful camping, and all those lakes for fishing, boating and swimming. Take those kayak lessons you've always wanted to, or just light a campfire and listen to the loons sing while the northern lights dance. For more information contact the park office at:

Makwa Lake Provincial Park
PO Box 39
Loon Lake, SK S0M 1L0
Telephone: (306) 837-2410
Fax: (306) 837-2415
You can link to their email from the SERM website at www.se.gov.sk.ca/saskparks.

MEADOW LAKE PROVINCIAL PARK

This enormous park, almost 1600 square kilometers in size, is the keystone to the north-west's recreational opportunities. From the many campgrounds and resorts in the park one can access an almost bewildering array of fishing, boating, golfing, hiking, canoeing, and sightseeing possibilities. This is a very complex park because of all the things going on throughout the park the whole year long; I'll try to simplify it by discussing each lake within the park individually, starting from east to west. There are three main entry points to the park, Hwy 4 via Dorintosh, Hwy 26 via Goodsoil, and Hwy 21 via Pierceland. The park administrative building is located at the entry gate on Hwy 4, and there is an entry booth on the Hwy 26 entrance; a secondary road 919 runs north to the Primrose Air Weapons Range above Cold Lake. As a general rule the roads in the park are all-weather gravel roads although some of the larger cottage subdivisions have paved access roads. The park is fully open from the May long weekend to the Labor Day weekend but it never really closes due to all the cottage subdivisions, ice fishing, snowmobiling and cross-country skiing that goes on.

SITES

As mentioned above, we'll start from the east at Waterhen Lake and run west to Cold Lake on the Alberta border. Hold tight, it's a long journey—we drove for over 400 km inside the park alone on the weekend we visited!

Waterhen Lake is accessed from Hwy 4 by driving past the park gate a couple of km then turning right on the gravel road (Hwy 904) at the T-intersection just across the Waterhen River. Follow the gravel road 20 km or so then turn right on the Waterhen Lake access road. As you drive up you'll see the park campgrounds directly ahead and two outfitters' developments, one on either side. There are 4 electrified sites and 24 non-electrified sites in the park portion of the development on the south side of the lake, renting from a self-registry kiosk; set up in the site of choice then fill out the envelope at the kiosk. The sites are naturally leveled and drained; built into mature jackpine and spruce forest they have good shade but little ground cover for privacy. The sites are generally large enough for modern units, and have wooden picnic tables and pole BBQs; firewood is available from a central bin. There are potable water taps and covered trash bins, and one dining shelter in the lawned day-use picnic area. Please note that this is bear country, so do not discard fish waste in the trash—use the fish-cleaning station at the boat launch instead. Toilet facilities are vault style and not really wheelchair friendly, and Tawaw Cabins has pay showers for their patrons. There is a small playground with swings and teeter-totters built into a sandbox. The boat launch and wheelchair-accessible fish-cleaning shelter are located beside Tawaw Cabins and are a shared facility. There are two privately owned outfitters, Tawaw Cabins and M & N Resort, both offering heated, furnished cabins and more electrified campsites. They also rent boats and motors, and both have a confectionary with simple groceries, branded clothing and fishing tackle. You can contact them directly at Tawaw Cabins, (306) 236-6716 and M & N Resort, (306)236-6718.

To get to Flotten Lake you must first drive past Jeannette Lake which has a simple boat launch, fish-cleaning table and picnic area with wooden picnic tables and pole BBQs but little else; there is no overnight camping. Located approximately 20 km north of Waterhen Lake on Hwy 904, Flotten Lake has two campgrounds and an outfitter; both campgrounds use a self-registration kiosk. Turn left past the resort to the south campground with its 23 non-electrified sites. They are built on both sides of the road bordering the lake, with the larger sites to the right along the lake while the ones to the left are built right into the mature forest at the base of a steep hill. There is a woodpile, trash hut and water tap beside the registry kiosk; bring an axe—the blocks of wood were quite large. All sites have picnic tables, pole BBQs, and are naturally leveled and drained. There is a fish-cleaning table beside site #17; the boat launch is located between here and the north campground. With the tall hill to the east both sides will be well shaded although the hillside camp sites will be better shaded through the day; they will also have a stunning view of the sun setting over beautiful Flotten Lake.

Driving a few km past the resort you'll see the turn for the north campground with its 25 non-electrified sites. They are set in two loops, all built in mature spruce and aspen forest so shade is good but privacy is poor due to a lack of ground cover. The sites are naturally drained and leveled and have picnic tables and pole BBQs. Toilet facilities are vault style, one set in each of the two loops in the north campgrounds, and there is a trailer dump station between the toilets, close to site #16. There is one centrally located trash hut and wood pile, and potable water taps are centralized in each loop.

Located between the north and south campgrounds is the public boat launch with a gravel slip and floating dock. You'll find a large parking lot, fish-cleaning table, vault toilets and potable water tap. As you can imagine fishing is very popular on this lake, with pike, walleye and whitefish commonly taken. There is a very thin beach at both campgrounds from which children can swim but there is no buoyed swimming area and you must supervise your own swimmers. You'll also find Flotten Lake Resort here with its cabins, private campsites, private boat launch and docks, and store. The store has a small line of groceries and camping needfuls; you can rent fishing boats and motors here as well. For more details, contact them directly at (306) 236-1940, or check out their website at www.flottenlake.com.

Across the road from the resort is the White Birch Hiking Trail. There is a good-sized parking lot and picnic area at the trail head where you'll find the trail brochures. It's a strenuous 2 km in length—certainly not wheelchair accessible, but a pleasant hour or so as you wander along the Flotten River. The trail brochure explains the sights at each of the numbered stations along the trail; there's even a boardwalk jutting into a muskeg so you can go feed the mosquitoes while trying to find bog orchids!

Greig Lake is located west of the T-intersection of Hwy 224 (the road running east-west through the park) and Hwy 4 from Dorintosh. This pretty lake houses a public campground, private cottage subdivision, and resort complex. You'll drive past the resort area to the campground office from which you'll be directed to your site. The campground has 149 sites of which 9 are full hook-up, 87 are electrified, and 53 are unserviced. This popular park has a reserve-a-site feature, with 31 sites set aside for reservations and the remainder available on a first-come, first-serve basis; there are also 8 sites available for seasonal rent. All sites are built into mature aspen forest with generally good ground cover. Some of the sites are relatively small although several are huge—two are wheelchair accessible with paved parking areas and pavement blocks covering the picnic area. The new area has the largest sites, and many sites have lakeside access—truly something for every camper! All the roads are paved and all sites are graveled with metal-framed picnic tables and pole BBQs. Toilet facilities vary from vault-style in the camping loops to the fully modern flush toilets and showers at the service center. You'll also find the coin-operated laundromat here (bring loonies and quarters), a recycling station and the firewood pile. There are two trailer dump stations, one at the entrance to the main camping loops and the other on the road to the new camping loop.

As you drive into pretty Greig Lake you'll pass the two group camping areas, "A" and "B." Of the two, "A" is smaller, long and narrow while 'B' is larger and more open. Both areas have vault toilets, wood piles, trash bins, a fire pit and dining shelter, a collection of pole BBQs and picnic tables, and potable water taps. All the roads are packed dirt. Just past this you'll find the huge lawn area with the ball diamond, its tall metal mesh backstop and grass infield, and the tennis court, which includes two basketball hoops in the fenced enclosure; bring your own equipment.

Just past the campground office is the turn to the public boat launch with its large parking lot, fixed dock and fish filleting facility. There is potable water here but no toilets. Although some fortunate campers may have lake access and can thus beach their boats by night, everyone is still expected to park their trailers in their sites or retrieve their boat daily. To the left of the boat launch is the public beach with a small playground and large, lawned day-use or picnic area. There is a buoyed swimming area and swim lessons are taught in July; contact the park office for details. There is a large parking lot beside the visitor's center which houses an interpretive center and meeting rooms. For the most part you will have to contact park staff at the campground entrance booth for assistance.

Located just to the right of the parking lot is Star's Place, the local outfitter. Here you'll find a friendly cup of coffee, fishing tackle and grocery items, gas, rental boats and motors and a wealth of information about all things Greig Lake! Contact them directly at (306) 236-3006 for details on their operation or to make rental arrangements. You'll find the Dutch Treat Mini-Golf course beside the excellent playground; you can call them directly at (306) 236-3800 for group bookings.

Located just past the resort street turn to the boat launch and campgrounds is the Hay Meadow Hiking Trail. These trails are groomed in winter for use as cross-country ski trails. A large map at the trail head details the many loops available, of which between 3 and 5 km are used in summer for hiking. There is a warm-up shelter beside the trail head, with a wood-burning stove and vault toilets. The potable water tap will not be working in the winter months.

Kimball Lake can be reached by driving west along Hwy 224 from Greig Lake. You'll pass a couple of scenic picnic spots, such as Rusty Lake with its picnic tables, Pole BBQ, simple boat launch and fish-cleaning table, but no overnight camping. Next is Rusty Creek (First Mustus Lake) which has similar facilities. Continuing a short way you'll find the Kimball Lake turnoff to 190 campsites, a private cottage subdivision and a resort. The campsites are spread out through 7 loops, not all of which will be open at the same time; they open areas based on demand so they may not have everything open on the May long weekend, as when we visited! Of these sites, only 42 are unserviced and some of these are quite small, suitable for tenting. The remaining sites are electrified and variable in size although generally suitable for the larger modern units. Two sites, #123 and 124, are paved throughout and wheelchair accessible. Most of the sites are back-in style although a very few are drive-by style. They are all built on gravel pads in mature aspen and birches, with excellent shade and adequate ground cover. All sites have metal-framed picnic tables and pole BBQs, with potable water taps scattered through the whole campgrounds. There are three strategically placed wood piles with recycling stations nearby. Toilet facilities are mostly flush-style with a few vault toilets in farther areas; there's one trailer dump station just past the permit office. The modern barrier-free service center has hot showers, flush toilets and the coin-operated laundromat; bring loonies and quarters. There are also free showers available in the beach changerooms. There is one very nice group camping area to the west of the main beach. It has 9 or so unserviced sites (picnic tables and pole BBQs) with vault toilets, a potable water tap, wood pile, dining shelter and trash bins. There's also a central fire pit and access to the beach area. There is a ball diamond in a nearby lawn and a tennis court with basketball hoops in a paved, fenced enclosure.

The beach simply has to be seen to be believed; people claim it's among the top 10 beaches in Canada and I can't argue. There's plenty of room on the beach and a buoyed (unsupervised) swimming area in which swim lessons are taught in July. The beach itself seems to curve forever around the lake, with clean, coarse sand, ideal for the beach volleyball, which seems popular here. The picnic area in behind it is well lawned and shaded amid tall spruce and pines, with picnic tables and pole BBQs; there is no wood provided as you are expected to use briquettes. There are two playgrounds to occupy little campers: a small one located on the eastern end of the day-use area has a climber and slide while the new and much larger creative playground is located beside the showerhouse and changeroom. There are vault toilets in the day-use area while the beach changerooms have flush toilets and barrier-free hot showers. A paved, wheelchair accessible walking path runs the length of the beach between lawn and sand from the parking lot to the store. The Kimball Lake store is located just on the edge of the beach with quite a spectacular view of the lake. You'll find they've got a pretty full selection of groceries, meat, clothing and confectionery items as well as grilled food and ice cream at the diner with its open-air patio. You can also rent boats, motors, canoes, water trikes, etc., from the busy store. There is ample parking both at the store and to the west of the picnic area, and at the boat launch, located west of the group camping area. There is a floating dock and gravel slip, but no marina facilities; you are expected to retrieve your boat nightly and store it in your site. The boat launch facility has a fish filleting table and water but no toilet facilities. Call the park office to reserve a site in this pretty campground so you can enjoy this beach!

Continuing west from Kimball Lake about 5 minutes you'll find little Vivian Lake with its 8 non-electrified sites. The road in is narrow and winding, built of sand right past the self-registry kiosk and into the campground. There are wooden picnic tables, pole BBQs and a wood pile but no potable water so camping prices are reduced here. Toilet facilities are vault-style, and the naturally drained and leveled sites are well shaded amid spruce and pines but there is little ground cover; as the sites are located around a small clearing this feels more like a cozy group camping area than anything else. There is a small boat launch and fish filleting table but no beach or playground equipment. Of interest is the Vivian Lake Hiking Trail with two loops for your afternoon stroll: the short one is 1.6 km (30 minutes) and the long one is 4.2 km (1.5 hours long). The trails are listed as easy although narrow. As you drive into the campground you'll note a road leading off to your right; this is the Tall Timber Trails riding stable. They organize guided trail or wagon rides in these scenic woods for individuals or groups; contact them directly for current information at (306) 236-5906; email at talltimbertrails@hotmail.com

Matheson Lake, hardly a rifle shot west of Vivian Lake, is larger, with its 42 unserviced sites. A self-registry kiosk is located just to your right as you drive into the first loop, #1–19, where you'll find the wood pile, trash bins, and recycling bins. All sites are back-in style, and built into mature coniferous forest with good shade and decent ground cover. Metal-framed picnic tables and pole BBQs are located at the back of the naturally leveled and drained sites, and potable water taps are located beside the vault toilets between sites #13 and 14. The second loop is much similar, with a water tap beside the vault toilets near site #26. As this loop is a bit larger there are a few sites available for seasonal rent. There's also a dining shelter and playground on the beach behind site #32. The beach itself has coarse, clean sand near the picnic area although the sand gets finer as you get into the water. There's a boat launch that shares the parking lot for the picnic and beach area. Here you'll find a trailer dump station, vault toilets, water tap, trash bins, pole BBQs and wooden picnic tables. The boat launch has a gravel slip with floating dock but no marina; retrieve your boat at night and store it in your site. The road past the parking lot takes you back to Vivian Lake by way of the Tall Timber Trails riding stable, listed above. This is a nice campground with fish in the lake and a nice beach with hiking trails close by; there's even a horse ride if you've a mind to!

Mistohay Lake is located 32 km west of the Hwy 4 intersection (or 16 km east of the Goodsoil entry gate). It has been referred to as a "Fisherman's paradise"! He was just coming in off the water with a nice catch of pike, which may have caused his enthusiasm. There are 20 non-electrified sites here in one bay-like loop, all built into mature aspen with some spruce and pines. Naturally leveled and drained, the sites have metal-framed picnic tables and pole BBQs, with excellent shade but little privacy although they are large enough to hold most modern units. The wood pile and trash hut are located across from the self-registry kiosk to the right as you drive in. There are vault toilets beside the trailer dump station across the entrance road from the kiosk, and water is provided from central taps. You'll find a picnic area and playground beside the boat launch; the picnic area has a dining shelter and the playground is split into two areas with swings in one and a slide in the other—both are built into sand boxes. We thought Mistohay Creek, a short distance west of the lake, was an interesting sight in the early spring; it was clear that the spring floods had quite the effect in the little river valley.

If you plan to visit Lac des Iles, you have a decision to make. The intersection between Hwy 26, north of Goodsoil, and the continuation west of Hwy 224 from Mistohay Lake (now Hwy 950—I

told you things could get overwhelming!) gives us a look at camping amenities on the north side of the lake or the south. We shall consider them from the north side first, beginning with Murray Doell Campground. You will find 134 sites in this reserve-a-site campground, of which 57 are electrified and 77 non-electrified. Of these, 20 electrified and 10 non-electrified sites can be reserved and a further 5 sites of each type are available for seasonal rent; call the park office for more details on either type. The sites are generally huge, certainly large enough for a modern unit plus boat trailer, and all built on gravel pads amid mature aspen and birch trees. The sites have good ground cover and are therefore quite private, for the most part, and all have a metal-framed picnic table and pole BBQ. There is a woodpile beside the self-registration kiosk, with trash huts and water taps scattered throughout the campground. Toilet facilities will generally be vault-style, with wheelchair accessible flush toilets and hot showers in the modern service center near site #1, which is probably the most barrier-free of the sites in this campground. There is a trailer dump station across the road from the self-registry kiosk. There are two dining shelters in the campground, one on a short road past sites #50 and 51, and one at the beach in the picnic area. Something of a rarity in this park, there are 8 streetlights in strategic areas to assist either in finding a toilet or losing the Milky Way, depending if you're looking up or down!

There is one group area available, which doubles as the overflow area in times of high demand. There are 10 unserviced sites here, with a central fire pit and dining shelter. All sites are well shaded and private, with separate water taps, vault toilets, trash bins, and wood pile.

The lake is a magnet due to the large, quiet beach with its lawn and picnic area. The parking lot is about 40 meters or so from the beach which is full of coarse sand (fine gravel, really) but clean. There is a boat launch to the far west of the campground with a cement pad, vault toilets, water tap and fish-filleting station located around a large parking lot. Fishing is supposed to be excellent on this lake with pike, walleye and whitefish commonly taken. A playground has been built beside the camp kitchen in the center of the park (near site #51) with a creative climbing structure built into a sand box. There is a small parking lot nearby, which also serves the small number of walk-in tenting sites along the beach. There is a road leading to Johnston Lake, accessed to the right of Hwy 950 as you approach the Murray Doell Campground turn, where you'll find a rudimentary boat launch and vault toilets but no other amenities.

If you are entering Meadow Lake Provincial park from the Goodsoil access on Hwy 26, you can turn west on the access to the south side of Lac des Iles. Here you will find two resorts, the first being Big Island Cove Resort which has light housekeeping cabins of various sorts, serviced campsites, a convenience store and boat/motor rentals. They are in the park but not of the park, as it were, so I won't go into great detail; you can contact them directly for current prices and reservations at (306) 238-4648, or check out their website at www.bigislandcove.com.

Continuing west on the same access one finds the Northern Cross Resorts, which has 70 campsites of which 25 are electrified as well as a variety of light housekeeping cabins. They also rent boats and motors from their lodge and store, and have an excellent beach and playground area. As with the other resort, they are in the park but not of the park so I won't discuss their operation in detail; contact them directly for current prices and reservations at (306) 238-4608 (May–August) or toll-free at (877) 597-3395 (September–April); check out their website at www.NCResort.com

Continuing your westward drive you'll pass little Lepine Lake which has no amenities although you can access it from the bridge across the river joining it to Pierce Lake. Just past that bridge is the access to the Howe Bay resort area. Here you'll find a private cottage subdivision and a resort, the Pierce Lake Lodge, which has taken over all the campsites once operated by the provincial park here. The lodge offers year-round cabins, summer camping in serviced and unserviced campsites, groceries, boat rentals and fishing supplies. Contact the Pierce Lake Lodge directly for current pricing or to make a reservation at (306) 839-4517.

Continuing on Hwy 950 will bring you to the intersection of Hwy 21 from Pierceland and Hwy 919, which continues north out of the park past Cold Lake to the Primrose Air Weapons Range. Along the way you'll pass the Sandy Beach campground access where you'll find 79 sites in total. Following the access north will take you straight to the lake and boat launch—guess what's very popular here! Take the campground turn to your right, past the Humphrey Hiking Trail and the trailer dump station to the left turn into the campground office from where you'll rent your site. The campground is laid out in 6 small loops to the right, with 33 non-electrified sites set up like small group areas. The last area to the right is the actual group area, used as an unserviced overflow when demand warrants. To the left of the campground office are 27 electrified sites as well as the 19 lakefront non-electrified sites. Although the campground has no reservation system, there are 10 sites available for seasonal rent. As a general rule, the sites to the east are more generously spaced and private while the western sites have better lake access.

All sites in the campground are built into mature aspen and birch forest, with good shade and privacy. The sites are leveled on gravel pads and have metal-framed picnic tables and pole BBQs. There is one firewood pile near site #30, and trash bins and potable water taps are scattered throughout the campground. Toilet facilities range from vault-style toilets in the campgrounds to wheelchair accessible flush toilets and hot showers in the service center in the field beside site #79. There is a turning loop and small parking lot at the end of the westmost camping loop, beside which is the ice cream stand. A small parking lot is accessed from the boat launch road, and serves the picnic area, play ground, and beach with its changerooms and vault toilets.

The boat launch has vault toilets, water taps and a fish filleting station. The nearby dining shelter also serves the beach and day-use area. The beach changerooms were locked during our visit in May, but would be open during July and August, the busiest times in this park. There is a volleyball court on the lawn behind the beach. The beach itself is somewhat narrow but long; there is a buoyed swimming area and the beach is unsupervised except when swim lessons are offered in July. The playground is reasonably large with swings and a wooden creative climber, all built into a large sand pit surrounded by grass. The Humphrey Lake Hiking Trail leads folks back into the woods on a delightful walk. The trail is narrow and not wheelchair accessible, and there were no trail brochures when we visited. The trail is moderately difficult with some slippery hills (when wet); Humphrey's Lake is a short 0.6-km hike, and the Tower Trail is a 3.2-km loop where you will find a viewing tower with a panoramic view of the local terrain.

Hirtz Lake, accessed from Hwy 919 west of Pierce Lake, has little to offer the camping public. The drive-in is on a sand road, narrow and about 1.5 km long, terminating in a small camping area with 4 non-electrified sites and a self-registry kiosk. To camp here you must be very self-sufficient and capable of "no-trace camping" as there are few amenities besides the naturally drained and leveled sites. There were wooden picnic tables and pole BBQs, but no drinking water; use the lake but you must be prepared to boil water first. There are vault toilets (one set), trash bins and a wood pile, but bring your axe—the blocks needed splitting! You'll find a rustic boat launch capable of launching/landing cartop boats or canoes but nothing larger unless the approach is dry. There was a small sand bar a few meters from shore at which several small boats were beached during our visit; there were no docks or marina facilities. Fishing is apparently good in this small, quiet lake. If you treat this campground as a wilderness area and are prepared to be self-sufficient you won't be far wrong!

After driving past Hirtz Lake you'll soon pass over Cold River, but be aware that the roads are in generally poor condition—this really seems like a logging road for bumps and soft, sandy spots. During our May visit, fishing was closed at Cold River to allow fish to spawn, and the boggy boat launch was essentially impassable. All the roads in the campground and access are built of sand and can be very soft; caution is advised. There are only 4 unserviced sites, rented from a self-registry kiosk on a discount basis, much like Hirtz Lake. There are vault toilets, wooden picnic tables and pole BBQs serving these naturally drained and leveled sites, all facing west across Cold Lake itself. There is one fire pit, and you'll need an axe to split the firewood supplied. There is a boat launch at the lake itself but it will not be suitable for a large boat which is a pity as this is a large lake and the fishing is reputed to be excellent. Much like Hirtz Lake, if you consider this to be wilderness camping and act accordingly you won't be far wrong. Just a reminder: if you get stuck here you'll be walking a ways to find help!

It is pretty much impossible to discuss this park without a section on the Waterhen River. For the canoeist this river is a magnet as you can find rapids and places to test your skill or you can paddle and drift down stream on a hot, lazy afternoon. There are lakes and streams in which to fish and out-of-the way places to camp. The provincial government has two documented canoe trips, #23 and #24, which discuss suggested maps, trip notes, and pick-up and drop-off points. One trip (#23) runs from Howe Bay on Pierce Lake to the bridge over the Waterhen River north of Goodsoil. The second trip runs from that bridge (as an alternate start-point) or First Mustus Lake to Waterhen Lake. As the government's brochures are far more complete than anything I could tell you I won't try to elaborate on these trips here; suffice to say that if you're considering a visit in the park and would like to spend a day or two canoe tripping, then you really should begin your planning here; there are designated backcountry camp sites along the Waterhen River and the park has a registration process to follow. Contact the park for more information. These excellent brochures can be downloaded from the SERM website at www.saskparks.netcanoe/, along with a host of other documented canoe routes. The park has also written a short brochure called *Canoe Routes of Meadow Lake Provincial Park*; contact the park office for a copy. If you'd like to rent equipment instead of bringing your own, contact Marlow Kayak and Canoe Rentals at (306) 236-4624, or by email at esau@sasktel.net.

HIKING TRAILS

Although I've written about this park's many hiking trails at each lake as they occur, a synopsis is worthwhile to keep it all straight! You'll find the SERM brochure, "Natural History Notes," an interesting companion for the general information it presents while hiking the woods. The park has written a brochure, *Hiking Trails of Meadow Lake Provincial Park*, with more extensive information and trails maps; I'll present the information in the same order as their brochure:

Hay Meadow Hiking Trail–Greig Lake–total length 4.8 km (about 1.5 hrs), moderate hike with some hilly sections.

Kimball Lake Hiking Trail–Kimball Lake–length (Raspberry Lake and back) 2 km (40 min.), around Raspberry Lake 6.5 km (2 hr), easy hike with narrow trail.

Vivian Lake Hiking Trail–Vivian Lake–short loop 1.6 km (30 min), around Vivian Lake 4.2 km (1.5 hr), easy hike with narrow trail.

Newbranch Hiking Trail–parking beside Hwy 224 across from Vivian Lake, 3 loops: parking lot to Matheson Lake 2 km (30 min one way), parking lot to Kimball Lake 6 km (2 hr one way), Peitahigan Loop 11 km (3.5 hr), all considered moderate hikes with some hilly terrain. There are also two backcountry camp sites along this trail; you must register with the park before you can access them.

Humphrey Lake Hiking Trail–Pierce Lake–two hikes: to Humphrey Lake 0.6 km (30 min loop), to the Viewing Tower 3.2 km (1.5 hr loop), moderate hikes with some slippery slopes through the hilly sections.

White Birch Hiking Trail–Flotten Lake–1.8 km (1 hr), moderate with some hilly sections.

CROSS-COUNTRY SKIING AND SNOWMOBILE TRAILS
"If you consider it a sport to gather your food by drilling through18 inches of ice and sitting there all day hoping that the food will swim by… You might live in Saskatchewan." (Jeff Foxworthy, live at the Northern Lights Casino)

Winter fun is certainly not forgotten in this park! Outside of the obvious ice fishing to be had at the many lakes and resorts there are several groomed cross-country ski trails available at Greig Lake. There is a warm-up shelter at the parking lot trail head, with a wood stove and wood supply, and another one near a junction map at the half-way point on the Spruce Bluff Trail. The park has a brochure detailing the trails with lengths, terrain marks and degree of difficulty to be expected; contact the park for a copy, or pick one up at the park entry gate.

Local snowmobile clubs also groom over a hundred kilometers of snowmobile trails all centered around Greig Lake. From here one can reach over 30 km west to just past Matheson Lake, looping back over the Waterhen River. Once again the park has written an excellent trail guide, available at the park entry gate or at Star's Place at Greig Lake; you can also contact the park office directly for a copy.

SERVICES
The park interpretive staff run a full slate of programs that are not only fun but educate campers about the beautiful forest they'll find themselves in. These sessions will take place all over the park throughout July and August, free for the asking; all you have to do is attend! Check with the park gate for a schedule of dates and places, or check any of the bulletin boards you'll find in campgrounds (usually at the service centers) throughout the park. The park also publishes (along with Makwa Lake Provincial Park, Bronson Forest Recreation Site and Chitek Lake Recreation Site) a wonderful magazine called *The Natural Choice*, with summaries of park regulations, advertising from local merchants, and articles on local events, natural history, or programs offered through these parks; pick up

your copy at the park entry gate or by contacting the park office.

When traveling in the area you'll note several excellent golf courses although none are actually in the park. The nearest would be 2 km south of the Lac des Iles park gate, just north of Goodsoil, with the Northern Meadows Golf Club. It is a championship golf course with pro-shop, equipment rentals and sales, branded clothing, licensed dining, bed-and-breakfast accommodation and camping. You can contact them directly at (306) 238-4653 or through their website at www.northernmeadows.com.

The towns of Meadow Lake, Goodsoil and Pierceland have all the shopping, mechanical, medical and worship services you could ask for among them, with the largest community being Meadow Lake. As you can see from this rather extensive write-up, this is a big, complex park with something going on pretty much the entire year. Several of the lakes have a "reserve-a-site" feature where you can reserve a site well in advance, which I highly recommend, particularly for the busy July and August long weekends. Many of the campgrounds also have seasonal site rentals which will also be popular for many patrons. For more information on these or any other services, contact the park office at:

Meadow Lake Provincial Park
PO Box 70
Dorintosh, SK   S0M 0T0
Telephone: (306) 236-7680
Fax: (306) 236-7679

Check their webpage by linking from the SERM website at www.saskparks.net; you can link to their email from that site as well.

NARROW HILLS PROVINCIAL PARK

Located approximately 135 km north-east of Prince Albert, this park offers its patrons a truly unique fishing experience. The conservation officers stock 60 lakes in the park and immediate area with many species of fish including many of the trout species that can be caught in the province. Although several of the lakes are large and support watercraft of all sizes, most are quite small with few boating amenities so all craft must be small enough to carry in. This means that the lakes retain their quiet tranquility while still delivering excellent fishing qualities. With all these small lakes dotting the park, hiking conditions are excellent although only one hiking trail has been established.

The park is 53,610 hectares in area and serviced by two main roads. Hwy 106, north from Smeaton, is paved right into the heart of the park, and I would recommend it for all seasons. Hwy 120, running north-east from Meath Park, is paved only as far as popular Candle Lake, and the last 45 kilometers are graveled. It is also heavily traveled by logging and pulp trucks, so the gravel portion can be quite rough at times. Although it is shorter than Hwy 106, I would still recommend the longer route for comfort and safety reasons. There is no entry gate, and park entry fees will be collected when reserving a campsite at one of the lakes. Park entry fees are $7 per day, $17 for 3 day, $25 per week, or $50 for the entire year. People transiting the park (driving to Creighton or visiting the children's summer camp, for instance) will not be levied a park entry fee.

The park is situated in the southern boreal forest, with evidence of ancient glaciation seen in the eskers and drumlins that adorn the park's topography. The major hill range is the Cub Hills, and two river systems drain the park: Caribou Creek and Stewart Creek; ultimately they join up with the Torch River and drain into Hudson's Bay via the Saskatchewan River—Lake Winnipeg—Nelson River route. The terrain has a predominantly sandy soil with few rocks although there are many marshy spots in low-lying areas. During your drive up, regardless of the route you take, you'll see how two major fires in the last 25 years have changed the face of the park. You'll pass by mature stands of jack pine that display lichen infestations, as well as tall aspens in the heavier, wetter soils. The burned-over areas are making a remarkable comeback, with dense pine forests filling in the blackened spots. These trees are free of the lichens damaging the older ones, demonstrating how fires are a natural part of a forest's vitality.

CAMPING

Several lakes offer a variety of camping amenities, from wilderness camping to electrified sites in full-service campgrounds. The largest lake in the park also holds the largest campgrounds, at Lower Fishing Lake. The park office can also be found here although it may not be open at all times. The lakes with campgrounds will be considered separately, from largest to smallest. The park staff has prepared a pamphlet detailing the fishing available within the lake, and the section for each lake has some simple data to assist you. There is a difference in what they expect of your abilities, though—when the park guide says "primitive camping" it means just that; they expect you to be self-contained and self-reliant. When it says "non-serviced camping," you will find picnic tables, vault toilets, firewood and pole BBQs but no running water. "Serviced camping" will include running water, electrified sites and possibly service centers with hot showers.

Lower Fishing Lake has by far the best amenities in the park as the campground boasts 81 sites, 30 of which are electrified, and is open from the Victoria Day weekend to the Labor Day weekend. Sites cost $20 per night for an electrified site, $15 per night, non-electrified. All sites are naturally leveled and drained, which shouldn't be a problem due to the sandy soil. Sturdy picnic tables adorn each site, as do pole BBQs. A reasonable map is available to show where everything is located. Firewood is available from central bins, for which no charge is currently levied. Those wishing to light a fire will be charged $3 per night, however, ostensibly to recover the cost of firewood and cleanup of the BBQ; besides, park regulations forbid bringing firewood into the park. Washrooms are modern, with flush toilets and running water. Showers are available at the service station. Potable water is piped to central taps. A trailer flush station is available, and most amenities are at least partially wheelchair accessible; there are no wheelchair accessible trails in the campground, however. The lake has by far the best swim beach in the park, wide and deep with delightfully clean sand and a shallow, shelving apron that seems to warm up nicely. A beach changeroom is available, but it does not have showers. A fine boat launch is available and fishing on the lake is excellent for pike and walleye.

The campgrounds is self-registering, so drive through and find a site then go back and fill out the envelope, pay up, and deposit it with payment in the slot provided. Note that site #60 (non-electrified) sits directly across the road from the campground service station, a wheelchair-accessible building with showers and modern toilets. Well treed and with fairly large spots, this park will fill up quickly, particularly on long weekends; as there is no site-reservation system, you may have to come up a day early to put your tent or unit down on a site to hold it.

Nearby is Pine Ridge Resort, which is open year-round. It has a small, private campground with 23 electrified sites for their patrons as well as 6 cabins for rent. Reservations are available as they are a private outfitter and not part of the park system. The resort also has boats/motors, paddle boats and canoes for rent, and a confectionary with shopping for souvenirs, bait and fishing tackle, as well as groceries, fuel and camping supplies. Prices and availability for this popular resort vary, so contact them early when planning your holiday. They can be contacted at:

Pine Ridge Resort (website: www.pineridge.8k.com)
P.O. Box 27
Smeaton, SK   S0J 2J0
Telephone: (306) 426-4123
E-mail: pineridge1@sasktel.net

Ispuchaw Lake is just 1 km north of the ZN Lake access, and is also approximately 1 km west of Hwy 106. At 142 hectares in area, it is bounded on the east shore by steep hills (15–22 meters from the waterline) and to the west by marshy shallows. There are 5 non-electrified sites costing $11 per night, with pole BBQs and heavy picnic tables. The camp sites are situated on top of a hill facing west, and a small beach is located at the bottom of that hill. This is also the water point for the lake's patrons; you can imagine how difficult fetching water is! Although I've never had any trouble with any of the lake water in this park, it is a fact of life that bacterial diseases are on the rise so I would recommend boiling lake water prior to drinking it. The campgrounds has no amenities other than a central firewood supply near the vault toilets, and the sites, although smaller than most, are set in mature jack pine forest so they are generally quite shady. The lake is popular for walleye and northern pike fishing, and is stocked every second year with walleye. The boat launch is at the bottom of the hill to the left of the campground and one must make a sharp turn at the bottom; only small trailers can make the turn effectively, and the boat launch itself is rather poor as it is simply packed sand. There is no boat dock.

Zeden Lake is located 1 km off Hwy 106, approximately 8 km south of the junction of Hwy 106 and Hwy 120. Also known as ZN Lake, it was named for a bush plane that was lost in the area, and is home to St. John Bosco Camp, a residential summer camp for children, along the north shore. Worship services are available in the camp's chapel; notices can be found in campground bulletin boards throughout the park. There are 14 non-electrified sites costing $11 per night clustered around the eastern end of the lake, along with a good-quality beach and a decent boat launch and dock. The lake itself is 29 hectares in area and is set among rolling hills to the north and south with a marshy end to the west. The facilities are primitive with no running water or showers and mature jack pine forest shades the sites from the east only as the lake allows cool westerly breezes to offset some of the sun's heat during those long, hot summer days. The campground is self-registering, with a park employee checking the sites twice daily as a rule. Fishing is supposed to be good for splake and tiger trout as the lake is stocked every second year with these species. I say "supposed to be good" as I've never caught anything there in five years of trying!

Baldy Lake is located 5 km off Hwy 106, just 6 km north of Caribou Creek Lodge. This 26 hectare lake is named for a man that lived at the southeast end of the lake. Apparently as bald as a cue ball, he was nick-named "Baldy" and this was "his" lake. You can still see evidence of a simple sawmill and old, rusting machinery at the site. It's a gentle hike along a fairly easy trail to the spot; you can't miss it! There are 8 non-electrified sites here, situated near the old road along the north shore of the lake. The campsites are fairly large as they really aren't well defined, but they are quite shady and well-drained on sandy soil. The picnic tables are quite sturdy, and the pole BBQs have been supplanted by a simple firepit on a couple of the sites. The lake provides drinking water, and firewood is available from a central bin near the vault toilets. The access road in the campgrounds is simply maintained, so tree roots and potholes have slowed traffic in the access points down to a crawl. The lake does have a primitive boat launch but no boat dock; due to marshy conditions I would recommend only small craft be launched here. The lake is populated with northern pike, walleye, and splake, and is stocked annually with walleye. I have rather fond memories of Baldy Lake, as it's one of the few I've actually caught fish in while angling in the Narrow Hills Provincial Park! I've had excellent success simply drifting along the reeds and casting from a canoe. There is a beach available, but it's approximately the size of your coffee table; as this is a very quiet lake that may not be a problem. As a side note, we picked several hats full of wild strawberries here, some as large as your fingernail, and feasted on wild strawberry pancakes the next morning and chocolate cake muffins laced with the berries for lunch. With fresh fish and such tasty treats, life was very good!

FISHING

As mentioned before, this park features fishing for so many species that it should occupy a book all its own. Although the provincial government's *Angler's Guide* has more detailed information on the numbers of fish stocked per lake and is updated annually, the park staff have prepared a highly useful pamphlet describing the myriad lakes in the park and the fishing to be had as well as the stocking regime. It includes information regarding the location, size, and stocking at over 60 lakes and streams both inside and nearby the park. Some of the fishing is for walk-in anglers only as few of the lakes have serviced boat launches. The pamphlet is not revised consistently, though, so take the information with some asperity. The road running into Lost Echo Lake, for example, is not maintained and the stretch leading down into the wilderness campgrounds is in very poor condition. Steep, deeply rutted and pitted, it can be difficult to get back to civilization. Just remember: if the lake data say "primitive camping," expect the road in to be rough, requiring off-road capability at the very least!

Although there are many lakes to fish and boat in, only two creeks drain the park into the Torch River, and neither of these could be considered truly navigable to motor boats. Canoeists will have trouble with them due to deadfall and beaver dams, so the only "river" canoeing available will be the creek between Upper and Lower Fishing lakes, and the Stewart Creek outlet to Lower Fishing Lake, and even then only for the first kilometer or so, depending on water conditions. Having said that, portaging a canoe into some of the smaller lakes (Pine Lake, for instance) will provide the only reasonable angling for those bodies.

All this taken aside, fishing is one thing this park does well. There is very little to compare with fresh-caught fish sizzling over a campfire as the cool mantle of dusk is falling. With the northern lights shimmering overhead and a loon's weird, echoing tremolo filling the lake one finds that magic that only the "silent spaces" can offer.

A couple of other fishing spots also offer wilderness camping—this means no amenities except for a vault toilet and a picnic table with pole BBQ. One such is MacDougall Creek, home to one of the few breeding populations of Western Brook Trout in the province. There is no site reservation system here, nor is there a kiosk onsite to pay camping fees. You can either pay the park staff when they drop by or pay at the Lower Fishing Lake office. The campground is the picnic area, and its two sites are naturally leveled and drained. It is well shaded, but with little understory there is minimal privacy between sites. It also has a fish filleting table a hundred meters or so from the picnic grounds, which may be a bit of a problem with wandering bears.

SNOWMOBILING AND CROSS-COUNTRY SKIING

The park is open throughout the year although the park office at Lower Fishing Lake is only open during the core summer months of May to September; the park office in Smeaton is staffed year-round. There are 8 snowmobile trails maintained in the park, varying in length from 4 to 70 km. As they follow the ridges and eskers and use the old cut lines and fire lines they are fairly easy to follow. The park has drawn up a useful map detailing the trails and the positions of lodges where food, fuel, and shelter can be found. Furthermore, the park operates two shelters in the park, one near the Grace Lakes campgrounds and one on the Falling Horse Creek Trail. Although neither has a stove or heater, they do offer shelter from inclement weather; if you wish to use the trails and shelters, you should check in with staff at either Caribou Creek Lodge and Pine Ridge Resort before you leave and upon your return, particularly if you intend to stay out overnight.

There are 3 ungroomed cross-country ski trails behind Lower Fishing Lake, each roughly 6–10 km long. The nearest parking is at Pine Ridge Resort, and you should note that snowmobiling is permitted on the Narrow Hills Trail. The terrain varies widely as you will be skiing up the esker ridge towards Grace Lake while on the Island Lake Trail and cutting through mature jackpine forest in lower, rolling hills.

For more information on any of these activities, contact the park office at the address above.

HIKING

The Gem Lakes area has the only regular hiking trail in the park, and is of interest as the series of small kettle lakes which comprise the Gems each has a slightly different mineral content so the lakes have different colors. The fishing is reported to be good (I've never caught anything there, but what do I know!) and the trail which wanders among the lakes holds a myriad of wonders in its grasp. There are a couple of wilderness-use-only campsites in the park as well as a vault toilet near the parking lot. One firepit and a picnic table are located near the boat launch on Jade Lake, but that's all the amenities you'll find. You won't really need a big boat here, either; the lakes are very small and a canoe is more than sufficient. It will also be a whole lot easier to portage from lake to lake as well! The trail is relatively short, a matter of 7 km or so, depending on the actual route you choose around the lakes, and it is fairly easy hiking although the trail does shrink in width from time to time. The glory of it is camping between Opal and Diamond lakes, or on Diamond Lake's north shore. The firepit beside Jade can also be used for camping although I prefer the north shore site myself. This is wilderness camping, so pack out what you pack in, and be prepared to harvest your own firewood.

The Narrow Hills Provincial Park is a delightful collage of water and sand sprinkled with forests and bogs, set in hills high enough to challenge. There is enough hiking to be done here to sate all but the hardiest, and I should know: for five years I wandered the paths and trails here leading a teens' hiking group for a local summer camp! Having said that, the park has not built many established hiking trials, expecting that you would rather explore the park's hidden secrets on your own.

The terrain is indeed varied as it ranges from black spruce swamp fringing esker ridges, and pines towering above jumbled hills. The predominant soil is sandy, so the forest canopy isn't overgrown except for the areas immediately bordering streams and the numerous bogs. These can be very dense forests, though, comprised of willows and alders beside the streams, and spruce mixed with tamarack in the bogs. Two main streams drain the park, the Falling Horse Creek and the White Gull River, leading into the Torch River which drains into the Saskatchewan River near Tobin Lake. As a result, river crossings will occur. Beaver dams are plentiful, but never seem to be around at the point you need them to cross the river, so you may have to get wet. As always, good maps are a must, and two general topographic maps should be obtained, with a scale of 1:50,000: 73 I/2 (Summit Lake) and 73 H/15 (White Gull Creek). Although not really useful for more than planning your trip, you may want to try 1:250,000–scale maps like 73-I (Wapawekka Hills) and 73-H (Prince Albert). All maps can be ordered from the provincial government; contact them for availability and cost at:

ISC Geospatial Data Products
300 - 10 Research Drive
Regina, SK   S4P 3V7
E-mail: ask@isc.ca
Home: 1-866-275-4721
Fax: (306)787-9220

Just south of the southeast corner of the park off Hwy 106, Hot Springs Lake has a southern marshy end about one-half the size of the lake proper, separated from it by sturdy beaver dam. The lake gets its name from the many mineral upwellings that dot the south shore; to the best of my knowledge, this is the only lake in the park that does have these mineral springs. The upwellings are characterized by iron oxides, and supposedly never freeze over, although I've never authenticated that story. There is a small campsite on the southwest shore that is served by a decent fair-weather trail. There are two trails seen from the Hanson Lake Road (Hwy 106), the left one curves around the north shore to an old logging operation, and the right one goes to an old public campground. The site had a picnic table, a firepit, a very boggy boat launch, and no toilet or garbage facilities. The campsite itself is dark due to the crowded trees, but is quite near the shallow spot used for a boat launch. You must cut your own firewood. Following a game trail that runs to the southeast brings you out to the beaver dam, across from which is a much better campsite. It has no facilities at all, but it is situated on a small promontory that catches the breezes. There are also fewer trees and so more sun. One needn't worry about meeting other campers here, as the fishermen will stay at the public site if they stay at this lake at all. Besides, the park has placed a sturdy berm across the access road to discourage vehicular traffic.

An easy day's hike to the east-northeast, as taken from the northeast corner of the lakeshore, brings you past Stewart Creek to the south end of Odell Lake. An old logging road runs most of the way, but it is wise to have a compass bearing ready to judge if a given branch in the road will take you to your destination. Few were the loggers who ran straight roads! The Stewart Creek crossing deserves some special mention as there is a hilly section just before the creek that was logged over about 30 years ago, and is excellent terrain for growing blueberries. Indeed, some of the finest berry-picking I did in the park was done right here. The road goes down to the creek, but can be very overgrown by willows; indeed, it resembles a marshy game trail right by the creek itself. This willow growth can be so dense that forcing a pack through is quite a chore. The creek was only about a meter deep all the times I crossed it, so your feet will get wet. Use extreme caution when forcing a crossing; as I only had to contend with a meter of water at that time and place, the conditions you see could be very different. As a side note, you'll want to take some precautions like putting matches, maps, and so on in protected places. A few minutes now will save no end of trouble if you get surprised.

In any case, about 50 meters from the creek's east bank a gently sloped clearing is a good place for a dinner break or a campsite. A group I led in 1977 found a decent stand of dewberries along the trail from the creek to the campsite, so getting water became a popular, if somewhat lengthy, chore! The site is open, and has good access to water and firewood.

The hike between this site and Odell Lake is mostly cross-country, although the old bush road weaves a ghostly (and sometimes visible) path among the trees. It is supposed to link up with the old Love Siding Road which runs from Lower Fishing Lake to Love, Saskatchewan. The upper portion of this road in now called the Esker Trail, and runs past Odell Lake. Still, a compass bearing is your best bet, and should bring you out on Odell's western shore. Even though it is a larger lake than many in the park, it still has the perpetual game trail running around it. Follow this trail to the east shore and the Esker Trail. About half-way up the east shore you'll find the campsite. It has a firepit with grate, a picnic table, a toilet, and a swamp whimsically called a boat launch. Do bring your own toilet paper as the CO's may not service this site any more. The Esker Trail, once used to link the loggers to the railroad, is now impassable to anything but an all-terrain vehicle for most of its length. Past the Grace Lakes, deterioration of the sandy hillsides has closed the road to cars, trucks and the like, and the CO's do not recommend anyone travel this road. They also make no effort to maintain it, which I believe to be a wise decision as the expense of repair would be very high, and I like the idea of areas accessible to hikers only.

Only a few kilometers north of Odell is the chain of small lakes known as the Grace Lakes. The Esker Trail joins Lower Fishing Lake to the two campsites here, so one can find mechanized campers here. Those contemplating the drive should be warned, though, the road is hilly and full of surprises. It is narrow, twisting, and has few places to turn around or meet oncoming vehicles safely. Trying to drive a motor home or tow a boat up here would be a difficult task, so caution is advised. I personally would not take anything larger than a half-ton truck up to the Grace Lakes, and nothing but my feet past them. The park provides a winter shelter here as well although it has no heater or stove. The Grace Lakes do offer one of the great panoramas in the park, however. During the day they command an astounding view of the Cub Hills, which you have just spent two days crossing. There are few things more beautiful in the park than watching the sun set over the Cubs, as seen from the overlook at the main campsite. The main, or upper, site has a small parking lot or overlook, several concrete firepits, a toilet, and a small enclosed cabin-style shelter. The number of picnic tables seems to vary; usually two or three can be found. The lower site, about 300 meters south of the main one, is much smaller and darker due to its tall trees. It has its own firepit, picnic table and toilet, and also has a rather steep area used as a boat launch. I would not recommend a boat larger than a canoe be launched in this chain of lakes, as it would be arduous to say the least.

Although a charming campsite in most respects, the Grace Lakes have one glaring drawback: the hill on which the campsites are located. From the upper site, the lakes are at least 60 meters down a steep and slippery hillside. Getting water requires near-heroic exertion and dexterity! Things aren't quite so bad at the lower site: the slope is only about 20 meters and not nearly as steep. Although there are sites across the lake, which have easier access to water, I chose not to use them as I thought the panorama made up for the trouble. A sturdy beaver dam exists across the creek joining the two lower lakes in the chain together. For those hikers coming directly across the Cub Hills from Mitten Lake or ZN Lake, this dam makes crossing the water barrier an infinitely easier process.

About 2 km north of the Grace Lakes is the Rat Lake overlook. This faces east, and shows you the somewhat marshy Rat Lake. It sits in its own swamp and is too mosquito-infested to be a comfortable camping lake. The overlook does show you a good view of the sunrise over the hill ranges to the north and east. Indeed, the second highest elevation lies off to the northeast, the Wapawekka Hills. Second only to the Cypress Hills in Southern Saskatchewan, these used to be inaccessible to any but the hardiest hiker. Now, a logging road runs to within a few hours hike of the summit. I suppose its called progress, but sometimes I wonder.

Meanwhile, back on the Esker Trail, a short hike north from the Rat Lake overlook brings you to tiny Mackay Lake. Stocked yearly with various salmonids, this lake has rapidly gained for itself the reputation of being a decent fishing hole. The enterprising resort owners at Lower Fishing Lake have even lugged a boat down to its shore, which you can rent; getting a motor down to the lake will be a chore, though, and getting it back up the hill even worse! The bank is steep, and the constant pressure of fisherman's feet has eroded the trail rather badly. An excellent campsite exists on the west shore for the weary hiker. Although it has no facilities, it has a certain charm of its own as it is open, spacious, and served by a cutline pushed in during the Fishing Lakes fire of 1977. This is perhaps the one drawback of the Mackay Lake campsite; the last time I was there I saw a small motor home pull in to set up camp. I would check with the park officers before attempting to drive in to this site—cutlines are not designed to be roads, and a travel ban may be in effect if the line has deteriorated.

As you continue hiking on the Esker Trail, you'll see the tall spire of the Fishing Lakes fire control tower. Although the conservation officers welcome visitors, they take an active dislike to anyone making an unauthorized attempt to climb the tower. It can be frightening to the uninitiated, and trying to rescue someone "frozen" on the ladder can be downright dangerous. I'm sure the CO's join me in saying "Stay off the tower!"

Continuing along the trail to Lower Fishing Lake we find the most heavily built up portion of the park. You can find almost any amenity here, including a hot shower, cabins for rent, the park office, and several excellent resorts and outfitters. These operations will provide a wealth of information about the park, and can provide a security service for vehicles left behind while you hike. Should your hike not be a full circle, they can also give you pick-up or drop-off service for a small fee. Any charges for these services are minimal. There is a park campsite here for those wishing to stay, providing the usual amenities including electrical hook-up for the "weekend warriors" and their mechanized invasion. It is for this very reason that I would continue another few kilometers west until I reached Nipawin Lake. It is tiny, has no amenities at all, and is usually deserted. It can be found just off the Lower Fishing Lake road, about 500 meters from its junction with the Candle Lake road. You may want to try your hand at a dawn fishing trip here; although the lake is tiny in size, some amazing fish have been caught here. Be forewarned, though, that the area used for a boat launch is just a marshy wallow.

A good day's hike to the west-northwest is beautiful Baldy Lake. Back in the 1970s the Hanson Lake road used to run around the west end of the lake. Now, the new road has been straightened so that it runs between Baldy and Lower Fishing Lake; you'll have to cross it to get to Baldy. A compass bearing is your best bet to get there, and the junction of the Candle Lake road and the Lower Fishing Lake access is the best aiming point. From time to time, an old game trail or bush road may run in the same direction, but you would be better advised to stick to your compass bearing. Getting to Baldy Lake is an interesting journey, as you must cross a steep series of hills to the northwest of Nipawin Lake. One young lady referred to these as "widow makers," and the name has since stuck. Not only are the hills tall, steep, and covered in slippery lichen, they are covered with a denser-than-average layer of deadfall. Once past the widow makers, though, the way is clear almost to Baldy. Tall trees, open forest floor, and few obstacles make this pleasant journey. The forest fire of 1977 swept through this area, but the system has made a brilliant recovery. Although the old trees are gone, the new growth covers much of the black; the ash and soot has given way to grass and lichen again.

From the southeast, Baldy Lake is a bit marshy but this soon gives way to much better terrain as you travel around the lake to the north shore. You will pass by a 1940s vintage logging camp, with traces of the operation all around. Legend has it that the owner of the mill was as bald as a cue-ball: "Baldy" was his nickname, this was "Baldy's" Lake, and the name has stuck. I don't know if this is true or not, but it's a fine story and I've never heard it disproved, either. Fine, open forest largely unhurt in the fire provides wonderful tenting sites, and the lake is largely deserted. The park has provided fire pits and wood, toilets and picnic tables along the northwest shore of the lake. Although no longer part of the Hanson Lake road, a fine all-weather road still joins the lake to the new road. By the way, the beach used to be better, but it is hardly used now and the shoreline is recovering from its previous heavier usage.

Leaving Baldy Lake, a short trip to the south along the old road leads to the Stickley Lake turnoff. Although I'm sure that there are many fine, primitive camping sites at Stickley, I've never used them. I prefer to camp at the old bridge over the creek feeding the lake. The old bridge has long since fallen down, so wheeled traffic stops here. It is a useful base point for a compass bearing to Lost Echo Lake, about 15 kilometers away. If you prefer, you can follow the old logging road west towards Lost Echo Lake until it takes a sharp north turn, towards Summit Lake. From this point, follow a compass bearing due west. You'll hit either the creek draining Lost Echo into Lower Fishing Lake, or Lost Echo itself. I should mention that a couple of old logger's huts were beside the trail about a kilometer or so before I made that turn into the bush. They were probably destroyed in the 1977 fire, but some remnants should be visible. The compass bearing is a simple one: due west will force you to hit water after a short time. If you hit the creek, follow it north until you come to the lake; if you hit the lake, follow it south until you come to the junction of the lake and creek. You'll find the best sites on either side of the creek at its junction with the bigger lake. I should mention that the trail running from Stickly to Lost Echo has no water along it, so fill all canteens before leaving the old bridge. As with all sun-drenched clearings in the park, a plethora of wild raspberry canes makes travel a slow if tasty trip along the old bush road.

Lost Echo Lake is comprised of two lakes: Little Echo to the south, and Big Echo to the north. The creek joining them is only about 30 meters long. The east bank used to be the site for my old hiking groups, while the west bank held a similar, stationary wilderness skills group. The west site is the better of the two as it is larger and gets more sun. Neither of these has any amenities at all; for the usual ones you have to hike about midway up the western shore where you find the public site. Served by a road from the Piprell Lake highway, this site has fire pits, picnic tables, toilets, and a boat launch. The road coming into the site may no longer be passable as severe rains in the late 1970s washed much of the road into the lake. What remains is an axle-bashing slope devoid of surface gravel. Although I'm sure a vehicle could still make it in, it won't be mine as I'm not sure the vehicle could get back out again!

Continuing north to Summit Lake is relatively easy as there are game trails running almost the entire way there. As always, keep track of your direction with a compass bearing, but you should have little difficulty. About three-quarters of the way up Lost Echo's eastern shore you should find a small pool halfway up a low hill. We called it "Happy-Face Pool" because of its shape, and my teeth still remember its achingly cold waters. The game trail following the creek turns east at Summit Lake, where many fine campsites exist. You can choose one here, or continue around Summit Lake to the northeast corner and camp there. A beaver dam gets you across the creek and the ubiquitous game trail keeps you moving north. I should point out that Summit Lake has a private cabin near the road. Although the lake and its shores are essentially public property, the cabin owner's facilities are most certainly not. If, for instance, you wish to use the outhouse, ask permission (if possible), and use your own paper; common courtesy demands no less.

A large clearing to the southwest of the lake is noteworthy as it offers a grand view of the hill range you've spent the last few days crossing. Climbing the hill from the creek into the clearing (which was logged over in the 1960s), one has a panoramic view of these very hills that prompted one young fellow to dig for his camera for that perfect shot. We had been hiking under a blazing sun after a re-supply following a lay-over, so the packs held an unaccustomed weight. After shooting a couple of frames, he remarked, "I intend to keep these until I have children, then I'm going to line them up and show them this place; if they don't start to cry, I'm going to hit them!" In truth, the crossing isn't all that bad but then I wasn't 13 years old, either! One other unique feature of this clearing is the echo effect. Facing towards the south, one can get a clear triple echo; on a good day, up to 5! It may be for this reason that Lost Echo gets its name, as the hills guard both its shores, but I've never managed to verify that.

To the northeast of Summit Lake lies the string of tiny lakes known as the Gem Lakes. The largest of these, Opal, has a picnic ground with tables, toilets, fire pits, and a decent boat launch. The last time I looked, overnight camping was not allowed at this site, and getting a motor boat into the other lakes would not be easy. As it isn't on park property, you should check with the park office prior to camping here. I used to lead groups to the top of the central hill separating the lakes so that our camp had the entire chain laid out at our feet. Getting water was a difficulty due to the steep hill, but the early morning sunrise with mist rising off the lakes is a rare pleasure. Besides, a small clearing on the hill crest turned out to be a marvelous blueberry pasture; having fresh berries to stir into the mornings pancake batter made the stay most enjoyable. I'll cook berries into my oatmeal and into bannock, but for my money, nothing can beat them in pancakes! As the Fishing Lakes fire spared this area, perhaps that little pasture still remains; I really should go see.

Retracing our steps to the old skills camp on Lost Echo Lake, we are ready for one of the better hiking trails the park has to offer. To the south (and a whisker west) lies Fairy Glen Lake. A compass bearing from the union of Lost and Little Echo Lake to the middle of Fairy Glen will bring you to an old logging road that leads directly past Fairy Glen Lake. This road, very overgrown, runs perpendicular to the bearing you've taken, so turn right upon reaching it. Should you miss the road due to the overgrowth, fear not as the compass bearing will see you safely there; the road offers a bit better hike. Following it for about an hour or so will bring you to a small but sturdy bridge over the creek feeding into the north end of Fairy Glen Lake. This makes a nice luncheon spot as water is close at hand, and the lake you can see just south of you is your destination. The trail continues west until it reaches the Piprell Lake road; turn left here and hike about a kilometer to the small clearing used as a camping spot. The Piprell Lake road will be your hiking highway for the next few days as it connects with both the Candle Lake road and the Hanson Lake road. The Fairy Glen campsite sits just beside this road, and offers little for the pampered camper. No facilities had been built into the site when I was last there in the mid–1970s, and I doubt that much has been done since. The Piprell Lake road wasn't much better than a quagmire at this spot, then, so be very aware that vehicular traffic may not reach into this area, when planning pick-ups or resupply. Mind you, that lack of traffic does make this a better-than-average hiking trail. You should note that many small trails and old logging operations used this road in its heyday, so keep a compass bearing handy should the trail decide to desert you! Continuing south for about 10 kilometers you will find yourself hiking parallel to the Candle Lake road, about 50 to 100 meters from it. So deceptive is the trail that you may not notice that the other road exists! You will cross a small bridge over an unnamed creek that, for identification purposes, my group named for itself. WOTS Creek has a good campsite, but there are no facilities. The site has been used so often by various groups from Saint John Bosco Camp that the firewood supply is drained, as is the so-called WOTS Lake site about 2 kilometers south of the creek site. For this reason, I would continue south along the road for another 8 kilometers or so to a less frequented site. The Piprell Lake road will cross the White Gull Creek, and a lovely campsite awaits the foot-sore hiker. An old trapper's cabin makes a picturesque backdrop, and decent water access and firewood supply make this an excellent stop. An access road connects this site to the Candle Lake road.

The bridge crossing the Candle Lake road over White Gull Creek is a good aiming point to send you northeast towards Ispuchaw Lake, also known as Calder Lake. If you prefer, hike north along the Candle Lake road until a lake becomes visible on the right; that's Ispuchaw, and it should be about 12 kilometers from the White Gull bridge. Following the game trail around the north end of the lake to the eastern shore brings you to a fine campsite with all the amenities, including leveled sites. A regular garbage pick-up lets you dump your unwanted bits, as do the toilets! There is a boat launch along the southeastern shore, but the road leading to it can be a bit dicey for larger vehicles. Past the boat launch is the private domain of Saint John Bosco Camp, which operates several tenting sites on a small promontory for their campers. The bulk of their operation is located at ZN Lake, 2 kilometers to the south on a fine, packed-sand trail.

ZN Lake, supposedly named for the call letters of a plane that went down in the area, has a lovely campsite on the southern shore complete with all the amenities usually offered by the COs. Unusual among northern lakes, this site offers a fine swimming beach, although no lifeguards or safety equipment is available. Most of the hiking I did in the park both originated and terminated at this beautiful lake, partly because of its central location, but also because I worked at the summer camp for 5 years!

From this lake you can either hike northeast to Upper Fishing Lake or south to Hot

Springs Lake. The entire trip used to take 7 or 8 days and covered 80 km or so. With a lot of wildlife to see and many splendid panoramas this hike was a real pleasure; the varied terrain made it a real challenge as well. If you wish to hike the backcountry in this park, please contact the park office well in advance with your planned itinerary, and definitely check in with them when you depart. Backcountry use may be limited or banned outright, if forest fire conditions warrant, so contacting the park prior to departure is not optional—it's for your own good. If they don't know you're there, they may send in fire suppression crews to put out your campfire and I doubt they'd be too happy with you!

SERVICES

With the exception of the restaurants and stores at Caribou Creek and Lower Fishing Lake, there is little to part you with your travel dollars. Major shopping and some mechanical service can be found in Smeaton, approximately 45 minutes drive south of the park, while the city of Prince Albert has all the shopping, medical, mechanical and worship services one could need. Besides all the natural delights the park offers, there is an interpretive program offered during the summer months, programming for which might include lessons on wilderness skills; check with the park office for details on dates and times. For information on this or any facet of this beautiful, natural park, contact the park office at:

Narrow Hills Provincial Park
P.O. Box 130
Smeaton, SK S0J 2J0
Telephone: (306) 426-2622, or toll-free 1-800-205-7070 (in Saskatchewan only)
E-mail: kkovar@serm.gov.sk.ca
Website: www.saskparks.netparkinfo

HOLY TRINITY ANGLICAN CHURCH PROVINCIAL HISTORIC SITE

Located within Lac La Ronge Provincial Park, the Holy Trinity Anglican Church (shown here, courtesy Sask Tourism) is important as the oldest building in what is now the province of Saskatchewan. Construction began in 1854 and was completed in 1860, complete with stained glass windows. It was once the focal point for the Anglican Church Missionary Society, a large organization that occupied a parcel of land across the Churchill River from the community of Stanley Mission. The wooden church and its ornate stained glass windows are all that remains of that organization although the church still functions as the focus of a faith community to this day. The cemetery is well kept and forms a record of the lives lived in this beautiful place. Accessible only by boat from the village of Stanley Mission, there are no amenities other than the Northern Store in the village, and the outfitters who service the anglers and hunters who travel here. Still, one cannot look at this gleaming white structure without a sense of wonder at the struggle to build it so long ago in such a distant place, and marvel at the spirit of a community that keeps it so beautiful for all to see. For more information on this historical building and the community it serves, contact the Lac La Ronge Provincial Park administration office at:

Lac La Ronge Provincial Park
P.O. Box 5000
La Ronge, SK   S0J 1L0
Telephone: (306) 425-4234
E-mail by linking from the website at: www.saskparks.net

You can also check out the Hamlet of Stanley Mission's fascinating website at: www.geocities.com/stanleymission00/

STEELE NARROWS PROVINCIAL HISTORIC PARK

This historic park, located at the narrows below Makwa Lake, approximately 25 km west of the village of Loon Lake on Hwy 699, commemorates the last battle in what is now known as the North West Rebellion. It seems peaceful enough now but on the still morning of June 2, 1885, this pastoral scene was rent with the sharp rattle of musketry and the shrill cries of the wounded. A company of mounted scouts, 75 strong, were sent in advance of the main body of General Strange's Alberta Field Force to locate Big Bear's Cree warriors, a force reckoned to be 300 strong, plus all their families and baggage train. The Crees also had a band of white captives taken from the massacre at Frog Lake and from the siege of Fort Pitt, some 27 people in all. Major Steele had brought his force up to the bottom of a wooded hill at daybreak, and could see the last of Big Bear's teepees still standing; the rest of the Crees were already crossing the narrows separating Makwa Lake (also known as Loon Lake) from smaller Tulibee Lake. Advancing in a skirmish line the scouts opened fire on the escaping rebels when Little Poplar, a Cree war chief, ran back to rally his warriors and take up the fight. Three Cree were killed and a handful wounded as well as 2 scouts and a North-West Mounted Police officer during the three-hour gun battle that followed. Eye witness accounts say that neither side would withdraw until the last cartridge was fired. The scouts, traveling light, didn't have unlimited ammunition supplies, and the Cree were fighting a rear-guard action to allow their families to escape. Nonetheless, brave men on both sides took the fight literally into the teeth of their foe, with one Cree warrior being shot only 10 feet from the scouts' skirmish line. With ammunition running low and the Crees withdrawing across the ford in good order after the non-combatants had crossed there was little left for Major Steele to do. Gathering his wounded, he withdrew towards Fort Pitt to await reinforcements.

His primary mission, finding Big Bear's Cree, was a success; his secondary mission of freeing the white prisoners was apparently a failure. What he could not know is that the rebels, now believing that the army would pursue them relentlessly, decided to split up with the Chipewyans heading west, the Wood Cree moving north with the prisoners, and Big Bear's Cree heading east. The Wood Cree thought the prisoners would be better off with them than with the more hot-blooded Plains Cree, so they began what must be considered an incredible march, walking across country all the way to Lac des Iles, in what is now Meadow Lake Provincial Park, before the prisoners could beg their release and walk back. Finally, exhausted, they stumbled back to Loon Lake where Middleton's men met them, ending their plight. In retrospect, they probably would have been released earlier had not one of their better friends, Cut Arm, a chief of the Wood Cree, been killed in the battle at what is now known as Steele Narrows. Furthermore, Wandering Spirit, a Plains Cree war chief and one of the instigators of the Frog Lake massacre, where 9 civilians were murdered, had forsaken Big Bear's band as he feared retribution for leading them into trouble; it is probable that he did not wish to relinquish the prisoners so easily and cowed the partially leaderless Wood Cree.

Today the battle and the brave men who fought here on both sides of the conflict are commemorated with a placard and interpretive signs on top of the very hill where they fought. There is a boat launch allowing access to Makwa Lake as well as a fish-cleaning station and trash bins. There is a parking lot and vault toilets but no potable water or overnight camping. The day-use area has two picnic tables and pole BBQs but no firewood supply. There are tall trees for shade, except on the top of the hill which is reached via 124 steps up a steep staircase. From here you have a panoramic view of the battleground, with interpretive signs to describe the action. For more information on this historic site, contact the park office at:

Steele Narrows Provincial Historic Park
P.O. Box 39
Loon Lake, SK S0M 1L0
Telephone: (306) 837-2410
Fax: (306) 837-2415

Or link to their email from the SERM website at: www.saskparks.net

PRINCE ALBERT NATIONAL PARK

Located approximately 90 km north of the city of Prince Albert on Hwy 2, there are two main entrances to the park. The old route (now referred to as the scenic route) winds through the aspen parkland forest to the South Gate on Hwy 263. You'll pass through the resort villages of Christopher Lake and Emma Lake on your trip north, and see some very pretty forest from your vehicle. The pavement is somewhat narrow and winding, though, so you may prefer the new route, turning left on Hwy 264 to the East Gate. You'll pass by a couple of private resorts (discussed elsewhere) and drive straight through to Waskesiu townsite. The park sits astride the transition zone between the aspen forest of the south and the boreal forest of the north so there is plenty of rich habitat to host a wide variety of plants and animals. It is one of the most southerly places in Canada where you can find permafrost, and is home to one of the few breeding colonies of white pelicans in the province. There are many hiking and biking trails, and there are a couple of very good canoe routes, particularly for novice to intermediate canoe trippers. Certainly not the least of the features of this park is Grey Owl, the erstwhile Englishman, Archie Belaney. You can hike or boat to his cabin at Ajawaan Lake. Campsites vary from primitive backcountry sites, well off the beaten path, to 4-star accommodation in Waskesiu townsite itself. In this park you can literally do it all: one night you can dine on fresh-caught pike with the Milky Way as your canopy, and thrill to the weird echoing tremolo of the loons as the northern lights dance; the next night you can dine on gourmet meals off fine china after a game of golf on one of the oldest and best-known courses in the province. The park is open year-round although the peak season is from mid-May until the end of September. A daily park entry fee is charged of $17.50 per vehicle (family or group) per day. Individuals are charged $7 per adult, $3.50 per youth; school groups have a cheaper rate (prices as of Spring 2006).

SITES

For your peace of mind, Prince Albert National Park is among the 18 national parks offering a campground reservation service. Campsites in Beaver Glen and the Trailer Park campgrounds can be reserved in advance by calling 1-877-737-3783 (1-877-RESERVE) or by emailing them at pccamping@pc.gc.ca; the park keeps some sites for the adventurous souls who don't feel the need to plan for accommodation. All backcountry camping, even at one of the wilderness campgrounds, is available on a strictly first-come, first-served basis—register and obtain a backcountry permit at the Information Center or for specific locations at the park entry gates. Backcountry camping fees will apply at locations where facilities and services are provided. As a side note, this is bear country: obtain a copy of "You Are In Black Bear Country" and follow the suggestions to minimize potential conflicts.

There are many places to camp in this diverse park, so I'll start with the southernmost and drive north along Hwy 263, as if you took the scenic drive into the park; why not—it's my favorite route!

There are 31 unserviced sites in the Sandy Lake campground of which 6 are tenting sites only; you walk up the hill to set your tent and have a great view of the lake! You'll see the campground to the left of the beach as you drive in from Hwy 263. There is a self-registry kiosk at the entrance, and one camping loop extending west along the bottom of the lake. All sites have wooden picnic tables and pole BBQs, with central bear-proof trash bins. Firewood is supplied in two main piles, one near the kiosk and another near the small parking lot for the walk-in tenting sites. Toilets are vault-style, several sets of which are scattered throughout the campgrounds. The sites can be close together with poor privacy or relatively spread out; the lower the number the closer the sites are together. Sites #8–18 are located on a small side spur, of which site #13 (right at the end of the turning loop) is perhaps the most private. The lake has an excellent beach with a wide lawn for picnickers, but no playground equipment. There is a good-sized parking lot serving this area, as well as a scattering of picnic tables and one camp kitchen. The beach is good for swimming with a buoyed but unsupervised swimming area. A boat launch offers anglers a chance at the pike in this lake, and the fish-cleaning station beside the trailer parking lot is proof that fish can be caught here; motor boats are allowed on this lake. A trailer dump station is located a few kilometers south of the campground on Hwy 263, near the park entry gate. In general, it's a pleasant, pretty lake with a small campground and good beach and day-use area.

Continuing north a few kilometers you'll see the access for Trappers Lake and its 10 unserviced sites, operated from a self-registry kiosk. Of these sites, 5 are available for individual rent; the others are in a gated group area which is available by reservation only. The gravel road in is narrow and winding so go slow; we saw a blue heron feeding in the small stream you'll cross a few hundred meters from the campground. All the sites here are built into mature jackpine forest so there is little ground cover but good shade. The sites are naturally leveled and drained, and have wooden picnic tables with pole BBQs. There are central vault toilets and bear-proof trash bins, one well-pump, two wood piles, a camp kitchen and a fish-cleaning table beside it. The lake is restricted to non-motorized boating only. It's a very small, clean campground, certainly private for small groups but there is no playground equipment.

A few kilometers north of Trappers Lake is the gravel access to one of my favorite camping spots, Namekus Lake. There are 21 sites here, of which 6 are for walk-in tenting only; a self-registry kiosk is located at the campground entrance. All sites are built in mature spruce and pines on gravel pads, with wooden picnic tables and pole BBQs. Some of the sites have great privacy from willows and alders; others are more open underneath the evergreens. There is a firewood supply and a well with pump; boil the water prior to use. All toilets are vault style, and there is no trailer dump station; use the one south of Sandy Lake or in Waskesiu at Beaver Glen Campground. There is a good beach which has a campfire ring nearby, perfect for latenight story-telling. There is no supervision for the beach, nor is there a buoyed swimming area. There is a beach parking lot but no boat launch as this is a non-motorized boating lake; a canoe is more than sufficient. As a side note, our family had excellent success fishing from our canoe a short distance off shore; the lads still remember it well! There is one camp kitchen but no playground equipment. This is a quiet campground, very clean and friendly, with good lake access and nearby hiking trails—it's my family's usual haunt when we're in the area!

As you drive the 10 km or so north from the Namekus turn toward Waskesiu, you'll cross the gravel Narrows Road leading 25 km or so around the south side of Waskesiu Lake toward the First Narrows; there are 3 excellent beaches and picnic spots along this road. Although there is no boat launch here, many people launch from the main Waskesiu marina or the Narrows marina, both privately operated, and then boat over to these out-of-the-way picnic areas. Here you can meet the rest of the family and set up for a day of fishing or tow sports, beaching your boat offshore and wading in or grounding it right on the sandy beach itself. There are vault toilets, bear-proof trash bins, a dining shelter or two (depending on which particular picnic area you choose), wooden picnic tables and pole BBQs, and a firewood supply. The 3 day-use areas are (from south to north as you drive along Narrows Road) South Bay, Trippes Beach, and Paignton Beach.

Once you've arrived at The Narrows you'll see the privately operated marina and store. Here you can make limited grocery and camping supply purchases as well as fishing license, tackle and watercraft rentals. This is a private marina, so there will be a fee levied for launching and retrieving your boat; the fee includes trailer parking. Note that if you'll be canoeing, there is no fee for launching across the beach; it's unsupervised and there is a buoyed swimming area. There is a fish-cleaning station beside the marina parking lot; motor boats are allowed on the lake and can be rented from the marina. The Narrows campground is a short distance away and has 87 unserviced sites operating from a self-registry kiosk. The sites are all built on gravel pads in a mature spruce and pine forest so you'll have excellent shade. All sites have wooden picnic tables and pole BBQs, and share access to water taps, bear-proof trash bins, and a firewood pile. Interestingly, the washrooms are solar-powered, supplying cold running water and flush toilets. There is a trailer dump station just beside the campground entrance. This campground, perhaps because of its distance from the resort village of Waskesiu, also has a large day-use area with picnic tables and a playground with swings. The beach, although small, is quite serviceable and has a large lawn area in behind for sun worshippers to enjoy a balmy summer's day. There is a campground host in attendance—check with the billboard in the registration area for dates and locations.

Instead of turning west off Hwy 263 at the Narrows road junction, continue north into the resort village of Waskesiu where you will find the two largest campgrounds in the park, starting with Beaver Glen Campground located on the northern edge of Waskesiu townsite. You can access it either from Waskesiu Drive to Ajawaan Street or (if you're coming from the east gate on Hwy 264) by turning west off Hwy 264 onto Ajawaan. Either way the park is well signed so you can't go too far wrong. The campground has an entry gate from where the helpful staff will rent you one of the 213 sites, of which 108 have electrical service; there are no full-service sites in this campground. The campground is arranged in 18 small loops accessed from a ring road which forms the perimeter of the campground itself. All sites are back-in style and built in a mature forest with excellent shade and ground cover. They feature wooden picnic tables, pole BBQs and gravel pads, and share access to centralized potable water taps, bear-proof trash bins and firewood. There are 5 service centers, one wheelchair-accessible, all with flush toilets and hot showers built in central areas to serve 3 or 4 camping loops each. There is a large, barrier-free open-air auditorium on the northern edge of the campgrounds from which the park interpretive staff offer free programming, most of which is not only entertaining but highly educational; check at the notice boards at the entry booth and the service centers for up-to-date schedules. Although you can comfortably walk from your campsite to the amphitheater, there is a parking lot available although it tends to fill quickly. A trailer dump station is located beside the perimeter road past the outdoor theater parking lot.

Located across Ajawaan Street from Beaver Glen Campground, there are 152 full-service sites available at the trailer park, renting from a gate entry booth. Although some of the sites are reasonably protected under pines and spruce (blocks G and H), most of the pull-through sites are built "herring-bone" style—from one end of the access road you can see pretty much the entire campground. Mind you, the license plates show that people from all over North America come here to enjoy their vacations. All sites have electrical, water, and sewer hookup and picnic tables. Roadways are paved in this campground, and all sites are wheelchair-friendly as they are well leveled with lawn in between. Trash bins are centrally located, as are the two wheelchair-accessible service centers with flush toilets and hot showers; there is one set of flush toilets serving blocks G and H. As this park is pretty much centrally located in Waskesiu townsite, there are walking paths leading from here to the main beach and day-use area as well as to the businesses of the downtown shopping core.

OTHER CAMPING

There are other smaller wilderness campgrounds scattered throughout the backcountry, all of which require a backcountry permit to use. As mentioned above, such permits are given on a first-come, first-served basis and sites cannot be reserved in advance. You must register at the information center on the day you are heading into the backcountry. If your favorite campsite is already full, park staff will help you with alternate plans. I personally have never had a problem getting the sites I wanted, but I have heard stories to the contrary. Mind you, talk to the park staff about your needs; you'll be pleasantly surprised at how flexible some things can be. Having said this there are innumerable backcountry campgrounds, both individual and group sites available for the discerning camper. Take a look at the map and you'll see them scattered over hiking trails and canoe routes throughout the park. What is it you want to see and do? Chances are there is a special place just waiting for you. These sites all have privy toilets, firewood supplies, bear caches, tent pads and fire pits; backcountry fees apply at these sites. In areas where designated sites are not provided, random camping without any facilities, services, or fees is also an option. You'll be looking for that hot shower when you get back!

HIKING

It is possible to hike for over 230 km one way in this park's extensive trail system as you access over a million acres of protected wilderness. The Waskesiu River Trail is barrier-free and most are well marked and maintained although some require more expert knowledge and understanding. Many of them become cross-country ski trails in winter for year-round backcountry access. Some of the more popular trails are self-guided and have brochures to assist you in understanding the features around you; park interpretive staff often lead guided excursions for interested folks—check with the entry gate staff or on bulletin boards for current interpretive scheduling. Many of the shorter, steep routes have staircases built in to assist you in climbing up or down some very steep hills. There's always the chance of spotting some of the local wildlife, if you're quiet, and you will see some truly pretty country. The park has a brochure and generalized map they will send you: the *Prince Albert National Park Official Visitor Guide*. Although useful to keep things in perspective, I wouldn't use it as a backcountry map; obtain a copy of the Prince Albert National Park map instead. Also known as "topographical map MCR 210," it has a scale of 1:125,000 and contour intervals of 50 meters. Also of great use is the PA National Park Trail Guide, available from the Friends of the Park Gift Shop, located on Waskesiu Drive. Please note that some trails are shared by hikers, bikers, and horses, but not all; this is where that trail guide comes in handy!

With these two resources in hand, a pair of comfortable hiking boots and your binoculars, you are indeed ready for the woods! Or, as my boys put it, "No better way to see the world than with two feet and a heart beat!" As the park has lots of information available (and you really should support the Friends of the Park by buying their trail guide), I won't go into detail here. The park gate staff will have all the information you require, so check with them regarding the latest trail conditions. The brochure and simple map published by the park organizes the trails based on which road they start from, so I will follow that here, beginning with (you guessed it) the south gate.

Trails accessed from Cookson Road:

Hunter's Lake Trail—16 km west of the south gate, 12 km one way; an overnight backcountry trail with moderate to strenuous hiking over fairly steep terrain, mostly in jack pine forest. There is a campsite at the end of the trail, just south of the junction with the Elk Trail, with fire pit and pit toilet; backcountry permit required.

Fish Lake Trail—11 km west of the south gate, 12 km one way; an overnight backcountry trail through rolling hills covered in aspen forest. There is a campsite at the end of the trail, just north of junction with the Elk Trail, with tent pads, bear cache, hitching rail, fire pits and vault toilets; backcountry permits required.

Trails accessed from Hwy 263:

Elk Trail—7 km north of South Gate, 39 km one way, an overnight (or possibly multiple nights) backcountry trail with moderate to strenuous hiking over fairly steep terrain, mostly aspen forest with some native fescue. There are some camping areas along the trail, with tent pads, bear cache, corral or hitching post fire pits and privies; backcountry permits are required.

Kinowa Trail—approximately 10 km north of south gate, parking at trail head, 5 km (1.5 hr) one way, moderate hiking in aspens and grasslands; terminus at Anglin Lake.

Anglin Lake Trail—11 km north of the south gate, 12 km one way, hiking through aspen and poplar forest.

Spruce River Highlands Trail—16 km north of South Gate, parking at trail head, 8.5

km (3 hr) loop; 1.5-km self-guided interpretive trail to lookout tower. This is a strenuous hike over steep hills.

Freight Trail—terminus either Narrows Road or just past Spruce Meadows Trail, on west side of Hwy 263. There is parking at either trail head or from 3 points along Hwy 263, 27 km (8 hr) one way, easy terrain. Plenty of wildlife and the trail's history make this an interesting hike.

Shady Lake/Height of Land Trail—This is short, a 1.7-km Shady Lake loop + 1.5 km Height of Land spur (2 hr total), but very strenuous—360 steps to ascend/descend! Westerly view from the Height of Land observation tower is nothing short of spectacular; parking at trail head.

Kingfisher Trail—2 trailheads, either from the Nature Center in the townsite or 2 km from Waskesiu; moderate 17- or 13-km loop, staircase in steep terrain, parking at trail heads.

Trails accessed from Narrows Road:

Amiskowan Trail—trail head 2.3 km west of the Hwy 263 junction. An easy 1-km (30 min) loop, this can be used as a self-guiding classroom as the numbered posts correspond to a teacher's guide. This is also the northern terminus for Freight Trail.

Ice Push Ridge—11 km down Narrows Road, 150m one way with an interpretive panel at the lakeshore.

Mud Creek Trail—trail head on the east edge of the South Bay day-use area parking lot. A short and easy hike, 2 km (1.5 hr) long; a self-guiding brochure is in a box at the trail head—please return it when you are done.

Treebeard Trail—trail head just south of the Narrows Campground on the Narrows Road. A short hike through moderate terrain, 1.2 km (1 hr), this trial can be slippery when wet. It is a self-guiding trail; return the brochure to the trail head box when you're done.

Trails accessed from Kingsmere Road/Hwy 264:

Boundary Bog—It is located just inside eastern boundary of the park on Hwy 264. A 2-km (1.5 hr) loop, over easy terrain with some stairs and a boardwalk onto the marsh. Parking at trail head as is the box with self-guiding brochures.

Red Deer Trail—the newest member of the trail system, this forms a complete loop around Waskesiu townsite and takes in a total of 17 km (8 hr) over three main spur trails. You can get on from the walking path between the beach and the parking lot and basically stay on it for the entire distance.

Waskesiu River Trail—Located about 6 km north of Waskesiu townsite on Kingsmere Road (the continuation of Hwy 264), it is an easy 2.5 km (1.5 hr) long, with the first 500 meters wheelchair accessible. Trail head is in a day-use area with wheelchair-accessible vault toilets, picnic tables and ample parking.

Narrows Peninsula Trail—Located 22 km north of Waskesiu townsite; the trail head is in the parking lot on the south side of the road. A moderate 3-km (2 hr) loop with some stairs, there is a small unsupervised swim beach at the turnaround point. Many ostrich ferns add an almost tropical quality to one part of the hike.

Kingsmere River Trail—Trail head in the day-use area parking lot, 32.5 km north of Waskesiu. Hike is an easy 1.5 km (1 hr) one-way along the river bank. The terminus is at the Southend campground on Kingsmere Lake; overnight camping is allowed by permit only. The day-use area has picnic tables, pole BBQs, firewood, privies, and a simple boat launch (small boats only).

Grey Owl Trail—Trail head is in the same parking lot as the Kingsmere River Trail; the two trails share a path for the first three hundred meters or so. The right-hand fork leads around the east side of Kingsmere Lake for a moderate 20 km (6–7 hrs) to the fork for Ajawaan Lake, upon which Grey Owl's cabin still sits. There are 5 campgrounds along the way, two of which can be reserved for groups; all the sites require backcountry permits, available from the park visitor's center in Waskesiu.

BOATING/CANOEING

With all this water, boating is extremely popular in the park, from power, paddle and sail boats to little canoes gently edging through the farthest reaches of the park. There are three marinas and boat launches on Waskesiu Lake: one at the Narrows Campground, one on the main body of Waskesiu Lake, and the other at the Hanging Heart Lakes. All three are operated by the same company so you can expect user fees to launch and retrieve your boat. They also have watercraft rentals, guided interpretive tours, and the Voyageur Canoe Adventure. They can be contacted directly for prices and reservations by telephone at (306) 663-1999 (summer) or (306) 763-1278 (winter); website is www.waskesiumarina.com and email is info@waskesiumarina.com.

Angling is also very popular, but provincial fishing licenses are not valid in the park; you must purchase a park fishing permit and adhere to the national park regulations. You'll find fish-cleaning stations near all the marinas; please clean your catch at these stations and not in your campsite as you may find a bear following the scent into the local trash. Even though these trash bins are bear-proof, you still don't want a close encounter of the ursine kind!

My personal favorite way to see the park is from a canoe, and there are several very good canoe routes established for backcountry use. Please note that both Kingsmere Lake and Crean Lake, where the best backcountry canoeing is available, can be dangerous in bad weather as they are both large enough to get serious waves building in windy conditions; it is very easy to swamp your canoe in such conditions so if you see thunderheads building, particularly to the northwest, head to shore! The park has published a visitor's guide which gives you some ideas on these routes as well as the best places to camp when stretching the paddle into a long weekend of camping. Please note that all backcountry camping areas require a permit, obtainable from the Information Center in Waskesiu townsite. Suggested canoe routes include:

Kingsmere Lake Access:

Bladebone Lake—You'll have to first cross Kingsmere Lake then turn west into the Bladebone River and follow it through the marshes and small lakes of the northwest corner of this area. There is some backcountry camping for which a permit is required and the trip is relatively easy although you will have to make a few short portages. You will certainly be alone though!

Lily Lake/Bagwa Lake—You can either portage from Kingsmere Lake into Clare Lake (there is a large red sign denoting the start of the portage) or you can canoe up to Pease Point and turn west into Bagwa Lake. There is camping at Southend Kingsmere Lake, Pease Point, and Lily Lake, all of which require a backcountry permit.

Grey Owl's Cabin—You must cross Kingsmere Lake to get to Ajawaan Creek, from which you will hike the last 3 km into little Ajawaan Lake to visit the recreation of Grey Owl's cabin. There is a dock and overnight camping nearby, for which you must have a backcountry permit.

Waskesiu Lake Access:

First Narrows/Kingsmere River—Launch your canoes across the public beach; there's a fee for using the boat launch and docks, then paddle past second narrows to the picnic area at the mouth of the Kingsmere River. You can access Kingsmere River by portaging over the berm, paddling upstream and use the rail portage to get you into Kingsmere Lake at the Southend Campground. If you wish to spend the night here you must obtain a backcountry permit.

King Island—Put in from Trippes Beach picnic area and paddle to the big island you see directly in front of you. There is a picnic area on the island and a hiking trail running around the island but no overnight camping is allowed.

Amiskowan Lake—Put in where the Narrows Road crosses Mud Creek; use the hiking trail parking lot. It's a circular route but the lake is hidden from road traffic for most of its circumference so it will feel like you're alone in the world; there is no overnight camping.

Red Wing Bay—Although the trip is a short paddle you'll still have to portage your canoe about 100 meters down the hill from the Kingfisher Trail pull-off south of Prospect Point on Hwy 263. Paddle south along the shore for about a kilometer until you see a foot bridge; portage your canoe over this bridge into the little marsh where you can drift and bird watch at your pleasure.

Waskesiu River—Put in at the marina, paddling east along the shore of Waskesiu Lake to access the river, then paddle downstream for about an hour or so. Don't be afraid to test the waters for hungry pike, and keep an eye out as this gentle stream often plays host to animals such as deer or moose, and many birds like eagles and ospreys, to name a few.

Crean Lake Access:

Hanging Hearts Lakes/Crean Lake—A short chain of three small lakes leads into much larger Crean Lake. You can put in at the Hanging Hearts Marina and paddle up to the campground, Crean Kitchen, to the left of Crean Lake as you round the western point. This and the three other campgrounds around Crean Lake require a backcountry permit for overnight use.

GOLFING

No discussion of this park would be complete without mentioning the famous Waskesiu Golf Club, home to the Lobstick tournaments. Built in the 1930s and designed by Stanley Thompson, the course is short (only 6300 yards from the championship tees) but precision is everything; a wandering shot puts you in real trouble on pretty well every hole. I know—I've been there! Players must take care as they are sharing the course with a herd of elk as well as a legendary fox that steals golf balls on one of the fairways! The fully licensed clubhouse features breakfast, lunch and supper in a beautiful building which has earned recognition as a heritage site. There is a pro-shop with club and cart rentals, lessons, and shopping for golfing equipment as well as branded clothing. With all of this, the course is still quite modest to play—only $36 for 18 holes and a large bucket of balls for the driving range is $7! For more information or to book your tee time (an absolute necessity), contact the course directly at (306) 663-5300 (in season). You can check out their fine website at www.waskesiugolf.com/, or snail mail at:

Waskesiu Golf Course
PO Box 234
Waskesiu Lake, SK   S0J 2Y0

Although Elk Ridge Resort and Golf Course are not actually in the park, it wouldn't be fair to not mention it as this is another truly beautiful golf course; you simply have to include it in your travel plans in this area. There are 27 holes, a full-featured pro-shop and licensed dining room and lounge. The resort, a 5-minute drive from Prince Albert National Park, has accommodation from cabins to condos. Contact them directly at:

Elk Ridge Resort
PO Box 130
Waskesiu Lake, SK   S0J 2Y0
Telephone: (306) 663-4653, Toll-free: 1-800-510-1824
Fax: (306) 663-5800
Website at www.elkridgeresort.com/
E-mail is info@elkridgeresort.com.

WASKESIU TOWNSITE AND SERVICES

One simply has to devote some time to a discussion of this remarkable place, likened to the "Banff of the Prairies." Sitting at one of the street-side cafes one can see the luxury cars heading up to the golf course and private cottages as well as the battered vans of the backpackers gearing up to head off to the backcountry! Here you'll find the Information Center, from which your questions will be answered and back-country permits issued. There is a Park Nature Center which has displays of animals and natural history as well as interpretive games for the younger crowd. There is a first-aid station at the Information Center whose well-trained staff can manage most minor injuries although for medical advice and treatment you'll have to go to Prince Albert, approximately an hour's drive south on Hwy 2. There is shopping galore, from souvenir-style trinkets to equipment for a back-country expedition. Grocery shops keep the back-country traveler in mind, so you can find dehydrated and other "backpack friendly" food as well as a full range of fresh, frozen and canned goods, and there is a post office to send postcards and letters back home. You'll also find many dining establishments, from fast food outlets to specialty ice cream shops, as well as fine dining at one of the several excellent hotels. Speaking of accommodation, there is everything from small, light house-keeping cabins to 4-star hotels. There is a cinema and a liquor store, and the RCMP office. Parking can be at a premium on the street, so many folks park a bit north of the shopping core at one of the beach parking lots and walk in. The beach itself is huge, and certainly the reason that this lake was used for recreation for so long. Extending from the breakwater in the south approximately a kilometer or so north to the end of the bay, the beach has deep, fine sand, groomed and cleaned regularly, behind which is a paved walking trail (part of the Red Deer Trail system, discussed elsewhere) and the huge expanse of lawn and trees which make up the day-use or picnic area. You'll find a large changeroom close to the downtown end of the beach, complete with hot showers for the weary backcountry enthusiast. (Lord knows how much I looked forward to lingering under the steady stream after canoeing 4 days around Kingsmere Lake!) As with other service centers in the park, these showers are free; you've paid to use them with your entry fees. The Waskesiu Community Association has an excellent website with contact information for all the shops and services in the town site. Contact them directly for more information at: www.waskesiu.org/, or by telephone at (306) 663-4522 to have a free copy of the Parks Canada Visitors Guide mailed to you.

One thing I haven't mentioned is the attention paid by the park to the First Nations presence this part of the world has enjoyed for centuries; it still holds a special cultural and spiritual place for local First Nations people. To this end, the park has partnered with local Aboriginal communities in creating the Paspiwin Cultural Heritage Site in the southeast corner of the park, on a site once occupied by the now-decommissioned bison paddock. The *Paspiwin* (Cree word meaning "survival") site hosts larger traditional cultural events in the park, such as powwows, cultural demonstrations, and an Aboriginal cultural youth camp. This partnership is celebrated yearly with events such as the National Aboriginal Day, Canada Day, the Aboriginal Artist's Fair, and the Children's Festival; plan on becoming part of this learning experience. Contact the park office for details on times and locations.

As you can see from this description, this is one very busy park: hiking and biking, boating and canoeing, fishing, bird watching, golfing, cross-country skiing and winter camping, animal watching, and interpretive programs to educate you on all of these aspects of the park (and more)—truly a recreational opportunity for every possible outdoors enthusiast. Waskesiu townsite has excellent shopping, accommodation and recreational opportunities. Summer is the peak season in the park, with all its many amenities open; winter takes on a slower pace but still offers excellent accommodation, dining, and recreational opportunities. For more complete information contact the chamber of commerce at:

Waskesiu Chamber of Commerce
P.O. Box 216
Waskesiu Lake, SK   S0J 2Y0
Telephone: (306) 663-5410
Fax: (306) 663-5448
E-mail: waskesiuchamber@sasktel.net
Website: www.waskesiulake.ca/

As mentioned above, campsites in Beaver Glen and the Trailer Park campgrounds can be reserved for your vacation: call 1-833-RESERVE. On a personal note, I have found that the smell of the pines and the soft sounds of the forest let my soul drink deep from a refreshing pool; I can see why Archie Belaney thought this place to be so special. For more information, contact the park office at:

Prince Albert National Park
PO Box 100
Waskesiu Lake, SK   S0J 2Y0
Telephone: (306) 663-4522
Fax: (306) 663-5424
E-mail: panp.info@pc.gc.ca

Website is: www.pc.gc.ca/pn-np/sk/princealbert/index_e.asp

Recommendations for Selected Stays

These lists are not intended to label any park as better than another, but rather to provide the reader with our view of what made these parks special and different from each other. For this reason, the sections are not presented as a limited list; there are more than 10 destination parks, for instance! These are not comprehensive lists, either; you may see a park listed here and wonder why that one gets mentioned while another isn't. The problem is one of excellence—with so many excellent parks to sort out, sometimes things will get missed; no slight was ever intended. Mind you, some of these sections could use a book of their own to do proper justice to the wealth of opportunities we have in this province: hiking trails, fishing, beaches, just to name a few! Another change from the previous edition is the removal of the playground list—most parks have undergone an extensive and expensive revision to their playground equipment. Large, colorful, creative climbers are now pretty much the standard although the size of the structure might be different. No matter which park you stay at (wilderness parks excluded), there will be something for the wee folk!

To use these lists you must first ask yourself what it is that you want out of your vacation. If you want a park with all the amenities and the hustle and bustle of a provincial or national park, then please don't go to Pine Cree! If, however, you want the peace and solitude of the forest with few amenities but acres of hiking and such, then Pine Cree is for you. We have included a short description for each section so that you will see what we mean by the heading. Some parks fit into several headings, and so are mentioned several times. I suggest that you decide what you want, then check the headings to see if one or two parks meet your criteria, then read those parks' write-ups (the page number is in parentheses). You might want to have a highway map handy to check locales as well.

DESTINATION PARKS

This is not a list of the "best" parks so much as it is a list of parks that are destinations in themselves. Some parks are places for you to camp overnight because you are on your way somewhere else, which is not in and of itself a bad thing, but some parks have made themselves into something more. They have plenty of facilities and activities, plus suitable campsites to make you want to stay for a week or more. The facilities are such that you can host family gatherings, weddings, reunions and the like in comfort and style; there will be camp kitchens and halls for rent or reservation. The complex of activities offered usually covers a wide range of age interests, so your whole family will most likely find something to do. Most of these parks will also be found in one of the other categories, giving you the chance to shorten your list of choices:

Atton's Lake Regional Park (160)
Brightsand Lake Regional Park (322)
Cypress Hills Provincial Park (58)
Duck Mountain Provincial Park (288)
Dunnet Regional Park (18)
Echo Valley Provincial Park (137)
Emerald Lake Regional Park (171)
Eston Riverside Regional Park (21)
Greenwater Lake Provincial Park (298)

Lac La Ronge Provincial Park (368)
Lac Pelletier Regional Park (29)
Lucien Lake Regional Park (255)
Macklin Lake Regional Park (179)
Manitou & District Regional Park (257)
Martin's Lake Regional Park (181)
Meadow Lake Provincial Park (384)
Memorial Lake Regional Park (185)
Moose Mountain Provincial Park (148)
Moosomin & District Regional Park (107)
Nickle Lake Regional Park (109)
Nipawin & District Regional Park (264)
Oungre Memorial Regional Park (111)
Prince Albert National Park (416)
Redberry Lake Regional Park (193)
Rowan's Ravine Provincial Park (312)
St. Brieux Regional Park (269)
Saskatchewan Landing Provincial Park (228)
Sturgeon Lake Regional Park (332)
Thomson Lake Regional Park (52)
Unity & District Regional Park (91)
Wakaw Lake Regional Park (114)
Wood Mountain Regional Park (55)
York Lake Regional Park (286)

WHEELCHAIR ACCESSIBILITY

Most provincial parks have made a concerted effort to have a barrier-free experience available. The historical and wilderness parks are obvious exceptions but even there you'll find some wheelchair-friendly amenities now and again. The provincial parks have built wheelchair accessible campsites and service centers and even established a few self-guided trails suitable for wheelchairs! Contact the provincial park of your choice for more information at 1-800-205-7070. The parks in this list will all have something for those requiring that level of service:

Anglin Lake Recreation Site (337)
Blackstrap Provincial Park (211)
Buffalo Pound Provincial Park (124)
Candle Lake Recreation Park (345)
Chitek Lake Recreation Site (352)
Cypress Hills Provincial Park (58)
Danielson Provincial Park (72)
Douglas Provincial Park (77)
Duck Mountain Provincial Park (288)
Echo Valley Provincial Park (137)
Emma Lake Provincial Park (363)
Good Spirit Lake Provincial Park (305)
Greenwater Lake Provincial Park (298)
Lac La Ronge Provincial Park (368)

Makwa Lake Provincial Park (378)
Meadow Lake Provincial Park (384)
Meeting Lake Regional Park (183)
Moose Mountain Provincial Park (148)
Narrow Hills Provincial Park (399)
Pike Lake Provincial Park (222)
Prince Albert National Park (416)
Rowan's Ravine Provincial Park (312)
Saskatchewan Landing Provincial Park (228)
The Battlefords Provincial Park (206)
Thomson Lake Regional Park (52)

HIKING

Most parks have some hiking in them to just wander about, but a few have made a concerted effort to provide trails or something extra special to see while you wander. A few had no trails but the opportunity to walk among the hills and coulees was so obvious that none were needed. Most provincial parks have some organized hiking trails; the ones included here have many trails, many of which are self-guided with brochures and points of interest to educate as you hike. There are trails in these parks for all age and activity levels—you just have to sort out what you want to see:

Carlton Trail Regional Park (90)
Cypress Hills Provincial Park (58)
Duck Mountain Provincial Park (288)
Douglas Provincial Park (77)
Herbert Ferry Regional Park (25)
Hudson Bay Regional Park (240)
Good Spirit Lake Provincial Park (305)
Grasslands National Park (87)
Jean Louis Legare Regional Park (27)
Kipabiskau Lake Regional Park (244)
Lac La Ronge Provincial Park (368)
Last Mountain Lake Regional Park (250)
Meadow Lake Provincial Park (384)
Moose Mountain Provincial Park (148)
Nipawin & District Regional Park (264)
Pasquia Regional Park (266)
Pine Cree Regional Park (43)
Prairie Lake Regional Park (45)
Prince Albert National Park (416)
Sask Landing Provincial Park (228)

BIRDING

By their very existence, our parks have become an oasis to birds, as the trees provide habitat not only for the birds but for the insects that they depend on for food. The lakes and streams provide further habitat, so that some parks have become major stop-over points for vast numbers of migrating birds. All parks will therefore have good to excellent bird watching opportunities, but some have better programming or bird lists to enhance the experience. For those people who thrill to expanding their "life list" or enjoy the variety of life, these parks offer something special:

    Brightsand Lake Regional Park (322)
    Last Mountain Lake Regional Park (250)
    Craik & District Regional Park (93)
    Good Spirit Lake Provincial Park (305)
    Grasslands National Park (87)
    Prince Albert National Park (416)
    Redberry Lake Regional Park (193)
    Saskatchewan Landing Provincial Park (228)
    Welwyn Centennial Regional Park (119)

SCENIC PARKS

Although the grain elevator will forever be thought of as the symbol of the Prairie Provinces, I did not include any municipal parks in this list as I equate scenery with open space. If you think of the prairies as flat and featureless, then you haven't seen the Cypress Hills or the Big Muddy Valley. If you think of the prairies as dull, you haven't sat beside a campfire on a northern lake, listening to the loons sing while the northern lights dance. These parks have some amazing sights for all to enjoy:

    Brightsand Lake Regional Park (161)
    Cabri Regional Park (11)
    Cypress Hills Provincial Park (58)
    Echo Valley Provincial Park (137)
    Eston Riverside Regional Park (75)
    Grasslands National Park (87)
    Herbert Ferry Regional Park (28)
    Lac La Ronge Provincial Park (368)
    Lady Lake Regional Park (147)
    Narrow Hills Provincial Park (399)
    Pine Cree Regional Park (19)
    Prairie Lake Regional Park (85)
    Saskatchewan Landing Provincial Park (228)
    St. Victors Petroglyphs Provincial Park (51)

GOLF COURSES

A great many of the province's parks have a golf course, often a sand-green course as they are so much easier to care for in this climate. The courses often have a clubhouse or a pro-shop, and host many tournaments over the course of the year. Some are difficult and some are easy, but the glory of most of them is that they provide a chance to get the family out golfing at a very reasonable price. A typical sand-green course costs about $6 per round, so one can afford to take the whole family out and make a day of it for about the same cost as for one person in the city. Some of these courses are famous for who built them, some for the view, some for the wildlife, and some just for the sheer fun value:

    Assiniboia Regional Park (12)

Battlefords Provincial Park (206)
Biggar & District Regional Park (162)
Carlton Trail Regional Park (90)
Cypress Hills Provincial Park (58)
Duck Mountain Provincial Park (288)
Emerald Lake Regional Park (171)
Eston Riverside Regional Park (21)
Fishing Lake Regional Park (237)
Greenwater Lake Provincial Park (298)
Hudson Bay Regional Park (240)
Kindersley Regional Park (177)
Lac Pelletier Regional Park (29)
Mainprize Regional Park (101)
Makwa Lake Provincial Park (378)
Manitou & District Regional Park (257)
Melville Regional Park (262)
Memorial Lake Regional Park (185)
Moose Creek Regional Park (105)
Moose Mountain Provincial Park (148)
Moosomin & District Regional Park (107)
Nipawin & District Regional Park (264)
Palliser Regional Park (39)
Pasquia Regional Park (266)
Prince Albert National Park (416)
Saskatchewan Landing Provincial Park (228)
St. Brieux Regional Park (269)
Silver Lake Regional Park (195)
Thomson Lake Regional Park (52)
Unity & District Regional Park (202)
Valley Regional Park, Rosthern (200)
Wakaw Lake Regional Park (274)
Woodlawn Regional Park (121)
York Lake Regional Park (286)

BASEBALL FACILITIES
Baseball in all its many current incarnations is a very popular sport in the province, and many of the parks have at least some equipment. Some parks, however, have set themselves up to be an excellent place to host a ball tournament. The actual size of the tournament, number of teams involved and so on, will determine which of these facilities would best suit you, but remember that they are popular venues for this sort of thing, and the prime weekends will be booked early:

Grenfell Regional Park (97)
Hudson Bay Regional Park (240)
Lucien Lake Regional Park (255)
Macklin Lake Regional Park (179)
Melville Regional Park (262)
Ogema Regional Park (36)

Radville-Laurier Regional Park (115)
Unity & District Regional Park (202)
Valley Regional Park, Waldheim (200)

WILDERNESS PARKS

For those of you looking for the campgrounds section (from the last edition), we came to the conclusion that since there are so many different needs for specific campgrounds (whether you're tenting or have a motor home—and what size of trailer, for instance), we've decided that all parks have sites suitable for the camping public, except for the wilderness parks where amenities will be few but you stand an excellent chance of being pretty much alone. There are other parks that have both: a back country and a front country. Only the wilderness parks are included in this list. These parks are all relatively accessible—only Athabasca and Wildcat Hill Provincial Wilderness Parks cannot be reached by road:

Clarence-Steepbank Lakes Provincial Park (355)
Clearwater River Provincial Park (359)
Grasslands National Park (87)
Pine Cree Regional Park (19)

COWBOY POETRY AND RODEO

The cowboy poetry phenomenon is growing as audiences become interested in the insights to be gained. I'll admit that poetry as a literary genre isn't for everyone, but if you do enjoy it, there are a few parks that have something to show. Rodeo is also popular, although not many parks have the local interest or infrastructure to host these exciting events. Mind you, some of the parks do it well:

Bengough Regional Park (14)
Hudson Bay Regional Park (240)
Sturgis and District Regional Park (273)
Wood Mountain Regional Park (55)

BEACHES

Not all lakes were created equally, and not all parks have developed them as completely as others. Almost all the parks we visited had a beach of some sort, but some people want to have beaches like the Caribbean or perhaps Le Cote d'Azure in France, and we can oblige at least a portion of that. The beaches here were all wide, had glorious sunning capability, wonderful water access, and filled with great castle-building sand! If you want a beach as your holiday destination, check these out:

Atton's Lake Regional Park (160)
Battlefords Provincial Park (206)
Brightsand Lake Regional Park (322)
Buffalo Pound Provincial Park (124)
Candle Lake Recreation Park (345)
Danielson Provincial Park (72)
Emma Lake Recreation Site (363)
Fishing Lake Regional Park

Leslie Beach (237)
Good Spirit Lake Provincial Park (305)
Greenwater Lake Provincial Park (298)
Katepwa Point Recreation Park (143)
Kipabiskau Lake Regional Park (244)
Leroy Leisureland Regional Park (253)
Makwa Lake Provincial Park (378)
Manitou & District Regional Park (257)
Martin's Lake Regional Park (181)
Meadow Lake Provincial Park (384)
Memorial Lake Regional Park (185)
Moose Mountain Provincial Park (148)
Moosomin & District Regional Park (107)
Nickle Lake Regional Park (109)
Redberry Lake Regional Park (193)
Regina Beach Recreation Park (156)
Rowan's Ravine Provincial Park (312)
Sandy Beach Regional Park (330)
Wakaw Regional Park (274)
York Lake Regional Park (286)

FISHING

Hidden underneath those calm waters there are a multitude of game fish all waiting to test your angling skill. Saskatchewan's waters are home to over 80 species of fish, from the smallest minnow to the mightiest trout. Some of our waters, such as Lake Diefenbaker in the middle of the province, are home to 20 or more species of game fish alone! Many of our wild fish populations are supplemented by fish grown at the provincial fish culture station located just east of Echo Valley Provincial Park in the Qu'Appelle Valley. In 2003, they supplied nearly 39 million fish to almost 250 bodies of water. If you're down visiting the park you can arrange for a tour of the hatchery; check the park write-up for details. More complete (and up-to-date) information can be found at their website, www.se.gov.sk.ca/fishwild/, or by contacting any Saskatchewan Environment office; check your telephone book for the nearest. These parks offer some of the finest sport fishing in the world, usually with an outfitter to rent boats, motors, and often guides as well:

Anglin Lake Recreation Site (337)
Buffalo Pound Provincial Park (124)
Chitek Lake Recreation Site (352)
Clarence-Steepbank Lakes Provincial Park (355)
Clearwater River Provincial Park (359)
Danielson Provincial Park (72)
Douglas Provincial Park (77)
Echo Valley Provincial Park (137)
Lac La Ronge Provincial Park (368)
Last Mountain Lake Regional Park (250)
Meadow Lake Provincial Park (384)
Mainprize Regional Park (101)
Narrow Hills Provincial Park (399)

Nipawin & District Regional Park (264)
Palliser Regional Park (39)
Prince Albert National Park (416)
Rowan's Ravine Provincial Park (312)
Saskatchewan Landing Provincial Park (228)

STAR-GAZING (ASTRONOMY)

I am very pleased to add this list to the book as it shows how visionary our park managers can be: they have decided to create "Dark Sky Preserves"—places where the night sky will not be polluted by waste light, places where you can still marvel in naked-eye views of the Milky Way, or pick out the constellations and asterisms (groups of stars familiar to us; usually they are parts of larger constellations) that are the guide-posts to the night skies. This is, of course, pleasurable to amateur astronomers and star-gazers. It is also much more natural for the animals in the parks. They are generally more active at night, so having all that waste light slows down their movements as they try to find food and water while avoiding hungry predators! The provincial parks are training their summer interpretive staff in guiding binocular "walking tours" of the night sky, and you can often find star charts in the handouts at the interpretive centers. The provincial parks will all become Dark Sky Preserves as time and resources permit, and the regional parks are becoming interested in the idea as well. I fully expect that the next edition of this book will have a lot more to say on the subject:

Cypress Hills Provincial Park (58)
Duck Mountain Provincial Park (288)
Greenwater Provincial Park (298)
Pine Cree Regional Park (19)
Rockin Beach Regional Park (47)

FIRST NATIONS

To learn about and understand our First Nations cultures is to touch the very face of history in this province. It was the First Nations people that made the fur trade work, and it was the fur trade that brought early commerce to the Great Plains. This early commerce, established in rudimentary trading posts or forts, became the bones upon which the earliest settlers built the agricultural base of our economy, which remains an important part of our lives to this day. Our parks give us a chance to see and learn about this important part of our mutual history together, whether it is through displays and explanations of artifacts or through colorful dance and drum ceremonies; you may even have a chance to learn some Aboriginal subsistence skills from the masters themselves. I feel privileged to offer these suggestions to those wishing to learn more about these fascinating people, their culture and history:

Battlefords Provincial Park (206)
Buffalo Pound Provincial Park (124)
Fort Carlton Provincial Historic Park (213)
Fort Pitt Provincial Historic Park (216)
Narrow Hills Provincial Park (399)
Prince Albert National Park (416)
Steele Narrows Provincial Historic Park (410)

Wood Mountain Provincial Historic Park (82)
Wood Mountain Regional Park (55)

In closing, I would like to thank you for allowing us to assist you with your vacations. I hope these ideas will shorten this massive province into a few areas of particular interest to you. The different levels of park systems in this wonderful province have an incredible variety to offer. In two camping seasons we saw every campsite in the province and we now have a short list of places we'll simply have to go back to see; one weekend is far too short a time to spend at some of our special places. What we did see in such a brief time we've captured here for you but it is only a shadow of what all the park staff, from the most grizzled senior manager to the newest summer temporary, have worked to prepare for you, their clients. For this reason we are ever grateful to the many people who took time out of their busy days to assist us with our inquiries by filling out our questionnaires and answering our questions when we visited, and by reviewing the material for accuracy before we sent it off to the publisher. For all of you who are thinking of spending your vacation time and dollars in the province, rest assured there is quite an adventure waiting for you out there! Go, find your own special retreats and let your work-weary cares drain away—Saskatchewan's many beautiful parks are waiting for you!

Index

A

Abbey, SK, 28
Acoose, 144
Ajawaan Creek, 417
Ajawaan Lake, 409, 416, 417
Alameda Dam, 120, 121, 159
Alameda, SK, 121
All Saints Anglican Church (Cannington), 141
Allen Sapp Museum (The Battlefords), 233
Allison's Store (Mouse Mountain), 159
Althouse Lake, 371
Amiskowan Lake (Prince Albert), 417
Amiskowan Trail (Prince Albert), 415
Anchor Marine (Kyle), 89
Anderson Point Campground (Anglin Lake), 343, 344, 345
Anderson Trapper's Cabin (Anglin Lake), 344
Andy Jumalt Hiking Trail (Pasquia), 284
Angler's Guide, 395
Anglican Church Missionary Society, 406
Anglin Lake (resort community), 343, 345, 414
Anglin Lake Cottage subdivision, 344
Anglin Lake Provincial Recreation Site, 343, 345, 422, 427
Anglin Lake Trail (Prince Albert), 415
Angus McGillis Heritage Site (Sylvan Valley), 49, 94
Antelope Lake Regional Park, 3, 4
Arborfield, SK, 282, 284
Aspen Campground (Good Spirit Lake), 320, 321, 324
Aspen Campsite (The Battlefords), 231
Aspen Crescent (Lac La Ronge), 370
Aspen Grove Campground (Cypress Hills), 60, 66
Aspen Grove Campground (Greenwater Lake), 313
Aspen Grove Group Camping Area (Douglas), 81
Aspen Grove Picnic Area (Blackstrap), 235, 236
Aspen View Campground (Echo Valley), 146, 147, 149
Asquith, SK, 185, 187
Assiniboia Aquatic Center, 5, 6
Assiniboia Regional Park, 5, 6, 424
Assiniboia River, 289, 290
Assiniboia Ski Club, 290
Assiniboia, SK, 5, 6, 49, 55, 94
Athabasca Eco Expeditions, 342
Athabasca Sand Dunes Provincial Wilderness Park, 329, 341, 342, 426
Athabasca Sand Dunes Provincial Wilderness Park brochure, 342
Atton's Lake, 176
Atton's Lake Golf Club, 176
Atton's Lake Regional Park, 175, 177, 421, 426
Aurora Houseboat (Nipawin), 280
Avonlea Creek, 12
Avonlea, SK, 12, 14, 36

B

Bagwa Lake, 417
Baker, Everett, 40
Bakers Coulee, 40
Bald Butte, 63, 68
Bald Butte Trail (Cypress Hills), 66
Baldy Lake, 395, 401
Ball Diamond Group Campground (The Battlefords), 231
Balsam Campground (Good Spirit Lake), 321
Bankside Lake, 329, 330
Bar-Bar (Moose Mountain), 164
Batka Lake, 307, 308, 310
Batoche, SK, 241
Battle Creek (Cypress Hills), 61
Battle of the Greasy Grass River, 95
Battleford (fort), 242
Battleford Trail, 85, 90
Battlefords, The, 193, 194, 209, 335, 336
Battlefords Provincial Park, The, 229, 233, 423, 425, 426, 428
Battlefords Tourism Guide, 233
Bayside Campground (Danielson), 76, 77
Beach Cafe (Greenwater Lake), 316
Beachside Rentals (The Battlefords), 232
Bear Claw Casino, 164
Beardy's Powwow, 238, 240
Bearpaw Campground (Sask Landing), 85, 86, 87, 88, 89, 91
Beaver Creek, 135
Beaver Glen Campground (Prince Albert), 409, 411, 412, 420
Beaver Lake Trail (Moose Mountain), 160, 162
Beaver Point (Athabasca Sand Dunes), 341
Beechy, SK, 42, 43
Belaney, Archie, 409, 420
Bengough Heritage Museum, 8
Bengough Regional Golf Club, 7
Bengough Regional Park, 7, 8, 426
Bengough, SK, 7, 8, 36
Benito cottage subdivision (Duck Mountain), 307
Bethany Seniors Lodge, 269, 271
Betty Lou boat tours, 43
Big Bear (Cree), 241, 407, 408
Big Echo Lake, 402
Big Island Cove Resort (Meadow Lake), 387
Big Jumbo Lake, 377, 378
Big Jumbo basin, 375
Big Muddy (Bengough), 8, 131
Big Muddy Valley, 424
Biggar and District Regional Park, 178, 179, 425

Biggar, SK, 178, 179
Birch Campground (Duck Mountain), 305, 306, 307, 308
Birch Crescent (Lac La Ronge), 370
Birch Forest Hiking Trail (Greenwater Lake), 315
Birch Forest Interpretive Trail (Moose Mountain), 160
Birch Lake, 356
Bison Observation Tower (Buffalo Pound), 74
Bison View Interpretive Trail (Buffalo Pound), 74
Blackstrap Provincial Park, 234, 237, 422
Bladebone Lake, 417
Blaine Lake, SK, 191, 199, 200, 201
Blood Red the Sun, 242
Bluebird Cafe (Regina Beach), 167
Boreal Forest Interpretive Trail (Duck Mountain), 308
Boundary Bog (Prince Albert), 415
Boundary Dam reservoir, 138
Bow Valley Park, 120
Brightsand Lake Regional Park, 180, 181, 421, 424, 426
Brightsand Lake Store, 181
Bronson Forest Recreation Site, 346, 347, 390
Brunyee Trail (Sask Landing), 91
Buena Vista cottage subdivision (Regina Beach), 165
Buffalo Pits (Waldsea Lake), 295
Buffalo Pound Provincial Park, 69, 75, 422, 426, 427, 428

C

Cabri Regional Park, 9, 11, 424
Cabri, SK, 9, 10, 11, 19
Cacti Trail (Douglas), 83
Calder Lake, 404
Calling Lakes, 146, 152
Cameron, William Bleasdell
  Blood Red the Sun, 242
Camp Easter Seal (Manitou), 273
Camp Tawow (Candle Lake), 350
Canadian Pacific Railroad (CPR), 95, 211, 301
Canadian Plains Research Center, 98, 360
CanAm Highway, 366
Candiac, SK, 113
Candle Lake, 392, 401, 403, 404
Candle Lake Recreation Park, 348, 352, 357, 422, 426
Candle Lake, SK, 348, 349, 350, 352, 355, 357
Candlelight Tours (Fort Carlton), 240
Cannington Manor Provincial Historic Park, 140, 141, 164
Canoe Rentals (Meadow Lake), 389
Canoe Routes of Meadow Lake Provincial Park brochure, 389
Canoeing the Churchill, 373
Canora, SK, 290, 326
Canwood Golf Club, 334
Canwood Regional Park, 333, 334
Canwood, SK, 333, 334

Caribou Creek, 392, 405
Caribou Creek Lodge, 357, 395, 396
Carlton Trail (Carlton Trail), 103
Carlton Trail (Touchwood Hills), 327
Carlton Trail Regional Park, 103, 104, 423, 425
Carlton Trail Walk (Fort Carlton), 239
Carlyle, SK, 140, 141, 157, 164
Carrot River, 282, 284, 329, 360
Carrot River Health Center, 284
Cassette Park (Woodlawn), 138, 139
Cavanaugh's Creek (Pasquia), 283
Cedar Cove Resort, 144, 145
Central Butte, SK, 84
Centre Campground (The Battlefords), 230, 231
Ceylon Regional Park, 105, 106
Ceylon Reservoir, 105
Ceylon, SK, 105, 106
Chamberlain, SK, 69
Chapel Gallery (in North Battleford), 233
Charles Harvey Program Center (Duck Mountain), 312
Chauvin, Alberta, 222
Chelan, SK, 313
Chipewyan people, 407
Chitek Lake Golf Course, 354
Chitek Lake Recreation Site, 353, 354, 390, 422, 427
Chitek Lake, SK, 353, 354
Christopher Bay (Kenosee Lake), 158
Christopher Lake, SK, 343, 345, 362, 363, 365, 409
Churchill River, 366, 372, 406
Clancy's On The Beach, 26
Clare Lake, 417
Clarence Lake, 355, 356, 357
Clarence-Steepbank Lakes Provincial Wilderness Park, 329, 355, 426, 427
Clark, Allan & Lorraine, 118
Clearview Campground (The Battlefords), 230, 231
Clearwater Lake, 358
Clearwater Lake Regional Park, 182, 184
Clearwater River Provincial Wilderness Park, 358, 359, 426, 427
Clunie, Jim, 259
Canadian National Railroad (CNR), 131
Cochin, SK, 208, 233
Codette Dam, 296
Codette Lake, 280, 296, 298
Cold Lake, 380, 387, 389
Cold River, 388
Conglomerate Cliffs (Cypress Hills), 68
Coronach, SK, 45
Coteau Bay, 76, 79
Coteau Creek Power Station, 79
Coulee Trail (Sask Landing), 90
Courtenay Lake, 373
Cove Resort (Greenwater Lake), 316, 319
Cowan, David Latimer, Constable, 241
Craik and District Regional Park, 107, 108, 424

Craik Reservoir, 107, 108
Craik, SK, 107, 108
Cranberry Campground (Greenwater Lake), 313
Crane Valley, SK, 36
Craven, SK, 133, 155, 165, 166, 168
Crazy Critters Mini-Golf (Greenwater Lake), 317
Crean Kitchen (Prince Albert), 418
Crean Lake, 416, 418
Cree Nation, 133, 152, 241, 296, 349, 360, 369, 375, 407, 419
Cree, Plains, 264, 407, 408
Cree, Wood, 407, 408
Creighton, SK, 392
Crescent Creek Valley, 109
Crooked Lake, 142, 143, 145
Crooked Lake Parks and Recreation Board, 144
Crooked Lake Provincial Park, 142, 145
"Cross-Country Ski and Snowmobile Trails" brochure, 309
Cruisers Family Restaurant (Moose Mountain), 160
Cub Hills (Narrow Hills), 392, 400
Cumberland House Hotel, 361
Cumberland House Provincial Historic Park, 360, 361
Cumberland House, SK, 360, 361
Custer, George A., General, 95
Cut Arm (Cree chief), 407
Cutknife Elks, 176
Cutknife, SK, 175, 177
Cutout Coulee Trail (Katepwa Point), 153
Cypress Hills, 40, 56, 400, 424
Cypress Hills General Store, 67
Cypress Hills Golf Resort, 64
Cypress Hills Interprovincial Park, 56, 60, 67, 68, 421-425, 428
Cypress Hills Resort Inn, 62, 64, 66, 68

D

D.A. Mackenzie Aquatic Center (Esterhazy), 109
Dakota peoples, 93
Danielson Provincial Park, 76, 77, 79, 80, 84, 422, 426, 427
Dar's Little Dipper, 67
Dark Sky Preserve, 44, 60, 428
Darlings Beach Campground (Lac Pelletier), 24
Darlings Beach, SK, 24, 25
Debden Community Center, 338
Debden, SK, 337, 338
Deer Camping Loop (Duck Mountain), 307
Deer Hollow Campground (Cypress Hills), 59
Delorme cottage subdivision, 231, 232
Department of Highways, 175, 262, 291
Diamond Lake, 397
Diana May Clay (Whitesand), 300
Dickens Lake, 373
Dickens, Francis, Inspector, 241, 242
Dickson Hardie Interpretive Center (Pasquia), 284
Diefenbaker Cottage Development, 37

Diefenbaker, John, Law Office, 293
Diefenbaker Lake, see Lake Diefenbaker
Dominion Telegraph company, 327
Don Allen cross-country ski trails (Lac La Ronge), 367
Don Allen Trails (Lac La Ronge), 367
Donald Gunn cottage subdivision (Good Spirit Lake), 321, 322, 323
Donald Hooper Loop (Greenwater Lake), 315
Dorintosh, SK, 380, 382, 391
Douglas Provincial Park, 78, 80, 82, 84, 422, 423, 427
"Douglas Provincial Park Nature Guide" pamphlet, 84
Douglas, T.C., 80
Dr. Brown Aquatic Center (Oungre Memorial), 127
Duck Lake, 238, 240
Duck Mountain Lodge, 305, 310, 311
Duck Mountain Provincial Park, 305, 307, 311, 312, 421-423, 425, 428
Duck Mountain Regional Park, 305, 309
Ducks Unlimited, 219
Dundurn, SK, 237
Dune Discovery Interpretive Trail (Good Spirit Lake), 322
Dune Hiking Trail (Good Spirit Lake), 323, 322
Dunes Hiking Area (Douglas), 83
Dunes Interpretive Center (Douglas), 83
Dunes Nature Center (Douglas), 84
Dunnet Regional Park, 12, 14, 421
Dutch Treat Mini-Golf Course (Meadow Lake), 383
Duval, SK, 264
Dwarf Mistletoe Management Project, 349
Dyke Trail (Buffalo Pound), 74

E

E.B. Campbell Dam, 360
Eagle Creek, 186
Eagle Creek Hills, 185
Eagle Creek Regional Park, 185, 187
East Trout Lake, 355, 357
Eastend, SK, 40, 41, 56, 68
Eastshore Rural Development Co-operative (ERDC), 133, 134
Echo Lake, 146, 149, 152
Echo Valley Mini-Golf course, 149
Echo Valley Provincial Park, 146, 151, 421, 422, 424, 427
Edmonton House, 103
"Educators Guide to Duck Mountain Provincial Park, The," 312
Elbow Harbor, 79, 80
Elbow Lakeside Marina, 81, 82, 89
Elbow Recreation Site, 80, 81
Elbow, SK, 78, 79, 80, 81, 82, 83, 84
Elk Camping Loop (Duck Mountain), 307
Elk Ridge Golf and Country Club, 344
Elk Ridge Resort and Golf Course, 418

INDEX • 433

Elk Trail (Prince Albert), 414
Elm View Campground (Buffalo Pound), 70, 71, 73, 75
Elmview Campground (Danielson), 76, 77
Elmwood Campground (Danielson), 78
Elmwood Campground (Rowan's Ravine), 168, 169
Elrose Golf Club, 189
Elrose Regional Park, 188, 189
Elrose, SK, 188, 189
Emerald Lake Regional Park, 190, 192, 421, 425
Emma Lake, 345, 364
Emma Lake Golf Course, 344, 364
Emma Lake Provincial Recreation Park, 362, 365, 422, 426
Emma Lake Resort, 365
Emma Lake, SK, 365, 409
Empire Road (Assiniboia), 5
Endeavour, SK, 261
Environment Canada, 79
Equestrian Camp (Sask Landing), 91
Equestrian Campground (Cypress Hills), 61
Ermine Trail (Echo Valley), 150
Esker Trail (Narrow Hills), 399, 400
Esterhazy Regional Park, 109, 110
Esterhazy, SK, 109, 110
Estevan Leisure Center, 138
Estevan, SK, 137, 139
Eston Riverside Regional Park, 15, 17, 421, 424, 425
Eston, SK, 15, 17
Etomante River, 254
Evergreen Golf and Curling Club (Nipawin), 280, 281
Exner Lake, 377

F

F.T. Hill Museum (Riverhurst), 39
Fairwell Creek, 63
Fairy Glen Campsite (Narrow Hills), 403
Fairy Glen Lake, 403
Falling Horse Creek (Narrow Hills), 397
Falling Horse Creek Trail (Narrow Hills), 396
Farwell's Trading Post (Cypress Hills), 64, 67
Federal Wildlife Sanctuary (Redberry Lake), 213
Fern's Grocery (Emma Lake), 365
Field Checklist of Saskatchewan Birds, The, brochure, 92
Fife Lake, 44
Fir River, 254, 255, 330
Firhead Lake, 329
First Mustus Lake, 383, 389
First Narrows (Prince Albert), 417
First Nations peoples, 67, 69, 93, 144, 155, 163, 232, 238, 272, 372, 374, 419, 428
Fish Creek Campground (Moose Mountain), 157, 158, 160, 162
Fish Hatchery (provincial), 150
Fish Lake Trail (Prince Albert), 414
Fisher Creek Campground (Candle Lake), 349

Fisheries Department (provincial), 129, 135, 336
Fishing Lake Lodge, 253
Fishing Lake Regional Park Authority, 251, 425, 426
Fishing Lakes (Narrow Hills), 403
Flintoft, SK, 55
Flotten Lake, 381, 390
Flotten Lake Resort, 381
Flotten River, 382
Foam Lake Golf and Country Club, 251, 253
Foam Lake, SK, 251, 252, 253
Fore Fun Mini-Golf (Duck Mountain), 311
Fort Battleford National Historic Park, 233
Fort Buford, Montana, 95
Fort Carlton, 103, 238, 239
Fort Carlton Provincial Historic Park, 238, 240, 428
Fort Garry (Winnipeg), 103, 327
Fort Pitt, 241, 242, 346, 375, 407
Fort Pitt Provincial Historic Park, 241, 242, 428
Fort Pitt Trail (Silver Lake), 218
Fort Qu'Appelle trading post, 155
Fort Qu'Appelle Visitors Guide, 152
Fort Qu'Appelle, SK, 146, 150, 151, 154
Fort San/Fort Qu'Appelle Highway, 148
Fort Walsh National Historic Site & Museum (Cypress Hills), 64, 68
Fossil House (Riverhurst), 39
Foster, Frank, 126
Fox Trail (Echo Valley), 150
Foxworthy, Jeff, 390
Fred Light Museum (The Battlefords), 233
Freight Trail (Prince Albert), 415
Frenchman River, 98
Friends of the Park Gift Shop (Prince Albert), 414
Friends of the Petroglyphs, The, 94
Frog Lake, 241, 407
Frog Lake massacre, 408
From's Lake Resort, 103
From, J.H., 103
Fudge Factory (Good Spirit Lake), 325

G

G & S Marina Outfitters (Rowan's Ravine), 170
Gardiner Dam, 76, 78
Geikie River, 373
Gem Lakes, 397, 403
Gift of Green Nature Trail (Pike Lake), 247
Glade Campground (Lac Pelletier), 24
Glaslyn, SK, 335, 336
Glenburn Regional Park, 193, 194
Glentworth, SK, 99
Glidden, SK, 27
Golf Kenosee Inc., 162
Good Spirit Lake, 324
Good Spirit Lake Golf and Country Club, 324
Good Spirit Lake Provincial Park, 320, 326, 422, 423, 424, 427
Good Spirit Lake Villas and Inn, 324
Goodsoil, SK, 380, 385, 386, 389, 391

Goodwin House (Sask Landing), 85, 90, 91, 92
Govan, SK, 133, 169, 264, 266
Grace Lake, 397
Grace Lakes, 399, 400
Grace Lakes campgrounds, 396
Grass River, 360
Grasslands National Park, 53, 54, 55, 97, 99, 100, 423, 424, 426
Gravelbourg, SK, 46, 47, 50, 52
Great Canadian Fossil Trail, The (Cypress Hills), 68
Green Hills Golf and Country Club (Greenwater Lake), 317
Greenwater Lake, 317
Greenwater Lake Provincial Park, 313, 315, 319, 421, 422, 425, 427, 428
Greig Lake, 382, 383, 390
Grenfell Regional Park, 111, 112, 425
Grenfell Regional Park Craft Shop, 112
Grenfell, SK, 112
Grey Owl, 409
Grey Owl Trail (Prince Albert), 416
Grey Owl's cabin, 416, 417
Grid Road 606, 35
Grid Road 637, 29
Grid Road 640, 301
Grid Road 649, 27
Grid Road 680, 221
Grid Road 693, 339
Grid Road 699, 375
Grid Road 793, 337
Grid Road 797, 242
Grid Road 798, 216
Gronlid, SK, 296, 298
Gull Lake, SK, 3, 4
Gunn Beach (Good Spirit Lake), 322
Gunn, Donald, 320

H

Habor Golf Club and Resort (Elbow), 83
Hafford, SK, 213, 215
Hanging Hearts Lakes, 416, 418
Hanging Hearts Marina (Prince Albert), 418
Harper's Store (Welwyn), 135
Hawkins Lake Hiking Trail (Greenwater Lake), 315
Hay Meadow Hiking Trail (Meadow Lake), 390
Hazelnut Grove Campground (Blackstrap), 234, 235
Hazlet Regional Park, 18, 19
Hazlet, SK, 18, 19
"Heading North 2004" brochure, 367
Hector Duncan Memorial Golf Tournament, 191
Height of Land Trail (Prince Albert), 415
Herbert Ferry Regional Park, 20, 21, 423, 424
Herbert, SK, 20, 21
Heritage House Museum (Avonlea), 13
Heritage Inn (Melfort), 297
Heritage Museum (Herbert), 21
Heritage Museum (Wakaw), 293
Heritage Museum (Willow Bunch), 23

Hermit's Cave, 41
Hidden Bay, 373
Hidden Valley Campground (Cypress Hills), 60
Hidden Valley Trail (Cypress Hills), 60, 64, 65
Highbush Interpretive Trail (Greenwater Lake), 315
Highland Interpretive Trail (Cypress Hills), 63
Highway 1, 152, 157
Highway 2, 5, 69, 291, 343, 362, 366, 409, 419
Highway 3, 254, 339
Highway 4, 24, 85, 92, 98, 178, 182, 189, 229, 335, 380, 382, 385
Highway 5, 251, 294
Highway 6, 262, 267, 275, 296
Highway 7, 195
Highway 8, 103, 104, 122, 136
Highway 9, 120, 140, 157, 160, 161, 164, 254, 260, 320, 329, 330
Highway 10, 277
Highway 11, 165, 223, 234
Highway 12, 190, 199
Highway 13, 5, 6, 33, 140
Highway 14, 178, 197, 225, 226
Highway 15, 210, 277, 327
Highway 16, 193, 218, 302
Highway 17, 216, 221, 242
Highway 18, 96, 97, 98, 99, 120
Highway 19, 80
Highway 20, 134, 155, 168, 264, 269
Highway 21, 346, 375, 380, 387
Highway 22, 109
Highway 23, 282
Highway 26, 380, 385, 386
Highway 28, 131
Highway 30, 15, 204, 242
Highway 31, 197
Highway 32, 9
Highway 34, 7
Highway 35, 126, 258
Highway 36, 22
Highway 37, 9
Highway 38, 313, 315
Highway 39, 116, 124
Highway 40, 175, 213, 221
Highway 41, 287
Highway 44, 76, 78
Highway 45, 210
Highway 47, 137, 142, 145
Highway 48, 113, 140
Highway 49, 289
Highway 54, 165
Highway 55, 279, 329, 333, 348, 355
Highway 56, 152
Highway 57, 305, 307
Highway 58, 46, 50
Highway 60, 243
Highway 80, 109
Highway 102, 366

Highway 106, 392, 394, 395, 398
Highway 109, 254
Highway 120, 348, 355, 394
Highway 210, 146, 148, 225, 226
Highway 212, 238
Highway 219, 37, 56, 76
Highway 220, 168
Highway 221, 56, 57
Highway 224, 382, 383, 385, 390
Highway 227, 56
Highway 229, 320, 325
Highway 247, 142
Highway 261, 85, 87
Highway 263, 362, 409, 410, 412, 417
Highway 264, 409, 412, 415
Highway 308, 135
Highway 310, 251, 252
Highway 312, 223
Highway 322, 168
Highway 332, 18, 129
Highway 334, 12
Highway 337, 131, 132
Highway 342, 182
Highway 343, 24
Highway 349, 262
Highway 358, 55
Highway 365, 272
Highway 368, 285
Highway 376, 194
Highway 377, 105, 106
Highway 378, 202
Highway 699, 407
Highway 904, 381
Highway 913, 355
Highway 919, 387, 388
Highway 927, 355
Highway 950, 385, 387
Highway 953, 343
Highway 955, 358
"Hiking & Scenic Drive" brochure, 316
Hiking Trails of Meadow Lake Provincial Park brochure, 389
Hilliards' Four Season Resort (Wapiti Valley), 297, 298
Hillside Nature Trail (Katepwa Point), 153
Hilltop Campground (The Battlefords), 230
Hilltop Campground (Buffalo Pound), 69, 231
Hilltop Campground (Greenwater Lake), 313
Hilltop Ski and Hiking Trail (Candle Lake), 351
Hirtz Lake, 388, 389
Holbein, SK, 339, 340
Hole-In-The-Wall Group Camp (Echo Valley), 148, 150
Holy Trinity Anglican Church, 406
Holy Trinity Anglican Church Provincial Historic Site, 406
Homestead Campground (Douglas), 83

Homestead Heritage Hiking Trail (Candle Lake), 352
Horizons Unlimited/Churchill River Canoe Outfitters, 373
Horseshoe Campground (Cypress Hills), 60
Hot Springs Lake, 398, 405
Howe Bay (Meadow Lake), 387, 389
Hudson Bay, 238, 329, 366, 392
Hudson Bay Regional Park, 254, 255, 423, 425, 426
Hudson Bay, SK, 254, 255
Hudson's Bay Company, 134, 155, 159, 241, 327, 358, 360, 372
　　Northcote, 360
　　trading post, 242, 327, 360
Humboldt, SK, 269, 271, 294, 295
Humphrey Hiking Trail (Meadow Lake), 387
Humphrey Lake, 390
Humphrey Lake Hiking Trail (Meadow Lake), 388, 390
Hungerford Lakes, 63
Hunter's Lake Trail (Prince Albert), 414

I

Ice Push Ridge (Prince Albert), 415
Imasees (Cree chief), 241
Imhoff art gallery, 375
Imhoff, Berthold von, Count, 181, 346
Information Center (Prince Albert), 417, 419
Information Services Corporation (provincial), 63
Interpretive Centre (The Battlefords), 231
Interpretive Center (Duck Mountain), 312
Interpretive Center (Greenwater Lake), 315, 316, 318
Irene's Boats (Pike Lake), 244
ISC Geospatial Data Products, 308, 330, 341, 398
Island Lake Trail (Narrow Hills), 397
Ispuchaw Lake, 394, 404
Ituna and District Golf and Country Club, 257
Ituna and District Regional Park, 256, 257
Ituna, SK, 257

J

Jackfish Lake, 207, 229, 310
Jackfish Lodge Golf Resort (The Battlefords), 229, 230, 232
Jacobsen Bay (Anglin Lake), 344
Jacobsen Bay Outfitters, 344, 345
Jacobsen Bay Trail (Anglin Lake), 345
Jade Lake, 397
Jasper Lake, 356
Jean-Louis Legare Regional Park, 22, 23, 423
Jeannette Lake, 381
Jiggy's Rentals (Good Spirit Lake), 323
Joe's Cabins (Candle Lake), 350, 351
John Diefenbaker Law Office, 293
Johnson, E. Pauline, 152
Johnson's Outfitters, 346, 347
Jonker, M.
　　The Sand Dunes of Lake Athabasca, 342
Jubilee Beach (Sylvan Valley), 48

Jumbo Beach (Makwa Lake), 376, 377, 378
Jumbo Beach Campground (Makwa Lake), 375, 377
Juniper Trail (Douglas), 83

K

K 'n N Kabins (Mainprize), 119
K.C. Beach Regional Park, 251, 252
Kamsack cottage subdivision, 310
Kamsack, SK, 305, 308, 311, 312
Karpan, Robin and Arlene
    Northern Sandscapes, 342
Katepwa Beach Golf Club, 154
Katepwa Beach, SK, 153
Katepwa Campground and Family 9 (Katepwa Point), 152, 154
Katepwa Hotel, 153
Katepwa Lake, 152
Katepwa Point Provincial Recreation Park, 152, 153, 154, 427
Kayak Club (Nickle Lake), 124
Keeway Group Campground (The Battlefords), 230, 231
Kelvington, SK, 319
Kemoca Regional Park, 113, 115
Kendal, SK, 113
Kenosee Inn Resort Hotel (Moose Mountain), 162, 163
Kenosee Lake Riding Academy (Moose Mountain), 163
Kenosee Lake, SK, 141, 145, 158, 162, 164
Kenosee Superslides (Moose Mountain), 160
Kevin Misfeldt Campground (Blackstrap), 234, 236
Kimball Lake, 383, 390
Kimball Lake Hiking Trail (Meadow Lake), 390
Kimball Lake store (Meadow Lake), 384
Kin Point (York Lake), 303, 304
Kindersley Regional Park, 195, 196, 425
Kindersley, SK, 195, 196
King Island (Prince Albert), 417
Kingfisher Trail (Prince Albert), 415, 417
Kingsmere Lake, 416, 417, 419
Kingsmere River, 417
Kingsmere River Trail (Prince Albert), 416
Kinistino, SK, 287, 288
Kinley, SK, 187
Kinookimaw Campground (Regina Beach), 167
Kinowa Trail (Prince Albert), 414
Kipabiskau Lake, 258
Kipabiskau Lake Regional Park, 258, 259, 423, 427
Kipabiskau Water Sports Club, 259
Kit Lake, 356
Kitchimanitou subdivision, 323
Kowalski Park (Struthers), 288
Kronau Reservoir, 129
Kronau, SK, 129, 130
Kuroki, SK, 251
Kyle, SK, 89, 90, 92, 182, 184

L

La Loche, SK, 358, 359
La Ronge Chamber of Commerce, 367
La Ronge, SK, 342, 366-371, 373, 374, 406
Lac des Iles, 385, 386, 407
Lac La Ronge Provincial Park, 366, 373, 374, 406, 422, 423, 424, 427
Lac La Ronge River, 369
Lac Pelletier Regional Park, 24, 26, 422, 425
Lady Lake Regional Park, 260, 261, 424
Lafleche, SK, 50, 52
Lake Athabasca, 329, 341
Lake Charron, 262
Lake Charron Regional Park, 262, 263
Lake Diefenbaker, 9, 20, 21, 37, 38, 42, 76-78, 80, 84, 85, 89, 90, 427
Lake Side Campground (Buffalo Pound), 70
Lake View Campground (Buffalo Pound), 71
Lake Winnipeg, 392
Lakeland Leisure Shop (Nipawin), 280
Lakeshore Foods (Douglas), 84
Lakeside Campground (Greenwater Lake), 313
Lakeside Campground (Lac Pelletier), 24
Lakeside Marina Service (Elbow), 78
Lakeside Service (Duck Mountain), 311
Lakeside Trail (The Battlefords), 231
Lakeview Golf Club (Macklin Lake), 197
Lakeview Hiking Trail (Moose Mountain), 158
Lakeview Picnic Area (Blackstrap), 235, 236
Lakeview Place (Waldsea Lake), 294, 295
Lakeview Trail (Moose Mountain), 160
Lakewoods Store (Nipawin), 280
Land of the Loon Resort, 344
Langenburg, SK, 103, 104
Larsen Field (Oungre Memorial), 127
Last Mountain House Provincial Historic Park, 134, 155, 156
Last Mountain Lake, 133, 165, 166, 168, 169, 264, 265, 266
Last Mountain Lake National Wildlife Area (NWA), 169, 264, 265, 266, 274
Last Mountain Lake Regional Park, 264, 266, 423, 424, 427
Last Mountain Sailing Club, 134
Last Oak Golf and Country Club, 144
Laurentian Mountains, 56
Laurier, SK, 131
Le Beau Village Museum (St. Victor), 94
Leask, SK, 190, 192
Lebret, SK, 152
"Legend of the Qu'Appelle Valley, The" poem, 152
Legare, Jean-Louis, 22, 54, 95
Lemsford Ferry Regional Park, 27, 28
Lemsford, SK, 27
Leoville, SK, 354
Lepine Lake, 387
Leroy Leisureland Regional Park, 267, 268, 427

Leroy, SK, 267, 268
Leslie Beach Regional Park, 251, 252, 253, 427
Lily Lake, 417
Limerick, SK, 55
Little Big Horn battle, 22, 54, 95
Little Country Grill (Victoire), 338
Little Deer Lake, 371
Little Echo Lake, 402, 403
Little Fishing Lake, 347
Little Fishing Lake Campground (Bronson Forest), 346
Little Fishing Lake Resort (Bronson Forest), 346, 347
Little Jumbo Lake, 375, 377
Little Kenosee Lake, 158
Little Loon Lake, 336
Little Loon Regional Park, 335, 336
Little Manitou Lake, 272
Little McLean Group Campground (Echo Valley), 149, 150
Little Poplar (Cree war chief), 407
Little Store With More, The (Greenwater Lake), 319
Lloydminster, SK, 216, 217, 222, 242
Loasby, Clarence, Constable, 241
Loch Leven Lake, 62, 63, 65
Loch Leven Marina, 65
Loch Leven Picnic Area (Cypress Hills), 65
Loch Lomond Lake, 65
Loch Lomond, SK, 57, 60
Lodgepole Campground (Cypress Hills), 59, 60
Lone Pine (Cree), 241
Lone Pine Campground (Cypress Hills), 60, 63
Long Creek (Oungre), 126
Long Creek Golf and Country Club (Dunnet), 14
Long Lake, 169
Lookout Point (Sask Landing), 91
Loon Lake, 407
Loon Lake Golf and Country Club, 376, 379
Loon Lake, SK, 242, 347, 375, 376, 379, 407, 408
Lost Echo Lake, 395, 401, 402, 403
Love, SK, 399
Lower Chalet Campground (Buffalo Pound), 72
Lower Fishing Lake (Narrow Hills), 357, 393, 396, 397, 399-402, 405
Lowland Trail (Blackstrap), 237
Lucien Lake Regional Park, 269, 271, 422, 425
Lucky Dollar Store (Victoire), 338
Lumsden Beach (Regina Beach), 165
Lussier Lake, 371
Lynwood Campground (Moose Mountain), 158
Lynx Lake, 371

M

M & N Resort (Meadow Lake), 381
MacDougall Creek, 396
MacFarlane River, 341
Macintosh Point (Emma Lake), 365
Mackay Lake, 371, 400
Mackay Lake campsite, 400

Macklin Lake, 197
Macklin Lake Regional Park, 197, 198, 422, 425
Macklin, SK, 197, 198, 222
MacSwaney's cabins (Nipawin), 279
Madge Lake, 305, 306, 308, 309, 310
Madge Lake Golf Resort, 310
Madge Lake Riding Stables, 308, 311
Maidstone, SK, 218, 220
Mainprize Regional Park, 116, 119, 425, 427
Mainprize, William G., Dr., 116
Mainstay Inn (Palliser), 39
Makwa Lake, 375, 377, 407, 408
Makwa Lake Provincial Park, 375, 379, 390, 423, 425, 427
Makwa Lake Resort, 379
Maltby House, 141
Man River, 330
Manito Lake, 221
Manitou and District Regional Park, 272, 274, 422, 425, 427
Manitou Beach Golf Club, 273
Manitou Beach, SK, 272, 273
Manitou Concessions (Good Spirit Lake), 325
Manitou Mineral Spa (Manitou), 274
Mankota, SK, 99
Maple Campsite (The Battlefords), 231
Maple Creek Hospital, 30, 56
Maple Creek, SK, 56, 65, 68, 94, 96
Maple Vale Campground (Buffalo Pound), 71, 73, 75
Marean Lake, 315, 317
Marean Lake Birding Trail, 315
Marina Mini-Golf (Sask Landing), 89
Marlow Kayak (Meadow Lake), 389
Marsden, SK, 221, 222
Marsh Boardwalk Trail (Buffalo Pound), 74
Martin's Lake Regional Park, 199, 201, 422, 427
Martin's Lake Regional Park Golf Course, 200
Master's Mini-golf (Mouse Mountain), 159
Matheson Lake, 385, 390
Matheson Point (Moosomin), 123
Mawka Lake, 379
Maymont Ferry, 194
Maymont, SK, 193, 194
McLaren Lake Regional Park, 29, 30
McLean, W.J., Chief Trader, 241
McLennan, David, 98, 360
McNab Regional Park, 275, 276
McNaughton Heights (Moose Mountain), 163
Meadow Campground (Lac Pelletier), 24
Meadow Hiking Trail (Meadow Lake), 383
Meadow Lake Provincial Park, 380, 386, 391, 407, 422, 423, 427
Meadow Lake, SK, 375, 379, 391
Meadows Campground (Cypress Hills), 59, 60
Meath Park (Candle Lake), 348, 355, 392
Medstead, SK, 336
Meeting Lake Regional Park, 202, 203, 423

Melfort Cross-Country Ski Club, 296
Melfort Mustangs Hockey Club, 298
Melfort, SK, 296
Melville Country Club, 278
Melville Regional Park, 277, 278, 425
Melville, SK, 142, 145, 277, 278
Memorial Lake, 204
Memorial Lake Regional Park, 204, 206, 422, 425, 427
Meota and District Golf Club, 208
Meota Regional Park, 207, 209
Meota, SK, 207, 209
Met Stadium (Woodlawn), 138
Mewasin Beach Campground, 377, 378
Mewasin Hiking Trail (Makwa Lake), 375, 377, 378
Midale, SK, 116, 118, 119
Middle Lake, SK, 269, 271
Middleton, Frederick, General, 407
Ministik Beach, 307, 309
Ministikwan Lake Campground (Bronson Forest), 346
Ministikwan Lake Lodge (Bronson Forest), 347
Minowukaw Beach (Candle Lake), 350, 351, 352
Minowukaw Campgrounds (Candle Lake), 348-352
Missinipe, SK, 366
Missinipe Campgrounds (Lac La Ronge), 371, 372
Mission Lake, 152
Mistasinihk Place (Lac La Ronge), 373, 374
Mistohay Creek (Meadow Lake), 385
Mistohay Lake, 385
Mistussinne, SK, 80
Mitten Lake, 400
Montmartre, SK, 113, 115
Moon Lake Golf and Country Club, 246
Moose Campground (Duck Mountain), 307
Moose Creek Golf Club, 121
Moose Creek Regional Park, 120, 121, 425
Moose Jaw Alpine Ski Association, 69, 73
Moose Jaw, SK, 69, 75
Moose Mountain Provincial Park, 140, 157, 164, 422, 423, 425, 427
"Moose Mountain Provincial Park Cross-Country and Snowmobile Trails" brochure, 161
Moose Mountain Provincial Park Recreation Hall, 164
Moose Trail (Anglin Lake), 345
Moosehead Inn (Moose Mountain), 164
Moosomin and District Regional Park, 122, 123, 422, 425, 427
Moosomin, SK, 122, 123, 136
Morin Lake Regional Park, 337, 338
Morin Lake Reunion Grounds, 338
Morin Lake Spawning Shoal, 337
Mount Blackstrap, 234, 237
Mountain Bike Trail (The Battlefords), 231
Mountain View Picnic Area (Blackstrap), 235, 236
Mrs. Bee's Doll House (Whitesand), 300

Mud Creek (Prince Albert), 417
Mud Creek Trail (Prince Albert), 415
Mulloch Lake, 371
Murray Doell Campground (Meadow Lake), 386
Murray Point (Emma Lake), 362, 364, 365
Murray Point Campground (Emma Lake), 362-365
Murray Point cottage subdivision, 362, 364
Musker Lake Trout Pond Trail (Candle Lake), 349, 352

N

Naicam Snowmobiling Association, 263
Naicam, SK, 262, 263
Nakota peoples, 93
Namekus Lake, 410, 411
Narrow Hills Provincial Park, 357, 392, 395, 397, 405, 423, 424, 427, 428
Narrow Hills Trail (Narrow Hills), 397
Narrows Campground (Prince Albert), 415, 416
Narrows Peninsula Trail (Prince Albert), 416
National Historic Park (Cypress Hills), 67
Natural Choice, The (magazine), 390
"Natural History Notes" brochure, 389
Nature Saskatchewan, 92
Nature Trail (Silver Lake), 219
Neilburg, SK, 222
Neis Beach (Emma Lake), 362
Nelson River, 392
Nelson's Fish and Chips (Regina Beach), 167
Nemeiben Lake, 367, 369
Nemeiben Lake Campgrounds (Lac La Ronge), 369
Nemeiben Lake Interpretive Trail (Lac La Ronge), 367
Newbranch Hiking Trail (Meadow Lake), 390
Nickle Lake, 124
Nickle Lake Regional Park, 124, 125, 422, 427
Nicolle Flats Interpretive Area (Buffalo Pound), 69, 74
Nicolle Homestead (Buffalo Pound), 74
Night Owl Camping Cabins (Pike Lake), 247
Nighthawk Campground (Sask Landing), 87
Nipawin and District Regional Park, 279, 281, 422, 423, 425, 428
Nipawin Lake, 401
Nipawin Wildlife Federation (NWF), 281
Nipawin, SK, 279, 281
Nipekamew Sand Pillars (Lac La Ronge), 366
Nobles Point Marina (Candle Lake), 351
Nokomis, SK, 264, 266
Norgrove Island, 317
North Battleford, SK, 207, 209, 215, 229, 233, 375
North Campground (The Battlefords), 230
North Meadows Golf Club (Meadow Lake), 391
North Saskatchewan River, 193, 238, 239
North-West Company, 152
North-West Mounted Police (NWMP), 54, 95, 241, 407
North-West Rebellion (Resistance), 238, 241, 346,

360, 375, 407
North-West Territory, 238, 241
Northcote (steam boat), 360
Northern Cross Resorts (Meadow Lake), 387
Northern Lights Casino (Meadow Lake), 390
Northern Lights pool (Melfort), 297
Northern Sandscapes, 342
Northwest Canoe and Kayak Club, 378
Notukeu Heritage Museum of Archaeology and Paleontology (Ponteix), 68
Notukeu Regional Park, 31, 32
Nut Point Campground (Lac La Ronge), 367, 368
Nut Point Trail (Lac La Ronge), 367, 369

O

Ochre Trail head (Nipawin), 281
Odell Lake, 398, 399
Ogema Regional Park, 33, 34, 425
Ogema, SK, 33, 34, 36
Ona's Campground (Lac Pelletier), 24
Opal Lake, 397, 403
Ormeaux, SK, 338
Ormiston, SK, 35, 36
Oro Lake, 35
Oro Lake Regional Park, 35, 36
Otter Lake Campgrounds (Lac La Ronge), 372
Otter Rapids (Lac La Ronge), 366, 372, 373
Otter Rapids Campground (Lac La Ronge), 371
Oungre Memorial Regional Park, 126, 128, 422
Oungre, SK, 128
Outlook and District Regional Park, 210, 212
Outlook, SK, 210, 212
Oxbow, SK, 120, 121
Oyama Regional Park, 129, 130

P

Paignton Beach (Prince Albert), 411
Painted Rocks (Dunnet), 13
Palliser Regional Library (Palliser), 14, 428
Palliser Regional Park, 37, 39, 79, 89, 425
Palliser Regional Park Board, 37
Palliser, John, 37
Papa Joe's Convenience Store (Bearpaw), 92
Paradise Hill, SK, 346, 347
Park Nature Center (Prince Albert), 419
Parks Canada Visitors Guide, 419
Parkview Golf Club (Shamrock), 47
Paspiwin Cultural Heritage Site (Prince Albert), 419
Pasqua Beach (Echo Valley), 148
Pasqua Lake, 146, 148, 149, 150, 152
Pasquia Golf Course (Pasquia), 282
Pasquia Gun Club (Pasquia), 255
Pasquia Regional Park, 282, 284, 423, 425
Paul Robertson Trading Post (Lac La Ronge), 374
Pease Point (Prince Albert), 417
Peck Lake, 347
Peck Lake Campground (Bronson Forest), 346
Pederson Place Building (Midale), 118
Peitahigan Loop (Meadow Lake), 390

Pelican Eco-Tours, 108
Pelican Picnic Area (Chitek Lake), 353, 354
Pelly Point Nature Trail (Duck Mountain), 308
Perdue, SK, 187
PFRA (Prairie Farm Rehabilitation Administration) dam, 50
Pickerel Point (Duck Mountain), 305, 307, 309, 310, 312
Pickerel Point (Moose Mountain), 161
Pickerel Point (Sturgeon Lake), 340
Pickerel Point Campgrounds (Duck Mountain), 309
Pickerel Point General Store (Duck Mountain), 306, 309, 311
Pierce Lake, 387, 388, 389, 390
Pierce Lake Lodge, 387
Pierce, Edward Mitchell, 140
Pierceland, SK, 380, 387, 391
Pike Lake Provincial Park, 243, 247, 248, 423
Pine Cove Resort, 377, 379
Pine Cree Main Campgrounds (Pine Cree), 40
Pine Cree Regional Park, 40, 41, 421, 423, 424, 426, 428
Pine Hill Campground (Cypress Hills), 57, 58
Pine Hill, SK, 57
Pine Lake, 396
Pine Point picnic area (Pike Lake), 245
Pine Ridge Resort (Narrow Hills), 393, 394, 396, 397
Pinelodge Service Center (Cypress Hills), 58, 60
Pipestone Valley reservoir (Moosomin), 122
Piprell Lake, 402, 403, 404
Pirie Field (Melville), 278
Point, The, Campground (Lac Pelletier), 24
Ponteix Town 'n Country Golf Club, 31
Ponteix, SK, 31, 32, 68
Poplar Campground (Duck Mountain), 305, 306, 308
Poplar Leaf Hiking Trail (Whitesand), 300
Porcupine Plain, SK, 319, 330
Porcupine Uplands (Greenwater Lake), 313
Prairie Lake Regional Park, 42, 43, 423, 424
Prairie Meadow Campground (Sask Landing), 88
Prairie Vista Interpretive Trail (Sask Landing), 91
Prairie Whispers Nature Trail (Rowan's Ravine), 171
Preeceville, SK, 260, 261, 290
Primrose Air Weapons Range, 380, 387
Prince Albert National Park, 343, 345, 409, 414, 418, 420, 422-425, 428
Prince Albert National Park Official Visitor Guide, 414
Prince Albert National Park Trail Guide, 414
Prince Albert, 204, 223, 330, 343, 345, 348, 352, 355, 357, 360, 362, 365, 366, 392, 398, 405, 409, 419
Prospect Point (Prince Albert), 417
Provincial Historical Park (Wood Mountain), 55

Q

Qu'Appelle, Diocese of, 141
Qu'Appelle River dam, 78, 80, 84
Qu'Appelle Valley, 80, 134, 144, 146, 148, 150, 152, 427

Qu'Appelle Valley Trail, 150

R

Rabbit Lake Heritage Society, 203
Rabbit Lake, SK, 202, 203
Radville Laurier Regional Park, 131, 132, 426
Radville, SK, 106, 131, 132
Rafferty Reservoir (Mainprize), 116, 117, 138
Rainbow Campground (Cypress Hills), 58
Rancher's Road Hill (Sandy Beach), 216
Ranger Bay (Duck Mountain), 310
Rankin's Campground (Buffalo Pound), 72
Raspberry Lake, 390
Rat Lake, 400
Raymore, SK, 327, 328
RB's Diner (Rowan's Ravine), 170, 171
RCMP, 125, 191, 201, 284, 419
Recreation Hall (Duck Mountain), 310
Recreation Hall (Good Spirit Lake), 325, 326
Recreation Hall (Greenwater Lake), 317
Red Deer Downs (Hudson Bay), 255
Red Deer River, 254, 255
Red Deer Trail (Prince Albert), 415, 419
Red River, 103, 239, 327
Red River Cart Trail (Fort Carlton), 238
Red Wing Bay (Prince Albert), 417
Redberry Lake Regional Park, 213, 215, 422, 424, 427
Redberry Pond Trout Fishery, 214
Regina Beach Campground (Regina Beach), 167
Regina Beach Provincial Recreation Site, 165, 167, 427
Regina Beach Yacht Club (RBYC), 166
Regina Beach, SK, 166, 170
Regina, SK, 107, 130, 152, 155, 156, 165, 167, 168, 172, 284, 308, 328, 330, 341, 398
Reindeer Lake, 366, 371, 373
Reserve-a-Site program, 248
Richmound, SK, 29, 30
Ridge Lake, 356
Ridges and Ravines Interpretive Trail (Sask Landing), 91
Riding Academy (Cypress Hills), 66
Rings, Ruts, and Remnants Hiking Trail (Sask Landing), 91
River Walk (Fort Carlton), 239
Riverbreaks Golf and Country Club (Palliser), 38, 79
Riverhurst Ferry, 37, 79
Riverhurst Lions Club, 39
Riverhurst Recreation Board, 39
Riverhurst, SK, 39, 79, 89
Riverside Campground (Sask Landing), 87
Robertdale Golf and Country Club (Radville Laurier), 132
Robertson, A.R., 132
Robinson Bay (The Battlefords), 231
Robinson Bay Campground (The Battlefords), 231
Rockglen, SK, 44, 45

Rockin Beach Regional Park, 44, 45, 428
Rodeo Ranch Museum (Wood Mountain), 53, 54, 55
Rosthern, SK, 223, 224
Rotary Park (Woodlawn), 138
Rotary Recreation Hall (Woodlawn), 139
Rothenburg Family Park (Emma Lake), 364
Rough Fescue Prairie Trail (Greenwater Lake), 316
Roughbark River, 117
Rowan's Ravine Provincial Park, 168, 172, 422, 423, 427, 428
Rowan, William, 168
Rowe, Stan
   The Sand Dunes of Lake Athabasca, 342
Royal Saskatchewan Museum, 284
Ruby Lake, 254
Rusty Coulee Marina (Palliser), 39
Rusty Creek (Meadow Lake), 383
Rusty Lake, 383
Rusty's Coulee (Douglas), 82
Rusty's Marina (Sask Landing), 89

S

Sacred Heart Parish (Montmartre), 114
Sagebrush Amphitheater (Sask Landing), 87
Sagebrush Campground (Sask Landing), 85, 86, 87
Sand Castles (near Beechy), 43, 79
Sand Dunes Interpretive Trail (Good Spirit Lake), 326
Sand Dunes of Lake Athabasca, The, 342
Sandy Bay Beach (Candle Lake), 351
Sandy Bay Campground (Candle Lake), 348, 350, 352
Sandy Beach Campground (Meadow Lake), 387
Sandy Beach Regional Park, 216, 217, 427
Sandy Lake Campground (Prince Albert), 410, 411
Sandy Ridge Campground (Good Spirit Lake), 321
Sandy Ridge Cottage Subdivision (Sask Landing), 86
Sask River Tours, 39, 79
Sask Tourism, 406
Sask Wildlife Trap and Skeet Club, 303, 304
Saskatchewan Beach, SK, 133, 134, 168
Saskatchewan Beach Regional Park, 133, 134
Saskatchewan Environment and Resource Management (SERM), 146, 151, 154, 164, 309, 310, 328, 341-343, 345, 359, 373-374, 379, 389, 391, 408, 427
Saskatchewan Express, 232
Saskatchewan Landing Golf Resort, 90
Saskatchewan Landing Provincial Park, 85, 90, 92, 422-425, 428
Saskatchewan Landing Provincial Park Marina, 82
Saskatchewan Parks and Recreation Association, 144
Saskatchewan Regional Parks Association (SRPA)
Saskatchewan River, 242, 279, 283, 296, 360, 392, 398
Saskatchewan Roughriders football club, 172
Saskatchewan, University of, 342
Saskatoon, SK, 37, 76, 107, 185, 187, 193, 215, 223,

234, 237, 240, 243, 248, 269, 270, 342
Saskin Beach, 251
Scott trout pond (Unity), 226
Senlac, SK, 222
SERM, see Saskatchewan Environment and Resource Management
Service, Robert, 148
Shady Lake Trail (Prince Albert), 415
Shady Lane Campground (Buffalo Pound), 71, 75
Shady Lane Campground (Danielson), 76, 77
Shady Lane picnic area (Pike Lake), 245
Shady Nook Campground (Cypress Hills), 60
Shamrock Regional Park, 46, 47
Shamrock, SK, 47
Shaunavon, SK, 40, 41
Shell Lake, 354
Shell Lake, SK, 190, 204, 206
Shell River, SK, 192
Shellbrook, SK, 192, 340
Silton, SK, 133, 134
Silver Lake, 218
Silver Lake Regional Park, 218, 220, 425
Sink Lake, 226
Sioux Nations, 22, 54, 95
Sitting Bull, Chief, 54, 95
Ski Hill (Buffalo Pound), 74
Sky Trail (Outlook), 211
Smart Trail (Sask Landing), 91
Smeaton, SK, 357, 392, 394, 396, 405
Souris River, 117, 124
Souris Valley, 126, 137
Souris Valley Communiplex, 127
Souris Valley Theater, 139
South Bay (Prince Albert), 411
South Campground (The Battlefords), 229, 230, 231
South Campground Recreation Hall (The Battlefords), 231
South Saskatchewan River, 9, 15, 27, 37, 85, 210, 243
Southend Campground (Prince Albert), 416, 417
Spiritwood Market (Good Spirit Lake), 325
Spiritwood, SK, 336
Sports Ground Area (Memorial Lake), 204
Spruce Bluff Trail (Meadow Lake), 390
Spruce Campground (Duck Mountain), 305, 306, 310
Spruce Crescent (Lac La Ronge), 370
Spruce Meadows Trail (Prince Albert), 415
Spruce River Campground (Anglin Lake), 344, 345
Spruce River Highland Trail (Anglin Lake), 345
Spruce River Highlands Trail (Prince Albert), 415
Spy Hill, SK, 104, 242
St. Brieux Regional Park, 285, 286, 422, 425
St. Brieux, SK, 285, 286
St. John Bosco Camp (Narrow Hills), 394, 404
St. Michaels Camp (Duck Mountain), 307
St. Victor Petroglyphs, 5
St. Victor Petroglyphs Provincial Historic Park, 48, 93, 94, 424
St. Victor, SK, 48, 49, 93, 94
St. Walburg, SK, 180, 181, 346, 347, 375
Stabler Point (Makwa Lake), 375, 377, 378
Stabler Point Campground (Makwa Lake), 376, 377, 378
Standard Hill Baseball Club, 220
Standing Buffalo Service Station (Echo Valley), 150
Stanley Mission, SK, 141, 366, 406
Star's Place outfitter (Meadow Lake), 383, 390
Steele Narrows, 242, 346, 375, 408
Steele Narrows Provincial Historic Site, 378, 407, 408, 428
Steele, Sam, Major, 407
Steepbank Lake, 355, 356
Steiesol Lake, 315, 317
Steiesol Lake Trail, 315
Stewart Creek (Narrow Hills), 392, 396, 398
Stewart Valley, SK, 92
Stickley Lake, 401, 402
Stony Rapids, SK, 342
Store and Shoreline Rentals (Mainprize), 119
Strange, Thomas Bland, General, 407
Strasbourg, SK, 172
Struan, SK, 187
Struthers Lake, 287
Struthers Lake Regional Park, 287, 288
Sturgeon Lake, 339
Sturgeon Lake Regional Park, 339, 340, 422
Sturgeon-weir River, 360
Sturgis and District Regional Park, 289, 290, 426
Sturgis Regional Park Board, 260
Sturgis Ski Hill, 290
Sturgis, SK, 289, 290
Sucker River, 369
Suffern Lake Regional Park, 221, 222
Summit Lake, 398, 401, 402, 403
Sunken Hill (near Beechy), 43
Sunnybank cottage subdivision (Mouse Mountain), 159
Sunset Campground (Cypress Hills), 60
Sunset Trail (Douglas), 83
Swift Current, SK, 24, 26, 85, 92
Sylvan Valley Regional Park, 48, 49, 93

T

T. Rex Museum (Eastend), 68
Tackle Box (Greenwater Lake), 316
Tall Timber Trails riding stable (Meadow Lake), 385
Tawaw Cabins (Meadow Lake), 380, 381
Taylor Field (Rowan's Ravine), 172
Tee-Pee Group campsites (Echo Valley), 148
Terrace Campground (Cypress Hills), 58
Terry Gould Foundation, 278
Thatcher, Premier Ross, 37
Theodore Reservoir (Whitesand), 299
Theodore, SK, 299
Thompson Bay (Athabasca Sand Dunes), 341

Thompson's Camps (Lac La Ronge), 372, 373
Thompson, Stanley, 418
Thomson Lake Regional Park, 50, 52, 422, 423, 425
Thomson Lake Regional Park Golf Course, 51
Tisdale, SK, 254, 258, 259
Tobin Lake, 280, 283, 398
Top of the Dam Café (Danielson), 78
Torch River, 392, 396, 398
Torch River Bridge (Candle Lake), 349
Touchwood Hills Provincial Historic Park, 327, 328
Tower Trail (Meadow Lake), 388
Trailer Park Campground (Prince Albert), 409, 420
Trailhead Nature Center (Pike Lake), 247
Tramping Lake, 228
Trans Canada Highway, 142, 157
Trans Canada Trail, 63, 74, 78, 84, 144, 153, 211, 307, 322
Trappers Lake, 410
Treebeard Trail (Prince Albert), 415
Trippes Beach (Prince Albert), 411, 417
Tugaske, SK, 84
Tulibee Lake, 378, 407
Tunnels of Moose Jaw, 75
Twin Lakes Trailblazers (Nipawin), 281
Twin Marine Boat (Nipawin), 280

U

Underwood Campground (Rowan's Ravine), 168, 169
UNESCO Biosphere Reserve, 213
Uniplex center (Elrose), 188, 189
United Church (Eagle Creek), 187
Unity and District Regional Park, 225, 226, 422, 425, 426
Unity, SK, 222, 225, 226
Upland Trail (Blackstrap), 237
Upper Fishing Lake, 396, 404

V

Val Marie, SK, 97, 98, 99, 100
Valley Regional Park (Waldheim), 223, 224, 425, 426
Valley Trail Group Campground (Cypress Hills), 60, 63
Valley View Campground (Echo Valley), 146, 147, 148
Victoire, SK, 338
Viewing Tower (Meadow Lake), 390
Vivian Lake, 384, 385, 390
Vivian Lake Hiking Trail (Meadow Lake), 384, 390
Voyageur Canoe Adventure, 416

W

Wadin Bay, 366, 371
Wadin Bay Campground (Lac La Ronge), 370
Wadin Bay Resort (Lac La Ronge), 371
Wakaw Lake, 292
Wakaw Lake Regional Park, 291, 293, 425, 427
Wakaw, SK, 271, 287, 291, 293
Waldheim, SK, 223, 224
Waldsea Lake, 294

Waldsea Lake Regional Park, 294, 295
Walsh, James, Superintendent, 95
Wandering Spirit (Cree war chief), 241, 408
Wapawekka Hills (Narrow Hills), 398, 400
Wapiti Lounge (Wapiti Valley), 296
Wapiti Valley, 298
Wapiti Valley Regional Park, 296, 298
Warlodge Campground (Cypress Hills), 57
Warner Rapids (Clearwater River), 358, 359
Warner Rapids Bridge (Clearwater River), 358
Waskahiganihk Family Restaurant (Cumberland House), 361
Waskateena Beach (Candle Lake), 350
Waskesiu Chamber of Commerce, 420
Waskesiu Community Association, 419
Waskesiu Golf Club, 418
Waskesiu Lake, 416, 417
Waskesiu Lake, SK, 418, 420
Waskesiu River, 417
Waskesiu River Trail (Prince Albert), 413, 415
Waskesiu, SK, 409, 411, 412, 413, 415-417, 420
Waterhen Lake, 380, 381, 389
Waterhen River, 380, 389, 390
Watrous, SK, 272, 273, 274
Watson, SK, 267, 275, 276
Welwyn Centennial Regional Park, 135, 136, 424
Welwyn, SK, 135, 136
Western Development Museum (in North Battleford), 233
Weyburn, SK, 124, 125, 126, 127
Whispering Pines Nature Trail (Cypress Hills), 63, 65
White Bear Golf Course (Moose Mountain), 162
White Birch Hiking Trail (Meadow Lake), 382, 390
White Gull Bridge (Narrow Hills), 404
White Gull Creek, 398, 404
White Gull River, 397
White Track Ski Hill (Buffalo Pound), 73
Whitegates Group Site (Duck Mountain), 307
Whitesand Regional Park, 299
Whitesand River, 299
Wildcat Hills Provincial Wilderness Park, 329, 330, 426
Wilkie Regional Park, 227, 228
Wilkie, SK, 227, 228
William Point (Athabasca Sand Dunes), 341
Willow Bunch, SK, 22, 23
Willow Campsite (The Battlefords), 231
Willow Crescent (Lac La Ronge), 370
Willow Dam reservoir (Assiniboia), 6
Windfall Trail (Cypress Hills), 62
"Winter Information—Cross-Country & Snowmobile Trails" brochure, 316
Wintergreen Nature Trail (The Battlefords), 231
Wolf Willow Trail (Douglas), 84
Wolverine Historical Society, 103
Wood Mountain Provincial Historic Park, 5, 54, 95, 96, 99, 429

Wood Mountain Recreation Club, 53
Wood Mountain Regional Park, 53, 55, 96, 99, 422, 426, 429
Wood Mountain, SK, 53, 55, 96
Wood Mountain Turf Club, 53
Wood River, 46, 47, 50
Woodland Nature Trail (Duck Mountain), 308
Woodland Trail (Good Spirit Lake), 322
Woodlands Trail (Cypress Hills), 62
Woodlawn Golf Club, 138
Woodlawn Regional Park, 137, 425
Woody's Field (Mainprize), 119
WOTS Creek, 404
Wymark, SK, 26
Wynyard and District Regional Park, 301, 302
Wynyard, SK, 301

Y

Yellow Creek, SK, 287
Yellowhead Highway (Highway 16), 251, 299
York Lake, 304
York Lake Golf and Country Club, 304
York Lake Regional Park, 303, 304, 422, 425, 427
Yorkton Canoe and Kayak Club, 303
Yorkton, SK, 254, 300, 303, 304, 320, 325
"You Are In Black Bear Country" pamphlet, 410
Youell Lake Trail (Moose Mountain), 160

Z

Zeden Lake (also ZN Lake), 394, 400, 404

PROVINCIAL & NATIONAL PARKS	CAMPING · RV · TOURS	DUMP STATION	FIREWOOD	FAST FOOD	STORE	TELEPHONE	SHOWER	MODERN WASHROOMS	SWIMMING	FISHING	BOAT LAUNCH	GOLF	HIKE-WALK TRAIL(S)	LAUNDROMAT	ACCOMODATIONS	WHEELCHAIR ACC	FUEL
ATHABASCA SAND DUNES PROVINCIAL PARK	-	-	-	-	-	-	-	-	-	✓	-	-	-	-	-	-	-
ANGLIN LAKE PROVINCIAL RECREATION SITE	25E · 53N	✓	✓	-	-	-	-	-	B	✓	✓	-	✓	-	-	-	-
THE BATTLEFORDS PROVINCIAL PARK	165E · 152N	✓	✓	✓	✓	✓	✓	✓	B	✓	✓	18G	✓	✓	✓	✓	-
BLACKSTRAP PROVINCIAL PARK	15E · 38N	✓	✓	-	-	✓	✓	✓	B	✓	✓	-	✓	-	-	-	-
BRONSEN FOREST RECREATION SITE	67N	✓	✓	-	-	-	-	-	B	✓	-	-	-	-	-	-	-
BUFFALO POUND PROVINCIAL PARK	100E · 108N · 2F	✓	✓	✓	✓	✓	✓	✓	B · P	✓	✓	M	✓	✓	-	✓	-
CANDLE LAKE RECREATION PARK	135E · 109N	✓	✓	-	✓	✓	✓	✓	B	✓	✓	9G	✓	✓	✓	✓	A · P
CANNINGTON MANOR PROVINCIAL HISTORIC PARK	Guided tour	-	-	-	-	-	-	-	-	-	-	-	-	-	-	L	-
CHITEK LAKE RECREATION SITE	25E · 25N	✓	✓	-	✓	✓	✓	✓	B	✓	✓	-	-	-	-	-	-
CLARENCE-STEEPBANK LAKES PROVINCIAL WILDERNESS PARK	6N	-	-	-	-	-	-	-	-	✓	-	-	-	-	-	-	-
CLEARWATER RIVER WILDERNESS PARK	17N	-	✓	-	-	-	-	-	-	✓	-	-	-	-	-	-	-
CROOKED LAKE PROVINCIAL PARK	28E · 44N	✓	✓	-	-	-	-	-	B	✓	✓	18G	✓	-	-	-	-
CUMBERLAND HOUSE PROVINCIAL HISTORIC PARK	-	-	-	-	-	-	-	-	-	-	-	-	-	-	-	-	-
CYPRESS HILLS INTERPROVINCIAL PARK	200E · 354N · 10F	✓	✓	✓	✓	✓	✓	✓	B	✓	✓	9G	✓	✓	✓	✓	A · D · P
DANIELSON PROVINCIAL PARK	48E · 43N	✓	✓	-	✓	✓	✓	✓	B	✓	✓	-	-	-	-	✓	-
DOUGLAS PROVINCIAL PARK	90E · 59N	✓	✓	-	✓	✓	✓	✓	B	✓	✓	9G	-	-	-	-	-
DUCK MOUNTAIN PROVINCIAL PARK	204E · 165N · 15F	✓	✓	✓	✓	✓	✓	✓	B · P	✓	✓	18G · M	✓	✓	✓	✓	A · P
ECHO LAKE PROVINCIAL PARK	176E · 132N	✓	✓	-	✓	✓	✓	✓	B	✓	✓	M	✓	✓	-	-	-
EMMA LAKE RECREATION SITE	28E · 22N	✓	✓	-	✓	✓	✓	✓	B	✓	✓	-	✓	-	-	-	A
FORT CARLTON PROVINCIAL HISTORIC PARK	15N	-	✓	-	-	-	-	-	-	✓	-	-	✓	-	-	✓	-
FORT PITT PROVINCIAL HISTORIC PARK	-	-	-	-	-	-	-	-	-	-	-	-	-	-	-	-	-
GOOD SPIRIT LAKE PROVINCIAL PARK	129E · 88N	✓	✓	✓	✓	✓	✓	✓	B	✓	✓	M	✓	-	-	-	-
GREENWATER LAKE PROVINCIAL PARK	144E · 42N	✓	✓	✓	✓	✓	✓	✓	B	✓	✓	18G	✓	✓	✓	-	L A · D · M · P
HOLY TRINITY ANGLICAN CHURCH PROVINCIAL HISTORIC SITE	Self guided tour	-	-	-	-	-	-	-	-	-	-	-	-	-	-	-	-
KATEPWA POINT PROVINCIAL RECREATION PARK	-	-	✓	✓	-	✓	-	-	B	✓	✓	9G	-	-	-	-	-
LAC LA RONGE PROVINCIAL PARK	90E · 146N	✓	✓	-	✓	✓	✓	✓	B	✓	✓	-	✓	-	-	L	-
LAST MOUNTAIN PROVINCIAL PARK	Tour services	-	-	-	-	-	-	-	-	-	-	-	-	-	-	L	-
MAKWA LAKE PROVINCIAL PARK	95E · 166N	✓	✓	-	✓	✓	✓	✓	B	✓	✓	9G	✓	-	-	✓	-
MEADOW LAKE PROVINCIAL PARK	298E · 565N · 9F	✓	✓	✓	✓	✓	✓	✓	B	✓	✓	M	✓	✓	✓	-	L A · M
MOOSE MOUNTAIN PROVINCIAL PARK	186E · 136N · 11F	✓	✓	✓	✓	✓	✓	✓	B · P	✓	✓	18G	✓	✓	✓	✓	A · D · P
NARROW HILLS PROVINCIAL PARK	30E · 91N	✓	✓	-	✓	✓	✓	✓	B	✓	✓	-	✓	-	✓	-	L A · D · P
PIKE LAKE PROVINCIAL PARK	125E · 100N	✓	✓	✓	✓	✓	✓	✓	B	✓	✓	9S · M	✓	✓	-	✓	-
REGINA BEACH PROVINCIAL PARK	-	-	-	-	-	✓	✓	✓	B	✓	✓	-	-	-	-	L	-
ROWAN'S RAVINE PROVINCIAL PARK	196E · 62N	✓	✓	-	✓	✓	✓	✓	B	✓	✓	M	✓	✓	-	✓	M
SASKATCHEWAN LANDING PROVINCIAL PARK	134E · 165N	✓	✓	✓	✓	✓	✓	✓	B	✓	✓	18G	✓	✓	-	✓	M
ST. VICTOR PETROGLYPHS PROVINCIAL HISTORICAL PARK	Guided tour	-	-	-	-	-	-	-	-	-	-	-	-	-	-	L	-
STEELE NARROWS PROVINCIAL PARK	Self guided tour	-	-	-	-	-	-	-	-	-	-	-	-	-	-	-	-
TOUCHWOOD HILLS PROVINCIAL PARK	Self guided tour	-	-	-	-	-	-	-	-	-	-	-	-	-	-	-	-
WILDCAT HILLS PROVINCIAL PARK	Self guided tour	-	-	-	-	-	-	-	-	-	-	-	-	-	-	-	-
WOOD MOUNTAIN PROVINCIAL PARK	Self guided tour	-	-	-	-	-	-	-	-	-	-	-	-	-	-	-	-
GRASSLANDS NATIONAL PARK	Guided tour	-	-	-	-	-	-	-	-	-	-	-	-	-	-	-	-
PRINCE ALBERT NATIONAL PARK	108E · 249N · 152F	✓	✓	✓	✓	✓	✓	✓	B	✓	✓	18G	✓	✓	✓	-	L A · M · P
REGIONAL PARKS																	
ANTELOPE LAKE	72E	✓	✓	-	-	✓	✓	✓	B	✓	-	9S	-	-	-	-	-
ASSINIBOIA	15E · 2N	✓	✓	-	-	-	-	-	P	✓	-	9G	-	-	-	-	-
ATTON'S LAKE	60E · 40N	✓	✓	✓	✓	✓	✓	✓	B	✓	✓	9G	✓	-	-	-	-
BENGOUGH	16E	✓	✓	-	-	-	✓	✓	B · P	-	-	9S	-	-	-	-	-
BIGGAR & DISTRICT	14E · 12N	-	✓	-	-	✓	-	-	-	-	-	9G	-	-	-	-	-
BRIGHT SAND LAKE	25E · 60N	✓	✓	✓	✓	✓	✓	✓	B	✓	✓	M	✓	✓	-	-	-
CABRI	64E · 11N · 50F	✓	✓	✓	✓	✓	✓	✓	-	✓	✓	-	-	-	-	-	-
CANWOOD	8E · 12N	-	✓	-	✓	✓	✓	✓	-	-	-	9S	-	-	-	-	-
CARLTON TRAIL	75E · 10N	✓	✓	-	✓	✓	✓	✓	B	✓	-	9G	-	-	-	-	-
CEYLON	21E · 16N	✓	✓	-	-	✓	-	✓	B	✓	-	-	-	-	-	-	-
CLEARWATER LAKE	15E · 14N · 30F	✓	-	-	✓	✓	✓	✓	B	✓	✓	9S	-	-	-	-	-
CRAIK & DISTRICT	40E · 9N · 6F	✓	✓	✓	✓	-	✓	✓	P	✓	-	M	✓	-	-	-	-
DUNNET	66E · 210N · 12F	✓	✓	✓	✓	✓	✓	✓	P	✓	✓	-	✓	✓	-	-	-
EAGLE CREEK	54E · 50N	✓	✓	-	-	✓	✓	✓	-	✓	-	9G	-	-	-	-	-
ELROSE	14E	✓	-	-	-	✓	✓	✓	P	-	-	-	-	-	-	-	-
EMERALD LAKE	14E · 6N · 18F	✓	✓	-	✓	✓	✓	✓	B	✓	✓	9S	-	-	-	-	-
ESTON	40E · 20N · 25F	✓	✓	✓	✓	✓	-	✓	P	✓	-	9G · M	✓	-	-	-	-
ESTERHAZY	33E · 9N	✓	-	-	✓	✓	✓	✓	P	✓	-	9G	-	-	-	-	-
FISHING LAKE - K.C. BEACH	67E	✓	✓	✓	✓	✓	✓	✓	B	✓	✓	-	-	-	-	-	-
GLENBURN	6E · 14N · 26F	✓	✓	-	✓	✓	✓	✓	P	-	-	9S	-	-	-	-	-
GRENFELL	23E · 15N · 9F	-	✓	-	-	✓	✓	✓	P	-	-	9G · M	-	-	-	-	-
HAZLET	12E · 20N	-	✓	-	-	-	-	-	-	-	-	9S	-	-	-	-	-
HERBERT FERRY	30N																